Canadian-Based Multinationals

THE INDUSTRY CANADA RESEARCH SERIES, together with a Working Paper Series and an Occasional Paper Series, are part of the Industry Canada Publications Program. This program sponsors and produces applied public policy papers intended to contribute to informed debate over issues relating to the department, especially micro-economic policy and analysis.

The views expressed in all the papers in this volume are the responsibility of the individual authors: they do not necessarily reflect the opinions or policies of Industry Canada or the Government of Canada.

GENERAL EDITOR: STEVEN GLOBERMAN

Canadian-Based Multinationals

The Industry Canada Research Series

The University of Calgary Press

© Minister of Supply and Services Canada 1994

ISBN 1-895176-49-2
ISSN 1188-0988
ID53-11-4-1994E

University of Calgary Press
2500 University Dr. N.W.
Calgary, Alberta, Canada T2N 1N4

Canadian Cataloguing in Publication Data
  Main entry under title:
  Canadian-Based Multinationals

    (Industry Canada research series, ISSN 1188-0988 ; v.4)
    Issued also in French under title: Les multinationales canadiennes.
      Includes bibliographical references.
      ISBN 1-895176-49-2

    1. International business enterprises—Canada. 2. Investments, Canadian—
    Foreign countries. I. Globerman, Steven.   II. Series.
    HD2809.C36 1994   338.8'8971   C94-910504-X

The University of Calgary Press appreciates the assistance of the Alberta Foundation for
the Arts (a beneficiary of Alberta Lotteries) for its 1994 publishing program.

EDITORIAL & PUBLISHING CO-ORDINATION: Ampersand Communications Inc.
COVER & INTERIOR DESIGN: Brant Cowie/ArtPlus Limited

Printed and bound in Canada

(∞)   This book is printed on acid-free paper.

Table of Contents

PART II ECONOMIC IMPLICATIONS

PART III BUSINESS IMPLICATIONS

PART IV   COUNTRY CASE STUDIES

PART V   FIRM STUDIES

PART VI   LESSONS

Preface

TRADITIONALLY, THE ATTENTION OF Canadian policy analysts, as well as that of the Canadian public, has focused primarily on foreign direct investment into Canada. Considerably less attention has been paid to the growing number of Canadian multinationals (MNEs) and their expanding roles in foreign countries. Given the increasing importance of Canadian direct investment abroad (CDIA) and the continuing globalization of Canadian MNEs, Industry Canada decided to undertake an in-depth analysis of the activities and performance of Canadian MNEs and their potential consequences for the Canadian economy. This work responds to Industry Canada's mandate to promote economic growth through the development of micro-economic (structural) analysis and policy recommendations concerning business organization, and the behaviour and strategies of firms.

At present, approximately 1,300 Canadian-based firms are operating abroad. The United States has been the dominant location for CDIA, but the diversification of destinations also increased significantly in the late 1980s.

For over a decade, the growth of Canadian direct investment abroad has outpaced the growth of foreign direct investment (FDI) into Canada. Between 1980 and 1992, the stock of CDIA increased from $27 billion to almost $100 billion. As a result, from 1970 to 1992, the ratio of CDIA stock to FDI stock in Canada rose from 23 percent to just over 70 percent. It is equally noteworthy that these trends have been pervasive across all major industries.

The expansion of activities abroad by Canadian-based multinationals is consistent with the experiences of other industrialized countries. Over the past decade, the phenomenal growth of FDI by firms from major industrialized countries has contributed to the globalization of world markets. In this context, foreign direct investment and trade have increasingly become complements rather than substitutes. Indeed, today one-third of international trade is intra-firm. This suggests that Canada's international competitiveness depends upon the expansion of activities of MNEs in Canada and of Canadian-based MNEs abroad.

This volume addresses the economic implications of Canadian-based MNEs with respect to capital movements, labour-market issues, technology and innovation, and taxation. In addition, it considers the foreign business strategies of two Canadian firms and includes two country studies. The country studies describe the experiences with outward investment in Sweden and Japan; the case studies deal with the international business activities of Northern Telecom and MacMillan Bloedel.

Following the development of a detailed research proposal by the Micro-Economic Policy Branch of Industry Canada, 21 specialists in the field of international economics were invited to present papers at a conference on "Canadian-Based Multinational Enterprises" held in Montreal in November 1993. The papers were subsequently developed and refined in light of comments received from the academic, government and business experts who participated in the conference. Steven Globerman of Simon Fraser and Western Washington Universities, served as General Editor. The final studies, together with the comments of the Rapporteur, are presented here.

The research assembled in this volume is mainly the product of work undertaken by academic researchers. Industry Canada staff, however, formulated and managed the project and provided constructive feedback throughout the process. Nevertheless, the papers ultimately remain the sole responsibility of the authors and do not necessarily reflect the policies or opinions of Industry Canada or the Government of Canada.

Industry Canada undertakes micro-economic studies on a wide range of issues to provide an analytical foundation for the Department's policies and programs. Research issues – and consequent publications – are determined in the context of the Department's strategic micro-economic policy priorities. The publications program – of which *Canadian-Based Multinationals* is the fourth volume in the Industry Canada Research Series – also includes a Working Paper series and a series of Occasional Papers. The aim in setting up the publications program has been to increase the Department's effectiveness in contributing to the national debate on micro-economic policy. We hope the distribution of pertinent research stimulates policy debate on important micro-economic issues confronting Canada and helps to build a shared vision of economic problems among the wider public.

I would like to take this opportunity to thank all of the authors for their work, particularly Steven Globerman in his capacity as both author and General Editor. I know that this volume will be of interest to the policy-making community as well as to everyone interested in economic issues here in Canada and abroad.

JOHN MANLEY
MINISTER OF INDUSTRY

Steven Globerman
Department of Economics
Simon Fraser University

1

The Public and Private Interests in Outward Direct Investment

INTRODUCTION

FOR WELL OVER A DECADE the effects of inward foreign direct investment on the host-country economy has waxed and waned as a prominent public policy issue in Canada and other countries. As a result of strong, albeit periodic, interest, a substantial literature has accumulated evaluating the determinants and consequences of foreign direct investment on the host economy.[1] In contrast, relatively little attention has been paid to the effects of overseas investment on the home country. To be sure, concerns have been raised from time to time about the effect of direct investment abroad (DIA) on employment in the home country,[2] and these concerns have given rise to several policy-oriented assessments of the activities of home-country multinationals.[3]

Despite the ambivalent empirical findings of the literature, governments have traditionally tended to favour and, indeed, in many cases to promote direct investment abroad.[4] Moreover, prominent assessments of the "competitiveness" of nations have suggested that the activities of home-country multinationals contribute in important ways to the international competitiveness of the home country. Porter's analysis is notable in this regard. For example, in his study of the competitiveness of the Canadian economy, Porter (1991, p.56) asserts that firms must compete with a "global" perspective, and he identifies this perspective as encompassing not only foreign sales but also the location of activities around the world. Porter assumes many potential benefits to the investing company, including lower costs, the stimulation of innovation and improved marketing. In turn, the presence of globally competitive firms in the home market contributes to a more "competitive" domestic economy by strengthening the aggregate skills of the "cluster" of domestic firms in related activities.[5]

In the context of what is arguably a favourable (albeit relatively unarticulated) view of direct investment abroad, the debate that surrounded the North American Free Trade Agreement (NAFTA) is instructive. Specifically, the concerns expressed by both American and Canadian opponents that the NAFTA would encourage a capital flight to Mexico belie the argument that direct investment abroad promotes the long-run economic welfare of the home country. Indeed, recent high levels of unemployment in the developed economies have sensitized labour unions and politicians to the worldwide competition for investment capital to the extent that the choice of where in the world domestically owned firms choose to install production capacity is likely to become an increasingly important public policy issue.

CANADIAN DIRECT INVESTMENT ABROAD

THIS SECTION OFFERS A BRIEF OVERVIEW of the main characteristics of Canadian direct investment abroad (CDIA) in order to put into context the relevance of the issue. The studies by Chow, and Rao, Legault & Ahmad in this volume form the basis for this overview.

Chow identifies the relatively rapid growth of CDIA in recent years. Specifically, the level of CDIA doubled between 1986 and 1992.[6] In doing so, it outstripped the growth of foreign direct investment in Canada. Indeed, the ratio of Canada's outward to inward direct investment stock increased from .23 in 1970 to .72 in 1992. Rao, Legault & Ahmad note that during the 1980s the stock of CDIA increased at a faster pace than the world's outward investment stock, as evidenced by the fact that Canada's share of the world outward direct investment stock increased from 4 percent in 1980 to more that 4.5 percent in 1990.

While this orientation of increased outward direct investment tends to characterize most major Canadian industries, the electrical and electronics products sector was the one with the highest propensity to invest abroad, where the measure of propensity is *investment abroad as a ratio of total assets*, However, the largest share of CDIA was concentrated in finance and insurance – representing one-quarter of the total CDIA at 1991 year end (Chow, this volume). Manufacturing's share of CDIA declined substantially between 1960 and 1991, although taken as a whole, manufacturing still accounts for the largest proportion (44 percent in 1991) of CDIA (Rao, Legault & Ahmad, this volume). Within the manufacturing sector, there was some broadening of industry representation. In particular, the share of technology-intensive industries in the stock of CDIA has increased substantially over the past 30 years.

The United States remains the major geographic location for CDIA, although the concentration of direct investment in the United States is decreasing, notwithstanding the fact that Canada's trade with the United States has become more concentrated over the past decade. The U.S. share of CDIA declined from a peak of 68.5 percent in 1980 to 58 percent in 1992. Interestingly, Canadian direct investment in Asian countries has not "taken off" with the rapid economic growth in that region; however, CDIA in Europe has become increasingly prominent, apparently in response to the formation of the European Community.

A noteworthy feature of the CDIA process is that there is a high concentration among a relatively small number of Canadian firms. Rao, Legault & Ahmad report that there are just over 1,300 Canadian-based multinational enterprises (MNEs), a total which represents less than .2 percent of all Canadian non-financial business establishments. Chow further notes that at the end of 1991 fully 93 percent of CDIA was held by slightly less than 15 percent of Canadian MNEs. In fact, the direct investment process is highly concentrated globally. Specifically, in 1992, the top 1 percent of MNEs accounted for almost 50 percent of the total world stock of outward direct investment (Rao, Legault & Ahmad, this volume).

These statistical analyses of CDIA highlight several characteristics. One is that conventional images of CDIA as being largely natural resource-based are incorrect and increasingly anachronistic. A second, related to the first, is that secondary manufacturing and service industries are increasingly prominent participants in CDIA. In these sectors market access is critical to exploiting fully latent economies of scale. Improved market access is particularly relevant for a small open economy such as Canada's. Indeed, Swedish direct investment abroad appears to have been driven by a similar motivation, and Sweden's is also a small, open economy. In contrast, Japanese direct investment abroad seems to be more strongly motivated by high domestic labour costs than is true for Canada or Sweden, although improved market access has clearly been of major importance in the automotive sector.

A FRAMEWORK FOR ASSESSING CDIA

IN ASSESSING THE LITERATURE on direct investment abroad and presenting an overview of this volume, it is useful to have a conceptual framework within which the private and public interests in direct investment abroad can be evaluated.

PRIVATE INTEREST MOTIVATIONS

AN UNDERLYING PREMISE to this conceptual framework is that firms will invest abroad if they expect such investments to increase their net present values or, equivalently, their long-run discounted profits. Increased net present value can, in turn, reflect an increase in net revenues and/or a decrease in the organization's cost of capital (for example, through a reduction in risk). A related premise is that firms will tend to ignore the effects of their direct investments abroad on third parties, and it is this phenomenon that primarily gives rise to the notion of "too much" or "too little" direct investment abroad being undertaken from the home country's overall social perspective.[7]

For the individual firm, expected increases in net revenues can result from lower costs and/or higher revenues. Opportunities to lower costs have been identified as a durable motive for direct investment abroad. Lower costs can be associated with a variety of factors: access to cheaper inputs such as natural resources, labour and management; avoidance of transaction costs such as tariffs and transportation; improved efficiency associated with the exploitation of economies of scale and scope; and the faster adoption of foreign-developed technology and related factors.[8]

Opportunities to increase revenues are less direct, but have also been noted in the relevant literature. They can be associated, for example, with an enhanced ability to serve customers by being proximate to them and therefore able to charge higher prices. They might also be associated with an enhancement of market power, for example, if direct investment abroad takes the form of acquisitions of foreign competitors. In these cases, home-country MNEs may be able to realize higher price-cost margins by exploiting market power.

The risk-reduction benefits of direct investment abroad are more subtle. Financial economists identify two kinds of risk: systematic and non-systematic. Systematic risk is associated with fluctuating business cycle conditions. Since specific economic activities are affected differently over the course of the business cycle, systematic risk can presumably be reduced by holding a diversified portfolio of businesses. To the extent that business cycle conditions are only imperfectly correlated across countries, additional diversification benefits can be gained, in principle, by holding a portfolio of businesses that is internationally as well as sectorally diversified.

If home-country MNEs are uniquely or even more favourably equipped to identify and take advantage of investment opportunities abroad, share-holders in those companies will recognize the risk diversification benefits provided by direct investment abroad. In turn, home country MNEs should enjoy lower costs of capital (and higher net present values) than purely domestic firms. On the other hand, if shareholders can invest abroad directly, for example by using mutual funds, with no higher cost or loss of efficiency, there would be no systematic risk reduction supplied by investments made by home-country MNEs and no increased valuation placed on the shares of those companies.

Non-systematic risk is, by definition, non-diversifiable. It reflects unique characteristics of a specific investment such as the potential for expropriation. To the extent that shareholders view foreign investments as being more risky (in the non-systematic sense) than domestic investments, direct investment abroad would reduce the capitalized value of the home-country MNE, all other things being constant. On the other hand, it is possible that many investors might view such attributes as the risk of expropriation as being lower abroad than in the home country. In these cases, direct investment abroad would reduce average risk for shareholders, and home country-based companies would be worth more to domestic investors.

In many cases the benefits derived from direct investment abroad can be obtained to a greater or lesser degree by other governance structures such as licensing, joint-venturing or other so-called strategic alliances. Presumably the firm undertaking the direct investment compares the various options and chooses the governance structure providing the greatest contribution to its long-run discounted profitability. In fact, relatively little is known about the precise nature of the potential trade-off between establishing overseas affiliates and entering into alliances such as joint ventures, a point discussed in some detail by Globerman & Wolf elsewhere in this volume.

Some observers of strategic alliancing argue that alliancing is primarily a second-best alternative to direct investment abroad given that host-country restrictions often exist on inward direct investment; however, as Contractor (1990) notes, such restrictions tend to be more relevant in the case of developing countries than in the case of developed countries. In the latter case, alliances are more likely to reflect other motives than circumventing host government restrictions on foreign control and/or ownership.

In some cases, as Globerman & Wolf note, alliances are undertaken for specific activities that are unlikely to become the focus of outward direct investment. In other cases, where direct investment is a plausible alternative, alliances such as joint ventures may be preferred because they involve more limited financial commitments, or lower transaction costs associated with merging entire organizations while learning takes place among the participants in the venture.

The disadvantages of alliances relate to problems associated with risks of opportunistic behaviour on the part of the parties to the alliance. Simply put, these parties have identical profit functions and, hence, have incentives to shift profits from other parties to themselves. This incentive, in turn, creates a need for parties to monitor each other's behaviour more closely than would be the case if the activities in question were undertaken by an integrated firm.[9]

Globerman & Wolf suggest that, given the concentration of CDIA in the United States, Canadian MNEs may have less incentive to undertake joint ventures that other MNEs. The United States imposes relatively few legal or regulatory restrictions on inward foreign direct investment. Moreover, Canadian firms tend to have a high degree of familiarity with the U.S. market.

Policy Implications

Presumably, private, for-profit organizations invest abroad when they expect such investments to increase their net present values; this is not to say that all direct investments are profitable or reduce risk. Indeed, evidence reviewed below suggests that certain classes of firms have experienced below-average returns on their direct investments abroad. In this regard, the case study of MacMillan Bloedel by Vertinsky & Raizada in this volume documents a number of the company's foreign direct investments that were unprofitable or undesirable for some other reason.

It is unclear how home-country governments might improve foreign investment decisions made by home-country firms. To the extent that information is imperfect and home-country firms are systematically ignorant about profitable opportunities abroad, there may be a role for home governments to play in identifying such opportunities. However, at least in the Canadian case, there is no evidence that home-country firms are systematically eschewing privately profitable direct investment abroad. Indeed, four studies in this volume are relevant to this point. Chow and Rao, Legault & Ahmad document the rapid growth rate of CDIA over the past decade. The case study of Northern Telecom by Amesse, Séguin-Dulude & Stanley documents Northern Telecom's direct investments abroad. And the study by Globerman & Wolf concludes that the modest amount of international joint-venturing done by Canadian firms reflects the advantage of direct investment over joint ventures for Canadian MNEs. It does not necessarily reflect an inefficient amount of strategic joint venturing.

The case studies of MacMillan Bloedel and Northern Telecom document that decisions to invest abroad are rooted each company's overall corporate strategy, and the ultimate success of the investment undertaken is importantly conditioned by the merits of the firm's corporate and competitive strategies. These studies provide no reason to believe that governments can improve on the strategies developed by private-sector managers. Rather, the relevant policy implication seems to be that home governments should try to ensure that home country firms enjoy access to the widest investment universe possible. In so doing, home-country firms would face minimal constraints in matching capital investment decisions to their corporate and competitive strategies.

PUBLIC INTEREST CONCERNS

FROM AN OVERALL SOCIAL PERSPECTIVE direct investments abroad are desirable if they improve net social welfare. In the absence of an explicit social welfare function, two primary attributes of social welfare are typically considered: real national income levels and distribution of national income. All other things constant, policies that increase the real income of domestic residents are desirable. Moreover, greater equality of income is preferred to greater inequality at all levels of national income.

To the extent that direct investment abroad increases the wealth of home country shareholders, *ceteris paribus*, it contributes to increased national income and is consistent with the public interest. The public interest in direct investment abroad may differ from the private interest to the extent that an increase in the expected wealth of domestic shareholders is more than offset by decreases in the wealth of other home-country residents. At a minimum, public policy makers may want to ensure that those domestic residents made worse off by direct investment are compensated. If compensation is difficult or costly, policy makers may want to discourage the relevant investments.

Alternatively, it is possible that direct investment abroad increases the expected wealth of domestic residents (other than domestic shareholders) so that foreign direct investments that are unprofitable *ex ante* promise to increase overall real national income. In this case, policy makers have a legitimate incentive to encourage the private sector to undertake more direct investment abroad than they otherwise would.

Externalities

The greatest potential source of a divergence between the private and public interests in direct investment abroad is the presence of external costs and benefits. Specifically, where certain effects of direct investment abroad are experienced by third-parties and are ignored by those undertaking the investment, significant external benefits or costs may create a divergence between the resulting private and social consequences.

In the foreign direct investment literature the externalities rationale for government intervention is frequently related to the issue of national competitiveness. Specifically, certain patterns of outward direct investment are seen as improving the ability of domestic firms generally to compete in international markets. Porter (1991) makes this argument in the context of Canadian multinational companies. He argues that foreign operations, particularly in the U.S. market, can strengthen the Canadian "diamond" by making available the services of skills that are not present in Canada on a cost-effective basis. Serving a sophisticated market of U.S. buyers at "close range" might also help keep Canadian firms apprised of the direction of global needs and stimulate the development of better products and services. However, Porter cautions against "over-reliance" on foreign technology and related skills which may adversely affect the innovative capabilities of the home country.

Porter's caution about excessive outward direct investment relates mainly to the potential for such investment to stimulate technological change abroad rather than in the home country. More typically, the argument is that outward direct investment stimulates innovation in the home country. One route is *via* its effect on research and development (R&D) spending. To the extent that outward direct investment stimulates net sales made by home-country companies, it provides a broader revenue base over which research and development expenditures can be amortized. Mansfield et al. (1982) have identified the stimulative effect that sales of foreign affiliates can have on research and development expenditures by the parent company, particularly in light of the general desirability of internalizing the results of research and development rather than licensing the new technology.

The case study by Amesse, Séguin-Dulude and Stanley documents how Northern Telecom's foreign investment activities stimulated research and development in Northern's central laboratory in Ottawa. Increased expenditures on promoting technological change, on R&D for example, presumably enhance the ability of the performing firms to introduce new and improved products and/or production techniques which, in turn, promote increased demand for their products in foreign and domestic markets and/or increase the profit margin that those firms can expect to realize on international sales. To the extent that the firms performing R&D capture all of the associated benefits, the linkage between direct investment abroad and technological change will be internalized in the decisions of home-country multinationals. However, to the extent that some of the benefits of R&D are captured by other domestic firms, the linkage is not completely internalized, and it might be concluded that there will be too little outward direct investment under the circumstances.[10] In fact, promoting increased outward direct investment is an unlikely policy response in this context. Rather, it would presumably be more efficient to stimulate increased domestic R&D more directly – through government subsidies or tax incentives, for example. Nevertheless, the existence of such externalities is a strong argument against the home government discouraging direct investment abroad.

Research and development expenditures are only one set of overhead activities that might be stimulated by outward direct investment. Others include industrial design, marketing, and trademark promotion. To the extent that these activities are characterized by economies of scale, sales in foreign markets offer a potentially larger revenue base over which to amortize such expenditures, thereby stimulating increases in those activities and greater firm-level advantages for the companies undertaking the activities. Again, if the benefits of the activities are less than fully captured by the relevant home-country multinationals, the indirect benefits of outward direct investment are realized by a broader set of domestic firms than the MNEs in question.

Another positive linkage between outward direct investment and the capabilities of domestic firms to introduce improved and/or cheaper products derives from the potential for the activities of home country MNE affiliates to accelerate the diffusion of new technology from foreign markets to the home country. The relevant notion here is that a physical presence in foreign markets facilitates faster and/or improved understanding of new technologies being used in those markets.[11] The Northern Telecom case study details how recently established R&D labs in the United States and Europe are expected to facilitate a reverse flow of technology back to the central R&D lab in Ottawa.

As noted earlier, Porter (1990) identifies the potential for direct investment abroad to weaken the innovative capabilities of the home country. This may be true if, for example, home-country affiliates relocate R&D activities to foreign affiliates. If the relocation of R&D leads to spillover benefits being captured by foreign-owned firms, the demand for products made by home-country firms might be adversely affected both in foreign markets and in the home-country market.[12]

Similarly, direct investment abroad might stimulate the faster adoption of new technology by foreign-based competitors. One possibility is that the physical presence of home-country affiliates in foreign markets facilitates "technological copying" by host-country firms – say through human capital transfers as employees in foreign affiliates relocate to domestically owned firms. Another possibility is that observing foreign affiliates using new technology might reduce the perceived risks that discourage host-country firms from adopting the technology. In either case, home-country firms may find themselves with reduced demand for their products in foreign and domestic markets at existing prices.

McFetridge (this volume) considers these possibilities in detail. He notes that R&D conducted in foreign affiliates can be geared toward "pure" knowledge creation or to specific manufacturing applications. While the former may give rise to spillover benefits captured largely by foreign-owned firms, appropriation of the latter may be restricted by its embodiment in firm-specific production techniques. Alternatively, R&D dedicated to manufacturing applications may assist foreign-owned firms to supply inputs more efficiently to the home-country MNE. In effect, the home-country MNE indirectly internalizes the benefits of R&D by enjoying lower costs of inputs and components. For example, R&D carried out in Northern Telecom's foreign-based labs has traditionally been focused on adapting products to accommodate the needs of foreign buyers; however, these labs are increasingly likely to undertake more knowledge-creating R&D, probably as part of a mandate to produce specific products for an international market.

Whether the potentially adverse effects of relocating R&D facilities abroad will justify home-government restrictions on outward direct investment is a speculative point regardless of its empirical magnitude, especially given the substantial administrative and other costs likely to be associated with monitoring investment behaviour and enforcing restrictions. In this regard McFetridge concludes that any losses to the home country due to increased leakages or foregone spillover benefits are likely to be small, relative to those that would be incurred if the foreign market were not served at all. More realistically, the existence of negative externalities would caution against the home government directly or indirectly encouraging direct investment abroad at the expense of investment in the home country.

Effects on Labour Markets

Most of the public policy concern about direct investment abroad has been (and continues to be) focused on its potential effect on the labour market. Specifically, as Gunderson & Verma (this volume) describe, the concern is that direct investment abroad will reduce the demand for domestic labour with resulting lower domestic wages and/or increased domestic unemployment (all other things constant). Even if the relocation of production abroad leads to higher profits for shareholders in the home country, the resulting redistribution of income from labour to capital might be socially undesirable; so might a redistribution from low-skilled to high-skilled workers. If labour markets fail to equate the supply of and demand for labour, there is also the fear that reduced demand for domestic labour may lead to prolonged periods of domestic unemployment with attendant social costs.

Gunderson & Verma offer a comprehensive overview of the potential domestic labour-market effects of direct investment abroad. They emphasize the well-recognized caveat that the long-run effects of direct investment abroad may offset the short-run effects. Many critics of outward direct investment discount this possibility by implicitly assuming that there is a fixed number of jobs in the economy, so that a loss of some existing jobs implies a reduction in aggregate employment. Gunderson & Verma refer to this assumption as the "lump-of-labour fallacy".

Gunderson & Verma also discuss the link between the "mix" of domestic jobs and direct investment abroad. The most typical argument is that direct investment abroad is associated with the loss of low-skill jobs in the domestic economy, as production activities are relocated abroad. At the same time, overhead and support occupations in activities such as R&D and marketing increase as the domestic firm grows larger through expansion in foreign markets. In effect, the international specialization of labour promoted by domestic MNEs is manifested in a replacement of low-productivity, low-wage domestic jobs by high-productivity, high-wage domestic jobs. While arm's-length exporting and importing also contributes to the international specialization of labour, the MNE is arguably a vehicle for accelerating and deepening this specialization.

To be sure, a different view of the home-country labour market effects of direct investment abroad has been offered; namely, that direct investment abroad leads to the relocation abroad of domestic manufacturing jobs paying above-average wages to be replaced by lower-paying manufacturing or service sector jobs. The study by Blomström & Kokko in this volume raises this concern in the context of Sweden, although the uneasiness is quite recent, and the relevant evidence is, at best, only suggestive.

To the extent that increased imports of foreign manufactured goods would lead to decreased demand for employees in home-country manufacturing industries, direct investment abroad could, at worst, be accused of accelerating a trend that would have occurred in any case. This relatively sanguine view is strengthened to the extent that above-average wages in domestic manufacturing industries are a function of union power rather than superior productivity. Nevertheless, it can be argued that the threat of job losses to domestic workers is greater precisely because MNE employers are relatively mobile. This greater mobility might, on the one hand, encourage increased productivity and workplace discipline. On the other hand, it might serve to discourage employee investment in on-the-job training or discourage emotional commitment to home-country MNE organizations with attendant adverse effects on productivity.

Gunderson & Verma also discuss the effects of direct investment abroad on home country labour-market institutions. They argue that inefficient labour market institutions will be threatened by such investment. If no useful "non-economic" objectives are served by these institutions, they should disappear. If broader social objectives are served, explicit subsidies may be required.

The labour-market effects of direct investment abroad will depend upon two factors: the importance of labour costs in the MNE's overall location decision; and the effect of actual and potential MNE decisions on the demand for labour. However, some of these effects may not be the result of the particular MNEs in question, but rather of a combination of events. For example, if many domestic MNEs decide to relocate simultaneously, the ensuing labour-market effects may lead to more prolonged periods of unemployment than would otherwise be the case. On the other hand, the mobility of MNEs' activities may lead to more efficient labour-market practices. For instance, the competitive discipline exerted on the labour market by direct investment abroad may spread to other domestically owned firms, thereby conferring external benefits to the labour market as a whole. In short, the labour-market effects of direct investment abroad may have social significance due to redistribution effects as a result of prolonged periods of unemployment and because of spillover effects associated with labour market adjustment processes.

Effects on Trade and Balance of Payments

The broad-based effects of direct investment abroad on the home country's trade and capital balances have long been a major focus of examinations of direct investment abroad. More recently the focus has been on the linkage between direct investment abroad and international competitiveness. This volume does not attempt to evaluate the various definitions of competitiveness found in the economics and business literature. Rather, it adopts as a policy premise (as elaborated upon by Rugman's study in this volume) that the competitiveness of firms will reflect their specific advantages which, in turn, will be affected by the specific advantages of the countries in which they do business.

Firm-specific advantages are, presumably, manifested in the ability of domestically headquartered producers to sell products at higher prices than their foreign-based counterparts and/or to sell greater quantities of output at the same prices charged by foreign-based rivals, all other things constant. These advantages will not necessarily be reflected in a growing trade surplus. For one thing, a substantial portion of exports to third countries may be made from foreign affiliates, rather than from the home-country affiliate. Also, fluctuating exchange rates should eliminate, or at least mitigate, persistent overall trade surpluses or deficits.

While international competitiveness is not necessarily linked directly to domestic trade balances, the international competitiveness of domestic firms could have broader social consequences beyond the profitability of those firms. Specifically, to the extent that enhanced advantages of domestically owned MNEs ultimately lead to improvements in the home country's terms of trade, either through increases in export prices (or decreases in import prices) denominated in the home country's currency or through appreciation in the home country's currency, real income gains can be bestowed on home-country consumers or factors of production in export industries.

To be sure, it is difficult to identify changes in the terms of trade as they relate to direct investment abroad. In particular, prices (including the exchange rate) are volatile and more subject to "overshooting" or "under-shooting" than real quantities of exports and imports. This may explain, in part, the focus on trade flows in previous studies of the effects of direct investment abroad on the home-country economy; however, a terms-of-trade rationale ultimately underlies a preference for technology-intensive or fast growing industries that characterizes a number of studies of international competitiveness. The (usually implicit) notion is that producers in these industries can charge above-average price-cost markups, thereby earning "quasi-rents" which support higher payments to domestic factors of production.

In his study for this volume, Graham discusses theory and evidence linking direct investment abroad and exports on the one hand, and direct investment abroad and domestic capital formation on the other. He suggests that the recent literature emphasizing the importance of external economies of scale as determinants of international production is likely to be more relevant than traditional models of international production, particularly when examining the linkage between direct investment abroad and trade for Canada. While this theory does not predict unequivocally that CDIA and exports will be complementary, it certainly implies this relationship.

Graham notes that if the domestic economy is already at full employment, increased exports will come at the expense of reduced production for the domestic market; however, sectoral shifts in output can imply higher wages and higher returns to capital. Because higher returns to capital stimulate increased domestic investment, the economy should be pushed onto a higher income growth path. To be sure, Blomström & Kokko caution against assuming that sectoral shifts in output associated with international specialization will necessarily lead to higher payments to domestic factors of production.

Government Taxes and Regulations

Early models of foreign direct investment stressed the role of imperfect capital markets in promoting direct investment abroad. In this view, MNEs earned economic rent by capitalizing on an ability to enter markets characterized by economic rent. Later models stressed the ability of MNEs to earn economic rent by creating and exploiting market power in international markets. In an earlier study, Horst (1976) raises the possibility that the higher domestic profits of U.S. MNEs reflect the potential for foreign investment to increase the domestic monopoly power of multinational firms.

In the relevant models, the distribution of the rents between host- and home-country residents depends in part on the tax policies of the home and host countries. In fact, whatever the source of any underlying economic benefits realized by MNEs, home-country governments must be concerned about whether and how their tax policies are affecting decisions to invest abroad. Governments must also consider the distribution of the "payoffs" from going abroad, especially as between host- and home-country factors of production.

As the study by Brean contends, government tax policy has both a positive and normative component with respect to direct investment abroad. The positive issue is whether government fiscal policy affects direct investment flows. In this connection, government fiscal policy might be thought of as the effective burden of domestic taxes levied on home country-based businesses net of the value of government services received by those businesses. The conventional wisdom is that MNEs will relocate economic activities, on the margin, from jurisdictions with relatively high effective corporate tax rates to those with relatively low effective corporate tax rates.

A closely related notion is that government regulatory policies will influence the geographical location of economic activity. Indeed, one important aspect of the recent debate surrounding the NAFTA is whether corporations in the United States and Canada will relocate production facilities to Mexico, where the enforcement of environmental regulations is perceived to be much weaker than in the United States or Canada. At the same time, mining companies in British Columbia have complained vociferously about how provincial government land use policies are driving local companies to relocate their mining and processing activities in Chile.

The normative issue is whether governments should intervene through fiscal policies either to promote or discourage direct investment abroad by home-country MNEs. Brean identifies and discusses a number of tax code features which can affect location decisions of MNEs, as well as the international competitiveness of home-country MNEs. In particular, Brean identifies the treatment of domestic R&D expenditures as especially important. He suggests that Canada's already favourable treatment of R&D be made even more favourable, for example, by raising and/or broadening the R&D tax credit base. Brean also indicates concern about transfer pricing practices being used by Canadian MNEs to reduce taxes paid by those firms. He sees the avoidance of arm's-length pricing on inter-company transactions as particularly inappropriate when home-country MNEs are exploiting abroad products developed in Canada with significant direct or indirect government fiscal support.

In substance, the literature directly or indirectly identifies various potential effects of direct investment abroad which can create a divergence between the purely private and the social benefits and costs of direct investment abroad. It also identifies the potential for direct investment abroad to have non-neutral effects with respect to income levels and other characteristics of home-country residents. Adverse distributional effects, along with any negative allocative externalities, could render specific patterns of direct investment abroad socially less desirable than would be suggested exclusively from the effects on the investing firms. Conversely, positive allocative externalities and/or favourable redistributive effects could enhance the overall desirability of specific investments. Whether third-party allocative effects or distributive effects are typically large enough to warrant government intervention is fundamentally an empirical issue. Findings bearing on the magnitude of the private and social effects of direct investment abroad are reviewed in the two sections following.

Private Effects of Direct Investment Abroad

STATED OR INFERRED MOTIVES for undertaking direct investment abroad offer a potential insight into the anticipated private effects of such investment. This section will review evidence bearing upon motivations for undertaking direct investment abroad, as well as the actual effects of direct investment on investors.

Motives For Direct Investment Abroad

EVIDENCE ON MOTIVES for undertaking direct investment abroad take two main forms: surveys in which managers are asked to explain their reasons for undertaking direct investment abroad, and statistical studies of foreign direct investment from the perspective of the home country, in which motives for investment are inferred from the statistical results.

Survey Evidence

A comprehensive summary of the relevant evidence is provided by Dunning (1993). Most of the relevant evidence he discusses comes from surveys of managers and suggests that there is a wide variety of influences on a firm's decision to invest abroad, and that the relevance of specific influences depends upon the nature of the direct investment. For example, the availability of resources at relatively low cost is a critical motive for resource-based direct investment abroad. Similarly, tax and other fiscal inducements offered by governments appear to be more important determinants of outward investment driven by a search for cost reduction than for investment motivated by other objectives.

Many factors are cited for market-seeking investments, including the size and growth of host markets relative to expansion opportunities in the home country, the relative costs of producing goods in different countries, the extent to which product adaptation and customization are required, and the need to diversify risks and cross-boarder transfer costs, including transportation costs and trade barriers.

For efficiency-seeking investments of the production rationalization type, the availability of indigenous resources and capabilities and the avoidance of cross-boarder transportation and other transfer costs are frequently mentioned. In particular, the availability of relatively low-cost skilled labour and relatively low transportation and communications costs are significant, as they reflect the importance of co-ordination in realizing efficiency gains from production rationalization. Finally, the evidence suggests that the acquisition of technology and market information has been a particularly important motive for strategic asset-oriented direct investment in the United States.

Dunning notes that only a few case studies and surveys specifically address the question of why firms undertake direct investment abroad rather than adopt some other mode of international business, such as licensing foreign firms to use their proprietary technology. The results along with other "casual empiricism" tend to support the internalization motive: i.e., firms choose to establish affiliates abroad in order to lower cross-border transaction costs. Elsewhere in this volume Globerman & Wolf provide additional case study evidence that firms often engage in joint ventures to facilitate learning about uncertain environments while mitigating large sunk cost investments associated with the learning process. In this context, direct investment becomes increasingly favourable over time as learning ensues.

A number of surveys identify motives for Canadian firms to undertake direct investments abroad. One recent study (Knubley, Krause & Sadeque, 1991) surveyed a cross-section of 23 Canadian firms with direct investments abroad. This study concentrated on larger firms, although there was considerable variation in firm sizes across the sample. Surveyed firms were asked to rate the importance of 17 factors in motivating their foreign investment strategy. No attempt was made to stratify responses by the nature of the direct investment undertaken: e.g. market expansion. The factors identified as being most significant were the perceived need for outward expansion; geographic product line diversification; and trade barriers and transportation costs. The next two factors cited were availability of skilled labour and favourable regulations abroad. Factors ranking particularly low in the survey included supplementing exports; forward and backward integration; and Canadian taxes and regulations.

Knubley, Krause & Sadeque compare their results with those of other Canadian surveys. They conclude that their findings are broadly consistent with those of previous studies, particularly with respect to the emphasis given by respondents to "pull" factors in the foreign environment rather than to "push" factors in the domestic environment. Their findings also agree with those of other surveys showing that trade barriers and transportation costs are important influences on the location decisions of Canadian multinationals.[13]

The relative importance of push factors should not be considered irrelevant. Certainly, if more favourable regulations abroad are a relevant stimulus, they represent an implicit mix of push and pull factors, since they are by definition more favourable than regulations established by Canadian policy makers. Moreover, at least one study cites push factors such as trade union attributes and relatively high unit labour costs in Canada.[14]

The case studies of Northern Telecom and MacMillan Bloedel in this volume provide additional evidence on motives for CDIA. In the MacMillan Bloedel case there are two dominant recurring motives for direct investment abroad: securing resources through backward integration; and securing markets through forward integration in order to gain the benefits of economies of scale. The need to exploit economies of scale has also been a strong motive for Northern Telecom to internationalize its operations. The need to be close to foreign customers in order to modify products quickly to their needs, as well as to avoid tariff and non-tariff barriers, motivated Northern's decision to serve foreign markets primarily through wholly owned affiliates. The Blomström and Kokko study notes that Swedish firms have been motivated to establish foreign affiliates for much the same reasons as Northern Telecom.

In summary, given the variations across surveys in research methodology, sample coverage and time periods, it is impossible to harmonize reported differences in motives for direct investment abroad; however, Canadian survey results do not seem anomalous. Given the historical prominence of natural resource-based MNEs in Canada, the search for lower cost resources might be expected to constitute an especially important motive mentioned by Canadian managers.[15] In fact, improved access to foreign markets also appears to be an important motive for direct investment abroad by Canadian resource-based companies, and (as elsewhere) it appears to be a dominant motive for direct investment abroad by non-resource based companies.

Statistical Evidence

Several empirical studies provide evidence that direct investment enhances the profitability of firms undertaking this investment. For example, Bergsten, Horst & Moran (1978) examined the period from 1965 to 1971 and concluded that higher foreign investment results in higher domestic profits. Wolf (1975) studied performance for two years, 1962 and 1966, and found that foreign investors were more profitable than non-foreign investors. Leftwich (1974), on the basis of 1966 and 1970 data, determined that multinational firms were more profitable than purely domestic firms. Severn & Laurence (1974) found that those with foreign investments were more profitable in 1965 that those without. While they concluded that R&D intensity, rather than foreign involvement, *per se*, explained the performance difference, it can also be argued that R&D performance is stimulated by foreign involvement.[16]

Daniels & Bracker (1989) considered whether (among other things) the association between dependence on foreign operations and profit performance is monotonic. They use a sample of 116 U.S. companies distributed over seven broad industrial groupings for the period from 1974 to 1983. They employ two measures of dependence of foreign operations: foreign sales as a percentage of total sales; and foreign assets as a percentage of total assets. In both cases, observations were classified into six intervals ranging from 0 percent to 10 percent to 50 percent and above. They found that returns on both sales and assets improved significantly with increased dependence on foreign production up through the 40 percent to 50 percent interval.

In a similar study, Geringer, Beamish & da Costa (1991) found that as the degree of internalization of MNEs reached higher values, performance (as measured by profit-to-sales and profit-to-total assets) also exhibited increased values but then peaked and exhibited diminished levels of performance. Consistent with other work in the strategic management literature, MNEs pursuing related diversification strategies over an extended period of time tended to achieve significantly superior performance.

To be sure, there are studies which conclude that there is no systematic relationship between profitability and international diversification.[17] However, these studies also tend to conclude that profit stability is significantly related to international diversification.

Several studies in this volume provide additional evidence on the effects of direct investment abroad on the profitability of MNEs. Rao, Legault & Ahmad find that the growth and productivity performances of outward-oriented Canadian-based firms, on average, tend to be superior to the performances of domestically oriented Canadian-based firms, which suggests that the profitability of outward-oriented firms should also be higher. Indeed, they find that outward-oriented firms outperformed domestically oriented firms by a large margin in terms of the average rate-of-return on capital from 1986 to 1991. The Rao, Legault & Ahmad findings contradict earlier findings by Corvari & Wisner (1991) that establishments of Canadian MNEs had lower labour productivity levels than national firms. It should be noted that the Corvari & Wisner analysis was based on a small number of Canadian MNEs. Moreover, there was substantial variance in their findings across industries.

In their study in this volume Ries & Head look at annual average returns on sales and assets for 1,070 publicly listed Japanese manufacturing firms during the 1980s. They classify this sample into MNEs and non-MNEs. MNEs have higher returns on sales and faster sales growth than do non-MNEs. Returns on assets are similar for both groups. After standardizing for industry, they find that MNEs have significantly higher returns on sales, although they have no different sales growth relative to non-MNEs.

Again, there is some Canadian evidence that direct investment abroad can be unprofitable *ex post*. Indeed, Vertinsky & Raizada document the significant losses experienced by MacMillan Bloedel on a number of direct investments abroad.[18] Chow notes that many smaller Canadian firms incurred losses on their foreign direct investments, especially in 1989 and 1990, while larger direct investors did not generate much profit from their substantial capital bases abroad.

In summary, outward direct investment appears to increase the profitability of companies; however, it is not always clear from the literature why this is so. In this regard, there is some evidence that the linkage between direct investment abroad and profitability is not uniform across industries. For example, Daniels & Bracker (1989) found that among the high-technology firms in their sample, there was no significant difference in profit performance between those with a high dependence on foreign sales as compared to those with a low dependence on foreign sales.

They explain this result in part by the relatively small share of total costs ascribable to R&D expenditures. Hence, spreading R&D costs over foreign sales is unlikely to reduce average costs by any significant amount. Furthermore, the "life-cycle" hypothesis argues that the home country is likely to be the most efficient production location for new products. Hence, producing new products in overseas affiliates will arguably dissipate the home-country advantages of technological leaders. By contrast, among very capital-intensive firms, a high reliance on either foreign sales or foreign production resulted in significantly greater returns on both sales and assets. Their explanation is that by the time firms are engaged in capital-intensive production, they are usually competing with fairly standardized products. Even with concurrent product differentiation strategies, competitive pricing is very important. In this regard, foreign sales may reduce average unit costs, and foreign production may enable the firm to acquire cheaper inputs.

In a related study, Kim & Lyn (1990) found that foreign firms operating in the United States are less profitable than randomly selected U.S. firms. These foreign-based multinational companies spend more on R&D and less on advertising than U.S. firms, an observation consistent with the hypothesis that overseas investment may not generate quasi-rents for firms involved in high-technology activities. Empirically, the excess market value for foreign-based multinational companies was related to three factors: leverage; liquidity; and firm size. The latter might be taken as a proxy for the presence of firm-level economies of scale.

Daniels & Bracker's (1989) analysis emphasized benefits associated with economies of scale and access to lower cost inputs. While economies of scale can be associated with production, they can also be associated with marketing activities. Their analysis begs the question, "Why do technologically intensive firms invest abroad if there is no 'profit-premium' compared to domestic investment?"

The case study of Northern Telecom provides some evidence on why a high-technology firm invests abroad. In Northern's case, the location of production facilities abroad facilitated market penetration since an ongoing and relatively close working relationship with local telephone company operators is required in the telecommunications equipment area. It is difficult to have an effective relationship which (in part) involves the ability to anticipate and meet customer requirements without a local presence.

Furthermore, it is beneficial to locate R&D facilities in the host country to adapt home-country-developed technologies to host-country customer requirements. In turn, the increased sales in foreign markets enables home-country MNEs to operate at a larger scale which facilitates increased R&D performance in the home-country affiliate.

In short, the Northern Telecom experience suggests that expansion of firm size in the telecommunications industry requires establishing foreign affiliates. Moreover, the increasing fixed costs associated with R&D activities are placing an increasing premium on attaining a large firm size. Hence, it may be that as R&D becomes more expensive in other high-technology industries, a positive relationship between returns on sales and assets and foreign sales and production will be more readily identifiable.

It may also be that studies focusing on profitability, which use equity capital as a base for standardizing earnings, obscure the identification of superior profits. This would be true if the advantages of multinational investment are "priced into" the securities of MNEs and significant changes in the degree of "internationalization" did not take place during the sample period. (Eddy & Seifert, 1989).

In summary, available studies tend to identify higher profitability and productivity associated with direct investment abroad. The causal link appears to be associated with improved efficiency which, in turn, may be at least partly the consequence of a more intensive exploitation of economics of scale and slope. Direct investment abroad does not seem to create any significant additional risks to shareholders. Indeed, it may provide some diversification of business cycle risks, although investors can probably enjoy most of these benefits already through portfolio investing. Taken as a whole, companies have incentives to make direct investments abroad which mitigates arguments in favour of government actions to promote such investment, especially given the potential for social rates of return to exceed private rates of return.

SOCIAL EFFECTS OF DIRECT INVESTMENT ABROAD

THE EMPIRICAL LITERATURE concerned with the broader social effects of direct investment abroad is relatively limited compared to the literature on the causes and consequences of inward direct investment. There is, however, some emerging consensus on several issues.

LABOUR MARKETS

AS SUGGESTED BY GUNDERSON & VERMA, the evidence on the effects of direct investment abroad on home-country labour markets is relatively consistent in identifying the differential effects on skilled and unskilled workers. For example, Campbell & McElrath (1990) concluded with considerable certainty that U.S. foreign direct investment abroad adversely affects the interests of low-skilled blue-collar workers while enlarging the opportunities for those classified as white collar or highly skilled. This raises the average skill level of the domestic labour force but may impose labour market adjustment problems. In a similar vein, Kravis & Lipsey (1990) found that the more a U.S. multinational firm produces abroad, the higher the average skill level of its U.S. employees. In their review of direct investment abroad from European countries, Buckley & Brooke (1992) interpreted the available evidence as suggesting that the jobs added or maintained by direct investment abroad are of a higher skill level than those lost. This suggests that foreign direct investment is an important mechanism for restructuring the home economy towards higher value-added activities.

The study by Ries & Head provides evidence for Japan that multinational expansion raises domestic wages. This result is strongly conditioned by the fact that Japanese electronics firms have transferred the less skill-intensive jobs to Southeast Asia. As discussed earlier, Blomström & Kokko note a recent concern that Swedish MNEs may be moving some higher value-added activities abroad. To the extent that this is true, it may reflect the relocation of activities where workers are being paid economic rent associated with union power rather than where highly educated workers are a relatively intensive factor of production. This would seem to explain why MacMillan Bloedel has also been relocating some of its relatively high value-added activities abroad.

There is less agreement on the effects of direct investment abroad on aggregate employment. Buckley & Artisien (1987) underscored the importance of assumptions about the substitutability of exporting for producing abroad in conditioning expectations regarding the overall effect of outward foreign direct investment on employment – an issue elaborated upon at length by Gunderson & Verma. In Buckley & Artisien's (1987) study of a variety of industries, they found that the substitution possibilities vary across industries and over time. In several cases, exports were replaced by direct investment with a consequent reduction in source-country employment. In other cases, the increase in balancing exports (sub-assemblies, intermediate goods, technology flows) compensated for the fall in final goods exports. In yet other cases, the ability of a direct presence to penetrate a previously closed market actually increased home-country employment. There are also cases where the multinational would have lost the market to competitors had it not invested, and so some job preservation took place. Some additional evidence on the substitutability of host- and home-country production is provided by Shepherd, Silberston & Strange (1985). They found that 50 percent of their U.K. MNE respondents thought they could have continued to export from the home market, while the other 50 percent thought they would have lost the foreign markets. Among those who felt that exporting could have continued, many felt that some reductions in exports would have taken place. The authors did not indicate whether the survey response results would have changed by shortening or lengthening the relevant time period.

In another European study, Buckley & Brooke (1992) concluded that the best set of assumptions is that foreign direct investment substitutes for exports in the short run, thus imposing employment losses on the source country; but in the long run it substitutes for investment by competing firms (home-country or otherwise) and thus preserves domestic employment. This tends to be the most prevalent view in the literature, although exceptions can be found. For example, Kravis & Lipsey (1990) found that the more a U.S. multinational produces abroad, the lower is its U.S. employment per dollar of output; however, it can be argued in these latter cases that domestic employment per dollar of output might have been even lower in the absence of outward foreign direct investment.

Through regression analysis, Rao, Legault & Ahmad show that total elasticities of Canadian exports with respect to the stock of CDIA is positive for two sub-periods: 1971 to 1980 and 1981 to 1989. This suggests complementarity between the two series. Elasticities of imports with respect to CDIA stocks are also positive, highlighting the fact that CDIA affects the mix of employment rather than the overall level. Further evidence supporting this interpretation is provided by Rao, Legault & Ahmad's finding that over the period from 1970 to 1991, CDIA had no significant relationship to capital formation in Canada.

As Gunderson & Verma conclude, to the extent that direct investment abroad accelerates adjustments in the home-country labour market, and to the extent that these adjustments are desirable in the long-run from the home country's perspective, it is difficult to argue that there are adverse social effects associated with direct investment abroad, at least with respect to the functioning of domestic labour markets. The Northern Telecom and MacMillan Bloedel case studies in this volume support this conclusion.

TRADE AND BALANCE OF PAYMENTS

THE EFFECTS OF DIRECT INVESTMENT ABROAD on trade and balance of payments may also differ across industries and over time, although the evidence is more ambiguous than in the case of the employment effects. The following factors condition the effects on the balance of payments:

- outflow of capital when the investment is made, although this is often largely financed from host-country sources;

- return flow of income in the form of dividends, license fees etc.;

- exports from the home country;

- imports from foreign affiliates;

- repatriation of capital from the sale of foreign assets.

In a world of floating exchange rates, any net effect on the balance of payments would presumably be manifested in a change in the terms of trade through appreciation or depreciation of the home currency.

In the case of the United Kingdom, the *Reddaway Report* (1967) found that new investment contributed a total net annual gain to the British balance of payments of £4 for each £100 invested abroad. This estimate was made on the basis of an assumption that if the direct investment abroad had not been made, foreign firms would have invested to serve the markets in question. Shepherd, Silberston & Strange (1985) noted that the greater part of direct investment overseas by U.K. firms had been financed by overseas borrowing and retained earnings. This, combined with the repatriation of a significant proportion of overseas' profits, made a positive contribution to the U.K. balance of payments. With respect to the effect on the trade account itself, the authors concluded that it is difficult to draw unequivocal conclusions other than that U.K. MNEs seem to prefer to export higher value-added products from the established U.K. home base.

There is also some evidence that Japanese direct investment abroad contributes to net exports from Japan. For example, Yamawaki (1991) examined the relationship between Japanese exports to the United States and the distributional activities of Japanese affiliates in the U.S. wholesale trade sector for 44 three-digit Japanese exporting industries. He found that the presence of U.S. distribution subsidiaries of Japanese manufacturing companies strongly promotes Japanese exports to the United States. Ishimine (1978) also concluded that Japanese foreign affiliates contribute to greater trade and foreign exchange earnings or savings through their local sales outlets and home-country sourcing of inputs.

In contrast, Ries & Head suggest that during the 1970s textiles plummeted as a share of all Japanese exports coinciding with a large increase in direct investment abroad by Japanese textile firms. They also suggest that foreign production substituted for exports in the 1980s, but that, on balance, the consequences of Japanese direct investment abroad may be greater for the composition of export products than for the total amount of exports. This is also the conclusion drawn for Sweden by Blomström & Kokko.

Evidence for U.S. MNEs is also broadly consistent with the interpretation that the mix of trade is more significantly affected by outward direct investment than is overall trade. For example, a comprehensive early study of U.S. MNEs by Bergsten, Horst & Moran (1978) concluded that the initial overseas investments of an American manufacturer tend to promote exports by developing foreign markets for U.S. products. Over time, however, foreign investment becomes less and less a complement and more and more a substitute for U.S. exports. Moreover, net exports may be influenced by the magnitude of outward foreign direct investment. Specifically, for 33 U.S. manufacturing industries, they found that in 1966 their measure of direct investment abroad was positively related to the export-to-shipment ratio. However, the square of the outward investment measure is negatively related to the export intensity measure. Horst (1976) also provided a qualified assessment of the linkages between direct investment abroad and exports; namely, that foreign manufacturing might be an alternative to U.S. production, while non-manufacturing activities tend to promote U.S. exports by expanding the market for U.S. goods.

Lipsey & Weiss (1981) found less equivocal evidence of a positive relationship between net exports and direct investment abroad by U.S. firms. Across 14 industries encompassing 44 destinations for 1970, they found that U.S. exports were positively related to the level of activity (output) of local affiliates of U.S. companies in 12 of 14 industries with respect to developed countries and in 11 of 11 industries with respect to developing country destinations. They also found that the exports of 13 other developed countries to the sample destination generally were negatively related to U.S. affiliate activity. They concluded that the foreign affiliate activities of U.S. firms appear largely to complement U.S. exports, and that the local sales of U.S. firms come largely at the expense of exports from third countries.

Graham's reading of the overall economic evidence is that it weakly supports the notion that direct investment abroad promotes net exports and makes a positive long-term contribution to the balance of payments of the home country. However, this conclusion is very sensitive to assumptions about what would happen to foreign markets if direct investment abroad did not take place. It is also qualified by conflicting findings for specific industries and for particular time periods. Graham also notes that the evidence does not identify whether increased direct investment abroad caused increased exports or whether both were associated with a simultaneous change in the production process. In sum, it seems prudent to carry over the conclusion from the Gunderson & Verma analysis of labour-market effects of CDIA. Specifically, the primary effect of CDIA is on the composition and aggregate volume of trade, rather than on the magnitude of Canada's net trade and payments balances.

TECHNOLOGICAL CHANGE

PERHAPS THE MOST WIDELY DISCUSSED linkage made between direct investment abroad and conventional notions of international competitiveness is related to the effect of direct investment abroad on technological change in the home country.[19] Unfortunately, the available evidence bearing on this linkage is quite limited. Some relates to the location of R&D facilities. For example, Mansfield, et al. (1982) affirmed the importance of decentralizing influences. Specifically, they found that the extent of geographic dispersion of R&D is positively related to the share of foreign affiliate sales in total company sales and negatively related to the share of U.S. exports. Nevertheless, they established that foreign sales and overseas investment are important in generating higher returns to

R&D. If firms were not permitted to utilize new technologies in foreign affiliates, R&D spending would fall by between 12 percent and 15 percent. If no foreign rents could be earned at all, R&D spending would be cut by between 16 percent and 26 percent. The size of the reduction across firms is positively related to the share of affiliate sales in total sales, among other things.

Hirschey & Caves (1981) affirmed the positive influence of the share of foreign affiliate sales and the negative influence of exports on the extent of the international dispersion of R&D performance for a sample of U.S. industries. Nevertheless, this does not mean that this leads to less overall R&D being performed in the United States. In this regard, Kotabe (1990) obtained a positive and significant relationship between import propensity and R&D intensity for a sample of U.S. MNEs. He interpreted his results as showing that the strategic readiness of U.S. MNEs to use their corporate resources to exploit the locational advantages of overseas markets does not impair their domestic innovatory capabilities. Findings drawing on U.S. data are reinforced by several non-U.S. studies. For example, Swedenborg (1985), drawing on the Swedish experience, concluded that whatever decentralization of R&D might have taken place, Swedish R&D intensity may be as much as 65 percent higher than it would otherwise have been in the absence of foreign production. Blomström & Kokko confirm that Swedish firms have continued to centralize R&D at home.

McFetridge offers a comprehensive assessment of the R&D activities of Canadian MNEs, where R&D is taken as an (admittedly) imprecise proxy for innovation activities. He puts the entire issue into perspective by recognizing that, with the exception of chemicals and allied products, CDIA is not in R&D-intensive sectors. A similar picture emerges if one examines the characteristics of the larger Canadian multinationals; however, with respect to smaller firms, direct investment abroad does appear to be a means of exploiting a technological advantage in foreign markets. Nevertheless, decentralizing R&D for purposes of foreign production tends to be characteristic of low R&D-intensity and low basic research-intensity industries, with Northern Telecom being a notable exception.

R&D undertaken in support of local production and market operations raises the greatest *a priori* concerns about technological spillovers benefitting foreign producers. Conversely, knowledge-seeking R&D tends to be motivated by the need for access to foreign networks, clusters or centres of excellence. This type of R&D promises to increase the extent to which the domestic economy is able to appropriate or draw from the international knowledge pool. McFetridge argues that as a well educated country with a small market, Canada should have a competitive advantage in knowledge-searching R&D Indeed, as noted earlier, Northern Telecom's overseas R&D activities are increasingly of the knowledge-seeking type.

In their case studies of international strategic alliances involving Canadian firms, Globerman & Wolf conclude that most of the alliances identified involved transfers of technology into Canada in exchange for improved market access. However, Corvari & Wisner (1991) cite evidence that Canadian parents were net importers of technology from their U.S. affiliates, using payments of royalties and license fees as a measure of technology flows. Therefore, outward investment by Canadian MNEs is associated with both inflows and outflows of technology, as appears to be true for outward investment by non-Canadian MNEs.

In summary, direct investment abroad appears to encourage some decentralization of R&D and also increased overall domestic expenditure on R&D. The R&D carried out within the MNE is differentiated across affiliates. Even knowledge-seeking R&D is likely to be specialized by affiliate in order to benefit from the unique skills and expertise possessed by the laboratories in different countries. This development is highlighted for Northern Telecom in the case study in this volume. This increased international specialization of R&D activities, as is the case for specialization of production activities, can be expected to improve the efficiency with which technological resources are used in both the home and host economies.

Direct investment abroad also appears to stimulate a two-way flow of technology between host and home countries. There is no basis for concluding that Canada is disadvantaged by the two-way flows associated with CDIA, or that Canada would be better off by restricting the technological activities of Canadian MNEs. Rather, as Brean argues, an agenda for promoting technological innovation in Canada is best pursued by making it attractive to develop and apply new technology in Canada.

CONCLUSIONS

EARLIER IN THIS STUDY, Porter's concerns about the possibility of "too much" CDIA were noted, as was Rugman's skepticism (this volume) as to whether there could ever be too much CDIA from an economic perspective. While a theoretical case can be made against CDIA, an even stronger theoretical case can be made in its support.

In the case of a small, open economy like Canada's, the role that CDIA plays in facilitating market access, with the associated exploitation of economies of scale and specialization, seems particularly relevant. In fact, available empirical evidence arguably supports a more complex assessment than either proponents or critics of CDIA usually provide. Specifically, CDIA appears to be more closely linked to changes in the *composition* of domestic economic activity than to changes in the overall *volume* of domestic economic activity. In particular, CDIA encourages increased domestic R&D, as well as increased employment opportunities for more highly educated workers. It also appears to encourage increased geographic specialization of production activities with associated efficiency gains for Canada.

Overall, the evidence bearing upon the economic effects of outward foreign direct investment appear to conclude that CDIA imparts net benefits to Canada over and above the benefits realized by the investors themselves. This assessment recommends against the Canadian government taking any action to restrict or otherwise discourage direct investment abroad. At the same time, there is no compelling or identifiable evidence that the externalities associated with CDIA abroad are sufficiently large to justify active government promotion of the phenomenon, especially given that such investment is usually profitable in an *ex ante* sense. Nonetheless, the evidence does support a policy conclusion that the Canadian government should continue to work toward international agreements that liberalize the international direct investment regime.

ENDNOTES

1 Seminal and comprehensive reviews of this literature are provided by Caves (1982) and Dunning (1993).

2 As a case in point, the relocation of the head office of Varity Corporation from Toronto to Buffalo, New York in 1991 ignited a firestorm of protest from the Ontario and federal governments, as well as from Canadian labour union leaders. Periodically, concerns have also been expressed about the performance of research and development in the United States by leading Canadian multinationals such as Northern Telecom and, more recently, the expansion of Northern's production capacity in the United States rather than in Canada.

3 For Great Britain, for example, see Reddaway, Potter & Taylor (1968). An overview of the U.S. debate is provided in Bergsten, Horst & Moran (1978). A Swedish assessment is found in Jordon & Vahlne (1981).

4 For a comprehensive historical overview of government efforts to promote the establishment of overseas direct investment, see Dunning (1993). The Ontario Premier's Council (1990) listed the lack of a healthy home base of indigenous multinational companies in non-resource industries as a major competitive weakness of the province.

5 While Porter does not cast his discussion explicitly in these terms, he is effectively positing the existence of significant external economies of scale in his description of clustering. Evidence bearing upon the existence of external economies of scale can be found in Porter (1990).

6 CDIA is defined as a 10 percent (or more) long-term equity stake in a foreign firm. The level of CDIA was $99 billion by the end of 1992.

7 In his contribution to this volume, Rugman posits that neoclassical economists are churlish to second-guess the merits of CDIA. In his view, Canadians must invest abroad to survive; however, he offers no convincing support for this assertion. Moreover, he implicitly assumes that all Canadian firms must invest abroad to survive – a patently insupportable assumption. While Rugman is justifiably concerned about possible interactions between domestic and foreign direct investment, he simply assumes that the two are always complements, thereby ignoring the possibility that in some circumstances they may be substitutes. Most studies in this volume treat the relevant interactions between domestic and foreign investment as an empirical issue rather that simply assuming that they are welfare enhancing.

8 While these motives are not mutually exclusive, individual motives tend to predominate in individual circumstances.

9 Indeed, it is these transactions' cost savings that underlie the internalization argument for direct investment. For a discussion of the internalization thesis, see Rugman (1980).

10 There is persuasive evidence of the existence of R&D spillover efficiency benefits. See, for example, Bernstein (1993).

11 This potential benefit is identified in Investment Canada (1990, p.54) as follows: "Depending upon the extent of decentralization, firms can gain better access to new technologies, new ideas and new sources of information about new inputs". Dunning (1993, p.338) notes another possible benefit: transfer of technology to host-country firms may facilitate cheaper production of inputs used intensively by the home country firms transferring the technology.

12 The prospect of competitive "damage" being inflicted on the home economy by the decentralization of R&D within the multinational is discussed in Dunning (1988).

13 For a brief review of other surveys, see Corvari & Wisner (1991).

14 See Rugman (1987). The importance of relative tax rates and other "government induced" business costs on the decision of Canadian firms to invest at home or abroad remains a particularly contentious issue. For example, Mintz & Halpern (1991) suggest that cross-border transactions between Canada and the United States are likely affected, to some degree, by tax provisions. On the other hand, Slemrod (1989) concludes that tax effects were not statistically significant influences on Canadian direct investment in the United States, even though they were significant for other countries. Brean (this volume) highlights the potential for relatively high personal tax rules in Canada to encourage the emigration of skilled employees, especially scientists and engineers.

15 For a description of the characteristics of the leading Canadian multinational enterprises, see Rugman (1987).

16 Evidence supporting the hypothesis that R&D expenditures are encouraged by foreign involvement is discussed below.
17 See Kim, et al. (1989) and Jung (1991).
18 It might be noted in this regard that "event studies" do not show any positive reaction in MacMillan Bloedel's stock price to announcements by the company of direct investments abroad. See Raizada & Vertinsky (this volume.)
19 Mansfield et al. (1982) found that in about half the cases studied, direct investment abroad by U.S. firms speeded up imitation of U.S. technology by foreign firms. At the same time, technological feedback from direct investment abroad was also considerable, especially for U.S. direct investment in Europe. See Mansfield & Romeo (1984).

ACKNOWLEDGEMENTS

I WANT TO THANK A NUMBER OF individuals who were of great assistance to me on this project. Among others, the staff at Industry Canada worked continuously with me at all stages. I would like to acknowledge the particular help of John Knubley, Mark Legault, Ross Preston, Someshwar Rao, Chris Roth and Don Wilson. Also, my special thanks to Chris Maule for comments on an earlier draft and to Daryl Madill and Brian Globerman for helpful research assistance.

Administrative, word processing and other technical support were cheerfully and competently provided, at different stages, by Linda Sheldon of Simon Fraser University and Kathryn Finn of Western Washington University. Alan Rugman and John Dunning made useful suggestions regarding the format of the conference, as well as participants to invite. Eunice Thorne and Ed Matheson of Ampersand were great professionals, as usual, in facilitating speedy publication.

During the first stages of the project, I was at Simon Fraser University. At later stages, I was at Western Washington University as the Ross Distinguished Professor of Canada-U.S. Business and Economic Relations. I would like to thank both institutions for their support.

Finally, a special note of appreciation to all the contributors to this volume and other participants in the associated conference — thank you all.

BIBLIOGRAPHY

C.F. Bergsten, C. F., T. Horst and T.Horst. *American Multinationals and American Interests.* Washington: Brookings Institution, 1978.

Bernstein, Jeffrey. "R&D Capital, Spillovers and Foreign Affiliates in Canada." In *Foreign Investment, Technology and Economic Growth.* Edited by D.G. McFetridge. Calgary: University of Calgary Press, 1991, pp.111-30.

Buckley, P. J. and P. Artisien. "Policy Issues of Intra-EC Direct Investment." *Journal of Common Market Studies*, 26, (1987): pp.207-30.

Buckley, P. J. and M. Z. Brooke. *International Business Studies: An Overview.* Cambridge, Mass.: Blackwell Publishers, 1992.

Campbell, D. C. and R. G. McElrath. *The Employment Effects of Multinational Enterprises in the U.S. and of American Multinationals Abroad.* Geneva: International Labour Office, Multinational Enterprises Program, Working Paper Number 64, 1990.

Caves, Richard E. *Multinational Enterprise and Economic Analysis.* Cambridge: Cambridge University Press, 1982.

Contractor, Farouk. "Ownership Patterns of U.S. Joint Ventures Abroad and the Liberalization of Foreign Government Regulation in the 1980s: Evidence From the Benchmark Surveys." *Journal of International Business Studies*, 1990.

Corvari, Ronald and Robert Wisner. "The Role of Canadian Multinationals in Shaping Canada's International Competitiveness," Report prepared for the Economic Council of Canada and Investment Canada, mimeo, July 1991.

Daniels, J. D. and J. Bracker. "Profit Performance: Do Foreign Operations Make a Difference?" *Management International Review*, 29, (1989): 46-55.

Dunning, John. "United Kingdom." In *Multinational Enterprises, Economic Structure and International Competitiveness.* Edited by John Dunning. Chichester: John Wiley and Sons, 1985, pp.13-56.

_____. *Multinationals, Technology and Competitiveness.* London: Allen and Unwin, 1988.

_____. *Multinational Enterprises and the Global Economy.* Wokingham, England: Addison-Wesley Publishing Company, 1993.

Eddy, A. and B. Seifert. "International Benefits and Foreign Acquisitions by U.S. Firms." *Management International Review*, 4, (1984): 27-35.

Froot, K. A. and J. C. Stein. "Exchange Rates and Foreign Direct Investment: An Imperfect Capital Markets Approach." *The Quarterly Journal of Economics*, 106, (1991): 1191-1217.

Geringer, J. M., P. M. Beamish and R. C. daCosta. "Diversification Strategy and Internationalization: Implications for MNE Performance." *Strategic Management Journal*, 11, (1989): 109-19.

Graham, E. M. and P. Krugman. *Foreign Direct Investment in the United States.* Washington, D.C.: Washington: Institute for International Economics, 1989.

Hirschey, R. C. and R. E. Caves. "Internalization of Research and Transfer of Technology by Multinational Enterprises." *Oxford Bulletin of Economics and Statistics*, 42, (1981): 115-30.

Horst, Thomas. "American Multinationals and the U.S. Economy." *The American Economic Review*, 66, (1976): 149-54.

Investment Canada. "International Investment: Canadian Developments in a Global Context." Working Paper 6, mimeo, 1990.

Ishimine, T "Performance Motivation and the Effects on the Balance of Payments." *Economia Internazionale*, 31, (1978): 46-64.

Jordon, J. S. and J. E. Vahlne. "Domestic Employment Effects of Direct Investment Abroad by Two Swedish Multinational." Working paper Number 13, Multinational Enterprises Programme, Geneva: International Labour OFfice, 1991.

Jung, Y. "Multinationality and Profitability." *Journal of Business Research*, 23, (1991): 179-87.

Kim, W. C., P. Hwang and W. P. Burgess. "Global Diversification Strategy and Corporate Profit Performance." *Strategic Management Journal*, 10, (1989): 45-57.

Kim, W. C. and E. O. Lyn. "FDI Theories and the Performance of Foreign Multinationals Operating in the U.S." *Journal of International Business Studies*, 21, (1990): 41-54.

Knubley, J., W. Krause and Z. Sadeque. "Canadian Acquisitions Abroad: Patterns and Motivations." In *Corporate Globalization Through Mergers and Acquisitions*. Edited by Leonard Waverman. Calgary: University of Calgary Press, 1991, pp.23-58.

Kravis, I. and R. Lipsey. "The Effect of Multinational Firms' Foreign Operations on Their Domestic Employment." National Bureau of Economic Research, Working Paper Number 2760, 1990.

Kotabe, M. "The Relationship Between Offshore Sourcing and Innovativeness of U.S. Multinational Firms." *Journal of International Business Studies*, 21, (1990): 623-39.

Leftwich, R. B. "U.S. Multinational Companies: Profitability, Financial Leverage and Effective Income Tax Rates." *Survey of Current Business*, (May 1974): 27-36.

Li, Jiatao and Stephen Guisinger. "How Well Do Foreign Firms Compete in the United States?" *Business Horizons*, 34, (1991): 49-53.

Lipsey, R. E. and M. Y. Weiss. "Foreign Production and Exports in Manufacturing Industries." *Review of Economics and Statistics*, 63, (1981): 488-94.

Mansfield, Edwin and Anthony Romeo. "Technology Transfer to Overseas Subsidiaries by U.S.-based Firms." *Quarterly Journal of Economics*, 95, (1980).

_____. "Reverse Transfer of Technology from Overseas Subsidiaries to American Firms." *IEEE Transactions on Engineering Management*, (August 1984): 610-27.

Mansfield, Edwin and Associates. *Technology Transfers, Productivity and Economic Policy*. New York: W. W. Norton, 1982.

Ontario Premier's Council Report. "People and Skills in the New Global Economy," Toronto: mimeo, 1990.

Porter, Michael. *The Competitive Advantage of Nations*. New York: The Free Press, 1990.

Porter, Michael and The Monitor Company. *Canada At The Crossroads*, Business Council on National Issues, mimeo, 1991.

Reddaway, W. B., S. T. Potter and C. T. Taylor. *The Effects of U.K. Direct Investment Abroad*. Cambridge, Mass.: Cambridge University Press, 1968.

Reddaway, W. B. "Effects of U.K. Direct Investment Overseas: Final Report." University of Cambridge, Department of Applied Economics, Occasional Papers, Number 15, Cambridge University Press, 1968.

Rugman, Alan. "Internalisation as a General Theory of Foreign Direct Investment: A Reappraisal of the Literature." *Weltwirtschaftliches Archiv*, Band 126, Heft 2, (1980): 365-79.

Rugman, Alan. *Outward Bound: Canadian Direct Investment in the United States*. Toronto: C.D. Howe Institute, 1987.

Severn, A. K. and M. M. Laurence. "Direct Investment, Research Intensity and Profitability." *Journal of Financial and Quantitative Analysis*, 9, (1974): 181-90.

Shepherd, D., A. Silberston and R. Strange. *British Manufacturing Investment Overseas*. London and New York: Methuen, 1985.

Swedenborg, Birgitta. "Sweden." In *Multinational Enterprises, Economic Structure and International Competitiveness*. Edited by John Dunning. Chichester: John Wiley and Sons, 1985, pp.217-248.

Slemrod, Joel. "Tax Effects on Foreign Direct Investment in the U.S.: Evidence from a Cross-Country Comparison." National Bureau of Economic Research Working Paper 3042, mimeo, 1989.

van den Bulcke, Daniel. "Belgium." In *Multinational Enterprises, Economic Structure and International Competitiveness*. Edited by John Dunning. Chichester: John Wiley and Sons, 1985, pp.249-280.

Wolf, Bernard. "Size and Profitability Among U.S. Manufacturing Firms: Multinational versus Primarily Domestic Firms." *Journal of Economics and Business*, 28, (1975): 1522.

Yamawaki, Hideki. "Exports and Foreign Distributional Activities: Evidence of Japanese Firms in the United States." *Review of Economics and Statistics*, 73, (1991): 294-300.

Part I   Evidence

Franklin Chow
Balance of Payments Division
Statistics Canada

2

Recent Trends in Canadian Direct Investment Abroad: The Rise of Canadian Multinationals

INTRODUCTION

CANADIAN DIRECT INVESTMENT ABROAD (CDIA) has grown rapidly in recent years. Since the mid-1980s the level of CDIA doubled to $99 billion by the end of 1992. This growth occurred during a time of trade liberalization marked by the formation or strengthening of trading blocs such as the Free Trade Agreement (FTA) and the elimination of the remaining internal barriers to European Community trade. Such developments provided Canadian enterprises with more opportunities to set up operations through direct investment abroad and to increase cross-border trade. Concurrently the competition for international capital intensified, induced by increased mobility of capital arising from the deregulation of financial markets in a number of countries and by spectacular technological advances in communications.

Historically, Canada has relied extensively on foreign investment for development capital. In its early years, a significant part of such investment was in the form of portfolio capital, especially from the United Kingdom and the United States. The mid-1950s saw a marked shift in patterns of foreign financing toward US direct investment in Canada, and this change predominated up to the mid-1970s. From that point, however, the sources of foreign capital became more diversified with foreign portfolio capital outpacing direct investment.[1]

It was not until the late 1970s that Canada began to establish direct investment in foreign countries on a broad scale. Until then, Canadian investment abroad had mainly been in the form of assets held by the federal government (international reserves and loans to other countries) and by Canadian banks (which had long since established operations abroad). Almost 95 percent of the C$ 45 billion increase in CDIA between 1986 and 1992 was financed through net capital outflows from Canada. Over three-quarters of this represented injections of working capital, with the balance used for the acquisition of existing businesses abroad. CDIA outstripped foreign direct investment in Canada, rising from 62 percent to 72 percent of foreign direct investment in Canada.

This study traces the profile and characteristics of Canadian direct invest-ment abroad, focusing on the years from 1986 to 1992. The analysis is in three parts. The first part deals with some general features of CDIA: its growth, largely financed by capital outflows from Canada; countries where CDIA is made; and industries into which CDIA is channelled. The next part focuses on Canadian direct investors: their country of control; the relative importance of CDIA in terms of their long-term capitalization; and the size of their direct investment abroad. The last part looks at the characteristics of foreign concerns: the size of the Canadian investment in these concerns; their various legal structures; their industrial pattern compared to that of the Canadian direct investors; and the importance of CDIA in relation to their overall long-term capitalization.

GENERAL CHARACTERISTICS OF CANADIAN DIRECT INVESTMENT ABROAD

GROWTH

BETWEEN 1985 AND 1992 Canadian direct investment abroad rose on average by 9 percent per year from $54 billion to $99 billion (Figure 1). Some 95 percent of the growth reflected direct investment flows from Canada, which averaged a net outflow of $6 billion a year. The remaining increase consisted of retained earnings and other factors (Table 1), although retained earnings were not a significant factor, as Canadian enterprises largely repatriated their foreign earnings through dividends or incurred large losses abroad. The write-downs of certain assets abroad also dampened the value of CDIA. In addition, currency fluctuations[2] also appear to have had a dampening effect on the CDIA position values. However, it is difficult to determine the precise effect over this seven-year period, due to the myriad of foreign currencies and currency movements.

The average net outflow of $6 billion a year from Canada masked very large two-way flows of capital into and out of Canada over the seven-year period under study. This period showed a spectacular increase in gross flows of direct investment compared to the previous seven years (Table 1).

From 1986 to 1992, net outflows accumulated to $42.6 billion, made up of gross outflows of $79.1 billion and gross inflows of $36.5 billion. Three-quarters of the gross outflows were for working capital, and the remainder was for the purchase of existing concerns abroad. Similarly, some 70 percent of gross inflows represented the return to Canada of funds advanced by Canadian enterprises. The balance represented proceeds from the sale of foreign concerns by Canadian direct investors to non-residents.

An analysis of the cumulative net outflow of $42.6 billion between 1986 and 1992 shows that over one-quarter of the outflow was by enterprises in the finance and insurance industry. The capital movements expressed in Table 3 are based upon the industrial sector of the Canadian direct investor (not upon

FIGURE 1

CANADIAN DIRECT INVESTMENT ABROAD, YEAR END POSITIONS, 1985-1992

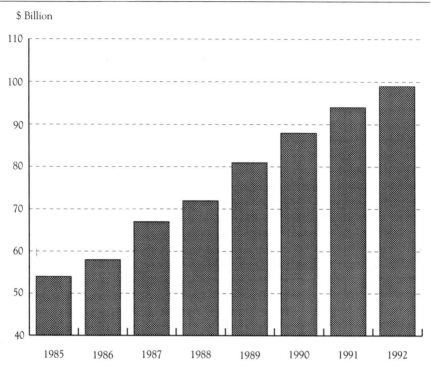

$ Billion

the industry of the recipient foreign entity) using the Canadian Standard Industrial Classification for Company and Enterprise statistics (SIC-C).

After the industrial sector, the next largest sector was construction and related activities with a net outflow of $8 billion to comprise 19 percent of the outflow. Electrical and electronic products followed with an outflow of $3.7 billion during the seven-year period to comprise 9 percent. Capital movements by the energy sector in Canada and by enterprises in the metallic minerals and metal products each comprised about 6 percent, with net outflows of $2.6 billion and $2.4 billion respectively.

GEOGRAPHICAL LOCATION AND INDUSTRIAL DISTRIBUTION OF CANADIAN DIRECT INVESTMENT ABROAD[3]

THE UNITED STATES has continued to be the predominant location for Canadian direct investment. However, in recent years there has been a gradual shift to European countries. From a peak of 69 percent at 1985 year end, the

TABLE 1

COMPONENTS OF THE INCREASE IN CANADIAN DIRECT INVESTMENT ABROAD,
1986-1992

COMPONENT	C$ BILLION	PERCENT
Net capital flows	42.6	95
Retained earnings and other factors	2.3	5
Total	44.9	100

share of direct investment accounted for by the United States steadily declined to 58 percent at 1991 year end. Estimates for 1992 indicate a relative shift in favour of investment in the United States, in spite of a mediocre earnings performance in that country and a relative decline in the United Kingdom, due largely to write-offs.

On an industrial basis, using the 1980 SIC-C, by far the largest share of CDIA was concentrated in finance and insurance concerns abroad, representing one-quarter of total CDIA at 1991 year end. The metallic minerals and products sector was next in size with 13 percent of CDIA. In the United States, CDIA was more diversified, industrially, with finance and insurance still leading, however, with 17 percent of the total, reflecting sizeable investments in banking and life insurance subsidiaries. Direct investment in other foreign countries was more concentrated, industrially, with some 35 percent in the finance and insurance sector, (largely banking). The metallic minerals and metal products sector followed with 14 percent. At the end of 1987, these two sectors, combined, accounted for 56 percent of direct investment, but their share had decreased to less than 50 percent by the end of 1991.

CHARACTERISTICS OF CANADIAN ENTERPRISES INVESTING ABROAD

CONTROL

MANY OF THE CANADIAN ENTERPRISES that have direct investments abroad are themselves controlled by non-residents. Table 4 shows CDIA according to the Canadian and foreign control of the Canadian enterprises.

From a peak of 37 percent in 1969, the proportion of CDIA ultimately controlled by non-residents declined dramatically to a low of 12 percent in 1986, and then increased to 18 percent at the end of 1991. The decline was due to factors such as the reclassification from foreign to Canadian control of two large enterprises in the early 1970s, and the inclusion in CDIA of the foreign operations of wholly-owned Canadian subsidiaries which were excluded from the Canadian direct investment series prior to 1979.[4] The latter offset somewhat the

TABLE 2

CANADIAN DIRECT INVESTMENT ABROAD, CUMULATIVE GROSS CAPITAL
MOVEMENTS, SALES, ACQUISITIONS AND OTHER FLOWS

FLOW	1979-1985	1986-1992
	($ billion)	
Gross Inflows		
Sale of existing interests to non-residents	4.1	10.1
Other inflows	11.4	26.4
Total Gross Inflows	**15.5**	**36.5**
Gross Outflows		
Acquisition of direct investment		
interests abroad from non-residents	6.6	18.1
Other outflows	32.6	61.1
Total Gross Outflows	**39.2**	**79.1**
Net Flows		
Net sales/purchases	-2.6	-7.9
Other net flows	-21.2	-34.7
Total Net Flows	**-23.7**	**-42.6**

TABLE 3

CANADIAN DIRECT INVESTMENT ABROAD, AGGREGATE NET CAPITAL MOVEMENTS,
BY INDUSTRY, 1986-1992 ($ MILLION)

INDUSTRY	AGGREGATE NET CAPITAL FLOW	PERCENT OF TOTAL
Food, beverage and tobacco	-1,238	3.0
Wood and paper	-1,563	3.7
Energy	-2,615	6.1
Chemicals, chemical products and textiles	-1,154	2.7
Metallic minerals and metal products	-2,379	5.6
Machinery and equipment	-245	0.6
Transportation equipment	-1,191	2.8
Electrical and electronic products	-3,701	8.7
Construction and related activities	-8,039	18.9
Transportation services	-2,519	5.9
Communications	-2,997	7.0
Finance and insurance	-11,109	26.1
Services to business	-911	2.1
Government services	0	0
Education, health and social services	-102	0.2
Accommodation, restaurants and recreation services	-1,512	3.6
Food retailing	-37	0.1
Consumer goods and services	-1,217	2.9
Total	-42,575	100

TABLE 4

DISTRIBUTION OF CANADIAN DIRECT INVESTMENT BY AREA OF CONTROL OF
CANADIAN ENTERPRISE, SELECTED YEAR ENDS (%)

YEAR	NUMBER OF CANADIAN ENTERPRISES		BOOK VALUE OF CANADIAN DIRECT INVESTMENT ABROAD	
	CANADIAN-CONTROLLED	FOREIGN-CONTROLLED	CANADIAN-CONTROLLED[a]	FOREIGN-CONTROLLED
1969	70	30	63	37
1970	68	32	65	35
1971	68	32	71	29
1972	64	36	81	19
1975	62	38	79	21
1980	74	26	83	17
1986	75	25	88	12
1989	73	28	85	16
1991	72	28	82	18

Note: [a] The direct investment assets of the Canadian chartered banks are included in the CDIA position data from
1983. If the assets of these enterprises are excluded from the CDIA book value totals for 1986, 1989 and
1991, the Canadian-controlled percentages for these three years would be, respectively, 87 percent, 83 per
cent and 80 percent.

acceleration of direct investment activity abroad by (largely Canadian-controlled) medium-size enterprises,[5] in the late 1970s. With the inclusion of the foreign corporate investment of the Canadian chartered banks beginning in 1983, the ratio of foreign-controlled CDIA touched 12 percent at 1986 year end, its lowest point. In the past few years, however, CDIA by foreign-controlled Canadian enterprises began to increase and reached 18 percent at the end of 1991. This was due to a number of factors such as the relative weakness of earnings and write-downs in foreign concerns controlled from Canada, notably in the real estate and merchandising sectors. Moreover, a number of U.S. corporations have restructured their operations in the past few years by recording their investment in third countries on the books of their subsidiaries in Canada.

CDIA RELATIVE TO LONG-TERM CAPITALIZATION
OF CANADIAN ENTERPRISES

A ROUGH INDICATOR OF THE PROPENSITY to invest abroad, rather than in Canada, is provided by relating Canadian direct investment abroad to long-term capitalization[6] of the Canadian direct investors. Based on the industrial sector of the Canadian enterprises (rather than of the foreign concerns), this new series (Figure 2) shows which of the Canadian sectors have devoted relatively more of their financial resources to investment in foreign countries.

FIGURE 2

CANADIAN DIRECT INVESTMENT ABROAD AND LONG-TERM CAPITALIZATION OF THE
CANADIAN ENTERPRISES, YEAR END 1991

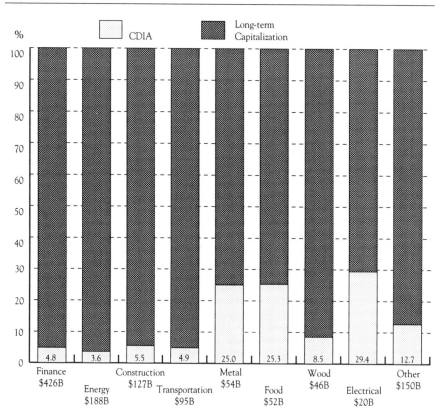

Electrical and electronic products, the sector with the highest propensity (29 percent) to invest abroad. The two next-largest sectors, with 25 percent each, were the food, beverage and tobacco sector and the metallic, mineral and products sector. The "other industries" category, covering such sectors as communications, transportation equipment, chemicals, and consumer goods and services, was also large, with 13 percent of their capital devoted to direct investments abroad. The proportion was 9 percent in the wood and paper sector. While finance and insurance comprise by far the largest category of CDIA, accounting for fully 25 percent of the total, the sector represents only 5 percent of long-term capital, lagging behind many other sectors. Finally, the construction and related activities sector, which includes real estate, also invested 5 percent of its long-term capital in direct investment abroad.

SIZE OF INVESTMENT BY CANADIAN ENTERPRISES

WHILE CDIA WAS RISING SHARPLY, the number of Canadian enterprises with direct investment abroad seesawed around a downward trend from a peak of 1,555 in 1985 to 1,396 at the end of 1991 (Table 5). During this period the average size of investment abroad by Canadian enterprises almost doubled from $34.8 million in 1988 to $67.7 million in 1991.

At the end of 1985, ten Canadian enterprises held direct investments of over $1 billion, comprising 40 percent of total direct investment. By 1991,

TABLE 5

CANADIAN DIRECT INVESTMENT ABROAD, BY AREA OF CONTROL AND BY SIZE OF INVESTMENT OF THE CANADIAN ENTERPRISE, YEAR ENDS 1985 AND 1991

SIZE OF INVESTMENT OF THE CANADIAN ENTERPRISE CONTROLLED IN:	1985		1991	
	NUMBER OF ENTERPRISES	$ MILLION	NUMBER OF ENTERPRISES	$ MILLION
Canada				
Less than $0	73	-864	85	-376
$0 - 999,999	405	135	350	103
1,000,000 - 4,999,999	306	709	209	536
5,000,000 - 9,999,999	90	627	89	641
10,000,000 - 24,999,999	104	1,564	74	1,219
25,000,000 - 49,999,999	61	2,227	65	2,367
50,000,000 - 99,999,999	33	2,332	39	2,715
100,000,000 - 299,999,999	47	8,036	51	8,815
300,000,000 - 499,999,999	11	4,302	13	4,828
500,000,000 - 999,999,999	11	8,001	17	11,182
1,000,000,000 and over	8	19,369	16	45,560
Sub-total	1,149	46,440	1,008	77,591
United States				
Less than $0	3	-46	9	-43
$0 - 999,999	105	24	52	15
1,000,000 - 4,999,999	49	115	30	74
5,000,000 - 9,999,999	23	165	22	160
10,000,000 - 24,999,999	19	295	25	432
25,000,000 - 49,999,999	12	412	13	514
50,000,000 - 99,999,999	11	719	16	1,159
100,000,000 - 299,999,999	–	–	–	–
300,000,000 - 499,999,999	6	1,307	20	5,677
500,000,000 - 999,999,999	–	–	–	–
1,000,000,000 and over	–	–	–	–
Sub-total	228	2,991	187	7,987

TABLE 5 (CONT'D)

SIZE OF INVESTMENT OF THE CANADIAN ENTERPRISE CONTROLLED IN:	1985		1991	
	NUMBER OF ENTERPRISES	$ MILLION	NUMBER OF ENTERPRISES	$ MILLION
All Other Foreign Countries				
Less than $0	16	-18	16	-38
$0 - 999,999	68	20	43	15
1,000,000 - 4,999,999	37	90	55	134
5,000,000 - 9,999,999	19	125	18	132
10,000,000 - 24,999,999	13	225	22	344
25,000,000 - 49,999,999	13	430	20	702
50,000,000 - 99,999,999	4	258	8	510
100,000,000 - 299,999,999	–	–	–	–
300,000,000 - 499,999,999	8	3,566	19	7,058
500,000,000 - 999,999,999	–	–	–	–
1,000,000,000 and over	–	–	–	–
Sub-total	178	4,692	201	8,857
All Countries				
Less than $0	92	-928	110	-457
$0 - 999,999	578	179	445	133
1,000,000 - 4,999,999	392	914	294	744
5,000,000 - 9,999,999	132	917	129	933
10,000,000 - 24,999,999	136	2,084	121	1,995
25,000,000 - 49,999,999	86	3,069	98	3,583
50,000,000 - 99,999,999	48	3,309	63	4,384
100,000,000 - 299,999,999	57	9,788	75	13,418
300,000,000 - 499,999,999	12	4,702	22	8,474
500,000,000 - 999,999,999	12	8,503	22	14,653
1,000,000,000 and over	10	21,587	17	46,575
Total	1,555	54,123	1,396	94,435

there were 17 enterprises in this size range, comprising virtually half of total Canadian direct investment abroad. There has not been a significant increase in concentration: enterprises with over $50 million of CDIA accounted for 15 percent of the number and 93 percent of the total value of CDIA at 1991 year end, compared to 9 percent and 88 percent in 1985.

SIZE OF INVESTMENT BY AREA OF CONTROL

AT THE END OF 1991, there were 1,008 Canadian-controlled enterprises that held $77.6 billion of CDIA. These enterprises represented 72 percent of the total number of enterprises (Canadian- and foreign-controlled) with CDIA, and as much as 82 percent of the total value of CDIA. Conversely, foreign-controlled enterprises accounted for 28 percent of the number of Canadian enterprises but less than 18 percent of total CDIA. In other words, the average size of CDIA by enterprises under Canadian control was, at $77 million, much larger than the average size of CDIA by foreign-controlled enterprises at $43.4 million.

Compared to the end of 1985, there was a drop in the number of both Canadian- and foreign-controlled enterprises at the end of 1991. Over the period, CDIA by Canadian-controlled enterprises fell from 86 percent in 1985 to 82 percent at the end of 1991. This decrease was taken up by CDIA by U.S.-controlled enterprises, which grew from 5 percent to 9 percent of the total, while the share of other foreign-controlled enterprises remained at 9 percent.

Canadian-controlled enterprises represent a substantial proportion of smaller firms with CDIA, in terms of both number of enterprises and book value. In the zero to under $1 million grouping, Canadian-controlled enterprises have consistently represented more than 25 percent of the total number of enterprises. With respect to the negative book value category, the Canadian-controlled companies have accounted for the bulk of the values, particularly in 1989 and 1990 when the negative values were sizeable. Negative values are due to both operating losses and extraordinary write-downs of assets, and may reflect a continuation of the problems in the petroleum and natural gas, and real estate sectors, (Richards, 1985).[7]

CHARACTERISTICS OF FOREIGN CONCERNS
SIZE OF CANADIAN DIRECT INVESTMENT IN FOREIGN FIRMS

BETWEEN 1985 AND 1991, the number of foreign concerns fell from 3,593 to 3,282 firms (Table 6). Each Canadian firm making direct investments abroad invested in an average of 2.4 foreign concerns at 1991 year end, a figure virtually unchanged from the average of 2.3 foreign concerns at the end of 1985. However, over this six-year period, the average size of the direct investment in foreign entities grew appreciably. From $15.1 million of CDIA at the end of 1985, the average size rose steadily to $28.8 million at the end of 1991.

At 1985 year end, there were 95 foreign concerns with over $100 million of direct investment from Canada, accounting for 66 percent of total CDIA. During the ensuing six years, the number of concerns abroad in this size group almost doubled to 181, and their share of CDIA increased to 78 percent of the total at 1991 year end. During this latter period, the greatest increase in CDIA was recorded in 1987, largely due to investment in the $100 million and over group.

At the other end of the size spectrum, over one-half of the foreign concerns had less than $1 million of CDIA at the end of 1985, with a negative book value of $1.5 billion. By the end of 1991, the number of firms in the group with less than $1 million of direct investment from Canada had decreased to 47 percent of the total number of foreign concerns, and their combined negative book value had declined to $1.3 billion.

TABLE 6

CANADIAN DIRECT INVESTMENT IN FOREIGN CONCERNS BY SIZE
AT 1985 AND 1991 YEAR ENDS

	1985		1991	
SIZE OF INVESTMENT IN THE FOREIGN CONCERN	NUMBER OF FOREIGN CONCERNS	C$ MILLION	NUMBER OF FOREIGN CONCERNS	C$ MILLION
Less than $0	307	-1,921	340	-1,643
0 - 999,999	1,514	453	1,185	339
1,000,000 - 4,999,999	863	2,044	720	1,814
5,000,000 - 9,999,999	288	1,995	277	1,991
10,000,000 - 24,999,999	285	4,431	295	4,689
25,000,000 - 49,999,999	150	5,231	176	6,307
50,000,000 - 99,999,999	91	6,395	108	7,561
$100,000,000 and over	95	35,496	181	73,378
Total	3,593	54,123	3,282	94,435

TYPE OF FOREIGN FIRMS

AT THE END OF 1991, 75 percent of the 3,282 foreign concerns were subsidiaries, 15 percent were branches and 10 percent were affiliates (see the
Appendix for a description of each type of foreign concern). Subsidiaries
accounted for an overwhelming proportion of the total book value of CDIA:
86 percent at the end of 1991. Affiliates comprised 11 percent of the value
while branches accounted for only 3 percent.

At the end of 1991, the foreign firms with the largest average CDIA
were in the United Kingdom ($45.6 million). followed by the United States
($34 million) and, far behind, the other countries ($19.6 million). Within
the last group, the average size of concerns in other European Community
countries (excluding the United Kingdom) was slightly higher at $20.5
million; and that for concerns in Japan was even higher at $37.4 million.

By 1991, the relative size of enterprises had changed significantly since
1987, when the average size of direct investment enterprises in the United
Kingdom was, at $25.2 million, slightly smaller than $25.8 million in the
United States. Over the next four years the dramatic 81 percent growth of the
average U.K. concern far outstripped the 32 percent increase in the U.S.
concerns, as companies appeared to position themselves to compete in the
more open trading environment in Europe.

At the end of 1987 direct investment enterprises in other foreign
countries averaged $14.1 million, or about 55 percent of the average size of
concerns in the United States. This ratio was maintained over the period, as
the U.S. concerns grew at about the same rate as those in other countries.

TABLE 7

PERCENTAGE DISTRIBUTION OF CDIA (STOCK) BY INDUSTRY OF ORIGIN AND DESTINATION, 1987 YEAR END

INDUSTRY OF FOREIGN CONCERN	INDUSTRY OF CANADIAN INVESTING ENTERPRISE															Total
	Food, Beverage & Tobacco	Wood & Paper	Energy	Chemicals, Chemical Products & Textiles	Metallic Minerals & Metal Products	Machinery & Equipment	Transportation Equipment	Electrical & Electronic Products	Construction & Related Activities	Transportation Services	Communications	Finance & Insurance	Accommodation, Restaurants, Recreation Services & Food	Consumer Goods & Services	Other	
Food, Beverage & Tobacco	46	0	0	0	0	0	0	0	0	0	0	0	0	0	0	8
Wood & Paper	0	80	0	0	0	0	0	0	0	0	0	0	0	0	0	4
Energy	3	0	90	7	2	0	3	0	1	3	0	0	0	0	4	9
Chemicals, Chemical Products & Textiles	35	1	5	76	0	1	7	0	0	0	0	1	0	4	0	8
Metallic Minerals & Metal Products	0	2	5	0	89	0	1	0	2	0	0	0	0	0	17	15
Machinery & Equipment	0	0	0	0	0	68	0	0	0	0	0	0	0	0	0	1
Transportation Equipment	0	0	0	0	0	0	79	0	0	0	0	0	0	0	7	1
Electrical & Electronic Products	0	0	0	0	0	0	0	98	0	0	1	0	0	0	0	5
Construction & Related Activities	0	9	0	0	1	0	0	0	76	0	0	3	0	3	12	8
Transportation Services	0	1	0	0	0	20	5	0	12	94	4	0	5	0	0	4
Communications	0	0	0	0	0	0	0	0	0	0	95	4	0	0	0	7
Finance & Insurance	2	4	0	15	4	11	5	0	3	2	0	90	0	4	3	22
Accommodation, Restaurants, Recreation Services & Food Retailing	0	0	0	0	0	0	0	0	0	0	0	0	94	0	0	2
Consumer Goods & Services	14	2	0	2	4	0	5	2	6	0	0	1	0	89	0	5
Other	0	0	1	0	0	0	0	0	0	0	0	0	0	0	56	1
Total	100	100	100	100	100	100	100	100	100	100	100	100	100	100	100	100

Almost 20 percent of the foreign concerns in other countries operated as branches, a much higher proportion than in the United States, reflecting unincorporated exploration and development activities, particularly in developing countries.

INDUSTRY OF ORIGIN AND DESTINATION

ANALYSIS OF THE INDUSTRIES of origin and destination of CDIA provides an insight into the motivations of Canadian enterprises for investing abroad (Tables 7 and 8). The industry of origin is the industry in which the direct investor is classified in Canada, while the industry of destination is the industry of the foreign concern, the basis on which CDIA is normally presented.

Gorecki[8] suggests that there are three types of linkages: horizontal, vertical and conglomerate.[9] A horizontal linkage, which shows an exact correspondence between the industry of origin and the industry of destination, would reflect a desire to exploit abroad that source of competitive advantage that the direct investor has mastered in Canada. A vertical linkage is signalled by the ownership of foreign concerns engaged in activities that exist either upstream or downstream from the activity of the Canadian parent. This may indicate a strategy to maximize the overall efficiency of the production and distribution of a product on a global scale. Conglomerate linkages occur when there is no relation between the industry of the investing enterprise and that of the foreign concern. This may merely indicate a strategy to diversify holdings across industries. Because of the design of the industry of origin and destination tables, it is easier to establish with confidence a horizontal linkage (if the industry of origin is the same as that of destination) than a vertical linkage, which can be viewed as a conglomerate.

There are extremely high horizontal linkages in CDIA which increased further over the period, from 81 percent at the end of 1987 to 85 percent at the end of 1991 (Table 9). In other words, the period from 1987 to 1991 was marked by a tendency to invest in industries of established expertise or to pull back from diversified investments in other sectors.

All sectors were highly integrated except for two: food, beverage and tobacco, and other industries (Tables 7 and 8). At the 1991 year end, horizontal strategies were predominant in the electrical and electronic products sector, with 95 percent of their CDIA in the same industry abroad; and in communications and transportation services with 99 percent and 98 percent of their CDIA in the same industry abroad respectively. None of the other 13 sectors fell below 58 percent, except for food, beverage and tobacco, and other industries, which had ratios of 56 percent and 48 percent respectively.

Horizontal investment may be a natural concomitant of the small size of the Canadian market and the maturation of Canadian companies – continued expansion results in the exploitation of foreign markets in order

TABLE 8

PERCENTAGE DISTRIBUTION OF CDIA (STOCK) BY INDUSTRY OF ORIGIN AND DESTINATION, 1991 YEAR END

INDUSTRY OF FOREIGN CONCERN	INDUSTRY OF CANADIAN INVESTING ENTERPRISE															
	Food, Beverage & Tobacco	Wood & Paper	Energy	Chemicals, Chemical Products & Textiles	Metallic Minerals & Metal Products	Machinery & Equipment	Transportation Equipment	Electrical & Electronic Products	Construction & Related Activities	Transportation Services	Communications	Finance & Insurance	Accommodation, Restaurants, Recreation Services & Food	Consumer Goods & Services	Other	Total
Food, Beverage & Tobacco	56	0	0	2	0	0	0	0	0	0	0	1	0	0	0	8
Wood & Paper	0	82	0	0	0	0	0	0	0	0	0	0	0	0	0	3
Energy	0	0	90	0	3	2	0	0	0	0	0	0	0	0	10	7
Chemicals, Chemical Products & Textiles	34	1	1	73	0	0	0	1	0	0	0	0	0	1	11	8
Metallic Minerals & Metal Products	0	0	2	0	88	3	0	0	2	0	0	0	0	0	6	13
Machinery & Equipment	0	0	0	0	3	58	0	2	0	0	0	0	0	0	0	1
Transportation Equipment	0	0	1	0	0	0	63	0	0	0	0	0	0	0	1	2
Electrical & Electronic Products	0	0	0	0	0	0	2	95	0	0	0	0	0	22	1	6
Construction & Related Activities	1	1	0	0	2	0	0	0	95	0	0	1	0	0	2	8
Transportation Services	0	0	0	0	0	0	0	0	0	98	0	1	5	0	0	5
Communications	0	0	0	0	0	0	0	0	0	0	99	1	0	0	0	8
Finance & Insurance	0	14	5	22	4	29	34	0	1	1	1	94	13	10	12	25
Accommodation, Restaurants, Recreation Services & Food Retailing	0	0	0	0	0	0	0	0	1	0	0	0	81	0	0	2
Consumer Goods & Services	8	1	0	1	4	8	0	1	0	0	0	0	0	67	10	3
Other	0	0	0	1	0	0	0	0	0	0	0	0	0	0	48	1
Total	100	100	100	100	100	100	100	100	100	100	100	100	100	100	100	100

TABLE 9

PERCENTAGE OF CDIA ACCOUNTED FOR BY HORIZONTAL INVESTMENTS BY AREA OF CONTROL, 1987 AND 1991 YEAR ENDS

ENTERPRISE	YEAR END	
	1987	1991
Canadian-controlled enterprises	82.1	88.7
Foreign-controlled enterprises	72.0	67.4
All enterprises	80.5	84.9

to mine the comparative advantage that has fuelled the growth of these companies in Canada. With respect to the manufacturing sector, the investment abroad may have been hastened by tariff and non-tariff barriers which restricted the flow of trade. Instead of exporting products from Canada, enterprises opted to establish smaller manufacturing replicas of themselves in the protected foreign market. Factors such as these have likely fostered the strategy to establish direct investment operations abroad similar to the firms' industrial activity in Canada.

AREA OF CONTROL OF CANADIAN ENTERPRISES INVESTING ABROAD

GIVEN THAT FOREIGN-CONTROLLED enterprises are international in their operations, it is expected that they are more likely than Canadian-controlled enterprises to diversify their holdings when investing abroad. Canadian-controlled enterprises, on the other hand, may be more likely to adopt conservative strategies characterized by investment in the industry of their expertise.

This is confirmed by the data in Tables 10 through 13, which show the percentage of CDIA by industry of origin and destination for both Canadian- and foreign-controlled companies for the 1987 and 1991 year ends. Investments by Canadian-controlled companies were more horizontal than those by foreign-controlled Canadian enterprises (82 percent compared to 72 percent at the end of 1987). This pattern was further accentuated over the next four years, when the percentages diverged further to 89 percent and 67 percent for the Canadian- and foreign-controlled enterprises respectively. The horizontal integration of Canadian-controlled companies was high in virtually all sectors except for the food, beverage and tobacco sector. Over the period, the more notable increases for Canadian-controlled enterprises were in construction and related activities, transportation equipment, chemicals, chemical products and textiles, and wood and paper. Besides a more cautious strategy for their new investments abroad pursued by Canadian-controlled enterprises in concentrating on their core activities, a number of factors may explain their increased horizontal integration: weak earnings of their foreign

TABLE 10

PERCENTAGE DISTRIBUTION OF CDIA (STOCK) BY INDUSTRY OF ORIGIN AND DESTINATION, 1987 YEAR END

Industry of Foreign Concern	Industry of Canadian Investing Enterprise															
	Food, Beverage & Tobacco	Wood & Paper	Energy	Chemicals, Chemical Products & Textiles	Metallic Minerals & Metal Products	Machinery & Equipment	Transportation Equipment	Electrical & Electronic Products	Construction & Related Activities	Transportation Services	Communications	Finance & Insurance	Accommodation, Restaurants, Recreation Services & Food	Consumer Goods & Services	Other	Total
Food, Beverage & Tobacco	46	0	0	0	0	0	0	0	0	0	0	0	0	0	0	
Wood & Paper	0	82	0	0	0	0	0	0	0	0	0	0	0	0	0	
Energy	0	0	90	10	2	0	10	0	1	3	0	0	0	0	0	
Chemicals, Chemical Products & Textiles	51	1	0	72	0	0	0	0	0	0	0	1	0	3	0	
Metallic Minerals & Metal Products	0	3	6	0	88	1	4	0	2	0	0	0	0	0	3	
Machinery & Equipment	0	0	0	0	1	72	0	0	0	0	0	0	0	0	0	
Transportation Equipment	0	0	0	0	0	0	63	0	0	0	0	0	0	0	9	
Electrical & Electronic Products	0	0	0	0	0	0	1	98	0	0	0	0	0	0	0	
Construction & Related Activities	0	11	0	0	1	0	0	0	71	0	0	3	0	3	16	
Transportation Services	0	1	0	0	0	0	0	0	0	94	0	0	5	0	0	
Communications	0	0	0	0	0	0	0	0	0	0	95	0	0	0	0	
Finance & Insurance	2	2	3	16	5	23	8	0	14	2	4	91	0	2	4	
Accommodation, Restaurants, Recreation Services & Food Retailing	0	0	0	0	0	0	0	0	0	0	0	0	94	0	0	
Consumer Goods & Services	0	1	0	0	4	4	15	2	8	0	0	1	0	91	0	
Other	0	0	1	1	0	0	0	0	0	0	0	0	0	0	67	
Total	100	100	100	100	100	100	100	100	100	100	100	100	100	100	100	100
Total Book Value ($ million)	7,389	2,415	4,004	1,325	9,628	653	307	2,911	4,937	2,031	4,580	12,947	1,633	798	602	56,161

TABLE 11

PERCENTAGE DISTRIBUTION OF CDIA (STOCK) FOR FOREIGN-CONTROLLED ENTERPRISES BY INDUSTRY OF ORIGIN AND DESTINATION, 1987 YEAR END

INDUSTRY OF FOREIGN CONCERN	INDUSTRY OF CANADIAN INVESTING ENTERPRISE															
	Food, Beverage & Tobacco	Wood & Paper	Energy	Chemicals, Chemical Products & Textiles	Metallic Minerals & Metal Products	Machinery & Equipment	Transportation Equipment	Electrical & Electronic Products	Construction & Related Activities	Transportation Services	Communications	Finance & Insurance	Accommodation, Restaurants, Recreation Services & Food	Consumer Goods & Services	Other	Total
Food, Beverage & Tobacco	47	0	0	0	0	0	0	0	0	0	0	3	0	0	0	100
Wood & Paper	0	74	0	0	0	0	0	0	0	0	0	0	0	0	0	100
Energy	7	0	90	0	0	0	0	0	0	0	0	0	0	18	0	100
Chemicals, Chemical Products & Textiles	0	0	1	85	0	0	11	9	0	0	0	0	6	0	0	100
Metallic Minerals & Metal Products	0	0	3	0	100	0	0	0	0	0	0	4	0	0	0	100
Machinery & Equipment	0	0	0	0	0	49	0	0	0	0	0	0	0	60	0	100
Transportation Equipment	1	0	5	0	0	0	86	0	0	0	0	0	0	0	0	100
Electrical & Electronic Products	0	0	0	0	0	0	0	86	0	0	0	0	0	0	0	100
Construction & Related Activities	0	0	0	0	0	0	0	0	97	0	0	0	0	0	40	100
Transportation Services	0	0	0	0	0	0	0	0	0	100	0	19	0	0	0	100
Communications	0	0	0	0	0	0	0	0	0	0	100	0	0	0	0	100
Finance & Insurance	2	19	0	10	0	0	3	6	3	0	0	73	0	0	35	100
Accommodation, Restaurants, Recreation Services & Food Retailing	0	0	0	0	0	0	0	0	0	0	0	0	83	0	25	100
Consumer Goods & Services	43	6	0	6	0	51	0	0	0	0	0	0	0	0	0	100
Other	0	0	0	0	0	0	0	0	0	0	0	0	11	23	0	100
Total	100	100	100	100	100	100	100	100	100	100	100	100	100	100	100	100
Total Book Value ($ million)	3,538	439	1,408	516	984	115	668	101	941	49	6	1,418	7	798	198	10,634

Table 12

Percentage Distribution of CDIA (Stock) for Canadian-Controlled Enterprises by Industry of Origin and Destination, 1991 Year End

Industry of Foreign Concern	Industry of Canadian Investing Enterprise															
	Food, Beverage & Tobacco	Wood & Paper	Energy	Chemicals, Chemical Products & Textiles	Metallic Minerals & Metal Products	Machinery & Equipment	Transportation Equipment	Electrical & Electronic Products	Construction & Related Activities	Transportation Services	Communications	Finance & Insurance	Accommodation, Restaurants, Recreation Services & Food	Consumer Goods & Services	Other	Total
Food, Beverage & Tobacco	56	0	0	0	0	1	0	0	0	0	0	0	0	0	0	8
Wood & Paper	0	95	0	0	0	0	0	0	0	0	0	0	0	0	2	3
Energy	0	0	89	0	0	4	0	0	0	0	0	0	0	0	11	5
Chemicals, Chemical Products & Textiles	43	0	3	98	0	0	0	0	3	0	0	0	0	0	10	8
Metallic Minerals & Metal Products	0	0	0	0	92	5	0	0	0	0	0	0	0	0	5	13
Machinery & Equipment	0	0	0	0	0	88	2	0	0	0	0	0	0	0	0	0
Transportation Equipment	0	0	0	0	0	0	90	0	0	0	0	0	0	0	0	1
Electrical & Electronic Products	0	0	0	0	0	0	6	99	0	0	0	0	0	27	0	7
Construction & Related Activities	0	1	1	0	1	0	0	0	95	0	0	1	0	0	0	8
Transportation Services	0	0	0	0	0	0	0	0	0	98	0	1	0	0	0	6
Communications	0	0	0	0	0	0	0	0	0	0	99	1	0	0	0	10
Finance & Insurance	1	0	0	0	5	0	2	1	1	1	1	94	0	12	10	24
Accommodation, Restaurants, Recreation Services & Food Retailing	0	0	0	0	0	0	0	0	0	0	0	1	93	0	0	2
Consumer Goods & Services	0	2	0	1	1	1	0	0	1	0	0	1	7	60	12	3
Other	0	2	7	1	1	1	0	0	0	1	0	1	0	0	50	1
Total	100	100	100	100	100	100	100	100	100	100	100	100	100	100	100	100
Total Book Value ($ million)	10,462	2,272	4,058	1,590	10,879	250	1,088	5,561	6,184	4,641	7,771	19,181	1,939	853	862	77,591

TABLE 13

PERCENTAGE DISTRIBUTION OF CDIA (STOCK) FOR FOREIGN-CONTROLLED ENTERPRISES BY INDUSTRY OF ORIGIN AND DESTINATION, 1991 YEAR END

INDUSTRY OF FOREIGN CONCERN	INDUSTRY OF CANADIAN INVESTING ENTERPRISE															Total
	Food, Beverage & Tobacco	Wood & Paper	Energy	Chemicals, Chemical Products & Textiles	Metallic Minerals & Metal Products	Machinery & Equipment	Transportation Equipment	Electrical & Electronic Products	Construction & Related Activities	Transportation Services	Communications	Finance & Insurance	Accommodation, Restaurants, Recreation Services & Food	Consumer Goods & Services	Other	
Food, Beverage & Tobacco	57	0	0	4	0	0	0	0	0	0	0	0	0	0	0	9
Wood & Paper	0	66	0	0	0	0	0	0	0	0	0	0	0	0	0	7
Energy	0	0	92	0	9	0	0	0	0	0	0	0	0	0	8	16
Chemicals, Chemical Products & Textiles	0	0	2	49	0	1	0	0	1	0	0	0	0	2	14	5
Metallic Minerals & Metal Products	0	0	0	0	71	0	0	21	0	0	0	0	0	20	10	12
Machinery & Equipment	0	0	0	0	0	39	0	29	0	0	0	0	0	13	0	2
Transportation Equipment	0	0	3	0	0	0	46	0	0	0	0	0	0	0	6	5
Electrical & Electronic Products	0	0	0	0	0	0	0	43	0	0	0	0	0	0	0	1
Construction & Related Activities	0	1	1	1	0	0	0	0	90	0	0	4	1	0	0	5
Transportation Services	0	0	0	0	0	0	0	0	0	100	0	0	0	0	0	0
Communications	0	0	0	0	0	0	0	0	0	0	100	0	0	0	0	0
Finance & Insurance	4	33	1	44	0	47	54	5	4	0	0	96	72	0	19	25
Accommodation, Restaurants, Recreation Services & Food Retailing	0	0	0	0	0	0	0	0	0	0	0	0	27	0	0	1
Consumer Goods & Services	39	0	0	2	20	13	0	2	5	0	0	0	0	100	0	11
Other	0	0	0	0	0	0	0	0	0	0	0	0	0	0	42	1
Total	100	100	100	100	100	100	100	100	100	100	100	100	100	100	100	100
Total Book Value ($ million)	2,659	1,633	2,725	1,624	2,669	414	1,707	395	792	23	4	1,371	433	184	212	16,844

53

concerns; debt problems in Canada compounded by the weakness of the Canadian economy, and the write-offs and even divestiture of investments abroad.

In contrast, foreign-controlled companies were much less integrated horizontally, except for those operating in the energy sector. Compared to 1987, the percentages of horizontal investment increased in seven sectors, remained the same in one, and decreased in seven others. The more noteworthy drops which showed more diversified investments abroad, were in the transportation equipment sector and the metallic minerals and metal products industry.

TOTAL FOREIGN CAPITAL CONTROLLED FROM CANADA

THIS ASPECT OF THE CAPITAL ABROAD controlled from Canada should not be confused with the control of the Canadian direct investor discussed earlier. The elements of capital abroad controlled from Canada comprises direct investment capital owned by the Canadian direct investor, plus, in the case of foreign subsidiaries, third-party long-term financing, covering debt and equity capital from all other sources. Third-party financing in affiliates and in branches is excluded from these elements.

Third-party investment includes borrowings by the subsidiaries from local banks in the host country, bond issues in that country, bond and bank borrowings

TABLE 14

CANADIAN DIRECT AND CONTROLLED INVESTMENT (STOCKS) ABROAD, 1979 TO 1991 YEAR ENDS ($ MILLION)

	A	B	C	D
YEAR END	DIRECT INVESTMENT	THIRD PARTY INVESTMENT	TOTAL INVESTMENT CONTROLLED (A + B)	CONTROLLED TO DIRECT INVESTMENT (C/A)
1979	20,496	13,584	34,080	1.66
1980	26,967	22,198	49,165	1.82
1981	33,847	30,922	64,769	1.91
1982	35,558	35,653	71,211	2.00
1983	39,859	33,699	73,558	1.85
1984	47,422	32,903	80,825	1.70
1985	54,123	38,186	92,309	1.71
1986	58,492	42,952	101,444	1.73
1987	66,794	43,557	110,351	1.65
1988	72,146	51,861	124,007	1.72
1989	80,779	62,194	142,973	1.77
1990	87,886	61,038	148,924	1.70
1991	94,435	50,982	145,417	1.54

from other countries (including Canada), and equity investments from portfolio investors in the host country and other countries. The mirror image of this liability approach is that total controlled investment (column C in Table 14) would be comparable to the long-term assets of the foreign subsidiaries.

Investment abroad controlled from Canada reflects the ability of foreign concerns to tap sources of capital other than the Canadian parent. This combination of elements is a rough indicator of the financial leverage used to increase long-term assets in foreign concerns at the disposal of the Canadian direct investor.

At the end of 1979, the ratio of controlled investment to direct investment was 1.66, i.e., a leverage two-thirds greater than direct investment (Table 14). The ratio climbed to 2.0 at 1982 year end, reflecting large acquisitions abroad which were financed from both Canadian capital outflows and foreign capital. This was the only year when third-party capital was greater than direct investment. The following years saw a contraction in the ratios to 1.54 at the end of 1991. The decline was due to a combination of factors including write-offs, bankruptcies, weak earnings and a pulling back of activities abroad. This relative decline in third party financing may explain the shift toward further funding from Canada as reflected in the substantial net outflows of capital over that period.

The ratios were higher for developed than for developing countries, with 1.58 and 1.33 respectively at the end of 1991. The controlled investment/direct investment ratio for investment located in the United States was the highest at 1.68, closely followed by the United Kingdom at 1.62. The latter ratio had declined considerably in the previous four years when long-term capital from third parties was almost as large as Canadian direct investment in the United Kingdom. The drop in the U.K. ratio was the result of the substitution of capital of third parties by capital from the Canadian direct investor in the electrical and electronic products sector. The ratios for direct investments located in Africa and Asia/Oceania both stood at 1.35.

CONCLUSIONS

THIS STUDY HAS FOCUSED on the dramatic growth in Canadian direct investment abroad between 1986 and 1992. Major highlights include:

- Capital flows into and out of Canada by Canadian multinational enterprises rose to massive proportions after 1986. From 1986 to 1992, the volume of CDIA transactions was more than double the gross flows between 1979 and 1985, gross outflows amounting to $79.1 billion and gross inflows to $36.5 billion.

- At the end of 1991 the United States remained the most favoured location for CDIA, accounting for 58 percent. However, from a peak of 69 percent at the end of 1985, its predominance had gradually fallen, while CDIA in the EEC had risen to 21 percent of the total by the end of 1991.

- By the end of 1991, almost one-quarter of CDIA was in the finance and insurance sector abroad. CDIA in the United States was much more diversified industrially than in other countries.

- Between 1986 and 1991, while the number of Canadian enterprises with direct investment abroad fell slightly, their average investment almost doubled to $68 million.

- Fully 93 percent of CDIA at the end of 1991 was held by slightly less than 15 percent of Canadian enterprises investing abroad.

- Almost one-fifth of CDIA was by enterprises controlled by non-residents by the end of 1991. This was down from a peak of 37 percent in 1969.

- Canadian enterprises with the highest relative propensity to invest abroad, as measured by the ratio of CDIA to their long-term capitalization, were in the electrical and electronic products sector (29 percent). They were followed by enterprises in the metallic and metal products sector and the food, beverage and tobacco products sector, with 25 percent each.

- Generally, Canadian enterprises invested abroad in the same industries in which they were engaged in Canada (exceptions were in the food, beverage and tobacco sector and in other industries). This horizontal investment pattern was more highly accentuated for Canadian-controlled enterprises than for foreign-controlled enterprises.

- The decline in third-party financing by the foreign subsidiaries in recent years may have contributed to additional funding from Canada, as reflected in the sizeable net outflows of direct investment capital.

Canadian enterprises channelled $43 billion in net capital flows abroad over the period between 1986 and 1992 in spite of the recession, which had a dampening effect on the economies of much of the industrialized world. Although they continued to favour the United States, Canadian enterprises also set up large operations in Europe to secure access to the expanding EC market.

In retrospect, the years between 1986 and 1992 proved to be a very turbulent period for Canadian direct investors. On the one hand, Canadian multinationals went abroad to a large extent to position themselves in foreign markets, especially those created by the integration of the European market and other free trade agreements. This translated into a rapid expansion of Canadian direct investment abroad, with large outflows of capital from Canada by the Canadian multinationals. However, the period also saw a drop in the number of Canadian enterprises conducting such investment abroad. Even after taking into account Canadian enterprises investing abroad for the first time during the period, the number of Canadian enterprises with direct investment abroad fell by 10 percent between 1986 and 1992. Many of the smaller direct investors incurred losses, particularly in 1989 and 1990, while the larger direct investors did not generate much profit from their substantial capital base abroad. In fact, a number of very large direct investors encountered serious operational problems, which considerably reduced the size of their foreign holdings and, in the process, affected their Canadian operations. On the other hand, the Canadian multinationals used that experience to learn the ropes of the foreign market, consolidating, restructuring and repositioning their activities and investments abroad.

The relatively faster growth of Canadian direct investment abroad over foreign direct investment in Canada has brought Canadian direct investment assets and liabilities into better balance. No longer mainly a recipient of foreign capital, Canada now acts as a provider of capital on the international scene. The resulting inter-corporate structure created by these international movements of capital may help to explain how Canada is affected by globalization through the behaviour of production, employment, investment and trade.

ENDNOTES

1 For more details about the growth of portfolio capital, see Laliberté, 1993.

2 As CDIA is valued from the books of the foreign concerns and denominated in foreign currencies, there is normally an exchange rate effect upon conversion to Canadian dollars from foreign currencies at the corresponding year-end closing exchange rates. A depreciating Canadian currency translates into a higher value for CDIA expressed in Canadian dollars. On the other hand, an appreciating Canadian dollar as compared to foreign currencies has a dampening effect on the CDIA positions when expressed in Canadian dollars.

3 See Rao, Legault & Ahmad, this volume, for more details about the geographical and industrial characteristics of CDIA.

4 See Statistics Canada Catalogue 67-202 (1992), p. 271, for more details of this conceptual change.

5 See Richards (1985), p. 9, for the role of medium-size enterprises in the tremendous growth in CDIA.

6 Long-term capital comprises shareholders' equity, deferred taxes and long-term debt.

7 See Richards (1985), p. 21, regarding losses by these two sectors.

8 See Gorecki (1990), pp. 23 and 24, for a description of the three types of linkages.

9 For additional details see Type of Foreign Concerns in the Appendix.

ACKNOWLEDGEMENTS

I WISH TO THANK Lucie Laliberté, the Director of the Balance of Payments Division, for suggesting our participation in the conference, Canadian-based Multinational Enterprises, and her many helpful comments. The contribution of my colleagues in the Division is also much appreciated, particularly, Linda Saikaley, Tai Hu, Emmanuel Manolikakis and Jill Watson.

APPENDIX: CONCEPT OF CANADIAN DIRECT INVESTMENT ABROAD

CANADIAN DIRECT INVESTMENT ABROAD is defined as investment made to acquire a lasting interest in a concern operating abroad with a view to have an effective voice in the management of that concern. The Canadian entity or group of associated entities that makes the investment is termed 'the Canadian direct investor'.

Having a lasting interest and a role in the management of the foreign concerns are the two key elements that distinguish direct investment from portfolio investment. The latter, which is more passive in nature, is concerned primarily about the safety and the return of the capital.

Direct investment is a balance of payments concept which has been defined by both the International Monetary Fund (IMF) and the OECD to ensure harmony of treatment among countries. According to this definition, the ownership of a 10 percent equity in a foreign firm establishes the presence of direct investment. Canada has generally adopted that threshold, except for a few isolated cases where direct investment was deemed to occur even with less than 10 percent equity ownership.

According to the IMF and OECD definition, direct investment also encompasses both long- and short-term capital. So far, Canada has considered only the long-term capital as direct investment: that is, long-term debt (bonds, debentures, loans, advances) and equity (common and preferred shares and retained earnings). A study over the period from 1987 to 1991 indicated that the inclusion of short-term capital would increase direct investment estimates by only 4 percent. For example, at the end of 1991, Canadian direct investment would amount to $98 billion, or $3.5 billion higher than the current estimates, made up of $1.5 billion of trade receivables and $2 billion of short-term claims on foreign concerns.

CANADIAN DIRECT INVESTMENT ABROAD – CAPITAL FLOWS AND POSITION DATA

THE MOVEMENT OF CAPITAL for Canadian direct investment abroad is part of Canada's Balance of Payments,[1] whereas the Canadian direct investment positions are part of Canada's International Investment Position.[2] The movement of capital includes cross-border flows which increase or decrease the amount of capital abroad owned by a Canadian direct investor. Such outflows include the increase in shares and the extension of long-term loans to foreign concerns. Conversely, inflows cover the redemption of shares in foreign concerns by the Canadian direct investor and the repayment of long-term loans. Over and above these flows to and from the foreign concerns, direct investment capital flows also include the acquisition or sale of foreign concerns by the Canadian direct investors. Finally, capital flows also cover share exchanges, although these do not strictly involve a flow of capital. Movement of direct investment capital is valued at transaction value as reported by the Canadian direct investors. If the flows are denominated in foreign currencies, they are translated at the noon average of the calendar quarter or month in which the transactions took place.

On the other hand, the position estimates of direct investment reflect, in addition to the cumulation of flows, a number of factors such as earnings retained in the foreign concerns, exchange rate fluctuations, valuation adjustments and other accounting adjustments. The position estimates are compiled on the basis of the financial statements of the foreign concerns and reflect the values owned by or accruing to the Canadian direct investors. As the balance sheet items of the foreign concerns are normally denominated in foreign currencies, the position estimates are converted to Canadian dollars at the end of the year and thus reflect the fluctuations of the Canadian dollar against these currencies.

The distinction between flow and position also extends to the industrial classifications. Direct investment flows are classified according to the industrial classification of the direct investors, since the data are obtained from the Canadian direct investors on a quarterly or annual basis. The stock estimates are, however, presented according to the industrial classification of the foreign concerns.

FOREIGN CONTROL OF CANADIAN DIRECT INVESTORS

MANY OF THE CANADIAN ENTERPRISES that have direct investments abroad are themselves controlled from abroad. In fact, for many years Canada has been used as a conduit country by foreign investors who set up Canadian companies to channel their investments to other countries. Until 1979 such investment, when conducted through wholly owned Canadian subsidiaries, was excluded from Canadian direct investment; it has since been incorporated into the CDIA series.

Whether controlled from abroad or from Canada, Canadian direct investors, in turn, often control the foreign concerns in which they conduct direct investment. Thus in addition to the capital they own in these foreign concerns, they also control the long-term capital which was financed from third parties in these concerns. This aspect of foreign capital controlled from Canada is discussed in the final section of this study.

TYPE OF FOREIGN CONCERNS

CDIA IS PRESENTED ACCORDING to three distinct types of foreign concerns: subsidiaries, affiliates and branches. *Subsidiaries* comprise companies that are wholly or more than 50 percent owned by the Canadian direct investors.

These also include the few Canadian incorporated companies whose business operations are entirely outside of Canada (referred to as extra-national companies).

Affiliates comprise companies incorporated abroad in which the Canadian direct investors have less than a 50 percent ownership of equity. These include a number of cases where the Canadian direct investors own a significant interest only in the preferred shares of a related company outside Canada. Such cases usually arise with foreign-controlled Canadian direct investors, where the two companies are related through ultimate common ownership by a foreign parent.

Branches comprise unincorporated investment abroad (of a direct investment nature) by Canadian incorporated companies. The investment abroad may be a manufacturing establishment or a merchandising or a distribution office located in the foreign country. Also included are interests such as leases, ventures and expenditures for exploration and development abroad by Canadian mining and oil and gas enterprises.

ENDNOTES

1 Refer to quarterly issues of Cat. 67-001, *Canada's Balance of International Payments*.
2 Refer to annual publications of Cat. 67-202, *Canada's International Investment Position*.

BIBLIOGRAPHY

Detailed Bench-mark Definition of Foreign Direct Investment. Paris: OECD, 1992, 2nd Edition.

Gorecki, Paul. "Patterns of Canadian Foreign Direct Investment Abroad." Statistics Canada, Analytical Branch, #33, 1990.

International Monetary Fund. *Balance of Payments Manual.* Washington, D.C.: IMF, 1977, Fourth Edition.

Laliberté, Lucie. "Globalization and Canada's International Investment Position." *Canadian Economic Observer*, April, 1993.

Richards, C.F.J. "Canadian Direct Investment Position Abroad: Trends and Recent Developments." Statistics Canada, mimeo, 1985.

Statistics Canada. *The Canadian Balance of International Payments and International Investment Position, A Description of Sources and Methods*, Catalogue 67-506E. Ottawa: Ministry of Supply and Services, 1981.

Statistics Canada. *Canada's International Investment Position, Historical Statistics, 1926 to 1992.* Catalogue 67-202. Ottawa: Ministry of Supply and Services, 1993.

United Nations Centre on Transnational Corporations. *The Determinants of Foreign Direct Investment.* New York: United Nations, 1992.

Someshwar Rao, Marc Legault & Ashfaq Ahmad
Industry and Science Policy
Industry Canada

3

Canadian-Based Multinationals: An Analysis of Activities and Performance

INTRODUCTION

THROUGH THEIR TRADE, investment and innovation activities, transnational corporations (TNCs) play an important role in sustaining Canada's economic growth and development, as they do in many other developed and developing countries. While some concern has been expressed about the oligopolistic characteristics of transnational firms and the markets in which they operate, there is strong evidence that during the post-war period TNCs have made significant contributions to the integration and prosperity of the world economies. This was achieved by improving the efficiency and the allocation of the world's productive resources, and by increasing the flexibility and adaptability of product and factor markets around the globe. This study supports this view in its examination of Canadian-based TNCs abroad.

According to the United Nations Centre for Transnational Corporations (UNCTC, 1993), there are at present over 37,000 transnational corporations world wide, controlling some 170,000 foreign affiliates. However, a small number of transnational firms represent half of the foreign activity of these firms. In 1992 the top 1 percent of these transnationals accounted for almost 50 percent of the total stock of world outward direct investment (US$ 2 trillion).

Canada's share of the world's transnational population is about 3.5 percent. Because of the rapid pace of internationalization of business by Canadian firms during the 1980s, the stock of Canadian direct investment abroad (CDIA) grew at a relatively faster rate than the global stock of outward direct investment. Consequently, Canada's share of world outward direct investment stock increased from 4.0 percent in 1980 to over 4.5 percent in 1990 (Rutter, 1992). In other words, Canada is today a major host and home country for foreign direct investment (FDI).

In the 1980s, a variety of interrelated trends in the world economy increased the pace of globalization by transnational companies. These trends included: shifts in the comparative advantage position of firms and nations; marked reductions in transportation and communication costs; rapid changes in product and process technologies; shorter product cycles; increased convergence of consumer tastes across countries; the emergence of newly-industrialized Asian countries as important forces in the world economy; the liberalization of trade, investment and financial flows; increased need for large investments in R&D and the increased uncertainty and risk associated with the returns on these investments; and fierce and increased international competition for markets. Furthermore, in order to stimulate growth of their economies, national governments focused their promotional efforts on attracting the investment and innovation activities of transnational corporations. All these developments both necessitated and facilitated the rapid pace of internationalization of business.

Transnational corporations are also becoming increasingly footloose by carrying out their production, sourcing, financing, investment and innovation activities on a regional and global basis. In fact, transnationals are increasingly oriented toward integrating their business activities on a global scale in an effort to improve efficiency, minimize costs, maximize performance and increase global market share.

Transnationals are adopting a range of complementary strategies for obtaining access to international markets and complementary new technologies, for improving their competitive position, and for properly managing the uncertainty and risk associated with huge investments in physical and human capital and R&D. These include mergers and acquisitions, greenfield investments, minority ownership, joint ventures and strategic alliances, subcontracting and licensing, among others.

In short, the role of transnational corporations in the world economy has increased dramatically over the past decade and this trend is expected to continue in the future. For instance, the stock of world outward direct investment increased almost fourfold from US$ 519 billion in 1980 to US$ 2 trillion in 1992, outpacing the growth in world output and trade. According to UNCTC estimates, transnationals account for over one-third of world private sector GDP.

Canadian transnationals have also actively participated in the globalization process; there are over 1,300 TNCs based in Canada today. As with global direct investment, the stock of CDIA increased rapidly in the 1980s, increasing from C$ 27 billion in 1980 to C$ 99 billion in 1992. Consequently, the ratio of CDIA stock to the Canadian foreign direct investment stock (CFDI) increased from 0.40 in 1980 to 0.73 in 1992.

The influences of FDI on the Canadian economy have been studied extensively (Investment Canada, 1992). By comparison, little attention has been devoted to studying the potential consequences of CDIA and its effect on Canada's competitive position and welfare. However, earlier research of Litvak & Maule (1981), Matheson (1987), Rugman (1987), and Knubley, Krause & Sadeque (1991) examined the motivations of CDIA in some detail.

The broad objectives of this study are to examine the recent trends in CDIA, to analyze the performance of outward-oriented Canadian firms and to assess the effect of their activities on Canada. In particular, our research attempts to answer the following questions:

- How has the geographic and industrial distribution of CDIA changed over the last 20 years?

- What factors account for the dramatic increase in CDIA?

- What are the characteristics of top Canadian transnational corporations?

- Does an increase in CDIA crowd out investment in Canada?

- Are exports and direct investment abroad substitutes or complements?

- How well are the U.S. affiliates of Canadian TNCs performing in the United States relative to those from other countries?

- Do outward-oriented Canadian firms perform better than domestically oriented firms?

- What are the possible costs and benefits of CDIA to Canada?

The organization of this study is as follows: the next section describes the recent trends in the geographic and industrial distribution of CDIA and identifies the broad macroeconomic factors that could explain the emerging trends. We go on to link the industrial and geographic distribution of CDIA to the structure and characteristics of the top outward-oriented Canadian firms. Next, we analyze the consequences of rapid growth of CDIA on a number of other economic indicators in Canada such as direct investment income, trade flows, foreign sales and competitiveness. The effect of CDIA on Canada's competitive position is analyzed by comparing the growth of sales and assets, productivity, and the profitability performance of the top outward-oriented Canadian companies *vis-à-vis* the top domestically oriented Canadian companies. The relative productivity, trade and R&D performance of the U.S. affiliates of Canadian TNCs, in relation to the affiliates of other countries in the United States, is also examined. Finally, we summarize our main findings and briefly examine their policy implications.

Our empirical analysis of the determinants of domestic capital formation in Canada and other G-7 countries suggests that an increase in direct investment abroad need not necessarily reduce investment in home countries. By the same token, our analysis indicates that trade flows and direct investment are complements rather than substitutes. More importantly, the growth and productivity performance of outward-oriented Canadian-based firms, on average, tend to be superior to the performance of domestically oriented Canadian-based firms. These results imply that an increase in CDIA could be of benefit to Canada.

CDIA Trends and Determinants

IN THIS SECTION WE EXAMINE the broad trends in world direct investment and Canadian direct investment abroad (CDIA). We then analyze the macro determinants of these developments and conclude with a discussion of micro factors, including the structure and characteristics of top Canadian-based TNCs. Before proceeding, however, a brief review of the major trends in world foreign direct investment (FDI) should be useful.

Global Trends

THE GROWTH OF WORLD OUTWARD INVESTMENT stock increased on average by over 10 percent per year between 1980 and 1992, almost double the rate of growth of world output and trade. Consequently, the stock of world outward direct investment increased from US$ 519 billion in 1980 to approximately US$ 2 trillion in 1992. The international production activities of TNCs generated about US$ 5.5 trillion of foreign sales in 1992, much of which is attributable to the large and growing role of intra-firm trade. According to the UNCTC estimates, TNCs account for about 80 percent of world trade.

Another global development has been the dramatic increase in the U.S. dependence on FDI in the 1980s. As a result, the U.S. share of world FDI stock increased from 16 percent in 1980 to over 25 percent in 1992, making the United States the largest host country of FDI in the period. In sharp contrast, Japan's share of world outward investment stock increased from a mere 4 percent in 1980 to almost 15 percent in 1992. A large portion of the increase in FDI in the United States came from Japan, raising the Japanese share of FDI in America from 6.2 percent in 1980 to 21.3 percent in 1991.

The rapid increase in world FDI has been accompanied by marked shifts in its industrial composition – away from primary and resource-based manufacturing industries toward services and technology-intensive manufacturing industries. These shifts have been pervasive across most industrialized countries. For instance, in six of the seven G-7 countries (excluding the United Kingdom), the share of service industries in FDI has increased considerably in the last decade (UNCTC, 1993; Ostry & Gestrin, 1993).

Huge investment/savings imbalances in the United States and Japan (as reflected by their current account imbalances), the large depreciation of the Japanese yen vis-à-vis the U.S. dollar, the threat of increased protectionism in the United States, and growing labour shortages in Japan all contributed to the emergence of Japan as a major home country and the United States as the largest host country of world FDI stock in the 1980s (Ostry, 1990; Dobson, 1993).

Large shifts in domestic economic activity toward service industries, rapid advances in information technology, privatization, and the liberalization of services' trade and investment (especially financial services) all help to explain the changes in the industrial composition of world FDI stock.

TRENDS IN CDIA

CANADIAN TNCS HAVE PARTICIPATED very actively in the process of globalization. Between 1980 and 1992 the stock of CDIA increased at a faster pace than world outward direct investment stock, reaching $ 99 billion in 1992. As a result, the Canadian share of world outward investment stock increased from 4.0 percent in 1980 to almost 5 percent in 1992. During this period the share of CDIA in Canadian GDP also increased from 8.7 percent to 14.4 percent. The increased outward orientation is pervasive across all major Canadian industries.[1]

Moreover, the relationship between CDIA and FDI stocks has become much more balanced in the last 25 years. The ratio of outward to inward investment stock increased steadily from 0.23 in 1970 to 0.72 in 1992.[2] Similar outward orientation has occurred in all major Canadian industries, although in the financial services and mining industries the stock of Canadian outward direct investment currently exceeds the corresponding stock of inward direct investment. For instance, in the financial services industry, the ratio of outward to inward direct investment stock increased from a meagre 0.47 in 1980 to 1.05 in 1991 (Figure 1). Similarly, Canada's investment relations with all its major commercial partners have also become more balanced during this period.

Geographic Distribution

As with trade, Canada's investment linkages with the United States are very strong, accounting for over 65 percent of Canada's inward direct investment stock. The United States is also the largest host country for CDIA. The U.S. share of CDIA declined significantly from its peak of 68.5 percent in 1980 to 58 percent in 1992.

The United Kingdom is the second largest host country to CDIA. More than 60 percent of the decline in the U.S. share of CDIA over the second half of the 1980s was captured by the United Kingdom. Its share of CDIA stock averaged 11 percent between 1986 and 1991, compared to the U.S. share of about 63 percent. Figure 2 shows an increase in the share of other E.C. countries, mainly France and the Netherlands, during this period.

Canadian investment in the Asia Pacific Rim, the fastest growing region in the world, increased markedly in the 1980s albeit from a very small base. For instance, the share of Japan and Singapore in CDIA increased from only 1.0 percent in 1982 to 3.8 percent in 1991.

FIGURE 1

RATIO OF STOCK OF CANADIAN DIRECT INVESTMENT ABROAD (CDIA) TO
FOREIGN DIRECT INVESTMENT (FDI) IN CANADA, 1980 TO 1991

Source: Industry Canada compilations based on Statistics Canada data.

Industrial Distribution

As with the world stock of outward direct investment, the share of primary
industries in CDIA has declined markedly over the last three decades. The
combined share of mining, petroleum and gas, and utilities declined from 36.5
percent in 1960 to 15.7 percent in 1991. Similarly, the share of manufacturing
sector declined from 55.9 percent in 1960 to 43.8 percent in 1991. Conversely,
the share of financial services increased from a mere 1.3 percent in 1960 to 30.2
percent in 1991. The share of other industries (largely other services) also
increased considerably (Figure 3). It is noteworthy that much of the change in
the industrial composition of CDIA has occurred during the last 10 to 12 years.

More than three-quarters of CDIA in the manufacturing sector is still
concentrated in resource-based manufacturing industries (mainly primary
metals, wood and paper products, and beverages). However, the share of
technology-intensive industries (mainly chemicals and chemical products, and
electrical and non-electrical machinery) has increased substantially over the

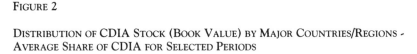

FIGURE 2

DISTRIBUTION OF CDIA STOCK (BOOK VALUE) BY MAJOR COUNTRIES/REGIONS -
AVERAGE SHARE OF CDIA FOR SELECTED PERIODS

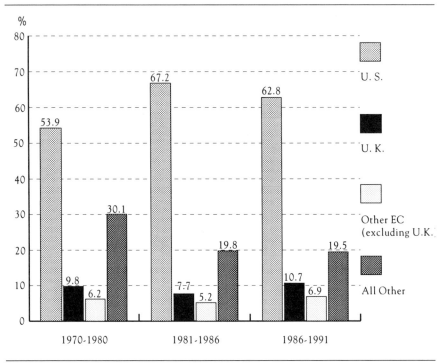

Source: Industry Canada compilations using data from Statistics Canada.

last 30 years. For instance, the share of chemicals and chemical products in manufacturing CDIA increased from a mere 2.6 percent in 1960 to 15.9 percent in 1991 (Figure 4).

The trends in the industrial composition of CDIA have also been pervasive in the outward investment patterns of all Canada's major commercial partners. The industrial distribution of CFDI stock experienced similar structural changes, although not to the same extent as CDIA.

REASONS FOR THE TRENDS

THE DISCUSSION SO FAR has identified three broad trends in CDIA: a much faster growth in Canadian direct investment abroad than in Canadian foreign direct investment (CFDI); a decline in the U.S. share of CFDI in the second half of the 1980s, largely in favour of Europe; and the increasing importance of

FIGURE 3

DISTRIBUTION OF BOOK VALUE (STOCK) OF CDIA BY INDUSTRY,
1960 AND 1991 (% OF TOTAL AND $ BILLION)

1960 CDIA Value = $2.5 Billion

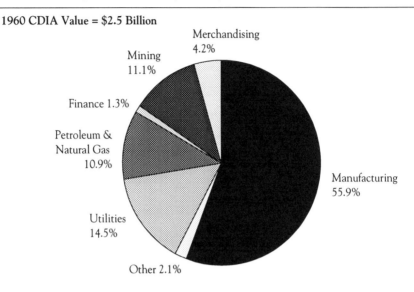

1991 CDIA Value = $94.4 Billion

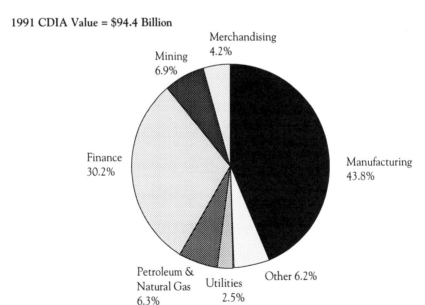

Source: Industry Canada compilations using data from Statistics Canada.

FIGURE 4

DISTRIBUTION OF BOOK VALUE (STOCK) OF CDIA IN MANUFACTURING,
1960 AND 1991 (% OF TOTAL AND $ BILLION)

1960 Value = $1.4 Billion

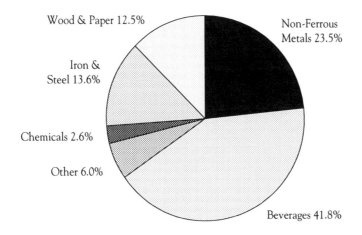

1991 Value = $41.4 Billion

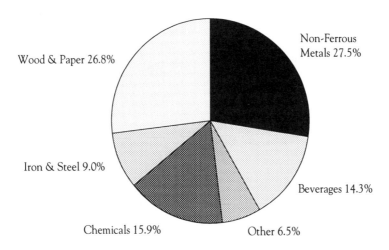

Source: Industry Canada compilations using data from Statistics Canada.

71

the financial services and the chemicals and chemical products industries. We now move to an examination of the roles of these global trends and the macro-economic factors related to their developments.

Motivations for Foreign Production

Transnational firms use direct investment as a primary vehicle for undertaking international production and innovation activities. They undertake FDI through a number of complementary strategies: mergers and acquisitions, greenfield investments, and minority ownership and strategic alliances, including joint ventures.

The motivations for international production have been extensively analyzed (Caves, 1982; Dunning, 1985; Cantwell, 1989; Rugman, 1987; and Globerman, 1993) and it is clear that foreign production permits firms to maximize the benefits from their ownership advantages by making more effective use of their (country-specific) locational advantages. The ownership advantages of firms include: up-to-date and superior technology, management know-how, large pools of capital and skilled labour, and a superior knowledge of markets and consumer tastes, as well as knowledge of emerging products and process innovations. Firms try to maximize the returns to these ownership advantages by undertaking production, investment and innovation activities in countries that offer superior locational advantages.

The country-specific advantages include factors such as the availability/proximity of natural resources and raw materials, availability of skilled labour, market size, proximity to larger markets, well developed physical and technological infrastructure, lower factor prices (labour and capital costs), flexible and dynamic factor and product markets, and competitive government incentives and market framework policies. In short, internationalization of production and innovation activities permits firms to minimize and diversify risks, minimize costs and maximize the benefits of ownership advantages.

A number of other complementary and interrelated global trends have both necessitated and facilitated the rapid expansion of direct investment and production by Canadian-based and non-Canadian-based transnationals, thus contributing to the creation of a cycle of globalization. These developments are: fierce and growing international competition for markets; removal of tariff barriers and the liberalization of capital flows across many countries; increasing use (actual and perceived) of non-tariff barriers to trade by national governments; increased risks and uncertainty associated with returns to large investments in physical capital and R&D; the presence of significant scale and scope economies; dramatic reduction in transportation and communication costs; and the emergence of niche markets.

Rapid Expansion of CDIA

The marked growth of CDIA stock relative to the growth of CFDI stock can be examined in terms of a number of important push and pull factors (Rugman, 1987). Deteriorating domestic economic conditions and unfavourable economic policies at home can push investments away from home countries and encourage firms to seek investment opportunities abroad. Conversely, a favourable economic climate and increased investment opportunities in foreign markets, rapid changes in technology, and firm-specific and country-specific comparative economic advantages can also pull investments toward host countries.

Among other factors, push and pull factors might include: an increased outward-orientation of Canadian firms (necessitated and facilitated by rapid structural changes in the global economy); relatively faster growth of real aggregate demand in Canada vis-à-vis other countries (especially the United States and the United Kingdom); large investment-savings imbalances in Canada and other industrialized countries; changes in the relative profitability position of various locations; variations in exchange rates and unit labour costs; increased use of non-tariff barriers (NTBs); and procedural protection in the United States and Europe 1992.

The effect of differences in the growth of domestic and foreign economic activity on the relative growth of CDIA stock can be analyzed in terms of two main variables: the growth of non-residential capital stock (nominal terms) in Canada and other countries (mainly the United States and the United Kingdom), and differences in the size of the elasticities of CDIA and CFDI with respect to domestic and foreign capital stock (including variations in these elasticities over time).

Taken by themselves, the growth rates of nominal stock capture only the effects of economic activity at home and abroad on CDIA and CFDI over time, assuming there are stable direct investment elasticities. Therefore, absolute differences in the sensitivity of CDIA and CFDI to changes in nominal capital stock and/or the relative variations in these elasticities of direct investment over time would affect the trends in CDIA and CFDI stocks differently, even without any differences in the growth rates of capital stock at home and abroad.

During the 1970s and the first half of the 1980s, the growth of capital stock in the United States (the largest host country of CDIA) was slightly lower than in Canada.[3] This implies that the differences in capital accumulation might not have contributed significantly to the rapid growth of CDIA during these two periods. On the other hand, some of the rapid growth in CDIA stock between 1986 and 1991 might be attributed to a faster growth of capital stock in the United States and the United Kingdom relative to Canada (Figure 5).

Thus, the differences in the size of the two direct investment stock elasticities and their relative variation over time could, to a large extent, explain the rapid expansion of CDIA stock relative to CFDI stock. The CDIA

FIGURE 5

AVERAGE ANNUAL GROWTH RATE OF PRIVATE NON-RESIDENTIAL CAPITAL STOCK
BY COUNTRY FOR SELECTED PERIODS (%)

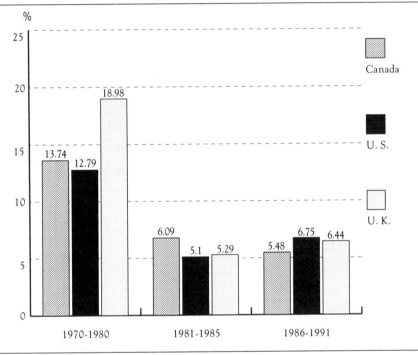

Source: Industry Canada compilations using data from Statistics Canada and OECD.

stock elasticity is well above the CFDI stock elasticity in all three periods. However, Table 1 shows that the gap between the two elasticities narrowed significantly over the second half of the 1980s. This development may also have contributed to slow the rate of growth of aggregate CDIA/CFDI ratio since the mid-1980s.

The higher sensitivity of CDIA stock to foreign economic activity relative to the sensitivity of FDI stock to economic activity in Canada could be due to a number of factors, some of which include: increased outward-orientation of Canadian firms; larger savings-investment imbalances in other countries; relatively faster rate of growth of real aggregate demand in other countries; and consistently higher rates of return on investment in other countries (probably due to lower production costs, a lower tax burden and larger investment subsidies). These propositions are generally supported by our empirical analysis[4] which also suggests three possible explanations for the elasticity gap: 1) the improved profit position in the United States and United

TABLE 1

ELASTICITY OF CDIA AND FDI TO PRIVATE NON-RESIDENTIAL CAPITAL STOCK, 1970 TO 1991

ELASTICITY OF CDIA TO FOREIGN PRIVATE NON-RESIDENTIAL CAPITAL STOCK

PERIOD	TOTAL	U.S.	U.K.	FRANCE
1970-1980	1.22	1.39	0.90	0.85
1981-1986	2.02	2.36	1.68	0.46
1986-1991	2.13	1.00	3.40	5.84

ELASTICITY OF FDI TO CANADIAN PRIVATE NON-RESIDENTIAL CAPITAL STOCK

PERIOD	CANADA	U.S.	U.K.	FRANCE	OTHER E.C.	E.C.	GERMANY
1970-1980	0.65	0.63	0.59	0.76	0.90	0.72	1.26
1981-1986	0.92	0.74	1.80	0.87	0.59	1.28	0.75
1986-1991	1.34	0.83	1.62	3.34	2.63	2.03	2.88

RATIO OF THE ELASTICITY OF CDIA TO THE ELASTICITY OF FDI

PERIOD	TOTAL	U.S.	U.K.	FRANCE
1970-1980	1.87	2.21	1.53	1.12
1981-1986	2.20	3.19	0.93	0.53
1986-1991	1.59	1.20	2.10	1.75

Source: Estimates based on data from Statistics Canada.

Kingdom relative to Canada (Figure 6); 2) the need for huge sums of foreign capital in the United States in the 1980s (as reflected by the large current account deficits) and; 3) restructuring/rationalization, due to the anticipated Canada-U.S. free trade agreement.[5]

It is also possible that changes in real aggregate demand, unit labour costs and exchange rates might not have played a significant role in the determination of trends in the elasticity gap. On average, there appears to be no significant difference in the growth of real aggregate demand in Canada and other countries, particularly the United States and Western European countries (Figure 7).

In general, trends in CDIA stock were not consistent with the observed trends of both exchange rates and unit labour costs (Figures 8 and 9). For instance, between 1981 and 1985, CDIA stock grew very rapidly, despite a large depreciation of the Canadian dollar and an improved cost position of Canadian exporters vis-à-vis international competitors.[6] Labour costs, however, are only a small (and declining) share of total production costs. Therefore, they are not expected to play a significant role in the locational decisions of Canadian TNCs, particularly in the industrialized countries. Thus, the greater

FIGURE 6

RELATIVE PROFITABILITY - GROSS OPERATING SURPLUS AS A % OF GROSS PRIVATE
NON-RESIDENTIAL CAPITAL STOCK, 1970 TO 1991

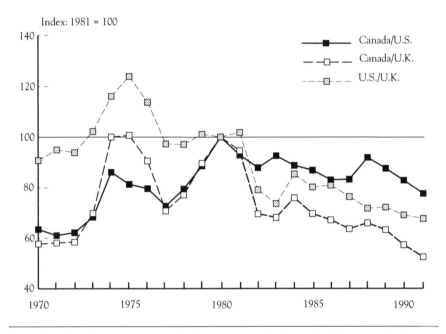

Source: Industry Canada compilations using data from OECD.

sensitivity of CDIA to the growth in foreign capital could be largely due to the
increased outward-orientation of Canadian TNCs which, in turn, could be
attributed to: the emergence of mature and strong Canadian firms; the
increased importance of scale economies; the threat of increased non-tariff
trade protection in the United States and fortress Europe; the need for market
diversification; and the emergence of niche markets.

In summary, pull factors appear to have contributed largely to the rapid
growth of CDIA stock relative to CFDI stock in the 1980s. These include a
greater outward-orientation of Canadian TNCs, a substantial need for foreign
capital in the United States, an improved profitability picture in the United
States and the United Kingdom, and a relatively faster growth rate of non-
residential capital stock in these two countries.

Increased Regional Diversification

The above framework can also be used to analyze trends in the geographic distribution of CDIA. Differences among host countries with respect to trends in economic activity, profitability, liberalization of trade and capital flows, exchange rates, threat of protectionism, availability of skilled people, factor costs, tax and regulatory burden, investment incentives, and the need for an increased and broader outward orientation by Canadian TNCs help to explain the temporal changes in the geographic composition of CDIA.

Real aggregate demand in the United States increased by 3.4 percent per year between 1980 and 1985, compared to only about 0.9 percent in the E.C. (Figure 7), suggesting that it may have contributed to the increased importance of the U.S. market to CDIA. The increased use of non-tariff barriers (NTBs) and the threat of increased protection in the United States might have also contributed to the rise in U.S. share of CDIA. On the other hand, a reversal of the GDP trends in the second half of the 1980s may also

FIGURE 7

AVERAGE ANNUAL GROWTH OF REAL DOMESTIC DEMAND FOR SELECTED COUNTRIES/REGIONS, 1972-1992

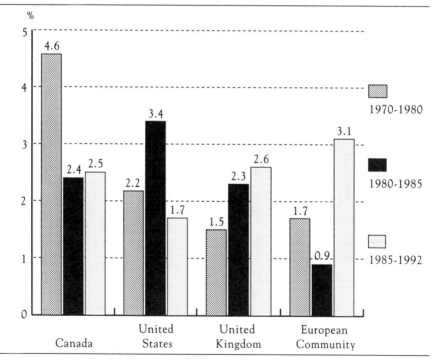

Source: Industry Canada compilations using data from OECD.

FIGURE 8

EXCHANGE RATES[a], CANADA, THE UNITED KINGDOM AND THE UNITED STATES, 1970-1992

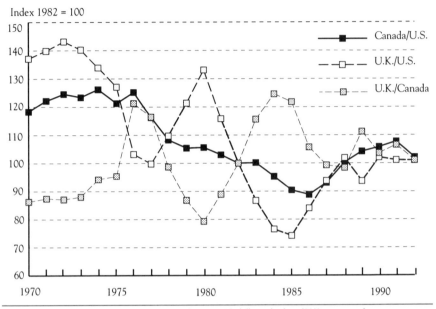

Note: [a] Value of U.K. and Canadian currency relative to U.S. dollar and value of U.K. currency relative to Canadian dollar.

Source: U.S. Dept. of Labor, Bureau of Labor Statistics.

have contributed to the growing importance of the E.C. to CDIA since 1986. A significant improvement in the relative profit position of the United Kingdom, the major host of CDIA in Europe, might also explain some of the increase in the share of CDIA going to the E.C. during this period (Figures 6 and 7).

The sharp increase in the sensitivity of CDIA to increases in capital stock in the United Kingdom and France during this period suggests that other factors could also have played a significant role in the growing importance of CDIA to Europe since 1986. These include expanded market opportunities associated with the formation of Europe 1992, the fear of fortress Europe, and the increased global orientation of Canadian TNCs.[7] Nonetheless, the relative trends in exchange rates and unit labour costs suggest that these factors may have played little or no role in influencing the trends in the geographic distribution of CDIA in the 1980s. As mentioned earlier, labour costs are a minor consideration for Canadian TNCs in their location decisions. Furthermore, labour and low-skill-intensive portions of the production chain are expected to move to the developing and newly industrialized countries with lower unit labour costs, rather than to high-wage economies like the United Kingdom and France.

FIGURE 9

RELATIVE UNIT LABOUR COST IN MANUFACTURING, CANADA, THE UNITED
KINGDOM AND THE UNITED STATES, 1977-1992

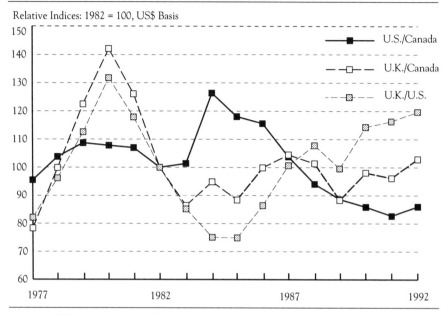

Source: U.S. Dept. of Labor, Bureau of Labor Statistics.

The Increased Importance of Services

The growing share of services and technology-intensive manufacturing
industries in the CDIA stock is consistent with the global trends discussed
earlier. Structural changes in the industrial composition of output in all
countries (the increased importance of service and technology-intensive
manufacturing industries in GDP and employment), the declining trend in
real prices of resources and resource-based manufacturing products, and the
liberalization of financial services help to explain the trends in the industrial
composition of world direct investment and CDIA stocks. However, resources
and resource-based manufacturing industries still account for a large share of
CDIA which primarily reflects the structure and characteristics of Canadian
TNCs, as discussed in the next section.

In short, our analysis suggests that a number of pull factors have
contributed largely to the rapid growth of CDIA relative to the growth of
CFDI in the last 20 years or so. We must allow, however, that the effects of
changes in exchange rates and unit labour costs have been difficult to assess
and that they may not have played a significant role in the determination of

TABLE 2

INDUSTRIAL DISTRIBUTION OF SALES, ASSETS, FOREIGN SALES AND FOREIGN ASSETS OF OUTWARD-ORIENTED CANADIAN-BASED FIRMS (%)

MAJOR INDUSTRY GROUPING	INDUSTRY	NO. OF FIRMS	TOTAL SALES (%)	TOTAL ASSETS (%)	FOREIGN SALES (%)	FOREIGN ASSETS (%)
Agriculture, Fish & Forestry		1	0.24	0.07	0.41	0.01
Mining		32	11.12	10.53	17.21	11.16
Construction		3	1.00	0.51	1.64	0.71
Labour-Intensive Manufacturing		12	8.49	5.04	13.01	8.94
	Textiles	2	0.76	0.32	1.27	0.63
	Clothing	0				
	Printing & Publishing	9	7.67	4.69	11.67	8.28
	Miscellaneous Manufactured Goods	1	0.07	0.02	0.07	0.02
Resource-Intensive Manufacturing		34	19.62	12.87	22.73	14.03
	Food & Products	4	5.07	3.64	8.56	7.27
	Tobacco	1	0.01	0.01	0.02	0.01
	Lumber & Wood	4	5.35	4.25	6.00	2.81
	Paper & Allied	7	4.41	2.57	4.34	1.81
	Petroleum Refining	0				
	Non-Metallic Minerals	3	0.58	0.33	0.30	0.18
	Primary Metals	11	3.48	1.80	3.03	1.73
	Fabricated Metals	4	0.71	0.28	0.48	0.22
Technology-Intensive Manufacturing		27	16.31	5.88	17.36	8.71
	Chemicals & Allied	4	0.60	0.28	0.87	0.36
	Rubber & Products	2	0.26	0.08	0.14	0.06
	Machinery excluding Electrical	5	2.22	0.94	4.21	1.57
	Computer & Office	2	0.37	0.13	0.63	0.23
	Electrical Products	3	0.15	0.07	0.10	0.05
	Communications Equipment	3	4.37	2.39	5.77	3.82
	Miscellaneous Electrical Products	1	0.14	0.08	0.09	0.04

TABLE 2 (CONT'D)

Major Industry Grouping	Industry	No. of Firms	Total Sales (%)	Total Assets (%)	Foreign Sales (%)	Foreign Assets (%)
	Motor Vehicles & Equipment	2	6.31	1.00	3.12	0.96
	Aircraft & Parts	3	1.41	0.66	1.81	1.12
	Light Machinery	2	0.48	0.26	0.62	0.51
Transportation		5	5.89	5.65	4.78	3.70
Communications		5	9.03	9.89	8.18	5.63
Utilities		1	0.77	0.57	0.11	0.02
Trade		14	13.52	2.79	7.17	2.24
	Wholesale Trade	7	5.77	1.49	3.81	1.33
	Retail Trade	7	7.75	1.30	3.37	0.91
Finance		12	11.97	45.10	5.14	43.49
	Depository Institutions	4	9.02	36.56	3.69	37.15
	Non-Depository Institutions	0				
	Securities & Brokers	0				
	Insurance	1	1.04	2.33	0.39	0.85
	Other Financial Services	7	1.91	6.22	1.06	5.50
Services		13	2.04	1.08	2.26	1.36
	Commercial Services	9	1.18	0.63	1.45	0.96
	Health Services	1	0.35	0.21	0.56	0.24
	Other Services	3	0.51	0.23	0.25	0.15
Total		159	100.00	100.00	100.00	100.00
Total (US$ million)			198,381	416,279	82,217	160,805

Source: Estimates based on data from Disclosure Inc.

CDIA trends. As discussed at the outset, however, our conclusions are largely tentative and a more rigorous empirical testing of our hypotheses is required.

THE ROLE OF TOP CANADIAN TNCS

ACCORDING TO THE UNCTC (1993) the top 1 percent of TNCs in the world own approximately 50 percent of the world's direct investment stock. A recent Industry Canada study (1993) also reported a similar concentration of economic activity by large firms in the United States and Canada. For example, in 1991 the top 1,000 North American firms had combined total assets and sales of US$ 9.2 trillion and US$ 4.4 trillion, respectively. Their combined sales accounted for nearly 50 percent of the gross sales of the three countries combined. Given their strong presence, the top 1,000 North American firms play a major role in shaping the comparative advantages and competitive positions of the three North American economies.

Although there are at present over 1,300 Canadian-based TNCs, accounting for 3.5 percent of all TNCs world wide, they represent less than 0.2 percent of all Canadian non-financial business establishments. This section analyzes the structure and characteristics of the top Canadian TNCs and relates them to the industrial and geographic distribution of CDIA, discussed earlier.

CHARACTERISTICS

USING THE DISCLOSURE/WORLDSCOPE GLOBAL DATABASE as the source, we developed a consistent set of data for 447 large Canadian-based firms. Of these, 159 firms are outward-oriented, i.e., firms with foreign assets and sales. The remaining 288 companies are domestically oriented (with no foreign assets or sales). A brief description of this database is given in the Appendix. Names and performance measures of the top outward oriented and domestically oriented Canadian based firms are provided in the longer version of this study, a forthcoming Industry Canada Working Paper.

Twelve of the 159 outward-oriented firms are foreign-controlled, i.e., more than 50 percent of their assets are owned and/or controlled by foreigners. The remaining 147 firms are domestically controlled, i.e., with more than 50 percent of their assets owned and/or controlled by Canadians.

The top 159 outward-oriented Canadian firms command enormous financial resources. Their combined total assets and sales in 1991 were US$ 416.3 billion and US$ 198.4 billion, respectively. Total foreign assets of these firms were US$ 160.8 billion or 39 percent of their total assets. Similarly, foreign sales account for 43 percent of their total sales (Table 2). More importantly, these top Canadian-based TNCs account for almost 50 percent of all the foreign assets of Canadian-based companies.

The foreign activities of the top Canadian firms are highly concentrated. In 1991, the top 20 firms contributed about 80 percent to the total foreign assets and sales of the top Canadian TNCs (Table 3). In addition, the top three firms in each major industry group account for nearly 75 percent of total foreign assets of all 159 top outward-oriented Canadian-based firms. Only nine of the top 73 manufacturing Canadian TNCs (Seagram Co. Ltd., Thomson Corporation, Northern Telecom, Noranda Inc., Bombardier Inc., Varity Corporation, Moore Corporation, Thomson Newspapers Ltd. and MacMillan Bloedel Ltd.) account for between 70 percent and 80 percent of the total foreign assets of the top manufacturing companies. Similarly, Alcan Aluminium Limited, Inco Limited, and Placer Dome Inc. hold 59 percent of the total foreign assets of the top 32 mining TNCs (Table 4).

The average annual sales and assets of top outward-oriented Canadian-based firms are US$ 1.2 billion and US$ 2.6 billion, respectively. However, the average firm size of the same firms, measured by either sales or assets, varies considerably across industries. For instance, the average annual sales range from a low of US$ 0.13 billion in miscellaneous manufacturing to a high of US$ 4.5 billion in depositary institutions (Table 5).

The average size of top Canadian firms is only half the American level in most industries. The size disadvantage is acute in mining, construction, resource- and technology-intensive manufacturing, and communications industries. Conversely, the average size of Canadian firms compares favourably with their U.S. counterparts in labour-intensive manufacturing and financial services (Industry Canada, 1993).

INDUSTRIAL DISTRIBUTION

THE INDUSTRIAL DISTRIBUTION OF FOREIGN SALES of the top outward-oriented Canadian firms is similar to the distribution of their total sales. The industrial composition of foreign and total assets are also similar. For instance, resources, resource-intensive manufacturing, and printing and publishing industries accounted for over 50 percent of the total foreign sales of the outward-oriented firms in 1991, compared with a share of 40 percent in total sales (Table 2). Equally important, the distribution of foreign assets of the top outward-oriented Canadian firms is similar to the industrial distribution of CDIA as discussed previously. The total foreign assets share of mining, resource-intensive manufacturing, printing and publishing, and financial services industries of the outward-oriented firms is almost 75 percent, similar to their share of total CDIA in 1991. Technology-intensive manufacturing, communication and transportation industries account for the rest of the foreign assets of the top Canadian TNCs (Table 2).

The top Canadian TNCs also play a vital role in determining the industrial distribution of total foreign sales of Canadian TNCs. Manufacturing industries account for 53 percent of the foreign sales of the top Canadian TNCs. Resource-intensive manufacturing and printing and publishing industries contribute over 70 percent to the total foreign manufacturing sales. Technology-intensive manufacturing industries account for

TABLE 3

TOP 20 OUTWARD-ORIENTED CANADIAN-BASED FIRMS

COMPANY NAME	MAJOR INDUSTRY GROUPING	INDUSTRY	FOREIGN ASSETS (US$ 000)	TOTAL FOREIGN ASSETS AS A % OF TOTAL ASSETS	U.S. ASSETS AS A % OF TOTAL FOREIGN ASSETS
The Bank of Nova Scotia	Finance	Depository Institution	32,770,742	41.52	n/a
Trilon Financial Corp.	Finance	Depository Institution	12,895,795	35.87	61.92
Royal Trustco Limited	Finance	Depository Institution	12,489,938	38.40	60.80
Seagram Co. Ltd.	Resource-Intensive Manufacturing	Food & Products	11,224,766	96.07	22.90
BCE Inc.	Communications		8,618,901	21.80	47.20
Thomson Corporation	Labour-Intensive Manufacturing	Printing & Publishing	7,591,114	92.96	62.91
Alcan Aluminium Limited	Mining		7,430,400	68.70	22.34
Northern Telecom Limited	Technology-Intensive Manufacturing	Communications Equipment	5,839,698	61.25	n/a
Carena Developments Limited	Finance	Other Financial Services	4,632,077	36.84	n/a
Canadian Pacific Limited	Transportation		3,987,406	22.39	80.55
Noranda Inc.	Resource-Intensive Manufacturing	Lumber & Wood	3,065,451	24.30	72.73
Varity Corporation	Technology-Intensive Manufacturing	Machinery excluding Electrical	2,235,079	75.26	n/a
Laidlaw Inc.	Transportation		1,835,687	50.17	98.87
Inco Limited	Mining		1,825,086	40.76	31.42
Bombardier Inc.	Technology-Intensive Manufacturing	Aircraft & Parts	1,780,214	68.12	49.42
First City Financial Corp. Ltd.	Finance	Depository Institution	1,586,732	33.13	99.40
Bramalea Limited (Canada)	Finance	Other Financial Services	1,565,188	28.58	98.11
Moore Corporation Limited	Labour-Intensive Manufacturing	Printing & Publishing	1,539,886	72.74	70.47
Cadillac Fairview Corporation	Finance	Other Financial Services	1,498,592	48.24	n/a
Thomson Newspapers Ltd.	Labour-Intensive Manufacturing	Printing & Publishing	1,403,963	83.37	n/a
Total			125,816,714		

Source: Estimates based on data from Disclosure Inc.

most of the remaining manufacturing sales (Table 2). This distribution is similar to the industrial composition of manufacturing sales of the U.S. affiliates of Canadian TNCs.

Similarly, the structure of non-manufacturing industries' foreign sales of the top Canadian firms has a major role in influencing the industrial distribution of foreign sales of all Canadian companies. For instance, the share of mining (17.2 percent), communication (8.2 percent), trade (7.2 percent), financial services (5.1 percent) and transportation (4.8 percent) industries account for over 80 percent of all the foreign sales of top Canadian TNCs outside manufacturing (Table 2). These industries are also the primary contributors to non-manufacturing sales of the U.S. affiliates of Canadian TNCs.

DEGREE OF OUTWARD ORIENTATION AND GEOGRAPHIC DISTRIBUTION

THE DEGREE OF OUTWARD ORIENTATION, as measured by the share of foreign assets in total assets, varies a great deal across industries, from a low of 1.4 percent in utilities to a high of 77.2 percent in food and food products industry. Given our comparative advantage, it is not surprising that Canadian firms in manufacturing (especially in printing and publishing, food and beverages, textiles and chemicals and chemical products) and mining industries are more outward-oriented than firms in other industries (Table 5). The United States accounts for 63.9 percent of all foreign assets and 64.7 percent of foreign sales of the top Canadian TNCs. Europe contributes between 27 percent and 30 percent to their foreign assets and sales. All other countries, mostly from Asia Pacific Rim and Latin America, account for the remaining foreign assets and sales of the top Canadian TNCs.

The U.S. share of foreign assets and sales of the top Canadian TNCs varies considerably across industries. In the case of assets, it varies from a low of 24.2 percent in motor vehicles and equipment industries to a high of 100 percent in transportation and electrical products (among others). Similarly, the U.S. share of foreign sales varies between 24.7 percent and 100 percent Table 5).

The overall concentration of foreign sales and assets in the U.S. market is greater than the average concentration of foreign sales and assets in the mining, food and products, paper and allied products, technology-intensive, depositary institutions and other services industries. On the other hand, firms in the textiles, tobacco, lumber and wood, metals, transportation, finance and service industries, among others, are more dependent on the U.S. market than the overall average. This greater reliance of Canadian firms in the finance and service industries is largely due to their close proximity to the world's wealthiest and most dynamic market and the greater need to service customers.

In summary, the top TNCs have played a dominant role in determining both the overall industrial and the geographic distribution of the foreign activities

TABLE 4

TOP THREE OUTWARD-ORIENTED CANADIAN-BASED FIRMS

Major Industry Grouping / Company Name	Industry	Foreign Assets (US$ 000)	Concentration of Foreign Assetsa (%)	Total Foreign Assets as a % of Total Assets	U.S. Assets as a % of Total Foreign Assets
Agriculture & Fish		17,862			
Fishery Products International		17,862	100.00	6.35	n/a
Mining		17,938,664			
Alcan Aluminium Limited		7,430,400	41.42	68.70	22.34
Inco Limited		1,825,086	10.17	40.76	31.42
Placer Dome, Inc.		1,337,329	7.45	83.37	n/a
Construction		1,138,991			
Coscan Development		713,840	62.67	64.59	100.00
United Dominion Industries Ltd.		410,390	36.03	46.98	68.50
Banister Inc.		14,761	1.29	10.33	n/a
Labour-Intensive Manufacturing		14,370,964			
Thomson Corporation	Printing & Publishing	7,591,114	52.82	92.96	62.91
Moore Corporation Limited	Printing & Publishing	1,539,886	10.71	72.74	70.48
Thomson Newspapers Ltd.	Printing & Publishing	1,403,963	9.77	83.37	n/a
Resource-Intensive Manufacturing		22,555,667			
Seagram Co. Ltd.	Food & Products	11,224,766	49.76	96.07	22.90
Noranda Inc.	Lumber & Wood	3,065,451	13.59	24.30	72.78
MacMillan Bloedel Ltd.	Lumber & Wood	853,858	3.78	25.84	87.16
Technology-Intensive Manufacturing		12,231,364			
Northern Telecom Limited	Communications Equipment	5,839,698	47.74	61.25	n/a
Varity Corporation	Machinery excl. Electrical	2,235,079	18.27	75.26	n/a
Bombardier Inc.	Aircraft & Parts	1,780,214	14.55	68.12	49.42

TABLE 4 (CONT'D)

MAJOR INDUSTRY GROUPING	COMPANY NAME	INDUSTRY	FOREIGN ASSETS (US$ 000)	CONCENTRATION OF FOREIGN ASSETS[a] (%)	TOTAL FOREIGN ASSETS AS A % OF TOTAL ASSETS	U.S. ASSETS AS A % OF TOTAL FOREIGN ASSETS
Transportation			5,950,390			
	Canadian Pacific Limited		3,987,406	67.01	22.39	80.55
	Laidlaw Inc.		1,835,687	30.85	50.17	98.87
	Trimac Limited		104,907	1.76	30.78	86.16
Communications			9,057,792			
	BCE Inc.		8,618,901	95.15	21.80	47.20
	Teleglobe Inc.		280,180	3.09	23.34	98.13
	Newbridge Networks Corporation		62,338	0.69	44.26	44.26
Utilities			34,139			
	Unicorp Energy Corp.		34,139	100.00	1.43	100.00
Trade			3,609,957			
	Onex Corporation	Wholesale Trade	813,469	22.53	73.61	100.00
	Loblaw Companies Limited	Retail Trade	488,049	13.52	23.89	100.00
	Scott's Hospitality Inc.	Retail Trade	394,204	10.92	49.29	49.47
Finance			69,940,722			
	The Bank of Nova Scotia	Depository Institution	32,770,742	46.85	41.52	n/a
	Trilon Financial Corp.	Depository Institution	12,895,795	18.44	35.87	61.92
	Royal Trustco Limited	Depository Institution	12,489,938	17.86	38.40	60.78
Services			2,179,166			
	Cineplex Odeon Corporation	Commercial Services	614,432	28.19	76.32	100.00
	Crownx Inc.	Health Services	392,577	18.01	44.46	100.00
	The Loewen Group Inc.	Commercial Services	352,764	16.19	79.09	100.00

Note: [a] Firm share in total foreign assets of all top outwardly oriented firms in industry.
Source: Estimates based on data from Disclosure Inc.

TABLE 5

GEOGRAPHIC DISTRIBUTION OF ASSETS AND SALES OF OUTWARD-ORIENTED CANADIAN-BASED FIRMS

MAJOR INDUSTRY GROUPING	INDUSTRY	NO. OF FIRMS	FOREIGN ASSETS TO TOTAL ASSETS (%)	FOREIGN SALES TO TOTAL SALES (%)	U.S. ASSETS TO TOTAL FOREIGN ASSETS (%)	U.S. SALES TO TOTAL FOREIGN SALES (%)
Agriculture, Fish & Forestry		1	6.35	71.61	41.91	44.84
Mining		32	40.92	64.13	88.28	77.64
Construction		3	53.68	67.68	69.11	57.03
Labour-Intensive Manufacturing		12	68.48	63.45	65.00	70.23
	Textiles	2	75.32	68.69		
	Clothing	0				
	Printing & Publishing	9	68.16	63.10	69.497	55.30
	Miscellaneous Manufactured Goods	1	38.91	43.17	63.83	66.58
Resource-Intensive Manufacturing		34	42.10	48.02	63.22	66.61
	Food & Products	4	77.22	69.91	42.27	52.66
	Tobacco	1	67.88	59.36	100.00	100.00
	Lumber & Wood	4	25.52	46.45	96.83	83.46
	Paper & Allied	7	27.24	40.78	60.68	62.52
	Petroleum Refining	0				
	Non-Metallic Minerals	3	21.14	21.24	100.00	100.00
	Primary Metals	11	37.16	36.10	68.48	79.10
	Fabricated Metals	4	29.96	28.30	100.00	100.00
Technology-Intensive Manufacturing		27	57.20	44.11	56.78	44.49
	Chemicals & Allied	4	49.97	60.12	77.05	83.67
	Rubber & Products	2	28.68	21.79		
	Machinery excluding Electrical	5	64.32	78.72	61.49	60.24
	Computer & Office	2	69.27	70.37	100.00	100.00
	Electrical Products	3	27.62	26.36	100.00	100.00
	Communications Equipment	3	61.80	54.75	45.92	52.20

TABLE 5 (CONT'D)

MAJOR INDUSTRY GROUPING	INDUSTRY	NO. OF FIRMS	FOREIGN ASSETS TO TOTAL ASSETS (%)	FOREIGN SALES TO TOTAL SALES (%)	U.S. ASSETS TO TOTAL FOREIGN ASSETS (%)	U.S. SALES TO TOTAL FOREIGN SALES (%)
	Miscellaneous Electrical Products	1	21.74	26.64	100.00	100.00
	Motor Vehicles & Equipment	2	36.87	20.47	24.20	24.74
	Aircraft & Parts	3	65.20	53.22	50.70	21.06
	Light Machinery	2	76.52	53.36	100.00	100.00
Transportation		5	25.29	33.63	100.00	100.00
Communications		5	22.00	37.57	50.46	77.42
Utilities		1	1.43	6.15	100.00	100.00
Trade		14	31.04	21.99	80.53	80.46
	Wholesale Trade	7	34.54	27.34	79.75	86.41
	Retail Trade	7	27.02	18.00	82.01	94.51
Finance		12	37.25	17.79	67.14	69.13
	Depository Institutions	4	39.25	16.95	63.09	56.59
	Non-Depository Institutions	0				
	Securities & Brokers	0				
	Insurance	1	14.04	15.58		
	Other Financial Services	7	34.16	22.91	96.33	99.59
Services		13	48.47	46.05	86.86	81.74
	Commercial Services	9	58.53	51.10	87.61	77.55
	Health Services	1	44.46	66.05	100.00	100.00
	Other Services	3	24.73	20.48	29.92	34.72
Total		159				
Average			38.63	41.44	63.90	64.73

Source: Estimates based on data from Disclosure Inc.

TABLE 6

AVERAGE FIRM SIZE BY SALES AND ASSETS OF OUTWARD-ORIENTED CANADIAN-BASED FIRMS

MAJOR INDUSTRY GROUPING	INDUSTRY	NO. OF FIRMS	SALES (US$ 000)	ASSETS (US$ 000)	EMPLOYMENT
Agriculture, Fish & Forestry		1	469,668	281,296	7,200
Mining		32	689,354	1,370,080	3,638
Construction		3	662,758	707,209	3,265
Labour-Intensive Manufacturing		12	1,404,231	1,748,782	12,101
	Textiles	2	757,871	672,529	6,400
	Clothing	0			
	Printing & Publishing	9	1,689,564	2,171,312	14,557
	Miscellaneous Manufactured Goods	1	128,950	98,519	1,400
Resource-Intensive Manufacturing		34	1,144,620	1,575,942	6,668
	Food & Products	4	2,516,671	3,784,660	8,500
	Tobacco	1	26,390	23,875	500
	Lumber & Wood	4	2,655,299	4,419,739	17,707
	Paper & Allied	7	1,248,781	1,530,611	7,665
	Petroleum Refining	0			
	Non-Metallic Minerals	3	384,457	460,901	3,199
	Primary Metals	11	627,522	679,911	4,264
	Fabricated Metals	4	351,382	291,140	2,806
Technology-Intensive Manufacturing		27	1,198,418	907,219	6,913
	Chemicals & Allied	4	298,368	288,189	2,252
	Rubber & Products	2	262,119	171,547	3,106
	Machinery excluding Electrical	5	879,989	783,891	4,706
	Computer & Office	2	368,091	268,930	2,250
	Electrical Products	3	96,837	98,836	983
	Communications Equipment	3	2,890,202	3,310,033	20,812
	Miscellaneous Electrical Products	1	274,013	316,190	1,959

TABLE 6 (CONT'D)

MAJOR INDUSTRY GROUPING	INDUSTRY	NO. OF FIRMS	SALES (US$ 000)	ASSETS (US$ 000)	EMPLOYMENT
	Motor Vehicles & Equipment	2	6,263,399	2,083,331	18,800
	Aircraft & Parts	3	929,528	920,752	9,486
	Light Machinery	2	476,463	535,016	5,000
Transportation		5	2,338,509	4,705,633	23,911
Communications		5	3,582,496	8,235,330	25,882
Utilities		1	1,522,142	2,387,365	
Trade		14	1,916,082	830,823	7,611
	Wholesale Trade	7	1,635,945	887,375	7,079
	Retail Trade	7	2,196,219	774,271	8,143
Finance		12	1,978,861	15,646,035	5,898
	Depository Institutions	4	4,473,494	38,048,594	14,829
	Non-Depository Institutions	0			
	Securities & Brokers	0			
	Insurance	1	2,063,623	9,686,097	9,161
	Other Financial Services	7	541,248	3,695,992	329
Services		13	310,832	345,833	6,033
	Commercial Services	9	259,425	293,552	3,611
	Health Services	1	698,332	882,990	31,800
	Other Services	3	335,886	323,624	4,711
Total		159			
Average			1,247,685	2,618,112	7,527

Source: Estimates based on data from Disclosure Inc.

of Canadian TNCs. These foreign activities are therefore responsible for the further integration of the Canadian economy, both within North America and in the world at large. Previous work (Knubley, Legault & Rao, 1994) has also demonstrated that the larger TNCs play a major role in the domestic economy.

Consequences of CDIA

HISTORICALLY, CANADA HAS RELIED heavily on FDI and foreign technology for its economic development. As a result, nearly 30 percent of the assets and sales of all non-financial corporations in Canada are now owned and controlled by foreign firms. In addition, in the manufacturing sector, which accounts for over 80 percent of Canadian merchandise exports, foreign-controlled firms contribute about 50 percent to its output and employment.

To date, there has been only limited analysis of the economic consequences of large and growing CDIA for domestic economic growth, jobs and real incomes in Canada. In public debate the subject has been largely forgotten, although when large outward investments are announced, concerns are always expressed about lost jobs and technology. The relatively scant literature on CDIA may reflect the fact that as an economic phenomenon it has only gained prominence in the recent past and its effect on activities at home and abroad has not yet been fully explored. The following section examines some of the issues concerning the potential effect of CDIA on the Canadian economy. The total effect of CDIA on the Canadian economy depends on the relative size of its direct and indirect influences on Canada's productivity, costs, trade, jobs, real incomes and the current account balance.

DIRECT EFFECTS

THE DIRECT CONSEQUENCES OF CDIA on the Canadian economy depend upon two opposing influences: domestic capital formation and direct investment income receipts.

Domestic Capital Formation

It is difficult to assess the direct effect of CDIA on investment expenditure and jobs in Canada. An increase in CDIA does not necessarily imply reduced investment spending in Canada for two reasons: first, an expansion of production and research facilities abroad (pull factors) may stimulate capital formation at home due to an improved international competitive position of Canadian firms and increased activity both at home and abroad. Second, reduced invest-ments at home by some firms may be offset by increased investment by Canadian and foreign firms. An increase in CDIA could reduce domestic capital formation only if the investments abroad are the result of increased barriers to Canadian exports in foreign markets (Caves, 1982). In short, if the increase in

CDIA is largely the result of new and improved investment opportunities abroad, it will have no direct negative impact on investment spending, and hence no effect on jobs and real incomes in Canada. On the other hand, if a weak domestic investment climate (push factor) is the main cause of a surge in CDIA, this could have an adverse effect on capital accumulation in Canada. However, possible offsetting investments by both federal and provincial governments and other private (domestic and foreign) investors could completely negate the effect of CDIA on domestic investment spending.

The rapid pace of expansion of CDIA in the 1980s coincided with a strong investment performance in Canada and the other G-7 countries. Our extensive regression analysis of the determinants of the trends in capital formation in Canada during the years between 1970 and 1991, disaggregated by major sectors, suggests that CDIA had no significant effect on capital formation in Canada. Similarly, our regression results for the United States, the United Kingdom, Germany and Japan for the same time period imply that direct investment abroad either had no significant influence or that it had a positive effect on domestic capital formation.[8]

Investment Income

Investment income associated with CDIA can contribute positively to the growth in output and employment in Canada by stimulating consumer and investment spending, and by having a positive effect on the current account balance, the exchange rate, and real interest rates.

Over the last 20 years or so, direct investment income has increased significantly in conjunction with the dramatic rise in the level of CDIA activity. It averaged C$ 3.91 billion per year between 1986 and 1992, compared to a meagre C$ 0.27 billion between 1970 and 1975. CDIA has therefore made a significant direct contribution to output and employment expansion in Canada (Figure 10). Moreover, the relationship between Canadian direct investment income receipts and payments has become more balanced in Canada's favour. The ratio of receipts to payments averaged 0.63 between 1986 and 1992, compared to only 0.25 between 1970 and 1975. These results imply that CDIA has also contributed significantly to improving Canada's current account position.

In summary, there is a priori either a positive relationship or no direct relationship between trends in CDIA and domestic investment spending. The limited empirical evidence from Canada and other host countries generally supports these hypotheses.

INDIRECT EFFECTS

IN ADDITION TO ITS DIRECT EFFECTS, CDIA can improve Canada's competitive position through its potentially positive influence on trade flows, the performance of Canadian TNCs at home and abroad, and by exerting positive spillovers on domestically oriented firms.

FIGURE 10

INVESTMENT INCOME FROM CDIA, SELECTED PERIODS

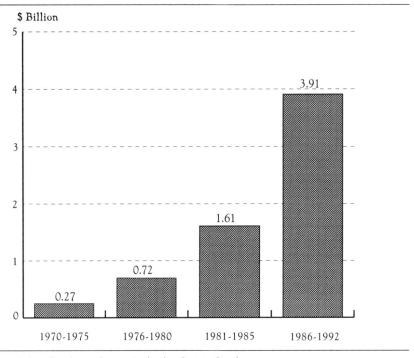

Source: Industry Canada compilations using data from Statistics Canada.

Trade Effects

Historically, trade and FDI have been viewed as substitutes for one another because much of the direct investment was the result of trade protection in host countries. It was argued that multinational firms were compelled to locate production facilities abroad in response to tariff and non-tariff barriers set up as impediments to make it difficult for them to serve international markets.

However, as already discussed, trade protection does not appear to have played any significant role in the rapid growth of the global stock of FDI over the last 15 years or so. Instead, the increased globalization of production is largely the result of the decisions of TNCs to diversify risk, minimize costs and maximize performance through increased specialization and to take advantage of scale and scope economies. The globalization strategies of transnational firms can therefore be expected to stimulate world trade, especially because of the increased intra-firm trade activities between parents and their subsidiaries (Rugman, 1987; Caves, 1982; Encarnation, 1993; and Globerman, 1993).

Increased world trade could in turn increase the level of world output and real incomes by improving the allocation of the world's productive resources, by reaping more effectively the benefits of scale and scope economies, by rapidly diffusing new and state-of- the- art technologies, by increasing innovation, and by improving the adaptability and flexibility of product and factor markets. In short, more and better investment linkages could strengthen the trade linkages between countries and set in motion a cycle of increased global economic integration which could improve the economic performance of all nations. By the same token, growth of CDIA can potentially strengthen the trade linkages between Canada and its trading partners, thereby improving our competitive position.

The past trends in CDIA and CFDI stocks, and Canada's exports and imports by industry and by major geographic region, suggest complementarity between trade and direct investment activity. Our estimates of total elasticities of Canadian exports with respect to CDIA stock for the two sub-periods – 1971-1980 and 1981-1989 are positive.[9] The total export elasticity averaged 0.48 during the second period, implying that a 10 percent increase in CDIA stock, on average, will increase Canadian exports by 4.8 percent. The trade elasticity is somewhat higher (0.67) in the manufacturing sector (Table 7). The decline in the magnitude of trade elasticities in the second period could be attributed in part to the slowdown in world output during this period.

Our estimates of Canadian import and total trade (exports plus imports) elasticities with respect to CFDI and total direct investment stock (inward plus outward) for the two sub-periods are also positive. As with the export elasticities, Table 7 shows that the import elasticities declined during the second period. However, on average, the import elasticity is significantly larger than the export elasticity. The difference in the two elasticities could be attributed to differences in the length of Canada's experience with the two types of direct investment activity; CDIA is a recent phenomenon relative to CFDI.

TABLE 7

ELASTICITIES OF TRADE TO INVESTMENT STOCK[a], SELECTED PERIODS

MAJOR INDUSTRY GROUPING	EXPORTS TO CDIA STOCK 1971-1980	1981-1989	IMPORTS TO CFDI STOCK 1971-1980	1981-1989	TOTAL TRADE TO INWARD & OUTWARD INVESTMENT STOCK 1971-1980	1981-1989
Manufacturing	1.12	0.67	1.67	0.89	1.48	0.79
Primary Metals	1.03	0.48	1.35	0.32	1.32	0.45
Wood & Paper	1.06	0.41	2.34	0.86	1.69	0.54
Chemicals	0.95	0.36	1.55	0.88	1.61	0.60
All Industries	1.02	0.48	1.86	1.26	1.56	0.82

Note: [a] Not controlled for the influences of other factors such as economic activity, comparative advantage and cost competitiveness.

Source: Estimates based on data from Statistics Canada.

Although our estimates of trade elasticities do not take into account the influence of other factors on trade flows, the results for Canada and other countries from other studies generally support the view that trade and direct investment are complements rather than substitutes (Rao & Lemprière, 1992; Graham, 1993; Blomström & Kokko, 1993; Ries & Head, 1993; and Lipsey & Weiss, 1981).

In short, an increase in CDIA could expand Canada's trade flows, primarily through increased intra-firm trade. For instance, intra-firm imports (imports from the parent company and from other foreign affiliates of the parent) accounted for 78 percent of all imports of U.S. affiliates of Canadian TNCs in 1990. Similarly, intra-firm exports (exports to the parent company and to other foreign affiliates of the parent) contributed about 50 percent to their total exports. As well as enhancing trade flows, increased CDIA could contribute to the expansion of foreign sales. As a matter of fact, the importance of foreign sales relative to Canadian exports has increased considerably over the last 15 years. For example, the ratio of sales made by Canadian subsidiaries in the United States to Canadian exports to that country increased from 0.72 in 1977 to 1.35 in 1990.

Performance of U.S. Affiliates: Canadian and Other Foreign Affiliates

In 1990, the American affiliates of foreign companies accounted for about 4.5 percent of employment and output of the U.S. non-bank private sector, compared with only 2 percent in 1977.[10] In addition, affiliates of foreign TNCs in the United States also make significant contributions to overall manufacturing output and the merchandise trade. For instance, they account for between 10 percent and 15 percent of all U.S. manufacturing assets, sales, employment and R&D. In addition, they contribute about 20 percent to total American merchandise exports and 35 percent to the imports.

Despite a dramatic increase in Japanese FDI in the United States, the U.S. affiliates of Canadian companies' share in total sales, employment and R&D of all American affiliates of foreign companies increased significantly between 1980 and 1990. In 1990, the subsidiaries of Canadian companies in the United States accounted for between 16 percent and 19 percent of employment, R&D and capital stock of all foreign subsidiaries in the United States (Figure 11).

The U.S. affiliates of Canadian TNCs also play a significant role in the American manufacturing sector. In 1990 they accounted for 22 percent of the capital stock, 14 percent of employment and 19 percent of R&D of all affiliates of foreign companies in U.S. manufacturing (Figure 12).

It can be persuasively argued that the large and growing share of the subsidiaries of Canadian companies in the United States is attributable to their strong productivity (labour and capital) performance *vis-à-vis* the American affiliates of other foreign companies, especially in industries in

FIGURE 11

CANADIAN SHARE OF FOREIGN AFFILIATE ACTIVITIES IN THE UNITED STATES, ALL INDUSTRIES, 1980 AND 1990

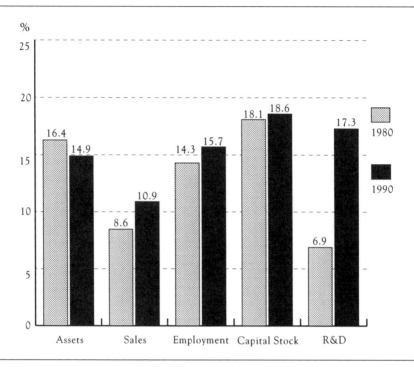

Source: Industry Canada compilations using data from the U.S. Department of Commerce.

which Canadian companies have a comparative advantage. For instance, after adjusting for differences in the industrial structure, labour and capital productivity of Canadian subsidiaries were well above the productivity levels of all the other American affiliates of foreign companies in both 1980 and 1990.[11] However, those productivity gaps have narrowed considerably over time (Figure 13). The narrowing of the productivity advantage can be partly attributed to the narrowing of the capital intensity and skill-level gaps between the Canadian and other foreign affiliates operating in the United States, perhaps due to the rapid growth of Japanese direct investment in the United States during the 1980s.

Manufacturing productivity advantage of Canadian subsidiaries in the United States is particularly strong in the following manufacturing industries: primary and fabricated metals, lumber and furniture products, paper and allied products, miscellaneous plastic products, and instruments and related products. Similarly, outside manufacturing, the productivity levels of

FIGURE 12

FIGURE 12

CANADIAN SHARE OF FOREIGN AFFILIATE ACTIVITIES IN THE U.S. MANUFACTURING
INDUSTRIES, 1980 AND 1990

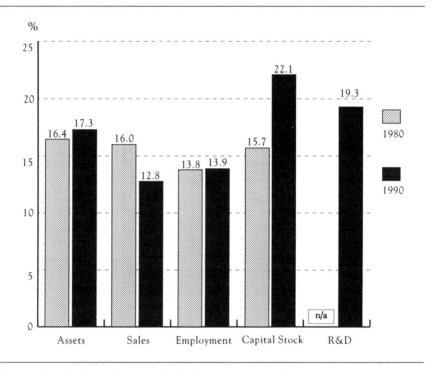

Source: Industry Canada compilations using data from the U.S. Department of Commerce.

Canadian subsidiaries are, on average, higher in mining, petroleum and insurance industries. On the other hand, productivity levels of Canadian subsidiaries in most service industries are generally lower.

The regression analysis for 1980 and 1990 of the pooled cross-section (comprised of 20 manufacturing industries for four countries) suggests that the superior labour productivity performance of Canadian subsidiaries can be largely attributed to the higher capital/labour ratio and the superior skill levels of the labour force (as reflected by the average wage rate).[12]

The trade performance of Canadian manufacturing subsidiaries in the United States compares favourably with the performance of all American affiliates of foreign companies. For example, Canadian subsidiaries exported 11.3 percent of their U.S. sales in 1990, compared with an export-to-sales ratio of 8.8 percent for all other foreign affiliates. However, the average export and import propensities of all the Canadian subsidiaries in non-manufacturing industries are considerably lower (Figure 14). This could be due to the

FIGURE 13

MANUFACTURING PRODUCTIVITY GAP[a], CANADIAN AFFILIATES VS OTHER
FOREIGN AFFILIATES IN THE UNITED STATES, 1980 AND 1990

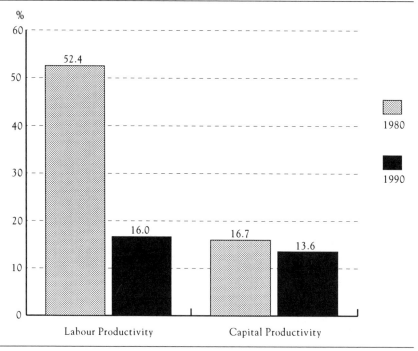

Note: [a] Percentage difference of productivity between Canadian and foreign affiliates, adjusted for difference
       in industrial structure. Positive value indicates Canadian productivity exceeds foreign productivity.
Source: Industry Canada compilations using data from the U.S. Department of Commerce.

establishment and effective use of wholesale trading houses by the Japanese
firms for purposes of promoting and expanding trade, as reflected by large
intra-firm trade, which biases upward the trade propensities of all countries
due to the large Japanese share.

Competitive Position of Outward-Oriented Canadian Firms

Internationalization of production and innovation activities can also improve
the competitive position of Canadian multinationals through secured and
improved access to foreign markets, physical and human capital, technologies,
and management and marketing practices. In addition, globalization allows
Canadian TNCs to enter into joint ventures, strategic alliances, and various
other vertical agreements with firms in other countries in order to minimize
costs and maximize performance.

FIGURE 14

TRADE PERFORMANCE OF FOREIGN AFFILIATES IN THE UNITED STATES, 1990

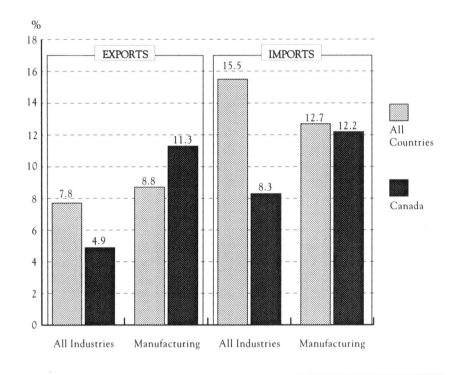

Source: Industry Canada compilations using data from the U.S. Department of Commerce.

This study shows that the growth and profitability performance of the outward-oriented Canadian firms is significantly better than the performance of the domestically oriented firms. This superior performance can, in turn, enhance Canada's competitive position both directly and indirectly. Thus, the increased globalization of Canadian firms may directly improve Canada's aggregate productivity and cost performance due to an implicit improvement in the allocation of productive resources. This would be reflected in an increased share of the factors of production (capital, labour and natural resources) being held by the outward-oriented firms.

An indirect contribution of outward-oriented firms to Canada's economic performance can also come through positive spillovers on the domestically oriented firms (for a detailed theoretical discussion of spillovers and a survey of available empirical evidence, see Bernstein, 1991). Vertical linkages between outward-oriented firms and small and medium-size domestically

TABLE 8

FIVE-YEAR GROWTH PERFORMANCE OF DOMESTICALLY ORIENTED AND OUTWARD-ORIENTED CANADIAN-BASED FIRMS, 1986-1991

MAJOR INDUSTRY GROUPING	NO. OF FIRMS		SALES GROWTH (%)		ASSET GROWTH (%)		EMPLOYMENT GROWTH (%)	
	DOMESTIC	OUTWARD	DOMESTIC	OUTWARD	DOMESTIC	OUTWARD	DOMESTIC	OUTWARD
Agriculture, Fish & Forestry	1	1		6.91		7.73		(3.49)
Mining	59	29	7.48	5.10	8.33	2.80	8.76	(4.66)
Construction	3	3	8.45	5.34	12.77	4.25	8.75	(0.19)
Labour-Intensive Manufacturing	2	12	(3.52)	12.14	0.95	19.74	(2.64)	5.77
Resource-Intensive Manufacturing	31	31	4.40	7.25	8.40	10.91	3.90	(0.41)
Technology-Intensive Manufacturing	10	24	4.24	12.22	2.96	14.88	(1.16)	3.58
Transportation	10	5	12.76	(1.04)	6.47	5.03	4.25	(0.17)
Communications	17	4	7.93	8.26	10.01	15.82	(1.04)	2.84
Utilities	19	1	4.46		6.18		1.41	
Trade	36	13	3.33	5.69	6.14	6.86	0.38	(4.42)
Finance	44	12	11.97	33.13	14.93	28.73	3.76	
Services	6	12	22.35	12.70	28.68	8.14	9.15	2.14
Total	238	147						
Average			7.03	8.96	10.63	14.93	2.73	0.73

Source: Estimates based on data from Disclosure Inc.

FIGURE 15

AVERAGE ANNUAL GROWTH OF OUTWARD-ORIENTED AND DOMESTICALLY ORIENTED CANADIAN-OWNED FIRMS, 1986-1991

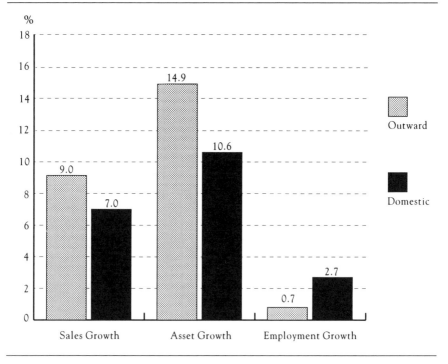

Source: Industry Canada compilations using data from the U.S. Department of Commerce.

oriented Canadian firms in the upstream and downstream industries can speed up the transfer of technology and the adoption of superior management practices. Such relationships can also facilitate rapid adjustment by domestically oriented firms to compete in international markets and promote interactions that can have a positive impact on the overall performance of domestically oriented firms.

While it is difficult to test the spillover thesis empirically, there is some indirect evidence to support this hypothesis. For instance, in both Canada and the United States the growth and productivity performance of industries with a high degree of outward-orientation (trade as well as direct investment) is, on average, superior to the performance of industries with lower degree of outward-orientation (ECAT, 1993; and Rao & Lemprière, 1992).

Empirical Evidence   To assess the empirical validity of the first hypothesis, the performance of the top outward-oriented Canadian firms was compared

FIGURE 16

PERFORMANCE OF OUTWARD-ORIENTED AND DOMESTICALLY ORIENTED
CANADIAN-OWNED FIRMS

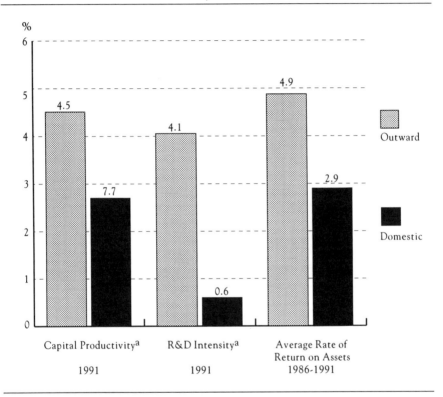

Note: [a] Capital productivity = sales/assets, R&D intensity = R&D/Sales.
Source: Industry Canada compilations using data from U.S. Department of Commerce.

with the performance of the top domestically oriented firms.[13] As expected, the performance of the outward-oriented firms was far superior to that of domestically oriented firms on the basis of several indicators (Figures 15 and 16). A similarly superior performance by Japanese TNCs relative to their domestic counterparts is reported in Ries & Head, (1993).

The average productivity of capital, as measured by the sales-to-assets ratio, of the outward-oriented firms is substantially higher (over 60 percent) than the productivity of domestically oriented firms. This superior performance is not due to difference in firm size, since the average firm size of the two sets of firms was more or less the same. More importantly, after controlling for inter-firm differences in the characteristics of the outward-

TABLE 9

R&D Intensity and Profitability of Domestically Oriented and Outward-Oriented Canadian-Based Firms

Major Industry Grouping	No. of Firms 1991		R&D as a % of Sales 1991		Return on Assets 1986-1991 (%)	
	Domestic	Outward	Domestic	Outward	Domestic	Outward
Agriculture, Fish & Forestry	1	1				6.57
Mining	59	29	0.98	1.83	5.50	5.18
Construction	3	3			6.93	3.07
Labour-Intensive Manufacturing	2	12		1.50	2.93	9.66
Resource-Intensive Manufacturing	31	31	0.35	0.46	5.21	6.00
Technology-Intensive Manufacturing	10	24	1.42	6.83	4.54	6.94
Transportation	10	5			2.71	4.75
Communications	17	4			8.89	6.00
Utilities	19	1			6.10	
Trade	36	13	0.62		5.45	5.93
Finance	44	12			1.26	2.35
Services	6	12	1.48	2.50	10.87	2.39
Total	238	147				
Average			0.63	4.12	2.93	4.88

Source: Estimates based on data from Disclosure Inc.

oriented and inward-oriented firms (such as firm size, the degree of leverage and the average growth of sales), the estimated marginal productivity of capital of the outward-oriented firms was calculated to be more than twice the productivity of the domestically oriented firms.[14]

In a majority of industries, the average growth of sales, assets, and productivity of the outward-oriented firms during the years between 1986 and 1991 was significantly higher than the growth record of the domestically oriented firms (Table 8). On average, sales and assets of the outward oriented firms increased by 9.0 percent and 14.9 percent annually, respectively, compared with 7.0 percent and 10.6 percent for the domestically oriented firms.

Outward-oriented firms also outperformed domestically oriented firms by a large margin in terms of the average rate of return on capital from 1986 to 1991 and the R&D performance (R&D/sales ratio), as may be seen in Table 9. However, the average employment growth of the outward-oriented firms during this period was significantly lower, implying a faster pace of adjustment and rationalization by the outward-oriented firms relative to the domestically oriented firms (Table 8). The difference in the pace of economic adjustment could well be a reflection of the fierce and intensified global competition for markets faced by the outward-oriented firms. Finally, the increased internationalization of production and innovation activities of Canadian firms does contribute to the enhancement of Canada's economic performance.[15]

CONCLUSIONS

THE ROLE OF TRANSNATIONAL CORPORATIONS in the world economy has increased dramatically in the past decade or so and this trend is expected to continue in the future. For instance, the stock of world outward direct investment increased almost fourfold from US$ 519 billion in 1980 to US$ 2 trillion in 1992, considerably outpacing the growth of world output and trade.

The effect of foreign direct investment on the Canadian economy has been studied extensively. By comparison, however, there has been little consideration of the potential consequences of CDIA for Canada. The broad objective of this study is to examine the recent trends in CDIA, to analyze the performance of outward-oriented Canadian firms, and to assess the impact of their activities on the Canadian economy.

Our major findings are:

- In the 1980s, Canadian TNCs actively participated in the process of globalization. From 1980 to 1992, the stock of CDIA increased at a faster pace than the global stock of direct investment as well as Canadian GDP, reaching C$ 99.0 billion in 1992. The increased outward orientation is pervasive across all major Canadian industries.

- The relationship between inward and outward direct investment has become much more balanced in the last 25 years. The ratio of outward to inward stock increased from 0.23 in 1970 to 0.72 in 1992. This trend is also pervasive across all major Canadian industries.

- The share of Europe and the Asia Pacific Rim in CDIA has increased significantly since 1985, primarily at the expense of a declining share of the United States. However, the United States is still the dominant location for CDIA.

- Resources, and resource-based manufacturing industries still account for over 40 percent of CDIA. However, the shares of financial services and technology-intensive industries (such as chemicals and chemical products, communication and communication equipment, and non-electrical machinery) have increased dramatically over the last 30 years.

- In the past 15 years, the relatively high sensitivity of CDIA to foreign economic activity, the higher profitability and faster rate of capital accumulation in the United States and United Kingdom relative to Canada, and the increased outward orientation of Canadian firms have all contributed to the rapid growth of CDIA.

- Similarly, a number of pull factors such as the fast rate of growth of real aggregate demand in Europe and the Asia Pacific Rim, the significant improvement in the relative profit position of the United Kingdom, the opportunities and fears associated with the creation of Europe 1992, and improvements in the U.S. savings-investment imbalance appear to have contributed to the recent decline in the importance of the U.S. market for CDIA. However, the U.S. continues to be the dominant location for CDIA. With the successful conclusion of the North American Free Trade Agreement (NAFTA), however, investment linkages between Canada and the United States could strengthen further in the future.

- The rising share of financial and technology- and information-intensive industries in world GDP, especially in the industrialized countries, partly explains the growing importance of these industries in CDIA.

- The foreign activities of Canadian TNCs are highly concentrated. The top 159 Canadian TNCs, identified in this study, account for about 50 percent of all the foreign assets of Canadian-based firms. In addition, about 80 percent of the foreign assets of the 159 Canadian firms belong to the top 20 firms.

- The industrial and geographic distribution of the foreign assets and sales of the top Canadian firms are similar to the distribution of CDIA and foreign assets of all Canadian firms.

- On average, the top firms are relatively more outward-oriented (as measured by the higher proportion of foreign assets and sales in their total assets and sales) in manufacturing (especially in printing and publishing, textiles and technology-intensive manufacturing) and in mining industries.

- A *priori*, there is either a positive or no relationship between trends in CDIA and domestic investment spending. Our econometric analysis of the determinants of domestic capital formation in Canada and the selected G7 countries supports this view.

- The investment income receipts associated with a rapidly expanding CDIA made a contribution to the real income growth and improvements in the Canadian current account balance during the 1980s.

- The increased outward orientation of firms could contribute significantly to the future enhancement of Canada's trade performance because of the complementarity between exports and CDIA. Moreover, CDIA contributes to the expansion of foreign sales. In fact, the importance of foreign sales relative to exports has increased substantially in the past 15 years or so.

- Our analysis indicates that the large and growing importance of Canadian TNCs in the United States can be attributed largely to the superior productivity performance of their subsidiaries in the United States relative to other foreign affiliates. Canadian subsidiaries outperform the affiliates of other foreign countries in the United States.

- The growth, productivity and profit performance of the outward-oriented Canadian firms, on average, has been superior to the performance of the domestically oriented firms.

- Between 1986 and 1991 employment growth in the outward-oriented firms was significantly lower than in the domestically oriented firms. This may be largely a reflection of greater restructuring and rationalization by the outward-oriented firms, due to intense global competition for markets measured in terms of costs, quality, variety and service. Nevertheless, over the longer term, the improved competitive position of outward-oriented firms might actually enhance their employment growth. In any case, an increase in outward direct investment is expected to be neutral with respect to the level of employment in the long run. However, the foreign activities of outward-oriented firms are likely to influence the composition of output and employment.

IMPLICATIONS

OUR RESEARCH SUGGESTS THAT the growing outward orientation of Canadian firms is mainly the result of new and improved economic opportunities abroad and a growing need to gain access to foreign markets and foreign technology. With such access Canadian firms should improve their cost and productivity performance. As Canadian firms become increasingly globalized, Canada's overall competitive position should also improve, as should its international commercial linkages.

Available evidence strongly suggests that the outward-orientation of Canadian firms will continue and probably intensify in the future. Recent trends in geographic and industrial distribution of CDIA are also expected to persist. However, significant changes to present patterns could occur if economic conditions in Europe deteriorate unexpectedly or if the NAFTA provides Canadian firms with a significant impetus to expand their activities in North America. Nonetheless, our conclusions as to the determinants of the trends in CDIA are only tentative; a more a rigorous empirical testing would be a useful next step.

Existing evidence also suggests that CDIA has a high potential to contribute to the expansion of trade and real incomes and help to improve Canada's competitive position and current account balance, efforts should be made through multilateral and bilateral negotiations to remove barriers to trade and direct investment flows.

Since the foreign activities of Canadian firms are highly concentrated, the activities and performance of the top Canadian TNCs are clearly important for enhancing Canadian trade and real incomes. A better understanding of the structure, characteristics, strategies, governance, and the determinants of the productivity and cost performance of the top TNCs could be useful in formulating effective public policies for improving Canada's competitive position.

ENDNOTES

1 For a descriptive analysis of trends in the micro aspects of CDIA, see Chow (1993) and Gorecki (1990). The paper deals with a variety of CDIA issues including the following: gross inflows and outflows of CDIA; the percentage distribution of Canadian and foreign controlled Canadian enterprises and CDIA; third party investments; long-term capitalization rate; size distribution of firms undertaking CDIA; and origin and destination of CDIA by industry.

2 CDIA and CFDI stocks are measured in book value rather than in market value terms. Consequently, CFDI stock might be underestimated relative to CDIA stock given that much of CFDI stock is of relatively older vintage than CDIA stock. Thus, the fact that CFDI is denominated in book value terms and not in market value terms means that the ratio of CDIA to CFDI stock is likely biased upwards.

3 Gross fixed non-residential capital stock data for the U.S. and U.K. were compiled from OECD publication *Flows and Stocks of Fixed Capital, 1964-1989*. Updates and revisions to the data were obtained directly from the Economic Statistics and National Accounts Division of the OECD. The data for Canada was obtained from Statistics Canada. The capital stock data used for the analysis were denominated in national currency units at current prices.

4 To make an empirical analysis of the broad macro-economic determinants of the rapid growth of Canadian outward direct investment stock relative to inward direct investment stock, we estimated two separate equations for CDIA and CFDI of the following form.

EQUATION I

$$\ln(CDIA) = a_0 + a_1 \ln(GDP^f/GDP^c) + a_2 \ln(PROF^f/PROF^c) +$$

$$a_3 \ln(EXCHR) + a_4 \ln(CAPSTK^f/CAPSTK^c) + a_5(TREND) +$$

$$a_6(DUMFTA)$$

EQUATION II

$$\ln(CFDI) = a_0 + a_1 \ln(GDP^f/GDP^c) + a_2 \ln(PROF^f/PROF^c) +$$

$$a_3 \ln(EXCHR) + a_4 \ln(CAPSTK^f/CAPSTK^c) + a_5(TREND) +$$

$$a_6(DUMFTA)$$

where,

$\ln(x)$ = The natural logarithm of the variable concerned.

CDIA = The stock of CDIA (in C$ billion).

CFDI = The stock of CFDI (in C$ billion).

GDP^f, GDP^c = Gross domestic product of foreign countries (United States and the European Community) and Canada, respectively (in US$ billion in price levels and exchanges rates of 1985).

PROF^f, PROF^c = The ratio of operating surplus to GDP, for foreign countries (United States and E.C.) and Canada, respectively.

EXCHR = The Canadian dollar per SDR (year-end rate).

CAPSTK^f, CAPSTK^c = Non-residential capital stock (private sector), for foreign countries (United States, United Kingdom, France, & Germany) and for Canada, respectively (in US$ billion).

TREND = Time trend.

DUMFTA = Dummy variable for Canada-U.S. Free Trade Agreement (0 = prior to 1985, 1 = for post 1985).

This specification allows for differences in the estimated elasticities of outward and inward direct investment stocks with respect to the independent variables.

The following are the final estimated equations, with the t-statistics of the estimated coefficients shown in parentheses.

EQUATION I':

$$\Delta lCDIA = \begin{array}{l} 0.06723 + 0.53123*\Delta lCDIA[-1] + 2.89831*\Delta lGDP^f[-1] \\ \;\;\;(2.0) \;\;\;\;\;\;\;(2.9) \;(2.8) \end{array}$$

$$+ 0.00876*\Delta lEXCHR[-1] - 1.60245*\Delta lGDP^c[-1]$$
$$\;\;\;(0.1) \;(2.1)$$

$$- 0.05959*DUMFTA$$
$$\;\;(2.5)$$

$R^2 = 0.58$ D.W.= 2.16   Estimation period = 1972-1991

Δl = The first difference of the natural logarithm of the variable concerned.

EQUATION II':

$$\Delta lCFDI = \quad 0.07597 - 0.31223*\Delta(PROF^f/PROF^c)$$
$$\quad\quad\quad\quad (15.8) \quad\quad (3.8)$$

$R^2 = 0.43$ D.W.= 1.39   Estimation period = 1971-1991

These two equations imply that the rapid pace of expansion of CDIA *vis-à-vis* CFDI in recent years is due to the relatively higher sensitivity of Canadian outward investment to foreign activity, the relatively higher profitability in foreign countries, and the greater participation of Canadian firms in the globalization process during the estimation period (as reflected by the differences in the constant terms).

The estimated coefficient for DUMFTA implies that, other things remaining constant, the FTA reduced the pace of CDIA, implying higher domestic participation by Canadian-based firms.

5 An indicator of aggregate profitability for the selected countries was measured by taking the ratio of gross operating surplus to gross domestic product (*National Accounts, Main Aggregates, Volume I, 1960-1991,* OECD). Operating surplus equals gross output at producers' values less the sum of intermediate consumption, compensation of employees, consumption of fixed capital and indirect taxes reduced by subsidies.

6 Nevertheless, changes in exchange rates directly affect the book value of CDIA stock denominated in Canadian dollars. An appreciation of the Canadian dollar will raise the CDIA stock; a depreciation of Canadian currency would have the opposite effect.

7 To analyze the changes in the regional composition of CDIA, we estimated an equation of the following form.

$\ln(CDIA^{US}/CDIA) =$

$$a_0 + a_1 \ln(GDP^{US}/GDP^{EC}) + a_2\ln(PROF^{US}/PROF^{EC}) +$$

$$a_3\ln(EXCHR^*)+ a_4(CABGDPUS) + a_5(TREND) +$$

$$a_6(DUMEC92)$$

where,

$\ln(x)$ = The natural logarithm of the variable concerned.

$CDIA^{US}$ = The stock of CDIA in the U.S. (in C\$ billion).

CDIA = The stock of CDIA (in C\$ billion).

GDP^{US}, GDP^{EC} = Gross domestic product of the United States and the European Community, respectively (in US$ billion in price levels and 1985 exchanges rates).

PROF^{US}, PROF^{EC} = The ratio of operating surplus to GDP, for the United States and the European Community, respectively.

EXCHR* = The U.S. dollar per U.K. pound sterling (average for year).

CABGDP^{US} = The ratio of U.S. current account deficit to U.S. GDP.

TREND = Time trend.

DUMEC92 = Dummy variable for the European Community 1992 (0 = prior to 1988, 1 = for post 1988).

The final estimated equation, with t-ratios in parentheses, is as follows:

$\Delta l(CDIA^{US}/CDIA)$

$$= 0.01627 + 0.02148*\Delta(CABGDP^{US}) - 0.06409*DUMEC92$$
$$\quad (2.2) \qquad (2.2) \qquad\qquad\qquad\qquad (3.3)$$

$R^2 = 0.38$ \qquad D.W.= 1.23 \qquad Estimation period = 1971-1991

The coefficients of the estimated equation imply that the recent decline in the U.S. share of CDIA can be attributed to the increased Canadian direct investment activity in the European Community associated with the formation of the E.C. 1992, and the improvement in the U.S. savings-investment imbalance as reflected in improvements in the U.S. current account position. These results also suggest that the U.S. share of CDIA will continue to decline in future unless the U.S. current account deficit position deteriorates.

8 To examine the relationship between changes in domestic capital formation and CDIA stock, we first computed the simple correlation coefficient between the two variables at the aggregate and sectoral (manufacturing, mining and financial services). The three sectors accounted for almost 85 percent of total CDIA stock in 1991. In all four cases, the correlation coefficient is large and positive and highly significant statistically. The simple bi-variate regressions suggest that CDIA stimulates rather than displaces capital formation at home.

However, once the influence of other factors (economic activity, profitability and technical change) on domestic capital formation is accounted for, the coefficient on CDIA is not statistically significant in all four equations. These results imply that on average an increase in CDIA neither crowds out nor stimulates capital formation at home.

The following are the regression equations of domestic capital formation in Canada from 1970 to 1990, with t- ratios in parentheses:

All industries: Canada

Δlcap =   1.48 Δlgdp + 0.08 Δldia + 0.0057 prf (-1) + 0.0044 prf (-2) +
          (2.25)   (0.55)   (1.63)   (1.04)

0.0029 prf (-3)+ 0.0008 * prf (-4) - 0.12
(1.98)   (1.98)   (1.72)

R^2 = 0.771   D.W. = 1.80

where:

Δl = The first difference of the natural logarithm of the variable concerned.

cap = Gross fixed non-residential capital stock.

dia = The stock of direct investment abroad.

prf = The ratio of profits to gross domestic product at factor cost (all industries or by sector).

Constant term in each equation represents the influence of technical change.

Manufacturing sector: Canada

Δlcap =   0.72 Δlgdp + 0.04 Δldia + 0.0071 prf (-1) + 0.0040 prf (-2) +
          (1.41)   (0.26)   (1.90)   (1.98)

0.0015 prf (-3) - 0.0004 prf (-4) - 0.11
(0.80)   (0.11)   (1.20)

R^2 = 0.511   D.W. = 1.18

Mining, Petroleum and Natural Gas sector: Canada

$$\Delta lcap = \quad 0.27\ \Delta lgdp - 0.09\ \Delta ldia + 0.0030\ prf\ (-1) + 0.0017\ prf\ (-2) +$$
$$\qquad\qquad (1.90) \qquad (0.96) \qquad (2.96) \qquad\qquad (2.08)$$

$$0.0001\ prf\ (-3) + 0.025$$
$$(0.15) \qquad\quad (1.44)$$

$$R^2 = 0.795 \qquad\qquad D.W. = 1.48$$

Financial sector: Canada

$$\Delta lcap = \quad 0.91\ \Delta lgdp - 0.097\ \Delta ldia + 0.0168\ prf\ (-1) + 0.0041\ prf\ (-2) -$$
$$\qquad\qquad (1.70) \qquad (1.22) \qquad\quad (4.12) \qquad\qquad (1.40)$$

$$0.0011\ prf\ (-3) + 0.0013\ prf\ (-4) - 0.099$$
$$(0.40) \qquad\qquad (3.06) \qquad\qquad (1.28)$$

$$R^2 = 0.827 \qquad\qquad D.W. = 1.82$$

Similar regressions were run for the United States, the United Kingdom, Germany and Japan at the aggregate level of industry. The following are the results of the regressions from 1975 to 1990 with the t-statistics of the coefficients in parentheses.

All industries: United States

$$\Delta lcap = \quad 1.33\ \Delta lgdp - 0.31\ \Delta ldia + 0.0089\ prf\ (-1) + 0.0142\ prf\ (-2) +$$
$$\qquad\qquad (3.54) \qquad (1.36) \qquad (0.89) \qquad\qquad (0.84)$$

$$0.0133\ prf\ (-3) - 0.75$$
$$(1.27) \qquad\quad (2.50)$$

$$R^2 = 0.745 \qquad\qquad D.W. = 2.20$$

where:

Δl = The first difference of the logarithm of the variable.

dia = The stock of direct investment abroad in units of national currency.

prf = The ratio of gross operating surplus to gross domestic product.

Constant term in each equation represents the influence of technical change.

All industries: United Kingdom

$$\Delta lcap = \quad 1.45\,\Delta lgdp + 0.10\,\Delta ldia + 0.0055\,prf\,(-1) + 0.0033\,prf\,(-2) +$$
$$\quad\quad (9.41) \quad\quad (2.63) \quad\quad (2.23) \quad\quad\quad\quad (1.61)$$

$$0.0001\,prf\,(-3) - 0.0040\,prf\,(-4) - 0.18$$
$$(0.04) \quad\quad\quad (1.44) \quad\quad\quad (3.42)$$

$R^2 = 0.971 \quad\quad D.W. = 1.44$

All industries: Germany

$$lcap = 0.14\,lgdp + 0.48\,ldia + 7.45$$
$$(0.76) \quad\quad (5.91) \quad\quad (4.64)$$

$R^2 = 0.995 \quad\quad D.W. = 1.42$

All industries: Japan

$$inv = 0.96\,gdp + 0.50\,\Delta dia - 11853.4\,trend + Constant$$
$$(8.82) \quad\quad (2.22) \quad\quad (6.36)$$

$R^2 = 0.992 \quad D.W. = 1.47$

where all variables are as previously defined for the United States, the United Kingdom and Germany, and where

inv = Gross fixed capital formation

trend = Time trend variable.

In conclusion, our regression results for Canada and the other G-7 countries suggest that the relationship between domestic capital formation and direct investment abroad is either not significant or positive.

9 These are total rather than partial trade elasticities with respect to CDIA. Hence, they are expected to be biased upward, because the influence of other factors on trade flows is not taken into account in computing these elasticities. Other determinants of trade flows include: economic activity; liberalization of trade barriers; technical change; cost structure; geographic and industrial distribution of exports and imports, exchange rate variability; capacity utilization, etc. However, the complementarity between Canadian trade flows and direct investment stocks (CDIA and CFDI), as found in our study, is consistent with the conclusions of other researchers (Graham, 1993; Rao & Lemprière, 1992a; Blomström and Kokko, 1993;

Ries & Head, 1993; Lipsey & Weiss, 1981; Hufbauer & Adler, 1968).

10 The data on U.S. affiliates of foreign companies were obtained from the U.S. Department of Commerce, *Benchmark Survey for 1980 and 1990*. The country of origin was determined using the criterion of Ultimate Beneficial Owner (UBO). The UBO consists of the person (or entity), proceeding up a U.S. affiliate's ownership chain, that is not owned more than 50 percent by another person (or entity); it consists of only the ultimate owner.

The industry details on labour and capital productivity, capital intensity, average wage, investment intensity, labour productivity-average wage gap, net income/sales ratio and export and import propensities (including intra-firm) for Canadian and other foreign subsidiaries in the United States for 1980 and 1990 are provided in a forthcoming Industry Canada Working Paper.

11 The effect of differences in industrial structure between Canadian and other foreign affiliates in the United States on *aggregate* labour and capital productivity of Canadian affiliates was measured in the following manner: first, the relative shares of sales and assets of all foreign affiliates in the United States were multiplied by the actual productivity levels of Canadian subsidiaries in *individual industries* to obtain pseudo-estimates of aggregate capital and labour productivity levels. Next, the ratio of actual to the estimated aggregate productivity levels was computed to account for the influence of the differences in industrial structure (for a detailed discussion of the methodology, see Rao & Lemprière, 1992b).

12 We estimated the sales-employment ratio (S/E) as a function of the capital-labour ratio (K/E) and the average wage rate (AW), a proxy for the skill level of the work force. Results for this equation in level and logarithmic form are as follows (the t-ratios are in parenthesis):

Level Equation:

$$S/E = \quad 35.26 + 0.49 \ K/E + 2.16 \ AW \qquad\qquad (1)$$
$$\qquad\qquad (4.38) \qquad (3.05) \qquad\qquad\qquad R^2 = 0.560$$

Logarithmic Equation:

$$\ln S/E = \quad 2.03 + 0.34 \ln K/E + 0.42 \ln AW \qquad\qquad (2)$$
$$\qquad\qquad (4.98) \qquad\quad (3.17) \qquad\qquad R^2 = 0.700$$

The two equations were estimated using the pooled cross-section (for 20 manufacturing industries for four countries (Canada, Germany, United Kingdom, Japan) and time-series data (1980 and 1990).

The two equations explain a large proportion (between 55 percent and 70 percent) of inter-industry and inter-country variance of manufacturing productivity levels. Equation (2) implies that a 10 percent increase in the

capital-labour ratio, other things being constant, will increase labour productivity by 3.4 percent.

13 To avoid any possible bias of intra-firm trade on the performance measures,
foreign-controlled firms are *excluded* from the two sets of examples.

14 Regression analysis was performed on the cross-section data for the outward-oriented and domestically oriented firms, grouped into 34 major
industries. We estimated the sales-employment ratio (S/E) as a function of
sales (S), equity as a percentage of total capital stock (EQ/CAP stock) and
the asset-employment ratio (A/E) for both domestically oriented and
outward-oriented firms. Regression results, with t-ratios in parenthesis, are
as follows:

Domestically oriented Firms

Level Equation

$$S/E = 200.28 + 1.44\ S + 1.26\ (EQ/CAP.\ STOCK) + 0.064\ (A/E) \qquad (1)$$
$$ (0.69) \quad (0.85) (31.20)\ R^2 = 0.845$$

Logarithmic Equation

$$\ln (S/E) = -1.57 + 0.26 \ln (S) + 0.22 \ln (EQ/CAP.STOCK) +$$
$$ (7.48) (2.81)$$

$$0.46 \ln (A/E) \qquad\qquad\qquad\qquad\qquad\qquad (1')$$
$$(11.23) \qquad\qquad\qquad\qquad\qquad\qquad R^2 = 0.500$$

Outward-oriented Firms

Level Equation

$$S/E = 77.50 + 1.24\ S + 0.93\ (EQ/CAP.\ STOCK) + 0.153\ (A/E) \qquad (2)$$
$$ (0.17) \quad (1.11) (13.64) \quad R^2 = 0.611$$

Logarithmic Equation:

$$\ln (S/E) = 0.84 + 0.034 \ln (S) + 0.23 \ln (EQ/CAP.STOCK) +$$
$$ (1.1) (2.30)$$

$$0.540 \ln (A/E) \qquad\qquad\qquad\qquad\qquad\qquad (2')$$
$$(16.10) \qquad\qquad\qquad\qquad\qquad\qquad R^2 = 0.684$$

All three variables are positively related to labour productivity in the two samples. However, only the coefficient of the asset-employment ratio is found to be statistically significant in the two level equations (1 and 2) and, as indicated above, it accounts for a high proportion of the equations' explanatory power (between 61 and 84 percent). Equation (2) implies that a one unit increase in the asset-employment ratio will increase labour productivity by 0.15, more than twice the size of the coefficient for the domestically-oriented firms. These results imply that marginal productivity of capital is considerably larger for the outward-oriented Canadian firms than for the domestically oriented Canadian firms.

Similarly, the asset elasticity is larger for the outward-oriented firms (see Equations 1' and 2'). The size of output (sales) elasticity in the two equations imply small increasing returns to scale.

15 Insufficient data precluded us from investigating the relative performance of subsidiaries of Canadian based TNCs in countries other than the United States.

ACKNOWLEDGEMENTS

WE ARE GRATEFUL TO Ross Preston, John Knubley and Steven Globerman for their support and their comments on the draft paper. We would also like to thank Chris Roth and Phillip Massé for their assistance throughout.

APPENDIX: DESCRIPTION OF THE MICRO DATA

TWO TYPES OF MICROECONOMIC ANALYSIS on Canadian-based TNCs are provided in this study. The first describes the characteristics, activities and performance of the top Canadian-based TNCs, drawing from the Disclosure/Worldscope Global Database. The second type of analysis describes the performance of the U.S. affiliates of Canadian-based TNCs, using data from the U.S. Department of Commerce. The first represents only a small sample of Canadian-based firms operating globally, whereas the second analysis represents the entire population of all affiliates of Canadian-based TNCs operating only in the United States. For these reasons the two approaches are not readily comparable; however, they do complement each other.

TOP CANADIAN-BASED TNCS

THE SAMPLE OF TOP 447 CANADIAN-BASED FIRMS was selected from the Canadian portion of the Disclosure/Worldscope Global Database. This database contains data on 9,832 public companies from 40 countries. The data for the Canadian-based firms were obtained from annual and periodic reports filed with all Canadian stock exchanges. Data on the federally incorporated private firms are supplemented by financial filings from the Department of Consumer and Corporate Affairs.

The following criteria were used by Disclosure to select the Canadian companies:

- Inclusion in Canada's national index (i.e. Financial Post 500).

- High profile or visibility of firm.

- Request for information by Disclosure clients.

Because of the *ad-hoc* nature of firm selection for the Disclosure database, as well as the small size of the sample, the firms used in this study may not accurately represent the population of all Canadian-based firms. However, it is not clear whether the sample of firms introduces any systematic bias into the results.

The 447 large Canadian-based firms were further divided into two broad groups: 159 outward-oriented firms and 288 domestically oriented firms – depending upon whether or not foreign assets were reported. Although this sample of 159 outward-oriented firms is small in comparison to the UNCTC list of 1,300 Canadian-based TNCs, the foreign assets of the 159 firms represents approximately 50 percent of the foreign assets of all Canadian TNCs.

The study also identifies the degree of outward orientation of the Canadian-based TNCs. It should be noted, however, that the financial statements of the firms do not all report foreign located assets and sales. For this reason, both the number of outward-oriented firms, as well as the degree of outward orientation, may be under-reported.

The study also distinguishes between Canadian-controlled and foreign-controlled Canadian-based TNCs. Foreign control was assigned whenever more than 50 percent of a firm's market capitalization was owned by foreign interests. As a result, 12 of the 159 outward-oriented firms are foreign-owned and 50 of the 288 domestically oriented firms are foreign-owned.

For analytical purposes, the top firms are grouped into 45 industries, according to their primary line of business, as determined by Disclosure's 1986 U.S. Standary Industrial Classification (SIC) system. The 25 manufacturing industries are further aggregated into three major groups: labour-, resource- and technology-intensive industries, similar to the Economic Council of Canada's (1992) aggregation, based upon factor input and technology intensities.

A definition of the financial variables as well as the calculated ratios contained in this study are available in the Industry Canada Working Paper, *Economic Integration in North America: Trends in Foreign Direct Investment and the Top 1,000 Firms.*

U.S. Affiliates of Canadian-Based TNCs

The data used to calculate the performance of U.S. affiliates of Canadian-based TNCs was drawn from the U.S. Department of Commerce Survey of foreign direct investment in the United States.

A U.S. affiliate is defined as a U.S. business enterprise in which there is foreign direct investment into the United States – that is, in which a single foreign person owns or controls, directly or indirectly, at least 10 percent of the voting securities if the enterprise is incorporated, or an equivalent interest if the enterprise is unincorporated.

In order to identify fully the nationality of ownership or control of the U.S. affiliates, as well as to establish which transactions are to be included in the reported transactions of U.S. affiliates, three concepts are used: foreign parent, ultimate beneficial owner (UBO), and foreign parent group. The foreign parent is the first person outside the United States in the U.S. affiliate's ownership chain which has a direct investment interest in the affiliate (10 percent rule as defined above). The foreign parent must be identified in order to ascertain that the foreign direct investment actually exists.

Proceeding up the affiliate's ownership chain, the UBO is the first person not more than 50 percent owned by another person. This is used to establish who owns and controls (and ultimately derives benefit from owning or controlling) the U.S. affiliate.

Finally, the foreign parent group consists of the foreign parent, any foreign person, proceeding up the foreign parent's ownership chain, who owns more than 50 percent of the person below it, up to and including the UBO, and any foreign person, proceeding down the ownership chain(s) of each of these members, that is more than 50 percent owned by the person above it. This last classification is used to distinguish between foreign persons that are affiliated with the U.S. affiliate (as either a parent, UBO, or other member of its foreign parent group) from those that are not.

The Bureau of Economic Analysis of the U.S. Department of Commerce publishes data on the following three groups of U.S. affiliates: all affiliates, non-bank affiliates, and bank affiliates. The data and analysis presented in this study reflects only the activities of non-bank U.S. affiliates.

Additional definitions of the U.S. affiliates of Canadian-based TNCs may be obtained from the following publication of the U.S. Department of Commerce, Bureau of Economic Analysis: *Foreign Direct Investment in the United States: 1987 Benchmark Survey, Final Results.*

BIBLIOGRAPHY

Blomström, M. and Ari Kokko. "Swedish MNEs: A Case Study." New York: National Bureau of Economic Research (mimeo), 1993.

Cantwell, J. *Technological Innovation and Multinational Corporation*, Oxford; Basil Blackwell, 1989.

Caves, R. *Multinational Enterprise and Economic Analysis*, Cambridge University Press, 1982.

Chow, F. "CDIA Patterns and Determinants." Ottawa: Statistics Canada (mimeo), 1993.

Corvari, R. and R. Weisner. "Foreign Multinationals and Canada's International Competitiveness." Ottawa: Investment Canada, Working Paper # 16, 1993.

Bernstein, J. I. "R&D Capital, Spillovers and Foreign Affiliates in Canada." In *Foreign Investment, Technology and Economic Growth*. Edited by D. McFetridge. Calgary: University of Calgary Press, 1991.

Dobson, W. "Japan's Trade and Investment in Eastern Asia." University of Toronto (mimeo), 1992.

Dunning, J. H. *Multinational Enterprise, Economic Structure and International Competitiveness*. Chichester: John Wiley & Sons, 1985.

ECAT. "A New Account of the Critical Role of U.S. Multinational Corporations in the U.S. Economy," 1993.

Encarnation, D. J. *Rivals Beyond Trade: America Versus Japan in Global Competition*. Ithaca, N.Y.: Cornell University Press, 1992.

Globerman, S. "CDIA: The Private and Public Interest." Vancouver: Simon Fraser University, (mimeo), 1993.

Globerman, S. "Foreign Direct Investment and 'Spillover' Efficiency Benefits in Canadian Manufacturing Industries." *Canadian Journal of Economics*, 12, 1 (1979).

Graham, E.M. "Canadian Outward Direct Investment: Possible Effects on the Home Economy." Washington, D.C.: Institute for International Economics, (mimeo), 1993.

Gorecki, P. "Patterns of Canadian Foreign Direct Investment Abroad." Ottawa: Statistics Canada, Analytical Studies Branch, # 33, 1990.

Gunderson, M. and S. Verma. "Labour Market Implications of Outward Direct Foreign Investment", University of Toronto (mimeo).

Hufbauer, G. C. and F. M. Adler. "Overseas Manufacturing Investment and the Balance of Payments," Tax Policy Research Study, No. 1. Washington, D.C.: U.S. Treasury Department, 1968.

Hymer, S. *The International Operations of National Firms: A Study of Direct Foreign Investment*. Boston, Mass.: MIT Press, 1976.

Investment Canada. "Business Implications of Globalization." Discussion Paper # 1990-V, 1990.

Industry Canada. "Economic Integration in North America: Trends in Foreign Direct Investment and the Top 1000 Firms." Working Paper 1, 1994.

Julius, D. *Foreign Direct Investment: The Neglected Twin of Trade*. Occasional Paper 33. Washington, D.C.: Group of Thirty, 1991.

Knubley, J., W. Krause and Z. Sadeque. "Canadian Acquisitions Abroad: Patterns and Motivations." In *Corporate Globalization Through Mergers and Acquisitions*, Investment Canada Research Series. Edited by L. Waverman. Calgary, University of Calgary Press, 1991.

Letto-Gilles, G. *International Production*. Polity Press, 1992.

Lipsey, R.E. and M.Y. Weiss. "Foreign Production and Exports in Manufacturing

Industries." *Review of Economics and Statistics*, 63, (1981).

Litvak, I.A. and C. J. Maule. *The Canadian Multinationals*. Toronto: Butterworths, 1981.

Ohmae, K. *TRIAD Power: The Coming Shape of Global Competition*. New York: The Free Press, 1985.

Ostry, S. *Government & Corporations in Shrinking World: Trade and Innovation Policies in the United States, Europe and Japan*. Council on Foreign Relations, 1990.

Ostry, S. and M. Gestrin. "Foreign Direct Investment, Technology Transfer and the Innovation Network Model," Toronto: University of Toronto (mimeo), 1993.

Parry, G. T. *The Multinational Enterprise: International Investment and Host-Country Impacts*. JAI Press Inc., 1980.

Rao, P. S. and T. Lemprière. "An Analysis of the Linkages Between Canadian Trade Flows, Productivity and Costs." Working Paper No. 46. Ottawa: Economic Council of Canada, 1992a.

_____. *Canada's Productivity Performance*. Ottawa: Economic Council of Canada, 1992b.

Rao, P. S. "Global (Stateless) Corporations and the Internationalization of Business: Implications for Canada and Canadian Marketplace Framework." Ottawa: Industry Canada, 1993.

Reich, R. *The Work of Nations*. New York: Vintage Books, 1991.

Ries, J. and K. Head. "Causes and Consequences of Japanese Direct Investment Abroad," Vancouver, B.C.: University of British Columbia, (mimeo), 1993.

Rugman, A. M. *Outward Bound: Canadian Direct Investment in the United States*. Toronto: McGraw-Hill Ryerson, 1987.

Rutter, J. "Recent Trends in International Direct Investment." Washington: United States Department of Commerce, International Trade Administration, 1992.

Safarian, A. E. *Multinational Enterprise and Public Policy: A Study of Industrial Countries*. Aldershott, U.K.: Edward Elder Publishing, 1993.

UNCTC. *World Investment Report 1993: Transnational Corporations and Integrated International Production*. New York: United Nations, 1993.

Vernon, R. "The Product Cycle Hypothesis in a New International Environment." *Oxford Bulletin of Economics and Statistics*, 1979.

Waverman, L.W. (ed). *Corporate Globalization through Mergers and Acquisitions*. Calgary: University of Calgary Press, 1991.

Part II   Economic Implications

Edward M. Graham
Institute for International Economics

4

Canadian Direct Investment Abroad and the Canadian Economy: Some Theoretical and Empirical Considerations

INTRODUCTION

THE EFFECT OF DIRECT INVESTMENT ABROAD (DIA) on the home nation's economy is a topic that has long been of interest to policy makers and to certain constituencies in many advanced nations. In Canada, the acceleration of the internationalization of Canadian firms that has taken place during the past ten years (Rao, Legault & Ahmad, this volume) and the creation of a Free Trade Area with the United States both raise the profile of this topic. Unfortunately, no theory or empirical evidence exists with respect to the effects of DIA on overall national welfare.[1] Also, much of the debate over DIA centres around distributional issues rather than overall welfare effects. These issues in turn rest on such questions as whether DIA and exports, or DIA and domestic capital formation, are complements or substitutes.

Distributional effects are important because in Canada (as in other nations that are home to DIA) much of the policy debate has centered around the concerns and claims of individual constituencies. For example, organized labour allied with left-of-centre constituencies in many countries, including Canada, worries about the effects of DIA on employment.[2] Their concern is that DIA reduces employment; this concern rests largely on unstated premises that DIA and exports, and DIA and domestic capital formation are substitutes rather than complements.

In a full equilibrium context it is easy to dismiss these worries because economic logic indicates that DIA should be employment neutral. That is, even if DIA affects exports or domestic capital formation, a net increase or decrease in either of these should have no long-term effect on overall levels of employment. Transitional effects can, of course, occur. For example, a decrease in demand for exports could reduce aggregate demand below full employment levels, inducing a reduction in output from full employment levels and hence temporarily reducing employment. But these effects are not long lived, and in time output and employment will return to full employment levels.

When claims are made that DIA will lead to job loss, however, these might be taken as shorthand for a more defensible and less simplistic position. If DIA reduces the demand for exports, and thus causes export-generating industries to shrink relative to the economy as a whole, workers displaced from these industries must relocate to jobs in import competing or non-traded goods sectors. This will, *inter alia*, create adjustment costs that must be borne by the economy. A longer-term effect is that in Canada many of these latter industries exhibit a lower marginal productivity of labour than do export industries, especially for jobs in the lower-skill category, and hence workers in these industries typically are paid lower hourly wages than workers in export industries. Therefore, the hourly incomes of at least some relocated workers would be reduced by DIA if this substitutes for exports.

Likewise, if DIA substitutes for domestic capital formation, then over time the stock of domestic capital per worker will shrink, relative to what it would have been in the absence of DIA. This reduction in capital deepening, *ceteris paribus*, would likely reduce the marginal productivity of labour and hence the wage rate.[3]

Either of these substitution effects, if they exist, could serve in the long run to reduce Canadian welfare by reducing income growth. However, and perhaps politically more important, they would have distributional consequences, with the factor share of labour falling relative to that of capital in the case of capital substitution, and the share of low-skill labour relative to that of higher-skill labour likely falling in the case of export substitution.

Later in this study I shall explore, in the context of Canada, whether DIA is likely to be a substitute or a complement for each of exports and domestic capital formation. One observation is that the structure of Canadian DIA and of the overall Canadian economy makes it extremely difficult to test these propositions for Canada alone. The section that follows argues that DIA and exports can be either substitutes or complements, as can DIA and domestic capital formation. However, both theory and international empirical evidence suggest that in either case a complementary relationship is a more plausible net outcome than a substitutive one. To the extent that this is the case, the concern that DIA will have a negative effect on the quality of employment in Canada is unwarranted.

However, before examining the substitutive/complementary issue, I first turn to an examination of what exactly are the determinants of Canada's trading and investment patterns. The case developed is that Canada's situation in this regard is not well served by existing theory, especially in the era of North American free trade, but that some new theoretical strands finding their way into the literature can help to illuminate these patterns.

CDIA AND CANADIAN EXPORTS

UNIQUENESS OF CANADA AND THE NEED FOR NEW EXPLANATIONS FOR CANADA'S TRADE AND INVESTMENT

AMONG THE ADVANCED INDUSTRIAL ECONOMIES, Canada is unique. Although one of the world's largest nations in terms of size of both economy and land area, Canada has only one land frontier: a very long border with the United States, a country roughly similar in terms of *per capita* level of economic development but ten times larger in terms of gross size. Furthermore, Canada's northerly location has resulted in by far the most of its economic activity being located within 100 km of the U.S./Canada border. One consequence is that the bulk of Canada's current international economic exchange is with the United States (almost 60 percent of the stock of its DIA, over 77 percent of its exports, and almost 63 percent of its imports), a pattern that was extant long before the two nations entered into a free trade agreement.[4] Another consequence is that the overall importance of trade and international investment (where the latter includes both DIA and direct investment in Canada) is at the high end of the distribution for the large industrial nations (Ostry, 1990).

Although the United States accounts for most of Canada's exports and DIA, the U.S. share on both measures has shrunk in recent years. It is noteworthy that the reduced U.S. share of Canadian DIA is accounted for largely by increases in the share held by nations of the European Union, especially the United Kingdom (Rao, Legault & Ahmad, this volume). However, except for investment and trade in products associated with natural resource industries, there is no obvious explanation to be found in neoclassical – Heckscher-Ohlin-Samuelson (HOS) – theory of international trade for the patterns of trade, such as they are, between Canada and the United States or the EC countries (e.g., the capital-to-labour endowments do not differ greatly between the two countries, and hence relative factor prices are not likely to differ greatly). Likewise, as has been well established (McFetridge, this volume), there is no obvious reason offered in classical theories of capital movement to explain Canada's DIA; these theories predict that a country with a high capital-to-labour ratio such as Canada would export capital to countries with a low ratio, rather than to other capital-rich countries such as the United States or the EC nations. The "newish" theories on economies of internalization as an explanation of FDI probably do better (Rugman, 1986) but, as argued below, they can be usefully supplemented by still newer theories. Indeed, of the trade and investment patterns of all of the industrialized countries, Canada's patterns might be best explained by newly emergent theories.

The argument to be developed here is that, to one looking for explanations of trade between Canada and the United States in particular, the new literature on the determinants of the geographical location of economic activity is likely to be much more useful than HOS theory.[5] The starting assumptions of this new "economic geography" theory that set it apart from HOS theory (and make the new theory, by and large, more relevant in the Canada-U.S. relationship than HOS theory) are:

- Much economic activity is characterized by scale economies that are external to the individual firm (HOS theory assumes constant returns to scale).

- Relative factor prices are equal across geographic space or, if inequalities appear, these are endogenously determined (HOS theory assumes the existence of 'nations' having unequal endowments of factors, and resulting differences in relative factor prices that drive international trade).

- Factors are mobile both geographically and across industries (HOS theory assumes that factors are mobile across industries but not across national boundaries).

In economic geography theory, as in HOS theory, the assumption is that products will flow across national boundaries if they are not hindered by barriers formed by national boundaries.

The two theories also differ in their treatment of logistical and transportation costs associated with these flows. In economic geography theory, these costs are integral to theory of the location of production. In standard HOS theory, by contrast, such costs are not really critical to the working of the theory and, indeed, in many expositions they are assumed to be zero.[6]

In terms of its usefulness for exploration of Canadian DIA, economic geography theory also has a major advantage in that, as will be argued shortly, it can be well integrated with modern organizational (OLI) theories of direct investment and the multinational corporation based on economies of internalization. Thus, the new theory, in addition to being driven by assumptions that seem more consistent with economic realities, such as those between Canada and the United States rather than those of HOS theory, is also a useful construct by which to examine relationships between DIA and trade.

Above all, economic geography theory is concerned with explaining the reasons for the existence of geographic clusters of economic activity. That economic activity is clustered geographically is, of course, not a new idea – indeed, the very existence of cities is one demonstration of clustering. But what drives the new theory is not the existence of cities *per se*, but rather the propensity of specialized and/or related activities to cluster in certain locations. For example, the U.S. semiconductor industry is very heavily concentrated in the famous "Silicon Valley" area south of San Francisco (although smaller clusters do exist in other areas, e.g. around Austin, Texas, Durham, North Carolina, and Orlando, Florida), and the North American auto industry has historically been clustered around Detroit, Michigan, and Windsor, Ontario. Indeed, this latter cluster straddles the Canada-U.S. border and hence has a significant effect on trade and investment between Canada and the United States in the automobile industry. These are only two examples of clusters of economic activity. Clusters of activity in many categories of product or service can be identified throughout the world (Porter, 1990).

Exactly why and how a cluster initially develops in a particular area is not fully understood, although within the new theory models have been developed that indicate that if factors of production are initially uniformly distributed across a geographical space, and if an activity characterized by localized external economies of scale of sufficient magnitude (discussed below) appears on the scene, at least some of these factors will migrate to one location to create one or more clusters of this activity. However, factors of production are not now, nor ever have been (including in colonial times), uniformly distributed across geographical space in either the United States or Canada. Thus, it is difficult on the basis of the theory to predict, *inter alia*, exactly when and where clusters of entirely new activities will develop. Indeed, the emerging literature on economic geography suggests that any explanation of why particular clusters are located where they are may owe as much to historic accident as to rigorous deduction.[7]

The new theory is more successful, however, in explaining the characteristics of an established cluster and how new clusters of an established economic activity arise apart from old ones. For example, (for reasons to be discussed shortly) an established cluster will tend to be stable as a result of incumbency advantages specific to its location. However, these incumbency advantages are not absolute, and as conditions change, new clusters of the same or similar activity might develop elsewhere.

Whatever the location-specific reasons for a cluster to develop initially in a particular location, the cluster typically owes its existence to a localized external economy of scale, i.e., some characteristic of the activity that enables operating units or "plants" (although in some cases a plant could be a single individual) to operate at a lower cost if these are located in close geographic proximity rather than widely scattered. (This type of scale economy must be distinguished from an internal scale economy, which determines the optimal size of an individual plant.) There are many reasons for the existence of localized external scale economies, but probably the most significant is the need for plants to have access to common pools of factors of production, especially specialized ones that meet the specific needs of the activity.

For example, for a plant to produce a specific product or service might require workers to have specialized skills not employed in other activities, but the plant's requirements for these workers might be subject to some seasonal or cyclical variation. Under these circumstances, there would be an economic reason for managers to locate such a plant where it could hire workers from (or release them into) a pool of individuals possessing the requisite skills. In the absence of such a pool, the firm would be forced either to: a) train new work-ers every time there was a requirement and to lay them off in the knowledge that they would not be available for rehiring when demand returned; or b) to retain unused workers during periods of slack demand. Either of these alternatives would be costly compared to being able to draw from or release into a common pool as conditions warranted.

But such a pool, if one were to exist, would be located where pre-existing plants were located. In such a location, workers possessing the specialized skills would be able to sell their services to multiple employers. This would be of advantage to the individual worker because any such worker who happened to be in the pool (i.e., for the moment at least, without employment) would face a lower expected duration of unemployment than if located somewhere where only one potential employer existed. But the very existence of a cluster of plants would reduce the likely duration (and cost) of unemployment from the level it would reach if there were only one plant, *if* plant activity at each plant were subject to fluctuation that was statistically independent of fluctuation at other plants. (Some fluctuation would not be statistically independent, e.g., that associated with general business cycles. However, some fluctuation would likely be statistically independent, e.g., if a particular firm secured a large contract, let only to one firm, that increased its business.)[8]

Thus, the existence of the pool of workers by itself creates an external scale advantage for plants that are close enough to draw from the pool (because the cost of training workers is minimized) and also creates an external scale economy for workers possessing relevant skills (because costs associated with being out of work are also minimized). Once in place, such external economies of scale can be difficult to reproduce elsewhere and hence are one source of the cluster's incumbency advantages.

In addition to pools of specialized factors, the cluster might have associated with it pools of complementary activities (e.g., the subcontracting of goods or services necessary for sustaining the main activities) which create additional localized external scale economies (and hence incumbency advan-tages) from which the cluster derives incumbency advantages.

Common pools into which multiple plants dip are not limited to labour pools. A particular economic activity might require, for example, certain specialized non-labour inputs (including, important service inputs) where it is more economical for a plant to contract out the service than to maintain an internal capability. This could be true, for example, if the efficient scale of production of the service were greater than the demands of one plant. In this case, one service provider could meet the needs of several plants. This implies that from the point of view of the plants using the service, an external economy of scale results from an internal economy of scale in the provision of the service.

In the case of activities involving advanced, rapidly changing proce-dures, information is often 'pooled'. The local external scale economy for such an industry results from informal information networking among the personnel of competing firms but who share information in a social setting. In these circumstances, all firms can benefit from shared information that is passed along the informal network.[9] The advantages created by external scale economies in no way conflict with the possibility that there might be, in a clustered activity, *internal* economies that compel plants to be held under common ownership.[10] The economics of the organization, centred around internalization, is a topic that lies at the heart of OLI theories of multinational enterprise (discussed below), but which has also been invoked to explain the existence of large firms operating multiple plants producing substitutable products and/or vertically integrated operations.[11] The core concept is that, for any of a number of reasons or some combination of these reasons (e.g., possession of proprietary technologies, need to maintain reputation based on quality standards), it is economically advantageous for multiple activities to be run as part of one organization, i.e., there is extant some economy of internalization.

But where an economy of internalization exists for some activity, a localized external scale economy can also exist at the level of the individual plant. In such cases, plants and related activities might be both clustered geographically and operated within a single organization or within a small number of organizations. For example, dozens of plants producing automobiles or automotive components are concentrated in the Detroit/Windsor area, but the final product is produced by only three firms, each of which operates multiple plants. In an extreme case, a single firm could own a multiple plant operation in a single cluster. In such a case, the external economies of scale would be entirely internalized within the organization, but they would still be external from the perspective of the individual plant.

Incumbency advantages created by external scale economies are reinforced by the fact that a cluster not only supplies goods and services but also demands them. If transportation and other transactional costs increase with distance, such costs are reduced to the extent that the goods and services produced in a cluster are also consumed there. The combined effects of "supply side" incumbency advantages (borne of economies of scale) and "demand side" ones (borne of logistical advantages) are such that, in formal models of clusters, these clusters become stable equilibria in the spatial co-ordinates of a suitable cartesian space.[12]

In the theory of economic geography, trade arises as a natural result of the clustering of activity: simply put, it is cost-minimizing to produce a particular good or service at one location and to ship the good or service to meet demand in outlying areas – which can include other clusters of economic activity. For example, the Detroit-Windsor area supplies automobiles to Toronto and New York, even though these two areas overall are much larger clusters of (other) economic activities than Detroit-Windsor. Likewise, financial services consumed in Detroit-Windsor may originate in Toronto and New York.

The trade thus generated can be in intermediate products. This introduces the possibility that, if there are extant in the production of some particular product or service both internal economies that span the vertical production process and (different) local external scale economies at the various vertical stages of production of the product, one firm might own upstream plants at one location and downstream plants at some other location, shipping intermediate goods from the former to the latter. Clearly, if the two locations are on opposite sides of a national boundary the two sets of economies (internalization and localized external scale) would then give rise to both vertical direct investment (in the sense used by Caves, 1971) and associated cross-border trade flows. The trade flows would then be two-way: intermediate goods would flow downstream, but finished goods would also flow upstream to meet the demands of local consumers in the upstream cluster. Also, these trade flows would be complementary to the direct investment. Indeed, without the investment, the trade flows would not exist.

As already mentioned, incumbency advantages are neither absolute nor time invariant. Growth in demand, or changes in transactional costs, can alter the situation to the extent that it becomes economical for a new cluster to develop apart from the original cluster. Indeed, in formal models of clustering, when the accumulated changes reach the point where a new cluster forms, the change is very dramatic: the optimal locations for both of the (now two) clusters are different from that of the original cluster, with the result that factors migrate away from the original location toward the new ones.[13]

Mathematical models from which such a result ensues embody concepts from chaos theory.[14] Formally, creation of the new clusters results from bifurcation of equilibrium points at which the clustering takes place. A "bifurcation" is the splitting of a single equilibrium point into several (usually three) new equilibria. Bifurcations typically occur when the value of some parameter reaches a critical point. In economic geography models the parameter most often represents total demand.

A simple case of bifurcation is the period doubling bifurcation that occurs when the parameter α of the logistics function $x_t = \alpha x_{t-1}(1-x_{t-1})$, a second-degree difference equation described in elementary chaos theory, reaches a certain critical value. (In fact, as described below, a series of bifurcations takes place as α rises above a critical point.) At the first bifurcation point two new stable equilibria arise in the immediate vicinity of the original one, while simultaneously the old equilibrium shifts from stable to unstable. The process is as depicted in Figure 1. As the parameter α increases past the first bifurcation, the loci of the new stable equilibria move away from the original equilibrium point until a new bifurcation occurs, whereupon two new stable equilibria appear in the immediate vicinity of each of the stable equilibria resulting from the previous bifurcation. These formerly stable equilibria again simultaneously shift to unstable. At the point of accumulation of the progression,

FIGURE 1

FIRST TWO BIFURCATIONS OF THE LOGISTICS FUNCTION $x_t = \alpha x_{t-1}(1-x_{t-1})$

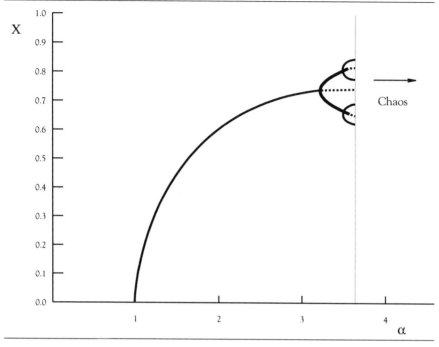

Note: The diagram indicates the location of equilibrium points x for the logistics function $x_t = \alpha x_{t-1}(1-x_{t-1})$ as a function of the parameter α for $\alpha \geq 1$; a solid line indicates a stable equilibrium and a dashed line indicates an unstable one. From $\alpha = 1$ to about $\alpha = 3.24$, there is only one stable equilibrium, but at this value of α the equilibrium splits (bifurcates) into two new stable equilibria and one unstable one. Then, at about $\alpha = 3.54$, each of the stable equilibria again splits. Only the first two bifurcations are shown, but higher order ones occur at values of α greater than 3.54 but less than 3.57. Indeed, the higher-order bifurcations occur at values of α following a simple convergent geometrical progression, with the parameter of the progression being equal to Feigenbaum's constant δ (≈ 4.6692). At the point of accumulation of this progression (at $a \approx 3.57$) there are no further bifurcations, and above this value of α the process becomes chaotic.

the entire phenomenon becomes chaotic! However, this is unlikely to occur in practice, at least for processes generating clusters of economic activity.[15]

This last statement is true because, among other reasons, in the real world frictional costs are likely to prevent old clusters of activity from disappearing altogether. In the formal models it is assumed that factors are clustered on a single point and move from an old equilibrium to a new one without cost, whereas in real life there will be substantial costs associated with the physical movement of capital and labour, and these costs will tend to keep capital and labour in place. Indeed, these adjustment costs give an existing cluster some incumbency advantage. Nonetheless, the models suggest that changing circumstances can cause the incumbency advantages of established clusters to erode to the extent that, over time, new clusters of an activity arise, and the importance of an old cluster declines. The theory predicts that if the critical parameter grows linearly, the bifurcations (new clusters) will occur increasingly rapidly.[16]

From an economic perspective, what is the reason for bifurcations – the creation of new clusters of economic activity for which incumbent clusters already exist? If (as I have been suggesting throughout) the cluster is based on the existence of a localized external economy of scale, then new clusters will occur when the demand for the end product produced within the cluster grows to the point where more than one cluster can be economically sustained. This would occur, for example, if cost curves of producers in the cluster were to reach a horizontal asymptote. But even if scale economies persist, costs cannot decline at a constant rate forever as scale is increased. Indeed, costs must eventually behave asymptotically even if they approach zero; otherwise, costs would eventually become negative, which is an impossibility.[17] As costs of producers in an existing cluster approach the minimum (even if asymptotically), there is little further economy to be achieved in expanding output at that cluster, and as demand continues to increase, logistical costs will eventually drive producers to create a new cluster in some location apart from the original cluster. Of course, if a point of maximum scale economy is reached such that output above that scale is subject to rising average costs, then it is clear that at some level of demand it would also be economical for one cluster to split into two.

The main point to be made from this discussion is that in economic geography models, the optimal location(s) of production shifts (shift) in response to demand increases rather than in response to changes in relative factor costs associated with the locations. However, once a cluster of activity is created, incumbency advantages will cause that cluster to continue to exist even if, in the face of increasing demand, it ceases to be the theoretically optimum location (or among the theoretic optima).

Important in the context of this study, changing advantages associated with a location do not necessarily imply changing advantages associated with ownership. Thus, organizational models of economic activity, especially the OLI variant associated with the explanation of direct investment and the multinational enterprise, can again be joined with the new economic geography theory.[18] Specifically, if there results a change in the optimal location of a cluster of economic activity (this locational advantage is the "L" advantage in "OLI") but no change in ownership and internalization advantages held by one or several firms (the "O" and "I" advantages in "OLI"), these might be expected to shift their operations from the old to the new location or, at least, to concentrate new additions to capacity at the new location. Such a shift in the location of a firm's operations to a change in locational advantage is envisaged, for example, by Dunning (1988), but he ascribes the shift to changes in relative factor prices (i.e., shifts in comparative advantage along HOS lines) without dealing with exactly why comparative advantage might shift from one place on the map to another in the first place. And, indeed, given that much of FDI in general, and CDIA specifically, flows from advanced nations to other advanced nations in which relative factor costs are not likely to be greatly different, it is difficult to see how this FDI could be driven by changing configurations of factor prices. By way of explaining FDI, economic geography theory holds a major advantage over OLI theory, as currently formulated, in that the former theory needs no recourse to (often implausible) shifts in classical comparative advantage for its motivation.

The reason why no such recourse is required is that if a national boundary separates the old cluster from the new one, direct investment can be driven by demand growth – i.e., exactly the same force that causes the new cluster of economic activity to arise – if the resulting shift in L advantage is independent of shifts in O and I advantages. Such direct investment would be horizontal, again using the terminology of Caves (1971). This line of reasoning appears to be especially suited to explaining horizontal direct investment between the Canada and the United States, where the long frontier and concentration (on the Canadian side, at least) of activity near the frontier would suggest that bifurcations would more likely straddle the border than occur entirely on one side or the other. The same line of reasoning might also help to explain direct investment within Europe and other advanced areas as well.

The bifurcation considered above is one where two clusters of essentially identical economic activity arise as the result of the splitting of activities formerly carried out in just one cluster. This implies that all operations in the vertical chain of production are performed in both locations. However, it is not out of the question that the bifurcation will affect only certain stages of the vertical production chain, e.g., that downstream operations undergo bifurcation but upstream operations remain clustered at the original site. Thus, bifurcation can result in partial geographic separation of vertical operations. In this context, my earlier remarks on the trade effects of such separation (i.e., that it creates two-way trade) may need some modification: e.g., if the bifurcation involves downstream operations, the trade effect may be that export of finished goods from the original site is replaced by export of intermediate goods. Because the bifurcation is driven by market growth, the total value of exports from the original location might grow, even though the unit value of exports would decline.

A few points in this new (and not yet fully developed) theory are of special relevance to policy makers, and I shall examine some of them before reviewing the empirical evidence.

First, according to this theory, growth of a region or nation is likely to be associated with direct investment into the region or nation. It should be noted that growth drives the investment, not the reverse. This observation is, if nothing else, consistent with poll results wherein executives of multinational firms are asked to rank the importance of factors affecting their decisions; market size and growth rates are consistently at or near the top of the list. It is possible that direct investment into a region, once it begins to arrive, will serve to help sustain growth of the region. But the fact remains that the growth must come first. This accords with recent experience in the United States, which attracted large amounts of direct investment during the late 1980s, after unusually robust growth – at least by U.S. standards – was registered earlier in the decade. It also accords with recent experience in China, where very robust growth again preceded a surge in direct investment. It follows that investment incentives offered to foreign investors in the absence of economic growth will not likely be effective to draw direct investment into a region or nation because in most cases these incentives could not be high enough to off-set the incumbency advantages of existing clusters of economic activity.

Second, the theory does suggest that as economic activity shifts from an old cluster to a new one, there will be some capture of markets by the new cluster that were formerly serviced from the old one. If there is a national boundary between the clusters, there will be a shift in trade patterns. Exports into the national territory of the new cluster from the national territory of the old cluster could be displaced and, indeed, the new cluster could begin exporting

FIGURE 2

HOW BIFURCATION ALTERS PATTERNS OF TRADE

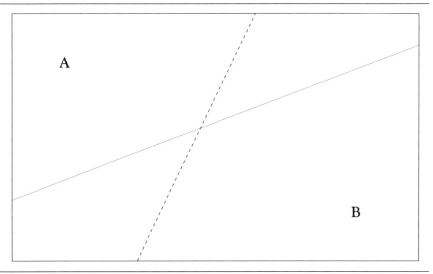

Note: The solid interior line represents a national boundary. A *priori*, the entire interior of the box is serviced by cluster A. Following the creation of cluster B, the market serviced by A is reduced to the territory left of the dotted line, and each cluster thus exports into the national territory of the other cluster.

into the national territory of the old cluster. However, as shown in Figure 2, the situation can be more complicated.

To the extent that DIA flows from the old cluster to the new one, it is true that the DIA would largely substitute for, rather than complement, exports.[19] However, the lost market share in this case is a foregone conclusion: it will be lost whether or not the DIA occurs because the alternative to DIA is that local firms, or direct investors from a third nation develop a new cluster. Also, exports that are displaced by the new cluster will to some extent be off-set by market growth in areas still serviced by the old cluster (Figure 2). Indeed, the fact that in this theory DIA is largely driven by market growth – or, to put it more strongly, the logic of the relationship between growth and DIA is more explicit in this theory than in others – can help account for the fact that most empirical evidence (see below) supports the proposition that DIA and exports are complements rather than substitutes. The reason for this is that while the DIA results in a loss of market share held by the old cluster (as compared to any particular firm), it does not necessarily lead to an absolute decline in exports from the cluster.

Economic geography theory might throw some light on a result obtained by Globerman (1985) showing that over the two decades from 1961 to 1981, new U.S. direct investment in Canada tended to be in industries with low revealed comparative advantage for Canada. Globerman finds this result to be inconsistent with OLI theory which, in its standard formulation, assumes that L-advantages are based on relative factor prices in accordance with HOS theory, and therefore that direct investment flows within an industry from countries with low or declining comparative advantage in an industry (but whose firms retained O-advantages) to countries with high or rising comparative advantage. However, under economic geography theory, as reinterpreted here in the context of OLI theory, direct investment between contiguous regions does not necessarily occur in industries where the receiving region has an overall comparative advantage in that industry. Within this new theory, again, shifts in the location of production come about primarily as a result of growth in demand rather than changes in relative factor cost.

Indeed, economic geography theory is perhaps better suited for explaining trade and investment between *contiguous* regions where the regions have similar incomes and relative factor prices but where they are divided by a political boundary, than for explaining trade and investment between nations that are geographically disjoint (even if income and relative factor prices are similar). Furthermore, this new theory is certainly best viewed as one that might cast light on trade and investment between nations at similar stages of develop-ment (i.e., it might not be particularly successful to explain commerce between the United States and Mexico, even though these are contiguous nations). Canada and the United States happen to be a case *par excellence* of nations whose economic activities are contiguous and whose incomes and relative factor prices are similar. To the extent that the new theory has merit at all (*inter alia*, it has not been subject to empirical testing), it will be applicable to the trade and investment between these two nations.

Finally, it should be noted that economic geography theory is a very new paradigm and has yet to be fully developed. Eventually, I suspect, it will become a very general body of theory of which those strands that are now know as "strategic trade theory" will be seen as special examples.[20]

EMPIRICAL EVIDENCE

THIS SECTION EXAMINES EMPIRICAL EVIDENCE bearing on the issue whether Canadian DIA and exports are substitutes or complements. Regrettably, as noted in the introductory section of this study, there is no wholly satisfactory empirical study of this issue. The theory presented immediately above suggests that, depending upon circumstances, the relationship could be either substitutive or complementary. Indeed, given the long frontier between the United States and Canada and the clustering of Canadian economic activity in close proximity to the border, the possibility that CDIA results from bifurcations of existing clusters of activity (or, put more prosaically, the establishment of new clusters of activities), and the fact that some CDIA is vertical and some horizontal, sorting out empirically the exact nature of the relationship is bound to be difficult.

Rao, Legault & Ahmad, for example, find that CDIA is associated with increases of both Canada's exports and imports. The same finding is reported with respect to foreign direct investment in Canada. The findings are aggregate and (apparently) based on time series analysis. The estimated elasticities of trade with respect to investment stocks (Rao, Legault & Ahmad, Table 7) are not controlled for the influence of factors such as economic activity, comparative costs, or other variables that could affect the outcomes, and thus must be seen as relatively crude estimates. Nonetheless, these results – that there is a positive relationship between CDIA (and Canadian inward FDI) and both imports and exports – are consistent with the theory presented above. The elasticities of imports with respect to CDIA were estimated to be higher than the elasticities of exports with respect to CDIA.

A study of some relevance to Canada is Blomström, Lipsey & Kulchyck (1988) which, *inter alia*, examined the effects of offshore production of Swedish-owned firms upon the exported manufactured goods of the home country (Sweden). Sweden, like Canada, is an advanced industrial economy located in close proximity to other (larger) advanced economies, and most of Sweden's direct investment is located either in these countries or in North America. Blomström et al. found that increases in this production are positively related to increases in exports for the seven industrial categories studied. Also, they showed that there was no propensity for this positive relationship to change as the foreign production grew.

Recent work by Bergsten & Graham (1994) produced roughly similar results for the United States. However, applying those results to Canada may not be altogether appropriate because Canada and the United States are not mirror images of each other and results that apply to the United States may not necessarily hold for Canada, despite their sharing of a long frontier. Although Canada is the United States' largest trading partner, it is not the largest nation in terms of investment stock. Nonetheless, the consistency of these results with those of Industry Canada make them worth reporting. Bergsten & Graham use a gravitational model to determine factors common to both trade in manufactured goods and investment stocks in the manufacturing sector held by the United States. Separate cross sectional regressions were run across 40 countries[21] for various years for exports, imports, and direct investment abroad as a function of total income of the host nation, per capita income of the host nation, and distance between that nation and the United States. The residuals for direct investment were then regressed on the residuals for exports and imports respectively. In both cases, for all years, the regression coefficients were positive and significant, indicating that there is a residual relationship between U.S. outward investment and both U.S. exports and U.S. imports that cannot be explained by the factors in the gravity model. Unlike the Canadian results reported by Industry Canada, however, Bergsten & Graham find that the elasticity of U.S. exports with respect to U.S. DIA is higher than the elasticity of U.S. imports with respect to U.S. DIA.

Bergsten & Graham also partitioned their country sample into regions (Western Hemisphere, Europe, and Asia). While the general results reported above held up for both Europe and Asia (i.e., U.S. outward FDI in these two regions was associated with both U.S. exports and U.S. imports of manufactured goods), they did not hold up for the Western Hemisphere. Here, the relationship between U.S. outward FDI and both U.S. exports and U.S. imports of manufactured goods was statistically insignificant. Bergsten & Graham attribute this result to import substitution policies that were prevalent in much of Latin America until quite recently.

Pearce (1990) followed an approach similar to that of Blomström et al. noted above. Pearce examined the exports and foreign production of 458 of the world's largest industrial MNEs for the year 1982. He found that increases in foreign production are generally positively related to increases in exports. This was especially true for intra-firm (as compared to inter-firm) exports, which tends to underscore the importance of vertical relationships among the various international affiliates of this sample of MNEs.

Earlier international studies of relationships between FDI and trade tend to confirm the findings of recent studies, i.e., that the relationship in net tends to be positive (more FDI is associated with more, rather than less, trade). In the late 1960s, in both the United States and the United Kingdom, for example, there was a period of official concern over the effects of outward FDI on the overall balance of payments on a current account basis. The effect of outward FDI on trade flows and the effects of financial flows were two concerns central to this issue. Two of the most careful studies of these effects were carried out under official auspices at that time and remain among the best empirical studies of the effects of FDI (Reddaway, et al., 1967 and Hufbauer & Adler, 1968).

Using somewhat different methodologies and coverage, both studies reached roughly similar conclusions, that on the basis of undiscounted cash flows the overall effects of outward FDI on the balance of payments were positive. That the effects of financial flows alone should be positive should not be a surprise to anyone; after all, a firm initiates any investment undertaking in the expectation that the investment will yield a positive return for the firm's shareholders, and ultimately that return must be reflected in dividend payments by the parent organization to those shareholders. Thus, to the extent that the shareholders of the firm are nationals of the home country, the returns accruing to the foreign affiliates of a firm must ultimately accrue to home-country nationals funded through the parent organization. However, both studies also indicated that outward FDI tended to stimulate exports (mostly of capital goods and intermediate goods) without an equivalent effect on imports.

In spite of this last effect, both studies found that new outward FDI projects tend to generate net cash outflows during their early years, so that on a balance of payments basis FDI tends to produce negative net cash flows during the years immediately following a direct investment. However, with time, cash flows tend to turn positive as the investment matures. The calculated "crossover" point for the average foreign direct investment undertaking – i.e., the elapsed time for which the cumulative effect on the balance of payments was zero – was calculated by Reddaway et al. to be about 14 years for the United Kingdom and by Hufbauer & Adler to be about nine years for the United States.

Other studies have yielded generally consistent results. Bergsten, Horst & Moran (1978), for example, found that the growth of U.S. affiliates abroad had a significantly positive effect on the growth of exports of the U.S. parent firms. Lipsey & Weiss (1981) also found that U.S. outward FDI was associated with increased U.S. exports, even after controlling for other effects (firm size, expenditures on R&D and marketing, etc.), but that the production of U.S. affiliates abroad substituted for exports to the host country of third countries. A later study by the same authors (Lipsey & Weiss, 1984) used data at the level of the individual firm to examine foreign production and U.S. exports in 14 industries in the manufacturing sector. They reported positive and significant relationships in 11 of these industries.

The international evidence thus largely supports the conclusion that DIA and exports are complements rather than substitutes. It is, however, important to put this conclusion into the context of the economic geography theory outlined earlier. As noted, the complementarity might be more an apparent result than a real one, in the sense that growth of production could be masking changes that occur in the production process, where the changes occur as the result of bifurcation and DIA flows associated with the bifurcation.

This conclusion is most likely to hold for analyses that are performed on the basis of time series (e.g., the Rao, Legault & Ahmad study in this volume, and the Blomström et al., 1988, results described above, as well as the Hufbauer & Adler, 1968, and Reddaway et al., 1967, studies) than ones that are based on cross-sectional techniques (as are the other studies cited).

Even so, the theory developed here is one in which DIA and associated trade flows are driven by economic efficiencies. There is nothing in the theory that would indicate that the patterns of trade that emerge from clustering of economic activity and bifurcations affecting these clusters are welfare reducing to regions possessing incumbent advantages. Indeed, the theory as presented in this study should be of comfort to Canada and Canadians, as it fails to sustain notions that DIA will lead to de-industrialization of existing clusters of activity. I shall return to this theme in the concluding section of this study.

CDIA AND DOMESTIC CAPITAL FORMATION

THE RELATIONSHIP BETWEEN DIA and domestic capital formation is a subtle and an indirect one. Alas, this fact does not prevent many an economist from positing the following simple relationship between the two using the national savings and investment identity

$$I - S \equiv NCF \tag{1}$$

where $NCF \equiv$ net flow of capital into a nation. Because DIA is a component of the NCF, some economists have been tempted to argue that[22]

$$\Delta DIA = \Delta I \tag{2}$$

If this relationship were true, it would imply that direct investment abroad was strictly a substitute for investment in the home economy. This would require, *inter alia*, that DIA have no effect on either domestic savings or on other components of capital flow into a nation. But that direct investment has no effect on other components of capital flow can be patently wrong. For example, if DIA is achieved by means of a takeover of an existing, ongoing firm in a foreign country by a Canadian firm, and the takeover is financed by selling bonds in that foreign country, the net flow of capital into Canada is zero (and thus neither I nor S is affected). In this case, the identity of equation (1) is satisfied by the selling of bonds resulting (in an accounting sense) in a capital inflow into Canada, while the DIA results in an equal and offsetting capital outflow. Indeed, in this transaction, domestic capital formation is not affected in either Canada *or* the host nation; all that happens is that the ownership of an existing firm changes hands.

In fact, CDIA occurs whenever Canadians acquire a sufficient equity interest in an economic activity outside Canada so that the Canadian owners are deemed to have control of that activity. Because equity is only one means by which firms can finance real capital formation, the above case is possible not only where DIA results in no capital formation (in either host or home country) but also where a firm under foreign ownership creates new real capital in the host country without there being any recorded flow of direct investment associated with the event. (This would happen, for example, if the firm were to finance new investment from its own holdings of cash or from the proceeds of a loan from local lenders). Thus, the statement that the relationship between capital formation and direct investment is indirect is true.

Nonetheless, in spite of the two examples just offered where there is no direct relationship between direct investment and any capital formation, most economists believe that there must be some such relation, even if it is indirect. But, because DIA is a source of financing for real capital investment rather than the investment itself, it is arguable that the link between DIA and capital formation in the home country is more likely to come by way of the savings component of the identity $I - S \equiv NCF$ than the investment component, namely, that direct investment reduces domestic savings needed to finance domestic investment. However, even assuming this to be true, it is still not clear whether reduced domestic savings would induce reduced domestic investment or domestic investment would remain constant and be financed through import of capital from abroad.

Whatever this relationship, it is bound not to be a very important one for Canada, simply because CDIA is lower relative to domestic capital formation in the Canadian economy. Table 1 offers two measures of this relationship for five recent years. During these years (1987-1991) CDIA as a percentage of gross fixed capital formation in Canada ranged from a high of about 8.8 percent in 1987 to a low of about 3.3 percent in 1990. Gross fixed capital formation, however, includes more than investment by business firms, and therefore a better indicator of the relative size of CDIA to Canadian domestic investment may be produced by calculating CDIA as a percentage of gross fixed capital formation by enterprises, also shown in the table. These percentages ranged from a high of about 15.9 percent in 1987 to a low of about 5.9 percent in 1990.[23] Thus, in recent years CDIA has amounted, even by this most generous measure, to somewhat less than one-sixth of Canadian gross fixed capital formation in any year.

With respect to comparable ratios for the three largest source nations (the United Kingdom, Japan and the United States) to direct investment during the past ten years, Canada's ratios are only slightly higher than those of either Japan or the United States but much lower than those of the United Kingdom (Table 2). With these remarks in mind, let us examine some results on CDIA and domestic capital formation reported in Rao, Legault & Ahmad (this volume). First, it should be noted that Rao, Legault & Ahmad agree that it is difficult to assess the impact of CDIA on domestic Canadian investment expenditure.

Rao, Legault & Ahmad then go on to conclude that while simple (bivariate) relationships between CDIA and domestic capital formation are

TABLE 1

CANADIAN DIRECT INVESTMENT ABROAD RELATIVE TO GROSS DOMESTIC FIXED
CAPITAL FORMATION, 1987-1991

	1987	1988	1989	1990	1991
	(C$ MILLION)				
Gross Fixed Capital Formation (GFCF)	116,717	132,790	145,902	141,486	132,383
Gross Fixed Capital Formation by Enterprises (GFCFE)	64,705	74,711	81,407	80,182	74,329
Canadian Direct Investment Abroad (CDIA)	10,271	7,098	6,126	4,715	4,922
	%				
CDIA/GFCF	8.80	5.35	4.20	3.33	3.72
CDIA/GFCFE	15.87	9.50	7.53	5.88	6.62

Sources: OECD, *National Accounts 1979-91* (for GFCF and GFCFE),
   IMF, *Balance of Payments Statistics Yearbook 1993* (for CDIA).

TABLE 2

DIRECT INVESTMENT ABROAD (DIA) AS A PERCENT OF GROSS FIXED CAPITAL
FORMATION (GFCF) AND AS A % OF GROSS FIXED CAPITAL FORMATION BY
ENTERPRISES (GFCFE) FOR FOUR MAJOR OUTWARD INVESTING NATIONS

	AVERAGES FOR 1987-1981	
NATION	DIA AS % OF GFCF	DIA AS % OF GFCFE
Canada	4.95	8.83
Japan	3.99	6.86
United Kingdom	17.70	34.30
United States	3.12	5.99

Source: Author's calculations, from data retrieved from sources of Table 1.

positive and significant, (suggesting that CDIA stimulates capital formation at
home rather than displacing it. Once the influence of other factors is taken
into account, however, the relationship between CDIA and domestic capital
formation is not statistically significant. These other factors include economic
activity, profitability, and technical change.

It is instructive to put these conclusions into the context of the economic
geography approach to the explanation of direct investment as discussed earlier.
The main point to emphasize here is that economic activity and technological
change are likely to be major drivers of direct investment, and therefore when

these are implicitly introduced into the Rao, Legault & Ahmad regressions, a problem of simultaneous determination results. Indeed, the theory predicts that rising demand determines the creation of new clusters of production of that for which demand is growing, and that to the extent that direct investment figures in the creation of the new clusters, increases in direct investment will be associated with growing activities and hence with increased domestic investment in these activities. In addition, as with exports, the connection between DIA and domestic capital formation becomes complicated. Horizontal bifurcation of economic activity implies a substitutive relation between DIA and identical activities at home, but (perhaps simultaneously) a complementary relation between this same DIA and related vertical activities (e.g., upstream activities in the home country might expand to meet the demand generated by downstream operations under home-country control). However, the growth that drives the bifurcation implies that, overall, capacity in the relevant activities is being expanded, even perhaps by firms in the original cluster. Advances in technology would, for the most part, increase the complementary aspect of DIA and domestic capital formation, largely because the change would likely result in old capital being replaced (everywhere) by new capital.

The result is that the simple bivariate results reported in Rao, Legault & Ahmad should not be dismissed out of hand. These indicate that growing CDIA is associated with growing activity in Canada, and that is exactly what the economic geography approach predicts (and suggests, indeed, that the two are inexorably linked). The relation between DIA and domestic capital formation, as noted above, will be some complicated mixture of substitution and complementarity, but the bivariate results reported in Rao, Legault & Ahmad suggest that the latter might very well dominate the former.

Conclusions

THE MAIN CONCLUSION TO BE DRAWN from this study is that Canadian direct investment abroad is likely to be healthy to the Canadian economy. There is no reason, on the basis of either theory or empirical evidence, to believe that CDIA displaces Canadian exports except as part of a natural process of economic growth. Neither is there any reason to believe that CDIA substitutes for Canadian domestic capital formation. CDIA does, where changing economic circumstances cause new clusters of economic activity to develop, enable Canadian-owned firms to retain ownership advantages. In a word, Canadians have no reason to fear that the economic future of Canada is compromised by the activities of Canadian-based multinational firms.

ENDNOTES

1 This situation can be contrasted with that in international trade, where theory – even taking into account the "new" international trade theory – overwhelmingly supports the proposition that open trade policies enhance national welfare. Although there are theoretical special cases where this proposition might not hold, these tend to be ones rather unlikely to apply in practice (Krugman, 1992). Of course politicians rarely accept uncritically the economic arguments for open-trade policy, and it remains an uphill battle for economists to make the case for such a policy. But, even so, theory (and empirical evidence – see Hufbauer & Elliott, 1994) rest firmly on the economists' side.

2 The organized labour position is stated in a classic article by U.S. labour leader Nat Goldfinger (Goldfinger, 1971).

3 Thus, if DIA and exports (or DIA and capital formation) were to be substitutes, the result could be adverse distributional effects, even if there were to be a net gain overall to the Canadian economy.

4 Of the 37.2 percent of CDIA that is not located in the United States, almost half – 17.3 percent – is located in European Union countries, a fact will be argued to bolster the main conclusions of this section.

5 An introduction to this new theory is found in Krugman (1991). This theory might also be useful to explain Canada's trading and investment patterns with other advanced nations – and, indeed, the patterns of trade and investment between advanced nations other than those of North America – but it is particularly likely to be useful in the Canada-U.S. context. See also Eaton, Lipsey & Safarian (1994a and 1994b).

6 There are, of course, variants of the HOS model in which costs of transport do appear; but these costs generally appear simply as minor complications to the model.

7 See, e.g., Krugman (1992).

8 The "chicken and egg" problem intrinsic in this situation – which comes first, the factor pool or the earliest plants? – is the factor that makes the problem of initial creation of the cluster difficult.

9 Eden (1991) emphasizes that certain technological changes, e.g., those associated with information technology (IT) and just-in-time (JIT) production, can lead to clustering of related economic activities. This is completely consistent with the general theory presented here; the combined impact of IT-JIT is to create (or strengthen) localized external scale economies.

10 The reader must note a terminological problem here: an "internal economy", as the term is used in the organizational economics literature, is not the same as an "internal economy of scale".

11 On the economics of the organization and internal economies, see, e.g., Williamson (1975) and Hart (1989), the seminal work in introducing the

concept of internal economy to the study of the multinational enterprise is Buckley & Casson (1976). Significant subsequent contributions have been made by Rugman (1980) and Dunning, whose works are cited later in the context of OLI theory.

12 In formal models, the clusters are concentrated on a single point in a phase space, obviously not a practical result!

13 This assumes that the factors are mobile; obviously, if one factor is immobile (e.g., land), the result would differ.

14 A mathematical introduction to chaos theory is Devaney (1989). A readable (i.e., non-mathematical) introduction is Gleick (1987).

15 As chaos is approached, the number of stable equilibria increases without bound, an unlikely result in a real economy. A necessary (but not sufficient) condition for the occurrence of chaos is that the unstable equilibria be dense in the chaotic region of the phase space, i.e., that in any subregion of this phase space, even a very small subregion, there be a countable infinity of unstable equilibria. Again, this is a condition that would be highly unrealistic in a real economy.

16 The reader is reminded that a linear growth process implies that the rate of growth is continuously *decreasing*.

17 These remarks are predicated on the notion that, subject to the external scale economy, average cost always declines with respect to output. The asymptotic nature of the costs is simply a reflection of the fact that eventually they must begin to decline at continuously decreasing rates if costs are not to fall below zero.

18 The OLI model is most closely associated with John Dunning (see, e.g., Dunning, 1980 and 1991) but is derived from earlier work on internalization. The OLI model is explained in greater depth by McFetridge elsewhere in this volume.

19 If the bifurcation affects only downstream operations, as noted earlier, the substitution is of intermediate goods for finished goods.

20 "Strategic trade theory", like economic geography theory, is built upon assumptions of increasing returns to scale. Unlike economic geography theory, strategic trade theory is based on very restrictive assumptions regarding the nature of these returns to scale and other aspects of the structure of production and consumption. Strategic trade theory is critically reviewed in Richardson (1990).

21 These countries account for over 95 percent of U.S. exports and U.S. DIA.

22 DIA is of course one of many such flows and, because it is an outflow rather than an inflow it must be given a negative sign, so that $NCF \equiv -DIA + \{other components\}$. Note that this is not a "straw man"; many an analysis of the effects of DIA on a home-nation economy has relied on this simple (but largely erroneous) reasoning. See, e.g., Musgrave (1975), a work that was widely cited in support of the Burke-Hartke bill, then

extant before the U.S. Congress, that would have greatly restricted U.S. outward direct investment.

23 For reasons already noted these ratios have something of the character of "apples to oranges" and they should not be over-interpreted. They are meant only to give an indication of the relative amounts of domestic capital formation in Canada and CDIA. It would be entirely wrong, for example, to assert (as some may be tempted to do) that in the absence of CDIA in 1987, Canada's investment by business firms would have been 15.9 percent higher than it actually was. To do so would be to miss the point of this discussion entirely!

BIBLIOGRAPHY

Bergsten, C. Fred, Thomas Horst and Theodore H. Moran. *American Multinationals and American Interests*. Washington, D.C.: Brookings Insitution, 1978.

Bergsten, C. Fred and Edward M. Graham. *Global Corporations and National Governments: Are Changes Needed in the International Economic and Political Order in Light of the Globalization of Business*. Washington, D.C.: The Institute for International Economics, (forthcoming).

Blomström, M., R. E. Lipsey and K. Kulchyck. "U.S. and Swedish Direct Investment and Exports." In *Trade Policy Issues and Empirical Analysis*. Edited by Robert E. Baldwin. Chicago: University of Chicago Press, for the National Bureau of Economic Research, 1988.

Buckley, Peter J. and Mark C. Casson. *The Future of the Multinational Enterprise*. London: Macmillan, 1976.

Caves, Richard E., "Industrial Corporations: The Industrial Economics of Foreign Investment." *Economica*, 38 (1971): 1-27.

Devaney, Robert L. *An Introduction to Chaotic Dynamical Systems*. Redwood City, CA: Addison-Wesley, 1989.

Dunning, John H. "Toward an Eclectic Theory of International Production: Some Empirical Tests." *Journal of International Business Studies*, 11, 1, (1980): 9-31.

_____. "The Eclectic Paradigm of International Production: A Personal Perspective." In *The Nature of the Transnational Firm*. Edited by Pitelis and Sugden. London: Routledge, 1991.

Eaton, B. Curtis, Richard G. Lipsey and A. Edward Safarian. "The Theory of Multinational Plant Location in a Regional Trading Area." In *Multinationals in North America*. Edited by Lorraine Eden. Calgary: University of Calgary Press, 1994a.

_____. "The Theory of Multinational Plant Locations: Agglomerations and Disagglomerations." In *Multinationals in North America*. Edited by Lorraine Eden. Calgary: University of Calgary Press, 1994b.

Eden, Lorraine. "Multinational Responses to Trade and Technology Changes." In *Foreign Investment, Technology, and Economic Growth*. Edited by Donald G. McFetridge. Calgary: University of Calgary Press, 1991.

Gleick, James. *Chaos*. London: Penguin Books, 1987.

Globerman, Steven. "Canada." In *Multinational Enterprises, Economic Structure, and International Competitiveness*. Edited by John H. Dunning. Chichester, England and New York: John Wiley and Sons, 1985.

Goldfinger, Nat. "A Labor View of Foreign Investment and Trade Issues." Commission on International Trade and Investment Policy, *United States International Economic Policy in an Interdependent World*. Washington, D.C., U.S. Government Printing Office, 1971.

Hart, Oliver. "An Economist's Perspective on the Theory of the Firm." *Columbia Law Review*, 89 (1989): 1757-74.

Hufbauer, Gary C. and Kimberly A. Elliott. *Measuring the Costs of Protection in the United States*. Washington, D.C.: Institute for International Economics, 1994.

Hufbauer, Gary C. and F. M. Adler. *Overseas Manufacturing Investment and the Balance of Payments*. U.S. Treasury Department Tax Policy Research Study No. 1. Washington, D.C.: U.S. Government Printing Office, 1968.

Krugman, Paul R. *Geography and Trade*. Cambridge, Massachusetts: The MIT Press, 1991.

_____. "Does the New Trade Theory Require a New Trade Policy?" *The World Economy*, 15, 4, (1993): 423-41.

Lipsey, R. E. and M. Y. Weiss. "Foreign Production and Exports in Manufacturing Industries." *Review of Economics and Statistics*, 63 (1981): 488-94.

_____. "Foreign Production and Exports of Individual Firms." *Review of Economics and Statistics*, 66, (1984): 304-08.

Musgrave, Peggy. Direct Investment Abroad and the Multinationals: Effects on the United States Economy. Washington, D.C.: U.S. Government Printing Office; monograph prepared for the U.S. Senate Committee on Foreign Relations, 1975.

Ostry, Sylvia. *Governments and Corporations in a Shrinking World*. New York: Council on Foreign Relations, 1990.

Pearce, R. D. "Overseas Production and Exporting Performance: Some Further Investigations." University of Reading Discussion Papers in International Investment and Business Studies, No. 135, 1990.

Porter, Michael. *The Competitive Advantage of Nations*. New York: The Free Press, 1990.

Reddaway, W. B., J. O. N. Perkins, S. J. Potter and C. T. Potter. *Effects of U.K. Direct Investment Overseas*. London: HMSO, 1967.

Richardson, J. David. "The Political Economy of Strategic Trade Policy." *International Organization*, 44, 1 (1990): 107-35.

Rugman, Alan M. "Internalisation as a General Theory of Foreign Direct Investment: A Reappraisal of the Literature." *Weltwirtschaftlichesarchiv* 116, 2 (1980): 365-79.

_____. "New Theories of the Multinational Enterprise: An Assessment of Internalization Theory." *Bulletin of Economic Research*, 38, (1986): 101-18.

Williamson, Oliver E. *Markets and Hierarchies, Analysis, and Antitrust Implications: A Study in the Economics of Internal Organization*. New York: Free Press, 1975.

Donald G. McFetridge
Department of Economics
Carleton University

5

Canadian Foreign Direct Investment, R&D and Technology Transfer

INTRODUCTION

THE PURPOSE OF THIS STUDY is to investigate the influence of Canadian direct investment abroad on the level of innovative activity in Canada and on the rate of productivity growth in Canada. This examination is motivated by the concern that technologies of Canadian origin are being exploited abroad rather than at home and that as a result associated rents and agglomeration economies are being lost to the domestic economy. While foreign direct investment (FDI) in high-tech industries is relatively new to Canada, there has been concern over the consequences for over twenty years and there is considerable literature on the subject. Indeed, it is ironic that while the United States was concerned that it was giving away technology transferred abroad by means of FDI, host countries such as Canada were concerned that they were not realizing any technological benefit. Of course, the general mercantilist concern with the export of technology has a lengthy history.

THE LOCATION OF INNOVATIVE ACTIVITY AND ECONOMIC GROWTH

THIS STUDY PROCEEDS ON THE BASIS of a taxonomy of the means by which Canadian firms can earn foreign income on technologies they have developed in Canada. First, the technology can be embodied in goods and services exported from Canada. In this case, ongoing development of the technology occurs in Canada and the widely cited but seldom measured agglomeration economies are realized in Canada. The Canadian firm also earns profits on these exports, part of which can be regarded as quasi-rents to its R&D effort. Foreigners also benefit to the extent that the price they pay for the Canadian good or service is less than the value to them of the new technology embodied in it. Foreigners can also reverse engineer; that is, copy the Canadian product once they have imported it.

A second option is to license the technology abroad.[1] This yields royalty income. The Canadian firm and its foreign licensees share in the ongoing development of the technology. Domestic agglomeration economies will continue to be realized, but likely to a lesser degree than in the first case. If ongoing innovation occurs at the production end as Jorde & Teece (1993) suggest, then the initiative could ultimately pass from the Canadian licensor to its larger foreign licensees.[2] The phenomenon of losing the initiative in co-operative arrangements with foreigners has been examined in the context of U.S.-Japan joint ventures by Lei & Slocum (1992).

A third option is to transfer the technology to foreign affiliates. This is the FDI option about which this volume is principally concerned. The Canadian parent realizes profits and royalties and retains control over the ongoing development of the technology. Development may occur in the affiliate if it is located in a larger market than the parent or if the product involved must be modified to suit the needs of foreign customers. To the extent that development occurs in the foreign affiliate(s), agglomeration economies will be realized abroad rather than domestically. In addition, leakage of technology from either foreign affiliates or licensees may be greater than if it had been retained in the home country.

The literature on the factors determining the choice among exporting, licensing, and foreign direct investment is well developed. According to the OLI paradigm (Dunning, 1977) exporting is chosen over technology transfer if domestic production is less costly than foreign production. Transportation costs, trade barriers (standards, local preferences and contingent protection), production costs and Teece's co-specialized assets enter this decision. The influence of these factors on the location of production depends on whether the domestic market is small or large relative to the foreign market(s).

Given the location of production abroad, the requisite technology can be transferred either internally, through FDI, or by means of a variety of arm's-length or partially arm's-length contractual arrangements. The choice of contractual form depends on the longevity and complexity of the transfer arrangement contemplated, that is, on the magnitude of the transaction-specific investment required.[3]

All this is well known. The Canadian parent will choose optimally from its private perspective. A small country parent will be more likely to opt for foreign production and foreign technology development and will probably not do as well privately as a large country parent. This can be aggravated (as Canadians are learning to their chagrin) by aggressive policies on the part of the large country.

The private and social *optima* need not coincide. It may be privately optimal to transfer the production of a large externality-generating activity abroad. In this case the FDI (or license) would not be socially optimal, at least from the point of view of the home country. To counteract this, the home country should subsidize the externality-generating activity. This may involve the subsidization, by various means, of both formal R&D and innovative activity in general. Of course, subsidies beyond formal R&D would run into trouble with the GATT and with U.S. countervail. Conversely, if domestic formal R&D goes abroad before it has had an opportunity to generate domestic externalities, the case for continuing to subsidize it is weakened.

It is important to understand that, while some forms of foreign sale of Canadian technology may be preferable to others from a domestic economic development point of view, foreign sales are almost always preferable to no foreign sales. That is, there are scale and substitution effects at work here. Measures to discourage FDI by Canadian high-tech companies might result in more domestic exploitation of the innovations that are produced but they would surely also result in fewer innovations being produced.[4] The issues, then, are:

- Does Canadian FDI have a significant technological component?

- Does technologically oriented Canadian FDI reduce the social return to innovative activity in Canada (that is, does the substitution effect dominate the scale effect)?

- Are there policy measures that can encourage Canadian firms to take account of domestic innovative externalities in their FDI decisions?

THE IMPORTANCE OF TECHNOLOGY TRANSFER AS A MOTIVE FOR CANADIAN DIRECT INVESTMENT ABROAD

CHARACTERISTICS OF CANADIAN FIRMS ENGAGING IN FDI

ACCORDING TO THE WIDELY ACCEPTED ownership location internalization (OLI) paradigm, the purpose of foreign direct investment is to facilitate the internal transfer of firm-specific assets to a foreign market. Thus, a possible motive for foreign direct investment by Canadian firms is to transfer Canadian-developed technologies or technological expertise abroad.

The general consensus has been, however, that technology transfer has not been an important motive for Canadian FDI. The industrial distribution of the stock of Canadian direct investment abroad as of the end of 1991 was as follows: beverages, 6.3 percent; non-ferrous metals, 12 percent; wood and wood products, 11.7 percent; iron and products, 4 percent; chemicals and allied products, 7 percent; other manufacturing, 2.9 percent; merchandising, 4.1 percent; mining and smelting, 6.9 percent; petroleum and natural gas, 6.3 percent, utilities, 2.5 percent; financial, 30.2 percent.[5] The composition of the stock has evolved over time, with the chemical and financial sectors becoming relatively more important and the beverage and utility sectors becoming less important.[6]

While these industrial categories are crude, they do show that, with the exception of chemicals and allied products, Canadian direct investment abroad is not in R&D-intensive sectors.[7] This is not to say that firms in the financial, wood products and ferrous metal and other sectors are not innovative. On the contrary, they are frequently innovative both as users of technological developments occurring elsewhere and in other ways (organization, marketing).[8] It can be argued, however, that while this innovative activity is important, it is unlikely to generate the kind of spillover benefits associated with the R&D-intensive sectors.

A similar picture emerges if the characteristics of the larger Canadian multinationals are examined. The type of firm-specific asset these firms are transferring abroad is more likely to be marketing expertise than new technologies. In his 1987 study, Alan Rugman reports that the 18 largest Canadian multinationals had relatively low R&D intensities (a mean of 0.8 percent if Northern Telecom is excluded). Rugman concludes that the advantages of these firms tended to be in marketing and distribution rather than new product development.

With respect to smaller firms, foreign direct investment does appear to be a means of exploiting a technological advantage in foreign markets. For example, Litvak & Maule (1981) found that, among a group of 25 small (sales under $100 million) Canadian firms with U.S. subsidiaries they surveyed in 1978, the possession of a superior technology was ranked highest as a reason for investing in the United States (Table 3, p. 42).[9] The authors also characterize the decision by one of their sample companies to establish a laboratory in Denver as being largely driven by technology-related considerations. Two particularly influential factors were the existence of a large number of government-funded and privately funded laboratories and the concentration in the Denver area of U.S. research, the company's area of expertise (pp. 46 - 7).

More recently, Gorecki (1992) has found that in 1986, among "large" Canadian firms (any firm with assets over $25 million), the probability that a firm is a multinational was .3397 among firms in high R&D-intensity (two-digit) industries and .1989 among firms in low R&D-intensity industries. Among "small" firms, the probability that a firm in a high R&D-intensity industry is a multinational was .0056 while the probability that a firm in a low R&D-intensity industry is a multinational was .0022. Thus, it appears that Canadian firms in the more R&D-intensive industries have a higher propensity to engage in FDI.

Gorecki's findings also point to the role of firm-specific assets in general as determinants of foreign direct investment. He finds that large firms in high advertising-intensity industries have a higher probability of being multinationals than large firms in low advertising-intensity industries (1992, Table 12). He also finds that large firms engaged in either related product or conglomerate diversification are also more likely to be multinationals than single product firms (1992, Table 9). This is consistent with earlier findings that the factors that drive firms to be multimarket firms domestically also drive them to be multinational firms.

Gorecki's findings with respect to the role of firm-specific assets in motivating foreign direct investment are supported by results reported in Table 8 of the Rao, Legault & Ahmad study in this volume. According to this table, Canadian firms with foreign assets (outward-oriented firms) are more R&D intensive in all industries than their purely domestic (no foreign assets) counterparts.

Corvari & Wisner (1991) have also analyzed the characteristics of Canadian-owned multinationals. They find that, on average, the margin on value added of the manufacturing establishments of Canadian-owned multinationals is slightly higher than the margin on value added of the manufacturing establishments of Canadian-owned firms with no foreign affiliates (1991, Table 2.3). When they disaggregate, the authors find that the multinationals' margin on value added is higher in three major groups – food and beverages, primary metals and fabricated metals – and lower in four others.

The margin on value added is defined as the proportion of value added accounted for by quasi-rents to tangible and intangible capital plus any economic rents ("excess" profit). A possible interpretation of the Corvari & Wisner finding is that Canadian-owned multinationals are no more intangible asset-intensive than Canadian-owned firms with no foreign affiliates. On the face of it this would contradict both Gorecki's findings and those of Rao, Legault & Ahmad (reported above). The different conclusions reached by Corvari & Wisner could be a consequence of the small size of their sample or of offsetting differences in tangible capital intensity or market power. In addition, advertising and R&D expenditures are generally not attributed to individual manufacturing establishments. In any event, none of the results presented by Gorecki, or Rao, Legault & Ahmad, or Corvari & Wisner constitutes a full test of OLI reasoning in that none holds constant locational factors such as transportation costs and trade barriers.

Therefore, insofar as its technological orientation is concerned, Canadian foreign direct investment has the following characteristics:

- An overwhelming proportion of the stock of Canadian FDI is accounted for by industries that are not technologically driven or, at least, not R&D intensive.

- Firms based in advertising or R&D-intensive industries have a higher propensity to engage in FDI (i.e., to have a foreign affiliate).

- Outward-oriented Canadian companies tend to be more R&D intensive than their purely domestic counterparts, although this difference can not be confirmed at the establishment level.

Characteristics of Canadian Direct Investment in the United States

THE PRECEDING SECTION CONCLUDES THAT the largest Canadian direct investments abroad have historically been in support of marketing and other non-technological firm-specific advantages. There is, however, a general tendency for firms in R&D intensive industries in Canada to be more active foreign investors, and there is survey evidence that smaller firms have invested in the United States in order to exploit their technological advantages more effectively in that country.

Of Canada's $31 billion net investment position in the United States, less than 10 per cent would normally be construed as being in R&D-intensive industries.[10] This includes chemical and allied products (0.81 percent), non-electrical machinery (1.12 percent), electrical equipment (4.68 percent), transportation equipment (0.35 percent), instruments (0.04 percent), business services (0.27 percent) and engineering services (0.11 percent).

The industries accounting for the largest percentage of Canadian investment in the United States are not R&D intensive. They include food and kindred products (16.30 percent), real estate (12.71 percent), insurance (10.47 percent), primary and fabricated metals (9.33 percent), printing and publishing (8.47 percent) and retail trade (7.74 percent). While firms in these industries are innovative in their own ways, it is doubtful that their presence generates significant technological spillover benefits to their American hosts.

The data on foreign direct investment in the United States indicate that foreign-owned manufacturing establishments as a group tend to account for a larger share of employment in the more R&D-intensive U.S. industries than in the less R&D-intensive industries (Howenstine & Zeile, 1992, Table F, reproduced in part as Table 1 below). Specifically, the correlation coefficient between industry R&D intensity and the employment share of foreign-owned manufacturing establishments is .286, and this is statistically significant. This is consistent with predictions derived from the OLI paradigm and with the empirical results obtained for other countries (Caves et al., 1980; Meredith, 1984).

Disaggregation by country of ultimate beneficial ownership reveals that it is German- and Japanese-owned establishments that tend to have a larger share of employment in the more R&D-intensive industries in the United States (correlation coefficients of .351 and .365 respectively).[11] There is no linear relationship between the employment share of Canadian-owned establishments and industry R&D intensity.[12] Examination of Table 1 suggests a possible reason for this result. As is the case with Germany, Japan and the Netherlands, the employment share of Canadian-owned establishments increases with industry R&D intensity until the 6 percent to 8 percent R&D intensity class is reached. The Canadian-owned share collapses

TABLE 1

AVERAGE EMPLOYMENT SHARES OF FOREIGN-OWNED ESTABLISHMENTS IN U.S. MANUFACTURING INDUSTRIES, GROUPED BY R&D ACTIVITY AND BY SELECTED COUNTRY OF ULTIMATE BENEFICIAL OWNERSHIP (UBO), 1987

	% INDUSTRY EMPLOYMENT ACCOUNTED FOR BY ESTABLISHMENTS WITH UBO IN:					
	ALL COUNTRIES	CANADA	GERMANY	JAPAN	NETHERLANDS	UNITED KINGDOM
All Industries	8.3	1.3	1.0	0.6	0.6	2.0
R&D EMPLOYMENT AS A % OF TOTAL EMPLOYMENT						
0.0 – 1.9 21 industries	6.6	1.0	0.3	0.4	0.3	2.2
2.0 – 3.9 15 industries	8.0	1.2	0.9	0.5	0.7	1.7
4.0 – 5.9 7 industries	8.0	0.9	1.3	0.7	0.5	2.0
6.0 – 7.9 7 industries	13.9	3.4	2.6	1.3	1.1	2.2
8.0 or more	8.7	0.3	1.3	0.8	0.8	2.0
EMPLOYMENT SHARE/ R&D-INTENSITY CORRELATION	.286[a]	.094	.351[a]	.365[a]	.233	-.044

Note: [a] Correlation is statistically significant at the 5 percent level.
Source: Howenstine & Zeile (1992), Table F.

in the highest R&D intensity class, and this collapse is more precipitous than is the case with Germany, Japan and the Netherlands. In contrast, British-owned establishments are equally prominent in all R&D-intensity ranges.

A plausible interpretation of these results within the context of the OLI paradigm is that British firms are transferring a mix of technological and non-technological intangible assets to the United States while German, Japanese and Dutch firms are primarily transferring technological intangibles. With the exception of the most highly R&D-intensive assets, technological intangibles are also relatively more important for Canadian firms.

Some evidence regarding the extent to which Canadian FDI may be supporting the transfer of other intangible assets to the United States is also provided by Howenstine & Zeile (1992, Table D). These authors find that the proportion of industry employment accounted for by foreign-owned establishments increases with industry "capital intensity". This is also true of Canadian-, German-, Dutch- and British-owned establishments.

Howenstine & Zeile measure capital intensity as the margin on value added (value added, less wages and salaries, expressed as a proportion of value added). As suggested above this could reflect quasi-rents to intangible technological or marketing (brand recognition) assets or to physical capital as well as economic rents ("excess" profits). To the extent that these margins reflect quasi-rents to intangibles, the Howenstine & Zeile findings are consistent with OLI reasoning.[13]

In sum, there is some weak evidence that Canadian-owned firms tend to be more prominent in moderately high-tech U.S. manufacturing industries than in low-tech U.S. industries, and that Canadian-owned firms tend to be more prominent in higher margin and possibly more intangible asset-intensive U.S. manufacturing industries.

The next question is whether Canadian FDI in the United States tends to be technologically-oriented *relative to other foreign investors*. The revealed comparative advantage of Canadian direct investors (RCAI) can be calculated using the value added (gross product) of foreign affiliates in the United States as reported in the *Survey of Current Business* (September, 1992). The RCAI in the *i*th industry is defined as:

RCAI$_i$ = (Share of Canadian-Owned Affiliates in all Affiliate Value Added in Industry i)/(Share of Canadian Affiliates in all Affiliate Value Added)

RCAI values for 1987 and 1990 are reported in Table 2. It is apparent that Canadian firms have a comparative advantage in printing and publishing (especially newspapers), retail trade, insurance, real estate, mining, transportation and communications and utilities. Canadian investors are at a comparative disadvantage in petroleum extraction and refining, non-electrical machinery, instruments, wholesale trade, and business services. It is also clear that RCAI values vary from year to year, so that it is unwise to draw inferences from all but the most extreme values.

With respect to whether Canada has a revealed comparative advantage in high-tech investment, there is little to indicate that this is the case. There is a clear comparative disadvantage in such R&D-intensive manufacturing sectors as non-electrical machinery and instruments, and services such as engineering and research. There is neither a comparative advantage nor disadvantage in electrical and electronic equipment.

Inferences regarding the technological orientation of Canadian direct investment in the United States can also be drawn from its interstate distribution as reported in the 1987 benchmark survey of foreign direct investment in the United States (U.S. Department of Commerce, 1990). The survey shows that Canadian affiliates accounted for the largest share of affiliate employment in (in descending order) Maine, West Virginia, South Dakota, Montana, Delaware and Vermont. Canadian affiliates accounted for the largest share of affiliate manufacturing employment in South Dakota, West Virginia, Delaware, Maine, Alaska and Idaho.

The interstate distribution of Canadian direct investment yields some interesting insights regarding whether Canadians are more inclined than other foreigners to invest in states bordering on Canada, in high-tech states or in low labour cost states. According to the survey, Canadian affiliates accounted for 16 percent of foreign affiliate manufacturing employment in the United

TABLE 2

REVEALED COMPARATIVE ADVANTAGE OF CANADIAN DIRECT INVESTORS IN THE
UNITED STATES

INDUSTRY	1990 SHARE (%)	1990 RCAI	1987 SHARE (%)	1987 RCAI
All Industries	16.16	1.00	18.38	1.00
Petroleum	5.05	0.31	3.60	0.20
Manufacturing	17.71	1.10	22.95	1.25
Food and Beverage	–	–	19.10	1.04
Primary Metals	17.54	1.09	16.18	0.88
Fabricated Metals	4.32	0.27	19.06	1.04
Machinery	11.25	0.70	14.29	0.78
Machinery excluding Electrical	3.06	0.19	–	–
Electrical Machinery	17.21	1.06	–	–
Textiles & Apparel	17.15	1.06	12.11	0.66
Lumber, Wood & Furniture	9.82	0.61	17.21	0.94
Paper & Allied	12.54	0.78	15.78	0.86
Printing & Publishing	50.64	3.13	56.87	3.09
Motor Vehicles & Equipment	10.15	0.63	–	–
Instruments	2.22	0.14	0.81	0.04
Wholesale Trade	3.79	0.23	5.92	0.32
Retail Trade	33.41	2.07	34.17	1.86
Finance except Banking	12.57	0.78	4.42	0.23
Insurance	28.89	1.79	23.35	1.27
Real Estate	28.73	1.78	44.43	2.42
Services	6.08	0.38	8.36	0.45
Business Services	3.61	0.22	2.01	0.11
Engineering	8.95	0.55	9.52	0.52
Accounting, Research Mgmt.	3.92	0.24	2.10	0.11
Mining	18.81	1.16	26.48	1.44
Construction	13.05	0.81	4.56	0.25
Transportation	28.06	1.74	27.90	1.52
Communications & Utilities	–	–	65.16	3.54

Note: Share is value-added of Canadian-owned firms as a percentage of all foreign-owned firms.
Source: U.S. Department of Commerce, "Gross Product U.S. Affiliates of Foreign Direct Investors, 1987-1990"
        Survey of Current Business, November, 1992; Tables 2.1 and 2.4.

States in 1987 and 16.4 percent of affiliate employment in the 11 border states, including Alaska. A simple comparison does not reveal any inclination of Canadian investors to concentrate on border states.

There are many ways of defining a high-tech state. It is defined here in terms of the interaction of patents per capita and aggregate industrial R&D spending.[14] By this measure, the five "highest-tech" states are California, New Jersey, Michigan, Massachusetts and New York. Canadian affiliates account for 11.5 percent of affiliate employment in these states, considerably below Canada's overall share.

Low labour cost states are defined here in terms of the interaction of the percentage of the labour force that is unionized and the percentage of the population that has completed high school. The states with the lowest value of this variable are South Carolina, Nebraska, North Carolina, Arizona and Utah. Canadian affiliates accounted for 19.6 percent of affiliate employment in these states, above Canada's overall share.

A more informative method of analysis is multiple regression. A regression of Canadian affiliate manufacturing employment share on the high-tech, labour cost and border state variables yields the following results:

$$\text{LOCSM} = -2.5 - .17(-5) \text{ INNOV} + .28(-3) \text{ LWS} + .61 \text{ BORD}$$
$$(2.48) \qquad\qquad (2.83) \qquad\qquad (3.40)$$

N=49; R-SQUARE ADJ. = .16   t-ratios in brackets
where:
LOCSM = log of the odds ratio of the Canadian share of affiliate
          manufacturing employment;[15]
INNOV = patents per head x industrial R&D spending
LWS = percent not unionized x percent not completing high school
BORD = one if state borders Canada, zero otherwise
MFS = proportion of state labour force in manufacturing

The multiple regression supports the conclusion that Canadian direct investment tends to be more prominent in the border states and in the less educated and less unionized states, and less prominent in the high-tech states than other foreign direct investment.

While Canadian FDI in the United States may be less oriented toward high-tech industries and states than other foreign investors, Corvari & Wisner (1991) and Rao, Legault & Ahmad (1994) have found that within many industries, Canadian-owned affiliates tend on average to be more R&D intensive than the affiliates of other foreign investors (Corvari & Wisner, 1991, Table 3.3). There are many possible explanations for this finding, including differences in affiliate scale and differences in home- and host-country market sizes with the R&D function not being perfectly divisible. Another possibility is that the United States is simply a more attractive site relative to the home country in the Canadian case than is the case with other foreign investors.

FDI AND THE TRANSFER OF TECHNOLOGY ABROAD

MOTIVES FOR INTERNATIONAL DECENTRALIZATION OF R&D

THERE IS NOW A SUBSTANTIAL BODY of evidence that the R&D function is becoming increasingly internationalized (Cheng & Bolon, 1993). It also appears, however, that this process has not proceeded very far (De Meyer & Mizushima, 1989; Patel & Pavitt, 1991).

TABLE 3

RATES OF GROWTH OF AFFILIATE SALES AND R&D SHARES, RELATIVE TO PARENTS,
U.S. MULTINATIONALS, 1982-1989

INDUSTRY	SALES SHARE (%)	R&D SHARE (%)
Petroleum and Coal Products	11.9	3.1
Grain Mill and Bakery Products	-9.1	26.2
Beverages	-34.3	127.3
Other Food and Kindred	2.6	32.0
Industrial Chemicals	21.9	32.2
Drugs	- 0.4	-8.6
Soap, Cleaners and Toilet Goods	11.3	113.2
Agricultural Chemicals	1.7	30.0
Chemical Products nec	36.1	44.7
Ferrous Primary Metals	75.5	319.6
Non-ferrous Primary Metals	-6.8	98.6
Fabricated Metal Products	-22.4	105.8
Construction and Mining Machinery	13.8	7.5
Office and Computing Machines	71.4	162.7
Farm, Garden and Other Machinery	67.4	103.3
Radio, TV and Communications Equipment	7.3	53.4
Electronic Components and Accessories	132.6	316.6
Household Appliances, Electrical Equipment nec	27.2	99.6
Transportation Equipment	7.0	-7.1
Textiles and Apparel	23.2	48.0
Lumber, Wood, Furniture and Fixtures	-8.1	110.6
Paper and Allied Products	88.5	182.1
Printing and Publishing	15.4	-24.1
Miscellaneous Plastics Products	135.6	276.3
Glass Products	-9.4	191.7
Stone, Clay, Other Non-metallic Minerals	45.2	-12.0
Instruments and Related Products	-23.6	27.0
Other Manufacturing	16.0	49.0
Durable Goods Wholesalers	-32.6	86.5
Computer and Data Processing Services	107.0	184.2
Business Services nec	19.9	169.2

Note: First Column = {[SA89/SP89] / [SA82/SP82] - 1} x 100 where SA = affiliate sales, SP = parent sales:
        Second Column = {[RA89/RP89] / [RA82/RP82] - 1} x 100 where RA is R&D performed for and by affiliates
        and RP is R&D of parents.
        nec = not elsewhere covered
Sources: U.S. Department of Commerce, *U.S. Direct Investment Abroad*, 1982 and 1989 Benchmark Surveys.

The perception of the extent of international R&D decentralization depends on the variable being measured (R&D or patents) and the nationality and industry of the firms being observed. The international distribution of corporate patent applications turns out to be more centralized than R&D spending (Casson, Pearce & Singh, 1992). Although now participating in the decentralization process, U.S. and Japanese multinationals have historically

161

had a greater tendency to centralize R&D in their home countries than have multinationals based in other countries, especially those with smaller home markets (De Meyer & Mizushima, 1989; Cantwell, 1993; Cheng & Bolon, 1993). The tendency to decentralize is greater in some industries, the most decentralized being food products, pharmaceuticals, and non-metallic minerals and the least decentralized being aircraft, professional and scientific instruments, and textiles (Cantwell, 1993, Table 2).

The industrial pattern of R&D decentralization by U.S. multinationals between 1982 and 1989 is reported in Table 3. The affiliates' share of R&D has grown most in electronics, miscellaneous plastics and ferrous metals and least in drugs, transportation equipment, stone clay and glass and printing and publishing.

The national pattern of recent R&D growth by affiliates of U.S. multinationals is reported in Table 4. It shows that affiliate spending has risen most in Japan, Ireland, Italy and the Netherlands and least (among OECD countries) in Turkey, Greece, Finland and Switzerland.

TABLE 4

SALES AND R&D GROWTH BY COUNTRY: AFFILIATES OF U.S. MULTINATIONALS, 1982-1989

COUNTRY	SALES GROWTH (%)	R&D GROWTH (%)	GERD/GDP (%)
Japan	126.5	792.9	2.8
Germany	58.2	60.0	2.7
France	70.9	56.9	2.3
Italy	84.9	162.0	1.1
United Kingdom	54.8	108.5	2.3
Canada	60.4	93.1	1.4
Spain	184.8	45.0	0.5
Australia	31.7	66.7	1.1
Turkey	172.7	0	0.2
Netherlands	64.6	464.6	2.1
Belgium	42.3	40.4	1.5
Sweden	22.8	10.7	2.8
Switzerland	8.9	-1.7	2.4
Austria	74.4	23.1	1.3
Greece	-20.0	0	0.3
Norway	3.3	5.9	1.6
Finland	91.9	-25.0	1.5
Portugal	145.8	100.0	0.4
New Zealand	45.8	33.3	1.0
Ireland	142.7	1,633.3	0.8

Source: OECD and U.S. Department of Commerce, U.S. Direct Investment Abroad, 1982 and 1989 Benchmark Surveys.

The fundamental forces leading to decentralization of R&D include:

- increased decentralization of production and marketing;

- improved information and communications technologies (that have facilitated international co-ordination and integration); and

- increased recognition of the scientific talent and resources for innovation that exist outside the home country.

The major factors inhibiting decentralization appear to be the diseconomies of small-scale R&D, communications and co-ordination costs and the similarity of foreign markets to the home market (Casson & Singh, 1993, Table 2). The requirements for critical mass in the R&D function vary, but they have been estimated at a technical staff of from 25 to 30 in paint and chemicals and 100 to 200 in pharmaceuticals (de Meyer & Mizushima, 1989). This would limit the number of Canadian firms that could make efficient use of multiple laboratories whether located in Canada or elsewhere (see Foreign R&D by Canadian Firms below).

There are two broad classes of foreign R&D. The first is the local production and market support operation. A support operation assimilates technology transferred from the parent, provides technical services for local customers and modifies product or process technologies to suit local (or possibly regional) customers or conditions. The location of local market support R&D is determined largely by the location of production.

The second broad class of foreign R&D has been known variously as a global or internationally integrated operation or, more recently, as knowledge-seeking R&D. An internationally integrated laboratory develops or participates in the development of technologies intended for use by the parent or by the company worldwide. The location of integrated or knowledge-seeking R&D tends to be influenced more by the need for access to local networks, clusters or centres of excellence (Fusfeld 1986, Cantwell 1989; Teece 1991). These local networks may involve any or all of advanced customers, suppliers or competitors, universities or research institutes.

Market support and knowledge-seeking R&D have different implications for both home and host countries. With respect to knowledge-seeking R&D, the implications for host countries are, first, that to attract multinational R&D operations, a country must have a critical mass of scientific expertise in the relevant area. Second, the benefit realized by the host country will depend on the extent to which knowledge-seekers also contribute to the local knowledge pool. If they serve merely as listening posts, they simply increase the extent to which the quasi-rents from domestic innovations are realized abroad. With respect to home countries, location of R&D abroad by domestic firms may increase the extent to which the domestic economy is able to appropriate or draw from the international knowledge pool. Thus, knowledge-seeking decentralization of R&D could entail domestic social benefits in excess of its private benefits.

Decentralization of R&D for purposes of foreign production or market support does not increase domestic withdrawals from the international pool of knowledge. Indeed, it may increase the leakage of domestic technology abroad.

This raises the possibility that foreign countries might use non-tariff barriers (procurement, standards, contingent protection) to induce firms currently attempting to sell in their markets to set up local production facilities. If local production requires local R&D and knowhow leaks out from either the production or the R&D operation, the parent loses profits and the parent's home country loses social benefits as compared with the exporting option. Specifically, the parent's home country foregoes any spillover benefits on production and R&D transferred abroad. While the parent firm's profits must be higher than if it had no access at all to the foreign market in question, its profits may be lower than if it had been able to export to that market.

RECENT EMPIRICAL EVIDENCE ON THE INTERNATIONAL DECENTRALIZATION OF R&D

RECENT STATISTICAL EVIDENCE on the factors bearing most prominently on the R&D location decision comes from Pearce (1992), Casson, Pearce & Singh (1992) and Casson & Singh (1993). Pearce finds that, with the exceptions of the pharmaceuticals and consumer chemicals industry, the office equipment industry and, to a lesser extent, the petroleum industry, the need to provide technical support to the local production unit or to modify or develop new products for the local market is much more important than the local scientific environment or infrastructure as a determinant of the decision to locate R&D facilities in a particular country.

Thus, according to Pearce, the industries oriented toward knowledge searching are pharmaceuticals and consumer chemicals, office equipment, and petroleum. The industries oriented towards local affiliate support are motor vehicles and components, metal products, and food, drink and tobacco (Pearce, 1992, Table 5.1). The local affiliate support industries tend to be the low R&D-intensity and low basic research-intensity industries.

Casson, Pearce & Singh (1992) present a similar picture of the knowledge searchers. They find that firms in the pharmaceuticals, professional and scientific equipment, and chemicals industries are more likely than others to be attracted to a foreign location because of the availability of professionals (1992, Table 6.6). They find that firms in the pharmaceuticals, office equipment, and chemicals industries are more likely than others to run an internationally integrated R&D operation (1992, Table 6.7). As a result of this integration, the distribution of patents of firms in these industries tends to be more centralized than in industries in which foreign R&D is more oriented to the solution of local process and product process problems (Table 6.8). This raises questions about the use of patent shares as measures of R&D decentralization as Patel & Pavitt (1991) have done.

The importance of supporting foreign production as a motive for decentralizing R&D is confirmed by Casson & Singh (1993) who also make use of the Pearce & Singh data. These authors find that the propensity to engage in overseas R&D is a function of the proportion of production that is overseas and of the scale of the parent's home R&D operation (Table 1). Given the relative importance of foreign production, parents in the chemical industry and parents based in small countries had a greater tendency to locate R&D overseas.

The number of foreign countries in which R&D is conducted is a function of the size of the firm and the proportion of production abroad and, given this, is higher in the pharmaceuticals, electrical engineering, and mechanical engineering industries. This provides a tentative indication that these industries are more inclined than others to locate their R&D with a view to tapping into local pools of knowledge. An alternative inference is simply that the number of foreign production sites (and thus opportunities for support R&D) associated with a given proportion of foreign production is higher in these industries.

Case study evidence confirms the importance of knowledge-seeking foreign R&D in the pharmaceuticals industry (Howells, 1990; Taggart, 1991; OECD, 1992, pp. 224-5). Dalton & Serapio (1993, p. 37) find that knowledge seeking is the dominant motive for the establishment of biotechnology R&D operations by foreign companies in the United States. These authors find that in the case of the electronics industry, acquiring technology and meeting customer needs are equally prominent motives for establishing a U.S. R&D facility. In the automotive industry, production support (meeting customer needs and meeting U.S. environmental standards) is the dominant motive.

More generally, the initial decentralization of R&D by U.S. companies is attributed by Fusfeld (1986, p. 132) principally to a desire to have "a window on foreign science". Fusfeld also notes, however, that the successful foreign R&D operations were associated with a manufacturing operation in the same country.

> From the view of research management, this correlation was to be expected. An industrial research laboratory does not exist in a vacuum. The interaction with a manufacturing arm provides some criterion for selectivity among the range of possible technical projects. It allows for feedback between technical approaches and manufacturing conditions. (1986, p. 133)

Other studies (OECD, 1992, p. 224) find that R&D is decentralized in order to take advantage of the accumulated expertise of foreign production affiliates in addition to local scientific expertise. The implication is that a statistical relationship between foreign production and foreign R&D does not necessarily imply that R&D is located abroad to support production. Foreign production also supports foreign knowledge-seeking R&D.

The mutually supportive nature of foreign production and foreign R&D is also empasized by De Meyer (1993), who finds that when asked why they have located R&D abroad, firms generally cite being close to customers, suppliers and manufacturing *and* being close to sources of technology and belonging to a network of ideas. The common factor is that both production support and knowledge-seeking involve faster learning on both the supply side and the demand side:

> Faster learning of more relevant information is, in our opinion, the key to explaining the internationalization of R&D. Learning about customer needs, monitoring the hot spots of the field to quickly learn about the most recent developments, and having access to the engineers and scientists who can process this information quickly is the objective of the internationalization process. (De Meyer, 1993, p. 44)

Some evidence regarding the factors bearing on the R&D growth of foreign affiliates of U.S. companies can also be gleaned from Tables 3 and 4 above. A regression of the change in affiliate R&D share on the change in affiliate sales share (using the data reported in Table 3) plus dummies reflecting the incidence of knowledge searching and production support behaviour, reveals that changes in affiliate R&D shares reflect changes in affiliate sales shares. Over the period from 1982 to 1989, there was no secular drift of R&D toward affiliates in the knowledge-searching industries.[16]

With respect to the international distribution of affiliate R&D growth, regression analysis of the data reported in Table 4 revealed a tendency for affiliate R&D spending to increase more in the more R&D-intensive countries and in the countries characterized by greater affiliate sales growth. This result is consistent with knowledge-seeking behaviour.

As a well-educated country with a small market, Canada should have comparative advantage in knowledge-searching R&D. In this case Canada should have a disproportionately large share of global industrial R&D in the knowledge-searching industries and a disproportionately small share in the local affiliate support industries. There is some evidence that Canada ranks relatively high as a location for basic industrial research and that the availability of qualified professionals has attracted R&D to Canada (Casson, Pearce & Singh, Tables 6.5 and 6.6).

FOREIGN R&D BY CANADIAN FIRMS

A RECENT CONFERENCE BOARD OF CANADA survey to which 151 companies located in Canada responded (Reitsma, 1993) reports that 58 percent of the responding firms perform some R&D in Canada. Among the firms performing some R&D in Canada, the mean percentage of R&D performed in Canada is 73 percent, implying that this group performs an average of 27 percent of its R&D abroad. The percentage performed abroad is expected to decline marginally over the next three years (p. 16). By way of comparison, Swedish multinationals performed 23 percent of their R&D abroad in 1987 (De Meyer, 1993, p. 42).

In their survey of the R&D laboratories of 500 major international firms, Casson, Pearce & Singh (1992, Table 6.4) find that the Canadian-owned firms in the group have 11 laboratories in Canada and one each in the United States and the United Kingdom. They then conclude from their statistical analysis that the foreign R&D of Canadian-owned firms tends to be oriented toward diversification that is, developing new uses for Canadian resources (1992, Table 6.5). This is a somewhat heroic conclusion to draw from observations on two foreign labs.

Some evidence on the location of the R&D activities of Canadian companies can be obtained from their annual reports and their 10K reports. The largest Canadian-owned industrial R&D performers are listed in Table 5. Northern Telecom is the largest industrial R&D performer in Canada by a considerable margin. According to its 10K report, its R&D expenditures totalled US$ 931 million in 1992 and US$ 948 million in 1991. Its wholly owned R&D affiliates employed 8,700 people as of December 31, 1992. Of this total 55 percent are employed in Canada, 29 percent in the United States and 16 percent in the United Kingdom.

TABLE 5

MAJOR CANADIAN-OWNED INDUSTRIAL R&D PERFORMERS

COMPANY	1992 R&D (C$ MILLION)	1992 R&D (% REVENUE)
Northern Telecom Ltd.	1,124.7	11.10
AECL	316.0	91.07
CAE Industries Ltd.	191.0	18.26
Ontario Hydro	183.0	2.36
Alcan Aluminium Ltd.	153.0	1.62
Hydro-Québec	140.9	2.07
Bell Canada	126.6	1.61
Inco Ltd.	55.3	1.79
Bombardier Inc.	53.7	1.76
B.C. Tel	52.0	2.55
Mitel Corp. Ltd.	46.5	11.45
Nova Corp. of Alberta	41.0	1.35
Newbridge Networks Corp.	29.5	16.24
Apotex Ltd.	27.4	12.63
Syncrude Canada Ltd.	26.0	1.74

Source: The Globe and Mail Report on Business Magazine, September, 1993, p.79.

The next largest Canadian (non-government) R&D performer is CAE Industries. It spent C$ 191 million on R&D in 1992 and C$ 173 million in 1991. CAE does not file a 10K report. Its annual report does not provide a breakdown of its total R&D. Given the company's customer-driven, development-oriented approach, considerable decentralization appears likely (Crawford, 1993). According to Lem (1993, p. B2):

> . . . CAE-Link Corp., the company's New York subsidiary and a major U.S. defence contractor, spent an undisclosed portion of that [$191 million] to develop the virtual anesthesiology system, designed to train medical personnel in the field of anesthetics.

Historically, Alcan has been a large Canadian R&D performer (Litvak & Maule, 1981; Rugman, 1985). It spent C$ 153 million on R&D in 1992. Alcan maintains two R&D laboratories in Canada (in Kingston, Ontario and Jonquière, Québec) and one each in Banbury, England and Cambridge, Massachusetts. The Jonquière lab is process and operations oriented. Kingston and Banbury are developing and improving aluminum alloys, fabricating processes and aluminum product systems, as well as exploring product opportunities. The purpose of the Cambridge lab is to explore product and process development. It thus appears to have a knowledge-seeking mandate. Additional development work occurs in the company's plants. Alcan has 100 fabricating plants in 18 countries and 14 smelters in five countries worldwide. Alcan also conducts (automotive) customer-oriented engineering at centres located in North America, Europe and Japan. Alcan illustrates the variety of influences on the location of technologically-oriented activities in a multi-national corporation. These include knowledge-seeking, production support and customer support.

Among the Canadian multinational companies with smaller R&D budgets, a variety of tendencies can be observed. Nickel producer Inco spent C$ 55 million on R&D in 1992, $44 million in 1991 and $40 million in 1990. Inco's central process research laboratory is located in Mississauga, Ontario. Inco also maintains research facilities at Port Colborne and Sudbury, Ontario, Thompson, Manitoba, Clydach, Wales and Acton, England. Inco operates refineries at Port Colborne, Clydach and Acton; and refineries and smelters at Sudbury and Thompson.

Moore Corporation, a producer of business forms, spent US$ 32 million on R&D in 1992 and $35 million in 1991. The company's R&D is conducted at its research center at Grand Island, New York. Moore has 52 plants in the United States, nine in Canada and 40 in other countries.

Forest products company MacMillan Bloedel spent C$ 20 million on R&D in 1992, C$ 17 million in 1991 and C$ 21 million in 1990. It conducts R&D on environmental protection, computer control and wood-based building materials development at its Research and Development Centre in Burnaby, British Columbia. Macmillan Bloedel also contributed US$ 3.5

million toward the research of the engineered lumber products joint venture Trus Joist MacMillan (TJM) of Boise, Idaho in which it has a minority interest.

These three companies illustrate some of the factors bearing on the location of research by Canadian companies. Moore does all its R&D in the United States presumably because a large fraction of its market is in that country. Inco and MacMillan Bloedel locate the bulk of their R&D in Canada in support of local production facilities and in all likelihood also draw on accumulated domestic expertise in metallurgy and forestry. Notice, however, that, in the case of MacMillan Bloedel, new product development at TJM is occurring in the United States.

FACTORS ASSOCIATED WITH THE TRANSFER OF TECHNOLOGY ABROAD

A SURVEY OF CANADIAN SMALL MANUFACTURING enterprises (SMEs) by Niosi & Rivard (1990) found that these firms typically transferred a proprietary technology to developing countries in order to secure a foothold or to increase exports to those countries. For SMEs producing or selling in industrialized countries, technology exchange and learning foreign technologies was also an important motive for technology transfer (1990, p. 1,535). Transfers to developing countries generally did not involve any equity involvement and where there was some equity involvement, it generally took the form of a joint venture. Transfers to developed countries apparently involved foreign affiliates somewhat more frequently.[17]

Litvak (1992) has monitored the fortunes of 29 Canadian SMEs over a 20-year period. As of 1991, 10 of the original 29 SMEs were still in operation as independent entities. Nine had failed and ten had been acquired by U.S. and European multinationals. Of the ten survivors, two had 1990 sales in excess of $100 million with the rest being under $50 million. The survivors have participated in alliances with foreign firms to obtain both technologies and access to markets (high tech markets are often subject to restrictive procurement policies). In Litvak's view, alliances are crucial to continued survival as independent firms.

The surveys of high tech SMEs have a number of interesting implications. First, a considerable proportion of the technology transfer activity of Canadian firms may not involve foreign direct investment. Indeed, the study of FDI may reveal little about technology transfer or, worse, it may lead to misleading inferences regarding the magnitude, nature and benefits of Canada's trade in technology. Second, the transfer of technology to less developed countries is generally for the purpose of supporting local production and is often induced by the commercial policies of the host country. Third, technology transfer to developed countries frequently involves knowledge seeking and it is likely that this type of arrangement, rather than R&D decentralization, is the predominant form of knowledge seeking.

FOREIGN R&D, TECHNOLOGY TRANSFER AND THE LEAKAGE OF TECHNOLOGY TO FOREIGNERS

FROM THE POINT OF VIEW of the parent's home country, the transfer of technology or the decentralization of R&D abroad may be costly because it reduces the ability of the home economy to appropriate the rents to its innovative activity. This would occur if the knowledge in question did not leak out or, at least did not leak abroad, if it were not transferred abroad. The classic form of leakage is *imitation* by competitors or potential competitors.

The question of whether the transfer of technologies abroad facilitates their imitation by foreigners was addressed by Mansfield et al. (1982). These authors found that, on average, the transfer of a technology had no effect on the speed at which foreign competitors were able to imitate it (1982, pp. 39-40).[18] There were, however, a few cases in which the speed of foreign imitation, especially of process technologies, was considerably accelerated by transfer (1982, p. 41).

The reason foreign imitation was generally not facilitated by transfer of a technology abroad is that the most frequent form of product imitation involves reverse engineering, which can be done on an imported product as easily as it can be done on one that is locally produced. The second most prominent means of imitation is to hire the personnel of the subsidiary. It seems reasonable to assume that hiring away key subsidiary employees would be easier for potential imitators than hiring the parent's key personnel and that this might, therefore, increase the ability of the host-country firms to imitate.

A more recent study by Levin, Klevorick, Nelson & Winter (1987) confirms the importance of reverse engineering as a means of imitating new product technologies. Of similar importance are independent R&D and licensing. Local production or R&D is not required for these means of local imitation. Hiring or conversing with employees of the innovating firm would require local production or R&D, but these methods are found to be much less effective means of imitation.

With respect to process innovations, independent R&D and licensing are the most effective means of imitation (Levin et al., Table 6). Hiring or conversing with employees are, again, less effective means of imitation. The implication of these findings is, again, that supplying foreign markets from foreign as opposed to domestic production and/or R&D facilities is unlikely to enhance significantly the ability of foreigners to imitate a new technology.

The Mansfield et al. study also estimates the magnitude of the spillover gains that accrued to British firms a result of local production by U.S. affiliates. Nearly half the British firms surveyed by these authors were not able to accelerate the introduction of any new products or processes as a consequence of spillovers of technologies transferred to British affiliates of U.S. companies. Almost none (2 of 68) of the British firms surveyed were able to accelerate more than 10 percent of their technology introductions as a consequence of spillovers from British affiliates of U.S. companies and none were able to accelerate more than 25 percent (1982, Table 2.8).

The implication of these results is that decentralization of production and R&D does not reduce appropriability significantly. This conclusion may not hold for other host countries and, indeed, even across industries or time periods in Britain. Cantwell (1992, p. 25) argues:

> In markets which without the entry of U.S.-owned affiliates would have been dominated by technologically strong British firms, U.S. investments injected a competitive stimulus which increased the rate of innovation throughout the relevant local industry. For example, in tyres, cleaning products and detergents, and domestic boilers, U.K.-owned firms became much more alert to the opportunities for technological change as a result of the U.S. affiliate presence. In terms of broader industrial groupings, whether measuring shifts in technological competitiveness by changes in the productivity differentials between U.S.-owned affiliates and local firms or using changes in the market shares of U.S. affiliates, it seems that there was some catching up by indigenous companies in rubber products and mechanical engineering in the 1940s and early 1950s. This is consistent with the case study evidence on tyres and boilers. However, it is not just a matter of benefits arising where U.S. entry broke up a local monopoly or a tightly collusive oligopoly. *By the 1980s it had become clear that, in general, beneficial spill-over effects result from inward direct investment through competitive imitation and accelerated learning, where there is a strong indigenous presence.* [italics added, references omitted]

What Cantwell is observing here is not so much reverse engineering as a demonstration effect. The presence of affiliates shows host-country firms that they can make better use of their existing innovative capabilities (shows them ways to increase the quasi-rents to their existing stocks of R&D capital).

Spillover benefits to host countries may take some form other than an increased ability to imitate home-country proprietary technologies. Other benefits may involve worker or supplier learning or the realization of agglomeration economies. In the case of supplier learning, foreign production is likely to rely, at least to some degree, on host-country suppliers for some inputs. In the course of their dealings with the local affiliate, these host-country suppliers may acquire knowledge which can be used to improve their existing products or produce new ones. As long as production continues in the home country, home-country suppliers will continue to benefit from this linkage. The difference is that foreign input suppliers now receive the same benefit.[19]

According to Cantwell (1992, pp. 25-6), British suppliers realized considerable benefits from their linkages with local affiliates of U.S. firms:

> In the case of suppliers it seems that the effect of the establishment and growth of U.S.-owned affiliates was most often in the form of widening rather than deepening the technological capacity of local firms from which they

purchased inputs. They were obliged to produce inputs of a kind and a quality not previously demanded by U.K.-owned firms, *and this required technical assistance from the affiliate.* However, while the emphasis in the impact of Japanese-owned affiliates was later to be on their component suppliers, U.S. affiliates appeared to have at least as great an effect on their customers. [italics added, references omitted]

The interaction between U.S. affiliates and their British customers also stimulated innovation in the capital goods industries in Britain in a way that imports from the United States could not have done:

> By comparison with exporting firms, U.S. affiliates were more likely to adapt their products to British requirements and *establish mutual beneficial understandings in combined new product development.* (Cantwell, 1992, p. 26) [italics added]

Insofar as affiliate-customer interaction is concerned, both the parent and the foreign customers would benefit if there were no interaction without the foreign production. Provided home-country production continues, home-country customers continue to benefit from supplier interaction with the parent, with the possible difference that host-country customers who may be their competitors may now be receiving similar benefits.

While conceding that interaction with subsidiaries yields benefits for host-country firms, Porter (1991) maintains that these benefits are less important than those realized by parent or "home base" country suppliers, customers and rivals:

> But the creation of skills and technology, and the location of home base activities on which they depend, has far different implications for national prosperity than being on the receiving end of ideas and skills created elsewhere. The externalities involved in creating skills and knowledge are local externalities within the diamond. There are also externalities involved in transferring knowledge and skills across countries within multinational networks, but these are different and carry less weight in national economic upgrading. (p. 80)

Even if the transfer of technology or the decentralization of R&D abroad were to result in speedier imitation by foreigners or loss of opportunities for home-country user-supplier interaction or home-country worker or professional learning, it is likely to be preferable from the point of view of both the home firm and the home country not to serve the foreign market at all. This was also recognized by Mansfield et al. (1982). These authors found that international technology transfer accounted for 30 per cent of the returns to home-country R&D (1982, p. 56).

Conclusions

IT IS REASONABLE TO CONCLUDE that an overwhelming proportion of Canadian direct investment abroad has been motivated by factors other than technology transfer. While there is some evidence that Canadian firms with innovative capabilities are more inclined toward foreign direct investment, and that the share of Canadian-owned firms in U.S. manufacturing employment increases (to a point) with industry R&D intensity, as foreign direct investors go, Canadians are not particularly R&D oriented.

Technology transfer or R&D decentralization in support of foreign production has probably not appreciably accelerated the rate at which host-country competitors are able to imitate specific home-country proprietary technologies. It may have had the effect of showing host-country competitors how to make better use of their own technological capabilities. Almost certainly technology transfer has increased the opportunities for mutually beneficial collaboration with host-country suppliers and customers. In some cases this may have reduced the opportunities for collaboration and learning available to home-country suppliers and home-country employees.[20] In other cases, particularly those involving knowledge-seeking R&D, the opportunities for home-country suppliers and employees may be increased.

Any losses to the home country due to increased leakages or foregone spillover benefits are likely to be small relative to those that would be incurred if the foreign market were not served at all. The appropriate policy responses of aggrieved home countries are, first, to work through multilateral channels to discourage the use of commercial policy to distort the choice between exporting and foreign production and, second, to ensure that the domestic technological environment remains attractive to both domestic and foreign firms.

ENDNOTES

1 The term 'license' is used here to represent the full range of governance structures short of full internalization (hierarchy). This could include joint ventures and various forms of alliances.

2 This could involve product or process improvements resulting from the interaction of the licensee with local customers or suppliers, from experience-related licensee improvements or from the combination of unique licensee knowledge or knowhow with licensor technology (see also Teece, 1991).

3 There is also an emerging theoretical literature on the amount of technology transferred (Wang & Blomström, 1992). Models of this nature generally involve a two-stage oligopoly game in which the disposition of second-stage oligopoly rents depends on both first-stage R&D by domestic firms and first-stage technology transfer by foreign affiliates. While many outcomes are possible, it may be that more technology is transferred to affiliates when domestic rivals are stronger. This conforms with Cantwell's (1992) view of British experience.

4 Professor Globerman has suggested that the substitution effect might be positive, that is, that foreign and domestic R&D might be complements rather than substitutes. This might be true of knowledge-seeking foreign R&D. This is discussed in "FDI and the Transfer of Technology Abroad" later in this study. Foreign and domestic production-support R&D would be complements rather than substitutes if foreign production is a complement to rather than a substitute for domestic production. This issue is addressed in Graham's study in this volume.

5 Statistics Canada, *Canada's International Investment Position.* Catalogue Number 67-202, May 1993, Table 10.

6 See Rao, Legault & Ahmad, this volume, Figures 3 and 4.

7 R&D-intensive sectors such as aircraft and parts, electronics, telecommunications equipment, instruments and machinery would all be included in the "other manufacturing" category in these data.

8 On the nature of innovation in non-R&D-intensive industrial sectors in Canada, see McFetridge (1993). Bresnahan (1986) has measured the spillover benefit realized by the financial sector in the United States as a result of the application of computer technology.

9 Possession of a superior technology was ranked "very important" by 21 respondents and "important" by four as a reason for investing in the United States. No other factor received as many first- and second-place rankings.

10 As at the end of 1986, according to the U.S. Department of Commerce (1990, Table I-3).

11 These correlations would be higher if "other transportation equipment", which is comprised largely of highly R&D-intensive defence production

from which foreign-owned firms are excluded, were dropped from the sample. The correlation aggregate foreign-owned employment share and R&D-intensity increase from .286 to .404 when this industry is dropped (Howenstein & Zeile, p. 53).

12 The correlation coefficient is .094. It is not statistically significant.

13 The caveat that an appropriate test would hold locational factors constant should be borne in mind.

14 Data are from U.S. Bureau of the Census, *State and Metropolitan Area Data Book*, 1991.

15 If the Canadian share of affiliate employment in the *ith* state is s_i, then the log of the odds ratio is:

$$LOCSM = \ln[s_i/(1-s_i)]$$

Unlike the share which is bounded at zero and one, the log odds ratio is continuous between plus and minus infinity. Regressions run using the share as the dependent variable yield the same inferences. Regressions are estimated using White's heteroscedasticity-consistent covariance matrix estimator.

16 The dependent variable in this regression is the rate of growth of the affiliate: parent R&D ratio (in the *ith* industry) over the period from 1982 to 1989. The independent variables are the rate of growth of the affiliate: parent sales ratio over the same period and a dummy variable equal to one if the *ith* industry is a knowledge-searching industry according to Pearce (1992) or alternatively to Casson, Pearce & Singh (1992). Neither alternative knowledge-searching dummy is statistically significant. The rate of growth of the ratio of affiliate-to-parent sales is statistically significant and the null hypothesis that its coefficient is one cannot be rejected. This implies that a one percentage point increase in the growth of the affiliate : parent sales ratio increases the affiliate : parent R&D ratio by one percentage point in both knowledge-searching industries and in the population at large.

17 The authors state that 11 of the 43 SMEs making transfers to developed countries had a foreign affiliate (p. 1,535). They do not indicate whether the affiliate was involved in the transfer.

18 Foreign transfer substantially hastened the spread of a small number of technologies but, on average, the hypothesis of no effect could not be rejected.

19 Given that home-country production has been replaced in part with foreign production, home-country suppliers will also learn less if learning is a function of the quantity of inputs supplied.

20 The emerging statistical literature on international R&D spillovers shows that Canadian firms realize spillover benefits from R&D done in the United States (Mohnen, 1992). Presumably, R&D performed in the

United States by Canadian firms would also yield spillover benefits in Canada. The question is whether these benefits are smaller than they might have been if this R&D had been done in Canada.

ACKNOWLEDGEMENTS

THIS STUDY WAS WRITTEN in part while I was the holder of the T.D. MacDonald Chair in Industrial Economics at the Bureau of Competition Policy. I would like to thank Jeffrey Bernstein, Lorraine Eden, Steven Globerman, John Knubley and André Raynaud for their comments. The views expressed are mine alone.

BIBLIOGRAPHY

Bresnahan, T. "Measuring Spillovers from Technical Advance: Mainframe Computers in Financial Services." *American Economic Review*, 76, (1986): 742-55.

Cantwell, J. "Innovation and Technological Competitiveness." In *Multinational Enterprises in the World Economy*. Edited by P. Buckley and M. Casson. Aldershot: Elgar, (1992), p. 20-40.

_____. "Multinational Corporations and Innovatory Activities: Towards a New, Evolutionary Approach." Reading, University of Reading, Department of Economics, Discussion Papers in International Investment and Business Studies, No. 172.

Crawford, M. "The Guys Who Came in from the Cold." *Canadian Business* (June 1993): 38-43.

Casson, M., R. Pearce and S. Singh. "Global Integration through the Decentralization of R&D." In *International Business and Global Integration*. Edited by M. Casson. London: MacMillan, 1992, p. 163-204.

Casson, M and S. Singh. "Corporate Research and Development Strategies: the Influence of Firm, Industry and Country Factors on the Decentralization of R&D." *R&D Management*, 23, (1993): 91-107.

Caves, R., M. Porter, A. Spence and J. Scott. *Competition in the Open Economy*. Cambridge: Harvard University Press, 1980.

Cheng, J. and D. Bolon. "The Management of Multinational R&D: A Neglected Topic in International Business Research." *Journal of International Business Studies*, 24, (1993): 1-18.

Corvari, R. and R. Wisner. "The Role of Canadian Multinationals in Shaping Canada's International Competitiveness" Ottawa, unpublished manuscript.

De Meyer, A. "Internationalizing R&D Improves a Firm's Technical Learning." *Research Technology Management*, 36, 4, (1993): 42-49.

De Meyer, A. and A. Mizushima. "Global R&D Management." *R&D Management*, 19, (1989): 135-46.

Dunning, J. "Trade, Location of Economic Activity and the Multinational Enterprise: A Search for an Eclectic Approach." In *The International Allocation of Economic Activity*. Edited by B. Ohlin, P. Hesselborn and P. Wijkman. London: Macmillan, 1977.

Fusfeld, H. *The Technical Enterprise*. Cambridge: Ballinger, 1986.

Gorecki, P. "Canada's Multinationals: Their Characteristics and Determinants." Ottawa: Statistics Canada, Analytical Studies Branch, Research Paper No. 52, 1992.

Howells, J. "The Location and Organization of Research and Development: New Horizons." *Research Policy*, 19, 4 (1990).

Howenstine, N. and W. Zeile. "Foreign Direct Investment in the United States: Establishment Data for 1987." *Survey of Current Business*, (October 1992): 44-76.

Jorde, T. and D. Teece. "Rule of Reason Analysis of Horizontal Arrangements: Agreements Designed to Advance Innovation and Commercialize Technology." *Antitrust Law Journal*, 61, (1993): 579-619.

Lei, D. and J. Slocum. "Global Strategy, Competence-Building and Strategic Alliances." *California Management Review*, 35, (1992): 81-97.

Levin, R., A. Klevorick, R. Nelson and S. Winter. "Appropriating the Returns from Industrial Research and Development." In *Brookings Papers on Economic Activity*. Edited by M. Baily and C. Winston. 3, 1987; pp. 783-820.

Litvak, A. "Public Policy and High-technology SME's: The Government Embrace." *Canadian Public Administration*,35 (1992): 22-38.

Litvak, I. and C. Maule. The Canadian Multinationals. Toronto: Butterworths, 1981.

Mansfield, E., A. Romeo, M. Schwartz, D. Teece, S. Wagner and P. Brach. *Technology Transfer, Productivity and Economic Policy*. New York: Norton, 1982.

Mc Fetridge, D. "The Canadian System of Industrial Innovation." In *National Innovation Systems*. Edited by R. Nelson. New York: Oxford, 1993; pp. 299-323.

Meredith, L. "Marketing Determinants of U.S. Direct Investment in Canadian Manufacturing Industries." *The Columbia Journal of World Business*, 19 (1984): 72-78.

Mohnen, P. *The Relationship between R&D and Productivity Growth in Canada and Other Industrialized Countries*. Ottawa: Canada Communications Group, 1992.

Niosi, J. and J. Rivard. "Canadian Technology Transfer to Developing Countries through Small and Medium-Size Enterprises." *World Development*, 18 (1990): 1,529-42.

OECD. *Technology and the Economy: The Key Relationships*. Paris, 1992.

Patel, P. and Pavitt, K. "Large Firms in the Production of the World's Technology: An Important Case of Non-Globalization." *Journal of International Business Studies* (1991).

Pearce, R. "Factors Influencing the Internationalization of Research and Development in Multinational Enterprises." In *Multinational Enterprises in the World Economy*. Edited by P. Buckley and M. Casson. Aldershot: Elgar, 1992, pp. 75-95.

Porter, M. *Canada at the Crossroads: The Reality of a New Competitive Environment*. Ottawa, Supply and Services, 1991.

Reitsma, S. *The Canadian Response to Globalization*. Ottawa: The Conference Board of Canada, Report 106-93, 1993.

Rugman, A. *Outward Bound*. Toronto: C.D. Howe Institute, 1987.

Rugman, A. and J. McIlveen. *Megafirms: Strategies for Canada's Multinationals*. Toronto: Methuen, 1985.

Serapio, M. and D. Dalton. "Foreign R&D Facilities in the United States." *Research Technology Management*, 36,.6 (1993): 33-39.

Taggart, J. "Determinants of Foreign R&D Locations in the Chemical Industry." *R&D Management*, 21 (1991): 229-40.

Teece, D. "Technological Development and the Organization of Industry." In *Technology and Productivity: The Challenge for Economic Policy*. Paris: OECD, 1991; pp. 409-18.

United States Department of Commerce. *Foreign Direct Investment in the United States 1987 Benchmark Survey*. Washington, D.C.: U.S. Government Printing Office, 1990.

Wang, J. and M. Blomström. "Foreign Investment and Technology Transfer." *European Economic Review*, 36, (1992): 137-55.

Morley Gunderson
Centre for Industrial Relations
University of Toronto

&

Savita Verma
Faculty of Administrative Studies
York University

6

Labour-Market Implications of Outward Foreign Direct Investment

INTRODUCTION

IN THE GENERAL CONTEXT OF LABOUR MARKETS the most worrisome issues surrounding outward foreign direct investment (FDI) centre on two main concerns. The first is that such investment is tantamount to exporting jobs. The second is that the threat of such capital mobility will inhibit a country from developing its own independent labour laws and regulations to the extent that they may deter inward foreign investment and even encourage further outward foreign investment. The purpose of this study is to provide a critical assessment of those concerns.

An assessment of the employment implications of foreign direct investment (both inward and outward) is a complex and difficult task because there is no straightforward or well-proven approach. As a result, existing empirical studies for individual countries and different time periods have come to different, sometimes conflicting, conclusions about the employment effects of foreign direct investment on home and host countries.

In estimating the effect of FDI on employment it is essential to distinguish between short- and long-term, and direct and indirect effects of FDI on home- and host-country employment. Various macro- and micro-economic factors, interacting in a complex manner, play an important role in determining the total and dynamic employment effects of FDI. It is also important to note that the long-term effects, which incorporate the indirect and dynamic effects, would be positive and could have considerably more influence than the direct and short-term employment effects.

The long term effect of outward investment on employment and wages in home countries will be quite different from the short-term effect because in the long term much of the effect of outward direct investment would be on real wages. On the other hand, in the short term the effect of outward direct investment will fall largely on employment, due to slower labour markets and exchange rate adjustment. Hence, the relative effect of outward investment on jobs and wages in home countries in the short-to-medium term will depend on the extent and speed of adjustment of real wages and exchange rates.

The total effect of outward direct investment on employment and wages in home countries is the sum of direct and indirect labour market effects. In the short term the direct effects will likely dominate. On the other hand, the indirect and dynamic effects will dominate in the longer term. The direct effects include possible crowding out of domestic capital formation and economic activity, and investment income receipts. The sign and size of the net direct effect of outward direct investment on employment and wages will depend on the relative weights of these two opposing effects. In contrast, the indirect effects could be positive and outweigh the direct effects, due to the trade- and efficiency-enhancing effects of outward direct investment on home countries.

In short, to assess the labour-market effects of outward direct investment on home countries is a difficult task. The results of such an exercise should be interpreted carefully and used with extreme caution because the methodologies used to compute the labour-market effects do not merit the degree of sophistication implied. A misinterpretation of the results could redirect attention from the key issue of an efficient and equitable labour market adjustment.

The objectives of this study are threefold: to review carefully the conceptual and empirical issues inherent in analyzing the labour-market effects of direct investment abroad on home countries; to provide a survey of the empirical research in this area; and to discuss their implications for the likely effect of CDIA on employment, wages and industrial relations in Canada.

Following a brief description of the nature of the concerns over outward FDI, we discuss a number of theoretical issues pertaining to the short-run and long-run effects of outward FDI on wages and employment, and the composition of employment. This is followed by an analysis of the effects of outward FDI on labour regulation. Empirical evidence is then discussed with respect to the effects of labour regulation on plant location decisions and outward FDI, as well as the job losses and gains associated with outward FDI. Evidence is also presented concerning the labour-market characteristics of Canadian outward FDI. We conclude with a critique of the current emphasis on the job content of FDI (and on trade in general) and a recommendation for focusing on adjustment issues rather than on job counting.

BACKGROUND ILLUSTRATIONS OF CONCERNS WITH OUTWARD FDI

THE NOTION THAT CANADIAN direct investment abroad (CDIA) is tantamount to exporting jobs is understandable in the context of the glaring publicity surrounding the closures of plants in Canada followed by their opening in the United States. The following newspaper headlines and statements clearly illustrate this perspective:

Throng of firms moves to U.S.to slash costs ... Tennessee waltz/parts maker Tridon left for the state, axing more than 500 Canadian jobs ... By last year, Canadian companies had invested $400-million U.S. to create 8,000 jobs in Tennessee, a stunning increase from $66.4 million and 2,000 jobs in 1980 (*Globe and Mail*, July 2, 1991).

The old south woos the great white north ... The southern states, having successfully raided their northern cousins in the early 1980s, are now looking to Ontario as the next logical place to go hunting for fresh investment... The northern states, which are close to large markets for Canadian companies, are hungry to replace plants that they had lost to the south years before. And Canada looks like ripe territory (*Globe and Mail*, July 3, 1991).

There are 52 Canadian firms now operating in North Carolina, employing 32,000 people — accounting for about 1 per cent of the state's total workforce (*Toronto Star*, December 2, 1991).

Auto parts makers driven to the United States (*Globe and Mail*, January 27, 1992).

[Varity Corporation of Toronto] **Shufflin' off to sample Buffalo's pleasures** (*Globe and Mail*, July 4, 1991).

The possibility that such plant relocations and investment decisions are influenced by the high costs attributable to Canadian labour laws and that these in turn may inhibit the different Canadian jurisdictions from developing their own independent regulations in this area (and perhaps in other areas of social policy as well) is also advanced in the media accounts:

Cheap land, low taxes and labour laws that favour management all help lure companies to the Tarheel State [North Carolina] (*Toronto Star*, December 2, 1991).

The dominant concern of the companies [117 foreign companies that have set up Canadian headquarters in southwestern Ontario] is government regulation, including labour regulations (*Toronto Star*, November 12, 1991).

Obviously, such newspaper accounts and media statements do not provide a comprehensive picture of the implications of foreign investment for the labour market. However, they do highlight the two main labour-market issues with respect to outward foreign direct investment: the potential loss of jobs, and the potential loss of control over domestic labour-market policy.

In Canada, these concerns over Canadian outward FDI are paramount under the North American Free Trade Agreement (NAFTA) with Canada, the United States and Mexico because there is general recognition that the

NAFTA has as much to do with investment as with trade. The mechanisms whereby agreements like the NAFTA affect foreign investment decisions are outlined in more detail in the next section. Suffice it to say at this stage that the main purpose of the NAFTA is to lock in the reforms that have been occurring in Mexico over the last decade and therefore to make it a more hospitable environment for investment, including investment from Canada or investment that otherwise might have gone to Canada.

It is noteworthy that over the past decade the Canadian preoccupation with FDI has shifted from a concern over *inward* investment to a concern over *outward* investment. From the labour market perspective, the former concern over inward investment had several causes. There might be a lack of control over the associated jobs if, for example, the best research and development and managerial jobs were being preserved for the home base, or if Canadian plants were being closed because the head office was responding to political pressure in the United States to keep open less efficient plants. There is often a perception that multinationals are less likely to be good corporate citizens and will pay little attention to the broader social issues of the communities in which they have made their investment. They are seen as more likely to send key head office personnel for stints in the host country and hence to inhibit the development of indigenous key personnel and entrepreneurial talent. Also, there is often concern that the importing of such foreign investment implies the importing of workplace practices and human resource policies that are not transferable and hence may lead to a clash of cultures. The divorce of ownership and control may also lead to more strikes as head offices, less familiar with the local scene and concerned that local settlements may spill over into plants elsewhere, adopt more intransigent positions.[1]

Those who oppose inward FDI into Canada because it imposes costs on Canadians while transmitting many of the benefits to the home country, also tend not to favour outward FDI because Canadians can reap the benefits while the costs fall on the host countries. Symmetry in the arguments suggest that outward FDI would keep the "good" jobs in Canada, or send key Canadian personnel to the host country for training, or that it would allow Canadian investors a higher return by not having to worry about being good corporate citizens. Such symmetry in arguments is not likely to be adhered to by those who oppose outward FDI. Rather, the opposition tends to be against both inward and outward FDI, as well as against free trade in goods and services.

However, this position need not imply an inconsistency. Opposition to outward FDI may reflect the perceived loss of jobs and loss of control over domestic labour market policy. Also, opposition to inward FDI may reflect the perceived loss of control over the behaviour of foreign investors. Nevertheless, it frequently happens that those who oppose inward FDI because it imposes costs on Canadians, tend not to follow the same argument and favour outward FDI because it yields symmetrical benefits to Canadians. To some extent the debate over the labour-market implications of outward FDI hinges on disagreement over theoretical inter-relationships, as discussed in the following sections.

THEORETICAL ISSUES

THE LINK BETWEEN FDI AND JOBS and labour-market policy can be illustrated by a discussion of the mechanisms whereby free trade affects FDI and the mechanisms whereby FDI affects jobs and labour-market policy. Although the emphasis in this study is on outward FDI, the effect on inward FDI is also discussed for purposes of completeness.

MECHANISMS THROUGH WHICH FREE TRADE AFFECTS FOREIGN DIRECT INVESTMENT

BY ELIMINATING TARIFF AND NON-TARIFF BARRIERS, free trade should reduce the need for inward FDI in the form of branch plants and subsidiaries as mechanisms for getting around tariff barriers. For example, with reduced tariffs there should be less need for U.S. multinationals to establish branch plants in Canada as an alternative to exporting into Canada. Exporting into Canada is now easier, although the threat of anti-dumping and countervailing duties can still make branch plants viable. The branch plants will undergo substantial restructuring (Crockell, 1987; Rugman, 1987; Rugman & Verbeke, 1988). They may be rationalized so as to specialize and develop the economies of scale necessary to compete on a global basis, although the strategic decision making and research and development will still be done largely in the home country. Branch plants may specialize by being given a world product mandate, in which case they will also be responsible for the strategic decision making and research and development of the product. Alternatively, they may be closed or relocated, with the production being done elsewhere (perhaps in the home country) and exported into Canada under the reduced tariffs.

In the above scenario, free trade should reduce *inward* FDI into Canada from the trading partners, since FDI is not required to jump the tariff barriers. Of course, the same applies to the other trading partners, and so there may be some increased inward FDI because it is now easier to export into their markets. As well, trade and FDI may be complements as multinationals maintain subsidiaries to facilitate specialization, intra-firm trade, a national presence, rationalization and the development of world product mandates (Safarian, 1985; Rugman & Verbeke, 1991).

The above scenario also implies that free trade should increase *outward* FDI from Canada into the trading partners, since it is now easier to invest or relocate plants in those countries and export back into Canada, given the lower tariff and non-tariff barriers.

Free trade will affect the trade and investment decisions of countries outside the free trade agreement as well as those of the trading partners within the free trade agreement. Specifically, other countries still face external tariffs from the trading bloc countries, and they may engage in FDI to get around those tariffs and to establish platforms within the trade bloc so as to export to the other countries within the bloc. As stated in Longair (1990) "foreign direct investment is the best strategic response when facing a regional integration of which you are not a member".

The NAFTA, for example, is likely to lead to considerable trade diversion as both Canada and the United States divert imports from low-wage Asian countries to Mexico, which also has a comparative advantage in low-wage labour (Leamer, 1991). To counter this tendency, Japan is likely to increase its FDI into Mexico (perhaps away from other low-wage Asian countries) and to use this as a platform to export into Canada and the United States. Some of that investment could be inward FDI into Canada as a platform to export to the United States and Mexico, but it is more likely that most would go into Mexico to take advantage of its low-wage labour.

Wage rates, however, are not the only factors influencing decisions about the location of investment. Unit labour costs, which take into account both wage rates and productivity, are a better measure of a country's labour advantage. The much lower productivity of Mexican labour greatly reduces the advantages of lower wage rates. In addition, other factors such as the availability of skilled labour; quality and quantity of infrastructure; proximity to raw materials, components, and markets are also important. Canada has an advantage in many of these other factors.

Free trade agreements like the NAFTA can also affect FDI more directly because of the national treatment provisions they contain – whereby members are not allowed to discriminate against foreign investment, but must treat it in the same way as investment from domestic sources. By reducing the barriers otherwise created against foreign investors, such provisions should increase both inward and outward investment, providing, of course, that reciprocal treatment is followed in practice.

Free trade agreements can also affect FDI less directly through a business climate effect. This occurs as free trade signals a commitment to a more open economy and to market forces. As indicated earlier, a main purpose of the NAFTA is to lock in the reforms and openness that have been occurring in Mexico over the last decade, and therefore to make it a more hospitable environment for foreign investment, including investment from Canada or investment that otherwise may have gone to Canada.

Free trade can also affect foreign investment indirectly through "integration effects" whereby exchanges in any of the components of goods, services, capital or labour, foster synergistic interactions that in turn encourage exchanges in the other dimensions. Exchanges in goods foster exchanges in other dimensions as wide ranging as tastes and technology. Organizations that develop corporate cultures amenable to international markets certainly find it easy to deal with the notion of outward direct foreign investment abroad.

In summary, free trade is likely to increase outward FDI because free trade makes it easy to export back into the source country of the FDI. As well, former artificial barriers to FDI may be reduced (i.e., as national treatment effects apply) and integration effects may also occur as exchange is fostered in other dimensions in addition to trade.

MECHANISMS THROUGH WHICH OUTWARD FDI LEADS TO JOB LOSSES

IN THIS AND THE FOLLOWING SECTION, emphasis is on the link between outward foreign direct investment, and wages and employment in the source country of the outward investment.

The discussion of the labour market effects that follows revolves around both wages and employment, recognizing that in the short run the main effect of outward FDI is on employment because nominal wages tend to be rigid and exchange rate adjustments are slow. In the longer term, real wages are more likely to adjust (through nominal wage changes diverging from inflation) as are exchange rates, with correspondingly reduced effect on employment. In the medium term, the effect on jobs and employment depends on the magnitude and speed of adjustment in real wages, and the exchange rate. The employment adjustment may also be greater in sectors with greater wage rigidity. In contrast, the negative wage adjustments associated with job displacement may be large when workers are displaced to other jobs. In such circumstances they may lose their industry-specific human capital or industry rents or an *ex ante* wage premium previously paid for the risk of job displacement.

The most obvious mechanism through which outward FDI affects domestic jobs is through the job content of that investment (i.e., the number of jobs embodied in the investment) had it occurred in the source country instead of the recipient country. This direct effect is consistent with the notion that outward foreign direct investment displaces (or is a substitute for) domestic investment and is tantamount to exporting jobs. As will be discussed later, the magnitude of the associated job loss can be approximated by various methods, including accounting procedures that show the relation between domestic investment and domestic jobs. Input-output procedures can also indicate the labour content of related effects on downstream producers who provide associated parts, supplies and services, as well as upstream producers who distribute and service the output.

This procedure of job counting has a certain appeal since it appears that if, for example, Canadian investors opened a factory in Mexico, that factory could have been located in Canada. While the number of associated job losses in Canada would likely be lower than the number of job gains in Mexico, given the higher capital/labour ratio in Canada, there would still be job losses in Canada. These would create further job losses from downstream and upstream producers.

Although naturally appealing, this line of reasoning is subject to the lump of labour fallacy which assumes there is a fixed number of jobs in the economy. This problem is outlined in more detail in the concluding section. Suffice it to say at this stage that while there can be an *accounting* relationship between outward FDI and the *potential* domestic job content of an investment, the behavioural or structural relationship between domestic jobs and outward FDI is not as simple as the accounting relationship suggests.

Outward FDI can also have an effect on the domestic work force through changes in capital : labour ratios. Other things being equal, outward FDI will lower the ratio of capital to labour in the source country of the FDI and raise it in the recipient country. This action, in turn, can lead to reduced labour productivity in the source country and increased labour productivity in the recipient country. Such productivity convergence can, in turn, lead to wage convergence between the two countries, although this may take considerable time, as the wage changes are likely to lag behind the productivity changes substantially. In the short run, any productivity decline in the source country that is not accompanied by a wage decline is likely to lead to reduced employment. In the longer run, wages are more likely to adjust to any productivity decline from a reduced capital : labour ratio; employment declines will be mitigated by such wage adjustments.

This scenario can be complicated by the nature of the investment. To the extent that the outward FDI is induced by the increased ability to export back into the source country of the investment (because of the reduced tariffs) the investment is most likely to be in manufacturing, since most traded goods are manufactured goods. As well, the investment is most likely to be in labour-intensive manufacturing, since that is the sector where the low-wage country has a comparative advantage. This means that the job losses associated with the investment are likely to be higher. However, to the extent that those jobs are of low value-added or productivity in Canada, their loss could raise Canadian labour productivity (as the composition of Canadian jobs shifts from low value-added to high value-added jobs). This, of course, accounts for part of the emphasis on the fact that the competitiveness of countries like Canada depends on the ability to restructure from low value-added to high value-added jobs.

Outward FDI can also have a negative affect on domestic jobs if a loss of technology is associated with the outward investment. This could occur, for example, if technology is capital embodied and is lost when the capital is exported. This in turn can reduce the productivity of home-country labour. To the extent that technology can be used more than once (e.g., through licensing or production of multiple units of high-technology equipment), it is not "used up" and thus lost when exported. Technology can be used many times, assuming that financial capital and other necessary factors are available. Furthermore, in the case of the NAFTA technology is unlikely to be an issue since investment is likely to be in jobs that do not involve innovative new technologies, but rather the transfer of technology already well established in Canada. To the extent that investment is likely to be in the low-wage, low-technology jobs, and that it spurs higher value-added investment in Canada, it should augment rather than reduce Canadian technology.

In summary, any negative effect on employment in the source country of the outward FDI is likely to occur through job losses associated with the displacement of domestic investment. As well, in the long run, any associated decline in capital : labour ratios in the source country or any loss of technology can lead to reduced productivity. These reductions, in turn, can lead to job losses in the short run if wages are rigid and possibly to wage reductions in the longer run when wages are more flexible. Behavioural relations are not well established, and there are offsetting factors that can reduce or negate wage and job losses and make it more likely that the job gains are high paying and the job losses are low paying.

MECHANISMS THROUGH WHICH OUTWARD FDI LEADS TO WAGE AND JOB GAINS

THE FOREGOING DISCUSSION referred to the mechanisms through which outward FDI could be associated with wage and job losses in Canada. There are other mechanisms whereby outward FDI can lead to more explicit wage and job gains in the country that is the source of the outward FDI.

Outward FDI ultimately leads to investment income receipts in the source country, the spending of which should enhance wages and employment. Outward FDI also leads to trade expansion through increased imports of capital and other inputs into the host country,[2] much of which is likely to be imported from the source country of the outward FDI. The complementary exports of capital and other inputs will increase employment in the source country of the investment. Fewer jobs are more likely to be created from the capital exports than lost from the forgone investment because the capital production is likely to be less labour-intensive than the production associated with the forgone investment, since the outward FDI is prompted to take advantage of the potential for labour-intensive production in the receiving country. However, the jobs associated with capital exports to the country receiving the FDI are likely to be higher-wage skilled jobs. Again, this is part of the restructuring towards higher value-added production in high-wage countries.

In addition to experiencing greater exports of capital and other inputs that go into the FDI, the source country of the outward FDI can expand its managerial and head office personnel associated with managing that FDI abroad. Some of this may be short run, associated with establishing the FDI; some may be long run, associated with the continued operation and co-ordination of that FDI. The magnitude of those head-office functions, however, depends on the degree of autonomy granted to the FDI abroad and on the degree of co-ordination required subsequently, even if there is a high degree of autonomy. In today's global market place, many head offices are evolving into operations more like holding companies, co-ordinating international networks of FDI throughout the world. Clearly, jobs are associated with such activities, and while they may be fewer in number than the jobs associated with the forgone investment, they are likely to be the higher-paid managerial, professional and administrative jobs, as well as jobs in research and development.

Outward FDI can also lead to trade expansion (with positive results on wages and employment) through indirect integration effects, as exchange is enhanced through synergistic interaction. Also, as discussed earlier, FDI and trade may be complementary, as FDI enhances trade flows especially through intra-firm trade between parent companies and their foreign affiliates. This can, in turn, contribute to increased productivity and competitiveness due to the improved allocation of resources, faster inflows of technology, increased specialization and improved economies of scale and scope. The competitiveness of Canadian firms engaging in CDIA may also be increased because outward-oriented firms may be more inclined to maximize the efficiency of their domestic and foreign operations. They may also impart positive spillovers, improving the performance of other domestically based firms through vertical linkages with firms in both upstream and downstream industries. These longer-run indirect effects of CDIA are likely to be manifest in an increased demand for the firm's products (and hence in the firm's demand for labour) with positive effects on wages and employment.[3]

In analyzing the labour market implications of outward FDI it is important to emphasize that the "counter-factual" for firms that do not invest abroad is not necessarily the *status quo*. Specifically, they may be adversely affected by increased imports, or they may even be driven out of business by high costs and low productivity. The ability of such firms to compete and survive may very well depend upon some degree of diversification through investment abroad.

In summary, outward FDI may have positive effects on wages and employment in the source country of the FDI through the spending of the investment income, as well as through trade expansion emanating from such factors as induced capital exports, intra-firm trade and integration effects. Positive effects may also be felt by managerial and head-office personnel who direct the outward FDI. In the long run, the domestic restructuring and outward-looking orientation should also increase efficiency and competitiveness with positive effects on wages and employment.

NATURE OF JOB RESTRUCTURING AND IMPLICATIONS OF EFFICIENCY WAGES

THE DISCUSSION SO FAR HAS EMPHASIZED that many of the job losses associated with the forgone investment related to outward FDI are likely to be in low-wage jobs, and many of the job gains (associated with induced capital exports and head office activities) are likely to be in high-wage jobs. For countries like Canada these wage and employment effects of investment are in the same direction as the wage and employment effects of free trade in general (Gunderson, 1993a). That is, the import competition will be from low-wage imports, and the export expansion will be associated with high-wage jobs.

It is possible that low-wage countries like Mexico may also have high-skilled work forces in certain areas such as software writing, engineering and automobile assembly. As emphasized by Betcherman (1993) the future cannot simply be extrapolated from the past, especially because low-wage countries are increasingly able to provide highly skilled work forces as well as investment and political stability. In such circumstances, higher-wage jobs in countries like Canada can be adversely affected by both the import competition and the capital flows to such high-skill, low-wage sectors. While this adverse effect is a possibility, the increased demand for labour in the low-wage countries should ensure that they do not remain low wage, although it may take considerable time. Furthermore, due to institutional and legal floors on wages in Canada, the wage costs of unskilled workers relative to skilled workers are likely to be higher in Canada than in Mexico. The empirical evidence (reviewed in Gunderson, 1993a) also indicates that the competitive threat for countries like Canada is potentially greatest at the low-wage unskilled level.

For these reasons, the wage and employment effects of outward FDI are likely to be in the same directions as those from import competition, having the greatest adverse effect at low-wage levels in Canada. These wage and employment effects of both trade and investment underline the key labour market issue – to facilitate the adjustment of labour from the affected low-wage import sectors to high-wage export sectors. This is as true for the wage and employment effects of outward FDI as it is for trade in goods and services.

Job restructuring from low- to high-wage industries also has implications for the payment of efficiency wages[4] – wages that firms voluntarily pay above the competitive norm to induce positive work behaviour by employees. Such positive behaviour includes reduced turnover and shirking and increased loyalty and commitment on the part of employees. The firm voluntarily pays the efficiency wage premiums because the cost of doing so is offset by the benefits of the induced positive work behaviour. The firm is indifferent as to incurring the cost of these higher-efficiency wage premiums on the one hand, and using other costly procedures to elicit positive work behaviour on the other hand.

While the firm is indifferent, employees who receive the efficiency wage premiums are not; the fact that they are better for receiving them motivates their positive work behaviour. The efficiency wage premiums are "prizes" which induce positive work behaviour; they are not merely compensating wages paid in return for more work effort or other factors that could conceivably increase the disutility of the work to the employee.

Because employers pay the efficiency wage premiums willingly and workers are better off receiving them, there are obvious welfare gains from having an economy with a large number of such "good" jobs.

Efficiency wage premiums are more likely to prevail in high-wage jobs partly because of the importance to the firm of eliciting positive work behaviour and deterring turnover of workers with specialized skills. Also, piece-work and other payment schemes amendable to measuring output are often less feasible in high-skilled jobs. To the extent that such efficiency wage premiums are more likely to be paid in higher-paying jobs, and that trade liberalization (or outward FDI induced by such trade liberalization) is likely to lead to a restructuring from low- to high-wage jobs, welfare is improved by the increased number of jobs that pay efficiency wages. There may therefore be some consolation in the fact that the job losses in low-wage sectors are unlikely to incorporate efficiency wage premiums, whereas the job gains in the high-wage sectors are more likely to do so.

In practice it is difficult to judge whether wage premiums are likely to be an important issue with respect to the wage and employment effects of trade liberalization and induced effects on outward FDI. There is controversy over the extent to which efficiency wage premiums do, in fact, exist, in contrast, for example, to simply reflecting union wage premiums that are not voluntarily paid. And even if they do exist, they are not necessarily greater in high-wage jobs. From a policy perspective, attempts to preserve such "good" jobs may simply lead to conventional (protectionist) measures to protect rents, especially because efficiency wage premiums are difficult to distinguish from other wage premiums. Given these complications, perhaps the sensible perspective is to indicate that trade- and investment-induced restructuring from low-wage to high-wage jobs may increase the use of efficiency wage premiums in countries like Canada, albeit this positive effect is questionable and unlikely to be large.

EFFECT OF OUTWARD FDI ON LABOUR REGULATION

THE DISCUSSION SO FAR has focused on the mechanisms through which outward FDI may be expected to affect wages and employment in the country from which the FDI originates. Specifically, the mechanisms centred on the job content of that investment, as well as on indirect effects associated with induced changes in productivity, technology, and imports of capital and other inputs.

HARMONIZATION PRESSURES

OUTWARD FDI CAN INDIRECTLY AFFECT wages and employment in the originating country by putting pressure on governments with respect to labour regulations and policies. These regulations are of interest in their own right, but they are also of interest because of their ultimate effect on the wages and employment they are often designed to regulate.

Outward FDI affects labour regulation in the originating country to the extent that labour regulations increase labour costs which, in turn, affect outward FDI (for example, through plant location and investment decisions). With rising levels of outward FDI and being free to invest where it suits them, employers can make a credible threat to locate their business and investment in jurisdictions that impose fewer regulatory costs. In other words, a country and different jurisdictions within a country will have more of an incentive to compete for new business if capital mobility through FDI is increased.

Opposition to free trade exists, in part, because of the perception that free trade will encourage outward FDI (because business can now more easily locate in the country of a trading partner and export back under the reduced tariffs), and this in turn will lead to a forced harmonization of labour laws. The fear has been that harmonization will be towards the lowest common denominator (i.e., jurisdictions with the lowest regulatory costs) as jurisdictions compete for investment by offering environments that do not impose excessive regulatory costs. The pressure caused by this threat of capital mobility can be increased by other trade-induced mechanisms. Specifically, labour policies in some sectors may be deemed unfair subsidies and therefore be under the potential threat of countervailing duties.

In contrast, increased trade brings increased exposure to the practices of trading partners, and this may encourage a convergence to best practices across the different countries. To the extent that such best practices involve reductions in excessive regulation, freer trade should lead to reduced labour regulation.

The effect of labour regulation on labour cost depends, in part, on the type of labour regulation and the purposes it serves.[5] Labour regulation that aims to improve the efficiency of labour markets can obviously survive the competitive pressures induced by the threat of capital mobility. Such could be the case, for example, with respect to the laws and regulations that set the basic legal structure within which private parties operate, or regulations and policies that correct for possible market failures. While there is little agreement as to the extent to which labour legislation can correct for possible market failures, examples of the latter could include valuable labour market information and provisions for advance notice requirements and general training. In contrast, labour regulation that reduces efficiency and protects rents will be under more pressure from the threat of capital mobility.

Labour legislation that serves a distributional or equity rationale, may also be under pressure from the threat of capital mobility and other trade-induced pressures. To the extent that the equity objective has a positive feed-back effect on efficiency (by providing adjustment assistance to persons who have been adversely affected by free trade, which may reduce their resistance to such a policy), there is no conflict between equity and efficiency. However, if the equity objective conflicts with efficiency (by providing income support that encourages people to stay in declining sectors or regions, for example), then it will be under pressure from the threat of capital mobility. Simply stated, business may be reluctant to locate investment in jurisdictions that have high regulatory labour costs, even if that regulation serves worthy distributional purposes. Obviously, if business people do not agree with the distributional objectives, the threat of capital mobility is even stronger.

In summary, capital mobility should lead to some harmonization of labour laws and regulations. Such harmonization, moreover, will be more closely keyed to the regulatory environment that imposes least cost on business. That is, with increased capital mobility there will be more inter-jurisdictional competition to attract business, and that competition will occur partly in the form of less labour regulation and fewer costly policies so as to attract investment. Although this scenario implies less labour market regulation, such regulation can still prevail if it serves an efficiency purpose, or if the jurisdiction is willing to pay to achieve other objectives such as equity. With greater capital mobility, however, the cost is simply more explicit: the potential for lost investment and possibly the jobs associated with that investment.

The internationalization of Canadian domestic policies, including labour-market policies, is likely to occur with or without the expansion of out-ward FDI. Since Canada depends heavily on foreign trade, inward FDI and foreign technology, the rapid pace of business globalization should lead to considerable convergence of policies across countries. It should also be empha-sized that such convergence need not be negative. Instead, it can reduce fric-tions among countries and facilitate the expansion of world trade, investment and technology flows. Furthermore, Canadian governments can protect the interests of Canadians from potentially adverse effects of convergence by playing an active role in international forums dealing with labour market and other policies (Betcherman, 1993).

EVIDENCE ON THE EFFECT OF OUTWARD FDI ON LABOUR REGULATIONS

ALTHOUGH CAPITAL MOBILITY can indirectly affect wages and employment (through restraints on labour laws and regulation), there is surprisingly little empirical information about the links between outward FDI and labour regulation. For outward FDI to affect domestic wages and employment through labour regulation, the following conditions must hold:

- Labour regulations must differ across the countries.

- These differences must affect labour costs.

- The resultant differentials in labour costs must affect FDI (through plant location and investment decisions, for example).

- The threat of such capital mobility must affect labour regulation (as through a harmonization of labour laws, for example).

As for the first link, and with respect to the NAFTA, it is reasonably well established that there is more labour regulation in Canada than in the United States (Betcherman & Gunderson, 1990). This is so with respect to a wide range of regulations: minimum wages; hours of work, overtime and leave policies; termination and layoffs; pay equity; workers' compensation and occupational health and safety; unemployment insurance; and regulations that facilitate and sustain collective bargaining. There is also general agreement that while Mexico has an extensive body of written labour regulations, these tend not to be enforced (Gunderson, 1993c). This is, of course, part of the rationale behind the pressure from the United States to include enforcement of labour and environmental issues as part of the NAFTA agreement – to reduce the competitive pressures from lower legislated environmental and labour costs that are further lowered in practice due to lack of enforcement of the legislation.

As for the second link – the effect of labour regulation on labour cost – there is even less systematic empirical evidence. Standard labour textbooks claim that minimum wages raise the wages of low-wage workers, that pay equity legislation raises the wages of women, and that collective bargaining legislation helps sustain unionization which, in turn, raises the wages of union workers by 15 percent to 20 percent. However, it is not clear how much of this is offset by other adjustments or by cost savings in other areas. Employers incur workers' compensation costs, for example, in return for not being exposed to the legal costs of the tort liability system, since workers give up the right to sue as an explicit *quid pro quo* for workers' compensation. Health and safety regulations also reduce occupational injuries and diseases, and save on workers' compensation and disability costs, especially in systems that are experience rated so that firms and industries with high accident rates pay higher premiums. Advance notice legislation may facilitate job searches and lower the recruiting cost of other employers. Unemployment insurance saves on the cost of a compensating wage premium that otherwise would have to be paid to cover the risk of unemployment or seasonal work; and workers' compensation saves on the cost of compensating wage premiums for otherwise uninsured risk. Lower wage premiums may also be paid by employers in a safer work environment that has been made so by enforced health and safety regulations; in return for pension benefits induced by pension regulations; and even in return for requirements to accommodate the needs of disabled persons in the workplace.

There is also little systematic information on the third link – the effect of regulatory labour costs on outward FDI through plant location and investment decisions – and that which exists is somewhat conflicting. Evidence that labour costs are an important determinant of plant location and investment decision has been documented in a number of interview and survey studies (reviewed in Carlton, 1979; Kieschnick, 1983; Litvak & Maule, 1981; and Williams & Brinker, 1985) with contrary results found in Forget & Denis (1985) and Ghandi (1990). Some survey evidence of Canadian firms suggests that regulation costs in Canada are not an important determinant of CDIA (Knubley, Krause & Sadeque, 1991). Overall their results suggest that foreign pull factors are more important than domestic push factors in influencing CDIA. Other evidence provided by Rugman (1987), however, suggests that unionization and labour costs are also important determinants of CDIA. Similarly, as pointed out by Betcherman (1993, p.7), the econometric literature[6] provides conflicting evidence as to the importance of labour cost as a determinant of FDI, in part because labour cost (average wage or average unit labour cost) is a poor measure of the true quality and competitiveness of a nation's work force.

There is also little systematic information on the fourth link: the effect of capital mobility on labour regulations. To some extent this reflects the difficulty of determining what factors influence legislators in establishing such laws, and regulators in applying and enforcing them. Labour regulation, of course, is also only one instrument that enables governments to attract business and investment. Taxes, public services, exchange rates and environmental and other regulations are other instruments. Also, multinationals may transplant their workplace practices into the countries in which they operate, thereby reducing the need for regulation.

Clearly, there is a lack of systematic evidence on any one – much less all – of the links, proving categorically that outward FDI indirectly affects wages and employment by altering labour laws and regulations. At this stage, the most that can be said with respect to each link is:

- Labour regulations differ substantially among Canada, the United States and Mexico.

- These differences probably affect labour costs, but the magnitude of that effect has not been determined.

- The legislated labour cost differences probably have some effect on plant location and investment decisions, although the evidence is scant and inconclusive.

- The effect of capital mobility on inducing changes in labour laws and regulations is unknown, although most attention is being paid to this issue in the political arena (for example, as an adjunct to the attention being paid to the harmonization of labour laws).

EMPLOYMENT EFFECTS OF OUTWARD FDI

THE INCONCLUSIVE EVIDENCE on the *indirect* effects of outward FDI on wages and employment through altering labour laws and regulations is matched by the inconclusive evidence on the more *direct* effect of FDI on wages and employment, largely through the job content of displaced investment. Several different empirical procedures have been used to relate outward FDI to its job content, and hence to provide estimates of the possible job loss associated with such displaced investment. These estimates are illustrated in the following recent studies, the first four of which refer to the expected impact of the NAFTA on U.S. FDI in Mexico, and ultimately on U.S. employment.

CYPHER (1992)

TABLE 1 ILLUSTRATES A SERIES OF CALCULATIONS extracted from estimates provided in Cypher (1992).[7] The first row sets out one set of hypothetical estimates of the increase in FDI expected to occur in Mexico between 1992 and 1997, with the second column indicating the additional amount ($17 billion) expected to be induced by the NAFTA. The subsequent NAFTA-induced changes shown in columns (2), (4) and (6) are the focus of the discussion here. Negative entries in the table indicate investment (and hence jobs) that are lost from the United States.

The calculation of U.S. job content related to investment is based on the fact that in 1990, every $1 billion (hereafter B) in economic activity (value added) is associated with 20,135 jobs. Since 63 percent of Mexican FDI originates in the United States (row 2), the NAFTA-induced investment is calculated as 0.63 x $17 B = $10.71 B (row 3). This implies a loss of 215,646 jobs over the five-year period (column 4) or an annual loss of 43,129 jobs.

Some of this potentially lost investment is offset by the fact that the investment involves capital imports into Mexico. Using the 1988 ratio of capital imports from the United States to FDI in Mexico of 0.053 (row 4), the additional NAFTA-induced FDI is calculated as 0.053 x $10.71 B = $0.901 B (row 5) of capital exports from the United States, with an associated creation of slightly under 4,000 jobs on an annual basis. The net investment shifted from the United States to Mexico is therefore $9.81 B (row 6) calculated by subtracting the induced capital export expansion (row 5) from the total investment shift (row 3).

Row 7 shows the induced output changes associated with that investment, based on the current capital/output ratio of 1.2 which implies that $17 B

TABLE 1

EFFECT OF THE NAFTA ON FDI AND JOBS[a] IN THE UNITED STATES (BASED ON CALCULATIONS IN CYPHER, 1992)

MECHANISMS THROUGH WHICH NAFTA CAN AFFECT FDI AND JOBS IN THE U.S.	EXPECTED FDI INCREASES 1992-1997 ($B)		JOB LOSSES (-) AND GAINS (+)			
			1992-1997		ANNUAL BY 1997	
	NORMAL (1)	NAFTA[b] (2)	NORMAL (3)	NAFTA (4)	NORMAL (5)	NAFTA (6)
INVESTMENT EFFECTS						
1. Increased FDI in Mexico[c]	-3.0	-17.0	-604,050	-342,295	-120,810	-68,459
2. x 0.63 Proportion from U.S.[d]						
3. = Investment shifted from U.S.	-18.9	-10.7	-380,552	-215,646	-76,110	-43,129
4. Row 1 x 0.053 ratio of U.S. Capital Exports : Mexican FDI[e]						
5. = Induced U.S. Capital Exports	+1.6	+0.9	+32,015	+18,142	+6,403	+3,629
6. Net Investment Shifted from U.S., i.e., Row 3 - 5	-17.3	-9.8	-348,537	-197,504	-69,707	-39,500
OUTPUT/EXPORT EFFECTS						
7. Increased Mexican Exports from Investment[f]	-25.0	-14.2				
8. x 0.64 exported to U.S.						
9. = Induced Exports to U.S.	-16.0	-9.1			-322,160	-182,557
10. Total Investment Shifts and Export Effects, Rows 6 + 9	-33.31	-19.21			-391,867	-222,057

Notes: [a] Negative entry indicates investment and jobs lost from U.S.; positive entry indicates gains. Job loss calculations based on each $1 billion of investment being associated with 20,135 jobs.
[b] Effect of NAFTA over and above the normal or baseline increases that are expected to occur without NAFTA. That is, columns (2), (4) and (6) indicate additional investment and jobs lost through NAFTA.
[c] Based on statements from President Salinas of expectations of annual increases of FDI of $6B per year, compared to the 1990 increase of $2.6B per year that is used for the normal or baseline expected increase.
[d] Based on ratio of U.S. : total FDI in Mexico.
[e] Based on ratio of Mexican capital imports from the United States (i.e., U.S. capital exports) : DFI of 2.04B : 38.40B = 0.053 in 1988.
[f] Based on capital output ratio of 1.2 : 1 which implies $30B of capital investment (row 1) is associated with $30B : 1.2 = $25B of additional output.
Source: Extracted from calculations in Cypher (1992).

of the NAFTA-induced investment would lead to output increases in Mexico of $14.17B (i.e., $17 : 1.2). It is assumed that all the FDI-induced output increase is exported, on the grounds that this is the objective of the Mexican government in attracting the FDI. The fact that 64 percent of Mexican exports now go to the United States (row 8) implies that $9.07B of the NAFTA/FDI-induced output increase will be exported to the United States (row 9). These additional imports into the United States imply a loss of

182,557 jobs associated with the cumulative investment that is expected to be in place by the end of 1997. Since these are associated with the cumulative investment, they are reported as annual job loss figures by 1997. Adding these to the job losses associated with the net investment shift from the United States implies an annual loss of 222,058 jobs (i.e., 182,557 + 39,501) for the United States by 1997, associated with the FDI induced by the NAFTA.

Obviously the assumptions underlying these calculations are open to question, as Cypher (1992) notes. Table 1, for example, does not show any employment gains to the United States associated with increased consumption exports to Mexico attributable to higher (Mexican) income levels resulting from the NAFTA. The point of the replication produced here is not to question those calculations, but rather to provide an illustration of how they are made. Our contention here (which is discussed in more detail later in this study) is not that the assumptions underlying the calculation are wrong, but rather that the job content analysis itself is not an appropriate procedure.

KOECHLIN & LARUDEE (1992A, B)

THIS STUDY IS AN ESTIMATE OF THE POTENTIAL job losses associated with the redirection of investment that may occur from the United States to Mexico as a result of the NAFTA. Their estimate of the extent of the increase in outward FDI from the United States to Mexico is based on two alternative procedures. The first applies the same proportionate increase in outward FDI from the United States into Ireland that occurred when Ireland joined the European Economic Community (EEC) in 1974. That proportionate increase (a factor of 3.8) was calculated by taking the deviation in the five-year moving average trend growth of U.S. FDI into Ireland that occurred after 1974. The authors argue that this is representative of the anticipated increase in U.S. FDI because both were prompted by access to a wider market.[8] This procedure yields a NAFTA-induced increase in U.S. FDI into Mexico of US$ 5.9B in 1992 or US$ 52.7B between 1992 and 2000. These figures represent the "high" investment estimates in Table 2.

The second procedure for calculating the increase in FDI from the United States to Mexico is based on estimates of the increases in U.S. outward FDI that occurred in response to the formation of the EEC in general, and to a measure (constructed by Koechlin & Larudee) of a favourable business climate. On the basis of data collected by the authors from 23 countries over the period from 1974 to 1984, they regressed outward FDI from the United States, using several independent variables believed to explain variation in outward FDI. These variables included a dummy variable for EEC membership, as well as a measure of a favourable business climate in the host country. The authors use the estimates from these two variables to capture the expected increase in U.S. investment into Mexico as a result of the NAFTA. This procedure yields a NAFTA-induced increase in U.S. FDI into Mexico of $3.5B in 1992 or $31.2B over the period from 1992 to 2000. These figures are given as the "low" investment estimates in Table 2.

Koechlin & Larudee assume that these increases in U.S. FDI into Mexico will result in an *equivalent* corresponding reduction of investment in the United States. They justify this assumption on two grounds. First, the reduced trade barriers will enable firms to locate in low-cost Mexico and service the large U.S. market. Second, the diversion of U.S. investment from other countries into Mexico will be more than offset by the diversion of foreign investment that formerly went to the United States and that now will go to Mexico.

The job losses associated with this lost investment in the United States is calculated by applying the capital : labour ratio to the lost capital investment. Two estimates of the capital : labour ratio are used. The first is based on projecting 1990 estimates of the gross value of capital assets per employee, which average $108,500 over the period 1992 to 2000. This implies that each $1B of capital investment is associated with $1B/108,500 = 9,217 jobs. The second estimate, based on Glickman & Woodward (1989) yields a capital : labour ratio of $120,000 per employee, which implies 8,333 jobs per $1 B of investment.

TABLE 2

EFFECTS OF THE NAFTA ON U.S. FDI AND JOBS
(BASED ON CALCULATIONS IN KOECHLIN ET AL.)

| | | U.S. JOB LOSSES | |
NAFTA INDUCED INVESTMENT SHIFT FROM U.S. TO MEXICO	INCREASED INVESTMENT ($B)	LOW: $1B = 8,333 JOBS[a]	HIGH: $1B = 9,217 JOBS[b]
	ANNUAL 1992		
Low: Based on Increased U.S. FDI into EEC	3.5	29,166	32,260
High: Based on Increased U.S. FDI into Ireland after joining EEC	5.9	49,167	54,380
	CUMULATIVE 1992-2000		
Low: Based on Increased U.S. FDI into EEC	31.2	259,990	287,570
High: Based on Increased U.S. FDI into Ireland after joining EEC	52.7	439,149	485,736

Notes: [a] Based on a capital : labour ratio of $120,000/worker, which implies $1B of capital is associated with 8,333 jobs as discussed in the text.
[b] Based on a capital : labour ratio of $108,500 per worker, which implies each $1B of capital is associated with 9,217 jobs, as discussed in the text.

Source: Extracted from Koechlin & Larudee, 1992a, 1992b, and Koechlin, Larudee, Bowles & Epstein, 1991.

These two alternative estimates of jobs per $1B of investment and the two alternative estimates of lost investment yield the four different estimates of job loss associated with NAFTA-induced U.S. FDI into Mexico, as summarized in Table 2. They range from approximately 29,000 to 54,000 on an annual basis (top panel), and 260,000 to 490,000 over the period between 1992 and 2000 (bottom panel).

As the authors of these studies recognize, their results are sensitive to the underlying assumptions. Two assumptions are particularly important: that outward FDI will lead to a corresponding reduction in domestic investment, and that existing capital labour ratios will remain fixed and thereby yield the corresponding job losses. Hinojosa-Ojeda & Robinson (1992), for example, argue that the NAFTA-induced investment changes are so small relative to the aggregate U.S. capital market that they are unlikely to have any effect at all on aggregate investment in the United States.

Faux & Spriggs (1991): Economic Policy Institute

Faux & Spriggs (1991) of the Economic Policy Institute utilize the Hinojosa-Ojeda/Mcleery (1990) computable general equilibrium model to simulate both the expected effect of the NAFTA on U.S. outward FDI into Mexico and the ultimate effect on U.S. wages and employment.[9] The expected effect of the NAFTA is captured by assuming that the resulting increased investor confidence would lead to a 10 percent reduction in the risk premium (differential returns to capital between Mexico and the United States) for U.S. investors by the year 2000. This is predicted to lead to a cumulative increase in U.S. FDI into Mexico of $44B, assuming that oil prices continue to rise.

In turn, this increase in U.S. FDI into Mexico is predicted to lead to 1,264,000 fewer jobs in the United States (551,000 or 0.45 percent fewer in the high-wage sector, and 713,000 or 4.95 percent fewer in the low-wage sector). It is also predicted to lead to 1,581,000 fewer Mexican immigrants into the U.S. as a result of improved economic conditions in Mexico, which largely offsets the potential job loss in the low-wage sector. Real wages in the United States are predicted to stay about the same in the high-wage sector (decline by -0.16 percent) and increase by 4.7 percent in the low-wage sector. This later effect reflects the reduced pressure on low wages in the United States from the reduction of Mexican immigration.

Prestowitz, Cohen, Morici & Tonelson (1991), Economic Strategy Institute

The Economic Strategy Institute estimated the potential effect of the NAFTA on FDI and jobs in the following fashion, as outlined in Prestowitz, Cohen, Morici & Tonelson (1991, pp. 45-63). Their first scenario involved the following assumptions and procedures.

1) A baseline (no NAFTA) investment scenario was estimated for the key manufacturing sectors in Mexico that account for most of the exports to the United States. This was done by assuming that they would have the same output-to-capital ratio as their U.S. counterparts, which enabled estimating the Mexican investment levels which were then projected to 1999.

2) The NAFTA was assumed to double this investment, based on public statements and recent trends.

3) This implies an increase of $25B to $46B of FDI in Mexican export-oriented sectors.

4) This will lead to an increase of $11B to $19B in U.S. exports of capital equipment, based on the fact that 60 percent of Mexico's imports of components and intermediate goods comes from the United States, falling to 50 percent by 1999.

5) Approximately 70 percent of the output ultimately resulting from this new investment will be exported to the United States, based on current figures from those sectors.

6) The potential employment effects of this FDI-induced trade is then estimated by using what the authors term "the standard economic formula holding that $1B worth of trade represents 30,000 jobs" (p. 47).

Using these assumptions, Prestowitz et al. estimate that the FDI-induced trade will ultimately lead to between 400,000 and 900,000 job losses in the United States by 1999. Initially, there will be job gains because of the initial surge in capital exports to support the FDI in Mexico. However, once that plant and equipment are in place and producing output (much of which will go to the United States), they will lead to greater imports into the United States. The hardest hit sectors in the United States will be auto parts, radio and television, and telecommunications.

Because of these potentially negative effects, Prestowitz et al. recommend trying to emulate the Japan-Thailand model whereby Japan has used Thailand as a low-wage investment platform for exporting to the rest of the world, thereby improving the competitiveness of both countries. They simulate this "win-win" scenario by changing two of the previous assumptions: first, the U.S. share of Mexico's exports falls from 70 percent to 50 percent and, second, the U.S. share of Mexico's imports of components and intermediate goods stays at 60 percent rather than falling to 50 percent by 1999. These seemingly small changes in what otherwise may appear to be innocuous assumptions lead to the substantial job losses of between 400,000 and 900,000 being converted to job gains of 225,000 to 264,000.

The authors suggest a variety of general policies that may be used to attain this win-win situation. Whether these policies are feasible or not, the analysis does highlight the importance of specific assumptions in making such job gain and job loss calculations.

EARLIER STUDIES AND OTHER PROCEDURES[10]

THE PREVIOUSLY DISCUSSED JOB CONTENT studies have all been applied to illustrate the potential effect of the NAFTA on U.S. FDI into Mexico, and the ultimate effect of this on U.S. employment. Similar job content methodologies had earlier been applied to analyze the effect of outward FDI in earlier periods. A U.S. Tariff Commission study (summarized in Dickens, 1988) indicated a wide range in the net job effects of U.S outward FDI in the 1960s. The net effects were: 1.3 million jobs lost (1.1 million gains less 2.4 million losses), assuming that all production associated with outward FDI could have been done in the United States with no shift in demand from other sectors; 400,000 jobs lost, assuming half of production could have been done in the United States; and a gain of 500,000 jobs, assuming the U.S. share of world trade did not change in the 1960s. The authors indicated that they perceived the later scenario to be most indicative of the effect of the outward FDI. Hawkins (1972b) also indicates a similar wide range of estimates and concludes that the best estimate is one where the job creation exactly offsets the job destruction. Buckley & Artisien (1987) find that the employment effects of outward FDI vary considerably over time and across industries in E.C. countries. Kravis & Lipsey (1990) find that the more a U.S. multinational invests abroad, the lower its domestic employment, although the counterfactual of even lower domestic employment without the outward FDI is a possibility.

A number of earlier studies also tried to estimate the extent to which foreign production from outward FDI substitutes for domestic production, based on estimates of production functions and the relative cost differentials across the countries (Adler & Stevens, 1974; Frank & Freeman, 1978). They arrive at an even wider range of estimates than those based on static assumptions with respect to substitutability of foreign for domestic production. In their analysis of E.C. countries, Buckley & Brooke (1992) conclude that outward FDI substitutes for exports (and employment) in the short run, but in the long run it substitutes for investment by competing firms, thereby preserving domestic employment. Other studies provide estimates indicating that outward FDI induces domestic production, exports and investment and hence employment (Bergsten et al., 1978; Henry & Willett, 1973; Horst, 1972 and 1978; Lipsey & Weiss, 1969 and 1981).

The study by Rao, Legault & Ahmad in this volume also provides evidence in support of the complementarity hypothesis. These authors indicate that "the rapid pace of expansion of CDIA in the 1980s coincided with a strong investment performance in Canada. Similarly, during this period, there is either a positive or no correlation between the trends in direct investment abroad and domestic capital formation in the G7 countries during the last 15 years or so". Graham (this volume) also cites earlier empirical evidence in favour of the complementarity hypothesis. In addition, he provides some tabulation of Canadian FDI in the United States, suggesting that FDI and exports are complements.

In their review of the literature of the impact of Swedish outward FDI on trade and employment, Blomström & Kokko (this volume) also find that outward FDI and exports are net complements, largely because the induced exports of raw materials and intermediate goods is larger than the reduced exports of finished goods. Specifically, the Swedish MNEs supplied components and raw material to their overseas affiliates which in turn concentrated on assembly and manufacturing. The jobs that were preserved in Sweden in the process tended to be in raw-material-based industries (metals, wood products and paper products) as well as ones involving considerable R&D.

Case studies of plant closings, where the plant has relocated in other countries, have often been used to demonstrate job losses. Overall, the case studies have been inconclusive in their evidence of the employment effects of outward FDI (reviewed in Bergsten et al., 1978; Caves, 1982; and Frank & Freeman, 1978). There have also been studies of the differences in employment growth across industries with different amounts of outward FDI. Some studies find slower employment growth in industries with high outward FDI (Jager, 1975); other studies find faster employment growth (Business International Corporation, 1972; Hawkins, 1972a; Kraseman & Barker, 1973).

After reviewing many of these earlier studies of the expected employment impact of outward FDI, Caves (1982, p. 137) notes that "The distributional consequences of foreign investment in the long run remain a strictly unsettled issue". He also concludes (p. 158) "The statistical evidence gives appreciable support to the complementary relationship...[between outward FDI and exports], and that mitigates the theoretical likelihood that investing abroad will be adverse to real wages in the home country". Dickens (1988, pp. 70-71) in his review states: "The wide range of estimates of net job creation suggests only the extent of our ignorance about this phenomenon. . . . The studies that have attempted to examine employment effects of FDI are all badly flawed to the point that they provide no useful estimate of the extent of displacement caused by direct foreign investment." Dickens also makes the important point that FDI would displace domestic workers only if it resulted either from foreign production that reduced domestic exports or from increased domestic imports. In either case, this effect would be picked up by trade displacement analysis; hence adding the effects of FDI to the effects of trade would be double counting.

While there is clearly no consensus on the employment effect in the domestic country of outward FDI (although a tendency to suggest it is employment enhancing in the long run), there is more agreement on its effect on the composition of the domestic work force. Specifically, it tends to be beneficial to higher-skilled, white-collar workers and harmful to lower-skilled, blue-collar workers (Buckley & Brooke, 1992; Campbell & McElrath, 1990; and Kravis & Lipsey, 1990). This conclusion highlights that the labour-market effects of outward FDI are similar to those of trade in general (more than 75 empirical studies, reviewed in Gunderson, 1993a). It also notes that while both outward FDI and trade are likely to have beneficial employment effects in the long run, they can create short-run adjustment problems and promote the growing wage polarization that is already occurring in countries like Canada and the United States.

LABOUR-MARKET CHARACTERISTICS OF OUTWARD FDI

EVEN IF IT WERE PERCEIVED TO BE methodologically sound to determine the potential wage and employment effects of CDIA by examining its labour content, systematic information is not available on the labour-market characteristics of all Canadian investment abroad. Information on the labour-market characteristics of Canadian FDI into the United States, however, is available, as illustrated in the following Tables. The tabulations simply illustrate the numbers and nature of the jobs associated with the investment.

Table 3 (last row) indicates that the total employment involved in Canadian FDI in the United States increased somewhat between 1985 and

TABLE 3

DISTRIBUTION OF CANADIAN EMPLOYMENT IN AFFILIATES IN THE UNITED STATES, 1985-1990, % BY U.S. INDUSTRY

INDUSTRY	1985	1986	1987	1988	1989	1990
Petroleum	0.91	0.66	0.37	1.21	1.54	1.47
Manufacturing	54.47	45.20	46.40	40.07	41.32	41.28
Wholesale Trade	4.02	3.72	3.09	2.47	2.69	2.80
Retail Trade	23.27	33.16	31.32	36.25	33.34	32.34
Finance[a]	0.58	1.09	0.32	0.33	0.25	0.59
Insurance	1.75	1.58	1.89	1.54	1.59	1.57
Real Estate	3.31	2.75	3.53	2.70	3.04	3.19
Services	5.01	5.63	5.68	5.71	5.60	6.28
Other	6.68	6.24	7.40	9.76	10.63	10.49
Total	100	100	100	100	100	100
Total Employment (thousands)	527.5	609.2	592.9	737.9	721.4	740.0

Note: [a] Finance does not include banking.
Source: Computations provided by Industry Canada, based on data from the U.S. Department of Commerce, Bureau of Economic Analysis.

TABLE 4

DISTRIBUTION OF FDI EMPLOYMENT IN THE UNITED STATES, 1989
% BY U.S. INDUSTRY

| | FDI EMPLOYMENT IN THE UNITED STATES | | COMPARABLE |
| | FROM ALL | FROM | EMPLOYMENT |
	COUNTRIES	CANADA	IN CANADA
Petroleum	3.01	1.54	0.41
Manufacturing	47.40	41.32	18.57
Wholesale Trade	8.84	2.69	5.54
Retail Trade	17.82	33.34	12.94
Finance[a]	2.10	0.25	3.52
Insurance	2.47	1.59	0.85
Real Estate	0.84	3.04	0.87
Services	10.21	5.60	49.41
Other	7.29	10.63	17.73
Total	100	100	100
Total Employment (million)	**4.51**	**.721**	**12.486**

Note: [a] Finance does not include banking.

Source: Computations provided by Industry Canada, based on data from the U.S. Department of Commerce, Bureau of Economic Analysis. Canadian figures from Statistics Canada, *Annual Estimates of Employment Earnings and Hours: 1983-1992.*

TABLE 5

DISTRIBUTION OF FDI EMPLOYMENT IN THE UNITED STATES, 1989,% BY REGION

REGION	CANADA	OTHER COUNTRIES
New England	6.54	6.41
Midwest	17.60	21.14
Great Lakes	13.96	17.73
Plains	5.97	5.07
Southeast	26.17	24.19
Southwest	8.40	8.46
Rocky Mountains	1.93	1.59
Far West	11.82	14.51
Other	0.47	2.26
Total	100	100
Total Employment (million)	**.721**	**3.79**

Source: Computations provided by Industry Canada, based on data from the U.S. Department of Commerce, Bureau of Economic Analysis.

1990, although the fluctuations are quite pronounced. Most FDI employment is in manufacturing, followed by retail trade. Obviously, CDIA in retail trade in the United States. is not likely to be associated with significant job loss in Canada, since those goods are largely consumed in the United States. Furthermore, if that specific investment were relocated to Canada, it would presumably displace other Canadian retail trade.

Table 4 (last row) illustrates that the FDI employment in the United States from Canada constitutes about 16 percent (i.e., 721,440/ 4,511,500) of all FDI employment in the United States. The 721,440 jobs associated with Canadian employment in the United States represent 6.78 percent of the total employment in Canada of 10.7 million in 1989. The industrial distribution of Canadian FDI in the United States (column 2) is fairly similar to the pattern from other countries (column 1), although retail trade is considerably more prominent in Canadian FDI, and wholesale trade and services are considerably less prominent. Compared to the industrial distribution of employment in Canada (column 3), however, Canadian FDI in the United States is disproportionately distributed in manufacturing and retail trade, and less in services.

Table 5 indicates that the regional distribution of Canadian FDI in the United States is similar to that from other countries, with about one-quarter of it occurring the Southeast. Whether this reflects the attraction of low-wage labour and few labour regulations in the sunbelt is open to speculation.

Table 6 shows that wages and salaries of Canadian affiliates in the United States are fairly similar to those from other countries, although wages

TABLE 6

ANNUAL WAGES AND SALARIES OF EMPLOYEES OF CANADIAN AFFILIATES IN THE UNITED STATES IN $US, BY U.S. INDUSTRY, 1989

INDUSTRY	ALL AFFILIATES	CANADIAN AFFILIATES
Petroleum	33,120	20,270
Manufacturing	28,880	33,250
Wholesale Trade	30,100	28,610
Retail Trade	12,570	13,710
Finance[a]	78,555	43,890
Insurance	31,510	34,960
Real Estate	23,600	21,920
Services	19,050	13,910
Other	33,840	31,930
Average	26,300	24,900

Note: [a] Finance does not include banking.
Source: Computations provided by Industry Canada, based on data from the U.S. Department of Commerce, Bureau of Economic Analysis.

and salaries in the petroleum, finance and service industries are substantially lower. Table 6 also indicates that the proportion of FDI employment covered by a collective agreement is roughly similar for Canadian FDI and for FDI from other countries, at about 19 percent. This is slightly higher than the overall U.S. rate of about 16 percent, but about half of the overall rate in Canada of around 40 percent.

The overall picture that emerges shows that approximately 700,000 jobs associated with Canadian FDI in the United States constitute about 16 percent of all FDI employment in the United States, and about 7 percent of employment in Canada. The numbers appear to be increasing, at least since the mid 1980s, although the yearly fluctuations are substantial. Most of the employment in Canadian FDI in the United States is in manufacturing and retail trade, with about one-quarter of it in the Southeast. The collective agreement coverage of that employment tends to be slightly higher than the U.S. average, but about half of the coverage in Canada (see Table 7).

This data may suggest the possibility that some of the Canadian FDI into the United States may be in response to the lower wages and less unionized and regulated environment, especially in the sunbelt.[11] If so, this could put pressure on Canadian governments to harmonize their labour laws and policies towards that lower level of regulation. However, such a conclusion is hazardous, because of the aggregate nature of the data and the lack of more direct information on the determinants of Canadian FDI abroad.

TABLE 7

PROPORTION OF FDI EMPLOYMENT IN THE UNITED STATES COVERED BY COLLECTIVE AGREEMENTS, 1987, % BY INDUSTRY

INDUSTRY	FROM ALL COUNTRIES	FROM CANADA	WITHIN CANADA
Petroleum	9.14	9.09	n/a
Manufacturing	22.45	23.26	45.1
Wholesale Trade	11.59	n/a	13.6
Retail Trade	20.71	n/a	17.0
Finance[a]	0.60	0.00	n/a
Insurance	0.23	n/a	n/a
Real Estate	n/a	n/a	n/a
Services	14.23	n/a	42.7
Other	n/a	28.84	n/a
Average	18.87	19.08	40.0

Note: [a] Finance does not include banking.
Source: Computations provided by Industry Canada, based on data from the U.S. Department of Commerce, Bureau of Economic Analysis. Figures for "Within Canada" are based on unpublished data from the Labour Market Activity Survey of the year 1988.

As noted in our introduction, the two main labour-market issues with respect to outward FDI are that such investment is tantamount to exporting jobs, and that it deters governments from developing their own independent labour laws and regulations. If the existing data on the labour-market characteristics of Canadian outward FDI are inadequate to test these hypotheses, what data is needed?

As discussed in the section on the effect of outward FDI on labour regulation, to test the hypothesis that outward FDI deters independent labour policies, it is necessary to have information on: 1) the extent to which labour regulations differ across countries; 2) the extent to which these differences affect labour costs; 3) the extent to which such labour cost differences affect FDI through plant location and investment decisions; and 4) the extent to which such FDI affects government decisions with respect to labour regulations. As indicated, we have remarkably little information on any of these links.

With respect to the other main labour market issue (the exporting of jobs) we argue that the focus should not be on empirical evidence that counts jobs lost or gained, but rather on adjustment issues.

CONCLUSIONS

IN ANALYZING THE POTENTIAL JOB LOSSES and gains associated with outward FDI from Canada to Mexico that may be induced by free trade agreements like the NAFTA, it is important to emphasize that much of that investment would likely occur even without the NAFTA. As well, much of it may simply reflect investment diversion from other countries that may have attracted the investment. This is analogous to the fact (on the product market side) that many of the increased imports into Canada will reflect trade diversion from low-wage producers in Asia and elsewhere, to importing from Mexico. The net effect of the NAFTA on increasing outward FDI may therefore be very small. Also, since Mexico is geographically closer than many other countries to which the investment may go, the induced increases in exports and head-office activities are more likely to spill back into Canada. Of course the United States is even better situated (geographically, culturally and linguistically) to take advantage of those feedback effects to capital exports and head-office activities.

It is tempting to regard the job content of outward FDI as jobs that are lost to Canada because the investment is not made in Canada. In that view, the repatriation of the approximately 700,000 jobs associated with Canadian FDI in the United States alone could represent the elimination of much of Canadian unemployment.

Our perspective is that, as appealing as it may be, this temptation should be resisted. It is tantamount to the lump of labour fallacy that assumes there is a fixed number of jobs in the economy, and that investing in another country is equivalent to exporting jobs. The job counting exercise and the lump of labour fallacy have a long history in labour economics. It was used to count the number of jobs displaced by mechanization and computers, but few would now say that we should not have accepted such technological change. It was used to count the number of "male" jobs displaced by females when they entered the labour force in larger numbers, but few would now say we should reduce female labour force participation to save male jobs. Such changes can bring adjustment consequences as particular individuals may well be displaced from specific jobs. But the number of jobs is not fixed, and acting as though it is fixed is likely to bring more severe adjustment consequences when the adjustments ultimately ensue if restructuring does not occur on a more continuous basis.

If a Canadian-owned factory is closed in the United States and re-opened in Canada, this move may obviously create jobs in a particular locality in Canada. However, it may also displace the output of other Canadian firms, with associated job losses. Also, if the Canadian factory is not competitive, the jobs created are not likely to be sustainable in the long run. In a dynamically changing economy the number of jobs is not fixed but is dependent upon a variety of factors, including the state of aggregate demand as well as the competitiveness of the economy. Our perspective is that focusing on the adjustment issues necessary to ensure competitiveness is likely to create more sustainable jobs in the long run.

The danger of the job-counting exercise is that it focuses attention on the symptom rather than the cause and so it may inhibit dealing with the underlying causes of job losses. Apart from important issues of aggregate demand, job gains and losses have to do with such structural issues as productivity, competitiveness, labour cost, and adjusting from declining to expanding sectors.

Refining the job-counting procedures is like taking a wrong number to 10 decimal points. It implies a degree of sophistication in the results that the underlying causal relations simply do not merit. It also redirects attention from the key issue of an equitable and efficient labour adjustment strategy, whether the pressure for that adjustment comes from free trade, global competition, technological change, the aging work force, the increased labour force participation of women, or outward FDI.

ENDNOTES

1 Of course, each of these concerns has a potential counterpart on the benefit side of the equation. Multinationals may behave as good corporate citizens because they are concerned with their image. The transfer of personnel and workplace practices can also have positive spillover benefits akin to technology transfers.

2 Graham & Krugman (1991) provide evidence from foreign direct investment in the United States indicating that such foreign owned firms have a higher propensity to import than do domestic firms. They did not have a propensity, however, to keep the 'good' high-paying jobs or research and development in their home country.

3 These longer-run positive effects are emphasized in the studies by Globerman and by Rao, Legault & Ahmad in this volume. The latter paper also provides empirical evidence on both the positive performance of outward-oriented firms and the fact that outward FDI does not seem to displace domestic investment.

4 In the general context of trade and industrial policy, efficiency wages are discussed in Dickens & Lang (1988) and in Katz & Summers (1989).

5 The likely effect of free trade on labour laws and regulations in Canada is discussed in Gunderson (1993b, c) in the context of the degree to which the legislation supports or conflicts with market forces. Betcherman (1993) also provides a discussion of global competition and labour law.

6 See, for example, Kravis & Lipsey (1982), Schneider & Frey (1985), and Wheeler & Moody (1992).

7 The presentation in Cypher (1992) differs from that given here, and occasionally there are small differences in some of the numbers.

8 This assumption may be questioned on the grounds that Ireland could give the United States a platform for exporting to the EEC, given the common external tariff that existed in all EEC countries against non-EEC countries. However, in the case of Mexico the tariff elimination means that the United States does not need to invest in Mexico to gain access to the Mexican market.

9 These results are discussed in Schoepfle (1991).

10 Many of these studies are discussed in Dickens (1988) and Caves (1982).

11 Some survey evidence suggesting that this is the case is provided in Williams& Brinker (1985).

ACKNOWLEDGEMENTS

FOR HELPFUL COMMENTS we are indebted to Gordon Betcherman, Steven Globerman and John Knubley, as well as other participants at the conference on Canadian-Based Multinational Enterprises. For assistance with the data we are indebted to Marc Legault.

Bibliography

Adler, M. and G. Stevens. "The Trade Effects of Direct Investment." *Journal of Finance*, 29 (May 1974): 655-76.

Bergsten, C., T. Horst and T. Moran. *American Multinationals and American Interests*. Washington, D.C.: Brookings Institution, 1978.

Betcherman, G. "Labour in a More Global Economy." Ottawa: Human Resources and Labour Canada, 1993.

Betcherman, G. and M. Gunderson. "Canada-U.S. Free Trade and Labour Relations." *Labour Law Journal* 41, (August 1990): 454-60.

Buckley, P. and P. Artisien. "Policy Issues of Intra-EC Direct Investment." *Journal of Common Market Studies*, 26 (1987): 207-30.

Buckley, P. and M. Z. Brooke. *International Business Studies: An Overview*. Cambridge, Mass.: Blackwell Publishers, 1992.

Business International Corporation. *The Effects of U.S. Direct Corporate Investment: 1960-1970*. New York: Business International Corporation, 1972.

Campbell, D.C. and R.G. McElrath. *The Employment Effects of Multinational Enterprises in the U.S. and of American Multinationals Abroad*. Geneva: International Labour Office, Multinational Enterprises Program, Working Paper Number 64, 1990.

Carlton, D. "Why New Firms Locate Where They Do: An Econometric Model. In *Interregional Movements and Regional Growth*. Edited by W. Wheaton. Washington, D.C.: The Urban Institute, 1979, pp. 13-50.

Caves, R. *Multinational Enterprise and Economic Analysis*. Cambridge: Cambridge University Press, 1982.

Crockell. H. "Managing Canadian Subsidiaries in a Free Trade Environment." *Sloan Management Review* 29 (Fall 1987): 71-6.

Cypher, J. "Labor Market Implications of the Mexico-U.S. Free Trade Agreement." Paper presented at the Allied Social Science Association Meetings, New Orleans, January 1992.

Dickens, W. "The Effects of Trade on Employment: Techniques and Evidence." In *The Dynamics of Trade and Employment*. Edited by L. Tyson, W. Dickens & J. Zysman. Cambridge: Ballinger, 1988, pp. 41-85.

Dickens, W. and K. Lang. "Why it Matters What We Trade: A Case for Active Policy." In *The Dynamics of Trade and Employment*. Edited by L. Tyson, W. Dickens & J. Zysman. Cambridge: Ballinger, 1988, pp. 87-112.

Faux, J. and W. Spriggs. U.S. Jobs and the Mexico Trade Proposal. Briefing Paper. Washington, DC: Economic Policy Institute, 1991.

Flanagan, R. *NAFTA and Competitive Adjustments in North American Labor Markets*. Vancouver: Fraser Institute, 1992.

Forget, C. E. and D. Denis. "Canadian Foreign Direct Investment in the United States: Reasons and Consequences." In *Outward Bound: Canadian Direct Investment in the United States*. Edited by A. M. Rugman. Toronto: C. D. Howe Institute, 1985.

Frank, R. and R. Freeman. "Distributional Consequences of Direct Foreign Investment." In *The Impact of International Trade and Investment on Employment: A Conference of the U.S. Department of Labor*. Edited by W. Dewald. Washington, D.C.: U.S. Government Printing Office, 1978.

Ghandhi, P. "The Free Trade Agreement and Canadian Investment in Northern New York." *Canadian Journal of Regional Science* 13 (Summer/Autumn 1990): 205-19.

Glikkman, N. and D. Woodward. *The New Competitors: How Foreign Investors are Changing the U.S. Economy*. New York: Basic Books, 1989.

Goreki, P. *Patterns of Canadian Foreign Direct Investment Abroad*. Ottawa: Statistics Canada Analytical Branch, 1990.

Graham, E. and P. Krugman. *Foreign Direct Investment in the United States*. Washington, D.C.: Institute for International Economics, 1991.

Gunderson, M. "Regional Dimensions of the Impact of Free Trade on Labour." *Canadian Journal of Regional Science*, 13 (Summer/Autumn 1990): 243-54.

Gunderson, M. and D. Hamermesh. "The Effect of Free Trade on the North American Labour Market." In *The Dynamics of North American Trade and Investment: Canada, Mexico and the United States*. Edited by C. Reynolds, L. Waverman & G. Bueno. Stanford, CA: Stanford University Press, 1991, pp. 225-40.

Gunderson, M. "Wage and Employment Impacts of Free Trade." Vancouver: Fraser Institute, 1993a.

_____. "Labour Market Impacts of Free Trade." Vancouver: Fraser Institute, 1993b.

_____. "Labour Adjustment under NAFTA: Canadian Issues." *North American Outlook*, 1993c.

Gunderson, M. and A. Verma. "Canadian Labour Policies and Global Competition." *Canadian Business Law Journal*, 20 (March 1992): 63-89.

Hawkins, R. U.S. Multinational Investment in Manufacturing and Domestic Economic Performance. Occasional Paper No. 1. Washington, D.C.: Centre for Multinational Studies, 1972a.

_____. Job Displacement and the Multinational Firm: A Methodological Review. Occasional Paper No. 3. Washington, D.C.: Centre for Multinational Studies, 1972b.

Herring, R. and T. Willett. "The Relationship between U.S. Direct Investment at Home and Abroad." *Rivista Internazionale de Scienze Economiche e Commerciale*, 20 (January 1973): 72-82.

Hinojosa-Ojeda, R. and R. McCleery. "U.S.- Mexico Interdependence, Social Pacts and Policy Alternatives: A Computable General Equilibrium Approach." *Estudios Economicos*, 5, 2 (1991).

Hinojosa-Ojeda, R. and S. Robinson. "Labor issues in a North American Free Trade Area." Paper presented at the Brookings Institution Conference on NAFTA: An Assessment of the Research. Washington, D.C., April 9-10, 1992.

Horst, T. "Firm and Industry Determinants of the Decision to Invest Abroad." *Review of Economics and Statistics*, 54 (August 1972): 258-66.

_____. "The Impact of American Investments Abroad on U.S. Exports, Imports and Employment." In *The Impact of International Trade and Investment on Employment: A Conference of the U.S. Department of Labor*. Edited by W. Dewald. Washington, D.C.: U.S. Government Printing Office, 1978.

Jager, E. and R. Kutscher. "U.S. Labor and Multinationals." In *U.S. Labor and the Multinational Enterprise*. Edited by D. Kujawa. New York: Praeger, 1975.

Katz, L. F. and L. H. Summers. "Can Inter-industry Wage Differentials Justify Strategic Trade Policy?" In *Trade Policies for International Competitiveness*. Edited by R. C. Feenstra. Chicago: University of Chicago Press, 1989.

Kieschnick, M. "Taxes and Growth: Business Incentives and Economic Development. In *State Taxation Policy*. Edited by M. Barker. Durham, NC: Duke University Press, 1983, pp. 155-280.

Knubley, J., W. Krause and Z. Sadeque. "Canadian Acquisitions Abroad: Patterns and Motivations. In *Corporate Globalization Through Mergers and Acquisitions*. Edited by L. Waverman. Calgary: University of Calgary Press, 1991, pp. 23-58.

Koechlin, T. and M. Larudee. "The High Cost of NAFTA." *Challenge*, (September-October 1992a): 19-26.

Koechlin, T. and M. Larudee. "Effects of the North American Free Trade Agreement on Investment, Employment and Wages in Mexico and the U.S." University of Massachusetts at Amherst, Economics Department working paper, 1992b.

Kraseman, T. and B. Barker. "Employment and Payroll Costs of U.S. Multinational Companies." *Surveys of Current Business*, 53 (October 1973): 36-44.

Kravis, I. and R. Lipsey. "The Location of Overseas Production and Production for Export by U.S. Multinational Firms." *Journal of International Economics*, 12 (1982): 201-23.

_____. "The Effect of Multinational Firms' Foreign Operations on their Domestic Employment." National Bureau of Economic Research Working Paper 2760, 1990.

Leamer, E. "Wage Effects of a U.S.-Mexican Free Trade Agreement." Paper presented at a conference on Mexico-U.S. Free Trade Agreement, Brown University, 1991.

Lipsey, R. and M. Weiss. "The Relation of U.S. Manufacturing Abroad to U.S. Exports." American Statistical Association Proceedings: Business and Economics Section, (1969): 497-508.

_____. "Foreign Production and Exports in Manufacturing Industries." *Review of Economics and Statistics*, 63 (November 1981): 488-94.

Litvak, I. and C. Maule. *The Canadian Multinationals*. Toronto: Butterworths, 1981.

Longair, J. "Economic Integration in a Multilateral World." *Canadian Business Review*, 17 (Summer 1990): 53-5.

Mead, W. *The Low Wage Challenge to Global Growth: The Labor Cost-Productivity Imbalance in Newly Industrialized Countries*. Washington, D.C.: Economic Policy Institute, 1991.

Prestowitz, C., R. Cohen, P. Morici and A. Tonelson. *The New North American Order: A Win-Win Strategy for U.S. Mexico Trade*. Washington, D.C.: Economic Strategy Institute, 1991.

Rugman, A. "Living with Free Trade: How MNC'S will Adjust to Trade Liberalization." *Business Quarterly*, 52 (Fall 1987): 85-90.

_____. *Outward Bound: Canadian Direct Investment in the United States*. Toronto: C.D. Howe Institute, 1987.

Rugman, A. and A. Verbeke. "Strategic Responses to Free Trade." In *Business Strategies After Free Trade*. Edited by M. Farrow & A. Rugman. Toronto: C.D. Howe Institute, 1988.

_____. "Foreign Direct Investment in North America: Current Patterns and Future Relationships in Canada, the United States and Mexico." Presented at a Conference organized by the Fraser Institute and the Centre for International studies at the University of Toronto, November 1991.

Safarian, E. "The Relationship between Trade Agreements and International Direct Investments." In *Canadian Trade at a Crossroads*. Edited by W. Conklin & T. Courchene. Toronto: Ontario Economic Council, 1985.

Schneider, F. and B. Frey. "Economic and Political Determinants of Foreign Direct Investment." *World Development*, 13 (1985): 161-75.

Schoepfle, G. "Labor Issues Related to a U.S.-Mexico FTA: A View from the North." Washington, D.C.: U.S. Department of Labor, Bureau of International Affairs, 1991.

Schoepfle, G. and J. Perez-Lopez. "U.S. Employment Effects of a North American Free

Trade agreement: A Survey of Issues and Estimated Employment Effects." Washington, D.C.: U.S. Department of Labor, Bureau of International Affairs, 1992.

Wheeler, D. and A. Moody. "International Investment Location Decisions: The Case of U.S. Firms." *Journal of International Economics*, 33 (1992): 57-76.

Williams, S. and W. Brinker. "A Survey of Foreign Firms Recently Locating in Tennessee." *Journal of Public, Urban and Regional Policy*, 16 (July 1985): 54-63.

Donald J.S. Brean
Faculty of Management
University of Toronto

7

Taxation and Canadian
Direct Investment Abroad

INTRODUCTION

TAXATION OF FOREIGN DIRECT INVESTMENT is a modern concern made complicated by an out-of-date tax: the corporate tax. Canada confronted this
issue earlier than most other countries. In the 1960s, the Carter Commission
came within a whisker of recommending the elimination of the corporate tax,
only to see a grand plan unravel by the complications caused by foreigners and
foreign-owned capital. Carter acknowledged the rude reality that a corporate
tax is the only practical way to tax income earned by foreign-owned business
in Canada. With limited scope to discriminate between foreign-owned and
domestic business, Carter reluctantly proposed to keep the corporate tax,
while confining corporate-personal integration to Canadian residents.

Compared to the problem of dealing with foreigners who establish
businesses in Canada, the question of how Canada ought to tax Canadian
direct investment abroad (CDIA) presents some relatively straightforward
options. Canada can double-tax such income, or relieve foreign taxes in some
fashion, or exempt the lot.

Canada has opted for the last method. To do otherwise would create the
formidable administrative challenge of chasing CDIA around the world for the
prospect of relatively little potential revenue. Moreover, since the countries in
which CDIA is invested are in a significantly more advantageous position to
tax income earned from CDIA, an advantage similar to the one Canada enjoys
in taxing inward foreign investment, if Canada were to be more fiscally aggressive toward CDIA, it would risk perpetrating international double taxation.

The general thrust of the following discussion of taxation of CDIA is
that current Canadian policy, which in some senses is remarkably simple, is
nevertheless reasonable in view of the complex and sometimes conflicting
objectives of corporate taxation in an open economy, where foreign direct
investment flows both ways. The policy challenge in the international dimension
of corporate taxation is to mitigate the distortive effects of tax on cross-border
investment without either compromising the integrity of the domestic tax

system, causing undue loss of revenue, or imposing unreasonable demands on tax administration. All open countries face a similar policy challenge. Many nations, Canada among them, have reached a practical common accord in these international corporate tax matters – each taxes the income from inward foreign direct investment in the same manner as domestic capital, while the income of outward foreign direct investment is not taxed by the capital-exporting nation.

From the premise that Canadian taxation of CDIA is generally not in need of wholesale reform – we cannot tax CDIA less and we ought not to tax it more – the analysis concentrates on the three-pronged topic of tax, international competitiveness and the so-called "new trade theory". Research and development, especially its sensitivity to taxation, emerges as the central theme of this study. Canadian taxation with CDIA in mind is advised to promote two objectives: first, to foster a domestic fiscal environment that encourages at-home development of the intangible assets of multinational enterprises (MNEs) and exportable technology and, second, to promote an international approach to Canadian corporate taxation that achieves proper fiscal compensation for foreign-source rents generated from Canadian technology.

The next section of this study outlines the objectives of and constraints on the taxation of internationally mobile capital (of which direct investment is one of two components). The other component, portfolio capital, consists of bonds and non-controlling equity. Portfolio capital is larger in volume than direct investment, it tends to be more sensitive to taxation, and it is a greater risk to national fiscal sovereignty. The line between direct investment and portfolio capital is unfortunately fuzzy, with the result that the difficulty in Canada's international tax policy is due largely to the lack of a clear distinction.

Most nations, including Canada, are both capital exporters and capital importers in *both* categories of international investment. This situation creates what may be described as the "policy parallax", in reference to conflicting national objectives in international tax affairs. This issue is the focus of the next section, where the discussion turns to the ways in which the relative importance that a nation assigns to various objectives are likely to change as that nation's international investment position changes.

This is followed by a selective summary, in point form, of empirical research on the effects of taxation on the investment, financing and intra-firm pricing decisions of multinational enterprise. Next there is a closer examination of international tax differentials and tax arbitrage. Tax-based policies that are inadvisable, either because MNEs are likely to neutralize the intended effects or because the net effects are negative for Canada, are distinguished from policies that are both feasible and worthwhile for Canada.

The next two sections introduce a modern case for pro-active tax policy toward CDIA, aimed at encouraging and capturing technological spin-offs from research and development (R&D) done in Canada while at the same time increasing Canadian tax revenue from rents earned through international production and marketing spawned by such R&D. The policy targets the nexus of technology, CDIA and taxation. In view of evidence presented that tax-based incentives for R&D in Canada are in fact both generous and effective, I recommend reforms of Canadian corporate tax policy – within international conventions for taxation – which result in reallocation of MNE income from foreign sources (where it is untaxed by Canada) to Canada, where it would be taxed. The final section offers my summary comments.

Canadian Taxation and CDIA

THREE KEY POINTS ABOUT CANADIAN TAX TREATMENT of direct investment abroad shape the following analysis. First, as mentioned, Canada does not tax foreign-source corporate income. Few nations do. Second, we could not effectively tax such income even if we wanted to. And third, all international tax issues are framed in a set of bilateral agreements. Each nation formalizes its relations in a network of tax treaties that represents a balance of competing fiscal and commercial interests. In the short term, Canadian freedom to revise policy is limited by the terms of our tax treaties (agreements we have made in the past) whereas in the longer term our international tax policy is constrained by the need to reach new agreements with other nations, or risk retaliation.

Before 1972, Canada was a tax haven. Dividends received by a corporation in Canada from a non-resident corporation that held more than 25 percent of its voting stock were not subject to further tax in Canada. This was a great enticement for tax planners. A Canadian corporation could easily establish a holding company in a tax haven and transfer ownership of its international assets to that holding company. Since the holding company satisfied the 25 percent plus rule, foreign source income could flow through it en route to Canada, where it was exempt from Canadian tax. Virtually all forms of foreign income, including interest, rents, and royalties were converted into tax-free dividends to the Canadian parent. In fact, the arrangement was so inviting that many foreign-owned firms in Canada channelled their worldwide income here.

While Canada could perhaps be blasé about foreigners arriving here to park income and savings away from taxes in their homelands, a more serious issue was that Canadian savings could (and did) flow abroad, earn income, and return to Canada with tax-exempt status.

To address this problem, Canada created the concept of foreign accrual property income (FAPI) and declared this category of foreign-source income to be taxable in Canada. FAPI includes virtually all forms of income except active business income earned by corporate affiliates, such as income from financial investments, real estate rental income, and most capital gains. A foreign affiliate is defined in the *Canadian Tax Act* as a non-resident corporation in which a Canadian taxpayer has an equity percentage of not less than 10 percent. The FAPI provisions go hand-in-hand with the foreign affiliate rule, since the focus is on an off-shore corporate tax liability.

The intent of Canadian policy is to identify the original sources of income flowing from (or through) a nonresident corporate affiliate and then to organize the dividend flow into Canada into active business income and passive or property income. Canada takes a hands-off territorial approach to income from direct investment and a residence approach – a worldwide claim – to the rest. Active business income of CDIA is dubbed tax-exempt surplus and, as the name implies, it is categorically free of Canadian tax.[1]

Canadian taxation of foreign-source income from portfolio investment is intended primarily to constrain opportunities to divert income and capital to tax havens. Foreign-source interest income of individuals and financial institutions, in particular off-shore branches of banks, is taxed in Canada on an accrual basis with credit for foreign taxes paid.[2]

Canadian tax policy with respect to foreign-source income begins with a distinction between portfolio and direct investment. Through the territorial approach, Canada allows CDIA to compete on an equal tax footing with domestic investors in foreign countries, as well as with other potential international direct investors resident in countries that, like Canada, do not tax their direct investment abroad. Canada promotes capital-import neutrality[3] for direct investment while containing domestic revenue loss through foreign portfolio investment.

Canadian policy seems consistent with a particular perception of Canada's place in the world. First, Canada is a major net importer of capital, since foreign savings are essential to the Canadian pattern of investment and consumption. Second, Canadian business has worthwhile direct investment opportunities abroad which, if exploited, can have potential feedback effects on the Canadian economy. In other words, foreign direct investment is apparently considered to be largely complementary to Canadian domestic investment. Third, Canadian foreign portfolio investment is unambiguously a substitute for portfolio investment in Canada; it is a drain on Canadian savings, and may be placed outside Canada to avoid Canadian tax. Finally, Canadian corporations are frequently involved in both foreign direct and portfolio investment, and the line between them is not always easy to draw.[4]

Whatever the empirical merits of each step of this argument – and they are for the most part far from clear – current policy generally makes most sense if these propositions are accepted: that net capital imports are essential in a macroeconomic context for external balance; that industry-specific direct capital exports are good; that out-bound financial portfolio investment is bad; and that it is difficult to tell the difference between good and bad outflows.

THE POLICY PARALLAX

IN INTERNATIONAL TAXATION, as in politics, where you stand depends on where you sit. International tax is all about potential gains and losses, and the distribution thereof. Each country's view of international tax relations

TABLE 1

CANADIAN TAXATION OF FOREIGN-SOURCE INCOME

TYPE OF FOREIGN SOURCE INCOME	WHEN TAXED	AMOUNT TAXED
Portfolio Dividends	When received in Canada	Gross dividends before withholding tax; foreign tax credit granted to maximum 15% of Canadian taxable income
Foreign Accrual Property Income (FAPI) of Controlled Foreign Affiliates	When earned by affiliate; no deferral	Taxpayer's participating percentage
Active Business Income of a Foreign Affiliate that is not a Controlled Foreign Affiliate	When paid in dividends to the taxpayer	Except where exempt by treaty, amount paid, grossed up for foreign corporate and withholding taxes
Tax Exempt Surplus	Not taxed in Canada	

depends on the gains that it stands to capture. Consequently the international dimension of each nation's tax policy is shaped by its net foreign asset position and, especially, the trend in that position.

The United States is often a pertinent point of reference for Canadian economic policy, either for comparison or for contrast. The United States is close and familiar and, of course, Canada and the United States generate the greatest bilateral volume of trade and investment in the world. Although in many fundamental respects our tax systems are similar, the U.S. and Canadian approaches to policy are significantly different on international tax matters.

For our focus on CDIA, the international dimension of U.S. policy – or how the United States taxes the foreign-source income of U.S. residents – is not a crucial issue. However, since the United States taxes CDIA on the basis of source, it is quite relevant to focus on the U.S. corporate tax applied within the country. CDIA in the United States bears U.S. tax. The United States extends "national treatment", which means that the U.S. corporate tax on U.S.-source income does not discriminate between domestic and foreign-owned companies.

There are two practical reasons for turning our attention briefly to the United States in our discussion of CDIA. First, about two-thirds of CDIA is in the United States. Thus the U.S. corporate tax is the source tax on the bulk of CDIA. Second, in recent years a significant amount of empirical research has been directed to the international dimension of U.S. taxation, encompassing taxation of foreign investment in the United States as well as U.S. investment abroad. Certain findings, especially concerning investment inbound to the

United States, directly concern CDIA or they capture tax-driven adjustments and manoeuvres by multinational enterprise in general.

The heightened American interest in international tax matters is easy to appreciate. The United States has the largest stock of investment abroad. This stock began to accumulate in the early part of the century and it swelled in the post-war period until the early 1980s. Since then, the tide has turned and the United States has become a major capital importer. In fact it is now the world's largest debtor nation.

As simultaneous creditor and debtor, the United States has encountered the international tax policy parallax. The United States finds itself trying to buttress its residence-based system in order to protect the integrity of domestic taxation, while at the same time tightening up on taxation of foreign firms in the country (as well as U.S.-based MNEs) and paying close attention to the effects of the international interaction of tax systems on investment in the United States.

IN A COMPLICATED WORLD, WHAT DO WE KNOW?

EMPIRICAL ANALYSIS OF INTERNATIONAL TAX ISSUES generally addresses a trio of questions. Virtually every open economy is interested in the answers.

- First, does the international structure of taxation influence the international allocation of capital? If it does, taxation is a potential cause of inefficiencies.

- Second, does the international mobility of capital erode national fiscal sovereignty, including the scope of nations to tax capital?

- Third, do transfer pricing and multinational corporate financial manoeuvering result in significant international income shifting?

For a variety of reasons, the empirical front of international tax research has been more active in the United States than anywhere else. Two major U.S. tax reforms within a decade, the first Reagan reforms of 1982 and *The Tax Reform Act* of 1986, provide a rich set of changes in tax structure, rates and regulations that serve the needs of empirical research. In addition, the U.S. tax authorities and The Bureau of Economic Analysis has redoubled its efforts to assemble data appropriate to the study of policy influences on international trade and investment. As mentioned, U.S. empirical research on international tax matters is often directly relevant to the Canadian issues at hand.

Among the pertinent empirical findings involving taxation and foreign direct investment based largely on the U.S. experience are:

- The interaction of source (e.g., U.S.) taxes and foreign residence (e.g., Canadian) taxes significantly affects foreign investment decisions (Scholes & Wolfson, 1990).

- Sub-national (state) tax considerations influence decisions as to where foreign investment is located in the United States (Hines, 1993b). This also appears to be the case for direct investment in the European Community (Guisinger & He, 1992).

- Tax considerations affect MNE decisions to export rather than to produce off-shore (Grubert & Mutti, 1991).

- MNEs, including Canadian firms in the United States, make extensive use of circuitous financial routes in and out of the United States for purposes of minimizing tax (Papke, 1989).

- Foreign source earnings flow to the United States without residual tax liability to the U.S. Treasury (Hines & Hubbard, 1990).

- Transfer pricing erodes the U.S. corporate tax base (Grubert, Morck et al.) In the United States the IRS consistently loses important cases in court (e.g., Bausch & Lomb and Sunstrand).

- Foreign-controlled affiliates in the United States report strikingly less taxable income earned in the United States than do their domestically controlled counterparts (Grubert et al., 1993). The lower reported rate of return is due in large part – but not entirely – to international income shifting.

- MNEs shift income out of high-tax countries into the United States and from the United States to low-tax countries (Harris et al., 1993).

- Foreign income of affiliates of MNEs is shifted among off-shore locations, from high-tax to low-tax countries (Hines & Rice, 1990; Grubert & Mutti, 1991).

- U.S. domestic spending on research and development by MNEs is sensitive to the net-of-tax cost of R&D as governed by the R&D write-off provisions in U.S. tax law. Revenue-enhancing regulations requiring MNEs to reallocate R&D expense in line with international production and/or sales, raise the effective tax on – and negatively affect – U.S. R&D spending (Hines, 1993a).

The American empirical studies indicate that foreign direct investment is sensitive to tax in a variety of ways. It appears that FDI enjoys several degrees of freedom – through financial adjustments and transfer pricing – to exploit tax differentials while mitigating the anti-investment effects of tax. Each of these empirical findings has relevance to our examination of taxation and CDIA.

TAX DIFFERENTIALS AND SUBSIDIES THAT ATTRACT CDIA

A PRESSING CONCERN FOR CANADA with respect to CDIA is whether domestic employment and output is lost as a result of corporate decisions to establish operations abroad rather than at home. The tax dimension is determined by whether the international structure of tax encourages or discourages CDIA. As noted earlier, current Canadian policy is designed to put CDIA on an equal footing with other firms abroad. However, there is no assurance that CDIA is on the same tax footing as comparable investment opportunities in Canada.

Canadian investment has an incentive to flow to countries with lower tax rates than Canada and a disincentive to flow to countries with higher tax rates. The U.S. studies confirm the general significance of the effect of international tax differentials on foreign investment decisions. In short, Canada's exempt surplus rules, which leave the tax borne by CDIA to be determined by the country in which it is placed, inevitably create a spectrum of domestic-offshore tax differentials for outward-looking Canadian corporate investors.

The empirical question is the strength of the off-shore pull on Canadian investment. There is little reason to think that the sensitivity of CDIA to international tax differentials is any less than in cases examined from the American perspective, especially in view of the (apparently failed) American attempt to establish capital export neutrality. Boskin (1987) estimates that when U.S. policy raises the after-tax return enough to prompt a dollar of increased domestic investment, it also attracts between 8 cents and 27 cents of U.S.-inward direct investment. U.S.-inward direct investment includes CDIA.

Shah & Slemrod (1992) provide additional evidence of the importance of the source tax rate for investment decisions by multinational enterprises. They focus on the finance of foreign direct investment in Mexico with a model that includes both source and residence tax rates, as well as regulatory factors in Mexico and indices of country risk. Their results indicate clearly that both financial transfers to subsidiaries in Mexico and the flow of reinvested earnings increase significantly in response to reductions in the Mexican corporate tax rate. Shah & Slemrod also find that the flow of finance to foreign investment is sensitive to the difference between the Mexican and foreign tax rates. Guisinger & He (1992) reach essentially the same conclusion in a study of a larger international cross-section of source countries.

A comprehensive study by the OECD (1991) computes marginal effective tax rates (METRs) on investment in and out of 14 different industrial nations. Fourteen nations produce 182 source/residence combinations plus 14 METRs for domestic investment. The computations indicate that the international variance of METRs from the perspective of countries-as-capital-exporters (for example the variance of METRs on Canadian investment in 13 foreign countries) is substantially greater than the METRs from the perspective of countries-as-capital-importers (for example the 13-country variance of METRs on foreign investment in Canada). These results suggest that the current transnational tax system is closer to being a source-based system than a residence-based one.[5] This conclusion, in turn, implies that the current system linking the countries examined is closer to achieving capital-import neutrality than capital-export neutrality.

It is an empirical challenge to estimate international differentials in the after-tax cost of capital that potentially divert mobile investment from one country to another. In a 1992 study, Shoven & Topper conclude that for a similar investment in Canada and the United States, the after-tax cost of capital is similar. This suggests that investment location decisions, at least between these two countries, are driven by productivity factors and not substantially by tax differentials.

Eden (1991) focuses on the complex interaction of tax, tariff, and transfer pricing effects on cross-border investment, intra-firm trade, and the incentive to shift income in order to minimize tax. Marginal effective tax rates appear to influence long-run production location decisions, whereas statutory tax rates and tariffs influence intra-firm trade patterns and financial flows. This is fundamental to the way multinational enterprises accommodate international tax differentials. Multinationals mitigate the effect of relatively punitive tax on their real investment decisions by shifting deductible costs, especially financial costs and intangibles, to the higher tax jurisdiction while reporting income in the lower tax jurisdiction. The effect is to "endogenize" marginal effective tax rates. When tax influences on real investment are absorbed by financial adjustment, marginal effective tax rates are lower than they might otherwise be.

Perhaps the most notorious example of tax-driven international financial structuring is the "double dip" devised by Canadian firms to finance off-shore investment.[6] The process begins when a Canadian firm borrows money in Canada and takes the usual interest deduction here: the "first dip". The funds are then transferred at zero interest to a financial subsidiary in a tax haven. The financial subsidiary, in turn, on-loans the funds at market rates to an operating subsidiary in, for example, the United States. The operating subsidiary takes the interest deduction in the United States: a "double dip", since this involves the same debt for which an interest deduction was previously claimed by the parent company in Canada. The U.S. interest payments accrue as tax-free income to the financial subsidiary in the tax haven. The income of the operating subsidiary (which has been spared some U.S. tax as a result of the interest deduction) can be repatriated to Canada as tax-free intra-corporate dividends to the Canadian parent under the exempt surplus provision. Furthermore, the interest income that accrues in the tax haven may also eventually be repatriated to Canada. The net effect is that CDIA is financed with Canadian debt capital which, because of the double deduction of interest, is effectively cost free to the corporation.

The double dip is an example of international tax arbitrage. It also illustrates how MNEs can take advantage of the (ill-fitting) international facets of two (or more) countries' tax systems. However, the double dip is not illegal, although perhaps it should be. To put finance-based international tax arbitrage beyond the pale of law, it would be necessary to establish tight international interest-tracing rules, a formidable task. While this theme is beyond the scope of this study, it nevertheless points up a serious weakness in applying the FAPI rules which, as mentioned earlier, are intended to define the boundary between off-shore active business income, which Canada has properly decided not to tax, and the rest, which it ought to tax.

International investment decisions driven by tax differentials are bound to become less significant as the differentials diminish.[7] There are clear indications that this is, in fact, occurring throughout the world (Carey et al., 1993). Also, in virtually every nation's tax mix, the corporate tax itself is declining in relative importance. In Canada, for example, the share of corporate tax in total federal government revenue dropped from 40 percent in 1960 to 30 percent in 1970, and to less than 10 percent today.

As one distorting effect diminishes, however, another inevitably rises to take its place. Cities, municipalities, states and provinces offer an enticing array of subsidies, grants and similar inducements to new investment. Capital grants, local tax relief, and all manner of location-specific and investment-specific inducements create a high degree of randomness to international investment. A recent striking example is the package of incentives offered to Dofasco of Hamilton and Co-Steel of Toronto by the State of Kentucky to build a new mill in that state. The Canadian pair received more than $140 million in incentives from the state, or about US$ 200,000 per job. The chief executive of Dofasco reported that, "We didn't approach the Ontario government. They just wouldn't have been able to compete."[8]

Foreign subsidies to CDIA are not necessarily bad for Canada. In the case of the steel example, Canada ought to regret Dofasco's play abroad only if Canada is, in fact, an efficient steel producer by world standards. If Canada is not an efficient producer, Kentucky may have enticed Dofasco from Korea rather than Hamilton. Canada would be worse off if we went tit-for-tat in international competition for industry, only to prop up production that is at odds with our comparative advantage.

In general, Canada should seek to be non-intrusive in taxation of Canadian business abroad, and it should avoid interfering with signals from world markets which identify international commercial opportunities. In those cases where rents are a prospect or where externalities are generated, however, there is some scope for more pro-active policy.

THE MODERN CASE FOR PRO-ACTIVE POLICY TOWARD CDIA

WHEN INTERNATIONAL BUSINESS allows pure profit, it is in each country's interest to try to capture that profit. A modern case for pro-active tax policy toward CDIA goes further to suggest public sector support of the industrial activities that create those rents. Domestic business activity that promotes rents to be earned abroad is often activity that has significant domestic benefit in the form of technological spin-offs.

New theories of imperfect competition in trade provide useful insights into the rent-generating processes of multinational enterprise. For example, the distinction between headquarter functions as compared to the off-shore production and marketing activities of multinational enterprise suggests a basis for targeting particular corporate activities for encouragement (Graham & Krugman, 1989).

Headquarter functions are associated with the development and control of firm-specific intangible assets – the *sine qua non* of foreign direct investment (Rugman, 1981) and the root of a firm's competitive position in world markets (Porter, 1990). Firm-specific intangible assets include protected patents and advances in technology, and unique management processes, as well as reputation and trade names. Headquarter services – and the cost of delivering them – are closely allied with the creation and protection of intangible assets. They also underlie the corporate proficiency to penetrate foreign markets.

To distinguish MNE product-specific operations, which necessarily involve investment abroad, from at-home activities that organize and control international production, is a step to designing a tax policy which maximizes the national gain from investment abroad. The gains derive from encouraging high value-adding headquarters activities while allowing corporations to seek out markets and production sites abroad in line with the economic efficiencies that they are in the best position to identify and exploit.

For example, it is one thing to provide an incentive to McCains to produce New Brunswick potatoes for export to France. It is quite another thing to encourage the Canadian development of McCains' technology to produce, process and market potatoes grown in France.

Similarly, it is one thing to provide export finance for Bombardier's urban transit projects in cities abroad; income accrues to Bombardier and its Canadian suppliers. It is quite another thing to structure the Canadian tax system in a way that encourages Bombardier to develop further and improve its position in urban transit technology.

For purposes of policy, CDIA ought to be viewed as a mechanism to deliver Canadian management and technology to the world. The greatest economic pay-off from CDIA is the innovation and technological advances developed at home in order to produce and market products effectively abroad. To achieve fair exchange, Canadian taxation should encourage the inflow of foreign-source intra-firm payments, such as royalties and management fees, for the use of Canadian-based technology and managerial services.

To support those industrial activities in Canada that are the foundation for successful rent-generating production and marketing abroad, it is not surprising that the focus must be on research and development.

THE NEXUS OF TECHNOLOGY, CDIA AND TAXATION

MOST ANALYSES OF INDUSTRIAL STRATEGY attach special importance to industries at the frontier of technological advance. The Report of the Premier's Council (Ontario), *Competing in the Global Economy*, for example, worked from the premise that:

> the industrial competitiveness of a nation today, more than ever before, is influenced by its capabilities in science and technology. Countries which support their science and technology effort with substantial and well-targeted resources are more competitive in international markets. (Vol. I, p.197)

That same Report goes on to document thoroughly the fact that Canada's science and technology performance is well below the level of other leading industrial nations.

Inventing Our Future: An Action Plan for Canada's Prosperity, the report of a blue chip private-sector task force convened by the federal government, also underscored the negative.

> Failure to invest more in technology was a significant reason for our negligible productivity growth in the past 10 years. ... Canada's performance in research and development lags behind our competitors. The initiative for change lies with the private sector. (p.18)

Multinational companies, like nations, face a constant competitive challenge that must be met through R&D. Numerous empirical studies, including Beaudreau (1989), confirm the correlation of international investment and such industry-specific variables as:

> R&D expenditures as a percentage of sales, professional and technical workers as a percentage of industry employment, and product-differentiating characteristics.

The microeconomics of so-called internationally fragmented industry (Markusen, 1992), with its focus on imperfect competition, protected technology and the effort to appropriate economic rent, may provide new meaning and guidance for interventionist policies. Fragmentation refers to the disentangling of complex production processes such as manufacturing an automobile (but also designing and engineering it) into component processes directed to the lowest-cost sites on earth.

The traditional case for subsidized factors of production is that they enable firms to reach economies of scale and production efficiencies that are otherwise unattainable. The modern case for subsidized R&D is that its social value exceeds its private value because of externalities and the difficulty of appropriating returns from private R&D. Public policy is necessary to counteract the private tendency to under-invest in R&D.

The nexus of technology, CDIA and taxation deals with R&D, rent generation and the non-appropriability issue in an international context. Public sector support of the domestic R&D effort of Canadian-based multinational firms offers two potential benefits even when the resulting industrial knowledge is used primarily to exploit commercial opportunities abroad. First, research-intensive activity in Canada has external effects within Canada, based largely on the technologically improved environment that R&D fosters. Second, the applied research in Canada strengthens the complementarity of CDIA and domestic production. For example, many of Canada's most rapidly expanding export groups, such as financial and telecommunications services, advertising, exported R&D, medical and safety equipment, and precision equipment are also among our most technologically sophisticated (Schwanen, 1993). As these export lines mature, they are likely to establish off-shore platform CDIA, for distribution and local marketing, that expands the international demand for both Canadian-sourced intermediate products and Canada-based headquarters activities.

In summary, while Canada does not (and should not and likely could not) tax CDIA, Canada nevertheless has an opportunity to use domestic tax policy to forge strong links between off-shore production or marketing and the domestic base of Canadian international business. Canada may also increase its domestic tax revenue in the process.

"Mais il faut cultiver notre jardin." (Voltaire)

CANADA BENEFITS SUBSTANTIALLY from CDIA through spin-offs from industrial research plus high remuneration to headquarters activities. One policy objective ought to be to ensure that these crucial managerial and research activities are encouraged in Canada. The policy prescription is to create an appropriate tax environment in Canada for both types of activity. Another policy objective ought to be to ensure that off-shore use of Canadian technology and managerial acumen generates appropriate payments to the source, and that such payments are taxable by Canada.

In fact, the Canadian tax system currently provides very favourable treatment for domestic corporate spending on the sorts of investments that are considered to be linked to research and industrial innovation. For example, we have generous allowances for investment in training, technical equipment and information technology, including capital cost allowances that equal or exceed the rate of technological obsolescence. Canada has a lower after-tax cost of capital for investment in domestic R&D than most other countries, including the United States (Bruce, 1992). Canada also maintains a liberal tax treatment of risk, and in this respect we appear to be in line with the United States (Shoven & Topper, 1992).

Tax incentives for R&D appear to work. Berstein (1986), focusing on Canada's R&D tax credit and special allowances, reports that when there is no growth in the economy, R&D increases by $0.80 for every $1.00 in government revenue forgone by the tax incentive. When the economy is in a growth phase, induced R&D expenditures increase by more than a dollar for each $1.00 of forgone fiscal revenue. In addition, the business fixed-investment tax credit is an indirect incentive that causes R&D expenditures to increase by about 10 percent of the increase in investment. The evidence provided by Berstein, when coupled with earlier empirical studies by Longo (1984) and Switzer (1984) demonstrating the relatively high social rates of return to R&D, leads to the conclusion that fiscal incentive for R&D is well worth the price. In view of the present discussion of the nexus of technology, taxation and CDIA, the pro-incentive stance is advisable for Canada if incentives for R&D lead to technologically advanced products or processes which, even if production and marketing are eventually shifted abroad, depend on Canada-based management and continued R&D.

One prickly problem, however, is that tax policy never provides absolute incentive; it provides only a relative incentive insofar as there is less taxation, or when one activity suffers less tax than another. As a result, tax-based incentives for R&D or any other target are generally effective only for firms that are in a taxable position to begin with.[9] Corporate tax incentives for R&D in particular may miss precisely those firms most likely to embody features of endogenous technical change: Schumpeterian entrants, small growing firms, or fledgling firms with problems of investible cash flow (Boadway, 1993). The question is whether such firms would find foreign sites more attractive for investment. Table 2 presents comparative descriptions of the tax treatment of research and development expenses in Canada, the United States, Japan, France, and Germany.

There is significant room for constructive tax change. To explore options in the international dimension, the focus turns to modifications of the Canadian corporate tax, targeting headquarters activities so that these become concentrated in Canada. The issue can quickly become complex.

Corporate expenses incurred in Canada are allowable deductions only against Canadian corporate revenue. When a Canadian corporate parent provides services to an off-shore subsidiary, the Canadian corporation usually levies a management fee to the subsidiary, which becomes part of the parent's (Canadian) income. Costs of providing the headquarters service are deductible in Canada to the limit of this management fee income. The value of that deduction depends on the Canadian corporate tax rate. Meanwhile the management fee is deductible by the subsidiary in the country where it is located. The deduction reduces the subsidiary's income and correspondingly reduces the (Canadian) tax-exempt surplus that can flow to Canada. In effect, the management fee renders foreign source revenue subject to Canadian corporate taxation. If the subsidiary is located in a country with a corporate tax rate that is lower (higher) than the Canadian corporate tax rate, there is an international tax bias against (in favour of) headquarters activity in Canada. In practice, Canadian parent firms tend to minimize management fees charged to subsidiaries in low-tax jurisdictions.

As the Canadian base for technology and headquarters services for CDIA expands, Canada ought to exert its residence status more forcefully in order to tax rents and revenues generated abroad. The policy objective is to increase the in-Canada taxable income of Canada-based corporate affiliates of multinational enterprises by requiring full measure for the technology and industrial services that they provide. Unilaterally, Canada could broaden the scope of charges to foreign affiliates for headquarters services and increase the valuation of technology transferred abroad. The point is to reduce foreign-source exempt surplus and to increase Canadian taxable corporate income through greater vigilance in valuation of Canadian-based intangible assets. On a bilateral basis, through renegotiation of tax treaties, Canada could also press for tax deductibility of royalty payments and cost-sharing charges in foreign host countries. This would reduce the off-shore after-tax cost of using Canadian technology and increase the intra-firm reverse flow of revenue to Canada.

Canada might also press for lower host-country withholding taxes on royalties, fees and similar charges remitted to the parent firm, a position that favours the technology-exporting nation. On the other hand, Canada imports a significant amount of foreign technology and currently defends the domestic corporate tax base by regulation intended to prevent arbitrary overstatement of outbound payments for intangibles provided by foreigners. Countries that currently confront tough Canadian policy toward technology imports are unlikely to take kindly to Canadian initiatives that may cost them with respect to Canadian technology exports. Canada's old net export position constrains policy options for the new.

Recent proposals in the United States for a thorough re-working of the international dimension of U.S. tax policy are motivated by considerations similar to those that we have suggested as being pertinent for Canada.

TABLE 2

TAX TREATMENT OF R&D EXPENSES, SELECTED COUNTRIES, CIRCA 1990

	UNITED STATES	CANADA	JAPAN	FRANCE	GERMANY
Normal rules for deductibility					
Expensing Capitalization, with depreciation or amortization	By election, all R&D may be expensed currently. By election, applicable to all R&D expense. Minimum amortization period is 5 years.	By election, all R&D may be expensed currently. By election, applicable to all R&D expense.	By election, all R&D may be expensed currently. By election, applicable to development research. Amortization period is 5 years or less.[a]	Ordinarily, all R&D is expensed currently. By election, but only if R&D is likely to be successful. Amortization period is 5 years.	Most R&D is expensed currently. Applicable to fixed or intangible assets acquired for consideration; and R&D for the extension or substantial modification of an existing product.
Special treatment of qualified expenses	None.	None.	First-year additional depreciation for high-technology companies located in "technopolis"; 15 percent for buildings and facilities, and 30 percent for machinery.	First-year additional depreciation: 50 percent for buildings used in R&D; 25 percent to 50 percent accelerated depreciation for new R&D equipment and tools.	First-year additional depreciation: 40 percent for movable fixed assets and 15 percent for immovable fixed assets.[b]
Tax credits	13.2 percent tax credit for excess of current R&D over base amount for that year; the credit applies to 100 percent of in-house R&D, and to 65 percent of contract R&D.	20 percent tax credit for current "net" R&D; the maximum credit is 75 percent of federal tax liability; carry-forward of 10 years, and carryback of 3 years for excess credits.[c]	20 percent tax credit for excess of current R&D over largest post-1966 R&D budget; small and medium-size firms can elect a tax credit of 6 percent of all R&D expense; maximum credit is 10 percent of total tax liability. In addition, a 7 percent tax credit for property used in basic technology; the combined maximum is 15 percent.	50 percent tax credit for excess of current R&D over average R&D in previous 2 years; maximum credit is FF 5 million.	Investment grant of 20 percent of the cost of assets for the first DM 500,000; 7.5 percent for additional cost of assets.[d]

TABLE 2 (CONT'D)

	UNITED STATES	CANADA	JAPAN	FRANCE	GERMANY
Normal rules for deductibility					
Inbound	30 percent unless reduced by treaty; typical treaty rates are 0 percent to to 10 percent.	25 percent unless reduced by treaty; 10 percent with United States.	20 percent unless reduced by treaty; 10 percent with United States.	33 percent unless reduced by treaty; 5 percent with United States.	25 percent unless reduced by treaty; 0 percent with United States.
Outbound	A sale of technology is taxable as the sale of a capital asset if technology was patented or patentable; otherwise taxable as ordinary income.	Taxable as ordinary income, or treated as disposition of capital asset with 75 percent of the gain included in ordinary income.	Taxable as ordinary income.	Taxable as ordinary income, but a reduced rate of 15 percent is applied under most conditions.[e]	Taxable as ordinary income, with a limited tax credit for foreign taxes paid.
Transfer pricing	Basic arm's-length standard with an additional "commensurate with income" test.	Arm's-length standard.	Arm's-length standard.	Arm's-length standard.	Arm's-length standard.
Cost-sharing agreements[f]	Cost sharing based on expected relative profits is permitted.	No regulations.	No regulations.	No regulations.	No regulations.

Notes:
[a] Development research is defined as research on new goods and new techniques, adoption of a new technique or new managing system, exploitation of resources, or development of a market.
[b] The asset must remain in the taxpayer's permanent establishment for at least three years. Movable fixed assets must be used 100 percent for R&D purposes, and immovable fixed assets must be used at least two-thirds for R&D purposes. Special depreciation is 10 percent if the immovable fixed asset is used between one-third and two-thirds for R&D purposes.
[c] "Net" R&D is all R&D performed by the corporation minus government or non-government assistance such as grants, contract payments and reimbursements under cost-sharing agreements.
[d] All assets must be held for at least three years. Two-thirds of real estate assets must be used for R&D. If the real estate is used between one-third and two-thirds for R&D, the investment grant is calculated on half of the cost. Tangible movable assets and intangible fixed assets must be wholly used for R&D to qualify for the investment grant.
[e] The reduced rate applies to intellectual property created by in-house development, to intellectual property acquired from third parties that was capitalized and acquired more than three years previously, and to a French parent company that receives royalties from a foreign subsidiary.
[f] All of the countries listed recognize cost-sharing agreements for tax purposes. The general rule is that the relationship between shared costs and allocated benefits must be reasonable and consistent.

Source: KPMG, "Tax Treatment of Research & Development Expenses," 1990.

Hufbauer (1992) recommends a structure that is remarkably similar to what Canada already has in place. Hufbauer wants the United States to move to the exemption (territorial) system, whereby dividends and interest paid by foreign subsidiaries to U.S. parents would not be taxed by the United States. This system, in turn, would allow the United States to dismantle its cumbersome system of foreign tax credits. Furthermore, deductions would no longer be allowed against U.S. income for losses incurred abroad.

Hufbauer also recommends, as a general rule, that all headquarters expense for activity carried out in the United States be allocated entirely against U.S. income. Headquarters expense comprises R&D as well as general and administrative expense, including the costs of corporate-wide accounting, engineering, legal and similar services. Under current U.S. tax law, headquarters expenses are divided between U.S. domestic- and foreign-source income. The portion allocated against foreign income may not be recognized as a deduction by the foreign countries concerned because the activity took place in the United States. As a result, U.S.-based multinationals may incur a tax disadvantage to headquarters activities in the United States. That disadvantage would be eliminated by full deductibility of all associated costs, although the disadvantage is removed at the expense of U.S. tax revenue.

In contrast to Hufbauer, our proposal to press for source-country deductibility of appropriate headquarters expense and similar intangibles through the tax treaty network is a more practical solution for Canada. It is practical insofar as the best solution – no allocation of headquarters expense to foreign subsidiaries, and agreement that royalties flow to Canada untaxed by foreign countries – is impractical.

Boadway & Bruce (1993) note that if the United States were to shift to the exemption system for foreign-source income, Canada could more effectively dispense corporate tax incentives. As it now stands, the U.S. system may neutralize the effect of a Canadian tax credit for, say, R&D undertaken in Canada by a U.S.-owned subsidiary. Such incentive is blunted by the U.S. foreign tax crediting arrangements, since a tax incentive in Canada gives rise to a higher tax liability on income repatriated to the United States.

In view of the fact that Canada currently offers generous tax provisions for R&D at both the federal and provincial levels, and that tax experts in the United States recommend radical structural change to their system, making their system much like Canada's, it is difficult to suggest more that Canada could do. For instance, the R&D credit could encompass innovative production activities in order to encourage so-called "shop-floor" research, and/or the range of eligible expenses could be appropriately broadened. Indeed, this is the direction of refinements and adjustments in recent Canadian policy initiatives. Clark et al. (1992) examine the motivation for recent changes to the Canadian scientific research and experimental development tax credits, and they address several key policy issues associated with their design.

Technical design issues, which inevitably have an important bearing on the effectiveness of tax-based incentives, include the question of whether incentives should apply to all R&D activity or only to the incremental portion, and whether tax credits that cannot be used by a performing business can flow through from the R&D performer to other investors.

As tax expenditures, it is likely that Canadian R&D incentives could be made more effective by focussing on the margin, as is currently done by the United States, Japan and France. These countries link their R&D tax credits to expenditures that exceed a specified base amount.[10] The problem with the incremental approach is that when an (incremental) credit is based on a moving-average of R&D, current R&D spending becomes linked to future tax credits: that is, R&D expenditures made today reduce tax credits in the future.[11]

R&D tax credits are a form of conditional finance. The incentives are attractive insofar as performing activity leads to tax relief. If a firm is non-taxable, however, a tax credit has no immediate value to the performing firm unless the R&D credit is refundable to the firm or the unused credit can flow through to taxable investors. Unused credits that flow through to investors are generally heavily discounted, and their value is therefore less than the fiscal cost to the government (Jenkins, 1990), making them a form of revenue leakage as well as an inefficient incentive. The Canadian system provides refunds rather than flowthrough of credits for scientific research and experimental development. Full refunds are extended to Canadian-controlled private corporations with taxable income under $200,000 on the credits earned in respect of the first $2 million of qualifying current R&D expense in a year. The limitation is based on size and reflects the fact that small firms are less diversified than larger firms, and their cash flow and other financing sources are generally more limited.

More creative policy might focus on persons – especially highly internationally mobile industrial scientists and technicians. It is well known that the Canadian taxation of individuals, inclusive of all direct and indirect taxes, social insurance payments and the like, weighs more heavily on persons in Canada than on persons similarly employed in the United States. To offset this tax bias against immigration (and in favour of emigration) of highly paid researchers, targeted corporate tax relief based on researchers' salaries could perhaps be introduced. Canada has done this in job creation programs where the target is often the marginally employable. A similar program ought to be targeted at the super-employable.

CONCLUSIONS

ALL CDIA IS NOT CREATED EQUAL. Some potential CDIA would better serve the nation if it remained at home. Investment that generates MNE intangible assets also produces location-specific spillovers in the form of industrial knowledge, agglomeration effects and innovative business role models. Canada is better off if these spillovers spill over at home. At a minimum, Canadian taxation ought not to be at odds with this activity.

Canada has chosen – reasonably, I believe – not to tax foreign-source income from active business activity. Canada should not endorse the position, however, that all foreign-source income from CDIA is transactionally determined in the off-shore sites where MNE products and services are produced and marketed. CDIA headquarters activity, within the larger set of intangible MNE assets, is a factor for generating rents around the world. Unfortunately, in the general nature of a production function with fixed costs – including co-ordinative headquarters costs as well as R&D – such costs tend to be arbitrarily allocated to various products or various places. Nevertheless, Canada should not allow Canada-based multinationals undue scope to write off headquarters expense and the cost of R&D undertaken in Canada. Rent-generating global management processes and intellectual property together represent intangible CDIA assets that are developed in Canada with significant fiscal support, which Canada is entitled to recover.

ENDNOTES

1 Like Canada, many countries, including Australia, France, Germany, The Netherlands, Sweden and Switzerland, do not tax corporate dividends repatriated from foreign sources. This territorial approach is generally limited to dividends paid from active business income earned abroad in countries with which the residence country has signed a bilateral tax treaty. In contrast to the simplicity of the territorial approach, countries that tax corporate income on a worldwide basis, primarily the large capital exporting nations, including the United States, Britain, and Japan, also provide credit (against the domestic tax liability) for foreign taxes paid. See OECD (1991) for detail.

2 Brean, Bird & Krauss (1991) deal with various theoretical and Canadian policy issues concerning taxation of international portfolio investment.

3 Capital-import neutrality relates to the situation in which in-bound foreign investment bears the same tax as the domestic investment with which it competes. When capital-importing nations do not discriminate one way or the other with respect to foreign investment, a sufficient condition for capital-import neutrality is that the residence country imposes no tax on the income from foreign investments of its residents: i.e., Canadian policy.

4 The recent federal budget (Department of Finance, February 1994) introduced a number of specific measures to sharpen the distinction – at least for tax purposes – between active and passive forms of off-shore

income earned by Canadian-controlled foreign affiliates. The amendments, effective for taxation years commencing after 1994, expand the categories of non-active income included in FAPI and which are thus taxable in Canada on an accrual basis. Rules are tightened with respect to off-shore property transactions, off-shore insurance arrangements, and the treatment of interest and rental income on indebtedness and lease obligations of persons resident in Canada. If, in any of these categories, more than 10 percent of the off-shore income of a Canadian-controlled foreign affiliate arises from non-arm's-length arrangements with the Canadian controlling firm, the (off-shore) income shall be treated as non-active business income. In addition, the recent budget broadens the definition of "investment business", introduces new limits on the extent to which business losses incurred in Canada can be deducted from FAPI, and takes action to control the use of tax havens by Canadian corporations and their foreign affiliates. On the latter point, a foreign affiliate will have "exempt surplus" only if the affiliate is resident in a country and has active income from a business earned in a country with which Canada has concluded a tax treaty.

5 In computation of METRs, the OECD study assumes that all foreign-source income net of source taxes is repatriated to the residence country. Since many nations in their sample provide foreign tax relief, including the United States, the United Kingdom, Japan and Germany, which extend the foreign tax credit, the residence policies unambiguously reduce the variance of METRs from the perspective of the average or typical residence country. Thus the finding that the variance of METRs from the residence perspective is greater than the variance from the source perspective is based on conservative assumptions.

6 This issue and similar international financial shenanigans are discussed at greater length in Brean (1984).

7 This would not affect the attractiveness of the double dip.

8 *The Financial Post*, 18 September 1993, p S21.

9 Canada's infamous scientific research tax credit involved a flowthrough provision to taxable companies and individuals in order to provide funds for research to tax-exhausted companies. The scheme was introduced in 1982, and it was to become one of the grandest fiscal fiascos of all time. Hundreds of millions of dollars of revenue poured out of Revenue Canada *via* the "quick slip" which, in effect, created a market for tax credits. Very little research ever materialized. Although the program was scrapped in 1984, several tax fraud cases are still in court.

10 When tax-based investment incentives are targeted at the margin – for example, when a tax credit is related to an increase in investment over some base amount – this may result in an investment pattern that is erratic or "bunched" as firms attempt periodically to show large increases.

11 Clark et al. (1992) suggest that a tax credit based on incremental spending

could actually discourage R&D in some cases. When a firm's desired level of R&D expenditure (in the absence of a tax credit) in a year is less than its average R&D expenditure in the previous base years, additional investment in the current year would not earn credits in the current year while it would reduce the base for credits in future years.

ACKNOWLEDGEMENTS

THE AUTHOR ACKNOWLEDGES helpful comments from Steven Clark, Lorraine Eden, Steven Globerman and Jack Mintz. Thank you.

BIBLIOGRAPHY

Beaudreau, Bernard C. "Entrepreneurial Ability, International Trade and Foreign Direct Investment." *International Economic Journal*, 3 (Autumn 1989): 1-22.

Berstein, Jeffrey I. "The Effect of Direct and Indirect Tax Incentives on Canadian Industrial R&D Expenditures." *Canadian Public Policy*, XII 3 (September 1986): 438-48.

Boadway, Robin. "Comments on 'The Cost of Capital and Competitive Advantage' (by Neil Bruce)." In *Productivity, Growth and Canada's International Competitiveness*. Edited by Thomas J. Courchene and Douglas D. Purvis. Kingston, Ontario: The John Deutsch Institute for the Study of Economic Policy, Queen's University, The Bell Canada Papers on Economic and Public Policy, 1993.

Boskin, Michael J. "Tax Policy and The International Location of Investment." In *Taxes and Capital Formation*. Edited by Martin Feldstein. Chicago: University of Chicago Press for the NBER, 1987, pp.73-84.

Brean, Donald J.S. *International Issues in Taxation: The Canadian Perspective*. Toronto: The Canadian Tax Foundation, 1984.

Brean, Donald J.S., R.M. Bird and M. Krauss. *Taxation of International Portfolio Investment*. Ottawa: Centre for Trade Policy and Law and The Institute for Research on Public Policy, 1991.

Bruce, Neil. "The Cost of Capital and Competitive Advantage." In *Productivity, Growth and Canada's International Competitiveness*. Edited by Thomas J. Courchene and Douglas D. Purvis. Kingston, Ontario: The John Deutsch Institute for the Study of Economic Policy, Queen's University - The Bell Canada Papers on Economic and Public Policy, 1993.

Carey, David, Jean-Claude Chouraqui and Robert P. Hagemann. "The Future of Capital Income Taxation in a Liberalised Financial Environment." Organization for Economic Co-operation and Development, Economics Department Working Paper Number 126; Paris: OECD / GD (93)3, 1993.

Clark, W. Stephen, Gerry Goodchild, Bob Hamilton and Bill Toms. "Canada's R&D Tax Incentives: Recent Developments." 1992 Conference Report: Proceedings of the Forty-

Fourth Tax Conference. Convened by The Canadian Tax Foundation. Toronto: Canadian Tax Foundation, pp. 32:1 - 32:29.

Department of Finance Canada. *Tax Measures: Supplementary Information (Supplementary Information and Notices of Ways and Means Motions of the Budget)*. Ottawa: Supply and Services, Feb. 22, 1994.

Drouin, Marie-Josée and David R. McCamus (Co-Chairs). *Inventing Our Future: An Action Plan for Canada's Prosperity* (A report of The Independent Steering Group on Prosperity). Ottawa: Government of Canada, 1992, Cat. No. C2-206/1992E.

Eden, Lorraine. "Free Trade, Tax Reform and Transfer Pricing." *Canadian Tax Journal*, 39, 1 (January-February 1991): 90-112.

Graham, Edward M. and Paul R. Krugman. *Foreign Investment in the United States*. Washington, D.C.: Institute for International Economics, 1989.

Grubert, Harry and John Mutti. "Taxes, Tariffs and Transfer Pricing in Multinational Corporate Decision Making." *The Review of Economics and Statistics*, 73 (May 1991): 285-93.

Grubert, Harry, Timothy Goodspeed and Deborah Swenson. "Explaining the Low Taxable Income of Foreign-Controlled Companies in the United States." In *Studies in International Taxation*. Edited by Alberto Giovannini, R. Glenn Hubbard & Joel Slemrod. Chicago: University of Chicago Press for NBER, 1993.

Guisinger, Steven and X.He. "Does Tax Neutrality Principle Matter? Fresh Funds Investment Versus Reinvested Earnings." Proceedings of The Academy of International Business; Baltimore, Md., 1992.

Harris, David, Randall Morck, Joel Slemrod and Bernard Yeung. "Income Shifting in US Multinational Corporations." In *Studies in International Taxation*. Edited by Alberto Giovannini, R. Glenn Hubbard & Joel Slemrod. Chicago: University of Chicago Press for NBER, 1993.

Hines, James R., Jr. "On the Sensitivity of R&D to Delicate Tax Changes: The Behavior of U.S. Multinationals in the 1980s." In *Studies in International Taxation*. Edited by Alberto Giovannini, R. Glenn Hubbard & Joel Slemrod. Chicago: University of Chicago Press for NBER, 1993.

Hines, James R. and R. Glenn Hubbard. "Coming Home to America: Dividend Repatriations by U.S. Multinationals." In *Taxation in The Global Economy*. Edited by A. Razin and J. Slemrod. Chicago: University of Chicago Press for NBER, 1990.

Hines, James R. and Eric M. Rice. "Fiscal Paradise: Foreign Tax Havens and American Business." National Bureau of Economic Research, Paper Number 3477. Cambridge, Mass: NBER, 1990.

Hufbauer, Gary C. (assisted by Joanna M. Van Rooij). U.S. Taxation of International Income: Blueprint for Reform. Washington, D.C.: Institute for International Economics, 1992.

Jenkins, Glenn P. "Tax Shelter Finance: How Efficient is It?" *Canadian Tax Journal*, 38, 2, pp. 270-85.

Lipsey, Robert and Merle Yahr Weiss. "Foreign Production and Exports in Manufacturing Industries." *The Review of Economics and Statistics*, 63 (November 1981): 488-94.

_____. "Foreign Production and Exports of Individual Firms." *The Review of Economics and Statistics*, 66 (May, 1984): 304-7.

Longo, Frank. "Industrial R&D and Production Activity in Canada." Ottawa: The Science Council of Canada, 1984.

Markusen, James R. *Productivity, Competitiveness, Trade Performance and Real Income: The*

Nexus Among Four Concepts. Ottawa: The Economic Council of Canada, 1992.

Organization for Economic Co-operation and Development. *Taxing Profits in a Global Economy: Domestic and International Issues*. Paris: OECD Publications, 1991.

Papke, Leslie E. "International Differences in Capital Taxation and Corporate Borrowing Behavior: Evidence From the US Withholding Tax." Paper presented to the National Bureau of Economic Research Summer Institute on International Taxation. Cambridge, Mass: NBER, 1989.

Porter, Michael. *The Competitive Advantage of Nations*. New York: Basic Books, 1991.

Rugman, Alan M. *Inside The Multinationals: The Economics of Internal Markets*. New York: Columbia University Press, 1981.

Scholes, Myron S. and Mark A. Wolfson. *Taxes and Business Strategy: A Global Planning Approach*. Englewood Cliffs, N.J.: Prentice-Hall Inc., 1990.

Schwanen, Daniel. *A Growing Success: Canada's Performance Under Free Trade*. The C.D. Howe Institute Commentary Series, No. 52 (September 1993). Toronto: C.D. Howe Institute.

Shah, Anwar and Joel Slemrod. "Do Taxes Matter For Foreign Direct Investment?" In *Fiscal Incentives for Investment In Developing Countries*. Edited by A. Shah. Washington, D.C.: The World Bank, 1992.

Shoven, John B. and Michael Topper. "The Cost of Capital in Canada, the United States, and Japan." In *Canada-U.S. Tax Comparisons*. Edited by John B. Shoven and John Whalley. Chicago: University of Chicago Press for NBER, 1992, pp. 217-35.

Switzer, L. "R&D and Total Factor Productivity Growth in Canada." Proceedings of The Canadian Economics Association; Guelph, Ontario; June 1984.

Part III   Business Implications

Alan M. Rugman
Professor of International Business
University of Toronto

8

Strategic Management and Canadian Multinationals

INTRODUCTION

BUILDING ON EARLIER WORK which has identified the nature and scope of activities of Canada's largest multinationals (Rugman & McIlveen 1985, Rugman & Warner 1989), this study elaborates on the strategic management decisions of Canadian multinational enterprises (MNEs). This requires first a brief review of the key literature in strategic management and then an attempt to adapt it for Canadian managers. In turn, this leads to consideration of the following two issues:

- Analysis of Porter's (1980) three generic strategies (cost, differentiation, and focus) and how they may apply to the strategic management decisions of Canada's MNEs.

- Reconciliation of Porter's (1986) home-based global strategy framework with his earlier work on the three generics.

This is done in order to relate his treatment of national responsiveness to other literature in the international business area, specifically that of Bartlett & Ghoshal (1989). This leads to the development of a new framework which distinguishes between non-location bound firm-specific advantages and location bound firm-specific advantages (the latter being in the form of national responsiveness). This framework (first developed by Rugman & Verbeke, 1992c) can be used to analyze the actual strategies of leading Canadian multinational enterprises. Specifically, a useful contrast can be drawn between the traditional economics-based analysis of cost and/or differentiation strategies and the newer managerial-based strategy of national responsiveness. This revised framework helps explain the investment decisions of Canadian multinationals, especially those operating mainly in the United States.

Simply put, the strategy of national responsiveness implies that a Canadian MNE can do well in a triad market like the United States only if it invests in understanding the U.S. market to the extent that it can outdo indigenous U.S. rival firms on their home turf. Examples are Canadian MNEs that develop managerial competencies in dealing with the U.S. legal and regulatory framework and/or adapt their products and services to meet the specific tastes of U.S. consumers. The very ability of Canadian MNEs to conduct such a policy of national responsiveness has been challenged by Porter (1991) and by Porter & Armstrong (1992), who argue that Canadian-based MNEs can at best achieve parity with U.S. firms by tapping into the U.S. market. This patronizing viewpoint has been questioned in earlier work (Rugman 1991, 1992) which developed an extension of Porter's (1990) "single-diamond" framework to make it relevant for small, open, economies, such as Canada's. The result was the Rugman & D'Cruz (1991) "double diamond", which implies that Canadian managers need to develop national responsiveness skills about the U.S. market in addition to building on their home base.

This study on outward investment focuses on market access issues and is a complement to that by Rugman & D'Cruz (1993b) that deals with the "five partners" framework of international competitiveness in Canada and its implications for inbound foreign direct investment Canadian investment abroad is viewed as a means of gaining access to larger triad markets, in particular, the United States. Here, we examine the managerial logic of various global strategies, how it applies to investments made by Canadian managers, and what this implies for Canadian public policy on investment.

Briefly, then, before managerial and public policy implications can be extracted, it is necessary to lay a sound foundation of the use of key strategic management concepts in a Canadian context. The five strategies developed here to summarize Porter (1980, 1986) can then be reconciled with the Bartlett & Ghoshal (1989) treatment of national responsiveness. This leads to two diagrams and a matrix wherein the concepts of one or multiple home-based diamonds are related to location bound or non-location bound firm-specific advantages, and a final matrix where the full range of strategies for Canadian MNEs is examined.

THE THREE GENERIC STRATEGIES

CONVENTIONAL ECONOMIC THINKING suggests that Canadian business derives benefits from access to a larger market (a triad market if the business is in the United States, as is two-thirds of Canadian business). In economic terms a Canadian manufacturer (or service provider) using this strategy will have the opportunity, through foreign expansion, to gain economies of scale in production and distribution. In a world where price matters, such scale economies are vital to the success of the manufacturer. But there are other ways of doing business. A second strategy, also recognized by economists, is to differentiate products (or services). Again, product differentiation (uniqueness of products and/or services offered by the firm) is helped immensely by gaining access to a large triad market. A third type of business strategy is to secure a global niche, or market segment, based on a "focus", with combinations of cost or differentiation skills.

These three types of business strategies have been advocated by Michael Porter (1980). Indeed, the cost, differentiation, and focus strategies are known in the business school literature as Porter's three "generics". For those who are unfamiliar with the strategic management literature, a useful way to visualize these three strategies is in Porter's 2 x 2 matrix shown in Figure 1.

Using two axes, one to represent strategic advantage (based on low cost or differentiation), the other to represent strategic target (scope of the product line; broad or narrow), it is possible to illustrate the three generic strategies, i.e., quadrant 1 for cost leadership and quadrant 3 for differentiation, with quadrants 2 and 4 for narrow (niched) product lines. There are, in fact, two sub-categories of niche: focus-cost in quadrant 2, and focus-differentiation in quadrant 4. The effective employment of these generic strategies requires that managers identify the source of their firms' competitive advantage, being aware of how these "core competencies" are to be created and managed over time.

To operationalize this Porter (1980) framework of business strategy, it is clear that business strategy consists of two basic choices for managers, as

FIGURE 1

PORTER'S THREE GENERIC STRATEGIES

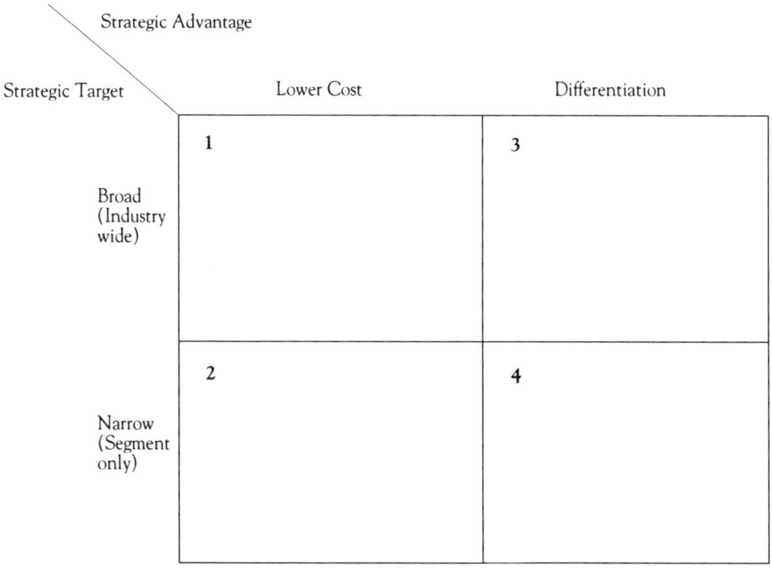

Source: Michael Porter (1980, 1985).

shown in Figure 1. First, there is a choice regarding the type of competitive advantage pursued; the choice is between low cost and differentiation. Second, there is a choice related to the firm's competitive scope. A firm's competitive scope reflects the breadth of its target market segments. The alternatives are a broad target, covering an entire industry or a narrow target, including only specific segments within an industry. The implication of Porter's three generic strategies framework is that managerial behaviour must be directed toward only one strategy, in order to avoid becoming "stuck in the middle". This approach to generic strategies has been the subject of extensive academic discussion (see Jegers,1993, for a summary). There has also been extensive discussion in the business strategy literature about the nature and relevance of core competencies (see Hamel, 1991, for a summary of some of these critical issues).

Porter (1980) also advocates the use of entry barriers to maintain competitive advantages, in his "five forces" model. He argues that a firm needs to gain a competitive advantage by holding market power over its suppliers, buyers, rivals, potential entrants and potential substitutes. It is a competitive framework where entry barriers are erected by scale, capital (financing) requirements, differentiation, cost of switching from both suppliers and buyers, and by government. Porter's five forces model is basically incompatible with the five partners co-operative framework of international competitiveness developed by D'Cruz & Rugman (1992a, 1992b, 1993). It is not necessary to dwell on the different approaches of these two models, since useful insights into Canadian management strategy can be obtained by adapting the Porter (1980) five forces framework into a relevant framework for Canadian-based managers. To do this requires two steps.

First, Porter's three generics must be transformed into truly global strategies; this leads to five generics. Second, Porter's use of the home-base diamond, from Porter (1990) must be emended to accommodate the reality of Canadian managers who have a "double-diamond" viewpoint; see Rugman (1991) and Rugman & D'Cruz (1991, 1993a). Since the latter issue has already been discussed in the literature, this study focuses on the former issue. To do this requires that Porter's three generic strategies be extended from the mainly domestic context of his 1980 book, to an international context, as undertaken in Porter (1986).

THE FIVE GENERIC STRATEGIES

PORTER (1986) EXTENDED HIS THREE generic strategies framework in order to take into account some of the complexities of global competition. As shown in Figure 2, his 1986 essay distinguishes between segment scope (many or few segments) and geographic scope (global or country-centered strategy). In Porter (1986) there are actually four dimensions of competitive scope (rather than two as in Porter 1980). The four dimensions are: a) segment scope (the range of segments the firm serves); b) industry scope (the range of related industries the firm competes in with a coordinated strategy); c) vertical scope (the activities performed by the firm compared to those done by suppliers and through channels of distribution); and d) geographic scope (the geographic regions in which the firm operates with a co-ordinated strategy). See Porter, 1986, p. 22.

Porter's (1986) framework provides four strategic options for a global industry: global cost-leadership or differentiation in quadrant 1; global segmentation in quadrant 2; protected markets in quadrant 3; or what he calls "national responsiveness" in quadrant 4. Global cost leadership and global differentiation are defined by Porter as "seeking the cost or differentiation advantages of global configuration/coordination through selling a wide line of products to buyers in all or most significant country markets". (Porter, 1986, p.47). Global segmentation is viewed as "serving a particular industry segment worldwide". (National responsiveness is discussed later).

Porter's three domestic generic strategies need to be extended to accommodate the issue of geographic scope in a global industry. The three initial generic strategies can be transformed into a set of five extended generic strategies, as done by Rugman & Verbeke (1993b), in Figure 3. Porter (1986) does not

FIGURE 2

PORTER'S GLOBAL STRATEGIES

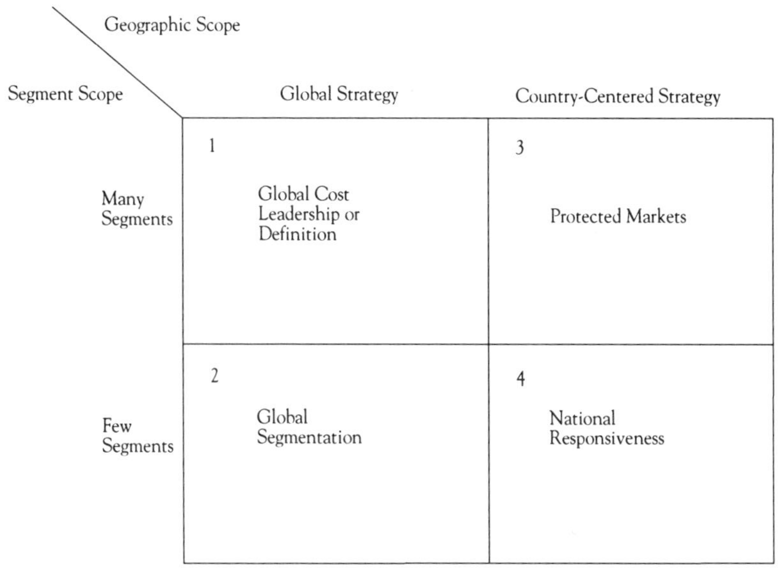

Source: Michael Porter (1986), p. 46.

FIGURE 3

THE FIVE EXTENDED GENERIC STRATEGIES

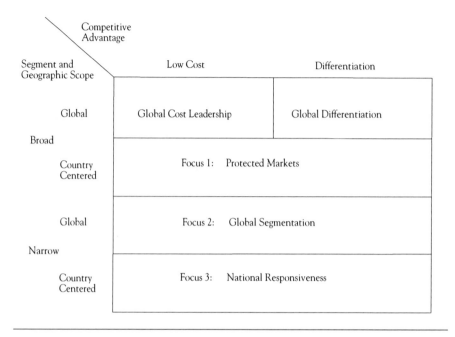

Source: Rugman & Verbeke (1993b).

develop this figure, nor does he uses the term 'extended generic strategies' in this international context. But given that global cost leadership, global differentiation and global segmentation are obviously the global versions of overall cost leadership, overall differentiation and focus, it is apparent that the set of five strategies described in Porter (1986, p. 46) cannot reflect anything other than generic strategies in a global industry.

There are two problems associated with this minor extension of Porter's five generic strategies framework shown in Figure 3. First, the basic choice of competitive advantage (cost leadership or differentiation) is actually used in only two of the five cases. In the three other cases (a protected market strategy, global segmentation, and national responsiveness) it appears that firms could become stuck in the middle if they pursue both cost leadership and differentiation simultaneously within the chosen geographic and/or market segment niche. Thus the initial three generic strategies framework described in Porter (1980) is inconsistent with the five generics of Porter (1986), since cost leadership and differentiation are not considered important enough to distinguish among all of the various strategies in the international context.

In practice it is very difficult to identify patterns in decisions and actions that are associated with only one type of competitive advantage. The strategic intensity (and related economic performance) of a dual focus on cost leadership and differentiation is much more important than the choice between the pursuit of a cost or a differentiation advantage (Reitsperger, Daniel & Tallman, 1993). For example, the three largest automobile manufacturers in the world, General Motors, Ford and Toyota, all pursue a combined cost leadership/differentiation strategy, in which economies of scope are relevant. It would be incorrect to argue that any one of these three firms has a substantially different emphasis on one of the two types of competitive advantage, compared to the two other firms. A dual focus on both cost leadership and differentiation is required across the various segments of the value chain.

A second and much more important problem, for public policy purposes, is that Porter's strategy of "protected markets" does not really fit with the other four strategies. In each of the other four cases (excluding protected markets) cost or differentiation advantages remain important, although, as already discussed, these two types of advantage do not appear to be mutually exclusive in the cases of global segmentation and national responsiveness. In each of these four cases efficiency (as measured by relative output/input differentials throughout the value chain) determines a firm's economic performance in terms of survival, profitability and growth.

In contrast, as Porter (1986, p. 48) himself recognizes, "protected markets strategies lack a competitive advantage in economic terms, their choice depends on a sophisticated prediction about future government behaviour". This suggests that Porter's extended framework of five generic strategies based upon two parameters (scope and type of efficiency-driven competitive advantage) is actually not able to handle the protected market strategy properly, despite this strategy being considered as one of the five generics by Porter himself. It is apparent that the Porter (1986) treatment of global strategy is logically inconsistent. Its relevance for Canadian international management is further devalued by the peculiar treatment of national responsiveness.

In defining national responsiveness Porter states that a firm aims to "focus on those industry segments most affected by local country differences though the industry as a whole is global" and meets "unusual local needs in products, channels and marketing practices in each country, foregoing the competitive advantages of a global strategy". (Porter, 1986, p. 48). Unfortunately, Porter then uses the term 'national responsiveness' to describe the behaviour of "domestic firms without the resources to become international as well as multinationals who lack the resources or skills to concentrate/co-ordinate their activities worldwide." (Porter, 1986, p. 48). Porter's view is thus in sharp contrast to most of the mainstream international business literature, e.g. Bartlett (1986), Bartlett & Ghoshal (1989), Rugman & Verbeke (1992b), which describes national responsiveness as a strategy that builds upon location-bound, firm-specific advantages (FSAs) of MNEs.

Properly interpreted, national responsiveness is a strategic alternative to other strategies based on globalization and integration; it builds upon firm-specific strengths, (see also Baden-Fuller &Stopford, 1991, 1993). National responsiveness is certainly not the result of a firm's internal weaknesses as alleged by Porter (1986). The "administrative heritage" of a firm, leading to national responsiveness, is just as valuable as one leading to global scale economies. In other words, the definition of national responsiveness used by Porter is inconsistent with other literature in international business and is misleading for policy purposes.

Due to the missing ingredients in Porter's work, the next section provides a bridge between Porter and the operationalization of strategy for Canadian firms. The missing link to be discussed is the nature of truly generic strategies – ones that generate efficiency-based rather than shelter-based firm-specific advantages. Efficiency-based FSAs are either non-location bound or location bound, where the latter type of FSA encompasses the national responsiveness strategy of interest to us.

FIRM-SPECIFIC ADVANTAGES AS GENERIC STRATEGIES

EVEN THOUGH DIFFERENT GENERIC STRATEGIES may be pursued simultaneously, their generic character should reflect the fact that they deal with a fundamentally different approach to competing and to achieving a satisfactory economic performance. Rugman & Verbeke (1990, 1992a) have demonstrated that the development and use of firm-specific advantages, or the lack of them, reflects the truly generic strategies between which firms are required to make a choice in each identifiable pattern of decision and action.

Firm-specific advantages include both proprietary know-how (unique assets) and transactional advantages with potential cost reducing and/or differentiation enhancing effects. In a number of cases it may be difficult to assess the actual effect of an FSA in terms of cost reduction or differentiation enhancement. Rugman & Verbeke (1991a) have suggested that in such cases the contribution of an FSA to "infrastructure development" of the firm should be considered. All strategies that build upon such FSAs or aim to develop new ones are classified as efficiency based.

In contrast, strategies that do not build upon FSAs to achieve a satisfactory economic performance in terms of survival, profitability, growth or any other goal considered relevant by managers, are classified as non-efficiency based or shelter based. If the economic performance of a firm or set of firms does not result from FSAs with cost reducing, differentiation enhancing or infrastructure building characteristics, its performance must result from shelter-based behaviour.

Shelter-based behaviour occurs in two important ways: first, when firms attempt to impose artificial costs or barriers to differentiation upon (foreign) rivals through government regulation (such as by tariff and non-tariff barriers);

and, second, when firms reduce the market incentives for cost reduction, differentiation enhancement or infrastructure building themselves (for instance, by collusive behaviour and cartel formation aimed primarily at exploiting the consumer) or limiting the potential effects of these incentives (for example, by government subsidies). In both cases, such strategies reduce workable competition in the short run.

Shelter-based strategies are often pursued in the context of international business, where firms located in a particular country may persuade public policy makers that protectionist measures will lead to higher economic welfare in terms of value-added creation or to a special type of public good in terms of the creation of domestic control over strategic sectors, technological spill-over effects, etc. This occurs even where such public goods may be non-existent or where shelter leads to a substantial reduction in consumer welfare. Rugman & Verbeke (1991b and 1991c) have demonstrated that such shelter strategies actually subvert policies aimed at achieving a level playing field and fair trade, as now frequently occurs in the United States and the European Community. In a similar way the recent international economic literature on strategic trade policy is a minor set of mathematical cases under sub-optimal conditions with little relevance and is not the basis for a successful long-run trade policy, as demonstrated by Krugman (1993).

This distinction between an efficiency-based strategy and a shelter-based strategy is the truly fundamental distinction in strategic management because each strategy builds upon different intellectual premises as to what constitutes the source of success. In the case of an efficiency-based strategy, consumer sovereignty ultimately determines whether or not the firm will be successful (except in the case of natural monopolies, few of which exist in an international context). Strong economic performance reflects the successful creation of value for customers. In contrast, shelter-based strategies reflect behaviour that reduces value for customers, compared to the situation where efficiency based strategies would prevail.

The importance of distinguishing between these two types of strategy results from the observation that different weapons are used and different rules of the game are followed in each case. Specifically, Canadian firms pursuing a conventional efficiency-based strategy, but faced with shelter-seeking U.S. rivals, may suffer in the short run, compared to a case where all competitors should be engaged in efficiency based behaviour. In the short run, U.S. shelter-based behaviour will reduce the opportunities for Canadian rivals not engaged in such behaviour to exploit their FSAs or develop new ones. There is a strategic asymmetry in the short run which can be minimized by a national responsiveness policy by Canadian MNEs. Furthermore, in the long run, shelter obviously works against the U.S. firms that build their economic performance on it. Thus it is always advisable for Canadian firms to follow efficiency-based strategies in both the short run and the long run.

Rugman & Verbeke (1993b) have outlined several reasons why shelter-based strategies may fail in the long run, leading to corporate inefficiencies and political dependence. For these reasons, due to the U.S.-Canadian size asymmetry, it is not useful for Canadian-based firms to use shelter as a strategic alternative. Porter's (1986) protected market strategy is both inefficient and irrelevant for Canadian managers. Unfortunately, they must compete with U.S. firms that rely on Porter more than on Rugman & Verbeke, and so until these methodological errors and triad asymmetries are more widely under-stood, there remains a problem that much U.S.-based strategic management thinking will be inappropriate for Canadian business. Fortunately, the actual managerial practices of Canadian firms seem to be more realistic than the advice they receive from Porter-type advisors.

In practice, it may not always be easy for outside observers to classify a specific pattern of managerial decision and action as efficiency based or shelter-based. There are five main dimensions to consider: need; managerial intent; organizational routines; outcome; and impact on performance.

Shelter-based strategies are used in international business only as the need arises. This occurs when there is an absence of strong FSAs that would allow firms to defeat rivals on the basis of the cost and differentiation characteristics of the products offered. An exception is the case of collusive behaviour when the various firms involved have strong FSAs (e.g., relative to foreign rivals) but attempt to extract rents from consumers through the elimination of competition. Shelter-based behaviour generally results from managerial intentions to engage in such a pattern of decision and action but may still contain an emerging component (see Rugman & Verbeke, 1991b). Specific organizational routines resulting in lobbying efforts may increase the probability of shelter-based behaviour. Just as in the case of efficiency-based strategies, the goals pursued may not be achieved. For example, government may refuse to provide shelter, thus affecting the firm's performance.

The study by Cho & Porter (1986) on the global shipbuilding industry demonstrates the problem in using Porter's extended generic strategies frame-work. For example, his analysis demonstrates that firms in the United Kingdom were not able to achieve a satisfactory economic performance after the mid-1950s in spite of strong government intervention in the form of subsidies. In contrast, Porter states that protected markets strategies in Japan after the Second World War led to a global cost leadership position. The reason for this disparity, of course, is that in the United Kingdom and other European nations, government support was used to provide shelter; that is, it did not lead to a more efficient exploitation of existing FSAs or development of new ones. In Europe (and North America), government support acts as an artificial substitute for strong FSAs and often results from firm lobbying. In contrast, Japanese government support programmes actually develop new FSAs and foster the long-run cost competitiveness/differentiation position of Japanese yards. In Japan, government support was used by shipbuilding companies as a complement to their existing FSAs and as a stimulus to generate new ones. As demonstrated in Rugman & Verbeke (1990) the more centralized nature of Japanese society leads to the development of FSA-generating strategies following protection, whereas in North America and Europe shelter-seeking lobbies capture the trade/protection decision making process, leading to inefficient outcomes.

OPERATIONALIZING GLOBAL STRATEGY

FROM THE VIEWPOINT OF A CANADIAN MANAGER, shelter-based strategies should be avoided, and firm resources should be directed to the development of sustainable firm-specific advantages within a triad framework. Most of the international business literature suggests that, within the efficiency-based patterns of decision and action, two managerial decisions need to be made.

The first decision concerns the type of FSAs to be developed or exploited, see Rugman & Verbeke (1992b). An important distinction exists between location bound FSAs (LB-FSAs) and non-location bound FSAs (NLB-FSAs). The former benefit a company only in a particular location (or set of locations), and lead to benefits of national responsiveness. In the context of international business operations, these LB-FSAs cannot be effectively transferred as an intermediate output (e.g. a tangible or intangible asset) or embodied in the final outputs of the organization, to be sold across borders. In contrast, NLB-FSAs are easily transferred and exploited abroad, whether in the form of intermediate outputs or embodied in final outputs. They lead to benefits of integration in terms of economies of scale and exploitation of national differences.

Many authors, including Bartlett (1986), Bartlett & Ghoshal (1989), Doz (1986), Ghoshal (1987), Kogut (1985a, 1985b), Prahalad & Doz (1987), and Roth & Morrison (1990), have provided the intellectual foundation that led to making this important distinction between two fundamentally different types of FSA (Rugman & Verbeke, 1991a, 1992a, 1992b).

The second decision is related to the number of home bases used by the firm. A 'home base' is defined by Porter (1990) as the nation where the firm retains effective strategic, creative and technical control. In addition, it is considered central "to choosing the industries to compete in as well as the appropriate strategy" (Porter, 1990, p. 599).

Rugman & Verbeke (1993a) have demonstrated that a firm may actually have several home bases contributing substantially to the development of new FSAs, and improving international competitiveness. It is important to distinguish between the existence of a single home base or multiple home bases in the pursuit of international competitiveness because it reflects the effect of the country-specific advantages (CSAs) of specific locations on strategic behaviour. A single home base implies the dominating impact of one set of national diamond characteristics on the firm's overall competitiveness. In contrast, with multiple home bases, competitiveness (both now and in the future) depends crucially upon decisions and actions taken in various locations as well as upon the characteristics of these locations. Canadian-based firms need to be in the latter camp; then they can be more nationally responsive to the U.S. market.

To the extent that the development and exploitation of NLB-FSAs requires co-ordination of decisions and actions across borders, a single home base requires direct, centralized control of all foreign operations. In contrast, in the case of a global subsidiary mandate the corporate headquarters role shifts toward "managing dispersed strategic processes, ensuring that subsidiary strategies continue to fit the overall corporation goals and providing the resources and freedom required to support the mandates" (Roth & Morrison, 1992, p. 718). In this case, typical home base activities are concentrated in the various nations where subsidiaries have received global subsidiary mandates.

Using the above analysis we can generate the two axes for Figure 4; number of home bases and either a LB-FSA or a NLB-FSA. In Figure 4, four important categories of efficiency-based strategies in global industries are apparent.

Patterns of decision and action in quadrant 1 of Figure 4 are typical for so-called 'multinational' firms, as defined by Bartlett & Ghoshal (1989). Here, the different operations in various countries are viewed as largely independent and build their performance on strengths in being nationally responsive.

FIGURE 4

PRINCIPAL CATEGORIES OF EFFICIENCY-BASED STRATEGIES

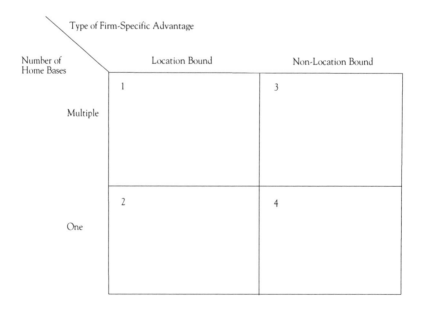

Examples of Canadian MNEs in quadrant 1 are Seagram's U.S. operations (accounting for about 90 percent of total sales) and Moore Business Forms, which is an extremely decentralized, polycentric, marketing firm.

In quadrant 2, competitiveness results from having only a single home base and building upon FSAs that lead to benefits of national responsiveness. Here, we find uni-national firms that attempt to remain competitive *vis-à-vis* global rivals in one nation or a limited set of nations. Examples are Moosehead beer exports from Atlantic Canada targeted at the U.S. market. Moosehead is more adapted to the U.S. market and sells better there than in many Canadian provinces.

Quadrant 3 reflects strategies aimed at achieving a superior economic performance through using multiple home bases, each of which builds upon NLB-FSAs. Firms with global subsidiary mandates, as described by Rugman & Bennett (1982), Poynter & Rugman (1983) and Roth & Morrison (1992), typically fall in this quadrant. Canadian MNEs in quadrant 3 are Northern Telecom and Alcan (to the extent that it is responsive to the U.S. environmental and regulatory climate).

Finally, quadrant 4 reflects behaviour typical for both the "global" firms and the "international" firms as defined by Bartlett & Ghoshal (1989). Global firms attempt to achieve global scale economies by producing primarily in a single country and exporting products globally as these embody the firm's NLB-FSAs. Examples are Molson and Labatt, both of which are exporting unadapted brand name products using a Canadian home base. Another example is Noranda, both Noranda Forest and Noranda Mines. International firms pursue international scope economies and/or benefits of exploiting national differences by transferring know-how across borders and/or by coordinating dispersed activities placed in different optimal locations. The dispersion of value activities implies global rationalization, whereby each subsidiary specializes in a narrow set of activities in the value chain, (Kobrin, 1991). There are few Canadian examples of this type of firm.

These four types of efficiency-based strategy appear to reflect the various archetypal firms engaged in international business as portrayed in the relevant literature. For example, the main characteristic of Bartlett & Ghoshal's (1989) "transnational solution" is the simultaneous occurrence of patterns of decisions and actions that fit into quadrants one and three of Figure 4.

The Figure 4 strategic alternatives also represent clearly identifiable patterns of decisions and actions in the pursuit of satisfactory economic performance. These patterns constitute alternatives among which choices need to be made, e.g., when reacting to an environmental change such as the EC 1992 programme or the North American Free Trade Agreement, even within a single strategic business unit. This framework is more relevant for the strategic management of Canadian multinationals than is the framework set out in Porter (1986).

FIGURE 5

STRATEGIES FOR CANADIAN MULTINATIONALS

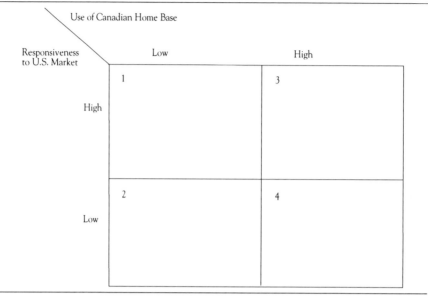

Source: Adapted from Rugman & Verbeke (1993a), Figure 1.

From the viewpoint of Canadian managers and policy makers the thinking in this study can be summarized in Figure 5. The concept of national responsiveness (to the U.S. market) is placed on the vertical axis, with high or low competencies for Canadian firms. The other axis represents the ability of the Canadian firm to derive competitive advantage from the Canadian home base.

Quadrant 4 of Figure 5 represents a Porter (1990) strategy of ignoring the U.S. market and using the single diamond home base as the primary route in developing non-location bound FSAs. Examples are Molson and Labatt, both of whom have concentrated on the Canadian beer market and just exported to the United States instead of building strengths in national responsiveness, e.g. by adapting their brands. Nova is another example.

Quadrant 1 is the opposite type of strategy, ignoring the Canadian home base and using only national responsiveness. This could generate a location-bound FSA and firms doing this would need to have very strong U.S. marketing programmes. Examples are Seagram and Moore Business Forms.

In quadrant 2, neither the Canadian home base nor the U.S. market is of strategic importance. Few, if any, Canadian-owned firms would be here, although this is a quadrant for an Ohmae (1990) type "pure" globalization strategy, i.e., one where global factor costs and global markets are all that matter. Here there are non-location bound FSAs. The Canadian firms in this quadrant, namely Inco, Varity, Domtar and former MNEs like Falconbridge and other one-dimensional resource-based firms, are in trouble.

The interesting strategic space in Figure 5 is quadrant 3. This is a double diamond area where both the Canadian home base and national responsiveness matter in the development of competitive advantage. There can be both location bound FSAs and non-location bound FSAs. This is the conceptual box of greatest benefit to Canadian multinationals in today's globalized but triad-based regional economic system. It is a box supported by the work of Bartlett & Ghoshal (1989), Rugman & Verbeke (1992b, 1993b), and Baden-Fuller & Stopford (1991, 1993) rather than by Porter (1986, 1990, 1991). The only Canadian MNE seriously attempting a quadrant 3 strategy is Northern Telecom. At least two others, Alcan and Noranda Forest, are beginning to build internal managerial strengths in dealing with the U.S. regulatory environment. Both have a long way to go before they are true quadrant 3 firms.

Commentators on this study have been struck by the operational paradox of national responsiveness. Here I have developed an asymmetrical strategic framework which suggests that Canadian managers can rarely achieve success in the United States without being nationally responsive, whereas American managers, on average, can get by without national responsiveness when doing business in Canada. The reason, of course, is that U.S. managers can choose a cost or differentiation strategy and beat the average competitor on a North American basis, virtually ignoring the marginal impact of the Canadian economy as it is one-twelfth the size of the U.S. economy. A successful U.S. business distributes its product across various U.S. regions in sequence and it usually treats Canada as just another region. The FTA and the NAFTA reinforce this strong single-diamond, home-base, strategic vision.

Yet none of this is as easy for Canadian managers doing business in the United States. While they still need to beat the average U.S. competitor on cost or differentiation margins, an additional requirement is that Canadians need to overcome discretionary entry barriers to the U.S. market. Such entry barriers can arise when discriminatory measures are introduced by U.S. governments, often at the behest of U.S. private sector rivals. Examples are the petitions for the use of U.S. trade law remedies against alleged subsidized or dumped Canadian products and the biased administration of such trade laws; (Rugman & Anderson, 1987, and Rugman & Verbeke, 1990).

While both the FTA and the NAFTA somewhat broadened the application of national treatment for Canadian investment in the United States (and for U.S. investment in Canada), there are many important derogations from this principle, not just in the sectoral exemptions listed in the NAFTA but also in the use of discriminatory rules of origin and exclusions for U.S. national security reasons (Rugman & Gestrin, 1993). For example, Canadian firms can be excluded from the U.S. research and development incentives offered to high-tech sectors, since the NAFTA lists R&D as an exemption from the national treatment provisions. In addition, U.S. anti-trust policy can be applied in a discriminatory manner against Canadian firms (Rugman & Warner, 1993). So important is this risk of loss of U.S. market access for Canadian firms that it becomes essential to develop a strategy of national responsiveness. Indeed, a Canadian firm that lives by the Porter cost or differentiation strategy alone will invite retaliation by its U.S. rivals, and if the U.S. firms lose market share, the application of punishing trade remedy laws becomes almost inevitable.

A related issue is whether the competitiveness of Canadian companies is weakened or strengthened by relocating critical value-chain activities to the United States. Porter (1990) and the Porter/Monitor (1991) study both argue that the core competitive advantage of a Canadian company must be drawn from the Canadian cluster of the home base diamond. While it would be theoretically simpler if this could occur, in practice it is observed that virtually all Canadian resource-based, manufacturing and service companies rely on access to the U.S. market for the success of their business; for example, on average over seventy percent of all sales of Canada's manufacturing firms occur in the United States. Given this dependence on the U.S. market, the contingent location of production and distribution in the United States (instead of in Canada alone) can never weaken the performance of Canadian firms, given the alternative, which is to lose access to the U.S. market and thereby go out of business.

This is why the neoclassical economics framework of social benefit cost analysis used elsewhere in this volume to evaluate the outward investment process is of limited value from the viewpoint of strategic management. The correct counterfactual is not investment, jobs, R&D, profits or other economic attributes in the United States versus these in Canada. Instead, it is a competitive business operating across the border, with the majority of sales in the larger triad market, versus no business at all. An example may help to illustrate the point.

In the forest products industry, MacMillan Bloedel and other British Columbia-based pulp, paper and newsprint producers export most of their production overseas. One of their largest markets is the State of California. Recently it has passed state laws requiring 50 percent recycled newspaper to be used in newsprint. The Canadian producers cannot afford to transport used newspapers back to British Columbia to their existing newsprint mills; therefore, to stay in business in California they must build new de-inking plants close to the "urban forests" of large U.S. cities. This is a classic case of a U.S. (sub-national) regulation leading to a switch of business modality from exporting to foreign direct investment.

What are the social costs of California's newspaper recycling laws? To a neoclassical economist they may be high, since investment, employment, R&D, etc. are lost to British Columbia and transferred to California. Yet to MacMillan Bloedel and other firms there is no choice; they must either become nationally responsive or lose the market. Given that from the firm's viewpoint there is no real or practical strategic option, except to play on this asymmetrical U.S. playing field, it seems churlish for economists to try to second guess the firm's strategic decisions. In summary, to remain internationally competitive Canadian firms need to have access to the U.S. market, and if their access by exports is threatened, they must achieve access by foreign direct investment and maintain the viability of such U.S. operations by an ongoing strategy of national responsiveness.

CONCLUSIONS

THE MAJOR POINT OF THIS STUDY is the asymmetry facing Canadian managers when making strategic management decisions. Unlike U.S. managers who can regard the Canadian market as a region of North America and legitimately proceed with strategic management decisions based on the three or five generics framework of Porter (1980, 1986), Canadian managers face a more complex task. As the U.S. market is 12 times as large as the Canadian market, Canadian investment abroad must be conceived and undertaken from a broader perspective than that of simply building on the small Canadian home base.

In short, in order to be successful competitors in the United States, Canadian managers need to have a national responsiveness mindset from day one of strategy design. They must not only achieve parity with rival U.S. firms in the U.S. market, but also outdo them in their U.S. home base. This is a classic case of the need for the national responsiveness strategy advocated by Bartlett & Ghoshal (1989). Even for resource-based commodity industries where only cost matters, to turn these commodities into products will require marketing and managerial expertise, mainly obtained in the U.S. market, not the Canadian.

The Canada-U.S. Free Trade Agreement and the NAFTA have not made strategic management decisions any easier for Canadian managers, although they may have done for U.S. managers. To an unfortunate extent many U.S. managers may view the FTA and the NAFTA as economic devices to integrate further the U.S. and Canadian strategic "space", leading to even further efforts to regard Canada as just another region of the U.S. market. This means that U.S. firms will follow cost, differentiation and/or focus strategies across the border without any thought of national responsiveness to Canadian conditions.

In contrast, most Canadian managers would probably regard the FTA and the NAFTA as, at best, partial institutional devices to put in place better rules for the operation of cross-border business activity. However, it is unlikely that many Canadian managers would regard the FTA and the NAFTA as giving complete free trade and unfettered access to the U.S. market. They would still regard the U.S. market as different from the Canadian market, with economic, political, legal, social and cultural differences. This asymmetric managerial information-processing capacity for Canadian managers, achieved through necessity, translates into a strategy of national responsiveness. On average, U.S. managers can get by without national responsiveness when doing business in Canada. But Canadians can rarely achieve success in the U.S. market without being nationally responsive.

On the basis of this emphasis on national responsiveness, it has been argued in this paper that there is not much that is "generic" for Canadian managers in the three or five generic strategies of Porter (1980, 1986). It is important to identify cost, differentiation and focus as relevant strategic options, but not in isolation from national responsiveness. There is an asymmetry for Canadian versus U.S. managers concerning the fundamental choices which need to be made between alternative patterns of decision and action. As a result, a distinction needs to be made between efficiency-based strategies and shelter-based strategies, and with no support being found for the latter, the generation of efficiency-based firm-specific advantages are the true generic strategies.

A new framework was developed which should be relevant for Canadian investment abroad. This relates the number of home bases (one or multiple) to the types of FSAs used (location bound versus non-location bound). This framework incorporates the Bartlett & Ghoshal concept of national responsiveness with Porter's generic strategies. In turn, this framework can be used to classify the actual strategies to be pursued by Canadian MNEs, relating the Canadian home base to national responsiveness in the U.S. market.

The implications for public policy of this analysis of the strategic management decisions of Canadian multinationals are simple. The United States is the key triad market for Canadian MNEs. The larger Canadian MNEs have been developing non-location bound FSAs based on Canada's strong resource base as well as location-bound FSAs of national responsiveness. Canadian government policy, at both federal and provincial levels, should be aware of, and supportive of, these joint strategies. By definition, these FSAs need to be proprietary to the Canadian multinationals; thus government policies must always be generally available to all firms and never discriminatory, since attempts to be selective would conflict with a firm's U.S. national responsiveness strategy. Recent policies to promote the FTA and the NAFTA are supportive of the framework proposed here. The revised framework for global strategy developed here should help to improve Canadian managerial practice and lead to more relevant strategic decision making by Canadian multinational enterprises.

ACKNOWLEDGEMENTS

MANY OF THE IDEAS IN THIS PAPER were developed with Professor Alain Verbeke of the University of Brussels; in particular, the second and third sections are our joint work. Helpful comments were also made by Steve Globerman, John Stopford, Mark Warner, Joseph D'Cruz, John Armstrong and John Knubley.

BIBLIOGRAPHY

Baden-Fuller, Charles and John Stopford. "Globalization Frustrated." *Strategic Management Journal* 12:7 (1991): 493-507.

_____. *Rejuvenating the Mature Business*. London: Routledge and Boston: Harvard Business School Press. 1993.

Bartlett, Christopher. "Building and Managing the Transnational: The New Organizational Challenge." In *Competition in Global Industries*. Edited by M.E. Porter. Boston, MA: Harvard Business School Press, 1986, pp. 367-404.

Bartlett, Christopher and Sumantra Ghoshal. *Managing Across Borders: The Transnational Solution*. Boston, MA: Harvard Business School Press, 1989.

Cho, S. D. and Michael Porter. "Changing Global Industry Leadership: The Case of Shipbuilding." In *Competition in Global Industries*. Edited by M.E. Porter. Boston, MA: Harvard Business School Press, 1986, pp. 539-68.

D'Cruz, Joseph R. "Business Networks for Global Competitiveness." *Business Quarterly*, 57, 4 (Summer 1993): 93-98.

D'Cruz, Joseph R. and Alan Rugman. *New Compacts for Canadian Competitiveness*. Toronto: Kodak Canada Inc., 1992a.

_____. "Business Networks for International Competitiveness." *Business Quarterly*, 56, 4 (Spring 1992b): 101-07.

_____. "Developing International Competitiveness: The Five Partners Model." *Business Quarterly*, 58, 2 (Fall 1993).

Doz, Yves. *Strategic Management in Multinational Companies*. Oxford: Pergamon, 1986.

Ghoshal, Sumantra. "Global Strategy: An Organizing Framework." *Strategic Management Journal*, 8 (1987): 425-40.

Hamel, Gary. "Competition for Competence and Inter-Partner Learning Within International Strategic Alliances." *Strategic Management Journal*, 12 (1991): 83-103.

Jegers, Marc. "Methodological Limitations of Porter's Three Generic Strategies Framework." In *Research in Global Strategic Management* Vol 4: Global Competition: Beyond the Three Generics. Edited by A.M. Rugman and A. Verbeke. Greenwich, Conn.: JAI Press, 1993, pp. 43-49.

Kobrin, Stephen J. "An Empirical Analysis of the Determinants of Global Integration." *Strategic Management Journal*, 12 (Special Issue 1991): 17-31.

Kogut, Bruce M. "Designing Global Strategies: Comparative and Competitive Value-Added Chains." *Sloan Management Review*, (Summer 1985a): 15-28.

_____. "Designing Global Strategies: Profiting From Operational Flexibility." *Sloan Management Review*, (Fall 1985b): 27-38.

Krugman, Paul. "The Case for Free Trade." *American Economic Review: Papers and Proceedings*, 83:2 (May 1993): 362-66.

Moon, Chang. "A Revised Framework of Global Strategy: Extending the Coordination-Configuration Framework." mimeo, University of the Pacific, Stockton, CA, 1992.

Ohmae, Ken-ichi. *The Borderless World*. New York: Harper Business, 1990.

Porter, Michael E. *Competitive Strategy: Techniques for Analyzing Industries and Competitors*. New York: The Free Press,1980.

_____. (ed.) *Competition in Global Industries*. Boston, MA: Harvard Business School Press, 1986.

_____. *The Competitive Advantages of Nations*. New York: The Free Press, 1990.

Porter, Michael E. and the Monitor Company. *Canada at the Crossroads*. Ottawa: Business

Council on National Issues and Minister of Supply and Services of the Government of Canada, 1991.

Porter, Michael E. and John Armstrong. "Dialogue on Canada at the Crossroads," *Business Quarterly*, 56, 4 (Spring 1992): 6-10.

Poynter, Thomas A. and Alan Rugman. "World Product Mandates: How Will Multinationals Respond?" *Business Quarterly*, 47, 3 (1983): 54-61.

Prahalad, C.K., and Yves Doz. *The Multinational Mission: Balancing Local Demands and Global Vision*. New York: The Free Press,1987.

Reitsperger, Wolf D., Shirley Daniel, and Stephen Tallman. "Integrating Generic Strategies: A Question of Strategic Intensity?" In *Research in Global Strategic Management* Vol 4: Global Competition: Beyond the Three Generics. Edited by A.M. Rugman and A. Verbeke. Greenwich, Conn.: JAI Press, 1993, pp. 65-79.

Roth, Kendall and Allen Morrison. "An Empirical Analysis of the Integration-Reponsiveness Framework in Global Industries." *Journal of International Business Studies*, 21, 4 (1990): 541-64.

_____. "Implementing Global Strategy: Characteristics of Global Subsidiary Mandates." *Journal of International Business Studies*, 23, 4 (1992).

Rugman, Alan M. "Diamond in the Rough." *Business Quarterly*, 55, 3 (Winter 1991): 61-4.

_____. "Dialogue on Canada at the Crossroads." *Business Quarterly*, 57, 1 (Summer 1992): 7-10.

Rugman, Alan M. and Andrew Anderson. *Administered Protection in America*. London: Croom Helm/Routledge, 1987.

Rugman, Alan M. and Jocelyn Bennett. "Technology Transfer and World Product Mandating in Canada." *Columbia Journal of World Business*, 18, 4 (1982): 58-62.

Rugman, Alan M. and Joseph D'Cruz. *Fast Forward: Improving Canada's International Competitiveness*. Toronto: Kodak Canada Inc., 1991.

_____. "The 'Double Diamond' Model of International Competitiveness," *Management International Review*, 33:2 (1993a): 17-40.

_____. "Business Networks and Strategic Management," In *Multinational Enterprises in North America*. Edited by Lorraine Eden. Calgary: University of Calgary Press, 1994.

Rugman, Alan M. and Michael Gestrin. "The Strategic Response of Multinational Enterprises to NAFTA." *Columbia Journal of World Business* 28, 4 (Winter 1993): 18-29.

Rugman, Alan M. and John McIlveen. *Megafirms: Strategies for Canada's Multinationals*. Toronto: Methuen Publications, 1985.

Rugman, Alan M. and Alain Verbeke. *Global Corporate Strategy and Trade Policy*. London: Routledge, 1990.

_____. "Environmental Change and Global Competitive Strategy in Europe." In *Research Global Strategic Management*, Vol. 2: Global Competition and the European Community. Edited by A.M. Rugman and A. Verbeke. Greenwich, Conn: JAI Press, 1991a, pp. 3-27.

_____. "Mintzberg's Intended and Emergent Corporate Strategies and Trade Policies." *Canadian Journal of Administrative Sciences*, 8, 3 (1991b): 200-8.

_____. "Trade Barriers and Corporate Strategy in International Companies." *Long Range Planning*, 24, 3 (1991c): 66-72.

_____. "Shelter, Trade Policy and Strategies for Multinational Enterprises." In *Research in Global Strategic Management*, Vol. 3: Corporate Response to Global Change. Edited by A.M. Rugman and A. Verbeke. Greenwich, Conn.: JAI Press, 1992a, pp. 3-25.

_____. "A Note on the Transnational Solution and the Transaction Cost Theory of

Multinational Strategic Management." *Journal of International Business Studies*, 23, 4 (December 1992b): 761-71.

_____. "Multinational Enterprise and National Economic Policy." In *Multinational Enterprises in the World Economy: Essays in Honour of John Dunning*. Edited by P.J. Buckley and M. Casson. Aldershot, U.K.: Edward Elgar, 1992c, pp. 194-211.

_____. "Foreign Subsidiaries and Multinational Strategic Management: An Extension and Correction of Porter's Single Diamond Framework." *Management International Review*, 33 (1993a Special Issue 2): 71-84.

_____. "Generic Strategies in Global Competition." In *Research in Global Strategic Management*, Vol. 4: Global Competition: Beyond the Three Generics. Edited by A.M. Rugman and Alain Verbeke. Greenwich, Conn.: JAI Press, 1993b, pp. 3-15.

Rugman, Alan M. and Mark A.A. Warner. "Strategies for the Canadian Multinationals." In *International Business in Canada: Strategies for Management*. Edited by Alan M. Rugman. Toronto: Prentice-Hall Canada, 1989, pp. 144-61.

_____. "Recent U.S. Protectionist R&D Policies: Are Canadian Multinationals Exempted?" University of Toronto, Faculty of Management, mimeo (December 1993).

Steven Globerman   *&*   Bernard M. Wolf
Department of Economics   Faculty of Administrative Studies
Simon Fraser University   York University

9

Joint Ventures and Canadian Outward Direct Investment

INTRODUCTION

THE RAPID PROLIFERATION of what have been variously identified as "strategic alliances" or "strategic partnerships" is arguably one of the most prominent developments in the business environment over the past decade. Since a large number of recently concluded alliances or partnerships involve firms with headquarters in different countries, it might be argued that the conduct of international business is changing in potentially profound ways.

The traditional focus of policy analysts has been on outward and (especially) inward foreign direct investment, partly because of traditional concerns about the 'sovereignty' of home country residents, and partly because of government fear of multinational enterprises (MNEs) dominating international trade and income flows. While a number of policy issues surrounding the direct investment process remain unresolved, the ostensibly growing prominence of international alliances raises a separate broad issue; namely, how does this alliancing activity alter or modify what we think we know about the direct investment process? A more specific issue is whether the alliancing process indicates a need for changes in public policy toward foreign investment activities of home country firms, where the latter include minority owned outward foreign investments.

It should be noted at the outset that this study focuses primarily on joint ventures as a specific form of alliance. There are several reasons for this. The first and perhaps most prominent is that data and case study information are more readily available for joint venturing activities than for other forms of alliancing. The second is that joint ventures clearly share several of the main characteristics of multinational investment. Most notably, they encompass equity ownership (albeit usually less than controlling ownership) in the partnering organizations. Furthermore, joint ventures encompass relational exchanges within the context of longer-term planning objectives, as distinct from exchanges in response to short-term opportunities for mutual gain (Mytelka, 1991).[1]

While strategic alliances presumably form a continuum with substitution possibilities across the range of alliances, the *a priori* substitution possibilities between non-equity based, specialized asset sharing arrangements such as technology transfer agreements and foreign direct investment are likely to be limited. Indeed, the strongest *a priori* substitution possibilities are arguably between equity-based joint ventures and foreign direct investment. Hence, identification of the determinants of alternative (to foreign direct investment) modes of international business is likely to be most successful if the focus is on joint ventures as the potential alternative.

This study addresses three interrelated questions:

- To what extent are international joint ventures substitutes for outward direct investment, and what factors condition the degree and nature of any substitutability?

- Do the extent and nature of international joint venturing activities being undertaken by Canadian firms raise any public policy issues?

- Are there grounds for Canadian government policies to promote or discourage international joint venturing by Canadian firms?

The study is organized as follows. The first section describes strategic alliancing activity broadly and joint venturing specifically and highlights the differences between international alliancing and foreign direct investment. The second section presents and discusses some data which offer a perspective on the magnitude and nature of alliancing activity (including joint venturing) and the participation of Canadian firms in this phenomenon. The third section assesses the relationship between alliancing, especially joint ventures, and foreign direct investment. The fourth section presents and discusses case studies of international joint ventures involving Canadian firms. The final section addresses potential public policy concerns associated with international joint venturing and offers a set of policy conclusions.

INTERNATIONAL STRATEGIC ALLIANCING AND INTERNATIONAL BUSINESS

WHILE OUR PRIMARY FOCUS is on the joint venture mode as an alternative to foreign direct investment, explicit and implicit hypotheses about the determinants of joint ventures are embedded in the broader literature on strategic alliances. Hence it is appropriate to review this broader literature in order to identify relevant hypotheses about joint ventures.

Despite a rapidly growing literature on strategic alliancing, there is still no well accepted definition of the phenomenon. This obviously complicates any effort to assess and synthesize the literature. It also underscores the importance of being explicit about the governance structure being compared to direct investment, since the comparison would not necessarily be expected to be identical for all forms of alliancing. In this latter regard a range of alliances, such as marketing agreements, technology exchange agreements and the like would seem on *ex ante* grounds to be related weakly, if at all, to foreign direct investment. On the other hand, international joint ventures and related equity cross-investments would seem to be closer in spirit to direct investment and, therefore, might arguably pose more of a challenge to the conventional wisdom surrounding the direct investment process.

It may be noted explicitly at the outset that it is difficult to draw a clear distinction between "outward" and "inward" alliances. Even when assets are created by an alliance and located in a specific locale, a variety of complementary activities may go on across borders with no clear identification of "host" and "home" participants. While this is also true to some extent even for foreign direct investment (FDI), the latter is more easily characterized by host and home country firms than, say, agreements to undertake and share research. Nevertheless, we shall try to keep as much as possible to the spirit of this volume by emphasizing joint ventures where Canadian firms invest in assets (tangible or intangible) located abroad. The qualifications and limitations associated with this focus are occasionally noted.

MOTIVES FOR ALLIANCING

VARIOUS MOTIVES FOR FORMING JOINT VENTURES have been suggested in the literature. The broad motives mentioned include: i) to acquire needed core competencies by pooling specific assets (or resources); ii) to operate in new markets which may encompass learning about those markets; iii) to diversify into new businesses; iv) to capitalize on economies of scale; v) to circumvent trade and foreign investment restrictions; and, vi) to influence industry structure or pre-empt competition.[2]

Many of these same motives have been suggested for direct investment abroad.[3] Why would a firm choose an international alliance (particularly a joint venture) rather than establish a wholly owned or majority-owned affiliate? One hypothesis is that restrictions on foreign ownership lead to the alliancing option being chosen as a "second best". Another hypothesis is that there are unique advantages to alliances which make direct investment a relatively weak substitute for alliances under specific conditions.

It is suggested that the unique advantages of joint ventures derive from specific trends in the economy which put a premium on the flexibility offered by alliancing. In particular, it is alleged that economic and technological changes are increasing the importance of speed and flexibility as key sources of competitive advantage. A related development is the increasing cost of maintaining technological competence, which also allegedly promotes the importance of sharing the costs of acquiring this competence and, indeed, of sharing the costs of learning more generally.

Ghoshal, Arinzen & Brownfield (1992) offer a representative statement of this broad motive for alliancing:

> Companies are confronted by the rapid globalization of markets and competition, the increasing importance of speed and flexibility as key sources of comparative advantage. . . . No one can do it alone. It costs too much to invest in certain technologies for one firm to finance it; the risks are too great for one firm to bear alone. . . . Global competition creates the simultaneous need for global scale-efficiencies, worldwide learning and local responsiveness. One response is specialization and contribution of best of breed to a strategic alliance rather than going it alone.[4]

Mytelka (1991) argues that in the face of financial and economic uncertainty and turbulence in the world economy and of parallel rapid and radical technological change, the 'new' forms of inter-firm agreements offer firms a way of ensuring, in a wide range of situations, a high degree of flexibility in their operations. Safarian (1991) also highlights the increased rapidity of technological change as placing a premium on more flexible and shorter-term arrangements than acquisitions.

Michalet (1991), among others, associates the advantages of alliancing with those of networking more generally. The main advantages are twofold: i) a reduction in costs resulting in an improvement in productivity due to more specialized components within the firm and ii) greater flexibility allowing for more rapid and extensive product differentiation and a more innovative attitude towards changes in the environment. In contrast to the global firm, i.e. the multinational enterprise (MNE), which favours the homogenization of products and processes worldwide, the network firm is able to adapt more easily to an increasingly diversified demand.[5]

In short, speed, flexibility and an increased need to pool financial resources and share information are cited as particularly important environmental motives for alliancing generally and joint ventures more specifically. However, as we shall discuss in more detail below, there has been only limited empirical examination of the presumed advantages of joint ventures. Moreover, even the theoretical arguments are subject to qualification. For example, it is not obvious why it would necessarily be faster to establish a joint venture than to acquire the potential joint venture partner, since establishing joint ventures usually requires a substantial amount of negotiation and legal formalization of the respective partners' obligations and responsibilities.[6]

The greater flexibility of joint ventures is presumably associated, at least in part, with avoiding certain sunk cost investments by sharing assets with joint venture partners. While it is relatively clear that sharing costs associated with overseas expansion reduces the absolute financial outlay required to enter markets, it is possible that sunk costs associated with exiting markets may be higher under the joint venture option. Specifically, it may be more difficult to liquidate assets in a joint venture if the latter "goes south" than it is to liquidate the assets of a wholly owned affiliate, since the value of assets tied up in a joint venture is dependent upon how the partner decides to use or dispose of its share of the venture.

The greater flexibility of joint ventures also rests on a claim that the benefits of sharing assets are becoming increasingly more specific. That is, complementarities which previously might have been captured through mergers or acquisitions are now more efficiently captured through joint ventures, since joint ventures obviate the need to expand the scope of a single management structure across a substantially broader range of business activity. Rather, some subset of the management of each joint venture partner needs to expand the scope of its focus to include the joint venture itself; however, the latter is presumably only a small expansion of the existing range of activities currently being managed. Hence, managerial diseconomies of scale that might be associated with gaining access to a relatively specialized asset by acquiring the entire organization may be mitigated by entering into a specialized joint venture.[7]

While quite plausible, this flexibility argument overlooks the fact that many foreign acquisitions and alliances involve affiliations with small companies whose values are, in fact, largely associated with ownership of certain specific assets. Moreover, host government policies may underlie any managerial diseconomies of scale associated with operating a network of foreign affiliates. In particular, to the extent that different governments impose conflicting requirements on the operations of a company's various foreign affiliates, any benefits of internalization may be more than offset by overhead costs required to remain informed of and to comply with different host government policies. On the other hand, as policies toward MNEs are harmonized through international trade agreements and treaties, direct investment abroad might be a net source of managerial economies of scale.

The financial benefits of establishing joint ventures and related alliances rather than establishing overseas affiliates are also arguably more subtle than typically represented. Two broadly related arguments are often made: it is cheaper to raise capital through alliancing; and it is less risky to invest through alliancing.

To the extent that one or the other party to a joint venture supplies financial capital to the partner, it reduces the need for the "non-contributing" partner to raise capital externally. If capital markets were perfectly efficient, it would be hard to see why capital raised from a joint venture partner would be cheaper than capital raised from broader equity issuances, e.g., selling common shares to public investors; however, a plausible argument can be made that capital markets are at least to some extent subject to information asymmetry. Specifically, potential outside investors may be misinformed about the expected returns and expected risks of specific ventures, whereas incumbent firms in related lines of business may be relatively well informed of these pitfalls. In this case, the firm in need of capital may find it cheaper to raise funds by dealing with knowledgeable investors, i.e., other firms. Moreover, taking in a well-known industry insider as an investor might serve as a credible signal to potential outside investors that the venture is credit-worthy and may therefore reduce future financing costs. This seems related to a motive adduced by Teece (1987) for alliances in high-technology industries; namely, smaller, less integrated companies are often eager to form joint ventures with established companies because of the name recognition and reputation spillovers the latter can provide.

To the extent that partners share the costs of a joint venture, there is some risk pooling for both parties. This seems to be what most proponents of the lower risk motive for alliancing have in mind. However, as noted above, risk also depends upon the characteristics of the investment, especially the "sunkness" of the relevant assets. In this context, entering a joint venture rather than establishing an affiliate might increase the overall risk of the venture itself, partly or completely offsetting any advantages of risk pooling. The higher risk of alliancing might be associated with a lower probability of success for the venture and/or a reduced potential for easy salvage of the assets in the venture.

It has also been argued that international joint ventures are less risky than establishing foreign affiliates because joint ventures involve fewer political risks given the preference of governments for participating in high-technology sectors through "national champions".[8] The relevance of sharing these risks through a joint venture of some sort becomes increasingly compelling the more limited the experience and knowledge one or another party has regarding the activities in question. In this case, the advantage of joint ventures would be primarily a function of host government policies.

This critical assessment of the reputed benefits of joint ventures is not academic nit-picking. To the extent that they are a preferred international business mode, joint ventures may convey benefits that would not otherwise be obtainable by home country participants. Furthermore, if some of the benefits are external to the home country participants in the alliance, an argument might be made for government encouragement of international joint ventures, especially if there is any reason to believe that home country firms are eschewing privately (and socially) beneficial joint ventures. The opposite policy conclusion would be drawn if joint ventures imposed net costs on the home economy. On the other hand, if they are primarily a second-best alternative to foreign direct investment, home country public policy might profitably focus on encouraging a liberalization of the international investment environment.

Possible Social Benefits and Costs of
International Alliances

THE POTENTIAL SOCIAL BENEFITS or costs of international joint ventures undertaken by home country firms clearly depend upon the nature of the joint ventures. For example, if a joint venture facilitates entry into new foreign markets by home country firms, it could promote improvements in a country's terms-of-trade. It might also encourage home country firms to undertake more R&D and innovation, since the relevant expenditures can be amortized over a larger volume of sales. These increased R&D expenditures can, in turn, generate external productivity gains for other home country firms.[9]

On the other hand, joint ventures whereby home country firms provide technology in exchange for access to foreign markets might accelerate the rate of innovation and technology adoption in foreign markets. This, in turn, might enable foreign firms to compete more successfully in international markets against home country firms with adverse effects on the home country's terms-of-trade.[10]

A more prevalent concern about joint ventures is that they may reduce competition in the domestic economy with associated adverse effects on rates of productivity growth and the ability of home country firms to compete against foreign-based firms. Two insights are relevant here: first, when profit streams of individual firms are linked through joint ventures or partial equity ownership, each firm will have an increased incentive to compete less vigorously and adopt behaviour conducive to joint profit maximization;[11] and second, Canada's *Competition Act* adopts a relatively benign attitude towards joint ventures.[12]

It may be noted that anti-competitive consequences of joint ventures do not require increased collusion subsequent to their formation, although joint approval of competitive initiatives is often a feature of joint ventures. In addition, an increased flow of information about the business plans of strategic partners could improve underlying information, thereby facilitating the co-ordination of capacity expansion, price changes and other potentially destabilizing competitive initiatives. While these concerns may be most directly relevant to joint ventures formed within Canada, "outward" alliances might lead to less competition within the Canadian market, e.g., through less aggressive exporting to Canada by foreign firms. On the other hand, if joint ventures promote the entry of imports into domestic markets or help strengthen the competitive capabilities of specific incumbent domestic firms, they may well promote competition in domestic markets.

There is relatively little published evidence on the social benefits and costs of joint ventures including their impact on competition in domestic industries. Several studies focus on the influence of joint ventures on the competitiveness of home country firms without ever explicitly identifying what is meant by "competitiveness". For example, Mowery (1988) finds no evidence that joint ventures between U.S. and foreign commercial aircraft firms erode the competitiveness of the U.S. commercial aircraft industry. Specifically, the flow of technology appears to be two-way. Moreover, while offshore production of aircraft components and assemblies may reduce the domestic content of each aircraft or engine sold, such teaming may also increase total sales of the final product, thereby creating or preserving jobs in the domestic industry as a whole. Mowery concludes that the imposition of controls or federal regulations on international collaboration, or on technology transfers within alliances, is undesirable. Rather, the U.S. government should address foreign trade-distorting policies which leave U.S. firms with no choice but to seek out a foreign partner for product development and manufacture.

Klepper (1988) in his study of the robotics industry concludes that international collaborations of all kinds may have enabled U.S. firms to develop a leading position in many of the control and software areas of the industry. While international joint ventures may have solidified the prominence of non-U.S. firms in robotic arm technology, it is not clear that any other policies could have mitigated this development without causing more serious problems than they were intended to cure. In a similar vein, Lynn (1988) concludes that while joint ventures with foreign steel companies may not have contributed to a resurgence of the U.S. steel industry, they may have helped slow its decline.

A comprehensive study of joint ventures in the automotive industry by Wolf & Globerman (1992) identifies a wide range of potential motives for alliances in the industry but draws particular attention to knowledge transfers. In particular, North American companies "learned about" lean production techniques from their Japanese counterparts, while at the same time the Japanese partners learned about the North American environment in which they were becoming increasingly important players.[13]

Alliances in the assembly sector of the industry arguably improved the efficiency of Canada's Big Three auto producers. Canadian parts suppliers also improved productivity and product quality by learning lean production techniques.[14] The authors find no basis for concluding that these alliances directly shifted production into or out of Canada, although without the efficiencies gained, Canadian production capacity would arguably have been reduced by international competition.[15]

Perhaps the most important conclusion of the Wolf & Globerman (1992) study is their finding that strategic alliancing in most cases increased competition in the North American automobile industry. Specifically, the market access provided by alliances with American-owned assemblers arguably lowered the costs of entry into North American markets for small Japanese assemblers such as Suzuki in its Canadian joint venture (CAMI) with General Motors. Indeed, in the early stages of entry, alliances lowered the costs of entry for larger Japanese suppliers such as Toyota, Mazda and Mitsubishi. At the same time, by enhancing the efficiency of North American procedures, alliances with Japanese companies may have enabled those producers to maintain a presence in the North American market. Moreover, there is little evidence of alliances leading to implicit agreements to share markets or to refrain from price competition, even among partners to a joint venture.[16] To be sure, many of these alliances would be considered, in our terminology, inward rather than outward, as they involved joint ventures and related investments within Canada. Nevertheless, if inward alliances raise few competitive concerns, one can be even more sanguine about outward alliances.

Next, we consider available evidence on patterns of strategic alliancing, including joint ventures, with a view toward gaining a perspective on the relative participation of Canadian firms and the potential arguments for government intervention.

TABLE 1

TRENDS IN THE GROWTH OF INTER-FIRM AGREEMENTS

AUTHOR AND TYPE OF AGREEMENT	'74	'75	'76	'77	'78	'79	'80	'81	'82	'83	'84	'85
Hladick (1985) Joint ventures by U.S. firms in high-income countries	37	14	16	15	14	27	34	40	35	–	–	–
Reseau, Milan (1985) Electronics	–	–	–	131	–	–	–	–	69	104	118	–
Hacklish (1986) 41 largest world merchant semi-conductor firms	–	–	–	–	2	1	4	22	19	16	42	–
Larea-Cerem (1986) Agreements involving European firms in R&D intensive industries	–	–	–	–	–	–	15	31	58	97	131	149
Venture Economics (1986) Corporate venture capital investment agreements	–	–	–	–	30	30	30	60	100	150	195	245
Schiller (1986) International agreements with small U.S.biotech firms	–	–	–	–	–	–	–	22	58	49	69	90

Source: Cited in Safarian (1991, Table 9). Original source: Chesnais, "Technical Cooperation Agreements Between Firms", OECD, *STI Review*, No. 4, 1988.

TABLE 2

INCREASE IN THE NUMBER OF INTER-FIRM AGREEMENTS BY FORM OF CO-OPERATION
(ABSOLUTE NUMBERS AND %)

MODES OF CO-OPERATION	BEFORE 1972	1973 – 1976	1977 – 1980	1981 – 1984	1985 – 1988	TOTAL
Joint ventures and research corporations	83	64	112	254	345	858
	53.2	41.8	23.6	20.8	17.8	21.6
Joint R&D	14	22	65	225	653	1,009
	9.0	14.4	13.1	20.9	33.7	25.5
Technology exchange agreements	6	4	33	152	165	360
	3.8	2.6	6.7	12.4	8.5	9.1
Direct investment (minority and cross-holdings)	27	29	168	170	237	631
	17.3	19.0	33.9	13.9	12.2	15.9
Customer-supplier relationship	5	19	47	133	265	469
	3.2	12.4	9.5	10.9	13.7	11.8
One-directional technology flows	21	15	71	259	271	637
	13.5	9.8	14.3	21.2	14.0	16.1
Total Number of Agreements	156	153	496	1,223	1,936	3,964

Source: Cited in Safarian (1991), Table 10. Original Source: J. Hagedoorn and J. Schakenraad, "Technology Co-operation, Strategic Alliances and their Motives: Brother, Can You Spare a Dime or Do You Have a Light?" Paper for SMS Conference, Stockholm, September 24-27, 1990.

TABLE 3

PATTERNS OF INTER-FIRM AGREEMENTS: GEOGRAPHICAL DISTRIBUTION

GEOGRAPHIC AREAS	HIGH-TECH INDUSTRIES		ALL INDUSTRIES	
	NUMBER	%	NUMBER	%
Intra-area				
U.S.	254	23.9	352	18.7
EC	150	14.1	282	15.0
Japan	18	1.7	59	3.1
Inter-area				
U.S.-EC	276	26.0	413	21.9
U.S.-Japan	141	13.3	202	8.6
EC-Japan	87	8.2	162	10.8
With other areas	135	12.8	413	21.9
Total	1,061	100.0	1,883	100.0

Source: Chesnais (1988) cited in Safarian (1991).

EXTENT AND NATURE OF ALLIANCING ACTIVITY

A REVIEW OF AVAILABLE information allows certain conclusions to be drawn about alliancing activity. One such conclusion is that joint ventures have ostensibly grown increasingly numerous in recent years. A second is that U.S. firms are especially prominent in international alliancing activity. Table 1 offers some support for the first conclusion. Specifically, it summarizes findings from various studies, all of which show a growth in inter-firm agreements in the 1980s compared to the 1970s.[17]

Table 2 provides similar evidence. Specifically, it shows that, compared to the 1970s, a dramatic increase in the absolute number of inter-firm agreements took place in the 1980s. It also shows a significant change in the nature of inter-firm agreements over time. In particular, the relative importance of joint ventures and research corporations decreased, while the relative importance of joint R&D increased substantially. Minority direct investments and cross-holdings also decreased somewhat in importance.

The emerging importance of joint R&D is underscored by the concentration of agreements in specific sectors. Safarian (1991) notes that about 40 percent of the agreements identified in Table 2 are in information technology industries, 20 percent in biotechnology, 10 percent each in new materials and chemicals and the remaining 20 percent in various manufacturing sectors.

The sectoral distribution of alliances suggests that U.S. firms should be heavily represented given the relatively large sizes of the information technology and biotechnology industries in the United States. Table 3 supports this inference. Specifically, it shows that the majority of both intra-national and international agreements involve U.S. firms. The prevalence of U.S. firms in inter-firm agreements is particularly noteworthy in high-tech industries. Table 4

TABLE 4

AGREEMENTS BY FRENCH FIRMS BY PARTNER'S NATIONALITY (%)

AEROSPACE/AIRCRAFT		INFORMATION TECHNOLOGY	
France	32	France	35
EC	32	EC	20
U.S.	23	U.S.	39
Japan	0	Japan	6
Others	11	Others	5
BIOTECHNOLOGY		MATERIALS	
France	35	France	21
EC	16	EC	18
U.S.	30	U.S.	32
Japan	7	Japan	11
Others	11	Others	18

Source: Mytelka (1991).

shows inter-firm agreements involving French firms by the nationality of their partners. In three industry sectors – information technology, biotechnology and materials – U.S. firms are the most prominent foreign alliancing partners, whereas other EC firms are most prominent in the case of aerospace/aircraft.

Given the high degree of uncertainty surrounding the success or failure of specific technological initiatives, technologically emerging industries such as biotechnology seem to be representative of sectors where firms seek to minimize sunk costs and pool risks. It is also a sector where asymmetric information might make it cheaper to raise capital from established firms rather than from outside capital markets. Certain segments of the information technology sector also seem to share similar characteristics with the biotechnology sector.

The prominence of technology exchanges indicated by the sectoral concentration of alliances and the relatively rapid growth of R&D alliances suggest that the welfare implications for the countries involved are principally related to technological externalities. They also suggest that joint ventures in these sectors are unlikely to raise anti-competitive concerns, as rapid technological change makes it unlikely that any set of firms can exercise market dominance for very long.

SOME DATA ON JOINT VENTURING BY CANADIAN FIRMS

CONCEPTUALLY, OUR FOCUS IN THIS SECTION is on international joint ventures (JVs) undertaken by one or more Canadian firms with the objective of expanding or enhancing that firm's (or firms') presence in foreign markets. As noted above, this is not always a straightforward task in practice. Specifically, inward alliances may be related to outward alliances. For example, a JV established in Canada between a Canadian firm and a foreign-owned firm might ultimately lead to a JV between those same firms outside Canada. In this case, a distinction between inward and outward investment is somewhat arbitrary. In other cases, alliances may involve no change in the geographical location of the relevant set of assets, e.g., an agreement to share R&D results, so that there is no direct linkage to international expansion by the Canadian company involved.

In order to be consistent with the literature on foreign direct investment, we consider a joint venture to be outward if it involves a Canadian firm locating assets in a foreign country. An inward joint venture involves a foreign-based company locating or acquiring assets in Canada.

Tables 5 and 6 report the number of joint ventures in the United States involving one non-U.S. partner over the years between 1981 and 1988. The presence of a Canadian or non-Canadian partner is indicated, as is the nature of the industrial sector to which the joint venture is classified. Given the relatively small number of JVs reported in the Tables, it seemed to make sense to aggregate the sectoral distribution of joint ventures into broader categories.[18] Clearly, these categories are somewhat arbitrary on the margin; however, they are meant to convey broad distinctions in the nature of the key competitive success factors underlying the various industries.

Several points seem to emerge from Tables 5 and 6. One is that JV activity increased somewhat in the second four-year period compared to the first four-year period, although the increase does not seem dramatic. A second point is that JVs involving Canadian parents were virtually unchanged between the two sub-periods. Over the same time period, JVs by European parents declined substantially; however, the most notable feature in Tables 5 and 6 is the explosion of joint ventures involving Japanese parents. A third point is that scale-intensive JVs tend to be the single most prevalent category in the U.S. sample. This result may strongly reflect the fact that transportation equipment is included in this broad category and joint ventures have proliferated in the automotive sector. The concentration of Canadian JVs in the scale-intensive and supplier-dominated sectors presumably reflects the relative importance of these sectors in Canada's manufacturing industries.

The relatively small number of service sector alliances is worth noting. This pattern is consistent with the relatively small amount of foreign direct investment that has traditionally characterized the service sector; however, service sector joint venturing seems to be accelerating, which would also be consistent with an increasing absolute and relative amount of direct investment in service industries.

Since data are unavailable concerning the magnitudes of the joint ventures reported in Tables 5 and 6, as well as the extent of joint venturing by Canadian companies in countries other than the United States, one must be very circumspect in drawing inferences from the available data; however, several cautious inferences seem appropriate. First, Canadian firms seem slightly under-represented in the United States in terms of joint-venture activity, at least relative to their share of direct investment activity in the United States. For example, over the years between 1981 and 1986, Canadian parents accounted for approximately 9 percent of the JVs reported in Tables 5 and 6. In 1987, affiliates of Canadian firms in the United States accounted for approximately 12 percent of all affiliate sales in the United States and 19 percent of all manufacturing affiliate sales.[19] A second is that Canadian firms seem particularly under-represented in the science-based and specialized supplier categories. We shall consider the implications of these observations later in this study.

By way of background, it might be useful to consider data on Canadian direct investment abroad over a similar period. Table 7 reports Canadian foreign direct investment abroad for the period from 1981 to 1988 classified as: i) complete or majority ownership; ii) minority ownership and, iii) unincorporated. The data in Table 7 indicate that all categories of direct investment abroad increased over the period with a slight relative increase in complete or majority ownership. To the extent that minority ownership and unincorporated status reflect joint venturing behaviour, rather than traditional direct investment abroad, the data in Table 7 further suggest that Canadian

TABLE 5

TWO-PARENT JOINT VENTURES IN THE UNITED STATES WITH ONE FOREIGN PARENT FORMED BETWEEN 1981 AND 1984

	INDUSTRY TYPE					
	SCIENCE-BASED	SPECIALIZED SUPPLIER	SCALE INTENSIVE	SUPPLIER DOMINATED	FINANCIAL SERVICES	OTHER SERVICES
PARENT COUNTRY						
Canada	3	1	10	1	1	1
Europe (total)	24	16	38	8	7	23
Austria	0	0	0	0	0	0
Belgium	3	0	0	0	0	0
Denmark	0	0	0	0	0	3
Finland	0	1	0	1	0	1
France	2	4	6	1	0	3
Germany (FDR)	6	5	6	3	2	7
Ireland	0	0	0	0	0	1
Italy	1	1	1	0	1	1
Liechtenstein	0	0	0	0	0	0
Luxembourg	0	0	0	0	0	0
Netherlands	1	0	4	0	0	0
Norway	0	0	2	0	0	1
Portugal	0	0	0	0	0	0
Spain	0	0	0	0	0	1
Sweden	3	3	4	1	0	2
Switzerland	1	0	0	0	0	0
United Kingdom	7	2	15	2	4	3
Japan	12	7	16	6	2	13
Australasia	1	1	1	0	0	1
Latin America	0	0	0	0	0	0
Africa/Middle East	1	0	1	0	0	0
USSR/Eastern Europe	0	0	0	0	0	2
Foreign, Unspecified	0	0	0	0	0	0
Total	65	41	104	23	17	63

Total: All Joint Ventures 313

Source: J. Michael Geringer, 1993.

firms have not embraced strategic joint venturing as a robust alternative to traditional outward direct investment. We consider this suggestion in more detail later.

RELATIONSHIP BETWEEN CDIA AND INTERNATIONAL JOINT VENTURING

ONE THEORETICAL CHALLENGE posed by international joint ventures is why such alliances are used as governance structures for international business. In particular, do they displace traditional direct investment abroad as

TABLE 6

TWO-PARENT JOINT VENTURES IN THE UNITED STATES WITH ONE FOREIGN PARENT FORMED BETWEEN 1985 AND 1988

	INDUSTRY TYPE					
	SCIENCE-BASED	SPECIALIZED SUPPLIER	SCALE INTENSIVE	SUPPLIER DOMINATED	FINANCIAL SERVICES	OTHER SERVICES
PARENT COUNTRY						
Canada	1	1	6	5	1	4
Europe (total)	8	10	19	17	5	17
Austria	0	0	0	0	0	0
Belgium	0	0	1	1	0	0
Denmark	0	0	0	1	0	0
Finland	0	0	1	0	0	1
France	2	2	0	1	2	5
Germany (FDR)	1	2	3	2	0	3
Ireland	0	0	0	1	0	2
Italy	0	0	1	1	0	2
Liechtenstein	0	0	0	0	0	0
Luxembourg	0	0	0	0	0	0
Netherlands	1	1	3	3	1	1
Norway	1	1	2	0	0	1
Portugal	0	0	0	0	0	0
Spain	0	0	0	0	0	0
Sweden	0	0	1	2	1	2
Switzerland	1	1	1	2	0	1
United Kingdom	2	3	6	3	1	6
Japan	29	22	64	21	3	32
Australasia	1	0	8	2	1	4
Latin America	0	0	3	0	1	0
Africa/Middle East	1	1	0	0	0	0
USSR/Eastern Europe	0	0	0	0	0	0
Foreign, Unspecified	0	0	0	0	0	0
Total	48	44	119	62	16	81

Total: All Joint Ventures 370

Source: J. Michael Geringer, 1993.

a means of undertaking international economic expansion by business, or are they largely complementary to direct investment?

A number of theoretical contributions have addressed this challenge. The main insights are summarized in Dunning (1993, p. 235). He notes that in imperfect markets ownership will be chosen if it is more likely to advance the firm's goals, to reduce perceived transaction costs (including risk) associated with governance, and/or to increase economic rent earned on the relevant set of activities; and if these benefits are not offset by the additional communications, organizational and production costs associated with internalization. Dunning also notes the benefits of sharing the uncertainty surrounding resource commitments.

TABLE 7

CANADIAN OUTWARD FDI, CLASSIFIED BY NATURE OF PARENT-AFFILIATE OWNERSHIP LINK, 1981-1988

| YEAR | INCORPORATED | | | | UNINCORPORATED | | |
| | COMPLETE OR MAJORITY | | MINORITY OWNERSHIP | | | | TOTAL |
	$ MILLION	% OF TOTAL	$ MILLION	% OF TOTAL	$ MILLION	% OF TOTAL	$ MILLION
1981	29,112	86	3,053	9	1,682	5	33,847
1982	31,439	88.4	2,315	6.5	1,804	5.1	35,558
1983	33,057	87.5	2,526	6.7	2,210	5.8	37,793
1984	36,178	82.0	5,470	12.4	2,471	5.6	44,119
1985	41,690	83.0	5,656	11.3	2,847	5.7	50,193
1986	44,693	84.1	5,564	10.5	2,916	5.5	53,173

Source: Gorecki, Paul K. *Patterns of Canadian Foreign Direct Investment Abroad*, Statistics Canada, Research Paper Series No. 33, 1990, Table 10.

While much has been written about the benefits of alliances under specific circumstances, relatively few studies have attempted to identify empirically the circumstances under which specific alliances, such as joint ventures, will be favoured relative to establishing wholly (or majority owned) affiliates. Perhaps the most comprehensive study is Auster's (1992) analysis of Japanese investment in the United States. In this study, she finds a predominance of technological linkages, e.g., technology licensing in emerging industries, joint ventures in growing industries and direct investment in maturing industries. This is consistent with her hypothesis that technological linkages will be most attractive in emerging industries as firms struggle to acquire technology, information and expertise and share cost and risk, yet retain flexibility. It is also consistent with the expectation that joint ventures should proliferate in growing industries because they offer a means of acquiring and expanding customer bases, yet reduce risk. In maturing industries, where firms' key competencies are more developed, direct investment allows the company to generate demand in new markets without the disadvantage of joint governance.

Auster's emphasis on risk-sharing as a dominant motive for alliancing, including joint venturing, does not receive robust support from several well-known surveys of alliances. In one survey, Marti & Smiley (1983) examined published reports of all cooperative agreements that were initiated in 1980 and reported in the European financial press. Through a combination of interviews and press reports, they identified a set of motives for the co-operative agreements. Risk sharing was cited in only 14 percent of the cases. Nevertheless, technology is clearly the important asset under alliancing, as technology transfers (either one-way or two-way) were cited as a motive for joint alliancing in 70 percent of the cases; however, the survey did not establish why alliances were chosen rather than another type of governance structure.[20]

In an empirical study of international strategic alliances formed between 1970 and 1982, Ghemawat, Porter & Rawlinson (1986) concluded that a quest to capture economies of scale was the single most important motive for alliancing in their sample. Market access was the next most important motive followed by technology development. Again, no attempt was made to evaluate why joint ventures or other forms of alliances were chosen in preference to another mode of international business.

Direct evidence on the choice of governance mode is provided by Gomes-Casseres (1989). In one study, the ownership choice between a wholly owned affiliate and joint venture is examined. Controlling for government influences on ownership patterns, the probability of an MNE concluding a joint venture was negatively correlated with its previous experience of operating foreign subsidiaries in the same sector and with its knowledge, of the country in which the joint venture was being contemplated. On the other hand, the size of the host country's industrial sector was positively correlated with the propensity of MNEs to conclude market-seeking joint ventures, particularly when the investing firm depended on the input of raw materials and the local partner could contribute marketing knowledge and skills.

In another study, Gomes-Casseres (1990) shows that the role of host governments was often critical in affecting the ownership structure of foreign direct investment. Holding other factors constant and assuming that some local ownership of foreign affiliates was desirable from the host government's viewpoint, the greater the bargaining power of governments, the more likely that joint ventures would be concluded.

Blomström & Zejan's (1991) study of the determinants of the owner-ship share of Swedish-owned foreign affiliates supports Gomes-Casseres' (1989) conclusion. Specifically, Swedish firms with only brief experience of foreign production and with highly diversified product lines were most likely to choose minority ventures; however, unlike Gomes-Casseres, they found that after a certain point, the size of a host country's market was positively related to the likelihood of a Swedish firm concluding minority joint ventures.

Indirect evidence on the relationship between joint ventures and alliances is provided in a study by Franko (1989). He argues that the move to acceptance of minority ownership positions was specifically a phenomenon of less developed countries (LDCs) and was concentrated in five specific countries. Barriers to complete merger (or takeover) of joint venture partners is especially marked in LDCs. Without necessarily gainsaying the importance of host government restrictions on foreign ownership as a motive for joint venture, Franko's conclusion that minority ownership is largely a phenomenon in LDCs seems belied by data presented in Tables 1 through 4.

Notwithstanding that joint ventures are prominent in developed countries, government restrictions on majority foreign ownership have traditionally been more relevant in the case of developing countries. For example, a survey by Beamish (1985) concluded that 64 percent of foreign firms questioned gave the need for partner skills as their main reason for concluding joint ventures in developed countries, while 17 percent mentioned government restrictions. Conversely, 57 percent of those seeking partners in developing countries thought government restrictions were the main reason, while 38 percent cited the need for local skills.

Contractor's (1990) study of U.S. joint ventures abroad provides additional evidence. He interprets data from the U.S. Department of Commerce's *Benchmark Surveys* as showing a small but unmistakable across-the-board reduction in the equity limits imposed on foreign investors in the 1980s. The result was a small but also unmistakable reduction in the proportion and share of sales of minority and 50-50 affiliates in all but a few nations. He also finds that host-government-imposed limits and performance requirements induce a greater use of minority and 50-50 affiliates in developed but particularly in developing countries. He finds indirect support for the hypothesis that joint ventures are increasingly maintained by the need for local help, synergies with local partners and minimum economies of scale – particularly in the large markets of OECD nations.

Several industry case studies also underscore the relevance of host government policies toward foreign ownership as an important conditioner of the choice of international business mode. For example, Pisano, Russo & Teece (1988) identify the importance of host government opposition to foreign takeovers of local telecommunications equipment suppliers as a motive for joint ventures and other collaborative arrangements in the industry.[21]

Mowery (1988) highlights the role of government policy in influencing collaborative ventures in the commercial aircraft industry. He argues that the decline in the relative size of the U.S. market for commercial aircraft and the steady growth of development costs mean that penetration of foreign markets is essential. Access to foreign markets by U.S. firms is often facilitated by enlisting a foreign firm as a partner in the development and production of an airframe or engine. To be sure, access to lower cost of capital and risk-sharing also apparently motivate U.S. firms to seek foreign partners; however, access to lower cost of capital itself apparently reflects, at least in part, host government policies. Specifically, a lower cost of capital is associated with foreign governments providing loans or other subsidies for a portion of the development costs incurred by their domestic aircraft firms.

In short, evidence on the extent and nature of the tradeoff between joint ventures and foreign direct investment tends to be limited and sometimes contradictory. However, it seems clear that host government policies affecting the possibility and profitability of operating wholly owned affiliates are clearly one important conditioning factor in many cases. It is also clear that direct investment (both inward and outward) and joint ventures are stimulated by opportunities and threats created by global competition. In a very broad sense, the lack of knowledge or familiarity with specific geographic and product markets (what might be called psychological distance) may predispose firms to choose joint ventures as an early entry strategy into international markets undergoing rapid structural change.

CASE STUDIES

IN THIS SECTION WE CONSIDER three industry case studies in order to gain some additional insight into the motives for and consequences of international joint ventures. The three industries are telecommunications services, automotive parts and software. All three industries have been characterized by a proliferation of international strategic alliances and therefore offer a potentially useful perspective on these issues.

It should be noted in advance that a substantial number of the cases discussed are not joint ventures in the traditional sense. Indeed, the case studies underscore the extraordinary variety of equity-based investments that firms are making which fall short of traditional foreign direct investments. In the software industry, many of the alliances are marketing agreements with no equity investments involved. They offer interesting counterparts to equity-based agreements in telecommunications that are negotiated, in part, to gain market access.

Telecommunications Services

A number of high-profile international equity-based alliances have been struck by Canadian telecommunications service-suppliers in the past few years. It may be noted that most of these alliances cannot be classified as 'outward' in the sense that we defined the term earlier; i.e., an alliance that is associated with increased Canadian ownership of assets abroad. Moreover, they are not joint ventures, strictly speaking. Rather, they primarily involve foreign firms taking minority ownership positions in the Canadian parent company or vice-versa. Nevertheless, the alliances are intended, in part, to enhance the ability of Canadian carriers to compete in both the domestic and foreign markets. Hence, they have potential implications for the competitiveness of domestic firms and are potentially instructive of the effects of joint ventures.

In one major alliance, AT&T acquired a 20 percent equity stake in Unitel. AT&T's stake was acquired from Unitel's two existing shareholders, Canadian Pacific Ltd. and Rogers Communications Inc., in exchange for long-distance switching machinery valued at C$ 150 million. The three companies also agreed to inject a total of C$ 200 million of equity into Unitel after the deal was completed.[22]

The 20 percent equity stake represents the maximum allowable foreign ownership share of a Canadian facilities-based telephone carrier under Bill C-62.[23] Hence, it is a moot point whether AT&T preferred a larger ownership interest in Unitel. AT&T's stated objective was access to customers. Specifically, Unitel will join AT&T's World Source partnership, a joint venture of Asian, North American and European carriers designed to offer common business long-distance services (including one bill in a currency of the customers' choice) to MNEs. The inclusion of Unitel offers a Canadian node to the World Source partnership – a node AT&T could not develop on its own, given Bill C-62.

Unitel's management also noted the advantage it gained in being able to offer access to World Service networking capabilities to Canadian businesses; however, the main advantages cited by Unitel were access to both AT&T's technology and sophisticated network services and AT&T management expertise.[24] In short, there would appear to be little concern about a technology leakage from Canadian firms to foreign competitors under this alliance.

The only potential concern raised by the AT&T/Unitel alliance is the increased likelihood that Unitel will buy its long-distance switching machines from AT&T rather than Northern Telecom. However, Unitel would be a relatively small buyer of Northern's equipment in any case, and so it is difficult to argue that Northern will suffer a significant loss of scale economies as a consequence.

In assessing the Unitel/AT&T alliance, market access (conditioned by government policy) was clearly the major motive. The alliance, if anything, will promote competition in domestic Canadian markets by strengthening Unitel's ability to compete against the incumbent carriers. There is no basis for any concern about adverse technological externalities for Canada.

Several major international joint ventures were also struck by Bell Canada Enterprises (BCE), the parent company of Bell Canada. In one deal struck with Britain's Cable and Wireless, BCE acquired 20 percent of Mercury Communications, Britain's competitive long-distance carrier, for approximately $960 million. Mercury is a subsidiary of Cable and Wireless. BCE was reported to be seeking easier access to emerging international markets in which Cable and Wireless participates, including several Asian countries.[25] Access by direct investment abroad would have involved greater initial outlays by BCE which was apparently a motive for the alliance; however, most foreign countries also have foreign ownership restrictions applying to facilities-based carriers, and so again the issue of BCE establishing a wholly or majority owned affiliate is arguably moot.

Cable and Wireless was reportedly interested in exploiting access to Northern Telecom's research and development labs. Specifically, it was interested in Northern's transmission labs in England.[26] There was also apparently a common interest in the cable television area, since BCE has a

30 percent stake in Videotron's British cable television subsidiary. In particular, Mercury wished to expand its access to local networks through cable television connections to customer's premises.

In another outward alliance BCE, in a consortium including MCI and two New Zealand companies, acquired Clear Communications, the alternative long-distance carrier to Telecom New Zealand. BCE owns 25 percent of Clear, while BCE and MCI together own 49 percent of the company.ˈ Again, concerns about control by foreigners appears to be an issue; however, the sharing of ownership between BCE and MCI seems, in part, motivated by an interest in sharing the costs of international expansion.

The motive for BCE's investment in Clear was, in part, to expand the scope of the international networking capabilities that BCE can offer its large business customers. There was also an expectation that the investment in Clear would be profitable in its own right. The joint ventures with Cable and Wireless and Clear Communications provide no grounds for anti-competitive concerns or uneasiness about adverse technological consequences for Canada.

Finally, as part of its membership in the Stentor alliance, BCE entered a joint venture with MCI to provide cross-border virtual private network services and high-speed private data network services.[27] In this case, BCE arguably enhanced its ability to offer state-of-the-art services to MNEs based in Canada. These include a streamlined 800 service to allow businesses with customers in Canada and the United States to answer toll-free calls from either country. Stentor will also gain access to MCI's advanced billing software. While Stentor could have developed the services itself, the alliance with MCI accelerated the timetable.[28] Stentor can offer its Canadian customers access to MCI's world-wide networking facilities as well. From MCI's standpoint, the main motive was apparently the extension of MCI's corporate networking services to Canada. The CEO of MCI also mentioned the possibility of Stentor helping MCI to compete in the market for local telephone service at some point in the future.

The Stentor/MCI alliance in combination with the Unitel/AT&T alliance might be seen as limiting the options available to Canadian subscribers. For example, it might imply that choosing Stentor as the domestic carrier obliges Canadian subscribers to use MCI as the carrier for international calls terminating in the United States, or in other countries where MCI has joint ventures with local carriers. Similar concerns might be expressed by Unitel customers. In fact, business subscribers are apparently looking increasingly for single-supplier communications packages, and so the joint ventures would seem to be an appropriate response to market forces. Moreover, they promise to accelerate the inflow of telecommunications technology into Canada.

In another newsworthy alliance, The Sprint Corporation agreed to buy 25 percent of Call-Net, a Canadian reseller of long-distance telephone services for $50 million. Under the agreement, Sprint will collect royalties on its products and services sold in Canada over 10 years and hold three seats on the Call-Net board. In turn, Call-Net will gain rights to much of Sprint's intellectual property and access to all of Sprint's network capabilities.[29]

The influence of government policy in the Call-Net/Sprint alliance is less clear than in earlier cases. Specifically, there are no foreign ownership limitations in Canada with respect to resellers. This is why Sprint's ownership could exceed the 20 percent limit set by Bill C-62; however, to the extent that Call-Net increasingly carries telephone calls over its own facilities, it might eventually be deemed a facilities-based carrier. A controlling ownership share by Sprint might therefore have limited Call-Net's ability to install its own capacity to process telephone traffic.

The implications of the Call-Net/Sprint alliance for the Canadian telephone industry are obvious. The ability of Call-Net to compete in the Canadian market has arguably been increased, thereby strengthening competitive forces in the domestic industry. The technology transfer is inward, and so concerns about adverse technology spillovers seem moot. Indeed, the alliance can be seen as accelerating the availability to Canadians of new services such as volume discounts and consolidated detailed billing.

In another alliance involving a Canadian reseller, LCI International, Inc. of Virginia agreed to acquire as much as a 50.1 percent stake in Canada's fifth-largest long-distance telephone reseller, STN, Inc. The agreement involves a bridge loan to STN to help finance soaring commission and marketing costs stemming from STN's rapidly expanding residential customer base. LCI has agreed to direct its Canadian calls through STN's network.[30] As in the preceding case, this alliance can also foster competition with established telecommunication carriers in Canada. It is not clear why in this case the American partner wanted a controlling ownership in the Canadian reseller. However, technology does not appear to have been an important asset in this alliance.

Finally it was recently announced that Canada's cellular telephone leader, Rogers Cantel Communications, Inc. is linking with U.S. cellular giant McCaw Cellular Communications, Inc. for a digital airplane cellular network across Canada. Rogers Cantel will buy 10 percent of privately held McCaw subsidiary Claircom Communications Group L.P. and will set up a new company called Air One Canada Communications, Inc. to extend Claircom's digital airplane cellular network across Canada. Claircom, in turn, will have a 20 percent stake in Air One. Rogers Cantel will build between 10 and 15 ground stations to service the network. Through its 10 percent stake in Claircom, Rogers Cantel reportedly hopes to reap profits from Claircom expansion into the air-to-ground market.[31]

The Cantel/McCaw link again underscores the role that alliances are playing in the diffusion of new telecommunication network services into Canada. For the U.S. partner, market access in Canada is clearly the primary concern. For the Canadian partner, access to trans-border service is the primary objective; however, Cantel's equity link to Claircom anticipates the potential for future ventures between the parent companies in the air-to-ground market. This link is particularly intriguing in light of the previously discussed Unitel/AT&T alliance. As previously noted, Rogers Communications is the parent of both Unitel and Rogers Cantel. AT&T, in turn, recently acquired McCaw Cellular. Hence, the Cantel/McCaw link might be construed as extending the community of interests between Rogers Communication and AT&T.

In summary, while there may be a variety of motives for the aforementioned alliances involving Canadian telecommunication companies, a dominant theme is market access, with the choice of the alliancing mode conditioned by government policy and by technology transfer. Specifically, larger ownership shares have been taken by U.S. firms when Canadian firms are not subject to the 20 percent foreign ownership limitation. Technology transfer is primarily associated with U.S. firms making specific network services available to Canadian carriers in exchange for faster access to Canadian customers. The opening-up of the Canadian market itself reflects recent Canadian regulatory initiatives to allow competition in public-switched long-distance service. U.S. carriers have had little experience in serving Canadian customers directly, since the regulated monopoly environment by definition precluded this ability to compete in Canada. Entering the Canadian market through an alliance rather than establishing a greenfield operation is therefore consistent with the premise that unfamiliarity with a market or technology promotes joint venturing in favour of direct investment, if all other factors are constant.

Some additional support for this interpretation is provided by BCE's recent acquisition of a 30 percent stake in Jones Intercable, Inc., a U.S. operator of 55 cable systems. A spokesperson for BCE said that the acquisition was designed to give BCE a presence in the United States home entertainment market without having to make a "blockbuster" investment.[32] Yet, controlling ownership is clearly anticipated as a possibility, since BCE also purchased an option to buy control of Jones Intercable. BCE's initial stake might be interpreted as a limited investment to test for complementarities in the emerging area of multi-media communications.[33] With additional information of a favourable nature, controlling ownership might be anticipated.

The alliances reviewed in this section offer no grounds for concern that Canadian competitiveness in the telecommunications industry is being eroded, or that domestic competition is being undermined. If anything, the opposite seems to be arguable.

Automotive Parts

Although technology is not moving as rapidly as in telecommunications, the automotive parts industry in North America is seeing a number of significant changes. The North American Big Three assemblers (GM, Ford and Chrysler) are adapting the "lean production" methods of the Japanese to achieve both higher quality and productivity.[34] The Big Three are in the process of out-sourcing more of their parts, reducing drastically the number of direct suppliers with whom they deal, expecting their suppliers (called Tier 1 suppliers) to provide systems instead of components, and demanding that suppliers have sufficient design and engineering capability to work with them on developing new vehicle models. At the same time GM has had to engage in considerable downsizing to make room for the Japanese assemblers whose market share through transplant operations and exports from Japan has risen to about thirty percent.

Along with the Japanese transplant assembly plants have come Japanese parts suppliers, often in joint venture arrangements with North American firms. The Japanese provide an environment for learning lean production and access to the Japanese assemblers, while the North American partners bring know-how of doing business in the region and access to the Big Three.

Following Japanese practices, the auto assemblers have all now opted for just-in-time (JIT) deliveries of parts, which requires parts manufacturers (especially of bulky items) to be located close to the assembler's plant. The combination of JIT and the location of the largest transplants in the Kentucky, Ohio and Tennessee area have made not only Canadian auto parts suppliers but others including American, Japanese and German firms want to locate there.

For original equipment auto parts, Canada and the United States have had an integrated market ever since the Canada-U.S. Automotive Pact was implemented in 1965. Some minor changes resulted from the Canada-U.S. Free Trade Agreement, and the North American Free Trade Agreement will result in Mexico becoming a third member of the market. Mexico is already seeing a boom in new auto parts plants.

Given this environment there has been a considerable shake out in the Canadian auto parts industry. Many smaller firms have opted to become tier 2 and tier 3 suppliers, selling components to tier 1 parts companies; others have closed, and still others have merged.

Despite a fairly lengthy period in which the Canadian dollar was arguably above its real value relative to the U.S. dollar, a number of Canadian-owned auto parts suppliers saw rapid growth and increased profitability. Of the four largest, three used joint ventures as part of their corporate strategy.

Magna International is by far the largest Canadian-owned original equipment auto parts manufacturer; with 1992 sales of C$ 2.4 billion, it ranks fifteenth in world sales. It ranked second in North American sales, excluding the parts subsidiaries of the Big Three. Magna has approximately 17,500 employees and 75 automotive parts manufacturing facilities (including nine joint venture facilities), 62 in North America (including one in Mexico) and eight in Europe, as well as five product-development engineering facilities. Approximately two-thirds of the company's consolidated sales in fiscal 1992 represented goods manufactured in Canada, of which approximately 60 per-cent were exported to the United States. Magna's recent expansion into

Europe will increase the importance of European sales. The company is divided into four core automotive groups, each responsible for providing assemblers with total systems capability in a specific area of the automobile.

Magna has a number of joint-venture or minority interest partners: one American, two Japanese, and three European. In the late 1980s, Magna sold a 23.3 percent share in Atoma International, its largest division, (accounting for 38 percent of Magna's 1992 sales) to Mitsibushi Trading Co. Its motives were to raise capital for expansion and gain access to the Japanese transplant market. A joint venture with Ford emerged in 1990, when Magna was forced to engage in massive financial restructuring. This involved selling an interest in two of its existing plants, one in Ontario and the other in Michigan, transactions that resulted in inward foreign direct investment and a reduction in direct investment abroad. Without Ford's infusion, Magna would not have been able to keep the two plants. Financial constraints were also the cause of Magna's opting out of a joint venture with Daiyko of Japan to supply CAMI, the GM-Suzuki joint venture in Ingersoll, Ontario. Magna's expansion into Europe was assisted by a joint venture with Vost-Alpine Stahl. In this instance, the joint venture fostered Canadian direct investment abroad.

In the case of the other joint venture with Ford, Magna's motive was to obtain technology in plastics production. Another joint venture with Webasco of Germany was undertaken to obtain access to the latter's expertise in sunroof production and led to the establishment of a plant in the United States. Similarly, seating system technology was obtained from Georg Grammar of Germany, which in turn received a five percent share of Magna's Atoma Division.

In late 1993, with Magna's operations profitable again, additional equity was issued in order to finance its European growth strategy. The aim is to strengthen its global position in the automotive market by laying a base for manufacturing in Europe that could, in time, equal its sales in North America. A further intention is to acquire European technology.[35]

Two European deals were made, giving Magna control of a manufacturer of steering wheels and airbags, and a producer of car mirrors.[36] In the first case, Magna acquired 60 percent interest in K.S. Automobile-Sicherheitstechnik (Germany) for C$ 60 million. While the move increased Magna's sales to the German auto makers, the primary motive was to obtain the airbag technology.[37] The airbag was one of only two major systems in an automobile interior that Magna did not manufacture.

Given the depressed state of the European auto parts industry, Magna was able to acquire its interest at far below replacement cost and much more quickly than it could replicate the technology. To provide additional cash to the seller, Metallgesellshaft, Magna agreed as part of the deal to take a 12.5 percent interest in the parent company, Kolbenschmidt, for C$ 40 million. Kolbenschmidt is primarily a manufacturer of pistons and aluminum blocks for vehicles – two products Magna does not produce in North America. The minority interest and first opportunity to acquire the rest give Magna an opportunity to decide whether it wants to expand into this niche of the auto parts business.

Magna's latest foreign investment was the acquisition of a 74 percent interest in the German-based Zipperle Group from Porsche of Austria.[38] The Zipperle Group, with two factories in Germany, one in Spain, one in the United Kingdom, and one in Czechoslovakia, is a maker of auto mirrors. Unlike the case of airbags, Magna already has the technology and facilities for this line in Europe. Although yet unplanned, further collaboration between Magna and the owners of Porsche (who have a large stake in Volkswagen) is possible. Magna obtained controlling interest in both these firms without paying in full. The minority partners are not expected to be active in these firms, so that these joint ventures do not involve "strategic partnering". Rather, they are for all practical purposes outward direct investments.

The Woodbridge Group, specializing in foam products, is Canada's second-largest auto parts company, with sales approaching C$1 billion in 1992 and ranking 26th in North American sales. Privately held, Woodbridge is itself a product of foreign disinvestment, a management buyout from Monsanto in 1978. Opel Germany and Inoae Kasei of Japan are Woodbridge's most important joint venture partners. The alliance with Opel is in Europe and is a plant within Opel's facilities. Clearly the motive was to capture a good part of GM Europe's seating business. With respect to the Japanese partner, Woodbridge's goals were to access Inoae's technology in instrument panels and gain assistance in selling to the Japanese transplants. Woodbridge had been working on similar technology, but acquiring it from the Japanese partner was faster and cheaper. The Woodbridge-Ionae joint venture established plants in both Canada and the United States. In Mexico, Woodbridge plays an opposite role, providing technology in return for facilities and sales assistance in the Mexican market.

ABC Group (also privately-held), makers of plastic and rubber auto parts, is the Canadian industry's fourth-largest firm. It, too, has European and Japanese partners; its joint venture with Woco of Germany has operations in Canada, Germany and Spain, while its operations with Nishikawa are in Canada and Japan. ABC wanted to combine its technology with that of its partners, with the result that the JVs would then service the markets of both partners in their respective countries.

The joint ventures discussed above were either financially or technologically driven. However, in some of the cases geographic unfamiliarity provided additional motivation. For ABC Group, its European and Japanese JVs provided an easy way to operate in those different markets. Magna indicated that had its management not had a Germanic heritage, it would have sought a joint venture partner to provide a smoother passage to doing business in Europe. Firms cited Mexico as an area where a joint venture partner would have been desirable, but in some cases a suitable permanent one could not be found.

The joint ventures of Magna, Woodbridge and ABC do not represent a large proportion of their businesses. Interviews with their executives suggested that "going alone" was the preferred route unless there were circumstances which made entry into a market quicker or cheaper and a suitably compatible partner could be found. A.G. Simpson, Canada's third-largest automotive parts manufacturer with sales of about $500 million in 1992, has no joint ventures.[39] Until quite recently it resisted foreign direct investment abroad, but in 1991, it acquired a plant in Michigan and now has greenfield sites under construction in Tennessee and Kentucky. For A.G. Simpson, there was apparently no lack of capital, no need for technology, no scale or scope economies and no unfamiliarity with the American market.

Although we have not made an exhaustive study of JV activity by Canadian independent auto parts suppliers, the evidence suggests that there is little relative to total foreign sales. In fact, joint ventures between American and Canadian automotive parts manufacturers are quite rare in the United States. In contrast, of the over 230 Japanese auto parts subsidiaries in the United States, over 75 are joint ventures with the United States as the foreign partner. What accounts for the difference? There seem to be four possible reasons. First, for the Japanese to operate in the United States requires a far greater change than for Canadian firms to operate there. Unlike the United States, Europe and the Far East represent the same degree of unfamiliarity for Canadian firms. The same applies to the United States for Japanese companies. On this basis one can speculate that increased investment in Europe and the Far East by Canadian auto parts firms would lead to relatively more joint ventures.

Second, MITI has encouraged Japanese auto parts suppliers investing in the United States to find local partners in order to make Japanese investment there more acceptable. Canada has no similar reason for encouraging its firms to carry out direct investment in the United States through joint ventures.

Third, in many instances, especially with the integrated Canadian-U.S. auto industry, exporting from Canada is still an option for servicing the American market, whereas exporting from Japan is more difficult.

Finally, about 70 percent of auto parts production in Canada is done either by the Big Three themselves or by subsidiaries of foreign controlled multinational enterprises. For these firms both outward direct investment and external joint ventures would be handled by the parent corporation. This, of course, does not preclude the subsidiary's benefiting from the parent's joint ventures.

In summary, a number of motivations are at work in generating joint ventures by Canadian auto competitors. An important theme is easing market access by the acquisition of a local partner. Less-than-controlling ownership is desirable when there is a lack of familiarity with the local market. In fact, only a small number of JVs involve Canadian auto firms, and the explanation may be that no government policy is required to induce more JVs, other than possibly making Canadian firms more aware of the opportunities in Europe and the Far East, where lack of familiarity with the markets could induce the channelling of a relatively higher proportion of direct investment abroad into joint ventures.[40]

Canadian companies that have undertaken JVs have been strengthened through additional financial resources, transferred technology, market access and so forth. Yet other firms (such as A.G. Simpson) have prospered without them. Moreover, the perpetuation of first-tier suppliers such as Magna, Woodbridge and ABC has strengthened the ability of their upstream suppliers and downstream customers to compete in the North American market. Specifically, the tier-one parts suppliers have put increased pressure on their tier-two suppliers to improve quality and reduce price, thereby playing the role of discriminating home country buyers, a part of the competitive "diamond" discussed by Porter (1990). Moreover, by strengthening the ability of specific Canadian companies to compete with the Japanese industry, the joint ventures described above may also have contributed to a more vigorous overall competitive environment for the North American automobile industry.

Software

The third Canadian industry case is software. Three rapidly growing companies, founded in the last eight years, are analyzed: Delrina (sales over C$ 50 million), Corel (sales over C$ 100 million) and ATI Technologies (sales over C$ 200 million). The industry is characterized by extremely short product life cycles; unless software is updated regularly, it becomes obsolete. For success in the industry, software must be on the leading edge and have a good distribution network. Ease of use with other leading software packages is essential for high-volume sales. Transportation costs for software products are minimal, and there are generally no trade barriers to shipments.

Toronto-based Delrina is the market leader in electronic business forms software and computer fax software. Its strategic alliances tend to involve marketing arrangements and/or technology collaboration. Most significant are a series of recently announced strategic alliances with telecommunication service providers, where Delrina is participating in the integration of PCs with communications offerings ultimately including multimedia information products. In this convergence of the telecommunications and PC industry (not dissimilar to the convergence of cable TV and telephone), the telecommunications service companies will provide improved messaging services such as enhanced fax, teleconferencing and electronic commerce. Delrina will build into its application products the capability to make it easy to use these enhanced services. By being part of these networks, Delrina is able to leverage its Winfax success in global communications.

Delrina's partners in the alliance are MCI's Global Messaging Services, Worldlinx Telecommunications, Inc., a Bell Canada subsidiary (both members of the MCI-Stentor alliance) and Vodata of the United Kingdom. For Delrina the alliance means not only selling more fax and forms software, but also moving into the broader communications markets. From the standpoint of the telecommunication communications companies, Delrina is an attractive partner because of its installed base of about three million sites and its ability to write easy-to-use software. Delrina also has joint development and marketing arrangements with network information-service providers such as NCR and GE Information Services. Delrina and the firms together create the technology for business forms, which the service providers package. Another form of joint marketing for Delrina is the bundling of "lite" versions of its software with the sale of PCs. Nearly 100 PC and modem manufactures, most based in the United States, are involved.

It might be noted here that in the cases cited above, Delrina is primarily selling a well-established product and technological capability to users. In this circumstance, alliances closer in spirit to arm's-length contracting might be expected and seem to be observable, especially since there are no restrictions on Delrina's ability to export from a Canadian base.

In other cases, Delrina has used direct investment abroad. For example, to expand its product line, Delrina purchased Amaze, Inc., a U.S.-based company, in October 1992. Amaze's software includes daily-planner and screen-saver packages. It is also a premier licensee of proprietary publishing content in the software industry. The acquisition of Amaze, rather than a joint venture arrangement, might reflect Delrina's comprehensive experience in the U.S. market, as well as the absence of any direct or indirect restrictions on foreign ownership in the U.S. software industry.

Ottawa-based Corel is a graphics and small computer interface product-development company. Both its widely acclaimed *Corel Draw* graphics software programme and its Corel interface software are market leaders. Corel has no foreign affiliates, other than an international sales subsidiary in Dublin, and no joint ventures. When it wanted to add to its software products, it purchased *Ventura Publisher* and *Ventura Database* and all related technologies from Xerox Corporation. This technology was effectively moved to Corel's home facilities.

Like Delrina, Corel has many cross-border joint marketing arrange-ments. They consist of agreements with original equipment PC manufacturers (such as Compaq), with graphic hardware manufacturers and makers of peripheral devices (such as NCR), all of whom bundle Corel Software with their products. As noted above, the nature of these types of exchanges are close to arm's-length transactions, and relatively complex governance structures such as equity joint ventures would not be expected.

ATI Technologies in Toronto manufactures and sells PC enhancements such as graphics, multimedia and communication products. Originally ATI's focus was hardware, but more and more the firm is developing integrated solutions combining both hardware and software products. Currently, 60 per-cent of ATI's research and development is devoted to software products.

ATI Technologies has not undertaken any foreign investment other than establishing regional sales and distribution offices in California and Germany. Its strategic alliances are also quite limited. Like Delrina and Corel, ATI's graphic accelerators are used by a number of PC manufacturers who advertise that their machines contain ATI products. In fact, one PC manufacturer accounted for 31 percent of ATI's sales in 1993. The other strategic alliance pursued by ATI is a two-way technology transfer through a joint development project with Intel involving the Shared Forms Buffer Interconnect (SFBI) multimedia specification. SFBI defines a method for combining full-screen, full-motion, graphics, and other multimedia functionality into a single, integrated multimedia system. For ATI, the alliance with Intel to develop this industry standard will mean that the company has 'first mover' advantages as the market for graphics accelerators (one of ATI's most important products) evolves to require multimedia functionality that will combine video acceleration, video compression and graphics functions. The ability to be the first to introduce new products into the market is a key competitive factor in the PC enhancement industry. The small size of this development project may explain why it was not organized as an equity joint venture.

Conclusions

THE RECENT PROLIFERATION of fact and opinion about international joint ventures is daunting. The rapid accumulation of literature on the subject gives the superficial impression that a major change in international business practices is taking place, and that firms (and national economies) not aggressively participating in this development will suffer grievous damage to their abilities to compete in international markets.

While joint ventures have not enjoyed the explosive recent growth that some other strategic alliances have, the substantial amount of joint venturing taking place poses a potential challenge to the traditional preeminence of MNEs as the major vehicles of international trade, as well as to the traditional preference of MNEs for controlling ownership of affiliates abroad. In fact, a judicious interpretation of what is still a relatively descriptive and often conflicting body of information might hold that traditional forms of FDI are in no imminent danger of being displaced by international joint ventures. Rather, international alliances, joint ventures included, may reflect (although certainly not totally) the emergence of specific new industries (e.g., biotechnology, information technology) and major new competitors (e.g., Japanese producers). In the latter case, host-government policies undoubtedly constrain the ability of Japanese producers to establish wholly owned affiliates, either by greenfield investment or by acquisition of existing domestic firms. The propensity of Japanese firms to seek international joint ventures may also reflect the psychological distance they confront when moving into new and far-flung geographic markets. Indeed, this psychological distance may also confront U.S. firms moving into new (to them) markets in Canada, such as long distance telecommunications.

In newly emerging industries such as biotechnology, joint ventures are an effective way to test for the existence of complementarities across partners while mitigating the need to sink relatively large costs in merging the partners. This motive is prominent in established industries undergoing significant change due to technology, government regulation and the like. Such changes have increased market entry opportunities across borders and across industry segments. In industries such as telecommunications, aircraft, and other technology-intensive sectors, government policies (especially foreign owner- ship restrictions) are also important influences on the margin, encouraging some joint venturing activity, although other motives are also at work. Nevertheless, as the recent takeover of McCaw Cellular by AT&T and BCE's purchase of Jones Intercable suggest, joint ventures may ultimately be superseded by full ownership, where government policy allows, once the extent of the complementarities is identified.

From a policy perspective, there is little reason to conclude that Canadian firms are not doing their fair share of international joint venturing. While they are less prone to engage in such alliancing than U.S. or Japanese firms, there are plausible reasons. In particular, the long-standing and over- whelming integration of the Canadian economy into the larger (and quite familiar) U.S. economy obviates the imperative for Canadian firms to under- take joint ventures in order to bridge psychological distances to its major foreign market. Moreover, the openness of the U.S. market to direct invest- ment by Canadian firms allows Canadian firms the freedom to establish wholly owned affiliates if they desire. For symmetric reasons, a rapid growth in joint ventures in Canada undertaken by U.S. firms would not be expected, and this is in fact the case.[41]

At a specific policy level, case studies of alliancing activity carried out by Canadian firms offer no basis for an argument that joint ventures have under- mined competitive forces in specific markets. Moreover, given our skepticism about international joint ventures emerging as a dominant mode of international business for Canadian firms, we are relatively sanguine about any future threats to competition that such joint ventures will generally pose. Nor is there any evident reason for concern about joint ventures leading to net technology outflows from Canada with attendant external costs for the domestic economy. If anything, international joint ventures seem to be associated with technology inflows into Canada.

Finally, there is no evident basis for the Canadian government to adopt a more interventionist posture towards international joint ventures. Rather, in common with other authors on the subject, we argue that policies toward international joint ventures are subsidiary to broader policies on investment and trade. Specifically, in an environment where MNEs can freely trade goods across borders and establish foreign affiliates where appropriate, it is more likely that international alliances generally, and joint ventures specifically, will be stuck at an optimal rate.

ENDNOTES

1 To be sure, other forms of alliances, e.g., R&D consortia, may also involve relational exchanges of a long-term and complex nature (Contractor, undated). However, data on such agreements are both difficult to obtain and relatively idiosyncratic to the specific arrangement.

2 The reader might consult overview studies such as Mowery (1988), and the papers in Mytelka, ed. (1991) and Contractor & Lorange, eds. (1988).

3 See Globerman, this volume.

4 The improved competence of potential subcontractors would reinforce this response.

5 Similar advantages of networking are cited by D'Cruz & Rugman (1993), although it should be noted explicitly that these authors do not necessarily equate alliances, such as joint ventures, to networks.

6 Safarian, op. cit., suggests that joint ventures may be faster to implement because in many countries acquisitions by foreign-owned firms may have to go through review and approval processes that are not required for joint ventures.

7 Teece (1986) makes this point in arguing that joint ventures are a means for a firm to obtain access to innovation-specific assets which are not vested in a stand-alone enterprise. In this case, acquisition of the asset could oblige the would-be acquirer to purchase an entire organization in order to gain access to the specific asset. Hennart (1988) also argues that joint ventures may be more efficient if indivisibilities due to scale or scope economies make full ownership of the relevant assets inefficient, or if acquisition of the firm owning the assets would entail significant management costs.

8 See Safarian (1991).

9 For evidence on the existence of spillover benefits to home country R&D expenditures, see Bernstein (1991).

10 This possibility has been highlighted by Reich & Mankin (1986). Also, see Lei & Slocum (1992) who argue that technologies are converging across industries. Hence, loss of skills and competencies suffered by home country firms in ill-founded alliances may have damaging collateral effects in related sectors as well. In the end, a strategic alliance may lead a domestic firm to relocate its headquarters abroad with the potential loss of externalities associated with a range of overhead activities.

11 See Reynolds & Snapp (1982).

12 See Waverman & Khemani (1993) who provide a theoretical overview of factors influencing the competitive implications of alliances.

13 As an aside, the authors found that alliances characterized by equity exchanges tend to be more complex and/or more extended over time. In this context, complexity may be thought of as the degree to which different parts of the organization are affected. Thus, the wider the organizational scope of the transactions involved, the greater the degree of cross-ownership.

14 For a discussion of the Canadian auto parts sector, see Wolf & Taylor (1991).

15 A number of specific case studies in the auto sector are discussed later in this study.

16 The authors caution that a continuation of the joint venturing phenomenon might at some point in the future raise competitive concerns. This point is underscored in Nohrie & Garcia-Pont (1991), who point out that alliances in the auto industry are consolidating firms into smaller numbers of "strategic groups".

17 Other studies pointing to the conclusion are cited in Contractor (undated).

18 The individual SIC codes corresponding to the broad groupings reported in Tables 5 and 6 are described in the Appendix. The grouping procedure is drawn from a paper by Pavitt (1984).

19 See Corvari & Wisner (1991, p. 33).

20 Hagedoorn (1993) also identifies technology partnering as the major motive for his sample of strategic alliances; however, another set of objectives that includes both market access and technology partnering (which demands a larger span of control by the company) seems to underlie joint ventures.

21 They also note that such arrangements may be especially efficient for pooling complementary assets which comprise a subset of the partners' overall assets.

22 See Surtees (1993a).

23 For a discussion of Bill C-62, see Schultz (1992).

24 Surtees, *op. cit.*

25 See Surtees (1992).

26 These labs were acquired as part of Northern's acquisition of STC PLC, a world leader in the design of submarine cables. Subsequent to BCE forming a joint venture with Cable and Wireless, Northern sold STC PLC to Alcatel of France.

27 Stentor is a domestic alliance of Canadian carriers who formerly operated as Telecom Canada.

28 See Surtees (1993).

29 See "Sprint To Buy 25 Percent of Canadian Long-Distance Company," *The New York Times*, August 5, 1993, C4.

30 McNish (1993).

31 McHugh (1993).

32 Surtees (1993c).

33 Additional synergies may be associated with the fact that Jones Intercable and BCE are partners in a British company that provides telephone and cable-TV service in London.

34 See Womack, Jones & Roos (1990).

35 The transportation costs and shipping time make it uncompetitive to ship most auto parts to Europe; therefore, some arrangement for European manufacturing is necessary.

36 Although both companies have European minority partners, control will be with Magna, and they will be treated as operating subsidiaries of Magna. See Dow Jones Service (1993).

37 Bidding for airbag contracts is normally done three to four years in advance.

38 See Pritchard (1993).

39 Hayes-Dana, approximately equal in sales to A.G. Simpson and with substantial Canadian shareholders, is not included as Canadian since it is controlled by Dana Corp. USA.

40 Although, there is no need for government intervention to foster more JVs, the auto parts trade associations in Canada, Mexico, and United States are trying to bring their members together to discuss intercountry co-operation.

41 For example, Geringer (1990) reports that there were 3,396 joint ventures in Canada in 1988, 3,407 in 1985 and 3,690 in 1981. The concentration of Canadian MNEs in extractive and resource-based sectors also conditions the results, as these sectors tend not to be alliance prone.

ACKNOWLEDGEMENTS

THE AUTHORS THANK the discussants Lynn Mytelka and Louis Hebert for helpful comments on an earlier draft. Useful suggestions were also received from Lorraine Eden.

APPENDIX:

CLASSIFICATION OF INDUSTRIAL SECTORS, TABLES 5 AND 6

Canadian Standard Industrial Classification Code (SICs)

1. SCIENCE-BASED
Drugs & Medicine (SIC 374), Chemicals (372-379), Other Electronic and Electrical Products (331-339), Refined Petroleum & Coal Products (361-369), Rubber Plastics & Synthetic Fibers (162 & 165)

2. SPECIALIZED SUPPLIER
Scientific & Professional Equipment (391), Telecommunications & Equipment (543-545), Aircraft & Parts (321), Machinery Industries (311-318), Computer Services (853), Engineering & Scientific Services (864), Printing & Publishing (286-289)

3. SCALE INTENSIVE
Mines (051-064), Metal Fabricating (301-309), Primary Metals (291-298), Crude Petroleum & Natural Gas (064), Basic Food Industries (101-104, 109), Non-Metallic Mineral Products (351-359), Electrical Power (572), Gas Power (574-579), Transportation (321-325), Other Transportation (326-329)

4. SUPPLIER DOMINATED
Food, Beverages & Tobacco (105-108, 151, 153), Wood-Based Industries (251-259, 261-268, 271-274), Other Manufacturing (399), Textiles (181-189), Leather (172-179), Clothing & Underwear (243-249), Transportation & Utilities (501-519, 572-579)

5. FINANCIAL SERVICES
Finance Industries (701-715), Insurance Carriers (721), Real Estate (735-737)

6. OTHER SERVICES
Community, Business & Personal Service Industries (801-899), Construction (400-421), Wholesale Trade (600-629), Retail Trade (630-699)

U.S. Standard Industrial Classification Code (SICs)

1. SCIENCE BASED
Drugs & Medicines (SIC 283), Chemicals (281-289), Other Electronic & Electrical Products (361-369), Refined Petroleum & Coal Products (461), Rubber, Plastics & Synthetic Fibers (301-308)

2. SPECIALIZED SUPPLIER

Scientific & Professional Equipment (381-387), Telecommunications & Equipment (401-407), Aircraft & Parts (372), Machinery Industries (351-359), Computer Services (737), Engineering & Scientific Services (871-874), Printing & Publishing (271-279)

3. SCALE INTENSIVE

Mines (101-149), Metal Fabricating (341-349), Primary Metals (331-339), Crude Petroleum & Natural Gas (131), Basic Food Industries (201-203, 208), Non-Metallic Mineral Products (321-329), Electrical Power (491), Gas Power (492-497), Transportation (371, 373-379)

4. SUPPLIER DOMINATED

Food, Beverages & Tobacco (204-209, 211-214), Wood-Based Industries (241-249, 251-259, 261-267), Other Manufacturing (391-399), Textiles & Apparel (221-239), Leather (311-319), Transportation & Utilities (501-519, 572-579)

5. FINANCIAL SERVICES

Finance Industries (601-628), Insurance Carriers (631-639, 641), Real Estate (651-655)

BIBLIOGRAPHY

Auster, Ellen R. "The Relationship of Industry Evolution to Patterns of Technological Linkages, Joint Ventures and Direct Investment Between US. and Japan." *Management Science*, 38, (June 1992): 778-92.

Bernstein, Jeffrey. "R&D Capital, Spillovers and Foreign Affiliates in Canada." In *Foreign Investment, Technology and Economic Growth*. Edited by D. G. McFetridge. Calgary: The University of Calgary Press, 1991, pp. 111-32.

Blomström, M. and M. Zejan. "Why Do Multinational Firms Seek Out Joint Ventures." *Columbia Journal of World Business*, 20, (1985): 13-20.

Contractor, Farok J. and P. Lorange (eds.). *Cooperative Strategies in International Business*. Boston: Lexington Books, 1988.

Contractor, Farok. "Ownership Patterns of US Joint Ventures Abroad and the Liberalization of Foreign Government in the 1980s: Evidence from the Benchmark Surveys." *Journal of International Business Studies*, 21, (1990): 55-73.

_____. "Between Markets and Collusion: The Implications of Joint Ventures for Public Policy and Regulation." Rutgers University Graduate School of Management; Working Paper Series, Updated.

Corvari, Ronald and Robert Wisner. The Role of Canadian Multinationals in Shaping Canada's International Competitiveness, Report Prepared for Economic Council and Investment Canada, mimeo, 1991.

D'Cruz, Joseph and Alan Rugman. "Business Networks, Telecommunications, and International Competition." University of Toronto, Faculty of Management, mimeo, 1993.

Dunning, John H. *Multinational Enterprises and The Global Economy.* Wokingham, England: Addison-Wesley, 1993.

Franko, Lawrence. "Use of Majority and 50-50 Joint Ventures by U.S. Multinationals During the 1970s: The Interaction of Host Country Policies and Corporate Strategies." *Journal of International Business Studies,* 20, (Spring 1989): 19-40.

Geringer, Michael. Trends and Traits of Canadian Joint Ventures, Working Paper Number 1990, IV, Investment Canada, 1990.

Ghemawat, Pankay, Michael Porter and Richard Rowlinson. "Patterns of International Coalition Activity." In *Competition in Global Industries.* Edited by Michael Porter. Boston: Harvard Business School Press, 1986.

Ghoshal, Sumantra, Breck Arinzen and Sharon Brownfield. "A Learning Alliance Between Business and Business Schools: Education as a Platform for Partnership." *California Management Review,* (Fall 1992): 50-67.

Gomes-Casseres, B. "Ownership Structures of Foreign Subsidiaries." *Journal of Economic Behaviour and Organization,* 2, (1989): 1-25.

Gomes-Casseres, B. "Firm Ownership Preferences and Host Government Restrictions." *Journal of International Business Studies,* 21, (1990): 1-22.

Hagedoorn, J. "Understanding The Rationale of Strategic Technology Partnering: Interorganizational Modes of Cooperation and Sectoral Differences." *Strategic Management Journal,* 14, (July 1993): 371-86.

Hennart, Jean-Francois. "A Transaction Cost Theory of Equity Joint Ventures." *Strategic Management Journal,* 9, (1988): 361-74.

Lei, David and John W. Slocum, Jr. "Global Strategy, Competence-Building and Strategic Alliances." *California Management Review,* (Fall 1992): 81-97.

Manti, P. and R.H. Smiley. "Co-operative Agreements and the Organization of Industry." *The Journal of Industrial Economics,* XXXI, (1983): 437-51.

McHugh, Michael. "Contel links with McCaw." *The Financial Post,* 9 November 1993, p 1.

McNish, Jacquie. "LCI Agrees to buy Stake in Long-Distance Reseller STN." *The Globe and Mail,* 19 October 1993, B13.

Michalet, Charles-Albert. "Strategic Partnerships and the Changing Internalization Process." In *Strategic Partnerships: States, Firms and International Competition.* Edited by Lynn Krieger Mytelka. London: Pinter Publishers, 1991, pp. 35-50.

Mowery, D.C. "Collaborative Ventures Between U.S. and Foreign Manufacturing Firms: An Overview." In *International Collaborative Ventures in U.S. Manufacturing.* Edited by D. C. Mowery. Cambridge: Ballinger, 1988, pp. 1-22.

Mytelka, Lynn Krieger, "Crisis, Technological Change and the Strategic Alliance." In *Strategic Partnerships: States, Firms and International Competition.* Edited by Lynn Krieger Mytelka. London: Pinter Publishers, 1991, pp. 7-34.

Nohria, Nitin and Carlos Garcia-Pont. "Global Strategic Linkages and Industry Structure." *Strategic Management Journal,* 12, (1991): 105-124.

Pavitt, Keith. "Sectoral Patterns of Technical Change: Towards a Taxonomy and a Theory." *Research Policy.* 13, (1984).

Reich, Robert and Eric D. Mankin. "Joint Ventures with Japan Give Away Our Future." *Harvard Business Review.* (March-April 1986).

Porter, Michael E. *The Competitive Advantages of Nations*. New York: The Free Press, 1990.

Reynolds, Robert J. and Bruce R. Snapp. "The Economic Effects of Partial Equity Interests and Joint Ventures." Department of Justice, Economic Policy Office Discussion Paper, mimeo, 1982.

Safarian, A.E. "Foreign Direct Investment and International Cooperative Agreements: Trends and Issues." Paper presented at Canada-Germany Joint Symposium, Competition Policy in an Interdependent World Economy, Institut for Wirtschaftforshung, Hamburg, 1991.

Schultz, Richard. "The New Canadian Telecommunications Legislation." McGill University Centre for the Study of Regulated Industries, Working Paper 92-58, Montreal: mimeo, 1992.

Surtees, Lawrence. "Unitel to speed up plans for long-distance services." *Globe and Mail*, 8 January 1993, B1.

_____. "Phone Companies seek long-distance affairs." *Globe and Mail*, 14 November 1992, B1 and B6.

_____. "Stentor alliances offers 2 new business services." *Globe and Mail*, 7 April 1993, B3.

_____. "BCE quits real estate and finance." *Globe and Mail*, 3 December, 1993, B4.

Teece, David. "Profiting from Technological Innovation: Implications for Integration, Collaboration, Licensing and Public Policy." *Research Policy*, 15,)1986): 285-305.

_____. "Capturing Value From Technological Innovation: Integration, Strategic Partnering and Licensing Decisions." In *Technology and Global Industries: Companies and Nations in the World Economy*. Edited by B. Gielle and H. Brooks. Washington, D.C.: National Academy Press, 1987.

Waverman, Leonard and Shyam Khemanu. "Strategic Alliances: A Threat to Competition?" University of Toronto and World Bank, mimeo, 1993.

Wolf, Bernard and Glenn Taylor. "Employee and Supplier Learning in the Canadian Automobile Industry: Implications for Competitiveness." In *Foreign Investment, Technology and Economic Growth*. Edited by D.G. McFetridge. Calgary, University of Calgary Press, 1991, pp. 279-316.

Wolf, Bernard and Steven Globerman. *Strategic Alliances In the Automotive Industry: Motives and Implications*, Ontario Centre For International Business, Research Programming Working Paper Number 62, May 1992.

Part IV   Country Case Studies

John C. Ries & Keith C. Head
Faculty of Commerce and Business Administration
University of British Columbia

10

Causes and Consequences of Japanese Direct Investment Abroad

INTRODUCTION

JAPAN IS TODAY THE LARGEST SOURCE of direct investment abroad (DIA) in the world. Over the seven-year period ending in 1992, Japanese investment averaged $45 billion annually, peaking at $67 billion in 1989 before falling off to $34 billion in 1992.[1] Among the explanations offered for this surge in investment are efforts by Japanese manufacturers to adapt to rising unit labour costs at home by moving production to low-wage sites. In addition, DIA is viewed as a means to circumvent barriers to Japanese exports raised by Western industrialized countries. How successful this large amount of direct investment abroad has been at maintaining Japanese competitiveness remains an open question, however.

This study explores the impact of Japanese direct investment on the Japanese economy by considering its effect on firms and workers in Japan. It also provides new econometric evidence on the firm-level determinants of Japanese investment abroad, which should help in assessing how well conventional explanations of this investment fit the actual experiences of Japanese firms. We also provide new evidence that the availability of internal funds acted as a constraint on attempts by Japanese firms to adjust to new economic conditions by moving production abroad.

This study is organized into four sections. The first describes important features of Japanese direct investment abroad; the next section develops a theoretical framework to assess the effects of DIA on welfare in Japan; the third section explores the relationship between DIA and firm performance, employment, wages, and exports; the fourth section uses regression analysis to determine the major factors that underlie Japanese outward investment; and the final section offers some concluding remarks.

Overview of Japanese Outward Direct Investment

WORLD OUTFLOWS OF DIRECT INVESTMENT abroad grew rapidly during the 1980s, registering an average annual growth rate of 29 percent from 1983 to 1989, and greatly exceeding the world growth rate for trade (9.4 percent) and gross domestic product (7.8 percent). Figure 1 shows Japan's position as the leading source country of direct investment abroad. It depicts the shares of average annual outflow of direct investment for top investing countries from 1984 to 1990. During this period, Japan averaged $25 billion or 19 percent of the world total, an amount well ahead of that of the United States and slightly above the amount invested by Britain. Other large European investors had smaller outflows during this period. In terms of stocks of DIA in 1989 (valued at 1989 exchange rates) Japan ranks second to the United States, with $254 billion of outward investment to $376 billion respectively. As shown in Figure 2, DIA for Britain and West Germany in 1989 was $212 billion and $110 billion respectively, with no other nation reaching $100 billion.

FIGURE 1

FDI OUTFLOWS, ANNUAL AVERAGES (US$ BILLION), 1984-1990

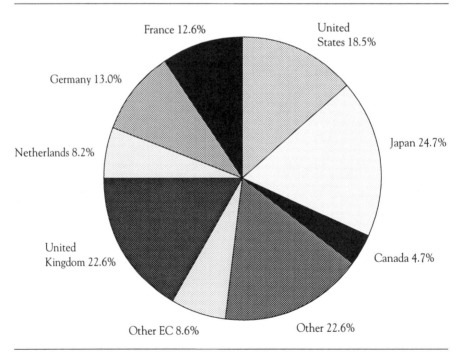

Source: UNCTC.

FIGURE 2

FDI STOCKS (US$ BILLION), 1989

US$ B

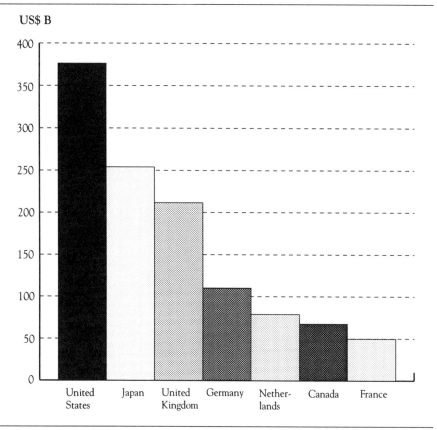

Source: UNCTC.

Japan's foreign investment performance is all the more remarkable in light of its geographic distance from the nations in which it invests. While much of European investment is in other European nations (for example, about 55 percent of the German and French stocks of DIA is within the EC) and 63 percent of Canadian DIA is in the United States, Japanese foreign investment travels far to reach host countries. The primary host regions for Japanese stock of DIA in 1990 were North America (44 percent), Western Europe (19 percent), and Southeast Asia (15 percent).

The geographic location and sectoral composition of Japanese DIA has changed over time. Table 1 shows the flows of DIA into the United States, Western Europe, and Southeast Asia between 1971 and 1992; Table 2 shows

TABLE 1

FLOWS OF JAPANESE DIRECT INVESTMENT ABROAD BY REGION, 1971-1992 (%)

	UNITED STATES	EUROPE	ASIA	OTHER
1971-1975	22.0	15.2	28.1	33.7
1976-1980	26.6	9.5	27.3	36.6
1981-1985	34.8	13.9	20.4	30.9
1986-1990	46.4	21.8	12.6	19.2
1991-1992	42.1	21.7	16.3	19.9

Source: Japanese Ministry of Finance

TABLE 2

FLOWS OF JAPANESE DIRECT INVESTMENT ABROAD BY INDUSTRY,[a] 1971-1992 (%)

	1971-1975	1976-1980	1981-1985	1986-1990	1991-1992
Manufacturing	33.3	36.7	25.1	25.1	29.5
Agriculture, Forestry, Fishery	2.0	2.7	0.7	0.4	0.1
Mining	25.1	15.4	9.9	2.1	3.0
Commerce	14.8	15.6	15.4	8.1	11.8
Banking, Finance, Insurance	8.0	5.5	17.9	24.5	12.6
Service[b]	n/a	n/a	n/a	15.0	15.8
Transportation	n/a	n/a	12.5	5.2	5.6
Real Estate	0.1	1.7	5.4	19.0	18.5
Others	16.7	22.4	13.1	6.8	3.1

Note: [a] Classification is according to the area of business in the host country.
        [b] Prior to 1986, services represented only 10 percent of accumulated FDI.
Source: Japanese Ministry of Finance.

its sectoral composition. In the 1970s, when a significant portion of Japanese investment was in either the manufacturing or mining sectors, Asia was the favoured location for Japanese investment. This pattern is consistent with the claim that due to the appreciation of the yen in the early 1970s and the removal of Japanese restrictions on DIA between 1969 and 1972,[2] the Japanese sought to secure access to vital raw materials and moved many of their manufacturing activities offshore. The 1980s saw a large increase in the share of investment going to developed countries in the West, particularly the United States. Since 1986, the United States has received almost half of Japan's DIA; Europe has received about 22 percent. Manufacturing continues to be an important sector for investment particularly in industries where the United States and the E.C. impose barriers on imported Japanese goods.[3] Other sectors where the share increased dramatically during the 1980s included banking, finance and insurance, and real estate. Investment in manufacturing and into Asia has resumed in the 1990s. Asia's share of investment has risen to 16.3 percent of total investment, with Indonesia and China being the chief recipients in 1991 and 1992. These trends support the hypothesis that Japanese manufacturers are again seeking low-cost production bases in response to the rising yen.

Table 3 sets out counts of manufacturing investments and the overseas employment figures for 17 manufacturing industries.[4] The electrical machinery industry has the dominant share of Japanese direct investment abroad, with the automobile industry in second place. Combined, these two industries account for over half the total employment of foreign Japanese manufacturing affiliates. The share of the total number of overseas investments held by the electrical goods industry is 27.2 percent; its proportion of overseas employ-ment is higher, at 39.9 percent. Investment by automobile companies increased dramatically during the 1980s, reflecting the imposition of voluntary export restraints in the United States and the E.C., but new investments by the electrical companies in the 1980s did not match their 1970s levels.

Table 4 shows the top 25 overseas investors among Japanese manufactur-ing companies in terms of employment abroad. While a few small firms appear on the list, the majority are large, well-known electrical goods or automobile producers. Many employ more workers abroad than at home and export sizable proportions of their output. Matsushita Electric Industrial, whose products are better known by brand names such as Panasonic and Quasar, heads the list with 65 foreign manufacturing affiliates as of 1989. The total overseas employ-ment of the 60 Matsushita affiliates that reported their employment figures is 46,791. With average assets worth $15.3 billion in the 1980s, Matsushita is one of Japan's largest manufacturers and has significant export business amounting to 31 percent of sales. Sanyo Electric, NEC, Hitachi, Sony, Nissan Motors and Toyota Motors are other household names that number among the top foreign investors. Minebea, a ball bearings manufacturer with assets averaging $1.8 billion in the 1980s, and Toray Industries, a synthetic fibre manufacturer with average assets of $4.7 billion, rank fifth and sixth respec-tively, and are the only manufacturers in the top eight outside the electrical equipment or motor vehicle industry. Table 4 also indicates that international investment activities have become significant parts of the operations of a number of major Japanese manufacturers.

THEORETICAL FRAMEWORK

THIS SECTION DEVELOPS THE THEORETICAL framework for assessing the consequences of increasing direct investment abroad.

Standard trade theory provides a useful framework for assessing the effects of movements of capital on national welfare, as well as their effects on factors of production. This theory, however, fails to distinguish portfolio

TABLE 3

INDUSTRIAL DISTRIBUTION OF JAPANESE FOREIGN MANUFACTURING INVESTMENTS

INDUSTRY	COUNT				EMPLOYMENT			
	1970-1979	1980-1989	TOTAL THROUGH 1989	%	1970-1979	1980-1989	TOTAL THROUGH 1989	%
			TOTAL	%			TOTAL	%
Food	28	61	100	5.4	8,380	7,066	19,318	2.9
Textiles	61	34	123	6.7	37,968	2,733	57,338	8.7
Pulp and Paper	5	11	18	1.0	1,689	1,906	4,984	0.8
Chemicals	73	139	240	13.1	10,911	11,248	26,556	4.0
Pharmaceuticals	12	20	40	2.2	3,018	3,144	7,068	1.1
Petroleum	0	0	0	0.0	0	0	0	0.0
Rubber	9	27	37	2.0	3,041	18,544	22,705	3.5
Glass, Cement	22	40	75	4.1	7,461	13,227	24,159	3.7
Steel	17	42	71	3.9	3,726	6,394	11,614	1.8
Nonferrous Metals	34	88	129	7.0	9,721	19,337	33,473	5.1
Machinery	54	109	188	10.2	12,499	25,849	45,088	6.9
Electrical	170	253	499	27.2	113,650	84,155	261,641	39.9
Shipbuilding	5	13	22	1.2	3,717	8,504	19,475	3.0
Automobile	44	129	189	10.3	19,341	63,854	97,461	14.9
Other Transport	1	4	5	0.3	156	206	362	0.1
Precision Machinery	24	28	59	3.2	10,842	3,841	15,997	2.4
Other Manufacturing	15	17	42	2.3	4,253	2,009	8,557	1.3

Note: Counts reflect the number of manufacturing investments where the parent has at least a 20 percent equity share and employment figures are reported. Employment shows the total number of employees in the affiliates surveyed.

Source: Toyo Keizai, Japanese Overseas Investment.

TABLE 4

TOP 25 OVERSEAS EMPLOYERS AMONG JAPANESE MANUFACTURERS,
ANNUAL AVERAGES, 1980-1989

COMPANY	TOTAL EMPLOYEES	COUNT[a]	EMPLRAT[b]	EXRAT[c]	ASSETS[d]	ROA[e]
Matsushita Electric Industrial	46,791	60	53.1	30.9	2,093	6.4
Sanyo Electric	28,493	43	45.3	49.2	788	3.9
Nissan Motor	26,587	8	33.5	51.3	2,473	4.9
NEC	18,164	22	32.5	29.9	1,621	4.9
Minebea	17,086	14	82.4	34.0	251	4.5
Toray Industries	16,255	22	62.9	23.3	642	5.3
Hitachi	14,725	17	16.1	28.8	2,484	4.6
Toyota Motor	14,499	18	17.6	41.4	3,512	7.2
Asahi Glass	13,587	19	59.4	8.8	635	6.2
Sony	13,400	10	45.2	65.7	944	5.9
Sharp	12,756	14	41.1	53.6	786	5.6
Suzuki Motor	12,694	15	50.2	45.8	335	3.0
Sumitomo Rubber Industries	9,930	4	67.2	23.8	176	4.7
Mitsumi Electric	9,918	12	83.7	33.9	49	3.9
Mitsubishi Electric	9,809	15	17.1	22.8	1,551	4.2
Alps Electric	9,769	11	60.0	29.4	206	5.6
Bridgestone	9,761	9	38.2	30.0	542	5.3
Honda Motor	9,564	22	24.2	67.7	1,005	5.7
Mitsubishi Heavy Industries	9,135	6	17.1	28.7	2,756	3.3
Toshiba	8,727	13	11.2	27.1	2,212	4.2
Fujikura	8,060	11	68.3	16.3	177	4.4
Toyobo	6,909	11	44.6	14.8	320	5.5
Toko	6,841	5	87.1	8.4	39	4.6
Ajinomoto	6,463	19	58.3	7.3	393	4.1
Yamaha Motor	6,040	15	37.7	61.9	233	3.8

Notes: [a] Number of overseas manufacturing investments where the parent has at least a 20 percent equity share and employment figures are reported.
[b] Ratio of overseas employment to domestic plus overseas employment.
[c] Ratio of exports to sales.
[d] Assets expressed as billions of yen.
[e] Return on assets.
Source: *Japanese Overseas Investment.*

investment from direct investment and generally assumes well-functioning competitive markets. The international business field has developed theories about the multinational enterprise that draw heavily on the industrial organization literature. This research augments standard trade theory by explaining how market imperfections underlie direct investment abroad. Here we consider both types of theory to provide a framework for assessing the effects of DIA on welfare in the home country.

Conventional trade theory makes strong predictions about the distribution of world production and the composition of trade. The theory of comparative advantage is captured by the Heckscher-Ohlin theorem, which demonstrates that countries will export goods that make intensive use of their relatively abundant factors. Relative abundance is defined in terms of both physical quantities and factor prices in autarky. In a two-factor world of labour, L, and capital, K, a country, J, is abundant in capital relative to country D if $L_J/K_J < L_D/K_D$. If consumers have identical and homothetic preferences, this implies that $w_J/r_J > w_D/r_D$ in autarky, or that real returns to labour are higher in country J than in country D, a result that reflects factor abundance in the two countries. In this simple scenario, country J will export goods that use capital relatively intensively, and country D will export labour-intensive goods. Vanek (1968) developed a less restrictive version that accommodates countries producing a variety of goods. Vanek's version demonstrates that the net factor content of trade (i.e., the factors embodied in exports less those embodied in imports) will reflect relative abundance.[5]

Greater output through specialization which increases world welfare is the compelling argument for free trade. The effect of free trade on the distribution of income within individual countries is addressed in the Stolper-Samuelson theory which states that *free trade raises the real returns of relatively abundant factors but lowers the real returns of scarce factors.* Accordingly, if Japan were relatively abundant in capital, then free trade would raise the real return to capital and lower the return to labour. Ultimately, trade would lead to factor price equalization where real returns to factors are the same across countries. A consequence of this theory is that there is no incentive for capital to move to even capital-scarce countries, and therefore there will be no foreign investment. However, even when trade barriers impede or eliminate trade, creating the possibility of differential real return to capital among countries, Mundell (1957) shows that factor-price equalization will occur when factors are mobile. Capital flows to locations where it can earn the highest return and eventually leads to equalized returns across countries. Mundell's insight is that capital mobility achieves the same outcome as free trade. Hence, free trade will lead to rising (or falling) returns to relatively abundant (or scarce) factors through free trade in either goods *or* factors. Free trade or capital mobility, therefore, accomplishes the same results: the nation achieves the gains associated with free trade, and tendencies towards factor-price equalization increase real returns for some factors and decrease them for others. Thus, traditional trade suggests that capital mobility should be viewed as positive but may lower returns to scarce factors in the source country.

Traditional trade theory fails to distinguish between direct investment and portfolio investment. According to trade theory, capital flows to regions where it can earn the highest return, ultimately equalizing returns everywhere. These returns do not relate to who manages the productive assets, and so trade theory offers no insight as to why these capital flows might be accompanied by the foreign investor's assumption of management control.

Most of the international business literature has focused on the reasons why firms choose to invest abroad. The theory of direct investment abroad considers the decisions of individual firms to access foreign markets through trade (imports and exports), licensing (contracting with foreign parties) or expanding their own operations across borders by means of DIA. The analysis considers heterogeneous firms with specific skills as compared to other domestic firms, as well as firms in other countries.[6] Its neglect of general equilibrium analysis can be justified in that DIA flows are small compared to those of portfolio investment,[7] and so it is the large volume of portfolio investment that equalizes equilibrium returns to capital and produces changes in comparative advantage. Direct investment is unlikely to have a significant effect on capital abundance, and even if portfolio investment equalizes returns to capital across countries, firm-specific advantages coupled with market imperfections will continue to provide opportunities to increase profits through direct investment.

The modern theory of the multinational has been formalized by Dunning, whose work in this area is referred to as the "eclectic" theory of the multinational enterprise.[8] The existence of three conditions leads to direct investment abroad: 1) ownership advantages, 2) locational advantages and, 3) internalization advantages. Ownership advantages provide a firm with the capability to compete in foreign markets. These can include access to a superior technology, advanced management skills, and the exploitation of economies of scale. Locational advantages, the second component, are associated with locating business activities abroad. These can include low costs and the circumvention of trade barriers. Low costs abroad may stem from relative factor abundance and therefore are perfectly consistent with standard trade theory. If relative abundance changes over time, manufacturing activities must adjust by moving to the locations that yield the lowest-cost production. As Mundell's (1957) analysis shows, capital movements may be a result of trade barriers, and so trade theory is also consistent with these locational advantages driving foreign investment. The third component, internalization advantages, determines whether a firm will restrict activity to its own boundaries rather than contract with foreign third parties. There are advantages to internalizing activities when a "fair" price cannot be negotiated due to market imperfections.[9] The existence of all three components predicts direct investment abroad. Ownership advantages give a firm the ability to compete in foreign markets; locational advantages imply that a firm is capable of conducting its business activity abroad; and internalization advantages ensure that a firm can undertake foreign business activity itself rather than contract it to an outside party.

While international business theory of foreign investment does not directly address its impacts on welfare in the source country, some implications can be drawn. First, DIA makes firms better off because a firm will employ DIA only if it expects that form of investment to yield higher profits than the other opportunities available to it. As with traditional trade theory, capital seeks its highest returns; the net result is higher profits, at least *ex ante*.

The effect of DIA on the returns to domestic labour tends to be similar to the effect of capital outflows on labour as predicted by traditional trade theory. For example, the effect of the appreciation of the yen on a firm's production decision is easily understood in a partial equilibrium framework. Consider a firm that sells its (differentiated) product in international markets and manufactures both at home and abroad. Assume that output at home and abroad is produced by capital and labour. The profit-maximizing firm will allocate production so as to equalize the marginal cost of producing at home and abroad. This implies that the marginal value product of labour will always be equal to the wage rate in each (perhaps different) location. When the home currency appreciates, the cost of employing workers at home increases, resulting in reduced home employment. This causes a decrease in production that raises commodity prices, thereby inducing the firm to expand production abroad. Therefore, currency appreciation leads to a substitution of labour from a home to a foreign affiliate, and if capital is a complementary input to labour, then the same substitution will occur for capital. This decrease in demand for domestic labour will have the effect of either lowering real wages or causing higher unemployment. Trade restrictions in foreign markets are likely to have similar adverse consequences for labour; by lowering the marginal value product of home workers, such barriers induce a substitution of foreign production for domestic production, thereby decreasing the demand for domestic labour and resulting in unemployment or lower wages. These effects can be attenuated if, as suggested in the Gunderson & Verma study in this volume, DIA raises the productivity of domestic workers.

THE EFFECT OF DIA ON WORKERS AND CORPORATE PERFORMANCE IN JAPAN

HERE WE EXAMINE SOME OF THE EVIDENCE on the effects of Japan's recent direct investment abroad on the profitability of Japanese firm operations and the employment opportunities of Japanese workers. The impact of DIA is inherently difficult to assess because the analyst lacks hard information and must therefore speculate about what would happen to firms and their employees if the government prohibited outward investment. It is also difficult to determine causality. The wages of domestic workers and the profitability of firms affect the incentives for outward investment while as DIA simultaneously affects worker welfare and corporate performance. Our approach does not resolve the issue; our focus is to compare the attributes of multinational and domestic-production-only firms. Our analysis of the employment, wage, and export consequences of DIA does pay special attention, however, to the performance of industries that employ large numbers of workers abroad: textiles, electronics, and transport equipment.

DIA and Firm Performance

TABLES 5A AND 5B COMPARE THE PERFORMANCE of multinational and non-multinational firms in Japan; they show the annual average returns on sales, and return on assets, and sales growth during the 1980s for 1,070 publicly listed Japanese manufacturing firms.[10] Japanese firms are classified as multinationals if they have at least one foreign manufacturing affiliate. This classification yields 488 MNEs and 622 non-multinationals among listed firms.

TABLE 5A

RELATIVE PERFORMANCE OF MULTINATIONAL AND
NON-MULTINATIONAL FIRMS IN JAPAN (%)

FACTOR	MULTINATIONAL (448)	NON-MULTINATIONAL (622)
Return on Sales		
Absolute Performance	5.38	4.70
Relative to Industry	1.10	0.92
Return on Assets		
Absolute Performance	5.07	5.08
Relative to Industry	1.02	0.99
Sales Growth		
Absolute Performance	6.93	5.85
Relative to Industry	0.99	1.01

Source: Authors' calculations based on data contained in Nihon Keizai Shimbunsha, Nikkei: *Annual Corporate Reports*, various years.

TABLE 5B

CORRELATION BETWEEN PERFORMANCE MEASURES AND NUMBER OF
MANUFACTURING INVESTMENTS OVERSEAS

FIRMS	RETURN ON SALES		RETURN ON ASSETS		SALES GROWTH	
	ABSOLUTE	RELATIVE	ABSOLUTE	RELATIVE	ABSOLUTE	RELATIVE
All Firms (1,070)	.008	.061[a]	.003	.093[a]	.157[b]	.016
Multinational Firms (448)	-.050	.037	.001	.148[b]	.216[b]	.036

Note: A multinational company is defined as a firm with at least one manufacturing investment overseas.
    [a] correlation coefficient significantly different from zero at confidence level of .05.
    [b] correlation coefficient significantly different from zero at confidence level of .01.
Source: Authors' calculations based on data contained in Nohon Keizai Shimbun Sha, Nikkei: *Annual Corporate Reports*, various years.

Table 5A shows that multinational firms have higher returns on sales and higher rates of sales growth than do non-multinationals. This can be seen from the numbers corresponding to absolute performance measures showing the return on sales averages of 5.38 percent for multinationals and 4.70 percent for non-multinationals, and sales growth averages of 6.93 percent for multinationals and 5.85 percent for non-multinationals.[11] Returns on assets are similar for both groups. Differences in performance measures, however, may simply reflect differences in industrial composition. To control for these, we calculated the performance of a firm relative to the average performance of firms in its industry and averaged the results across the two sets of firms. These calculations reveal than while multinational firms tend to have high levels of sales growth, they do not have high sales growth relative to others in their industry. Conversely, the relative return on sales for MNEs is significantly higher (1 percent level of significance) than that of non-MNEs.

Table 5B shows the correlation between firm performance and the extent of multinational activity as measured by the number of manufacturing investments. The calculations reveal that the relationship between the amount of DIA and performance varies depending on whether we evaluate absolute performance or relative performance. The first four columns, showing Return on Sales and Return on Assets, indicate that absolute return on sales and absolute return an assets do not correlate to the number of overseas manufacturing investments. There is, however, a positive correlation when relative performance is considered. Sales growth exhibits the opposite relationship. Absolute sales growth is positively related to counts on investments, but growth relative to the industry average is not. This pattern is similar to the one in Table 5A and indicates that while firms in fast-growing industries tend to invest abroad, such foreign investment is not associated with faster growth relative to the industry.

As a whole, the performance of Japanese multinationals does not appear to be much different from that of Japanese non-multinationals, but there is evidence that multinational activity is associated with relatively high return on assets and sales within some industries. One explanation is that capital market imperfections prevent some firms from investing abroad, which causes them to perform less well than firms that were not constrained. We explore the relationship between internal funds and DIA in the next section, but our analysis cannot determine whether multinational activity causes higher returns on assets and sales because the correlation may result from ownership advantages that lead to high levels of performance and foreign investment. The evidence, however, is at least consistent with the hypothesis that direct investment improves firm performance.

DIA, EMPLOYMENT AND WAGES

AT FIRST GLANCE, Japan appears to provide an unpromising case study for assessing the effects on workers of direct investment abroad. As measured by the aggregate unemployment rate, Japan has been a labour-scarce nation throughout the entire period during which it has established its overseas manufacturing facilities. With an unemployment rate hovering at just over 2 percent during the 1980s (and even lower during the 1970s), the labour market could easily absorb any workers released by multinationals. However, a concern has emerged throughout the developed nations over the sectoral composition of jobs, particularly with respect to declining manufacturing employment. Partly in response to the appreciation of the yen, there is now a growing worry in Japan over the 'hollowing out' of manufacturing firms. This section examines the increase in overseas employment by Japanese firms and considers evidence that overseas employment has affected the structure of employment and/or the compensation to Japanese workers.

Figure 3 illustrates the steady growth in the share of Japanese multinationals' employment accounted for by workers outside Japan (of whom all but a few managers are non-Japanese). The figure presents both the average share and the quartiles of the distribution. Aside from the upward trend, the

FIGURE 3

SHARE OF EMPLOYEES OVERSEAS (FIRMS WITH ONE OR MORE BRANCHES BY 1990)

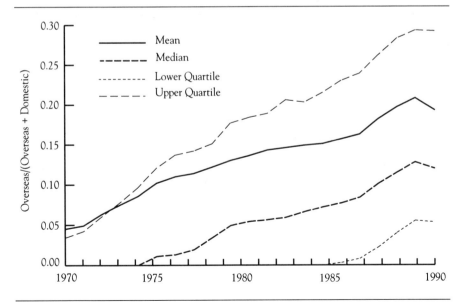

Source: Toyo Keizai, *Japanese Overseas Investment*.

JAPANESE EMPLOYMENT ABROAD SINCE 1970

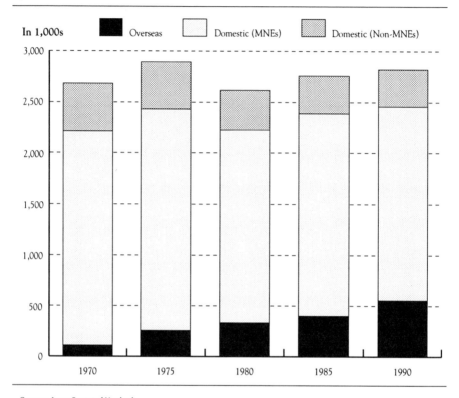

Source: *Japan Statistical Yearbook*.

most noteworthy aspect of the plot is the skewed nature of the distribution. As late as 1976, over half the firms that would ultimately invest abroad (see endnote 4) still confined their production activities to Japan. By that time, however, a small number had already established significant overseas beachheads and a full 25 percent of the sample had overseas employment shares in excess of 10 percent. By 1990 the average share had risen to about 17 percent, with a quarter of the firms employing more than 26 percent of their total work force abroad. Since the domestic employment figures include headquarter employees engaged in accounting, marketing, and research, these figures clearly understate the portion of production workers located outside Japan, and so the potential for significant effects of DIA on Japanese workers now appears to be more serious.

The rising share of overseas employment begs the question of what is happening in absolute terms to domestic employment. On the one hand, we can pose a "reallocation" hypothesis that protectionism overseas and rising

FIGURE 4B

TRENDS IN THE COMPOSITION OF THE JAPANESE WORK FORCE SINCE 1970

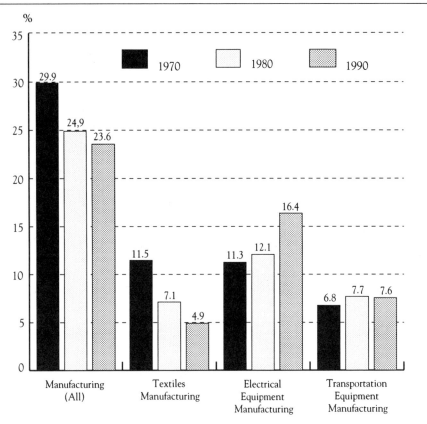

Source: *Japan Statistical Yearbook*.

Japanese wages have caused Japanese firms to substitute foreign workers for domestic ones.[12] A more optimistic perspective would stipulate that the most competitive Japanese firms have embarked on expansion programs both at home and abroad, with disproportionate expansion overseas. Figure 4A shows that among manufacturing firms listed on the Tokyo Stock exchange, domestic employment has remained fairly flat. However, the firms that became multinational between 1970 and 1990 have increased their share of domestic employment (listed firms only) from 82 percent to 84 percent. Meanwhile, the total employment of these firms, including their foreign branches, has risen steadily since 1980. Thus, the data presented so far provide no evidence of pure reallocation of employment.

TRENDS IN RELATIVE INDUSTRY WAGES SINCE 1970

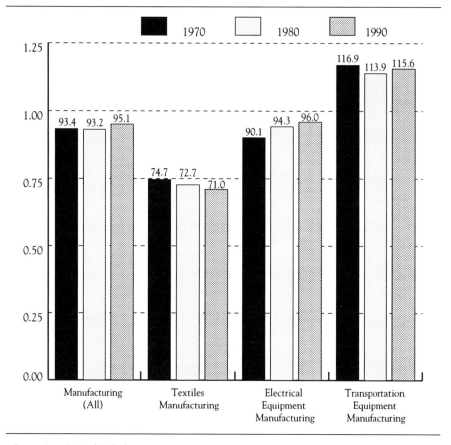

Source: *Japan Statistical Yearbook*.

Table 3 reveals that Japanese employment abroad has been concentrated in three major industries: electrical, automobile and textile. In the 1970s, Japanese textile firms created nearly 38,000 jobs overseas, while in the 1980s, the auto industry created over 60,000 such jobs. In both decades, electronics firms made the largest contributions to overseas employment. This suggests that we shall find the strongest effects of overseas investment concentrated in these three industrial sectors.

Figure 4B shows trends in the composition of the Japanese work force since 1970. The first set of bars shows that Japan, like most other OECD nations, has experienced a decline in the manufacturing share of employment. While this decline might indicate that the developed countries are generally

FIGURE 5B

RELATIVE WAGES OF MNE EMPLOYEES

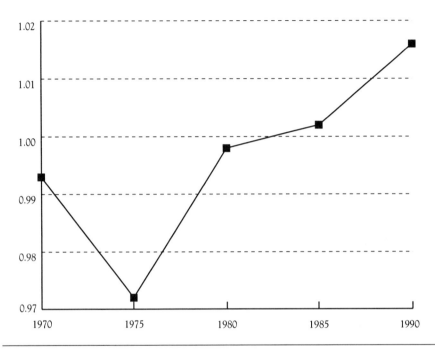

Source: *Japan Company Handbook.*

shifting employment to developing nations, continued productivity improve-ments in manufacturing reduce the number of manufacturing workers required for given levels of consumption.

The three sets of bars on the right side of Figure 4B suggest mixed effects of DIA on employment. In the textile industry, employment shrank sub-stantially in absolute terms and also as a share of all manufacturing. The largest part of the shift coincided with the increase in direct investment abroad by Japanese textile firms such as Toray Industries. A somewhat different pattern occurs in electronic equipment. There, growth abroad was accompanied by continued expansion at home. In transport equipment, the substantial overseas expansion that occurred in the 1980s may have dampened growth in domestic employment. It was during the 1980s that automobile firms created two-thirds of the total foreign jobs.

In addition to having employment effects, the reallocation hypothesis leads one to expect declining relative wages in those sectors where firms use the threat to move employment overseas as leverage against their domestic

FIGURE 6A

GROWTH IN EXPORTS PER EMPLOYEE

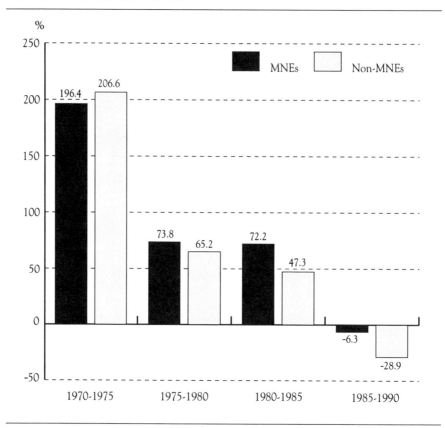

Source: *Japan Company Handbook.*

work force. Figures 5A and 5B show that, aside from the textile industry, if anything, multinational expansion raises domestic relative wages. Figure 5A reveals that the differences between industry wages far exceed the differences over time. As has been documented in the United States and in other nations, there are substantial inter-industry wage differentials as well. (Transport equipment workers, for example, earn one of the highest wages in the United States.) Direct investment abroad has not had any notable effect on that pattern. The rise in electronics wages supports the conventional view that Japanese firms have transferred their less skill-intensive jobs to Southeast Asia, triggering a corresponding rise in the average skill level of their domestic employees. Although real wages in electronics rose by 85 percent between 1970 and 1990, labour productivity rose by over 700 percent! Meanwhile, in

FIGURE 6B

EXPORTS PER EMPLOYEE

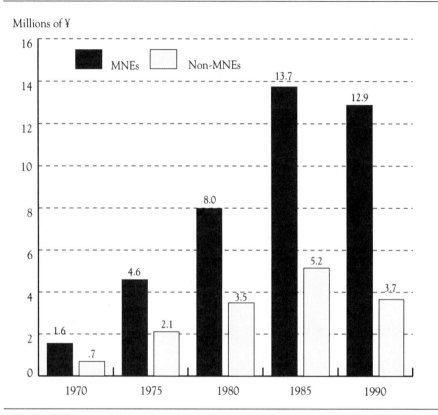

Source: *Japan Company Handbook*.

textiles, real wages increased by 63 percent, while labour productivity rose by 109 percent. Although unit labour costs declined in both industries, the cost reductions in the textile industry appeared inadequate to maintain employment levels. Japanese textile workers lost their competitive advantage to other Asian producers as Japan's comparative advantage shifted to more sophisticated goods such as electronics.[13]

Another potential consequence of foreign investment is the reduction of wages within particular firms that establish overseas manufacturing capabilities. Such effects should be limited, since employees are typically assumed to be mobile across firms in the same industry. However, if workers make firm-specific investments or are generally tied to particular firms by an ethic of lifetime employment, their wages may be vulnerable. To examine

FIGURE 7A

EXPORTS BY INDUSTRY

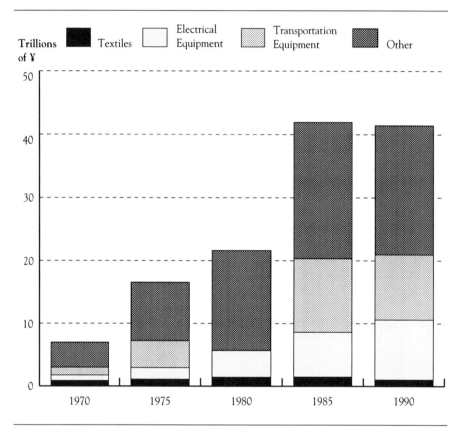

Source: *Japan Statistical Yearbook.*

this hypothesis we compared the average domestic wage (the total wage bill divided by the number of employees) of employees of firms that had made an overseas investment by 1990, with the domestic wages of firms that retained all production in Japan. Figure 5B shows that the average wages are approximately the same. (The gradual rise in MNE employee wages between 1975 and 1985 was very small.) A study of U.S. firms by Kravis & Lipsey (1988) found similar, but stronger, results and argues that the rise in compensation per employee occurs as the home-country skill intensity rises.

Most of the evidence reported in this section argues in favour of a view of the Japanese internationalization process as a source of overall net benefit, rather than cost, to Japanese employees. The textile sector is the major exception. In that case the predictions of the reallocation hypothesis appear

FIGURE 7B

EXPORT SHARES RELATIVE TO TOTAL EXPORTS

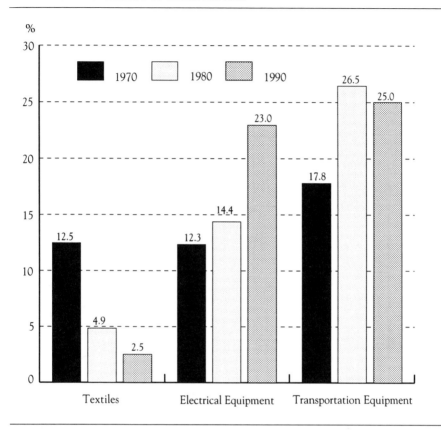

Source: *Japan Statistical Yearbook.*

to be consistent with the evidence: increasing overseas employment, declining employment and relative wages at home.

EFFECTS OF DIA ON EXPORTS

IF DIRECT INVESTMENT ABROAD serves solely to reallocate production overseas, there should be evidence of this in the pattern of Japanese exports. Figures 6A and 6B chart the export performance of Japanese multinationals (as of 1990) relative to solely domestic producers. During the 1970s, all Japanese firms experienced high levels of growth in exports per employee. However, the firms that went on to become multinationals started with, and maintained, approximately twice the export-to-employee ratio of purely domestic producers. This suggests that these firms had a more international focus even prior to investing abroad. In the late 1980s, when the appreciating yen hurt exports, Japanese multinationals watched their exports per employee decline by 6 percent, while non-multinationals experienced a 29 percent decline. Under the reallocation hypothesis the multinationals might have been expected to take the lead in serving foreign markets through foreign production while redirecting their remaining domestic production toward the domestic market. Instead, the data suggest that high-export orientation contributed to firms' decisions to invest abroad, and that these investments may later have helped them to maintain export markets for core components to be assembled overseas.

With respect to the industry composition of Japanese exports, Figures 7A and 7B indicate that in conjunction with other substantial overseas investments, the Japanese electrical equipment industry experienced steady export growth in both absolute and relative terms after 1970. There is some evidence of reallocation in the case of textiles and transport equipment. During the 1970s, textile exports plummeted as a share of all Japanese exports. In the 1980s, we see some indication that foreign production may have been substituted for exports in the auto industry.[14]

Research in (and cited by) Kravis & Lipsey (1988) corroborate the evidence presented here that foreign production often complements rather than substitutes for domestic production for export. This is most evident in the electronics industry. In the case of textiles, Japanese firms continue to reallocate production abroad as the domestic sector continues to decline steadily by almost any measure.[15] The difference between the performances of the two sectors suggests that the home-country effects of outward investment are more likely to be positive (in terms of employment and export performance) in dynamic industries (where expansion of overseas employment may cause a change in the skill composition within particular firms or industries), but they do not simply move jobs overseas.

EFFECTS OF DIA ON DOMESTIC SPILLOVERS AND ECONOMIC RENTS

THE STUDY BY BLOMSTRÖM & KOKKO in this volume argues that DIA influences the patterns of production within some industries, which may affect national welfare. If positive technological spillovers are associated with manufacturing activities in these industries, then moving production abroad could result in a loss of these spillovers. This is especially so when research and development and other innovative activities move abroad. Fujita & Ishii (1991) studied the investments of the nine top Japanese electronic firms and found that of the 123 R&D facilities established by these firms between 1976 and 1990, only 28 were located overseas and these were concentrated in the United States (13 plants) and the E.C. (7 plants). During this period, these firms also established 337 production plants, of which 203 (or 60 percent) were located overseas. It appears that while Japanese electronic companies rapidly increased their overseas production, most of their R&D activity stayed at home, suggesting that the potential loss of technology spillovers in the electronics industry is probably not an important concern for Japan.

Another way changes in production activity brought about by DIA can influence home-country welfare is if particular stages of the manufacturing process confer rents to labour in the form of higher wages. DIA that moves these stages offshore can result in lower welfare at home. However, there is little evidence in the case of Japan that many "desirable" jobs move abroad with DIA. Our analysis of wages revealed that, with the exception of textiles, the relative wages of manufacturing firms and industries with high levels of DIA remained high. Furthermore, Fujita & Ishii (1991) show that electronic companies establish new "trial factories" in Japan that develop new products and processes, and (arguably) require skilled labour, while they frequently build mass-production factories abroad. Coupled with their findings that Japanese firms site almost all new R&D plants in Japan, their evidence indicates that "desirable" production activities are not moved offshore.

There is also evidence suggesting that management and professional jobs are usually not transferred to foreigners as a result of DIA. This phenomenon is important to Japan to the extent that these occupations pay high wages and support the accumulation of human capital. A study by the U.S. Department of Labor (1993) concludes that Japanese affiliates in the United States employ a relatively low proportion of professional and managerial workers and a relatively high proportion of production workers.[16] Moreover, in an earlier volume in this series Westney provides evidence that approximately one-half of the managers in foreign affiliates of Japanese companies are Japanese nationals. Again, the available evidence suggests that DIA does not result in losses of desirable jobs to foreigners.

The existence of agglomeration externalities (benefits associated with firms locating in geographic proximity) can involve costs associated with moving production abroad that are not completely internalized by firms. For instance, if a major manufacturer decides to relocate a factory abroad, it may impose a cost on related and supplier firms. While relocation may be a wise decision for the major manufacturer, it may be harmful overall to Japan due to losses incurred by the related and supplier firms. While Head et al. (1993) argue that these externalities appear to exist for Japanese firms, we have not attempted to measure these costs in this analysis.

DETERMINANTS OF OUTWARD DIRECT INVESTMENT

THIS SECTION UTILIZES A TIME SERIES on the investment activities of Japanese manufacturing firms to explore empirically the factors that underlie Japanese foreign investment. The analysis has two objectives. The first is to contribute to the understanding of the determinants of foreign investment and provide information on whether conventional explanations of Japanese direct investment are consistent with the empirical evidence. The second, which is most relevant to welfare in Japan, is to determine whether capital market imperfections inhibit direct investment abroad by Japanese firms by evaluating whether company liquidity and wealth facilitate invest-ment. Capital market imperfections may well provide a rationale for policies easing financial constraints.[17]

Market imperfections stemming from asymmetric information (where creditors cannot easily determine the quality of a firm's investment projects) may limit the amount of investment financed by external funds (i.e., debt and new equity issues). Increases in internal funds (including the market value of liquid assets) can increase investment (domestic and abroad) by means of two mechanisms:

- A more liquid balance sheet can lower the effective cost of external financing. A lower cost of capital will result if the cost of external funds increases in the total amount of the external funds provided to the firm. This will occur if creditors believe the risk of their loan increases with the amount of borrowing by the firm from external sources.

- Firms in a credit-rationed position (i.e., one in which no external source is currently willing to lend more at any interest rate) could use internal funds directly or as collateral to secure addi-tional loans.[18]

In other words, firms do not face a perfectly elastic supply of capital. Note that liquidity effects are not based on the notion that capital markets are internationally segmented. Neither do they imply that the demand of an individual firm is large enough to affect the market price of external funds. Rather, liquidity becomes a matter for concern when a firm cannot borrow as much as it wants at prevailing interest rates. The study by Blomström & Kokko in this volume also points out that credit market imperfections might cause direct investment abroad to crowd out invest-ment at home.

Empirical analysis has attempted to verify the positive relationship between internal funds and direct investment abroad. Caves (1990) shows that retained earnings, which generate internal funds that can be used for investment, are positively (but not significantly) related to the propensity of firms to make foreign investments. Belderbos & Sleuwaegen (1993) find that liquidity has a positive influence on investment by Japanese electronic firms in the West (Europe and North America) but not in Southeast Asia, whereas Drake & Caves (1992) find a negative and significant relationship between

Japanese industry's retained earnings and Japan's foreign investment share in the United States. Tan et al. (1993) studies the timing of Japanese investment in the United States and Canada, and identifies inconclusive empirical relationships between cash on hand and the likelihood of early investment.

The real exchange rate may have two effects on DIA. Froot & Stein (1992) argue that credit market imperfections may generate a linkage between the real exchange rate and direct investment flows. They posit that if a firm must finance a percentage of its foreign investment with internal funds, then the appreciation of the real exchange rate expands the amount of internal funds denominated in the foreign currency and increases the likelihood that the firms will invest abroad. Thus, real appreciation of the yen will result in greater wealth for Japanese companies, which increases their likelihood of direct investment. Changes in the real exchange rate will encourage outward investment not only because of the wealth effects postulated by Froot & Stein, but also because they will lead to relatively high production costs in Japan. There are many reasons why international factor prices do not equalize in the short or even the long run.[19] In particular, the existence of non-traded factors of production such as labour means that factor prices may differ across countries. The propensity of Japanese firms to invest abroad may increase as Japanese labour becomes more expensive. Indeed, Japanese scholars have identified yen appreciation and concomitant higher wages in Japan as a primary reason for Japanese foreign investment.[20] If firms seek low wages by going abroad, labour-intensive firms might be expected to be deeply influenced by movements in the exchange rate.

Japanese firm networks can also play an important role in a firm's overseas investment strategy. Financial *keiretsu* are conglomerate groupings organized around a main bank and a large trading house (*sogo shosha*) and formally linked by the cross-shareholding of stock. While direct business activities between financial *keiretsu* groupings are usually limited, they may facilitate information exchange. Hoshi et al. (1991) have shown that membership in a financial *keiretsu* eases liquidity constraints on investment, perhaps because such memberships mitigate information asymmetries between investors and creditors.

Earlier empirical studies also suggest other variables that are likely to influence the decision to invest abroad.[21] These studies employ characteristics of firms or industries, most often focusing on investment in the United States and Europe. Firm size has consistently been found to be positively associated with direct investment. For U.S. companies, Grubaugh (1987) shows this positive relationship, while Juhl (1979) makes the same finding for German companies. Belderbos & Sleuwaegen (1993) find that size is an important determinant for investment by Japanese electronics firms in both Southeast Asia and the West (Europe and North America). Tan et al. (1993) demonstrates the importance of size for the early entry of Japanese electronic firms in North America.

The intensity of research and development has also been shown to be positively related to foreign investment. High R&D expenditures can create ownership advantages which are likely to be internalized through DIA because they are difficult to contract to outside parties. Studies of U.S. investment corroborate this view. Belderbos & Sleuwaegen (1993) find this relationship for Japanese electronics firms investing in the West but not for investors in Southeast Asia. Kogut & Chang (1991) analyze industry counts of Japanese entries in the United States and find that Japanese R&D expenditures have a positive influence on investment. They also show that joint ventures tend to be concentrated in industries where the U.S. R&D intensity is higher than Japanese intensity, indicating that this form of investment may in part be motivated by desires to source U.S. technology. This finding is corroborated in Yamawaki (1992). Similarly, advertising and marketing intensity, which can lead to hard-to-transfer ownership advantages, has been found to be a positive determinant of investment, although empirically not all studies detect a strong relationship.

Export tendencies can also be significant factors underlying foreign investment. Firms that export intensively might use direct investment abroad as an alternative to exporting. While a negative relationship might be expected if the two modes are substitutes, in the short run we found that the exporters are the firms making the direct investments. There is also the view that foreign investment and trade are complements, a proposition supported by our analysis in the previous section, which would lead to a positive relationship. Drake & Caves (1992) find Japanese share of exports to be a significant, positive determinant of Japanese share of industry-level foreign investment in the United States.

We extend our empirical analysis of the determinants of DIA by analyzing DIA investment decisions of listed Japanese firms. Our dependent variable is the annual count of manufacturing investments for each firm between 1970 and 1989. We then match those counts to characteristics of the firm at the time (or shortly before the time) of investment, and use econometric analysis to estimate the relationship between the counts and firm characteristics. The firm attributes considered are the size of the firm, measures of wealth and liquidity, advertising and R&D intensity, and export intensity. We also consider exchange rate movements.

Our panel data set provides valuable time series information which has not been considered by other researchers using firm-level data. Some of those studies (Belderbos & Sleuwaegen, 1993, and Grubaugh, 1987) classify firms as multinational or non-multinational while others (Swedenbourg, 1979) proxy multinational activity by the overseas production ratio. These studies then match current firm characteristics to these dependent variables. Our approach is superior in that it allows us to match investments with firm characteristics at the time of overseas investment. This is particularly important if characteristics change over time.

We specify a Poisson regression to estimate the relationship between manufacturing investment counts and firm characteristics, a method commonly employed to fit count data such as the number of patents.[22] The basic Poisson specification is

$$Prob(n_{it}) = \frac{e^{\lambda_{it}} \lambda_{it}^{n_{it}}}{n_{it}!}$$

where the number of events for firm i at time t, λ_{it}, is Poisson distributed and the parameter λ_{it} is specified to be

$$\lambda_{it} = \exp(X_{it}\beta)$$

where X_{it} is a matrix of characteristics for firm i at time t, and β is a vector of parameters. In our model, n_{it} is the number of manufacturing investments for firm i in year t. All publicly listed Japanese firms are considered, including those that never make overseas investments. The explanatory variables, X_{it}, include measures of wealth and liquidity, the ratio of production labour costs to total labour costs, Japan's real exchange rate, and other variables shown in previous studies to be important.[23]

Three measures of liquidity are considered. Following Hoshi et al. (1991), CASHFLOW is defined as income after tax plus depreciation less dividends. This measures the annual flow of cash into the firm. A stock measure, CASH, is calculated by summing cash and marketable securities, which represents the stock of liquid assets on hand. In addition, a measure of wealth, STOCKVAL, is calculated by considering the market value of stocks held by each firm. This is calculated as the amount of investments in securities plus holdings of stocks of affiliated firms. Since these stocks are valued at acquisition cost, we multiply by the value-weighted index of the Tokyo Stock Exchange (TOPIX) to estimate the market value of these stock holdings.[24] All these measures are normalized by dividing by assets. CASH and STOCKVAL are lagged an additional year to represent the position of firms entering in the year they make the investment. If firms must rely partly on internal funds to finance their foreign investment, these variables will be positively related to investment.

Many scholars consider some Japanese DIA to be motivated by the desire to access low cost labour. We calculate PLSHR as the ratio of the cost of production labour to total labour costs. One minus this ratio was used by Belderbos & Sleuwaegen (1993) to represent human capital which was positively associated with DIA. Their argument is that high levels of human capital lead to ownership advantages. Accordingly, we predict this variable will have a negative relationship to investment abroad (as it is one minus Belderbos & Sleuwaegen's variable). However, we posit that as the yen appreciates, firms with high ratios of PLSHR will be induced to locate their production overseas. The basis for this hypothesis is that DIA allows firms to substitute foreign production labour for domestic production labour, whereas it is difficult to shift selling, general and administrative tasks overseas. To investigate the effect of real exchange rate movements on production-labour intensive firms, we use PLSHR_RER as the product of the two variables. Since the appreciation of the yen has a positive value in our exchange rate index, this variable is expected to enter with a positive sign. As a separate item, we also include the real exchange rate, RER, as it has been found to be significant by other researchers.

TABLE 6

ESTIMATED COEFFICIENTS

VARIABLE	1970-1979	1980-1989
CONSTANT	-5.01	-10.72
	(-2.88)	(-15.16)
LASSET	0.54	0.65
	(15.76)	(24.57)
RDINT	0.0014	0.0002
	(0.81)	(0.13)
ADVINT	8.69	3.80
	(3.87)	(1.89)
EXINT	0.99	-0.16
	(3.53)	(-0.70)
RER	-3.79	0.003
	(-2.63)	(0.01)
CASHFLOW	5.56	3.12
	(6.94)	(7.36)
CASH	-0.33	-0.40
	(-0.40)	(-0.94)
STOCKVAL	1.41	0.11
	(4.76)	(3.20)
PLSHR	-5.09	-2.36
	(-2.26)	(-2.82)
PLSHR_RER	4.02	1.08
	(2.07)	(2.69)
LOG LIKELIHOOD	-1744.8	-2444.6
OBSERVATIONS	8788	9406

Note: T-statistic in parenthesis.
Source: Authors' calculations based on data contained in Nihon Keizai Shimbunsha, NIKKEI: Annual Corporate Reports, various years.

Firm size, as measured by the log of assets (LASSET), is added, as well as R&D to sales, and advertising to sales (RDINT and ADVINT, respectively) to explore whether these hard-to-transfer ownership advantages contribute to overseas investment.[25] In other studies these factors have been shown to have a positive effect on DIA. We also include the ratio of export to sales, EXINT, to see if export-oriented firms are more likely to invest abroad. Finally, seventeen (industry) dummy variables are added to control for industry differences.

TABLE 7

ESTIMATED COEFFICIENTS FOR INDUSTRY DUMMY VARIABLES

INDUSTRY	1970-1979	1980-1989
Food	0.28	0.88
	(0.82)	(3.09)
Textiles	1.00	0.66
	(3.13)	(2.13)
Pulp and Paper	-0.43	0.05
	(-0.81)	(0.12)
Chemicals	0.45	1.18
	(1.44)	(4.46)
Pharmaceuticals	-0.40	0.44
	(-0.85)	(1.21)
Rubber	0.49	1.62
	(1.05)	(4.99)
Glass, Cement	0.51	1.05
	(1.40)	(3.48)
Steel	-0.24	0.54
	(-0.62)	(1.79)
Nonferrous Metals	0.70	1.54
	(2.08)	(5.60)
Machinery	0.63	1.36
	(1.96)	(4.93)
Electrical	1.23	1.49
	(4.01)	(5.48)
Shipbuilding	-0.67	0.42
	(-1.23)	(1.11)
Automobile	0.46	1.54
	(1.36)	(5.50)
Other Transport	-1.28	0.31
	(-1.23)	(0.55)
Precision Machinery	0.90	1.20
	(2.40)	(3.62)

Notes: T-statistic in parenthesis.
     The omitted industry group is the "other manufacturing" industry, so the coefficients reflect industry effects relative to this industry.

The Poisson regression equation is estimated separately for the 1970s and 1980s to determine if the parameters change over time and to check the robustness of our results. Table 6 lists parameter estimates for the firm variables; Table 7 shows the coefficients for the industry dummies. The most noticeable result is the tremendous importance of firm size (assets) on the probability of investment. If ownership advantages underlie firm size then, clearly, these ownership advantages are instrumental in operating overseas. This finding is common to most empirical studies of firm determinants of DIA.

Advertising intensity is estimated to be positively and significantly related to overseas investment, although its importance diminishes over time. R&D intensity, while having the expected positive sign, is not a significant variable in the regressions. Lall (1980) points out that these proxies for ownership advantages are most powerful when they are related to those of firms in host countries. To the extent that Japanese investment in the 1980s shifted away from Southeast Asia to more highly industrialized Western countries, the diminishing importance of these proxies for ownership advantages may reflect the fact that high levels of these variables for Japanese firms do not translate into ownership advantages for investment in the West. Export intensity was important in the 1970s, but the high levels of exports compared to sales during the 1980s were not associated with manufacturing DIA.

Cashflow is found to be important in both periods. Similarly, the value of stocks is also estimated to increase significantly the probability of DIA. The stock of cash and marketable securities on hand, however, does not have a significant influence in the regression. Nonetheless, the weight of the evidence is that liquidity and wealth are associated with direct investment abroad. Thus, it appears that firms that do not have internal funds are constrained from investing abroad. Belderbos & Sleuwaegen (1993) found this result to hold for electronics goods firms that invest in the West but not for those classified as Southeast Asia investors. These findings indicate that liquidity constraints generally exist for Japanese firms investing abroad.

As previously mentioned, Hoshi et al. (1991) show that affiliation with a financial *keiretsu* reduces the need to rely on internal funds for investment. We test this proposition with regard to DIA by re-estimating the equation and allowing for *keiretsu* firms to have their own coefficient values for these liquidity and wealth variables. A likelihood ratio test does not reject the hypothesis that the two equations yield the same fit at the 20 percent significance level. There is no strong evidence in our data, therefore, that *keiretsu* help to overcome liquidity constraints on investment.

The share of cost of production workers to total labour cost is estimated to have a negative relationship to investment for both periods. This is consistent with the view that this variable is an inverse measure of advantages stemming from human capital. However, when we apply this ratio with the real exchange rate we find a positive relationship in both periods. Thus, while firms with high ratios of domestic production workers are generally less likely to go abroad, they are more likely to invest in manufacturing subsidiaries overseas when the yen appreciates. This result supports the hypothesis that DIA is one way for labour-intensive firms to respond to increases in the relative wages of domestic workers.

We also allow for a non-interactive effect of real exchange rates and obtain mixed results. During the 1980s the real exchange rate had a positive, but insignificant, effect on the propensity to invest abroad as predicted by the Froot & Stein (1991) model. The negative and significant coefficient obtained for the 1970s contradicts the intuition that yen appreciation leads to more DIA regardless of production labour intensity. However, this perverse result appears to occur only with respect to the early years of direct investment when the Japanese government was liberalizing regulations at the same time that the Bretton Woods exchange rate regime was collapsing. The negative exchange rate effect becomes insignificant when we begin estimation in 1973.[26]

Table 7 shows the estimated coefficients for the industry dummy variables. The omitted group is the "other manufacturing" industry, and so the coefficients reflect industry effects relative to this industry. They measure the average propensity of firms in an industry to invest abroad (relative to the omitted industry) after controlling for the effects of firm characteristics measured by the other explanatory variables. Between 1970 and 1979, the electrical industry had the largest coefficient, followed by textiles. During the 1980s, many more industries recorded average investments higher than the "other manufacturing" industry, and the coefficients for electronics and textiles are therefore no longer as prominent relative to the coefficients for other industries. After controlling for firm characteristics, firms in the rubber industry and the automobile industry generally are more likely to invest abroad than electrical firms. The result for the automobile industry partly reflects the widespread adoption of voluntary export restraints (VERs), making DIA necessary. VERs on automobiles might also explain some of the rubber industry result, in that tire makers constitute an important component of that industry and may well be following automobile producers abroad. Similarly, the large positive coefficients for the machinery and precision machinery industries may reflect VERs placed on machine tool exports to the United States. Finally, it appears that the industry dummy variables partly reflect barriers imposed on Japanese exports.

CONCLUSIONS

OVER THE PAST DECADE direct investment abroad has been an integral component of the strategies of Japanese manufacturing firms. During the 1980s, Japan's top manufacturers established hundreds of overseas manufacturing subsidiaries employing over 250,000 workers, and our analysis shows that Japanese multinational firms enjoyed high returns and large volumes of exports. Moreover, they appear to have been better able to maintain their domestic labour force than non-multinational firms. Consequently, we find no evidence that high levels of direct investment abroad impose costs on domestic labour. Although unemployment in Japan is low, real wages have continued to rise, even in industries with large amounts of investment abroad. Concerns about losses of R&D spillovers associated with moving business activities overseas are also unfounded, as Japanese firms appear to be keeping most of their research activities at home.

While we cannot answer the question of whether workers and firms are better off with DIA than they would be without it, there is no evidence to suggest that it has been harmful. Indeed, the only case where DIA has coincided with poor domestic industry performance is in textiles. However, the international history of the textile industry suggests that high-wage countries cannot maintain high levels of competitiveness in textile production. Japanese multinationals such as Toray Industries may at least preserve a share of the industry profits by maintaining control of production while economic forces promote its reallocation to low-wage nations.

Our econometric study on the determinants of DIA shows the importance of liquidity in financing investment abroad. This suggests that capital market imperfections induce Japanese firms to rely on internal funds in order to invest overseas. As in previous empirical work on DIA, our results demonstrate the strong relationship between firm size and outward investment, and we find that firms with high advertising intensity have a higher propensity to invest abroad. Our results also show that firms with high proportions of production labour costs to total labour costs invest abroad when the yen appreciates.

The Japanese experience suggests that Canada need not fear DIA. Japanese firms invested abroad in order to expand their aggregate business activities; there is little evidence documenting adverse effects on the domestic work force. However, the pattern of steady employment and wage growth in Japan is at least partly attributable to Japan's tight labour market, a characteristic that is not shared by the Canadian economy. Thus, Canadian DIA could well have some detrimental effects on the domestic work force. Our analysis shows that DIA is associated with firms that perform strongly in terms of return on assets, growth, size, exports and employment creation. However, the causation is not very clear. For instance, the high levels of DIA could be partly a consequence rather than a source of firm-competitive strength.

ENDNOTES

1 Aggregate FDI data used in this study are from Japan's Ministry of Finance. There are two limitations in the data. First, they measure notifications, and so the actual expenditures might come much later, if at all. Second, while they include loans from Japanese parents to overseas affiliates, they do not account for repayment of these loans. Both these effects tend to overstate the actual amount of DIA.

2 The yen appreciated by 19 percent in real trade-weighted terms over the two years following the abandonment of the dollar peg in 1971. See Komiya (1986) for further details on the deregulation of Japanese direct investment abroad.

3 North America and Europe implemented quantity restrictions (usually referred to as "voluntary export restraints") for automobiles, machine tools, colour television sets and other goods. Anti-dumping duties on a number of other products also provided an incentive for "tariff-jumping" investments. In addition, European countries imposed local content legislation that encouraged direct investment by parts suppliers.

4 These data are derived from a complete listing, compiled by Toyo Keizai, of Japanese firms' direct investments abroad as of 1990. While they provide more sectoral detail than is available from the Ministry of Finance, capital amounts are reported with a number of idiosyncrasies that limit comparability. Hence, we rank industries by the number of foreign investments (we use this count measure in the regression section as well) and the corresponding number of employees.

5 Deardorff (1982) establishes the Heckscher-Ohlin theorem for many goods and unequal factor prices.

6 This is in stark contrast to traditional trade assumptions that technologies are identical and homogeneous in the first degree (i.e., doubling inputs doubles outputs) in each country.

7 According to the United Nations Centre on Transnational Corporations (1991, Table 15), outside of Europe, direct investment as a proportion of gross domestic capital formation is low, usually less than five percent. Even in Europe, where inter-regional flows of direct investment are high, this proportion is under 20 percent. The importance of direct investment flows to capital formation, however, has been increasing with time.

8 A comprehensive treatment of this framework is found in Dunning (1993).

9 Issues pertaining to internalization closely parallel those concerning the theory of the firm in the field of industrial organization. Williamson (1975) contains a good summary of reasons why a firm prefers to expand its activities rather than contract through the marketplace.

10 In order to control for differences in borrowing, return on assets is calculated by adding net profits and interest payments, then dividing by assets. This approach is used by Nakatani (1984). Return on sales are

operating profits divided by sales, and sales growth is the annual growth rate of sales.

11 These difference are significant at a 1 percent significance level.

12 This reallocation hypothesis is consistent with the theory discussed previously.

13 While these trends in labour productivity are striking, cautious inter-pretation is required, since measured labour productivity depends on capital investment as well. Another interpretation of the preceding facts is that labour productivity in the textile industry stagnated (in relative terms) as firms ceased to invest domestically.

14 Within the transport equipment industry, ship exports peaked in 1975, motor vehicle exports peaked in 1985, and exports of parts for motor vehicles peaked in 1990.

15 A recent *Business Week* article (August 30, 1993, "How Badly Will Yen Shock Hurt?") reported that the leading Japanese textile firm, Toray Industries, which already employs 16,000 workers outside Japan (see Table 4), plans to raise foreign production as a percent of foreign sales from 13 percent today to 40 percent ten years from now.

16 Specifically, the proportion of employment of managerial and adminis-trative workers for Japanese manufacturing establishments is 4.9 percent and 9.9 percent for professional, paraprofessional, and technical workers, while it is 73.5 percent for production and related workers. These figures compare to 6.3 percent, 12.2 percent and 65.1 percent for all U.S. establishments. These differences are even more pronounced in the transportation-equipment industry, where Japanese establishments have 85.7 percent of the employment in production compared to 60.5 per-cent for all U.S. establishments.

17 The econometric analysis does not analyze the sensitivity of the deter-minants of Japanese DIA to the location of the investment. A recent paper by Belderbos & Sleuwaegen (1993) provides this type of analysis for the Japanese electronics industry. They classify Japanese firms into three types – purely domestic, Asia-bound, and West-bound (Europe and North America) – and relate firm characteristics to the probability of being each type. We include discussion of their findings in the evaluation of our regression results.

18 Credit-rationed equilibria may arise due to the adverse selection problem. The only firms willing to borrow at high interest rates are the ones that know they have a high likelihood of default and consequently are precisely the firms the creditor wishes to avoid.

19 Trade theory assumes free trade, identical and homogeneous technologies, incomplete specialization, the absence of factor intensity reversals, and perfect competition to generate factor price equalization, conditions that are likely to be violated in the real world.

20 For example, see Komiya (1986).

21 An excellent summary of the factors that influence Japanese investment into the United States is contained in Caves (1993). The United Nations Centre on Transnational Corporations (1992b) provides a review of the literature on the determinants of foreign investment.

22 See Hausman et al. (1984) for a discussion and evaluation of this method.

23 All the explanatory variables are lagged one year, since the investment date usually corresponds to the date operations started, which is later than the date the subsidiary was established.

24 Investment in securities is not a pure measure of stockholdings, as it includes non-stock investments. We are implicitly assuming that it is a good proxy for actual stock holdings.

25 We use the average R&D/sales ratio from the period 1985 to 1990 for R&D intensity, and so it does not vary across time for each firm. These data, from in the *Japan Company Handbook*, are taken from a survey and considered to be more reliable than the accounting R&D figures.

26 In the restricted 1973-1979 sample, all other variables retain their approximate magnitudes and statistical significance levels except for PLSHR and PLSHR_EX, which maintain their signs but are no longer significant.

ACKNOWLEDGEMENT

THE AUTHORS WISH TO THANK Wendy Dobson, Steven Globerman, and other conference participants for their helpful comments.

BIBLIOGRAPHY

Belderbos, Rene and Leo Sleuwaegen. "Japanese Firms and the Decision to Invest Abroad: Business Groups, Regional Core Networks and Corporate Development." mimeo, Erasmus University Rotterdam, Tindergen Institute, 1993.

Deardorff, Alan V. "The General Validity of the Heckscher-Ohlin Theorem." *The American Economic Review*, 88, 5 (1982): 941-57.

Caves, Richard E. "Japanese Investment in the United States: Lessons for Economic Analysis of Foreign Investment." *The World Economy*, 16, 3, (May 1993): 279-300.

Caves, Richard E. "Exchange-Rate Movements and Foreign Direct Investment in the United States." In *The Internationalization of U.S. Markets*. Edited by David B. Audretsch and Michael P. Clandon. New York: New York University Press, 1990, pp. 199-228.

Drake, Tracey A. and Richard E. Caves. "Changing Determinants of Japanese Foreign Investment in the United States." *Journal of Japanese and International Economies*, 6, (1992): 228-46.

Dunning, John. *Multinational Enterprises and the Global Economy*. Wokingham: Addison-Wesley Publishing Co., 1993, Ch. 4.

Froot, K.A. and J.C. Stein. "Exchange Rates and Foreign Direct Investment: An Imperfect Capital Markets Approach." *The Quarterly Journal of Economics*, 106 (1991): 1191-1217.

Fujita, M. and R. Ishii. "Location Behavior and Spatial Organization of Multinational Firms and Their Impact on Regional Transformation in East Asia: A Comparative Study of Japanese Korean, and U.S. Electronic Firms." *ICSEAD Intermediate Research Report*, University of Pennsylvania, 1991.

Grubaugh, Steven G. "The Determinants of Direct Foreign Investment." *Review of Economics and Statistics*. (1987): 149-52.

Head, C. Keith, John C. Ries and Deborah Swenson. "Agglomeration Benefits and Location Choice: Evidence From Japanese Manufacturing Investments in the United States", mimeo, Faculty of Commerce, University of British Columbia, 1993.

Hoshi, Takeo, Anil Kashyap and David Scharfstein. "Corporate Structure, Liquidity, and Investment: Evidence From Japanese Industrial Groups." *Quarterly Journal of Economics*, (1991): 33-60.

Hausman, Jerry, Bronwyn H. Hall and Zvi Griliches. "Econometric Models For Count Data with an Application to the Patents-R&D Relationship." *Econometrica*, 52, 4 (1984): 909-38.

Juhl, P. "On the Sectoral Patterns of West German Manufacturing Investments in Less Developed Countries: The Impact of Size, Factor Intensities and Production." *Weltwirtschaftliches Archiv*, 15 (1979): 508-19.

Kogut, Bruce and Sea Jin Chang. "Technological Capabilities and Japanese Foreign Direct Investment in the United States." *The Review of Economics and Statistics*, (1991): 401-13.

Komiya, Ryutaro. *The Japanese Economy: Trade, Industry and Government*. Tokyo: University of Tokyo Press, 1986, pp. 111-55.

Kravis, Irving and Robert Lipsey. "The Effect of Multinational Firms' Foreign Operations on Their Domestic Employment." *NBER Working Paper #2760*, 1988.

Lall, S. "Monopsonistic Advantages and Foreign Investment in U.S. Manufacturing Industry." *Oxford Economic Papers*, 32 (1980): 102-22.

Mundell, Robert A. "International Trade and Factor Mobility." *The American Economic Review*, (June, 1957): 321-35.

Nakatani, Iwao. "The Economic Role of Financial Corporate Grouping." In *The Economic*

Analysis of the Japanese Firm. Edited by M. Aoki. Amsterdam: Elsevier Science Publishers B.V. (North Holland), 1984, pp. 227-58.

Rugman, Alan, ed. *New Theories of the Multinational Enterprise.* London: Croom Helm, 1982.

Swedenbourg, Birgitta. *The Multinational Operations of Swedish Firms: Analysis of Determinants and Effects.* Stockholm: Industrial Institute of Economic and Social Research, 1979.

Tan, Benjamin, Ilan Vertinsky, John Ries and C. Keith Head. "Entry Timing of Japanese Firms in the United States and Canada", mimeo, Faculty of Commerce, University of British Columbia, 1993.

Toyo Keizai Inc, *Japan Company Handbook*, various issues, Tokyo.

Toyo Keizai Inc. *Japanese Overseas Investment.* Tokyo: Japanese Overseas Investment, (Japanese language) 1990, (English language) 1992/3.

United Nations Centre on Transnational Corporations. *World Investment Directory 1992, Volume 2 Developed Countries.* New York: United Nations, 1992a.

United Nations Centre on Transnational Corporations. *The Determinants of Foreign Direct Investment: A Survey of the Evidence.* New York: United Nations, 1992b.

United States Department of Labor, Bureau of Labor Statistics, *News* (New Research on Occupations in Foreign-Owned Manufacturing Establishments in the United States). USDL 93-455, October 27, 1993.

Vanek, Jaroslav. "The Factor Proportions Theory: The N-Factor Case." *Kyklos*, 21 (1968): 749-56.

Williamson, Oliver. *Markets and Hierarchies: Analysis and Antitrust Implications.* New York: Free Press, 1975.

Yamawaki, Hideki. "International Competitiveness and the Choice of Entry Mode: Japanese Multinationals in U.S. and European Manufacturing Industries", mimeo, Department of Economics, Université Catholique de Louvain, Belgium, 1992.

Magnus Blomström   &   Ari O. Kokko
Professor of Economics   Assistant Professor   **11**
Stockholm School of Economics   Stockholm School of Economics

Home-Country Effects of Foreign Direct Investment: Sweden

INTRODUCTION

THE HOME-COUNTRY EFFECTS of foreign direct investment (FDI) continue to be debated, especially in smaller OECD economies with large outflows of FDI. In Sweden, the topic attracts particular attention for good reasons. Swedish multinational enterprises (MNEs) occupy a dominant position in the Swedish economy, accounting for almost half of total manufacturing employment. Also, the flows of Swedish outward investment have been much larger than flows of inward investment: between 1981 and 1990, the sum of Swedish investment abroad was more than five times larger than inward FDI (OECD, 1993). Consequently, much work has been done analyzing the effects of Swedish investment abroad on the Swedish economy. The extensive literature includes a large number of academic studies from various universities and research institutes, as well as several comprehensive reports by government committees.

The purpose of this study is to examine two issues related to foreign investment by Swedish multinationals: first, the effects of outward FDI on domestic investment, exports and employment and, second, the effects on the domestic economy of the increasing division of labour between the parents and foreign affiliates of Swedish MNEs. Here, we summarize and synthesize the existing empirical evidence on these matters (much of which has hitherto been available only in Swedish) and discuss some possible long-run effects that have not received much attention in the literature. We also make some specific comparisons with the Canadian situation.

The remainder of this chapter is organized as follows: the next section outlines the motives for Swedish FDI and provides some descriptive statistics; the following section examines the evidence of the effects of FDI on Swedish investment, exports, and employment; while the final section focuses on some possible effects on domestic industry structure. There are also a summary and conclusion.

THE MOTIVES AND PATTERNS OF SWEDISH FDI

SWEDEN HAS A LONG TRADITION of foreign direct investment and multinational firms in the manufacturing sector. The oldest Swedish MNE dates back to the 17th century. Indeed, several of today's leading Swedish multinationals had established foreign operations before the First World War, and 18 of the country's 20 largest MNEs have been multinational for over three decades (Swedenborg et al., 1988).

Throughout the history of Swedish FDI, the main ownership advantages of the country's multinationals have been related to technologies based on domestic natural resources. Olsson (1993) identifies two types of development paths that were already emerging at the beginning of the 20th century. One group of Swedish multinationals based their competitiveness directly on local raw materials, such as wood and ferrous metals, and stayed close to their original industries. Others built on the long Swedish tradition of metal manufacturing, originally based on the exploitation of local sources of high-quality iron ore. Over the years these MNEs upgraded their operations to more advanced industries, including the manufacturer of sophisticated machinery and transport equipment. This pattern of using technology as the main competitive advantage is still discernible, although some firms now rely more heavily on their sales networks rather than on their initial technological assets (Olsson, 1993).

The motives for foreign production have remained largely unchanged over time. According to Jordan & Vahlne (1981), Swedish firms have typically established foreign affiliates to reduce transportation costs, to avoid trade barriers and to get closer to their customers. Close customer relations have been necessary in order to adapt products suitable for particular markets or specific national product standards, as well as to avoid discrimination against foreign producers (as in public procurement, for example). The foreign operations of Swedish multinationals have seldom been undertaken to secure access to foreign raw materials, and access to cheap foreign labour has generally not been an important consideration, except in the garment industry after the 1960s (Swedenborg, 1979).

Some of the motives underlying FDI in the late 1980s appear to differ from those of earlier periods, however. A new reason to establish foreign affiliates – industry's need to accommodate the increasing likelihood of a single European market that might exclude Sweden – coincided with reductions in Swedish controls on international capital movements, extremely high liquidity in Swedish firms, and a strong krona, to create a boom of outward investment.[1] This boom has had a significant effect on the overall structure of Swedish FDI and may also have changed the character of some home-country effects as we discuss later.

Swedish firms with foreign production facilities are concentrated in manufacturing and include more than 100 corporations. As Table 1 shows, these firms dominate the Swedish manufacturing sector. In 1986 domestic

MNEs accounted for almost half of Sweden's manufacturing employment and 90 percent of its commercial R&D expenditure. There are no data on the domestic MNEs' share of total production, but it may be observed that they have supplied well over half of total Swedish manufacturing exports since 1970. It is also useful to note that the population of Swedish multinationals is dominated by a relatively small number of large and old firms. In 1986 the 20 largest corporations accounted for 90 per cent of the foreign production and the foreign employment of Swedish manufacturing MNEs; the 10 largest corporations by themselves recorded more than 75 per cent of the total (Swedenborg, et al., 1988).

Table 1 also shows that the importance of the domestic Swedish market for the multinationals' operations is diminishing, and that the firms are gradually becoming more international. The Swedish share of the MNEs' total employment and output (including both parents and affiliates) fell from approximately 70 percent in 1970 to 60 percent in 1986. Employment in foreign production affiliates increased from 182,090 to 259,820 during the same period. Since 1986, the absolute and relative importance of foreign operations has increased further as a result of the investment boom of the late 1980s – the flow of outward FDI from 1986 to1990 was almost five times higher than that between 1981 and 1985. Preliminary reports using the latest available data indicate that the total employment of foreign affiliates reached above 450,000 and the Swedish share of the MNEs' production fell to below 40 percent by 1990 (Andersson, 1993).

The sectoral distribution of the foreign production of Swedish firms in 1970 and in 1986 is presented in Table 2.[2] In both years non-electrical and electrical machinery were the most important sectors, in terms of employment as well as assets (although the relative importance of non-electrical machinery is declining) but the shares of paper products and transport equipment

TABLE 1

SWEDISH MNES AND THE SWEDISH ECONOMY: SOME DESCRIPTIVE STATISTICS

	MANUFACTURING EMPLOYMENT (%)		MANUFACTURING OUTPUT (%)		INDUSTRIAL R&D (%)	
	1970	1986	1970	1986	1970	1986
Swedish MNEs' share of Swedish activity	43	48	n.a.	n.a.	70	90
Swedish share of Swedish MNEs' activity	69	59	72	61	83	86

Source: Calculated from Swedenborg (1973) and Swedenborg, et al. (1988).

TABLE 2

SECTORAL DISTRIBUTION OF SWEDISH MANUFACTURING FDI,
PRODUCING AFFILIATES (%)

	EMPLOYMENT		TOTAL ASSETS	
	1970	1986	1970	1986
Food Products	1	1	1	1
Textiles	2	1	1	0
Pulp and Paper	2	3	7	3
Paper Products	2	8	3	11
Chemicals	14	11	8	10
Metals	10	9	13	7
Non-electrical Machinery	43	34	43	36
Electrical Machinery	18	22	16	19
Transport Equipment	2	7	4	9
Other	6	4	6	3

Source: Swedenborg, et al. (1988), *Den svenska industrins utlandsinvesteringar 1960–1986*, Industrial Institute of Economic and Social Research, Stockholm, Table 3.4.

increased significantly during the period. Comparable data on FDI stocks for more recent years are not available, but information on FDI flows from the Swedish Central Bank suggests that the shares of pulp and paper, paper products, machinery, and transport equipment industries have increased since 1986, particularly in the E.C. region (Andersson & Fredriksson, 1993, p. 44).

Table 3 presents some data on the geographical distribution of Swedish FDI in 1970, 1986 and 1990. The E.C. countries and the United States were the main locations for Swedish investment during this period, although the Latin American share was also relatively high. Table 3 shows a reduction in the overall E.C. share of investment between 1970 and 1986, but a large increase thereafter. (The E.C. share of employment in Swedish foreign affiliates increased to 56 percent by 1990.) The employment share of North American affiliates also grew continuously (to 22 percent in 1990), whereas the shares of EFTA, other developed, and developing countries fell.

The continuous growth of the foreign subsidaries of Swedish multinationals raises important questions regarding the effect of outward FDI on Sweden and the Swedish component of the MNEs' operations. One cause for concern is that the competitiveness of Sweden as a nation, on the one hand, and the competitiveness of Swedish multinationals, on the other hand, have developed differently over time. Between the mid-1960s and the mid-1980s, Sweden lost more than 20 percent of its share of world exports of manufactured goods, whereas the export shares of Swedish multinationals (including both parents and affiliates) increased over the same period (Blomström & Lipsey, 1989). The reason is that the exports from foreign affiliates increased

TABLE 3

GEOGRAPHICAL DISTRIBUTION OF SWEDISH MANUFACTURING FDI,
PRODUCING AFFILIATES (%)

| | EMPLOYMENT | | | TOTAL ASSETS | |
	1970	1986	1990	1970	1986
EC6	45	36	-	47	36
EC3	12	11	-	11	10
EC12	60	51	56	-	-
EFTA	10	8	5	10	8
Other W. Europe	1	3	-	1	2
United States	5	19	-	7	30
Canada	2	2	-	5	3
North America	7	21	22	-	-
Other developed	5	4	3	4	3
Latin America	12	12	-	12	8
Africa, Asia	8	5	-	3	1
Developing	18	17	13	-	-

EC6 = Belgium, France, Germany, Italy, Luxembourg, Netherlands
EC3 = Denmark, Great Britain, Ireland
EC12 = EC6 + EC3 + Greece, Portugal, Spain
EFTA = Austria, Finland, Iceland, Norway, Switzerland (+ Portugal for 1970 and 1986)
Other Western Europe = Greece, Malta, Spain, Turkey
Other Developed = Australia, Japan, New Zealand, South Africa
North America = Canada, United States
Developing = Africa, Asia, Latin America

Source: Swedenborg, et al. (1988), *Den svenska industrins utlandsinvesteringar 1960-1986*, Industrial Institute of
Economic and Social Research, Stockholm, Table 3.5, and Andersson and Fredriksson (1993).

faster than the exports from the Swedish parent companies. Does this trend suggest that Swedish exports are being replaced by goods produced abroad by Swedish affiliates, and that foreign jobs substitute for Swedish jobs? These questions are examined in the next section.

EFFECTS ON HOME INVESTMENT, EXPORTS AND EMPLOYMENT

ANALYZING THE INTERACTIONS between domestic and foreign operations, Stevens & Lipsey (1992) consider the topic in the light of two related questions. First, are there financial interactions that come about because investments in different locations compete for scarce funds and, second, are there production interactions because FDI may either substitute for home exports or increase home exports of components and intermediate goods used by the foreign affiliates? It is appropriate to distinguish between these two types of interaction here before proceeding further.

FINANCIAL INTERACTIONS

IN THE DEBATE ON FINANCIAL INTERACTION, it is often argued that domestic and foreign investment may be substitutes when the multinationals' capital costs are not constant. If the cost of borrowed funds increases as the firm becomes more leveraged, then the MNE's alternative projects (foreign and domestic) will compete for access to relatively cheap internally generated funds. The decision to invest scarce resources abroad may thus reduce the likelihood for concurrent investments in the home country, and *vice versa*. However, restrictions on inter-national capital mobility, vertical integration and other complementarities between domestic and foreign production are likely to dilute this effect, so the degree of substitution constitutes an empirical question.

Evidence from the United States, presented by Stevens (1969), Ladenson (1972), Severn (1972), and Stevens & Lipsey (1992), suggest that there is indeed some substitution between domestic and foreign investment by U.S. firms. McClain (1974)[3] argues that the same holds true for multinationals from the United Kingdom, and Belderbos (1992) points to a similar pattern for Dutch MNEs. It is easy to summarize the Swedish evidence regarding this type of financial interaction, since the only study to address the question explicitly is Svensson (1993b), quoted in Andersson & Fredriksson (1993). Comparing the capital stocks of Swedish MNEs in British, French, German, Dutch, and Swedish machinery industries in 1976, 1986, and 1990, Svensson found that increasing relative profitability in any one of the countries was negatively relat-ed to investments by Swedish MNEs in the other countries. He went on to argue that this implies some substitution between foreign and domestic investment because of financial or other resource constraints, but to look at country totals begs the question of what happens at the firm level.

It should be noted here that until 1986, capital market regulations limited the opportunities for Swedish MNEs to finance FDI from Sweden. Consequently, the degree of substitutability between Swedish and foreign investment opportunities was probably low before that time. After 1986, how-ever, the behaviour of Swedish MNEs may have become more like that of multinationals from other countries. In fact, there is an on-going public debate in Sweden about whether the low level of domestic investment in the early 1990s is partly due to the high indebtedness of Swedish multinationals, inherited from the FDI boom of the late 1980s.

PRODUCTION INTERACTIONS

QUESTIONS REGARDING THE EFFECT of FDI by Swedish firms on Swedish exports and employment have occupied much more prominent positions on the Swedish research agenda, and several detailed studies are available. These represent business-oriented analyses as well as econometric studies, which means that there is some variation in methodology and generality of results. Typically, the more business-oriented authors have attempted to examine what happens in specific cases when investment abroad is not possible (available), whereas the econometric studies have tried to detect the overall relationship between FDI and exports in larger samples of firms or industries.

Jordan & Vahlne (1981) is an example of the former approach. The authors compare the domestic employment effects of foreign direct investment with alternative ways to exploit the competitive advantages of a sample of Swedish firms. The options considered are exports from Sweden, licensing, and minority joint ventures. Their analysis attempts to take into account several factors that may influence Swedish exports and employment in the medium term. These factors include estimates of the market shares that can be captured under the optional strategies, differences in the ability to face and solve customer problems in the relevant markets, flows of royalties and license payments (which influence the opportunities to undertake R&D) and differences in related product sales under the optional strategies.

Jordan & Vahlne's overall conclusion is that foreign direct investment (FDI) has positive effects on Swedish exports and employment because the establishment of foreign affiliates typically leads to large increases in the foreign market shares and in exports of intermediate products to affiliates. The driving force is the existence (or fear) of various types of trade barriers that would limit the market shares if export were the only available option. Moreover, foreign direct investment is connected with higher royalty and license payments (from affiliates) and higher exports of related products. Foreign production is judged by Jordan & Vahlne to be particularly beneficial for low-technology products with high transportation costs. However, the results rest on specific assumptions about export survival rates (i.e., the parts of the affiliates' market share that can be served by home exports). In some cases, using standardized products as an example, the assumed survival rates are as low as 2 percent to 8 percent. In a related government research report (SOU 1981:33), Vahlne & Sölvell studied a larger sample of firms and obtained similar results, with the summary conclusion that FDI is a necessary strategy for the survival and international competitiveness of Swedish firms.[4] Foreign direct investment is complementary to Swedish exports and employment because without it the foreign market shares of Swedish firms would have been much lower.

It is obvious that the assumptions about export survival rates are of central importance for the outcome, and it is therefore interesting to compare Jordan & Vahlne's (1981) estimates with data from other sources. To begin with, it can be noted that many other business-oriented case studies have also been based on very low survival rates. For instance, Stobaugh et al. (1972), who studied nine U.S. firms, concluded that their entire foreign markets would have been lost within five years in the absence of FDI. A problem with these studies is that the estimates of survival rates are often based on surveys and interviews with company officials, who naturally are interested in "portraying their foreign activities in as favorable a light as possible *vis-à-vis* their impact on the domestic economy" (Frank and Freeman, 1978, p. 9).[5]

An alternative is provided by Frank & Freeman (1978), who set up a model for the U.S. economy wherein survival rates are explicitly calculated from data based on costs and revenues. The model yields estimates of survival rates ranging between 20 percent and 40 percent, depending on the industry. However, the authors rule out shifts in market size that are "occasioned by the establishment of a foreign subsidiary" (p. 35), which means that their figures are likely to be on the high side: the establishment of an affiliate may lead both to shifts in the demand curve and increases in market shares. They also calculate a short-run 'break-even' survival rate for the U.S. economy in 1970 that would lead to equally large export displacement and export stimulus from FDI. This break-even estimate is 11 percent (p. 62): foreign direct investment will stimulate domestic exports if the surviving market shares are smaller, but FDI will reduce exports if they are larger. Using their own best estimates of survival rates, they concluded that foreign direct investment has substituted for U.S. exports, and that the net employment effect of FDI is an annual loss of between 120,000 and 160,000 jobs (p. 62).[6] It should be noted that the generality of these results is also uncertain, since the period under examination may not be representative (this was the peak of the U.S. firms' internationalization process). Still, a Swedish government research report (SOU 1981:43) looking at an FDI project in West Germany (made by the packaging firm PLM) applies the model using Swedish data. The results suggest a survival rate of between 15 percent and 50 percent, which means that the project is likely to substitute for home exports. This stands in sharp contrast to PLM's management estimates of survival rates of close to nil, which imply that the project would have stimulated Swedish exports.

The problem of assessing survival rates does not usually arise in econometric studies. Instead, these typically employ regression analysis to determine the relationship between exports and various firm, industry, and country characteristics – controlling for as many other determinants as possible, the focus is on the partial effect of FDI (measured, for example, as the stock of foreign assets or the value of foreign production). A negative coefficient for FDI implies that foreign production substitutes for exports, whereas a positive sign suggests that complementarity – the stimulus to home exports of intermediate and other related products – is more important in aggregate. It can be noted that most U.S. studies of this type, including Horst (1974), Bergsten, Horst & Moran (1978), Kravis & Lipsey (1988), and Lipsey & Weiss (1981, 1984) conclude that the complementarities have tended to outweigh the substitution effects. Yet, there are differences between the competitive advantages of Swedish and U.S. multinationals and it may not be possible to generalize results across countries. Moreover, there is good reason to examine the Swedish studies separately, since many of them include interesting methodological innovations and employ more detailed and disaggregated data than are available elsewhere.

The most comprehensive econometric analyses of the Swedish FDI-trade relationship are presented in Swedenborg (1979 and 1982) Blomström, Lipsey & Kulchycky (1988) and Svensson (1993a). The studies are all based on a detailed data set on Swedish multinationals collected by the Industrial Institute for Economic and Social Research (IUI) in Stockholm, but there are significant differences in methodology and results.

The major innovation in both of Swedenborg's studies is that she bases her analysis on 2SLS (two-stage least squares) estimations, in order to avoid the bias that comes about because both foreign production and exports may be affected by the same omitted variables. The first stage estimates the size of foreign production as a function of various firm, industry, and host country characteristics. The second stage estimates exports from the Swedish parent company with the first-stage fitted values of foreign production as one of the independent variables. In Swedenborg (1979) the focus is on a sample of approximately 100 Swedish manufacturing MNEs with more than 300 foreign affiliates in 1974. Her findings suggest that foreign production had no significant overall effect on the exports of Swedish parents that year. However, the aggregate results hide two significant, but opposite, effects. Foreign production appears to substitute for some exports to sales affiliates and non-affiliated customers in the host country, but there is a concurrent (larger) positive effect on the exports of goods to producing affiliates (both intermediates and finished products).[7] Swedenborg (1982) adds observations for three more years (1965, 1970 and 1978) with similar results. The effect on total exports is still not statistically significant, but there is a clear pattern when complementary and substituting exports are examined separately. A one-dollar increase in foreign production is found to result in a 12-cent increase in exports to producing affiliates, but only a 2-cent fall in exports to other customers in the host country – i.e., a net export gain of 10 cents.

Blomström, Lipsey & Kulchycky (1988) argue that Swedenborg's results are uncertain because her first-stage estimates have low explanatory power so that much of the relevant variation in the affiliates' production is neglected in the second stage. They examined Swedish exports and foreign direct investment for 10 aggregate industry groups in 1978, as well as changes between 1970 and 1978, in a conventional OLS (ordinary least squares) framework. By focusing on changes in the variables they hoped to eliminate the impact of the omitted variables that simultaneously affect foreign production and exports but not those that affect changes in production or exports. Moreover, they looked at total Swedish exports in each industry rather than only the parent corporations' exports. This means that they may have captured some instances where the affiliates' activities replaced other firms' exports but also cases where FDI facilitated other Swedish firms' exports to the host market. The latter situation may occur if foreign production familiarizes the host country with Swedish products, or if the affiliates transfer information about the host country's business environment back to Sweden. Nevertheless, the findings in Blomström, Lipsey & Kulchycky (1988) differ little from those presented by Swedenborg (1979 and 1982). There are no signs of substitution between Swedish exports and foreign production for any of the industries included – if anything, the authors find a larger complementary effect – and there is no evidence that large foreign production in a country reduces that country's subsequent imports from Sweden.[8]

A recent study by Svensson (1993a), using unpublished data from the latest survey of Swedish direct investment abroad (for 1990), challenges the results of the earlier research. Svensson argues that it is necessary to account for the foreign affiliates' exports to third countries because they are likely to substitute directly for parent exports. By doing this, he determined that there may well be substitution between Swedish investment abroad and exports from Sweden. However, his results are not comparable to those of the earlier studies. While Swedenborg (1979, 1982) and Blomström, Lipsey & Kulchycky (1988) examined the effect of production by Swedish foreign affiliates on the *absolute* value of exports from Swedish parent companies or the country as a whole, Svensson investigates the effect of FDI on the *ratio* between parent exports and the company's (parent plus foreign affiliates) sales. Since foreign direct investment typically increases the denominator of his dependent variable, there is good reason to expect a negative estimated effect of FDI even if nothing at all happens with parent exports.[9] Thus, what Svensson finds is simply that exports from the home country become relatively less important when the size of foreign operations increases.

We can summarize the debate on production interactions by noting that the earlier studies have found either no effect on home-country exports or a somewhat higher level of home-country exports as a result of Swedish firms' investment abroad. Judging from these results, Swedish FDI does not appear to be detrimental to Swedish exports. However, it must be noted that the examination of financial and production interactions omits some important aspects of the effects of FDI on the home country. For a more complete analysis, therefore, we turn our attention to another set of issues that, until recently, has been neglected in most studies: the structural effects that come about because FDI influences the composition of home-country exports.

EFFECTS ON THE HOME COUNTRY'S INDUSTRY STRUCTURE

TO DATE, THE STRUCTURAL EFFECTS OF FDI on the home country have received relatively little attention in the international debate, and the few studies that are available have focused on a limited set of issues. A number of studies have examined the relationship between FDI and profits (or, in general terms, market power) in the home country, and have concluded that internationalization typically strengthens the domestic market position and the firm characteristics that made it possible to undertake FDI in the first place (Cohen, 1972; Pagoulatos & Sorensen, 1976; Bergsten, Horst & Moran, 1978; Hirshey, 1982; and Benvignati, 1983). The MNEs' profitability is improved through their ability to "achieve greater vertical integration (utilizing cheap labour and/or raw materials), spread joint costs across a larger base, diversify portfolios across different economies and markets and reduce tax liabilities" (UN, 1993, pp. 73-74). Higher profits, in turn, stimulate investments in R&D and marketing, and enhance the oligopolistic nature of the industries where multinational corporations typically operate. Other researchers have discussed the impact of foreign direct investment on the composition of domestic labour demand (Hawkins, 1972; U.S. Tariff Commission, 1973; Frank & Freeman, 1978; and Gunderson & Verma in this volume). The picture emerging from these studies is that there is a shift in the demand for labour favouring white-collar employees at the expense of blue-collar workers, arguably because multinational firms tend to export production activities while concentrating management, marketing, and R&D at home.

Only a few Swedish studies have examined this kind of issue in detail – one exception is a government research report dealing with the effects of investment abroad on the structure of the Swedish labour force (SOU 1983:16) – but the awareness of the importance of structural effects is growing. The consequences of FDI on the composition of export products – shipments of intermediate inputs and other complementary products to affiliates replacing exports of finished products to other customers – may well be more conspicuous than the effects on the total amount of exports. Below, we discuss first the type of operations Swedish MNEs are likely to retain in Sweden; then we try to identify possible effects of this change in production structure.

PRODUCTION LOCATED IN SWEDEN

TRADE THEORISTS CONTEND THAT the international division of labour within multinational corporations (under free trade) should conform to the factor endowments of different production locations (Dunning, 1993). The factor requirements of different stages in the production process vary, and each separate stage should be located where the most intensively used inputs are most abundant.

Traditionally, Swedish comparative advantages have been based on natural resources such as timber, mining, and hydro-electric power, and products developed from these assets continue to be important Swedish exports. According to Blomström, Lipsey & Ohlsson (1990), Sweden's comparative advantages vis-à-vis other OECD countries are still in products with low R&D content, many of which are based on the country's indigenous natural resources. Raw-material-based industries (metals, wood products, and paper products) are particularly prominent in Swedish exports to the E.C., whereas imports from the E.C. are largely made up of engineering products (machinery, electronics, and transport equipment). This pattern persists even though since the mid-1970s the R&D expenditures of Swedish firms (in percent of value added) have been among the highest in the world.

Theory suggests, therefore, that the production undertaken at home by Swedish multinationals should also capitalize on Sweden's comparative advantages and focus on products with relatively low R&D content. The production of Swedish affiliates located in other industrialized countries should have some bias toward high-tech products (although transport costs and various types of market imperfections may muddy the picture somewhat). Unfortunately, this hypothesis cannot be tested directly. There are no comprehensive data available on the factor contents in the MNEs' foreign and domestic production, nor is detailed information available on what specific products parents and affiliates are actually manufacturing.

However, trade data seem to confirm that the division of labour between parents and affiliates is becoming more accentuated, and that the degree of specialization in home production is increasing. The intra-firm trade between parents and affiliates has always made up a large share of the Swedish parents' total exports, but the importance of these flows increased significantly during the late 1980s, particularly for E.C. affiliates. About one-third of the parent exports to the six original E.C. members went to producing affiliates in 1986, but as shown in Table 4, that share increased to nearly one-half by 1990. The rates of increase in intra-firm exports to affiliates located in the other E.C. countries were equally large, although deriving from lower initial levels. At the same time, there were marked changes in the structure of these exports. Whereas intermediates and finished goods accounted for roughly 50 percent each in 1986, the share of intermediates grew to nearly 75 percent by 1990. The affiliates' exports back to Sweden also increased during the period, accounting for almost a fifth of their total sales in 1990 (Andersson, 1993, p. 6).

It appears clear that Swedish parent companies are concentrating their efforts on production of intermediate inputs. What can we say about the characteristics of these products? Because of the lack of data on product categories and factor intensities, some authors have used information on other aspects of MNE operations in their efforts to answer the question. Andersson (1993) notes that the labour productivity of E.C. affiliates increased at an average annual rate of 5.5 percent between 1986 and 1990, while the parents' productivity growth rates were negative. He posits that this was caused mainly by a shift in the location of the Swedish MNEs' various production stages. Earlier, most of the value added was produced by the parent company and many affiliates functioned as relatively simple assembly plants. More recently, he argues, affiliates have taken over some of the more skill-intensive aspects of the production process, and parents are specializing in simpler, raw-material-based operations at lower levels of the value-added chain. Andersson also

TABLE 4

PARENT EXPORTS TO PRODUCING AFFILIATES AS A SHARE OF
PARENT'S TOTAL EXPORTS TO REGION, 1974-1990 (%)

	EC6	EC3	OTHER EC	EFTA	NORTH AMERICA	OTHER OECD
YEAR						
1974	34.8	15.1	28.8	16.9	17.1	46.4
1978	26.5	17.1	12.2	11.3	23.9	17.0
1986	30.5	12.7	19.8	9.2	14.7	30.7
1990	46.0	23.2	27.0	5.1	17.2	31.4

EC6 = Belgium, France, Germany, Italy, Luxembourg, Netherlands
EC3 = Denmark, Great Britain, Ireland
Other EC = Spain, Portugal, Greece
EFTA = Austria, Finland, Iceland, Norway, Switzerland
Other OECD = Japan, Australia, New Zealand

Source: Andersson (1993), Table 3.

examines firm-level data for the years between 1974 and 1978, and between 1986 and 1990, in a regression analysis, and finds a significant negative relation between labour productivity growth in parents and increases in the share of intermediate goods in the parents' total exports to their E.C. affiliates. From this, he concludes that FDI is now causing Swedish production to become more specialized in raw-material-based production with relatively low value added.

Given the lack of direct evidence, this conclusion must be interpreted with caution. Swedish productivity growth may have been low for reasons that have nothing to do with the division of labour between MNE parents and affiliates – for instance, the incentives to work hard have probably been weak in Sweden because of the high income taxes and the compressed wage structure. It can also be argued that imperfections in the Swedish market have motivated MNEs to move operations abroad, so that the causality runs from events in the home country to MNE behavior, rather than the opposite. Nonetheless, it is interesting to note that the only available study of the employment structure in Swedish MNEs outlines a picture that is at least partly consistent with Andersson (1993). Increasing foreign production in Swedish MNEs was apparently already accompanied by lower skill requirements in home-based production in the early 1980s – the largest MNEs employ a lower share of qualified production workers than Swedish industry on average (SOU 1983:16, p. 172). This result partly contradicts Gunderson & Verma's discussion of labour market implications elsewhere in this volume, where the emphasis is on an expected shift towards more qualified jobs in the home country.

In addition to the suspected specialization in intermediates with low value-added and high raw material content, Swedish MNEs have also retained most of their technology production at home. Over four-fifths of the MNEs' R&D expenditures in 1990 were still undertaken in Sweden, although the affiliates' share of R&D has increased slightly since 1986 (Andersson, 1993). The focus on R&D is also apparent in the MNEs employment structure. The largest MNEs employ higher proportions of R&D personnel than do other Swedish firms (SOU 1983:16, p. 172), which is consistent with the predictions for Canada by Gunderson & Verma in this volume.

As a result of this concentration of research efforts, Sweden has one of the world's highest rates of R&D expenditure, along with Japan, Germany, Switzerland and the United States. However, there is a contradiction between the intensive research efforts and the large export shares of products with low R&D content. Why have exports not shifted towards more R&D intensive products during the past decades? One possible answer is that the resources spent on R&D have been wasted, but this is inconsistent with the observation that the competitiveness of Swedish MNEs has increased over the recent past. Another explanation is that Swedish R&D has been directed mainly toward rationalizing techniques for the production of low-tech manufacturing, such as pulp and paper. A third argument is that the MNEs have not found Sweden to be the most suitable location for their high-tech production – the fruits of the MNEs' Swedish research efforts have instead been exported for use by foreign affiliates (Blomström, 1990). This explanation is consistent both with the hypothesis that the operations at the MNEs' home-bases are shifting to intermediates with lower value-added, and some new case study evidence for MacMillan Bloedel, a Canadian-based multinational. The Vertinsky & Raizada study in this volume suggests that MacMillan Bloedel's market-seeking investment abroad has meant that some of its most important innovations are now exploited abroad, although the company's R&D is still largely concentrated in Canada.

Thus, the limited evidence we have about the type of production located in Sweden suggests a somewhat peculiar pattern. On the one hand, there is some concentration on the production of intermediates which, according to some authors, are characterized by relatively low value-added and high raw material content. On the other hand, there is also a focus on technology production, which is where Swedish MNEs have their firm-specific competitive advantages. It is possible that this peculiar pattern appears only in advanced countries with abundant natural resources but not in advanced countries with comparative advantages in human capital and technology, where the advantages of both the country and the MNEs are likely to coincide. Hence, the pattern in Sweden (and perhaps Canada as well) may differ from that of countries that are poor in natural resources, such as Japan, the Netherlands and Switzerland.

Effects of Increasing Specialization

The foregoing discussion implies that Swedish multinationals are concentrating their home production in two areas: R&D and intermediate products. Since the MNEs' location choices are based on profit maximization, it can be assumed that their decisions derive from the fact that private gains are to be made from specialization. It is not equally obvious what the net effects are for Sweden. One reason is related to the characteristics of markets and production processes. Differences in market structure allow some industries to charge higher prices and generate larger profits than others, and differences in technologies mean that some types of production processes are connected with positive external effects and spillovers. The effect of FDI on the home country may be beneficial if production processes with high profits and positive externalities are retained at home, but effects are likely to be less advantageous if these are among the activities that are moved to foreign affiliates. Another reason is that it is impossible to identify any alternative to the continuing internationalization of Swedish multinationals. Would the MNEs be able to retain the present production volumes and market shares if they were not allowed to continue the specialization of their Swedish operations and the expansion of their foreign production, or would they be out-competed by foreign rivals?

Consequently, very few studies have examined the home-country effects of FDI from this perspective, and there is no generally accepted notion of what industries are most beneficial, what kinds of externalities are relevant, how important they are in quantitative terms, and how they compare with the gains from specialization identified in neo-classical trade theory. The sole exception seems to be a consensus that FDI has allowed Swedish MNEs to grow larger and spend more resources on R&D than would otherwise have been possible, and that this has had a positive impact on Sweden's scientific and technological capability (Håkansson, 1980). Our discussion of the possible long-term effects of increasing specialization is therefore rather speculative, and the ensuing paragraphs may perhaps be best seen as an agenda for future research.

The view that the decisions taken by MNEs to concentrate R&D in the parent company are beneficial for Sweden is seldom questioned, as noted above, and there is no need to repeat the arguments as to why R&D may be connected with positive externalities. Instead, it is interesting to note that the recent debate has raised several questions about Sweden's ability to benefit from the potential R&D spillovers in the long run.

First, the debate has revealed deep-seated anxieties that R&D is moving abroad, and the foreign affiliates' share of Swedish MNEs' total R&D expenditure did, indeed, increase slightly between 1986 and 1990. It is not yet clear whether this is a stable trend (with the affiliates' share of R&D remaining more or less stable between 1970 and 1986) but the recent changes do call attention to the question, "What determines the location of R&D?"

Specifically, it is argued that R&D has been cheap in Sweden because the salaries of scientists and engineers have been low compared to those paid in other OECD countries (Blomström, 1990). But low salaries have another effect as well. They reduce the incentives among young people to invest in higher education, and so skilled labour is becoming more scarce. Sweden is therefore losing its position among the countries with the highest levels of education and skill in manufacturing, and it may be difficult for the country to retain its comparative advantage in R&D if the present trends continue.

A second cause for concern is the absence of a shift in total Swedish exports toward more high-tech products over the past decades, despite the very high R&D expenditures (Blomström, Lipsey & Ohlsson, 1990). As discussed earlier, this may indicate that Swedish research results are not exploited at home, but rather are exported to foreign affiliates where production is located. This leads us to the question, which activities yield the most positive externalities: production of high technology (i.e., R&D) or high-technology production? This may be a more general problem than the one raised earlier, but it may also be more relevant for Canada, judging from the study of MacMillan Bloedel by Vertinsky & Raizada in this volume.

Finally, for Sweden to benefit from the potential R&D externalities, it is necessary that there be a population of local firms able to absorb spillovers (Kokko, 1992). However, if MNEs actually do concentrate their Swedish operations on fewer and less advanced intermediates, this may have a profound impact on thousands of their non-multinational suppliers and sub-contractors in Sweden. Overall, there is already a downward trend in the number of sub-contractors, and the share of inputs purchased in Sweden is also falling (Braunerhjelm, 1991). Further increases in Swedish investment abroad and a continuing specialization of Swedish production could increase this trend, since many of the suppliers and sub-contractors may lack the resources to follow the MNEs abroad. This effect of FDI on industry structure therefore raises questions about the possibilities of absorbing the spillovers from the R&D efforts made by MNEs in the future. The emergence of a more concentrated industry structure may have other implications as well – as we discuss below.

The possible consequences of a stronger bias towards production of interme-diate products with low R&D content have been discussed only briefly in the Swedish literature, but most of the comments point in the same direction: there are serious doubts about the advantages of this development. One reason for the apparent skepticism is the worry that the MNEs' decisions concerning production locations may have been motivated partly by various market imperfections that have distorted factor prices. This would also tend to distort the resulting division of labour and motivate policies to remove the imperfections. In fact, current unemployment rates (over 8 percent of the labour force is unemployed and another 5 percent to 6 percent is engaged in various public programs compared with average unemployment rates of between 1 percent and 3 percent over the past decades) testify that problems of this kind are serious since all markets do not clear.

Nonetheless, the possibility that market structure and different types of externalities are important has also figured in the debate. For instance, Andersson (1993) departs from the assumption that increasingly Swedish MNEs are specializing in simple, raw-material-based products. He argues that there are differences between markets for simple intermediates, and markets for more advanced and differentiated finished goods. For the first group of products, there is already fierce price competition, and the entry of new producers from the newly industrialized countries (NICs) and the emerging market economies of Eastern Europe, is likely to add to the pressure. Continued competitiveness in these industries will require cost reductions and perhaps a decline in real wages as well. By contrast, the markets for advanced finished products are more oligopolistic and are generally characterized by higher profits, faster product development, and more room for increases in real wages. This implies that the pattern of specialization will be a determinant of the distribution of income between capital and labour. That outcome, along with a bias towards production of intermediates, may then be contrary to Sweden's national objectives, although it is optimal from the standpoint of Swedish multinationals. The main caveat is that we do not know exactly how production is divided between parents and affiliates: as noted earlier, there are no detailed studies of the characteristics of the products made in the two types of firms. So, even if there is a bias towards raw materials, it is not obvious that these industries have less room to manoeuver than other advanced industries facing competition from American, European and Japanese rivals. This is especially relevant considering that the exports from MNE parents to their affiliates are intra-firm transactions. The prices and competitive conditions in parallel arm's-length markets may not apply, and intra-firm trade may even be an effective way to exploit domestic raw materials.

Nevertheless, it is easy to envisage other effects pulling in the same direction. For instance, it has been shown that the prices of raw material-based intermediate products are often more sensitive to changes in business trends than those of advanced finished products. The case of Finland, whose exports have traditionally been much more biased towards intermediates based on forest products and metals than Sweden's, provides a relevant example (Haavisto & Kokko, 1991). The value of Finnish exports has always dropped rapidly during the troughs of the international business cycle, and the resulting crises in the country's balance of payments have necessitated recurrent devaluations. In fact, the Finnish ten-year devaluation cycle (with major currency devaluations in 1949, 1957, 1967 and 1977-1978) correlates closely with the major depressions in the European economy during the post-War period.[10] Devaluations are seen to be the only possible policy response, simply because the size of the export sector makes it imperative to uphold international competitiveness, often at the expense of other objectives. Income distribution is one of the other goals that is sometimes sacrificed because devaluations typically benefit capital owners at the expense of wage earners. Hence, there may be cause to be wary about increasing dependence on raw materials to the extent that recurrent changes in exchange rates (or volatile exchange rates) are contrary to other political or economic objectives: again, the caveat is that increasing specialization on intermediates must not mean more dependence on raw materials.

Finally, there is reason once again to consider the effects of specialization on the sub-contractors and suppliers of MNEs. When the parent company specializes in the production of some of the intermediate inputs used in its final products, fewer components are made in Sweden, and the motivation to engage Swedish suppliers is reduced. The number of suppliers employed by Swedish MNEs has also declined rapidly in recent years, as noted earlier. Moreover, few domestic (non-multinational) suppliers and sub-contractors have the capability to follow the MNEs abroad, as shown by Braunerhjelm (1991). Examining a sample of 140 Swedish sub-contractors, he notes that only 4 percent of their output is shipped to Swedish MNE affiliates abroad, while Swedish MNEs at home account for 43 percent of their sales. This means that a continued division of labour along the lines discussed above – even one that is successful enough to increase total employment in Swedish industry – may have a profound impact on the structure of Swedish industry. It is conceivable that the present population of manufacturing firms (which is now made up of few large MNEs and thousands of smaller sub-contractors and suppliers) may be replaced by a structure with the same number of MNEs (that may perhaps be even larger than they are today) but with a significantly lower number of smaller firms.

We have already noted that this kind of development might reduce the opportunities to benefit from R&D-spillovers but there may also be additional effects on growth rates, for example. It is generally believed that small- and medium-size firms were instrumental in generating economic growth in the United States and the United Kingdom during the 1980s, and that they have played major roles in the development of new high-tech industries all over the industrialized world. Recent empirical studies have also demonstrated that the growth of the firm tends to decrease with firm size and firm age (Evans, 1987; Hall, 1987; Dunne, Roberts & Samuelson, 1989). The link between firm size and growth in Sweden may be different from that outlined by these studies, but any significant correlation provides a good enough reason to think twice about the possible effects of FDI on the home country's economic structure.

CONCLUSIONS

THIS STUDY SET OUT TO SUMMARIZE THE RESEARCH on the effect of Swedish investment abroad on Swedish investment (generally), exports, and employment, and to discuss some of the effects of the division of labour between MNE parents and their foreign affiliates. The only available study on the relation between investment abroad and investment at home suggests some weak substitution, because of constraints on the firms' financial assets or other resources. In reviewing the literature on the relation between foreign investment and home-country exports (and employment) we found that the net effect seems to be one of complementarity. Foreign production substitutes for some home exports of finished goods, but the advantages of market proximity allow foreign affiliates to capture a larger market share than the parent can achieve, exporting from Sweden. The resulting increases in the parent's exports of intermediate and related products are large enough to make up for the lost exports of finished goods.

We also noted that the effect of FDI on the structure, rather than on the volume, of Swedish exports may be important. Instead of shipping finished products to foreign consumers, increasingly, parents are shipping intermediate products to their foreign affiliates. There are no data on product categories or the factor content of the parents' and affiliates' production, and so it is not possible to draw any definite conclusions regarding the characteristics of these intermediates. Nonetheless, some authors argue that the division of labour may entail increasing specialization of Swedish manufacturing on products with relatively low value-added and low R&D content. There is, in addition, a concentration of R&D activities in the home country of the multinational corporation.

Few studies have hitherto examined the effects of FDI in terms of its impact on the structure of exports, and so there is a paucity of relevant information on the topic. Our discussion of the possible long-term effects of increasing specialization has therefore been rather speculative and has focused on some topics for future research. The questions raised concern the possibilities to benefit from potential R&D externalities, the impact of an increased raw material bias on income distribution and exchange rate volatility, and the consequences for industry structure and growth rates. Some of these effects are potentially important, not only for Sweden but perhaps for Canada as well.

ENDNOTES

1 It is useful to note the difference between the Swedish response to European integration and some North American reactions to the NAFTA. The fear that Sweden would perhaps *not* join the European Community contributed to the surge of Swedish investment in E.C. countries during the late 1980s, whereas the North American debate in 1993 revealed concerns about the opposite reaction, i.e., massive outflows of investment ("the great sucking sound") as Canada and the United States join the NAFTA. This illustrates a fundamental difference between the motives for FDI in the two regions: Swedish MNEs are still concerned mainly about market access abroad, whereas North American MNEs already have access to their most important markets (i.e., their home markets), and they worry more about production costs.

2 Most of the data on Swedish MNEs are obtained from comprehensive surveys conducted by the Industrial Institute of Economic and Social Research (IUI) in Stockholm. These surveys were conducted every fourth year between 1970 and 1990 (except for 1982), but detailed information on the results of the 1990 survey are not yet available.

3 As quoted by Caves (1982, p. 166).

4 The SOU publications are government committee reports on various topics: the ones referred to in this paper are all based on investigations by the Direct Investment Committee 1977-1983.

5 Interestingly enough, the prevailing view of the Swedish labour movement is also that FDI is "necessary and positive for the overall competitiveness of the firms, and generates spillover gains to the domestic branches of the corporations" (Hjalmarsson, 1991, p. 256).

6 Another illustration of how results depend on assumptions about export survival rates is provided by the U.S. Tariff Commission (1973) where the employment effects of FDI are analyzed. Assuming 100 per cent survival rates, the Commission estimates that the total impact of U.S. Foreign direct investment in 1970 was a loss of 1.1 million jobs. Assuming a 50 per cent survival rate reduces the estimated loss to 400,000 jobs. Finally, the effects are recalculated on the assumption that U.S. exporters would maintain the shares of world trade they held in 1960-1961 (i.e., before the rapid expansion of American investment abroad that took place during the 1960s). The result is a net job gain of 500,000 U.S. jobs (Frank & Freeman, 1978, Chapter 11).

7 Swedenborg claims that a one-dollar increase in foreign production stimulates 15 cents' worth of exports to the producing affiliate, but substitutes for 9 cents' worth of exports to other firms in the host country (Swedenborg, 1979, pp. 215-217).

8 Blomström, Lipsey, and Kulchycky (1988) also include some 2SLS estimates similar to those of Swedenborg (1979 and 1982). Their 2SLS

regression yield somewhat larger positive coefficients for the effect of foreign production on Swedish exports than what their OLS regressions do. This is contrary to Swedenborg's findings (although she only looked at the parents' exports from Sweden) and possibly an indication that foreign production may have some positive external effects on other Swedish exporters.

9 Apparently, Svensson (1993) divided his original dependent variable (parent exports) by the size of the MNE in order to avoid heteroscedasticity.

10 Trade with the Soviet Union exerted a countercyclical effect on Finnish exports after the mid-1970s, which led to a change in the export structure and reduced volatility during the 1980s, until the collapse of the Soviet Union in 1991 (Haavisto & Kokko, 1991). The picture has now reverted to that before 1980: consequently, the most recent European depression has forced a large devaluation.

ACKNOWLEDGEMENTS

WE ARE GRATEFUL TO Steven Globerman, Keith Head, John Knubley and Robert Lipsey for their valuable comments on an earlier draft of this study.

BIBLIOGRAPHY

Andersson, T. "Utlandsinvesteringar och policy-implikationer." Supplement 3 to SOU 1993:16, Nya villkor för ekonomi och politik. Stockholm: Allmänna Förlaget, 1993.

Andersson, T. and T. Fredriksson. Sveriges val, EG och direktinvesteringar. Supplement 7, EG-konsekvensutredningen, Samhällsekonomi (Fi 1993:06), Stockholm: Allmänna Förlaget, 1993.

Belderbos, R.A. "Large Multinational Enterprises Based in a Small Economy: Effects on Domestic Investment." Weltwirtschaftliches Archiv, Band 128, 1992, pp. 543-57.

Benvignati, A. Domestic Profit Advantages of Multinationals. Washington, D.C.: U.S. Federal Trade Commission, 1983.

Bergsten, C.F., T. Horst, and T.H. Moran. American Multinationals and American Interests. Washington, D.C.: The Brookings Institution, 1978.

Blomström, M. "Competitiveness of Firms and Countries." in Globalization of Firms and the Competitiveness of Nations. Edited by J. Dunning, B. Kogut and M. Blomström. Crafoord Lectures 1989, Lund: Lund University Press, 1990.

Blomström, M. and R.E. Lipsey. "The Export Performance of U.S. and Swedish Multinationals." Review of Income and Wealth, Series 35, (1989): 245-64.

Blomström, M., R.E. Lipsey, and K. Kulchycky. "U.S. and Swedish Direct Investment and Exports." In Trade Policy Issues and Empirical Analysis. Edited by R. Baldwin. Chicago: University of Chicago Press, 1988.

Blomström, M., R.E. Lipsey, and L. Ohlsson. "What Do Rich Countries Trade with Each Other? R&D and Composition of U.S. and Swedish Trade." Banca Nazionale del Lavoro Quarterly Review, 173, (June 1990): 215-35.

Braunerhjelm, P. Svenska underleveratörer och småföretag i det nya Europa: Struktur, kompetens och internationalisering. Research Report No. 38, Stockholm: Industrial Institute for Economic and Social Research, 1991.

Caves, R.E. Multinational Enterprise and Economic Analysis. Cambridge: Cambridge University Press, 1982.

Cohen, B.I. "Foreign Investment by United States Corporations as a Way of Reducing Risk." Discussion Paper No. 151, Economic Growth Center, Yale University, 1972.

Dunne, T., M. Roberts, and L. Samuelson. "The Growth and Failure of U.S. Manufacturing Plants." Quarterly Journal of Economics, Vol. 104.

Dunning, J.H. Multinational Enterprises and the Global Economy. Wokingham: Addison-Wesley, 1992.

Evans, D.S. "Tests of Alternative Theories of Firm Growth." Journal of Political Economy, 95, (1987): 657-74.

Frank, R.H. and R.T. Freeman. Distributional Consequences of Direct Foreign Investment. New York: Academic Press, 1978.

Haavisto, T. and A. Kokko. "Politics as a Determinant of Economic Performance: The Case of Finland." In Diverging Paths: Comparing a Century of Scandinavian and Latin American Economic Development. Edited by M. Blomström & P. Meller. Baltimore: Johns Hopkins University Press, 1991.

Håkansson, L. "Multinationella företag: FoU-verksamhet, tekniköverföring och företagstillväxt." SIND 1980:4, Stockholm: National Industrial Board, 1980.

Hall, B.H. "The Relationship Between Firm Size and Firm Growth in the U.S. Manufacturing Sector." Journal of Industrial Economics, 35, (1987): 583-606.

Hawkins, R.G. Job Displacement and the Multinational Firm: A Methodological Review.

Occasional Paper, No. 3, Washington, D.C.: Center for Multinational Studies, 1972.

Hirschey, M. "Market Power and Foreign Involvement by U.S. Multinationals." *Review of Economics and Statistics*, 64, (1982): 343-46.

Hjalmarsson, L. "The Scandinavian Model of Industry Policy." In *Diverging Paths: Comparing a Century of Scandinavian and Latin American Economic Development*. Edited by M. Blomström and P. Meller. Baltimore: Johns Hopkins University Press, 1991.

Horst, T. "American Exports and Foreign Direct Investments." Discussion Paper No. 362, Harvard Institute of Economic Research, 1974.

Jordan, J.L and J.E. Vahlne. "Domestic Employment Effects of Direct Investment Abroad by Two Swedish Multinationals." Working Paper No, 13, Multinational Enterprises Programme, Geneva: International Labour Office, 1981.

Kokko, A. *Foreign Direct Investment, Host Country Characteristics, and Spillovers*. Stockholm: Economic Research Institute, 1992.

Kravis, I. and R.E. Lipsey. "The Effect of Multinational Firms' Foreign Operations on Their Domestic Employment." NBER Working Paper No. 2760, 1988.

Ladenson, M.L. "A Dynamic Balance Sheet Approach to American Direct Foreign Investment." *International Economic Review*, 13, (1972): 531-43.

Lipsey, R.E. and M.Y. Weiss. "Foreign Production and Exports in Manufacturing Industries." *Review of Economics and Statistics*, 63, (1981): 488-94.

Lipsey, R.E. and M.Y. Weiss. "Foreign Production and Exports of Individual Firms." *Review of Economics and Statistics*, 66, (1984): 304-08.

McClain, D.S. "Foreign Investment in United States Manufacturing and the Theory of Direct Investment." Ph.D. Dissertation, Massachusetts Institute of Technology, 1974.

OECD. *OECD Reviews on Foreign Direct Investment: Sweden*. Paris: OECD, 1993.

Olsson, U. "Securing the Markets. Swedish Multinationals in a Historical Perspective." In *The Rise of Multinationals in Continental Europe*. Edited by G. Jones and H. G. Schröder. London: Edward Elgar, 1993.

Pagoulatos, E. and R. Sorensen. "International Trade, International Investment and Industrial Profitability in U.S. Manufacturing." *Southern Economic Journal*, 42, (1976): 425-34.

Severn A. "Investment and Financial Behavior of American Direct Investors in Manufacturing." In *The International Mobility and Movement of Capital*. Edited by F. Machlup, W. Salant and L. Tarshis. New York: NBER, 1972.

SOU 1981:33. *Effekter av investeringar utomlands*. Stockholm: Liber Förlag, 1981.

SOU 1981:43. *De internationella investeringarnas effekter*. Stockholm: Liber Förlag, 1981.

SOU 1983:16. *Sysselsättningsstrukturen i industriella företag*. Stockholm: Liber Förlag, 1983.

Stevens, G. "Fixed Investment Expenditures of Foreign Manufacturing Affiliates of U.S. Firms: Theoretical Models and Empirical Evidence." *Yale Economic Essays*, 8, (Spring 1969): 137-200.

Stevens, G.V.G. and R.E. Lipsey. "Interactions between Domestic and Foreign Investment." *Journal of International Money and Finance*, 11, (1992): 40-62.

Stobaugh, R.B. and Associates. U.S. Multinational Enterprises and the U.S. Economy. Boston: Harvard Graduate School of Business Administration, 1972.

Svensson, R. *Production in Foreign Affiliates-Effects on Home Country Exports and Modes of Entry*. Licentiate Thesis, Gothenburg: Gothenburg University, 1993a.

Svensson, R. "Domestic and Foreign Investment by Swedish Multinationals." Working Paper No. 391, Stockholm: Industrial Institute of Economic and Social Research, 1993b.

Swedenborg, B. *Den svenska industrins investeringar i utlandet*. Stockholm: Industrial Institute of Economic and Social Research, 1973.

Swedenborg, B. *The Multinational Operations of Swedish Firms*. Stockholm: Almqvist & Wicksell International, 1979.

Swedenborg, B. *Svensk industri i utlandet. En analys av drivkrafter och effekter*. Stockholm: Industrial Institute for Economic and Social Research, 1982.

Swedenborg, B., G. Johansson-Grahn, and M. Kinnwall. *Den svenska industrins utlandsinvesteringar 1960-1986*. Stockholm: Industrial Institute of Economic and Social Research, 1988.

UN. *Transnational Corporations from Developing Countries*. Transnational Corporations and Management Division, New York: United Nations, 1993.

US Tariff Commission. *Implications of Multinational Firms for World Trade and Investment and for U.S. Trade and Labor*. Report to the U.S. Senate Committee on Finance, February 1973.

Part V Firm Studies

Ilan Vertinsky & Rachana Raizada
Forest Economics and Policy Analysis Research Unit
The University of British Columbia

12

MacMillan Bloedel: Foreign Investment Decisions and their Welfare Consequences

INTRODUCTION

THE FOCUS OF THIS CASE STUDY is the foreign direct investments (FDI) of MacMillan Bloedel (MB), a Canadian forest products multinational. The methodology of a case study allows us to identify the function of "specific context" in shaping FDI decisions and their consequences. We begin with an historical overview of MB's FDI, identifying the changes in the company's internal and external environments that have led to shifts in its FDI strategies.[1] In the next section we use econometric methods to test hypotheses that emerge from the historical review about the determinants in MB of motives to invest (specifically in the United States) and the consequences of the investment. Data limitations and the idiosyncratic nature of many FDI decisions, however, leave much unexplained. We then look at a number of detailed examples of foreign investment within four classes of dominant motives: a) efficiency seeking, b) resource seeking, c) market seeking and, d) risk reduction. The theoretical and normative implications of each experience is then analyzed and measured against concepts drawn from Dunning's Eclectic Theory (Dunning, 1981 and 1988). Next we summarize the welfare implications for Canada of MB's FDI. We conclude with some general observations and suggest some lessons that can be learned by other resource companies from the MacMillan Bloedel experience.

A BRIEF HISTORY OF A CANADIAN MULTINATIONAL'S ADVENTURES IN FDI

MACMILLAN BLOEDEL IS AN INTEGRATED forest products company[2] based in the province of British Columbia (B.C.), Canada, where its head office and approximately two-thirds of its productive assets are located. It also has integrated forest product operations in the United States. In 1991, MB was the thirteenth largest forest products company in North America and the twenty-ninth largest in the world (based on 1990 revenue). MB's corporate specific assets are largely sector-specific. It is therefore necessary to understand the nature of the sector in order to understand MB's strategic decisions over the years.

In the mid-1960s, after several decades of predictable business cycles, the forest industry in North America entered a period of high and irregular fluctuations in the demand and prices of some of its major products. During "down" periods in the forest product business, cost competitiveness is a key to firm survival; in boom years concerns over fibre supply dominate.

> Perhaps more than in most other industries, the location of production plays a key role in determining the ability of a forest products firm to compete in particular markets. Access to basic raw material (wood fibre) is a function of both the physical environment and the regional and national regulatory regimes which govern harvesting and determine the cost of fibre and the security of access to it. (Booth & Vertinsky 1991:906)

Regulations determine the costs of other major production factors. The international scope of the market means that monetary policies affect exchange rates, and trade policies affect both cost structures and market access of producers, depending on the location of production. In a study of strategies and performance of North American forest companies, Booth & Vertinsky (1991) concluded that geographical diversification is associated with lower fluctuations in rates of return but at a cost of lower rates of return. Geographical diversification is a significant determinant of growth of sales, serving as a means of alleviating fibre constraints and ensuring market access. Since economies of scale are important in most of the industry's market segments, growth is often vital in preserving cost competitiveness – by magnifying resource-seeking investments.

Preoccupation with securing access to raw material and intermediate goods motivates backward vertical integration. Forward vertical integration in the industry often yields scale economies, cost savings and market security (Globerman & Schwindt, 1986). Thus, an examination of MB's FDI reveals recurring strategic themes: securing resources through backward integration and forward integration to secure markets and gain the benefits of economies of scale. While these strategies appear to be vital to maintain the firm's competitiveness, they also imply a tendency to seek FDI opportunities, especially when local fibre supplies are insecure or constrained, or protective trade policies threaten exports to large markets.

The following sections provide an overview of the evolving pattern of MacMillan Bloedel's FDI over the 30-year period from 1963 to 1992. (The investments referred to here are summarized in the Appendix.) The starting point is 1963, since that is the year in which MB made its first foreign direct investment, having settled down after a merger[3] For the purposes of this analysis, the following 30 years have been broken into five periods of six years each. There are certain defining characteristics for each of these periods, either in terms of the development in the external market in which the firm operates, or in the internal environment that affects decision making.

Period 1: 1963-1968

Having grown to its limits on the coast of British Columbia, MB took its first successful step into FDI in 1963, with the acquisition of two corrugated container producers in the United Kingdom. By 1964, MB was Canada's largest integrated exporter of forest products, and 75 percent of its total sales were to foreign countries.[4] In 1965, due to the unfavourable expansion climate in B.C., MB turned its investment attention to the U.S. South, which had become competitive in the production of low-cost pulpwood. In 1966, after re-examining the value of captive markets, MB concluded that in the long run, a captive market strategy offered the best security.[5] Accordingly, the company entered the U.S. packaging business by acquiring corrugated container plants which would provide it with a captive market for linerboard from its planned forest products complex at Pine Hill, Alabama. The company's move to the United States was the first of its kind by a B.C. wood products company.[6]

Also in 1966, MacMillan Bloedel finalized an agreement with one of Britain's largest softwood importing firms (Montague L. Meyer Ltd.)[7] to enter into a distribution venture that would "jerk the U.K. softwood trade into the seventies."[8] This venture involved the construction of central distribution terminals at the ports of Newport and Tilbury in the United Kingdom for the reception, storage and distribution of MB's shipments from B.C., providing customers with better service and decreasing importing costs. Later in 1966, MB withdrew from membership in a newsprint marketing consortium and established its own distribution subsidiary in Australia (MB Pty. Ltd.) in order to develop a strong MB identity and keep tighter control over its marketing arrangements. In 1967, through MB Pty. Ltd., MB took its first step in producing wood products in Southeast Asia by investing in a logging venture on Bougainville Island. In its annual report for 1967 MB announced that in light of its expansions in B.C. and Alabama, its forest resources were sufficient to meet its foreseeable needs.

Between 1963 and 1968, the composition of MB's markets changed: sales of lumber and plywood to the United States had increased from 29 percent in 1964 to 41 percent; and to Japan from 8 percent to 14 percent. Sales to the United Kingdom fell from 22 percent to 9 percent and in Canada from 22 percent to 15 percent. Pulp and paper sales fell to 8 percent in the United Kingdom from 11 percent, but grew from 7 percent to 11 percent in Japan. Many of MB's major foreign investments during this period constituted forward vertical integration and so were motivated by the possibility of acquiring captive markets (e.g. the corrugated container firms in the United Kingdom and the United States). The distribution partnership in the United Kingdom was expected to reduce transportation costs and increase sales and profits as MB penetrated further into established U.K. trade channels. Investments such as MB Pty. Ltd. were undertaken for the explicit purpose of expanding sales to growing markets. Whether for the purpose of acquiring captive markets, or simply expanding sales, all of these investments can be characterized as market seeking. In effect, the company was expanding through a strategy of forward integration by acquiring partial or full control over the markets for its products. The Pine Hill investment and the logging project on Bougainville Island were undertaken mainly to expand MB's raw material base. Although these investments simultaneously provided MB with new markets and the risk reduction benefits associated with geographical diversification, their primary contribution lay in access to additional forest resources.

Period 2: 1969-1974

The passing of the owner-manager era was formalized in 1970 when H. MacMillan and W. VanDusen resigned from MB's board,[9] – a change that was influential in allowing the company to diversify. In 1969, when Ian Brand was appointed Director of Far East Development, MB's Chairman commented:

> Creation of this new position is an indication of the growing importance the company attaches to the Far East as a market for its products, and as a region for future expansion."[10]

During 1973, the Canadian Transport Co., an MB subsidiary, transformed itself from a carrier of MB's forest products into a general shipping line and one of the largest dry-cargo ship operators in the world. MB's most radical move in this period was the organization of the Ventures Group, in 1974, to represent its investment interest in companies unrelated to its core business, many of which were high-risk businesses unlikely to turn an early profit. Ownership varied from majority to minority positions, although even in the latter case the interest was usually of sufficient size to provide a major voice in the operation and activities of the companies.[11] Although operated separately, these ventures were so diverse that they consumed a disproportionate part of management time.[12]

In 1971, *The Financial Post* applauded MB's geographical diversification suggesting that it had "shrewdly been buying into a number of foreign markets and lessening its dependence on the volatile B.C. economy".[13] By 1974, MB defined itself as an multinational company with majority interests in manufacturing operations in Europe, Southeast Asia, the United States and Brazil. The company's investments at this time were focused on the geographical diversification of its raw material base through access to tropical hardwood forests in Brazil, Malaysia, Indonesia and the Philippines. Interestingly, MB went ahead with these investments, even though by then its Bougainville venture had ended disastrously, having been MB's first attempt at operating in these unfamiliar regions. These investments can be characterized as resource seeking. Meanwhile, in the United States, MB's investment strategy was largely centred on the synergies to be gained from integrated operations. The acquisition of additional corrugated container plants (the Hankins Container Division of the Flintkote Company) whose strategic benefits were derived from integration with operations at Pine Hill can be described as an efficiency-seeking investment.

Period 3: 1975-1980

MacMillan Bloedel faced its first-ever loss ($85 million) in 1975, when a global recession began and demand for its products fell in all markets.[14] The timing of MB's entrance into the global shipping business was unfortunate, and the transportation division contributed $46 million to the loss. Domestically, the company was faced with one of the costliest strikes in its history.[15]

As a result of the shipping debacle, MB's top executives, the Chairman, and President, were fired. After joining the company in September 1976, MB's new CEO defined the company's goals as focusing capital spending on modernization to bring increased productivity and profits; improving the debt-to-total-capital ratio, and concentrating on the company's traditional business areas. Between 1972 and 1975, the company had averaged only $50 million a year on capital spending in B.C.[16] and its competitive advantage had been adversely affected.

In 1976, MB was thoroughly studied by the federal Royal Commission on Corporate Concentration. In it's submission to the Commission, MB argued that the forest products industry was competitive on an international basis, and large size was essential to compete internationally.[17]

When a new five-year capital expenditure program was drafted in 1977, only 25 percent was allocated to operations outside British Columbia. The program would permit MB to harvest and convert its full annual allowable cut from its existing timber base in the province.[18] In 1979, after experiencing its best year ever, MB increased this program by 50 percent to $1.5 billion, and in 1980, despite the lumber market recession, the company announced a new five-year capital expenditure program totalling $2 billion.[19]

Throughout most of the 1970s, MacMillan Bloedel continued to be one of the least profitable of the integrated forest companies in British Columbia.[20] By 1980, MB had recovered from its disastrous début in the shipping business and had decided to rebuild its competitive strengths in its B.C. forest operations. Investment expenditure, after 1975, marked a shift from the *direct growth* strategies of the past to *indirect growth* strategies aimed at increasing profits and sales through productivity improvements and reduced costs. Most of the company's foreign investments were not performing well, and businesses in the Ventures Group were incurring losses. MB spent much of this period divesting itself of these businesses while keeping corporate management busy with domestic affairs such as the leadership changes and an attempted takeover.

Period 4: 1981-1986

Early in 1981, prospects of forest product companies for the rest of the decade were generally regarded as favourable by forest industry analysts and investors due to previously announced modernization programmes.[21] As a result, MB again became the focus of a takeover.[22] British Columbia Resources Investment Corporation (BCRIC), which held 20 percent of MB, fought for control before losing to Noranda Mines, which bought 49 percent of the company for an estimated $626 million.[23] Soon afterward, the worldwide recession of the early 1980s led to a collapse in market pulp pricing, echoing the chaos of the mid-1970s.[24]

In 1982, MB's return on invested capital was -2.6 percent[25] The company responded by moving out of low- or no-profit dimensional lumber into high mark-up products such as specialty lumber cuts for the Japanese market[26] with the result that many money-losing operations were closed and unprofitable foreign investments sold. In 1982, MB thus moved to a "radically decentralized management structure aimed at ridding the company of its top heavy bureaucracy".[27] These changes were widely attributed to Noranda's control.

Effective July 1, 1983, MB transferred its Canadian packaging plants to MacMillan Bathurst Inc., a newly formed, 50 percent-owned, joint venture with Consolidated Bathurst Inc. This pooling was intended to rival Domtar, Canada's largest manufacturer of corrugated containers.[28] On October 1, 1983 it transferred its U.K. packaging plants to MacMillan Smurfit SCA Ltd., a newly formed 50 percent-owned joint venture with the Jefferson Smurfit Group Ltd. and Svenska Cellulosa Aktiebolaget (SCA) of Sweden. The divestment of the packaging activities to alliances with competitors took place in response to highly competitive market conditions in the packaging business; MB did not have the resources to compete alone and needed these partnerships to retain its declining market share.

MB's rigorous cost-cutting and debt-reduction efforts paid off in 1986 when it ranked first in the world among forest product companies on the basis of earnings.[29] Since 1980, it had reduced its work force by 40 percent, the largest drop of any forest producer in North America. MB's performance was deemed "spectacular", especially since other forest product companies were still struggling to show increases.[30]

Period 5: 1987-1992

In 1988, MB's profits reached a high of $329.8 million and, at 19 percent of 1988 equity, the company's debt ratio was the lowest in a decade. As soon as MB announced it was "completely recovered and poised for growth",[31] there was another recession, and in 1991 the company was faced with its worst-ever financial result. By now, MB was confronted with new competitive challenges. In 1980, only 22 percent of its operating assets were located in the United States, as compared to 30 percent by 1991. Exchange rates therefore became an increasingly important determinant of MB's performance and investment decision making in this period.[32] The strength of the Canadian dollar during the recession period aggravated the impact of exchange rates.[33]

Environmental imperatives in various forms constituted the other major competitive challenges of this period. In MB's major newsprint market, the U.S. west, environmental dictates came in the form of increased demand for recycled newsprint. Compared to the U.S. companies, which had easy access to 'urban forests' of waste newspaper, MB was at a disadvantage. Although MB tried to face this challenge by locating near the urban forest (through a proposed recycled newsprint venture with a German company), a combination of poor markets and other environmental challenges left it with insufficient capital to finance this expansion. In July 1992, the government raised environmental standards for MB's aging pulp mill at Port Alberni, requiring MB to provide secondary treatment for all the mill's effluent.[34] Table 1 shows MB's capital expenditure by function over this period. Drastic increases in environmental expenditures came at the expense of business maintenance and expansion, and modernization. Finally, the security of MB's forest resources, a key factor determining its international competitiveness, was threatened by environmental pressure groups. In 1988, environmental groups in B.C. targeted approximately one-third of the remaining old growth in MB's Alberni Region Tree Farm License 44 alone, which implied a decrease in the annual harvest from this region of almost 25 percent.[35] MB had already lost between 3 percent and 5 percent of its annual allowable cut, and another 15 percent was in dispute.[36]

TABLE 1

MacMILLAN BLOEDEL'S CAPITAL EXPENDITURE BY FUNCTION, 1987-1992

YEAR	MAINTENANCE OF BUSINESS		EXPANSION AND MODERNIZATION		ENVIRONMENT		TOTAL
	C$ (M)	%	C$ (M)	%	C$ (M)	%	C$ MILLION
1992	68	28.7	23	9.7	146	61.6	237
1987	153	59.7	74	28.3	29	11.5	257

Overview

During the first two periods, that is, from 1963 to 1974, MB evolved from a national B.C.-based company dependent on its large export markets, to a multinational firm with manufacturing operations all over the world. MB concentrated its investment efforts on *direct growth* strategies: vertical integration (backward and forward), horizontal expansion and geographical diversification, and risk reduction (unrelated diversification). The period between 1963 and 1968 was for the most part one of market seeking investment. MB's investments between 1969 and 1974 can be classified as resource seeking, efficiency seeking, and motivated by risk reduction (unrelated diversification). However, not all the investments made in these periods were successful, from either a strategic or a financial viewpoint. By diverting capital from its competitive strengths in forest resources to unrelated business segments and to distant geographic regions where it had little management expertise, MB diluted its overall competitive position. Changes in world markets, in home-country environmental factors, and in the economic circumstances of host countries were instrumental in influencing the progress of various investments. The investments themselves had an effect on the company's internal resource position through their subsequent financial performance and their interdependency. Although most of MB's investments looked advantageous from a perspective of prior information supporting impressive estimates of returns, in many cases their unsuccessful implementation or an incorrect estimate of the risk involved led to their failure. External environmental conditions (such as the recession in 1975 following MB's heavy investment in the shipping business) exacerbated the effect of these investments on MB's financial position. MB reacted by refocusing its investment attention in the latter three periods on *indirect growth* strategies[37] aimed at strengthening its existing competitive advantage through the improvement of its existing resource base.

The next three periods clearly demonstrate the impact of business cycles on investment. Even though MB entered each period in a strong position, a combination of adverse economic conditions and changes in its internal resource position negatively affected the company's financial and operating performance. Over the years from 1975 to 1992, MB divested itself of virtually all of its foreign manufacturing investments, except those in the United States and its equity stake in Koninklijke Nederlandsche Papierfabrieken N.V. (KNP) in Holland. By the end of each of these periods, MB had recovered financially from adverse market conditions, and by the end of the fourth period in particular, MB was in an exceptionally strong financial position, having achieved its targeted debt/equity ratios (25 percent at the top of a business cycle and 35 percent at the bottom). The final period brought new competitive challenges in the form of various environmental imperatives and the increased effect of fluctuations in exchange rates.

Basic Patterns of MB's FDI and its Effect on Corporate Performance: Preliminary Models

WHILE THE PRECEDING HISTORICAL REVIEW suggests that the pattern of FDI followed by MacMillan Bloedel was determined by a variety of objectives reflecting different strategic contingencies, a systematic pattern of investment in market development and resource seeking is evident. Now, by focusing on the relation between MB's investments in the United States and those in Canada, we attempt to test empirically the extent to which these and other motives may explain the geographical pattern of investment. The difficulty of using econometric techniques in the context of a single-firm case study lies in the serious limitations of the data base. Only simple models can be estimated, and these are therefore vulnerable to specification biases. Although the models we estimate in this study are under-specified in most cases, we do not expect significant correlation between the error term and the dependent variables used. The analysis thus provided is exploratory and the conclusion should therefore be viewed as tentative.

The first hypothesis we test is that the relative division of assets between Canada and the United States depends on the relative competitiveness of each region, i.e., the relationship between average regional costs of production determined by local fibre, energy and labour costs, and cost of transportation to the market. For each region we compute competitiveness indexes for producing bleached softwood kraft pulp and softwood lumber. Each index relates production costs in the U.S. south to the production costs on the B.C. coast. All costs have been converted to U.S. dollars. Data were available for the period from 1973 to 1991.

The model specified is

$$USCAN_t = b + a_1 \, CINDEXL_t + a_2 \, CINDEXP_t + \varepsilon_t$$

where

$USCAN_t$ is the ratio of U.S. to Canadian assets at time t;

$CINDEXL_t$ is the relative competitiveness index of B.C. coastal lumber producers relative to U.S. south producers at time t;

$CINDEXP_t$ is the relative competitiveness index of B.C. coastal bleached softwood kraft pulp producers relative to producers in the U.S. South at time t.

The estimated equation obtained after transformation is:[38]

$$USCAN_t = 0.11 - 0.0013 \text{ CINDEXL} + 0.0028 \text{ CINDEXP}$$
$$(-0.74) \qquad\qquad (2.09)$$

The adjusted R^2 was 0.24.

To interpret the result, the nature of investment by a resource company in the forest product sector must be considered. Production of dimension lumber or other solid wood substitutes is typically located near the resource. Thus, if it is cheaper to produce in one region, a rational producer who is contemplating expanding production is likely to shift investment to the region where production is more competitive. Indeed, the results of our estimate suggest that investment flow patterns reflect shifts in competitiveness so that the firm increases its investments in the more competitive region (in our model a negative coefficient of CINDEXL, although not significant, signifies higher investment in the more competitive region): i.e., as Canadian competitiveness declines, more of the assets shift to the United States.

Expansion of capacity in the pulp and paper sector can increase pulp production or integrate forward by producing paper and other products. If the firm intends to expand production of market pulp, it is likely to invest in the region where pulp production is more competitive. However, if the major motive of the investment is to add value and secure market for pulp, then the relationship may be reversed. A firm with a higher home advantage (i.e., operating in a competitive environment) in the production of pulp will have an advantage in expanding operations in a targeted market over a local firm whose sources of fibre are more expensive. Thus, the positive coefficient of CINDEXP may reflect the fact that MB's move to the United States in the pulp and paper sector is motivated by a desire to secure markets and is strengthened as its Canadian competitiveness improves. (The home location advantage in fibre becomes an ownership advantage in other locations.)

While the above model focuses on investment pull variables (i.e., variables that attract investment to a region), we also test some propositions with respect to push variables (i.e., variables that encourage investment to exit from a region). The labour climate in B.C. is often cited as a risk factor which encourages local multinationals to seek foreign production sites. We thus investigate the relation between days lost to strikes in B.C. (an indicator of labour climate) and MB's relative investment flows to the United States and Canada.

The following model was estimated (Adjusted R^2 = 0.22)

$$\frac{CHUS}{CHCAN_t} = 1.29 - 0.72 \ 10^{-3} \ STRIKA_t$$

where:

$\dfrac{CHUS}{CJCAM_t}$ is the investment flow to the United States over the invest-

ment flow to Canada in year t.

$STRIKA_t$ is the number of days lost to strikes in B.C. in year t.

The Durbin-Watson statistic is 1.34, indicating no problem of serial correlation, but the sign of the equation does not support our expectation that an adverse labour climate will lead to capital flight. It appears that industries tied geographically to a unique resource (e.g. old growth forests) may combat an adverse labour climate by shifting to more capital-intensive modes of production locally (thus reducing the adverse impact of concessions made to labour) rather than abandoning the resource and seeking opportunities in other regions.

We also attempt to investigate the effects of other types of environmental risk (e.g. government regulatory changes), but the constraints of data prevent proper testing. It does appear, however, that (at least in the short run) local investment often increases to deal with the adverse effects of new regulations that impose constraints on the flow of FDI. In the long run we expect push variables to play a significant role, especially when resources are depleted.

Finally, we examine two propositions dealing with the relation between foreign direct investment and corporate performance. Using accounting data (ROI) we find no significant connection between the ratio of domestic and foreign assets and firm profitability. We also use financial market data to assess whether information about MB's commitment to make foreign investments resulted in abnormal profits. Event study methodology with both pooled and individual events yielded no significant results (i.e., within a reasonable window around each FDI event, no significant abnormal profits could be attributed to the event after adjustment was made for other factors that might have influenced share prices).

It appears that while the FDI of a resource company is often motivated by the search for resources and markets for growth, the profit consequences to the firm depend to a large extent on the specific context of the decision to invest, the details of the implementation, the tolerance of the firm to risk, and the horizon used for the evaluation. Next, we provide (through case analyses) a context-rich investigation of some of MB's major investments and their effects on the firm.

SELECTED FOREIGN INVESTMENTS BY MB: ANALYSIS

FOREIGN DIRECT INVESTMENT is a multifaceted phenomenon, and in order to understand its effect on the firm, it is necessary to relate specific FDI decisions to the motives underlying them and their firm-specific contexts. In the following examples we analyze a number of MB's FDI ventures by the principal dominant objective categories identified earlier:

- efficiency seeking;
- market seeking;
- resource seeking;
- risk reduction (unrelated diversification).

These examples were chosen either because they are representative of MB's investments in that category, or because they had a significant effect on MB's subsequent foreign investment policy. Rather than identifying context-free relations, the emphasis here is on the specific external and internal contingencies that affected the firm's decision to invest, the modes of implementation and the consequences of the decision to the firm. The investments in each category are analyzed within the framework of Dunning's Eclectic Theory (1981, 1988).

Table 2 provides a partial list of ownership-specific advantages (OSAs) and location advantages (LAs) important to the assessment of FDI in a forest products company. OSAs are assets: 1) to which the firm's competitors do not have access and, 2) which differ from location-specific inputs because the MNE possessing them can exploit them *wherever it wishes*. Thus, this kind of endowment is mobile between countries but not between firms.[39] Location advantages can be used by MNEs only in the location in which they are sited. However, *some LAs may be internalized by firms, and once that internalization takes place, they may be used by the firm wherever it wishes to do so.* That is, in such circumstances, an LA changes into an OSA. For factors marked with a √ only under location advantages, the implication is that the firm must move to the location to take advantage of that factor. For factors marked with √ only for ownership-specific advantages, the implication is that those factors can be used by the firm wherever the firm can find the best use for them. Location advantages (or disadvantages) can accrue at home and in host countries. If they are LAs of the host country, then they operate as pull factors; if they are location disadvantages of the home country, then they operate as push factors.

An internalization advantage (IA) relates to the cost advantage or strategic benefit that can be realized by the firm if it buys (all or part of) the asset it is seeking to use. An IA differs from both an LA and an OSA, since an IA is a process advantage which cannot be separated from the act of investment. An IA is realized by a firm when it builds on its OSAs or internalizes certain kinds of LAs. The *process* implication of IAs is: since they do not exist *a priori* (to the act of investment), the firm cannot assess the potential consequences of these advantages prior to the act of investment. Moreover, these advantages can change in the course of the internalization process.

TABLE 2

OWNERSHIP-SPECIFIC AND LOCATION ADVANTAGES

FACTORS	OWNERSHIP-SPECIFIC ADVANTAGES	LOCATION ADVANTAGES
Access to primary raw materials	√	√
Access to skilled labour	√	√
Access to financial capital	√	√
Access to transportation facilities	√	√
Abundant wood supply		√
Cheap energy sources		√
Low labour costs		√
Low transportation costs to market		√
Low (other) input costs		√
Infrastructure provisions		√
Large market size and high growth rate		√
Avoidance of tariff and non-tariff trade barriers		√
Similarity to home culture		√
Agglomeration advantages		√
Proximity to home culture		√
Favourable exchange rates/exchange rate stability		√
Tax and government spending benefits		√
Political risk benefits (including land tenure and stumpage policies)		√
Management experience (all functions)	√	
Proprietary technical knowledge	√	
Reputation, brand recognition or loyalty, trademarks, etc.	√	
Economies of scale	√	
Vertical integration advantages	√	
Advantages from multinationality	√	
Distribution networks	√	

EFFICIENCY-SEEKING INVESTMENTS (TYPE 1)
Hygrade Corrugated Cases and Cooks Corrugated Cases (U.K.)

In 1963, MB's agents in the United Kingdom were bought by a competitor. On learning that its main linerboard customers in the United Kingdom would be lost as part of the transaction, MB moved quickly to ensure its continued markets for linerboard in that country. MB acquired the preferred and ordinary shares of Hygrade Corrugated Cases (of Southall, Middlesex) and the ordinary shares of Cooks Corrugated Cases (of Hatfield, Hertfordshire). Ownership was secured on January 2, 1964, and the acquisition was proclaimed by MB's chairman as:

... an important milestone in the history of the company since it is the first time the company has expanded its manufacturing facilities outside Canada."[40]

The two newly acquired companies brought with them an important proportion of the total linerboard and corrugated paper sales in the United Kingdom and their acquisition by MB secured markets for these products and also constituted an important extension of MB's activities. At the time, MB's Packaging Group in Canada consumed 58,418 tons of paper and board stock annually, of which 30,034 tons were supplied from MB's own mills.

In 1964 MB decided to expand Hygrade through construction of a new corrugated box factory at Weston-Super-Mare. Construction of another new plant at Bishop Auckland in the north was scheduled to start shortly thereafter. These two plant expansions, which were to cost over $5 million, reflected MB's confidence in the market future of the United Kingdom. The following year was difficult, however, for both Hygrade and Cooks, due to poor economic conditions. To remain competitive, the two companies had to buy increasing amounts of U.K.-produced raw material obtained from waste, manufacture of which was encouraged by a November 1964 import surcharge in the United Kingdom that affected paper and paperboard. By 1966, although the corrugated container business in the United Kingdom was even more competitive, the new plant at Weston-Super-Mare (which had opened in 1965) was operating satisfactorily, and construction began on the plant in the north. In October 1967, Hygrade and Cooks (now 5 plants) were amalgamated as MB Containers Ltd. in order to realize economies and to facilitate administration of the entire organization.

On October 1, 1983, MB transferred its U.K. packaging plants to MacMillan Smurfit SCA Ltd., a newly formed 50 percent venture with the Jefferson Smurfit Group Ltd and Svenska Cellulosa Aktiebolaget (SCA). The merger stemmed from the recession and lower British output which had reduced demand for corrugated boxes. Large investments in capacity in the 1970s were followed by the recession, and the companies were forced to merge in order to preserve strength in the marketplace.[41] The joint venture was expected to establish a wider customer base and a better geographic spread throughout Britain, as well as to gain access to raw materials through MB's acreage in Canada. However, a decade later, in February 1993, MB sold its share in the venture to the Jefferson Smurfit Group, which had already acquired SCA's shares in 1986. The motivation for this investment had always been to secure a market for MB's linerboard. When MB closed down its linerboard machine at Port Alberni, there was no need to continue with the earlier arrangement.

The Hankins Container Division of the Flintkote Co. (U.S.)

In the late 1960s, MB began to acquire packaging plants in the United States. In 1966 it acquired plants in Jersey City and in Baltimore, and in 1971, a third plant, located in Odenton, Maryland. These acquisitions were part of a strategy to secure a low-cost leadership position in the U.S. packaging business; they were also a strategic element in MB's overall plan for the United States, which centred on its integrated forest products complex at Pine Hill, Alabama. The smaller plants were to be important captive markets for linerboard from the Pine Hill complex, which included a linerboard mill. After acquiring full control of the complex in 1970, MB was responsible for all the linerboard production of the group and needed additional captive markets. By November 1971, MB was considering the acquisition of the Hankins container division of the Flintkote company, which consisted of 10 plants located in the United States. At this time the profitability of the highly integrated containerboard industry was very low, and a captive market strategy promised to provide the company with a stable outlet for its production. In 1971, MB's fifteen packaging plants consumed over 295,000 tons of paper and board, of which more than 57 percent came from MB's own mills.

In 1970 the profitability of the Hankins division was above the industry average, an important consideration in view of MB's need for profit stability. Its 10 well-maintained plants, ideally located to serve markets, provided a basis for future expansion and produced a varied product mix with emphasis on value-added specialty businesses. By acquiring the Hankins plants, MB could divert Pine Hill linerboard sales from the lower mill-net export markets to better mill-net domestic markets. The benefit of diverting sales from less profitable markets was estimated to have a potential of about $1 million/year at $10/ton on a volume of 100,000 tons. In addition to the sales accruing from the mill-net effect, an additional 30,000 tons could be sold in the average year, thus improving the operating ratio by about 8 percent. In total, the integration benefits were calculated at $1.5 million/year before tax.

MB was faced with two investment alternatives: acquiring the Hankins plants for cash or undertaking a joint venture. Ultimately the plants were acquired, which permitted integration with MB's other U.S. operations. At this time, Flintkote was negotiating long-term contracts with its suppliers, and MB needed to make a decision before these contracts were concluded. The Hankins division was acquired by MB from Flintkote on June 16, 1972, for approximately C$ 31 million. This acquisition was a significant milestone in MB's U.S. packaging strategy, as the company now operated 17 corrugated container plants in North America and the United Kingdom. During 1972, MB's packaging operations achieved a 46 percent increase in sales over 1971, three-quarters of which was attributed to the Hankins acquisition. In 1978, the first full year of integration of linerboard and packaging operations, sales reached record levels of $352.4 million, compared with $307.5 million in 1977.

Two years later MB sold three of its U.S. packaging plants (at a profit of C$ 7.1 million), since they did not form any vital link in MB's integrated businesses. In 1983, when MB transferred its U.K. and Canadian packaging plants to two joint ventures (MacMillan Smurfit and MacMillan Bathurst respectively), the U.S. plants constituted the major packaging facilities that MB was continuing to manage on its own. Since acquiring these plants in 1972, MB had spent U.S.$34 million on their modernization and expansion. By 1983, 92 percent of MB's containerboard and packaging capacity was located in the United States.

Analysis of Type 1 Investments   MB's major FDI in this category was in its packaging division and was concentrated within two foreign countries, the United States and the United Kingdom. Corrugated container plants utilize linerboard, and the acquisition of such plants constituted forward vertical integration for MB, assuring the company of captive markets for its linerboard. Type 1 investments are characterized as "efficiency seeking" because the key to their implementation lies in 100 percent control. With full control of the new plants MB could fulfil its strategic objectives and fully integrate the newly acquired plants.

Location Advantages   Both the United States and the United Kingdom had attractive location advantages. The two countries had always been traditional markets for MB in this segment, and they accounted for a large proportion of MB's total sales. As a Canadian company, MacMillan Bloedel had strong cultural ties to both the United Kingdom and the United States. However, since MB did not have integrated operations in the United Kingdom, it was easier for it to withdraw from that market than from the U.S. market.

Industry Characteristics   Containerboard is a capital-intensive business, with a low rate of turnover-per-dollar-invested and very little product obsolescence. The low value/bulky weight nature of containerboard is such that it cannot be easily transported over long distances. For this reason, containerboard must be manufactured near its final destination. Because Canada lacks a large market for containerboard, MB had to look for other markets.

Ownership-Specific Advantages   MB had a well-defined strategy with respect to its packaging segment: it wanted to retain a leadership position in the United States. The existence of the forest products complex at Pine Hill was an important ownership-specific advantage held by MB, in that the Pine Hill packaging plants were assured of an economic and stable supply of linerboard, the most important raw material.

Internalization Advantages   Acquisition constitutes complete internalization. MB's American and British acquisitions in the packaging segment could be integrated with its other investments in these countries. Consolidating the Hankins plants with MB's linerboard facilities in Alabama gave the Hankins plants a guaranteed supply of linerboard and removed their vulnerability to short-term fluctuations in linerboard prices. This acquisition also enabled MB to improve the efficiency and operating ratio of its linerboard mill.

Consequences for Home Country   Since production of containerboard requires market proximity, FDI provided MB with opportunities for market growth while offering economies of scale and networks for its domestic production facilities. The evidence indicates that in Western Canada, plant size is constrained by the thinness of the market (Schwindt, 1977, p. 122); therefore by investing in these facilities abroad, MB was able to take advantage of scale economies, sourcing some of its domestic plants through its lower cost foreign production centres.

RESOURCE-SEEKING INVESTMENT (TYPE 2)

As WITH MOST RESOURCE-BASED COMPANIES, MB has always been preoccupied with securing its (timber) resource supplies. Initially, its focus was on domestic supply, and in 1963, MB implemented an intensive forestry program designed to increase the sustained yield from the company's timberlands by 15 percent within ten years. This *indirect growth* option (discussed above) was aimed at increasing the productivity of MB's timber resources. However, the program was not successful, partly due to biological conditions in the Pacific Northwest and partly because of economic considerations such as insecurity of tenure. As an indirect growth option, intensive forestry was found to have definite limits in providing an alternative for MB to make up for fibre shortages. Therefore, seeking resources in foreign locations through FDI became an important strategy to ensure future growth.

Pine Hill Complex (U.S.)

MB began to look outside Canada for fibre sources as early as 1963. Earlier, it had applied for timber rights near Kitimat, B.C. to support a pulp-lumber complex there, but the provincial government had declined to grant rights to all the pulpwood requested. Thus, not only did the location advantages of the U.S. South operate as a pull factor in influencing this investment decision, but the location disadvantages in B.C. also operated as an important push factor.

Early in 1965, through the efforts of its vice-president of corporate development, who was familiar with the U.S. South, MB bought an option on a mill site on the Alabama River, allowing it access to the sea and world markets.[42] Initially, MB made two separate investments at Pine Hill, Alabama. On January 1, 1966, the company announced a wholly owned greenfield investment, MB Products (MBP), to engage in logging, sawmilling and plywood manufacture, as well as the supply of chips to MB United (see below). The estimated $20 million cost was to be financed largely by a Municipal bond offer.

The larger of MB's two initial investments at Pine Hill, MB United (MBU), involved the construction of a linerboard mill in partnership with the United Fruit Company of Boston. Linerboard had become a fast-growing product, but replacing its only linerboard machine at Port Alberni with a larger model would not have been consistent with MB's long term project plans there.[43] Since 1963, MB had considered a linerboard mill at Pine Hill to be a good investment; the only real problem was the lack of a market for the product. That picture changed with the possibility of United Fruit becoming a partner. As the world's largest banana merchant, United Fruit used 150,000 tons of linerboard in its containers each year.[44]

Total investment requirements of MB with respect to its integrated U.S. operations were U.S.$ 53.997 million. It was estimated that the return on investment (ROI) would be slightly greater than 10 percent if MB sold only 80 percent of the output from the linerboard mill. ROI would be 14.8 percent if all the output were to be sold, which was the more likely scenario. The acquisition of the packaging plants in New Jersey and Maryland (discussed earlier) through a separate investment was a key consideration in the overall strategy for Pine Hill.

On January 15, 1966, MB announced the formation, with United Fruit, of MacMillan Bloedel United Inc., with United holding 40 percent and MB holding 60 percent of MBU. The companies were to build a $60-million plant, two-thirds larger than the linerboard mill at Port Alberni. Initially a mill with a capacity of 340,000 tons-per-year was considered, but this plan was later scaled down to a 270,000 tons-per-year mill. Even though the smaller mill would increase total costs to $1.50/ton, the penalty associated with operating below capacity with the larger mill would have been even greater. MB prepared plans and specifications for the mill and supervised construction, starting in mid-1966, plant start-up was scheduled for mid-1968. Later MB would supervise and operate the mill, for which it would be paid 1.5 percent of the sale price of linerboard sold by MBU. The project was conceived as a:

> true joint venture with each partner responsible for the fixed costs related to their share of the capacity and entitled to dividends based on the volume taken as if two separate mills existed. Thus United was getting a 108,000 ton mill but with the know-how and cost advantages associated with a 270,000 ton mill. (Memo from Corporate Archives)

The Alabama investment was, in fact, more or less self-financing for MB in the long run. The venture was capitalized at $5 million, of which MB's share was $3 million. An Alabama Industrial Development Board issued 20-year bonds of $50 million at a low (4 percent) interest rate with provision for issuance of additional bonds in case of cost over-runs. The leveraged position of MBU had serious implications: a projected cash investment by MB of $10.74 million was expected to generate annual cash earnings of $7.058 million, a staggering return. However, MB's share of the total debt diminished its ability to borrow by 1.5 times the amount guaranteed.

The board of MBU was comprised of five directors, three nominated by MB and two by United Fruit. MB was firm from the outset that it wanted a majority position on the Board. It was agreed that the principals would share

MBU's output, with United purchasing 60 percent and MB 40 percent during the course of every fiscal year. This agreement whereby United Fruit was obliged to buy a certain proportion of the mill's output was intended to ensure a secure market for the mill's product. Profitability rested on the assumption of captive markets. In addition, MB was aware from the outset that it should not put United in a position where it would have to sell spot tonnage on the open market.

> If United could not take its full requirements and w[ere] to operate on a marginal basis, this could be a disruptive influence on the total market. (Memo from Corporate Archives)

Despite MB's best intentions, United was eventually obliged to sell its share of output from the joint mill on the open market and buy its own requirements elsewhere because it found it more economical to do so.[45] Finally, in 1970, MB bought United's share, taking sole control over what would eventually become a successful integrated forest products complex.

Expansion of the Pine Hill Complex   By December 1971 MB had developed a comprehensive plan for the Alabama complex: its main objective was to assume a leadership position in the U.S. packaging industry. One of the main problems facing MB was the need to acquire linerboard outlets. This need led to negotiations with companies requiring linerboard, and the resulting acquisition of the Hankins division of Flintkote in 1972. This acquisition improved profit stability through fuller integration of the Pine Hill linerboard with higher value domestic consumption by Hankins.

In 1980, MB announced a five-year capital expenditure program totalling C$ 2 billion, designating the expansion of the Pine Hill facility (at a cost of US$ 274 million) as the largest single project in the plan. The next year, after being adversely affected by the recession, the company had to scale back these ambitious plans; only the Pine Hill project continued as planned. The expansion was completed in 1983, with the start-up of a new corrugating medium line, described by MB as a "final step in making Pine Hill a total fibre utilization complex". It is noteworthy that MB decided to go ahead with this project, at a time when it was being forced to cut costs and reduce capital spending in Canada. This course was justified on the ground that the MB board was convinced that the U.S. corrugated box industry was on the verge of a technological breakthrough which would utilize the company's new pulping technology.[46]

On December 31, 1984, MB acquired the assets of two additional corrugated container plants in the United States in order to increase further the degree of integration of the Pine Hill containerboard operation. In 1988, MB went on to approve the spending of US$ 17 million for Phase II of a program, begun in 1987, to improve the quality of Pine Hill's linerboard. In early 1989, the expenditure of a further US$ 62 million was approved for Phase III of the project which, in addition to quality enhancements, would also increase annual capacity by 70,000 tons. By December 31, 1990 U.S.$ 51.9 million had been spent on Phases II and III of this program.

Opportunities in Southeast Asia and South America   After start-up at Pine Hill in 1968, MB began to look even farther afield for fibre sources. By February 1970, because of high construction costs and the local (B.C.) labour situation, MB had decided not to become involved in any additional major pulp projects in British Columbia. The company had suffered substantial cost overruns in its major projects in B.C. due to the low productivity of construc- tion labour; in addition, the B.C. government was inviting foreign companies to come to the province to exploit its forest resources because it feared that the market power wielded by the established companies was too great.

In December 1966, a consulting firm, the Tuolumne Corporation, conducted an exploratory study for MB, focusing on regions capable of supplying 700,000 cubic metres of timber on a sustained yield basis. The study identified 10 countries for which it assembled infrastructure indicators, forest resource information (often incomplete due to lack of data), and information on the social, economic and political environment. The Australian trust territory of Papua and New Guinea was ranked first with respect to short-term profit potential.

Bougainville Development Corporation (Solomon Islands)

In September 1965. MB received a proposal from an Australian company, Development Finance Corporation (DFC), for a two-stage project involving logging and, eventually, sawmilling on Bougainville Island (one of the Solomon Islands) in the Australian trust territory of Papua and New Guinea. DFC was a financing development company that wanted to organize a consortium (Bougainville Development Corporation, or BDC) of a limited number of well-known companies experienced in aspects of the international timber trade. It wanted a North American member who would be the exclusive selling agent for BDC products in selected American markets. The other markets for this project would be Australia, New Zealand and Japan. Initially DFC indicated that MB would have to commit around C$ 120,000 to the venture. Some top managers at MB at the time held a strong belief in the future growth potential of this area. Timber stands in these areas of Southeast Asia were close to the large markets of Japan and China. MB was

> . . . impressed with the potential of Malaysia and New Guinea as being in a good position to supply the exotic woods for consumption by billions of people in the Far East. (Memo from Corporate Archives)

The main problem with New Guinea was that despite its large forest resources, it had a poor economic infrastructure. As for the proposed site, there was no road and only a limited water supply, although it did have adequate harbour facilities. MB wanted to be the developer and equity holder, although it acknowledged that it had no expertise in the logging, milling or marketing of tropical woods. In addition, MB was not happy about the prospect of participating with five other companies.

By October 1966, the feasibility or profitability of a specific venture on Bougainville or a general venture in Papua and New Guinea had still not been fully assessed. It was estimated that C$ 1.8 million would be required to develop any venture to its full potential. The main problem was that 32 percent of the timber was on soft ground, for which there was no known logging method. Moreover, the matter of government/labour stability was in doubt. An earlier New Guinea report suggesting that Australia would be under considerable pressure to give New Guinea independence if the project went ahead, raised the possibility of political strife. The report stressed that caution should be used in listening to New Guinea people who discounted the problems of getting wood out of the forest. However, on the positive side the project appeared to have the potential to be a successful venture which could lead MB to share in 50 billion board feet of timber close to the Far East population. The *Tuolumne Report* also provided support for the short-term profit potential of investments in Papua and New Guinea. Investment in this venture would familiarize MB with logging and management requirements in this area and would provide it with tropical logging know-how in the event of future investments in this region. The project was described as a "gamble which could pay off handsomely if it were successful, without too much being lost if it were not". The economics of Bougainville depended on the assumption that it would be a "well managed company".

By June 1967, MB had indicated to DFC that it was prepared to participate, and DFC agreed to MB's stipulation that the person in charge of the project be an "MB production man". The joint venture would require $2.5 million, of which MB's share was (Australian)$ 630,000 which gave MB 32 percent of the equity.[47] DFC was responsible for raising the remaining capital from other sources. The agreement was signed in July 1967, and MB decided to make the investment through its wholly owned Australian subsidiary, MB Pty. Ltd. MacMillan Bloedel would have one person on the Board and would send additional experienced employees from B.C., if necessary, to oversee logging operations. Return on investment was anticipated at 23 percent after tax. By the end of July, MB had paid in its capital. In August 1967, the BDC forecast for the fiscal year ending June 30, 1968, was production of 9 million board feet and a before-tax profit of A$ 50,000; the projected figures for 1969 were 25 million board feet and A$ 500,000. BDC began operations earlier than planned in order to protect its rights to the concession. By doing so, it was offered additional concessions but decided against taking them until the first one turned a profit.

From the beginning, the project did not proceed as planned. In January 1968, operations for the previous four months showed losses of $14,000, but by then these results were considered better than expected. MB wanted Bougainville to be profitable before expanding its interests elsewhere, partly because MB considered Bougainville an experiment to determine whether viable and profitable operations could be conducted in the Far East. Although MB knew about the lack of infrastructure on the island, it was unprepared for the extent to which this factor would impede project implementation.

On March 11, 1968, a report from management in New Guinea stated:

> I cannot give you any costs, because I have none. There is a big labour problem, the native operators have the maturity of children. On the brighter side I have six European operators who are outstanding. I need more of them, but I cannot get approval for the housing they will require. I estimate that in twelve months of native operation, every machine would break down. Moreover, there is bad weather and problems with road construction. (Memo from Corporate Archives)

In 1969, as a result of its inexperience in tropical hardwood logging under such poor conditions – no roads, bad weather, unskilled labour – MB finally divested itself of this investment.

Embrasca (Brazil)

Brazil had ranked ninth with respect to short-term profit potential among the ten countries identified by the Tuolumne Corporation study in 1966. In May 1972, MB's interest in Brazil was revived, following a proposal sent to it by the consulting firm A.D. Little Inc. (ADL). Executives at MB were favourably disposed toward Brazil by then.[48] ADL outlined Brazil's location advantages: the economy was growing fast, and a new entrant could capture 20 percent of the containerboard market. Existing forests were unsuitable for commercial use, but biological conditions allowed for the fast growth of some valuable species and reforestation was a national priority, encouraged through fiscal incentive programs. A 20-percent return and ownership of one-third of a forest asset was possible on a small capital investment. The profit potential from future mill operations was maximal with such an economical and assured supply of fibre. Downside risks were minimal since the forest asset could be sold at a profit. Brazil's geographic location was good for domestic and export markets and it had the appropriate infrastructure for forest development.

Total logging costs including land and planting of the investment were estimated at $12 per 100 cubic feet in Brazil in contrast to $30 per 100 cubic feet in British Columbia. MB believed that if its strategy required more long-fibre pulp or hardwood pulp capacity, Brazil should be a contender long before any part of Canada or the United States. In October 1972, after a preliminary visit to South America, MB appointed a joint MB-ADL study team for a reconnaissance survey of Brazil. An MB executive on leave in Brazil submitted an informal assessment of the survey results to MB management prior to the investment decision. He had strong reservations regarding the survey results and disagreed with them in many instances.[49] As a result of unexpected Brazilian press publicity in November 1972, MB received numerous proposals from Brazilian investors. One of these came from Brascan, a Canadian company with a 70-year history of successful operation in Brazil, thorough local knowledge of politics and business, and a reputation of operating in the Brazilian interest. Its excess earnings in Brazil, which it could not repatriate to Canada for five years, would provide investment capital. The main drawback was that an MB-Brascan association might portray a strong Canadian (i.e., "foreign") image, although the reconnaissance survey had recommended entering Brazil with a strong partner based in Brazil to provide strategic, political and financial advice and leadership in attracting investors. In June 1973, MB and Brascan signed an interim letter of understanding, to combine efforts to study the feasibility of entry alternatives for a proposed joint venture (51 percent MB and 49 percent Brascan).

In December 1973, the MB-ADL team submitted a final project proposal to MB's Board for a reforestation project in Brazil which would eventually be the basis for an integrated forest products complex. Capital requirements were estimated at $18.2 million for the first two years, with a peak investment level of $17 million in the third year. Profits from planting and harvesting would decrease the net capital requirement to $4.7 million in 1985, when the plantation was ready. At 350,000 acres, it would be approximately the size of MB's two tree farm licenses (TFLs) in the Alberni area.

Establishing the plantation under the tax incentive programme suggested an after-tax discounted cash flow (DCF) of 10 percent. Without the incentives, the return would still be 10 percent, but the capital requirements would be $44.7 million rather than $4.7 million. The estimated returns on any future pulp mills and sawmills were 15 percent and 25 percent after-tax DCF respectively (assuming 50 percent export of pulp and local sale of all lumber at conservative prices). A pulp mill could be established, at the earliest, in 1982; the first sawlogs could be produced in 1991, and payback was to occur in 1987.

The most attractive plantation site was Joinville, a coastal mill site with adjacent forests, well located to serve export and domestic markets. The MB-ADL report compared Brazil with Alabama, concluding that the cost of land in Joinville was one-fifth that of Alabama. Productivity was four times as high; thus, for each dollar invested in land in Joinville, MB would get 20 times more wood per year than it would by investing in Alabama.

The MB-ADL report recommended Brascan as the partner because it would let MB handle project management from planting to marketing, and it had a high degree of influence and was sufficiently well-connected in Brazil to provide assistance when needed. Other potential partners offered MB a different kind of investment opportunity, such as direct capital investment as a means of early entry to manufacturing and marketing of forest products.

The report further recommended that the project commence as early as possible in 1974, since time was of the essence because land availability was decreasing fast, prices were increasing, and other firms were studying venture opportunities. The incentive programme was already seven years old, and even during the time that MB had been conducting the feasibility studies, the incentives had been reduced from 50 percent to 25 percent. The sense of time pressure would continue to characterize decision making on this investment. In early 1974, MB and Brascan began negotiating the final joint-venture agreement, and even though by April it seemed that Brascan might withdraw, negotiations did continue. MB insisted on having exclusive control of sales from the joint venture, fearing that products from the venture might be competing in the same market if they were sold by more than one partner in the venture, thereby jeopardizing the profitability of the investment. (MB had had some previous unpleasant experiences in this respect with its United Fruit partnership.) Given MB's marketing strengths in the form of its worldwide marketing organization and wide range of large customers who would sign long-term contracts, MB believed that it was in a better position than Brascan to control the marketing aspects of the venture.

In July 1974, MB announced that it had reached agreement on "Embrasca" with Brascan; the final agreement was signed in late August. The partners were to plant extensive pine and eucalyptus forests which would be the base for the eventual development of an integrated forest products complex. MB would hold 51 percent and Brascan 49 percent in Embrasca, the holding company. Embrasca acquired a subsidiary "Comfloresta" to function as the planting company (i.e., Comfloresta would buy land and carry out planting on a contract basis). MB and Brascan would hold 29 percent (all the common stock with voting rights) of Comfloresta, and Brazilian investors who were contributing their tax incentive funds would hold 71 percent (preferred, non-voting stock). Brazilian investors would participate in both the plantation and manufacturing complex. Embrasca would own approximately 25 percent of the forest when it was completed in 1985, and the fiscal investors would own 75 percent. The value of the forest, in 1985, was conservatively estimated at between $95 million and $100 million, assuming that neither land nor wood values increased. Embrasca's Board was to have five members; MB would nominate three and Brascan two. At this time, in 1974, it was thought that total share ownership would require funding in the amount of $10.9 million. Between 1974 and 1976, MB with Brascan, invested C$ 8 million in Brazil .

MB's investment experience in Brazil did not turn out well. By April 1975, the *pro-forma* of the original feasibility study had to be updated. Land acquisition in Brazil had not proceeded as planned, and registration of areas proved to be a slow and time-consuming task. The weather was bad for the first three months of 1975, and there were difficulties in obtaining labour. Operation start-up was slower than anticipated, and in 1974, there was a reversal of Brazil's previously favourable trend towards lower inflation rates. The costs of acquiring the necessary land and the costs of clearing, planting and maintaining the forest also increased significantly. However, revenue from fiscal incentive funds also increased, offsetting many of the cost increases.

The revised *pro-forma* estimates of peak investment requirements increased from US$ 16.7 million for 1976, to US $20 million in 1977. By that time a total of 57,000 hectares of land had been purchased, representing 46 percent of the objective. Project economics were also adversely affected by changes in the land use assumptions. The lowland areas, which were more difficult to work, now constituted a greater proportion of the land, which led to a lower plantable ratio and higher costs. In the highlands, the amount of attractive land available within economic distance of preferred mill sites had decreased from the original 70 percent to 30 percent. MB was in direct competition with other companies for land acquisition and was forced to negotiate agreements with other buyers. The project would now have to be based on 12 percent less land than originally estimated. It was concluded that the original *pro-forma* had:

> . . . clearly imposed criteria too optimistic for prevailing conditions, and had over estimated the speed with which an efficient organization could be assembled to execute the project. (Memo from Corporate Archives)

By December 1975, MB's Board began to question the company's financial ability to continue its Brazilian activity, especially when the construction of a pulp and paper complex would require large capital outlays, but it concluded that the project was still justified. Start-up difficulties were thought to be over; by the end of 1976 the investment would be 99 percent complete, and since withdrawal could not be effected before the end of 1976, it would make little economic sense to withdraw at the end of the cash outflow period without waiting for the cash inflow to begin. Moreover, withdrawal might damage MB's reputation and would not solve the problem that originally motivated the investment: the need for additional fibre sources. Since the project was designed to carry itself financially through the acquisition of investors after 1976, MB decided to continue its participation.

In 1976, net losses were 9.76 million cruzeiros compared to projected after-tax profits of 1.729 million cruzeiros. Embrasca had made significant progress with respect to the volume of plantation production obtained, but costs were 13 percent over planned levels, partly due to inflation. In December 1976, the Brazilian government announced a series of administrative acts and legislative changes to the fiscal incentives in reforestation activities that affected the 1977 plan.

In 1982, MB assumed 100 percent control of Embrasca. Losses in 1982 amounted to $1.8 million; 1983 losses were $4.7 million. By December 1983, total losses since entering Brazil in 1974 were $13 million. By December 1986, MB's share of losses in its Brazilian subsidiaries since the original acquisition amounted to $21.8 million. In 1987, MB sold its Brazilian investments to Brascan for $10.9 million.

Recycled Newsprint Joint Venture (U.S.)

The Western United States had traditionally been MB's largest and most important newsprint market, but MB's market share in this region had been declining steadily. By 1991, California had increased its already stringent requirements for recycled content in newspapers,[50] which constituted a significant location disadvantage for MB, since it was faced with a shortage of waste newsprint in B.C.[51] For the first time in 35 years, the United States was producing more than half of its newsprint requirements in large low-cost mills with access to recycled fibre at a decreasing cost. These mills were operating largely with non-unionized labour and were not closing down due to strikes. This high degree of reliability made them the preferred supplier over Canadian companies. It was for these reasons that MB was considering California as a potential newsprint production base, even though it was scheduled to close one of its newsprint machines at Powell River, B.C. in March 1992, and was due to close another within a year.[52]

In 1991, MB joined forces with Haindl Papier GmbH of Germany to study the feasibility of establishing a recycled newsprint mill in California. The project involved building a C$ 1.5B newsprint mill, with the first stage requiring C$ 454 million in capital. Although the facility would be equally owned, MB would depend on Haindl for expertise in recycled newsprint. The partnership with Haindl was described by MB's CEO Robert Findlay to be ". . . a key to the project. Haindl has been producing recycled printing papers in Europe since the 1960s and has been a leader in both the process and the technology".[53]

California has significant location advantages such as low input costs, low transportation costs to market, large market size, geographic proximity to consumers, cultural familiarity and protection against exchange rate fluctuations. However, MB was unprepared for the bureaucratic problems associated with operating there.[54] After incurring its worst-ever loss of $94.3 million in 1991, MB finally decided, in September 1992, to postpone financing the project "until newspaper prices improve substantially". It announced that until then it had no capital even for the first $500 million stage.[55] At the time of this writing, the investment is on hold.

Analysis of Type 2 Investments   MB's resource-seeking investments were in large part spurred by its commitments to buyers. Through its Harmac, B.C., facilities, MB was reputed to be a reliable market pulp supplier[56] and a number of customers (including KNP) had grown to expect MB to be their major supplier.[57] MB was therefore committed to a certain amount of pulp production and attempted to find suitable locations where pulp mills could be built. A pulp and paper study by MB determined that there are few economic timber resources on which a pulp mill using between 750 and 1,000 tons per day can be based. Access to timber resources is either too costly by reason of remoteness and government royalties (the case for most Canadian sites) or too politically insecure and with high infrastructure costs (the case in most developing countries). MB therefore invested in low-cost natural forest resources where it could find them or, in the case of Brazil, where it could create them. More recently, the environmental imperative has led to the emergence of a new type of raw material in the form of recycled fibre from the "urban forest". While natural forests in other regions of the world provide a new competitive challenge with the introduction of technology such as thermo-mechanical pulping (TMP), which allows many different tree species to be used for fibre requirements, urban forests also constitute a significant source of artificial fibre which is likely to become more important in the future.

Location-Specific Advantages In searching for access to foreign fibre resources, MB decided to move its investment location decisions from the U.S. South to Southeast Asia and Brazil. It began with the most familiar areas and gradually moved farther afield. The transition from the U.S. South to Southeast Asia was eased through a partnership with Jardine Matheson, a firm with extensive knowledge of the area. This partnership (MacJard) will be discussed later. The main advantage of all these locations was the availability of low-cost forest resources, but many locations had extensive disadvantages (poor infrastructure and tropical climates) which were either not immediately apparent or grossly underestimated. Only the Pine Hill complex was located in a culturally similar, economically developed area in geographic proximity to a major market. Other location advantages of Pine Hill were coastal access (which decreased transportation costs), low-cost financing and the availability of qualified labour.

Ownership-Specific Advantages At the time when the investments were made, MB's ownership-specific advantages (OSAs) were not well suited to either the Southeast Asian or the Brazilian investment opportunities. These investments can be seen as attempts to transfer what MB thought to be non-location-bound OSAs, but which were in reality very strongly location-bound OSAs. MB's forestry expertise lay in the capital-intensive manufacture of softwood-lumber forest products in temperate climates. Its attempts to transfer this knowledge to areas characterized by a completely different set of location factors have not been successful. Also, although MB's business partners in these ventures (Development Finance Corporation and Brascan), had extensive local business knowledge of the respective areas in which they operated, they lacked manufacturing experience in forestry. Moreover, although MB was responsible for the technical (production and marketing) aspects of these ventures, it was not able to transfer its knowledge in these respects from the Canadian context to a foreign context. If MB and Haindl do eventually proceed with their recycled newsprint venture, MB will be largely dependent on the technological expertise of its partner, since it does not count a strong base in recycled newspaper technology among its ownership-specific advantages.

Internalization Advantages   Internalization advantages accrue according to the extent to which the venture is internalized. All the investments examined in this category were initiated as joint ventures, and MB insisted on a majority position in each case. In some of these areas there were externally imposed limits on internalization advantages because government policies restrict the degree of internalization. In the other cases (e.g., Embrasca and Bougainville) the costs to MB of complete internalization would have been too high and beyond its resource capabilities, both financially and in terms of knowledge of local business conditions. Pine Hill became successful only after MB took total control and reaped the subsequent integration benefits.[58]

The success of MB's Pine Hill investment rested on the synergy between OSAs, LAs, and IAs. Many of MB's OSAs could easily be transferred to Pine Hill. Location advantages of Pine Hill such as cultural and technological similarity and geographic proximity to markets facilitated easy transfer of MB's managerial and technical expertise. MB already had market knowledge of the United States and experience in selling to that market through its sales offices in New York and Alabama. The implementation of this investment took place at a strategic time, for MB was the first B.C. company and one of the earliest Canadian companies to establish manufacturing operations in the United States. Very favourable financing conditions were offered to MB at Pine Hill, and by establishing itself as a new entrant MB benefitted from the resulting barriers to entry.

Consequences for Home Country   Since the home advantage for the B.C. forest sector is based on its natural resource supply, resource development abroad by MB can be viewed as having the potential to erode the competitive edge of the forest sector in British Columbia. This assertion, however, assumes that if MB had not invested in resource development abroad no other firms would have done so. However, there is compelling evidence to the contrary. Indeed, in several instances MB moved to pre-empt rivals from securing access to particular resources. Since MB was constrained from expanding its resource supply domestically (mainly by government policy), it had to ensure its access to resources abroad. Its behaviour, however, confirms that it had a strong commitment to its core assets in British Columbia (despite newspaper contentions to the contrary). Indeed, in periods of retrenchment it sold some of its assets abroad, despite their profit-making potential, in order to secure capital needed at home. The investments in the United States, however, became a key component of its core assets and are considered to be a very important part of the company's overall corporate strength. The resource-seeking investments in the United States were aimed at strengthening other market- and efficiency-seeking investments. The ability of the firm to exploit its OSAs through FDI and generate a flow of dividends to Canada appears to be strong in the familiar environment of developed countries. The company's experience in developing countries appears to highlight the risks of FDI in those countries.

MARKET SEEKING INVESTMENTS (TYPE 3)

MacMillan Jardine (Hong Kong/Japan)

In 1962, Japan lifted restrictions on pulp imports. At that time, MB sold newsprint to Japan through its membership in the Export Sales Company,[59] an export cartel. In 1963, for the first time, lumber shipments to Japan exceeded those to the United Kingdom, and so MB decided it could gain significant strategic benefits in Southeast Asia by selling all its products through one organization to this increasingly important far eastern market.

In October 1963, after visits to the area, MB formed a marketing partnership with Jardine Matheson and Co. Ltd., a very well established and famous trading house in Hong Kong.[60] Early in 1964, MacMillan Jardine Ltd. (MacJard) was incorporated in Hong Kong as a joint venture. As soon as MB could terminate arrangements with existing agents, MacJard was to be both the exclusive sales agent for all MB products in the Far East and MB's area representative in the reporting of marketing intelligence for the pulp and paper segment. The partnership was intended to progress from that of a sales vehicle to that of MB's primary investment vehicle in Southeast Asia. MacJard set up its own subsidiary in Japan, known as MacMillan Jardine (Japan) Ltd. [MacJard (Japan)].

It took about two years for MB executives to begin to feel dissatisfied with the partnership. MacJard personnel had failed to comply with requests for information and had not, as originally expected, "enthusiastically generated ideas and opportunities that could benefit MB in the long run". Channels of communication and organization had not been well defined, and MB eventually realized that:

> Western management principles do not apply in Japan; Nanjo (the manager) must be allowed to develop his staff in his own Japanese way. He will respond to Western thinking but we must let him do it in his own way and at his own speed. (Memo from Corporate Archives)

To get closer to MacJard, the two companies exchanged personnel, sending Canadians to MacJard (Japan), and bringing Japanese workers to Canada. Subsequent meetings between MB and MacJard personnel emphasized that there should not be an "agent-principal" relationship between the two organizations. The use of the term 'agent' was just legal phrasing, which should not set the operating climate. MacJard personnel were to see themselves as MB's partners, express themselves freely and recognize their important position in MB's marketing effort, a suggestion they accepted with enthusiasm. By 1968, MacJard's profits were US$ 902,000 compared to U.S.$ 212,000 in 1964. Selling expenses per US$ 100 sales value had decreased from .72 in 1964 to .54 in 1968. MB enjoyed a strong position and a good reputation in the Japanese lumber market and therefore decided to look at other avenues for expansion.

By 1969, MB's major North American competitors (Boise-Cascade, Weyerhaeuser, Georgia-Pacific and U.S. Plywood-Champion) had also entered Southeast Asia. MB therefore re-evaluated Southeast Asian investment opportunities with respect to its corporate goals which were: 1) to maintain it's traditional leadership role in the forest industry; 2) to increase the extent of its geographical diversification with pioneering investments in these developing countries; 3) to provide ROI greater than 12 percent; 4) to establish a base for the pursuit of profitable business opportunities not necessarily directly related to the forest industry. By January 1969 it was decided that MacJard would be MB's investment vehicle in Southeast Asia. In April 1969 MB and MacJard established a joint Task Force with the following objective:

> To identify for MacJard profitable investment opportunities primarily in Malaysia and Singapore, secondarily in Indonesia. The opportunities are to be in areas of the timber industry-forestry development, logging and wood products manufacture; but this will not exclude identification of profitable investments in other industries should they become apparent to the Task Force. (Memo from Corporate Archives)

The criterion for inclusion of opportunities was an after-tax return of between 20 percent and 30 percent "after full and realistic consideration of all the risks involved".

In 1970, MB's capital share in MacJard was just under $1.9 million, and MacJard operations were to provide the funds for projects in Southeast Asia. In the same year, following recommendations by the joint Task Force, MB invested through MacJard in a profitable logging operation in Malaysia (Mentiga Forest Products).

By 1971, MacJard represented MB as well as the Export Sales Company (the export cartel that MB belonged to in 1962) for the sale of newsprint to Hong Kong, Indonesia, Japan, Malaysia and Thailand, and for the sale of pulp to Taiwan and Japan. On January 1, 1971, the hardwood lumber business of Jardine Matheson and Company was merged into MacJard Ltd., extending MacJard's business into the marketing of hardwood logs, lumber and veneer products in Japan and other Pacific areas. In 1972, MacJard extended its activities to a logging operation in Indonesia (P. T. Sangkulirang), in partnership with the Indonesian Navy and a subsidiary of Unilever.

Although MB exited this partnership (and the investments in Malaysia and Indonesia) in 1982, for "ethical reasons",[61] this initial marketing experience in Southeast Asia paved the way for MB to gain access to two specialty markets in Japan: specialty grade newsprint and specialty lumber. There was a 3.9 percent duty on specialty grade newsprint, in addition to non-tariff barriers such as the close ties between Japan's newspaper publishers and their domestic suppliers.[62] After extensive market analysis and technical refinements, MB became the first foreign supplier in this market.

In 1985, MB opened wholly owned lumber distribution offices in Japan (MB Building Materials or MBKK). Three months later, a re-valuation of the yen effectively doubled Japanese labour costs, bringing them into line with North American labour costs. Location advantages and investment timing were ideal. The change in the value of the yen gave MB's competitive position a tremendous boost at the same time that the company was improving its penetration of the Japanese market.[63] As a result, by 1993 Japan was MB's leading lumber market, with sales representing 40 percent of the company's total lumber sales.

Although MB's share of the total volume of the Japanese lumber market is relatively small, it's share of the high-value end of the market is significant. MB now has an important ownership-specific advantage in selling to Japan. It's Alberni Pacific sawmill is the first coastal sawmill certified to grade lumber to Japanese standards. Since this lumber requires no further grading before distribution in Japan, it can be used in homes being constructed with government mortgages. MB's largest ownership-specific asset, which it uses in the Japanese market, is its control over the high quality of its product. This control is possible because of MB's integrated structure: it holds the rights to quality fibre, and it has its own manufacturing facilities, shipping company and distribution facilities.[64]

KNP (Holland)[65]

In October 1965, MB made it's first entry into the (European) Common Market by investing $15 million in a 36 percent interest in Koninklijke Nederlandsche Papierfabriek (KNP), the Dutch fine-paper manufacturer. As with most of its other investments, MB would have preferred to hold a majority position. The investment came about through the efforts of Larry Harris, vice president of the pulp and paper group, in his search for captive markets.

> My whole point in foreign acquisitions was to get an interest in a company and have it absorb our raw material. I had been selling pulp in Holland to KNP, and thought it would be good for a first shot into Europe. They were growing, they were good, and they wanted to put in a new paper machine (which would increase their consumption of pulp).[66]

KNP is located in Maastricht, a strategic position for access to the countries of the Common Market. MB's equity in KNP would strengthen customer-supplier relationships and enable KNP to expand its manufacturing facilities. The MB investment would go toward a new mill at Lanaken, Belgium, with a capacity of 60,000 tons per year, which would, in turn, increase pulp purchases from British Columbia. The move also constituted horizontal diversification for MB, since it had only limited experience in the fine paper business.[67] An agreement between MB and KNP guaranteed KNP management complete independence; thus MB could only exercise its rights as a shareholder in exceptional cases (e.g., liquidation of the company). Soon after MB bought a stake in KNP, the two companies agreed on joint participation in a separate project (Celupal) in Spain.

Initially, MB was optimistic about its investment. Examining KNP's performance on September 30, 1966, MB believed that it was doing well in the face of increasingly competitive markets and rising labour costs. However, by October 1966, conditions throughout Europe were becoming more difficult, and KNP had to make price concessions to maintain its position in the German market. But there were other serious problems within KNP.

For generations KNP had been a family-controlled firm. However, on January 19, 1967, MB's director on the KNP board reported his lack of confidence in the family's management of the company. Besides having to contend with a power struggle within its top management, KNP had a weak financial position and was forced to devise a new capital expenditure and financing plan for the 1967-1971 period. By January 1967, profits were down, and the estimated costs of the new mill at Lanaken had increased by $1.8 million. MB suggested hiring McKinsey & Company, a consulting firm which it had itself employed in 1962. It argued that McKinsey should go into KNP because "they have no idea what an organization should be, by today's standards". The family that controlled KNP was opposed to using McKinsey, and it was eventually decided that retaining McKinsey would not be economical.

In 1970, MB increased its share in KNP to 41 percent, and this share was further increased to 46 percent in 1973; MB's share then fell to 45 percent in 1974, and, finally, to 44 percent in 1975. In 1978, MB lost $4.5 million through its European investments which included equity stakes in KNP and two other companies, GEC and Celupal. MB's share of losses in KNP alone amounted to $4.1 million in 1978, and to $7 million in 1979. Despite the losses MB incurred, these investments were important to MB. On September 6, 1979, MB's world ranking relative to those of other forest product companies rose from 11th to 10th through consolidation of the sales of KNP, GEC and Celupal. However, it remained the 11th in terms of assets, and 13th in terms of profits, irrespective of the consolidation.

In February 1980, MB considered taking a majority position[68] in KNP, in contrast to being a majority shareholder with a 46 percent interest. KNP was seen as a company with significant potential, but which would have to make major changes to realize that potential. KNP was in a strong position relative to its Scandinavian competitors and had profitable fine paper machines at Lanaken and Maastricht, technological and marketing competence in the fine paper segment, low-cost production and a strong balance sheet. However, too much of KNP's management time and resources were tied into its unprofitable packaging group. There was a lack of strategy, little investment in upgrading productive assets, and management skills were uneven. KNP had continued to perform unsatisfactorily, and since 1974, its earnings under North American GAAP had been very low. It had paid no dividends since 1975, and planned none for 1980. Return on investment, measured by dividends to investment costs, averaged 3 percent between 1974 and 1979. If MB were to increase its investment in KNP, it would further increase its foreign currency exposure, which would, in turn, affect its profit and loss statements.

The advantages to MB of its investment in KNP were: 1) a semi-captive market for Harmac pulp; 2) provision of information regarding the changing finish of European fine paper; 3) access to technical expertise in printing and writing papers; and, 4) indirect participation in fine paper expansion. The disadvantages to MB of its investment in KNP were: 1) a low return on the substantial amount of capital committed; 2) insufficient influence over management decisions and strategic directions; 3) a pulp contract which tied both its hands; and, 4) under-utilized potential of the MB-KNP relationship. This last was the most significant disadvantage.

Later in 1980, MB finally decided against taking a majority position, electing to increase its KNP holding to 48 percent. This share was to remain more or less constant until 1985-1986, when MB was forced to sell shares to raise cash, and its holding fell to 25 percent. Later, when its financial position improved, MB began to buy KNP shares as they became available. On January 3, 1989, MB subscribed and paid for an additional 5 percent common share interest in KNP at a cost of $46.7 million, giving it a stake of 30.6 percent. In early 1993, KNP announced a merger with Buhrmannn-Tetterode VG which would increase its presence in the European marketplace. Today, MB owns 16 percent of this new larger entity and expects its original investment to increase significantly in value. This investment proved very fruitful for MB in the 1980s, as the high quality standards set by KNP were instrumental in helping MB to establish guidelines for the quality of its own products. Recently, the CEO of MB confirmed that it will sell its shares in the merged firms if its target price is met.[69]

MacMillan Rothesay Ltd. (Germany)

In June 1968, MB had a problem. Two companies were fighting for a leadership position in the coated paper market in Germany. One was KNP, in which MB had a significant equity stake; the other was Feldmühle Aktiengesellschaft, one of the EC's largest producers of paper and board, but also one of MB's major pulp customers. Another complicating factor was that the president of Feldmühle, Helfried Krug, was conducting a running feud with George Haindl, president of Haindl Papierfabrieken, another leading German company, with whom MB also had a pulp contract.[70] In February 1969, MB met with Feldmühle. At the meeting, Krug emphasized that the "bigs" could not continue to fight the "bigs". Feldmühle proposed that MB and Feldmühle jointly set up a new company – MacMillan Rothesay Ltd. (MRL) – which would own the Rothesay Paper Corporation (RPC), a newsprint producer located in Saint John, New Brunswick, in which Feldmühle already had a 40 percent equity stake. The joint company would sell 100,000 tons/year of pulp to Feldmühle. Feldmühle and MB would also be partners in another machine at Lanaken. (Feldmühle did not then know that MB was already installing a machine at Lanaken with KNP.) The final element of the proposal was the joint exploration of other European investment opportunities.

On July 17, 1969, Feldmühle sent MB a draft letter of intent in which MB was given a choice of holding 49 percent, 50 percent or 51 percent of the equity. Feldmühle suggested paying MB a fee to operate the mill. ROI was estimated at between 11 percent and 14 percent on an investment of between $14 million and $17 million, assuming an increase in newsprint prices by 1972, the successful installation of a second newsprint machine, and the verification of assumptions relating to sales volumes. Due to prevailing market conditions, the second newsprint machine would have to be flexible: i.e., capable of producing groundwood and newsgrade specialties, in addition to standard grades. A flexible second machine would provide MB with additional product as well as geographic diversification. In financial terms, the investment was considered attractive if the output could be marketed in an "orderly fashion".

The venture offered MB a potentially good strategic fit with its other operations. The company would gain both an important Canadian east coast newsprint base and a captive market for pulp from its Harmac mill. The future success of the joint venture would hinge on MB's marketing and management strength. Feldmühle held 4 percent of KNP which, combined with MB's 36 percent holding, gave them a significantly strong position in KNP and would provide MB with further diversification in this region. Finally, the long-term Feldmühle pulp contract would fit the strategic goal of reducing dependency on open market pulp sales, although the increased newsprint tonnage would represent an increased commitment by MB to commodities.

On August 5, 1969, MB sent Feldmühle a draft letter of intent regarding a) Rothesay participation, b) a long-term pulp contract, and c) harmonizing, extending and complementing European business done by Feldmühle and KNP, about which discussions were to commence in 1970. The Board would consist of four members, two nominated by MB and two nominated by Feldmühle. MB would hold 51 percent of the equity and Feldmühle the rest, the initial common equity being $20.2 million. MB would manage the mill, for which it would receive a management fee, and would commence construction of the second newsprint machine. Although the two parties entered into an informal agreement on August 28, 1969, it was subsequently decided that a formal joint venture agreement would be necessary. The deal was finally closed in December 1969.

In 1970, MB contemplated a merger with Feldmühle. Ironically, it was now the existence of MacMillan Rothesay Ltd., the venture with Feldmühle, which did not fit with the merger objectives and was a strong disincentive to the merger. Feldmühle's interest in Rothesay (newsprint) and a 25 percent interest in Intercontinental Pulp were not compatible with MB's criteria for reducing dependence on commodity products, and locations outside B.C. could pose a significant conflict of interest. While the possession of 50,000 tons to 100,000 tons of captive pulp was one of the main attractions of a merger with Feldmühle, its unimpressive 6 percent growth in sales and no-growth profit performance from 1963 to 1967 were not compatible with MB's profit objectives. Furthermore, there was also no basis for predicting an improvement in Feldmühle's performance. Feldmühle's heavy commitment to producing fine paper for the printing and publishing industries put it in direct competition with KNP in western Europe. Finally, a merger with Feldmühle would place a major block of MB stock in the hands of the Flick family (the owners of Feldmühle), a position MB wanted to avoid. Eventually, the merger negotiations were abandoned.

1971 was a difficult year for MRL. The new company faced an unsteady product demand at a time when it was experiencing start-up problems with its second machine. Feldmühle was under the impression that the United States was to be the main market for the new company's product. Initially, Europe, and other off-shore markets were considered only as substitute outlets. However, when market prospects changed because European markets began to offer better profit prospects, MB wanted to sell the Rothesay production in European markets. This plan clashed with Feldmühle's European newsprint distribution interests, which had recently widened. The U.K. and Irish markets had become more important to Feldmühle since their entry into the Common Market. In September 1973, in a letter to MB, Helfried Krug expressed his disappointment in MB's management of the venture:

> Many hopes and expectations have failed to come true since we so hopefully set out on our partnership. I have in mind the problems encountered in selling the output from the second paper machine, stemming from the change in currency relations but also from the poor performance of the sales organization. I also think of the really inadequate planning and construction work with ensuing production problems, the frequent but unfortunately unnecessary changes in management, and last but not least the whole complex of barge operation which falls significantly short of expectations in terms of profitability.

By October 1973, after investing $18.1 million in the new MRL, MB had incurred a loss of $10.7 million (after deferred taxes) due to soft newsprint markets, difficulties with the start-up of the second newsprint machine, a strike, and costs for chemical pulp and power that were higher than anticipated. Feldmühle regarded MRL as a purely financial investment, since it did not tie in directly with the company's other businesses. By dissolving the agreement, MB would be free to make investments which it considered necessary to improve MRL's competitive position. MRL had a good strategic fit with MB's other business interests, and prospects of a turnaround at the Rothesay mill looked favourable. As a result, in December 1973, MB bought Feldmühle's 49 percent stake in MRL for $17.5 million. The return on this investment was estimated at 11.5 percent (DCF after tax). Although the mill was operating well, it was forced to buy its chemical pulp on the open market, and this was a serious competitive disadvantage. However, the installation of a new thermo-mechanical groundwood facility could decrease chemical pulp requirements and improve the mill's return on investment to 13.5 percent. Now, with full ownership, MB was free to invest in MRL without having to consider the wishes of a partner. However, soon after buying Feldmühle's equity in MRL, MB sold 35 percent to Simex, a Spanish government corporation, in the hope that this new partnership would stimulate newsprint sales to the Spanish market.

In July 1981, MB sold the MRL pulp mill for $145 million after buying out the 35 percent held by Spanish concerns,[71] thus easing the pressure caused by the financing costs of MB's expansion program. MB rationalized the sale by explaining that it was trying to concentrate on integrated locations so as to reduce its reliance on outside pulp suppliers.[72] The Rothesay mill had to buy 20 percent of the pulp needed to make newsprint. Furthermore, the company would need more wood to justify pulp production, and this wood was unavailable.

Trus Joist MacMillan (U.S.)[73]

In the early 1970s, MB's R&D department began to develop its engineered wood technology with a view to producing alternative wood products that would compete with other materials used in the construction industry. Its first product in this program was waferboard, marketed under the trade name ASPENITE™. The world's first waferboard plant was operated by MB at Hudson Bay, Saskatchewan, and is still operating profitably today, although it no longer has the technological lead it once enjoyed. In retro-spect, the company failed to exploit its early leadership due to its inexperi-ence in both new product management and proprietary technology. On the positive side, the technological know-how accumulated by MB in this area enabled it to bring another innovation from the research lab to production. This unique reconstituted lumber product, *Parallam*, was the result of almost 20 years of research and development at a cost of more than $52 million.[74] *Parallam* is a very strong, uniform, structural wood product which is based on softwood, but is not dependent on old growth and can also utilize residues from veneer plants.

In 1987, MB announced plans to commercialize *Parallam*. An existing prototype plant in New Westminster, B.C., was expanded, and a new plant was to be built in the United States at Colbert, Georgia. The commercialization of *Parallam* presented MB with a dilemma: as opportunities for additional manufacturing capacity arose, the growth in business would consume more cash than it generated. The market for engineered wood products had been growing at an annual rate of over 20 percent, and further growth was forecast. However, for MB, this meant that the engineered wood business would have to compete with other demands for corporate capital,[75] many of which were environmental imperatives that could not be postponed.

The *Parallam* plant in New Westminster began commercial production in 1988, and made its first official contribution to sales in the building materials segment in 1989. A further $1.2 million was invested in the New Westminster plant to increase its capacity. The Colbert plant was completed in July 1990, at a cost of US$ 68.6 million. In 1990, MB began construction on another manufacturing plant near Deerwood, Minnesota (at a cost of US$ 74 million) to produce another new engineered wood product, PSL 300™. The product was to be used in housing construction and MB had an assured source of raw materials from the state of Minnesota. The PSL 300 plant went into production at the end of 1991.

Despite the accolades that *Parallam* had received, its sales were running well behind production.[76] In 1990, annual production was only 57,400 cubic feet, compared with the planned 475,000 cubic feet. In order to realize the full potential of this product, MB decided to transfer its *Parallam* operations to a joint venture with Trus Joist International of Boise, Idaho (TJI). TJI was the largest North American producer of engineered wood products, including a product that competed with *Parallam*. TJI had been in operation since 1960, and had an excellent reputation with architects and engineering groups in North America. It was thought that MB's new technology combined with TJI's sharp focus and established position in the market would be an excellent combination for increasing market acceptance of the product, and thereby the rate of production.

On October 1, 1991, MB signed an agreement with TJI to form a limited partnership to produce and market a wide range of engineered wood products. The venture, which would control approximately $350 million in assets, was to be named Trus Joist MacMillan Ltd. (TJM) and was to be headquartered in Boise. MB's *Parallam* operations at New Westminster, B.C. and Colbert, Georgia, previously included in the building materials segment, were transferred to the new partnership, as was the plant at Deerwood, Minnesota, which had not yet started production. TJI would contribute its 11 plants. With 51 percent ownership, TJI would be the managing partner of TJM, and MB would hold the remaining equity. MB would provide TJM with ongoing R&D.

TJM would provide MB with a wider range of laminated products for its wood products distribution segment to sell across North America. Any future investment by TJM would be "where the company has a competitive advantage. The U.S. site has an advantage as long as the United States is the largest market."[77]

Analysis of Type 3 Investments   There are several strategies to improve market access and develop market potential. Since 1963, MB has used FDI to strengthen distribution networks, acquire market knowledge, create captive or committed markets, and facilitate relationships with clients through local manufacturing.

Location Advantages   Location advantages for this category relate to the potential for market growth in a particular location and barriers to imports. Barriers to imports include regulatory barriers (e.g., tariff and non-tariff barriers), market information barriers, and technical and other barriers to competitiveness. The nature of the investment indicates the type of barrier it is meant to overcome. In some cases MB's foreign investments reflected the need to secure market access by serving customers from local plants. In other cases the investments were motivated by both technical factors (such as the bulky nature of the product) and the need to improve customer services. In still other cases, local manufacturing helped to secure the flow of products from threats of tariff barriers (e.g. plywood). Investment in production facilities was also a means to secure markets for raw materials and intermediate products. This was certainly the case with attempts to create markets for pulp. Dealing with more remote and less familiar markets required the strengthening of distribution networks (often through partnerships with distributors with strong local distribution networks).

Ownership-Specific Advantages and Internalization Advantages   A large proportion of the market-seeking FDI of MB was in the form of joint ventures or partnerships. Local market knowledge and reputation can be acquired by selecting a local partner with an established reputation in marketing channels. Arm's-length transactions (i.e., using local agents) limit the extent to which MB might have utilized the strategic assets possessed by its partners. The use of partnerships as a mode of entry allowed for quicker market access than might have been obtained if MB had entered these markets on its own.

Consequences for Home Country   Generally, market-seeking FDI should improve home welfare by securing higher prices for domestic production and providing potential for growth at home. Clearly, the potential for growth of production at home may be smaller if, to achieve market access, production facilities are located abroad. It may be argued, for example, that the joint venture to produce *Parallam* in the United States may have meant that the technologies developed by MB were used to generate jobs abroad. However, the case history showed that there were difficulties in penetrating the market and that in this case FDI helped create new markets for *Parallam* which might not have existed without the joint venture. Consequently FDI, while not creating employment at home, did help to sustain a continued R&D activity at home and thus promoted the further development of Canadian technological capability. Also, the dividends generated by this successful investment did contribute directly to the welfare of Canadians, who own the majority of MB shares. There were also some indirect benefits to the competitive position of MB, as it could transfer certain successful managerial and production practices to its Canadian plants from the plants in the United States.

RISK REDUCTION INVESTMENTS (TYPE 4)

INVESTMENTS IN THIS CATEGORY are designed to diversify business and thus decrease risk.[78] Many such MB investments have been opportunistic and were made in areas where the company had little experience. Others were extensions of some subsidiary functions (e.g. shipping) where MB had some experience.

Northside and Northpoint (Australia)

Early in 1970 Jardine Matheson offered MB an investment proposal involving the construction of an office/hotel complex in Sydney. The project company, Northside Gardens Investments Pty. Ltd. (Northside) was to be capitalized at A$ 2 million with an estimated total cost of A$ 8 million. Jardine had successfully completed other real estate projects in Australia, and MB had confidence in its partner. It was concluded that since real estate was booming in Sydney, MB would receive a good return on a modest investment. MB could participate with or without a debt-financing obligation. It chose to participate with a debt-financing obligation of A$ 1.2 million (C$ 1.44 million) because of a higher return (after tax DCF) of between 11 percent and 19 percent as compared to 4 percent with no debt. Although MB was uncomfortable about this debt obligation, which would adversely affect its own borrowing capacity, it approved the project since, in the words of a company executive,

> . . . there is a good future in the general relation with Jardine Matheson in these areas and as this is our first venture with them in Australia I think we should go ahead even though there is a debt obligation.

Jardine Matheson & Co. (Australia) Pty. Ltd. was to hold 51 percent of Northside. MB was to make an initial contribution of A$ 400,000 (C$ 480,000) for a 20 percent stake, and other Australian interests were to hold 29 percent. Construction was to begin in March 1971, and be finished by June 1973.

In June 1970, the Australian economic outlook was not favourable. Government policy over the next few months would have an adverse effect on availability of domestic funds for commercial development. Despite this situation, on June 19, 1970, following MB's investment in Northside, a second proposal was received from Jardine with respect to a property development

project in Sydney, Northpoint Properties Pty. Ltd. (Northpoint), for the construction of an office building. The project was to start in December 1971, be
completed by December 1973, and be leased by September 1974. Jardine
would contribute 80 percent of the equity and 71 percent of the loan
funds. MB would contribute 20 percent of the equity (A$ 95 million) and 29
percent of the loan funds (A$ 2.85 million), an unfavourable stipulation for
MB.[79] If costs increased, participants would be required to increase their equity
and loan contributions proportionately. Jardine would contribute land (on
which it would make a capital profit of $1.23 million in which MB would
not participate), while MB would contribute cash. A conservative estimate of
the return on equity (ROE) was 15.2 percent before tax, and a non-conserva-
tive estimate was 52.9 percent. MB could nominate one director to the Board.
MB compared size, cost and expected profit to its Vancouver building and,
concluding that Northpoint was more profitable, decided to participate.

By November 1972, the Northside project budget had increased to
A$ 10 million. MB was now worried about the stipulation in the original
agreement relating to loan guarantees, which would decrease its borrowing
capacity.[80] When the project was finally complete in December 1973, total
costs were A$ 12.68 million. The outlook for Northpoint was even less
promising. The economics of the project had been adversely affected by
increasing material costs and interest rates, an oversupply of office space,
unprecedented wage rate increases, and unavailability of overseas borrowing.
Serious problems in the design of the foundation had also caused delays in the
construction schedule. A decision had to be made with respect to continuing
the project.

MB decided to continue on the assumption that going forward was the
only way to realize any value from the project. Since estimated costs (now at
A$ 20 million) were too high for MB and Jardine, they decided to bring in a
50 percent equity partner. However, the prevailing economic and political
scene in Australia exacerbated the problems of locating a new partner. To
complete the construction, Jardine and MB established a A$ 15 million
credit line. MB would have to guarantee its share of the A$ 15 million
loan (A$ 3 million = C$ 4.35 million) through an unrestricted subsidiary. In
March 1975, construction on Northpoint was still not complete, and MB was
having difficulty obtaining up-to-date information on the project from Jardine.
MB eventually disposed of these two investments in 1978, at a significant loss.

Analysis of Type 4 Investments   MB's investments in this category
have been extremely unsuccessful and short lived. They include incursions
into transportation, real estate development and a number of other unrelated
businesses. Although there was a valid strategic rationale for these investments (reduced risk and therefore greater profit stability in the highly cyclical
forest industry), MB did not have the expertise to manage them. Even so, MB
took interests that were sufficiently large to provide it with a strong voice in

the operations of these companies. As a result, the capital and management time tied up in these investments weakened MB's competitive position in its main business segment. Moreover, the welfare consequences of these investments were negative in that they added significantly to MB's losses. Indeed, MB's investments in shipping continued to contribute to its losses until 1979, after an initial loss of $46.3 million in 1975.

Welfare Implications of MB's FDI for Canada

IN HIS STUDY ELSEWHERE in this volume, Globerman provides a comprehensive summary of the effect of overseas investment on the home country. Empirical evidence on this topic has concentrated on the effect felt by the home-country labour market. While the evidence generally shows a positive effect on skilled workers in contrast to a negative impact on low-skilled workers, the aggregate employment effect is less clear. The MB experience appears to contradict this pattern and perhaps reflects the experience of resource-intensive industries where most value-added operations have been moving closer to the market, while the core resource-intensive operations have been kept at home. This has meant a shift in employment of skilled workers from home to jobs abroad, while relatively low-skilled jobs have remained at home. (However, these jobs command relatively high wages because of the capital-intensive nature of the industry and unionization.) This phenomenon is similar to the Swedish experience reported in Blomström & Kokko, 1993. As in Sweden, where the share of resource industries in the economy is significant, some R&D activities remain at home, although the production activities they serve have moved abroad.

The Welfare Consequences of MB's Outward FDI for Canada

THE MNE'S OBJECTIVE OF PROFIT MAXIMIZATION is thought to be consistent with the social objective of welfare maximization (Horstmann & Markusen, 1989) with profit remittances making a positive contribution to the home country's wealth. In this respect, many of MB's investments failed to return a profit, and in some cases, by the time MB disposed of the investments (Embrasca and Bougainville, for example) their cumulative effect on MB was negative with respect to profit contributions. Some of these investments made no contribution to MB's profits during the entire time that MB's capital was tied up in them. Indeed, the negative welfare effects of these investments are higher if the opportunity costs of the capital investment is taken into account. The higher the profits of a multinational company from its consolidated operations, the higher the taxes it will pay in its home country. Given that many of MB's investments were eventually written off after incurring cumulative losses, it can be concluded that they adversely affected MB's overall profit position thereby reducing the amount of tax paid in Canada. MB's unrelated diversification investments also made negative welfare contributions in this respect. The question of profit repatriation (and foreign restrictions on it) was not an important factor in MB's case, since many of MB's investments in countries with these restrictions were sold before they reached any stage of profitability.

Of the investments which did not incur losses (e.g., MacMillan Jardine and KNP), the profits were often used toward further capital expansions related to those investments in the foreign countries in which they were located. MacMillan Jardine, explicitly established as MB's investment vehicle, was motivated by the idea that any cash it generated would be used toward further expansion in Southeast Asia. It can now be argued that through the MacMillan Jardine investment, MB at least did not have to utilize its own funds for expansion, since MacJard generated the investment funds. However, in considering the subsequent performance of these investments, it can be seen that when the investments incurred substantial cost overruns (e.g., Northside/Northpoint), MB was forced to give parental guarantees for loans and this, in turn, had a serious adverse effect on the company's borrowing capacity.

Barriers to trade prevent exports. Therefore, FDI complements exports rather than replacing them, since these export markets would be lost anyway had they not been reopened through FDI (Globerman, 1985). In this respect, MB's FDI made some positive welfare contributions. By establishing a plywood plant at Pine Hill, MacMillan Bloedel was able to establish a foothold in this market. Without this investment MB could not have competed in the U.S. plywood market largely because tariff barriers frequently made exports of plywood uneconomical. Similarly, the investment in KNP (i.e., one of MB's captive market strategies) was instrumental in providing a market for pulp exports from Canada. It should be noted that the captive market strategy is useful only in reducing transaction and market search costs. In a commodity market non-price characteristics play less dominant roles than in markets where products are differentiated. Knowledge of foreign markets gained from a presence in them through FDI may contribute to market development. For example, MB was able to be the first foreign supplier of specialty grade newsprint to Japan, despite tariff and non-tariff barriers to trade, because of its presence in Japan and its previous direct experience with the Japanese market.

Outward FDI contributes to home-country welfare by providing both growth opportunities for home-country suppliers of capital equipment and possible advances in their technological prowess, depending on the extent to which secondary processing activities are undertaken in the home country (Dunning, 1981, p. 326). Although one cannot draw conclusions in this respect based on the FDI activities of one firm, it is interesting to note that

Canada's competitive advantage in the pulp and paper equipment industry lies mainly in the equipment used to produce commodity products. Canada is world competitive in mechanical pulp machinery and capable in chemical pulp machinery. It has only limited capabilities in tissue, and virtually no capabilities at all in paper finishing equipment.[81] Over the last 30 years, Canadian performance in this industry has declined significantly.

Concerns have been raised that FDI leads to the "export" of jobs (Rugman, 1987, p. 44). However, it can be concluded that the Canadian economy has not suffered (direct) negative welfare consequences as a result of jobs being exported by MB. Outside Canada, only the United States and the United Kingdom accounted for large numbers of MB employees (e.g., in 1979, of a total of 24,500 employees, 16,300 were located in B.C., 3,500 in the United States and 1,800 in the United Kingdom). Given that the investments in these countries made important contributions to MB's overall operations, foreign employment in this case can be seen as necessary to strengthen MB's overall competitive position. MB has traditionally made an important contribution to the B.C. economy in terms of employment, but between 1980 and 1986, it reduced its work force by 40 percent.[82] It is interesting to note that in 1991 MB was achieving about the same output as in 1983, with 40 percent fewer workers.[83] Similar losses of employment were experienced by British Columbia firms without FDI; such losses are a natural outgrowth of productivity increases due to technological progress in a highly competitive global market.

With respect to the quality of employment, the move to produce value-added products close to the market while retaining resource-intensive operations at home, may have had adverse affects to the extent that jobs requiring skills were created abroad and not at home. It is not clear, however, that those jobs would have been created at home. Indeed, it is possible that in the absence of market access created by FDI, the levels of resource intensive operations at home may have been reduced and high- paying jobs may have been lost.

The welfare implications with respect to technological competitiveness are mixed. It has been suggested that by engaging in FDI, MNEs have directed their energies away from technology-innovating activities in their home countries, and have improved the international competitiveness of the host country at the expense of firms in the home country (Dunning, 1981). However, in MB's case it appears that outward FDI has also increased R&D at home to serve foreign production facilities. MB, which has little experience in the area of new product management, has now transferred the patents for its most important innovation in decades (*Parallam*) to the joint venture TJM, which is managed by TJI, and in which MB has a minority interest. This was necessary to ensure the product's commercial success in the market with the most potential (the United States). This success has supported continued R&D activity in Canada. Some of TJI's management experience and skills in production processes were transferred to MB's Canadian operations, thus improving their competitiveness. The wisdom of transferring some R&D activities to foreign locations (e.g. the establishment of a research laboratory at Pine Hill) is more open to question. However, this can be a source for reverse transfer of technologies[84] where home operations can benefit from U.S. research skills and expertise.

A final argument against FDI is that it directs capital expenditure away from the home country. Between 1965 and 1975, only half of MB's capital spending went into British Columbia.[85] Following its first loss in 1975, MB redirected its capital toward improving the productivity of its operations in B.C. and the United States. In the late 1970s and throughout the 1980s, MB made a sustained effort to re-affirm its B.C. identity. In recent years, however, the choice has been between the United States and Canada – and MB management has clearly favoured the United States.

> When we make any large investments, we'll put them where we can get the best return. That's not in B.C. and its probably not in Canada.[86] (Memo from Corporate Archives)

If we assume perfect capital markets, MB's FDI need not have any significant effect on its decisions to invest in Canada. Reduced investment in Canada may merely reflect investment saturation in the Canadian forest sector and decline in the marginal returns of investment opportunities (brought about, for example, by resource constraints) or other push factors (e.g., the regulatory environment).

If MB relies on internally generated cash flows, capital budget-constraints arguments can be raised with respect to the effect of FDI on investments in Canada. This case study, however, shows that MB diverted capital to Canada to cope with problems of competitiveness and environmental regulation. Despite corporate announcements to the contrary, the fibre resource in Canada appears to be a core strategic asset to be utilized. When competitiveness in using the resource declined, the company invested to restore competitiveness. However, resource constraints (which inhibit growth prospects domestically) induced the company to invest abroad. Similarly, to ensure growth, market-seeking investments received priority.

Conclusions

A NUMBER OF CONCLUSIONS can be drawn from MB's experience with respect to foreign investment policy by resource-dependent companies. Forest product companies operate in highly cyclical markets. As a result, they tend to invest during boom periods when they have good cash flows. However, in down periods, when faced with severe capital constraints, they lack the resources to continue their commitment to the newly made investments.

When banks refuse to extend credit, investment abroad is made at the expense of domestic investment, competing for internally generated funds. As a last resort, foreign assets are often sold to create a source of liquidity. Without continued commitment many ventures fail. A resource company facing a fluctuating market may therefore tend to treat its non-core foreign assets in much the same way that a portfolio investor treats a portfolio – as MB did. The use of non-liquid assets to make up for cash flow shortfalls, however, is an expensive way to finance operations.

MB's experience also reveals that at least in the case of a resource company, some critical OSAs are location-bound. MB's technical knowledge and expertise in forestry, derived in temperate forests harvesting softwood, was inappropriate for managing tropical forests with hardwood harvests.

MB's market-seeking investments were largely successful, although its experience shows that in a competitive commodity market captive buyers do not guarantee market access. Special relationships with buyers, while not guaranteeing sales, allow a firm both the advantage of better communications (thus permitting improved service) and some reduction in transaction costs. Indeed, having a special relationship with KNP (a demanding customer) allowed MB to improve both its product quality and its competitiveness.

MB's experience also indicates that through joint ventures a company can acquire strategic assets that it cannot possess by itself. Thus, for example, the marketing skills of Trus Joist International complemented MB's technical skills in producing and marketing *Parallam* in the United States.

Perhaps the most important lesson to be learned from MB's experience is that unrelated diversification by a firm is often a costly enterprise. Risk reduction is probably best left to individual and institutional portfolio investors. On the other hand, FDI that is directed to improve efficiency through integration appears to be successful.

Finally, FDI is a strategic tool which allows a resource company to grow by improving access to markets and also to new resource sources. It allows ownership-specific advantages to be utilized and new advantages derived from foreign operations to be created. MB's experience, however, shows that FDI is a risky strategy that can lead to significant losses to both the company and the welfare of the country. A major problem faced by a resource company is the cyclical nature of the market, which often strains the patience and long-term perspective that FDI in the resource sector requires. Perhaps the experience of MB with KNP proves that a long-run commitment may ensure eventual pay-off. Indeed, the ownership of a significant share of KNP offers MB opportunities to capitalize on the strength of its alliance with the largest paper-producing company in the world. A recent announcement by MB's CEO, however, appears to suggest that this strategic opportunity created by FDI for long-term repositioning of the company in global markets has a lower priority than the opportunity to realize capital gains from the sales of the shares.[87]

ENDNOTES

1 Much of the material in this section has been drawn from MacMillan
 Bloedel Corporate Archives, interviews with MB personnel and MB
 Annual Reports.
2 MB produces lumber, panelboards, engineered wood products, kraft pulp,
 newsprint, groundwood printing papers, fine papers, containerboard and
 corrugated containers.
3 In 1951 the firm of Bloedel, Stewart & Welch merged with the H. R.
 MacMillan Export Company, established by Harvey R. MacMillan. In
 1960, MacMillan & Bloedel merged with the Powell River Company Ltd.
 to form MacMillan, Bloedel & Powell River Ltd. which changed its name
 to MacMillan Bloedel Ltd. on May 10, 1966.
4 MB sold 80 percent of its market pulp; 93 percent of its newsprint; 43 percent of its kraft paper and paperboard; 85 percent of its lumber; 23 percent
 of its plywood and 86 percent of its cedar shingles to foreign markets.
5 MacKay, 1982, p. 269.
6 *Financial Post*, January 1, 1966, p. 19.
7 Montague Meyer, the company chairman, was the same person who had
 co-operated with Harvey MacMillan in founding the H. R. MacMillan
 Export Company.
8 *Canadian Forest Industries*, June, 1966, p. 25.
9 MacKay, 1982:281.
10 *MB News*, June, 1969.
11 These ventures included: an 83 percent interest in Walpole Woodworkers
 Inc. of Walpole, Massachusetts, a fencing and garden furniture producer;
 an interest in Energex of San Diego, California, a small company making
 burners to convert waste wood into hot gas energy for sawmills. In
 December 1974, this investment was converted into a 28 percent interest
 in Industrial-America Corp. of Jacksonville, Florida for $4.7 million. A
 subsidiary of Industrial-America developed real estate in Florida (*Wall
 Street Journal*, December 26, 1974, p. 11). MB also acquired interests in
 Dominion Aircraft Corp. Ltd.; Hovair Ltd., which was developing a new
 type of hovercraft; 80 percent in Unidrug Systems; a plastics plant in
 Edmonton; and 50 percent of Montebello Metal Ltd. of Hawkesbury,
 Ontario, which made metal tubes for toothpaste (MacKay,1982:292).
12 MacKay, 1982, p. 293.
13 *Financial Post*, October 2, 1971, p. 13.
14 *Financial Post*, April 10, 1976, p. 26.
15 *Financial Post*, September 13, 1975, p. 11.
16 *Financial Post*, March 5, 1977, p. 11.
17 *Globe and Mail*, January 14, 1976, p. B9.
18 *Globe and Mail*, February 24, 1977, p. B8.
19 *Financial Post*, November 29, 1980, p. 23.

20 *Financial Post*, November 29, 1980, p. 23.
21 *Financial Times*, March 26, 1981, p. 26.
22 *Globe and Mail*, March 12, 1981, p. B1; *Financial Times*, March 12, 1981, p. 29.
23 *Pulp and Paper Factbook*, 1982-83, p. 82.
24 *Pulp and Paper Factbook*, 1982-83, p. 68.
25 *Canadian Business*, July, 1991, p. 45.
26 Ibid.
27 *Financial Post*, January 23, 1982, p. 1.
28 *Globe and Mail*, June 7, 1983, p. B8.
29 *Pulp and Paper International*, 1987, p. 57.
30 *Globe and Mail*, August 1, 1986, p. B3.
31 *Financial Post*, March 27, 1989, p. 25.
32 Price Waterhouse estimates that every one-cent drop in the Canadian dollar against its U.S. counterpart adds $240 million in pre-tax profits to the industry's collective income statements. However it adds that this is "not enough to be material in the long run." *Globe and Mail*, November 3, 1992, p. B8.
33 *Canadian Business*, July, 1991, p. 47.
34 *Financial Post* Daily, July 27, 1992, p. 6.
35 *Pulp and Paper Journal*, April 1990, p. 9.
36 *Canadian Business*, July 1991, p. 47.
37 This includes investments geared towards increasing profits indirectly through cost reductions, new product development, and product/process productivity improvements.
38 Since a problem of serial correlation was present, we have used the Theil & Nagar (1961) transformation of the independent variables. The Durbin-Watson statistic for the transformed model was 1.07.
39 Dunning points out that many of today's ownership advantages of firms are a reflection of yesterday's location advantages of countries; although their origin may be linked to location specific endowments, their use is not so confined.
40 MacKay, 1982, p. 250.
41 *Globe and Mail*, July 28, 1983, p. B7.
42 MacKay, 1982, p. 261.
43 Ibid.
44 Ibid.
45 This was because the original agreement called for both parties to pay the lowest prevailing market price for linerboard (bought from the mill) in the geographic market area served by the mill.
46 Pulp and Paper International, September 1984, p. 38.
47 On April 24, 1967: A$1=C$1.22
48 An inter-company memo points out that the Brazilian government has a highly sophisticated Finance Department. Planned inflation of between 18

percent and 20 percent per year is accepted and the cruzeiro is devalued at regular intervals. In Mexico, no one would want to build newsprint mills because the price level would probably be controlled by the government.

49 IBDF (the Brazilian government agency which granted approvals) had 1,200 projects valued in excess of $100 million, and it was unlikely that this scale of incentives could be sustained for as long as ten years.

50 It had legislated purchasing preference for recycled paper in state agency contracts, and required publishers and commercial printers to buy at least 25 percent of their newsprint with at least 40 percent recycled content, to be increased to 50 percent recycled content by the end of the decade. From the *Globe and Mail*, September 25, 1992, p. B3.

51 Although MB was involved in a recycling project with Fletcher Canada, this joint operation, Newstech, already absorbed all the waste newsprint from the urban Vancouver area. Thus a shortage of waste newsprint for B.C. producers led to MB's decision to "serve the recycled market from the urban forest of recycled papers in California, rather than ship the waste stream back to B.C." From the *Globe and Mail*, September 25, 1992, p. B3.

52 *Globe and Mail*, April 10, 1992, p. B5.

53 *Globe and Mail*, September 25, 1991, p. B3.

54 MB and Haindl spent several million dollars trying to get the project permitted (without having yet succeeded). Even before the decision was made to go ahead with the project, environmental groups were already suing MB.

55 *Financial Post* (daily), September 25, 1992, p. 14.

56 In 1975, it was marketing 450,000 tons of bleached market pulp per year; 100,000 to KNP/Celupal; 200,000 to approximately 20 long-term buyers concentrated in the EEC; 80,000 to Japan; and 70,000 to U.S./Australia.

57 At this time, MB believed that few paper companies would be left by the end of the next 10 years, and that surviving pulp suppliers would have to make long term contracts or equity arrangements with surviving paper makers.

> Basic pulp and paper strategy in the free world revolves around the fact that the company which can control a portion of the pulp market can control a portion of the paper market, this is especially true in the fibre deficit area of the EEC. Outlets for bleached softwood pulp (market and integrated) to 1985 indicated that there will be a growing shortage based on the fact that capacity will have to expand by 5 million tons between 1978 and 1985."

58 The first stage, when MB took United as a partner, was necessary in that it is unlikely that MB would ever have made the move to the U.S. South without a partner.

59 The members of the Export Sales Company were MB, British Columbia Forest Products, and Crown Zellerbach. Membership was divided equally

among the three partners, but the tonnage split was on a 60-20-20 basis with the major share going to MB.

60 The Jardine Matheson Company had been agents for the original H. R. MacMillan Company in the years between the wars.

61 In 1978, the United States passed the *Foreign Corrupt Practices Act*. Since MB filed returns with the SEC in the United States, its concern that certain practices (e.g. bribery) which were common in Southeast Asia (and often resorted to by Jardine Matheson), might lead to legal problems under this *Act*, motivated it to exit the MacJard venture, as well as the other investments made through this partnership in Mentiga Forest Products and P.T. Sangkulirang.

62 *Globe and Mail*, June 24, 1985, p. B15.

63 *MB Journal*, May 1993, p. 4.

64 *MB Journal*, May 1993, p. 4.

65 Strictly speaking, this is not a foreign *direct* investment, as MB does not have management participation. However KNP plays an important strategic role in MB's operations.

66 MacKay, 1982, p. 260.

67 *Financial Post*, October 9, 1965.

68 Under Dutch law at the time, taking a majority position of 50+ percent made a company a subsidiary, but did not in itself provide control. Control was derived from ownership of 75+ percent of shares when a company's articles could be modified so that the 75+ percent shareholder had the right to appoint the Management Board which effectively ran the company.

69 The rationale offered for this sale was that KNP did not fit with MB's core business. The desire for improved liquidity could also be a reason for attempting to sell.

70 Krug had already made a proposal to George Haindl, but things had ended badly when negotiations fell through.

71 Financial Post, July 4, 1981, p. 5

72 *Globe and Mail*, June 26, 1981, p. B3; Financial Post, July 4, 1981, p. 5.

73 Some of the information on this case is from O. Fergacs, *UBC Business Review Journal*, 1993, pp. 25-27.

74 It is interesting to note that this excessively long development period caused a great deal of controversy within the company. From O. Fergacs, *UBC Business Review Journal*, 1993, p. 26.

75 O. Fergacs, *UBC Business Review Journal*, 1993, p. 26.

76 *Vancouver Sun*, June 18, 1991, p. C1.

77 *Globe and Mail*, June 18, 1991, p. B1.

78 It is interesting to note that, typically, diversification can be left to the individual portfolio investor or institutions which can probably do it more efficiently. However, Canadian laws impose constraints on the ability of pension funds and registered retirement funds to diversify abroad. These constraints can be relaxed by investment in a Canadian corporation with a

large share of foreign direct investment. Thus FDI may serve to increase demand for MB shares by institutional investors.

79 At the time, A$1 = C$1.18.

80 MB's borrowing capacity depended on the total amount of assets in excess of 250 percent of funded debt. Because a guarantee constituted funded debt and brought with it no corresponding assets, a $2 million guarantee used up $5 million of assets, whereas a straight loan would only require an asset margin of $3 million, since the proceeds of the loan would appear on the asset side.

81 Canadian Pulp and Paper Equipment Industry, Working Paper, Monitor Company Inc., 1991.

82 *Globe and Mail*, August 1, 1986, p. B3.

83 *Canadian Business*, July 1991, p. 47.

84 See Mansfield & Romeo, 1984.

85 MacKay, 1982, p. 316.

86 *Canadian Business*, July, 1991, p. 44.

87 Roberts (1993) argues that one of the main justifications MB could have used for maintaining its investment in KNP was to help maintain the option of producing printing and writing paper in the future. The fact that MB does not consider KNP to be a core asset suggests that MB will not be participating in the fastest growing segment of the pulp and paper industry.

Appendix: Major Investments, 1963-1991

Date	Investment Name (% ownership)	Location	Investment Type	Fate
1991	Joint venture with Haindl Papier GmbH (50%)	California, U.S.	2	In September 1992, faced with severe capital constraints, MB decided to postpone proceeding with this investment, which is still on hold.
1991	Trus Joist MacMillan (49%)	Idaho, U.S.	2	TJM continues to be a profitable and successful venture.
1975	Delta Industries Inc. (100%)	Mississippi, U.S.	1	Integrated with MB's U.S. operations on acquisition.
1975	Habitant Shops Inc. (100%)	Michigan, U.S.	4	These firms were not profitable and were absorbed by MB's building products group in 1976.
1974	Scotpack Ltd. (100%)	United Kingdom	1	Integrated with MB's U.K. packaging operations on acquisition.
1974	Embrasca (51%)	Santa Catarina, Brazil	2	MB took sole control in 1982. It accumulated losses of over $20 million before disposing of this investment in 1987.
1974	Pagdanan Timber Products (40%)	Philippines	2	This investment was not profitable for MB, and it was sold in 1982.
1973	GEC (40%)	France	3	MB withdrew from this investment in 1979, after having written it off in 1977.
1973	Canadian Gulf Lines (100%)	Texas, U.S.	4	MB disposed of this investment in 1977.
1972	Hankins Container Division (100%)	U.S. (10 locations)	1	These corrugated container plants continue to play an important role in MB's integrated U.S. operations.
1971	P.T. Sangkulirang (25%)	Indonesia }	2	Both these investments were made through the MacJard partnership. Although Mentiga was profitable, MB sold these investments in 1982.
1970	Mentiga Forest Products (30%)	Malaysia }	2	
1970	Northside Gardens Investments Pty. Ltd. (20%)	Australia }	4	These two investments were not profitable. and MB disposed of them in 1978, after incurring significant losses.
1970	Northpoint Properties Pty. Ltd. (20%)	Australia }	4	
1969	MacMillan Rothesay (51%)	New Brunswick, Canada	3	In 1973, MB took sole control of MRL, but soon afterward sold a 35 percent interest to Simex. In June 1981, after buying the 35 percent held by Simex, it sold this investment.

APPENDIX: MAJOR INVESTMENTS, 1963-1991 (CONT'D)

DATE	INVESTMENT NAME (% OWNERSHIP)	LOCATION	INVESTMENT TYPE	FATE
1967	Bougainville Development Corporation (32%)	Papua and New Guinea	2	This investment did not perform well and was written off in 1969.
1966	MacMillan Bloedel United (60%)	Alabama, U.S. }	2	Management of these investments was integrated in 1969.
1966	MB Products Inc. (100%)	Alabama, U.S. }	2	MB took over sole control of the complex in 1970, and it continues to be MB's most important investment in the United States.
1966	MacMillan Bloedel Meyer Ltd. (58%)	United Kingdom	3	In its early years this partnership made an important contribution to MB's U.K. distribution strategy. MB sold its share to its partner in 1988.
1966	MB Pty Ltd. (100%)	Australia	3	MB's Australian distribution subsidiary continues to serve that market.
1966	Celupal (37.5%)	Spain	3	This investment did not do well over the long run and was sold in 1988.
1965	KNP (36%)	The Netherlands	3	This investment continues to play an important role in MB's European strategy.
1964	Hygrade Corrugated Cases Ltd. (100%)	United Kingdom }	1	In October 1967, these two companies were amalgamated. On October 1, 1983, the plants were transferred to a joint venture, MacMillan Smurfit SCA, in which MB held 50 percent. In February 1993 MB sold its share in MacMillan Smurfit.
1964	Cooks Corrugated Cases Ltd. (100%)	United Kingdom }	1	
1963	MacMillan Jardine (51%)	Hong Kong/Japan	3	Prior to its dissolution in 1982, this partnership made an important contribution to MB's Far East marketing effort.

BIBLIOGRAPHY

Blomström, Magnus and A. Kokko. "Home-Country Effects of Foreign Direct Investment: Evidence from Sweden," paper presented at the Conference on Canadian Direct Investment Abroad, November 8-9, 1993, Montreal, Canada.

Booth, D. and I. Vertinsky. "Strategic Positioning in a Turbulent Environment: An Empirical Study of Determinants of Performance in the North American Forest Products Industry." *Forest Science*, 37, 3 (1991): 903-923.

Dunning, J. H. *Explaining International Production*. London: Unwin Hyman Ltd., 1988.

———. *International Production and the MNE*. London: Allen & Unwin, 1981.

Globerman, S. "Direct Investment, Economic Structure and Industrial Competitiveness: The Canadian Case." In *Multinational Enterprises, Economic Structure and Industrial Competitiveness*. Edited by J. H. Dunning. London: John Wiley, 1985.

Globerman, S. and R. Schwindt. "The Organization of Vertically Related Transactions in the Canadian Forest Products Industry." *Journal of Economic Behaviour and Organization*, 7 (1986): 199-212.

Horstmann, I. J. and J. R. Markusen. "Firm Specific Assets and the Gains from Foreign Direct Investment." *Economica*, 56 (1989): 41-8.

MacKay, D. *Empire of Wood: The MacMillan Bloedel Story*. Vancouver: Douglas & McIntyre, 1982.

Mansfield, E. and A. Romeo. "Reverse' Transfers of Technology from Overseas Subsidiaries to American Firms." *IEEE Transactions on Engineering Management*, EM-31, 3 (1984): 122-27.

Roberts, D. "Comments on MacMillan Bloedel, A Case Study of Decisions to Invest in Foreign Locations and Their Welfare Consequences", presented at the Conference on Canadian Direct Investment Abroad, November 8-9, 1993, Montreal, Canada.

Rugman, A. *Outward Bound: Canadian Foreign Direct Investment in the U.S.* Toronto: C.D. Howe Institute & Washington D.C.: National Planning Institute, 1987.

Rugman A. and A. Verbeke. "A Note on the Transactional Solution and the Transaction Cost Theory of Multinational Strategic Management." *Journal of International Business Studies*, 23, 4 (1992): 761-71.

Schwindt, R. "The Existence and Exercise of Corporate Power: A Case Study of MacMillan Bloedel Ltd." Royal Commission on Corporate Concentration, *Study No.15*. Ottawa: The Queen's Printer, 1977.

Theil, H. and A. Nagar. "Testing the Independence of Regression Disturbances." *Journal of the American Statistical Association*, 56 (1961): 793-806.

Fernand Amesse, Louise Séguin-Dulude & Guy Stanley
Centre d'études en administration internationale
École des Hautes Études Commerciales

13

Northern Telecom: A Case Study in the Management of Technology

NORTHERN TELECOM IN THE GLOBAL TELECOMMUNICATIONS MARKET

IN 1991, THE TOP 50 MANUFACTURERS of telecommunications equipment in the world had combined annual sales of US$ 109.8 billion; the top six manufacturers accounted for 54.4 percent of that total. Clearly, the industry is characterized by high market concentration. Table 1 shows that in 1991 Alcatel was comfortably in first place, followed by AT&T and Siemens; Northern Telecom ranked fourth, ahead of NEC and Ericsson.[1]

The telecommunications market is comprised of three broad sectors of approximately equal size: switching, transmission and customer premises equipment. Switching systems, especially central office switches, are distinguished by the greatest market concentration and the highest barriers to penetration (such as the very high cost of research and development). The world's top six producers also dominate the central office switch market with 75 percent of world sales.[2]

TABLE 1

SALES BY WORLD'S LEADING TELECOMMUNICATIONS COMPANIES, 1991 (US$ MILLION)

COMPANY	COUNTRY	SALES (TELECOMMUNICATIONS)	TOTAL SALES
Alcatel	France	14,791	19,532
AT&T	United States	12,274	44,694
Siemens	FRG	9,882	43,994
Northern Telecom	Canada	8,183	8,183
NEC	Japan	7,514	28,883
Ericsson	Sweden	6,878	7,572

Source: "Dossier..." Telecoms Magazine, 1992, p. 38.

Digital technology precipitated a sharp escalation of R&D costs for switching systems. To illustrate, the development cost of a digital central office switch is now between US$ 600 million and $1.2 billion; this range is approximately 100 times higher than the cost of developing an electromechanical switch.[3] Since only very large manufacturers can afford to make such sizable investments, market concentration has increased even further in recent years.

> The modern digital central office switch is the locomotive of the information age. There were 26 world-class telecommunications equipment makers when the first digital central office switching systems came into service in the late 1970s. By 1984, the number had dropped to 18. Peter Huber, author of the Justice Department's 1987 Huber Report, believes there will be about six in the next decade or so. And by the turn of the century, according to a privately circulated report by Mitsubishi, there may be only three companies, none of them American, with the size and strength to stay in the business: Northern Telecom, Siemens and NEC. (Grigsby, 1989, p. 34)

As Table 2 indicates, the "big six" make substantial R&D investments in each of the product categories. Such huge R&D investments support a global approach to new equipment design and a domestic approach based on product adaptation and differentiation. As C. A. Bartlett (1986) points out, central office switch manufacturers must not only contend with the growing pace and complexity of world-wide technological change, they must also meet the high costs of adapting their products to meet different national regulations and standards and specific customer needs.[4]

Faced with development costs that a domestic market is less and less able to sustain, the product adaptation costs and constraints dictated by domestic

TABLE 2

R&D EXPENDITURES BY PRODUCT CATEGORY AND AS A PERCENTAGE OF SALES BY SEGMENT, IN US$ MILLION

COMPANY	CENTRAL OFFICE		TRANSMISSION		CUSTOMER PREMISES EQUIPMENT	
	$	%	$	%	$	%
Alcatel	350	12	154	8	228	9
AT&T	227	6	286	9	1,133	11
Siemens	339	16	126	7	562	9
Northern Telecom	377	13	203	20	131	10
NEC	209	14	203	10	183	8
Ericsson	404	18	52	4	57	10

Source: NGL Consultants Ltd., 1991, p. 35.

standards, regulation, and the purchasing policies of the major common carriers, the leading manufacturers have had to target regional markets. Currently, there are three large regions where a few suppliers enjoy market dominance: for all practical purposes the North American market is shared by AT&T and Northern Telecom; the European market is served by Alcatel, Siemens and Ericsson; and the Japanese market is supplied primarily by the big four of the NTT Family – NEC, Hitachi, Fujitsu and Oki Electric. The major manufacturers' markets, which were originally domestic, have become regional and are gradually becoming global as these producers seek to expand into the three large regions of the triad (Ohmae, 1985).

Northern Telecom's experience exemplifies this model of development, particularly as its small domestic market compelled it to play by the rules of international competition. As Dunning (1991 and 1993b) has shown, multi-national corporations based in small countries tend to have decentralized manufacturing and R&D, since the scale of their foreign operations often surpasses their domestic operations.

In the section that follows we address the questions: How did Northern Telecom become a major industry player? Why and how was the international-ization of its R&D, manufacturing and markets accomplished? Finally, what has been the impact of Northern Telecom's internationalization on the Canadian economy and, more specifically, what are the benefits to Canada of foreign direct investment by Northern? We begin with some general comments based on our analysis of the Northern Telecom case and draw a number of general conclusions.

At the outset, Northern Telecom needed a solid strategy of market penetration for the entire North American market for its central office switches and private branch exchanges (PBXs). In this connection, its success in the U.S. marketplace has stemmed from its decision to decentralize its manufacturing and R&D in order to establish close relationships with major U.S. customers. Northern was successful in creating an interactive network by effectively integrating its manufacturing, engineering, product adaptation, financing and marketing operations. Decentralizing R&D to the United States was essential for Northern Telecom. Without decentralization Northern Telecom would have been unable to adapt its products to specific U.S. market conditions and customer needs and thereby achieve high sales in the vast U.S. market. In this instance, foreign sales served to finance *all* of Northern Telecom's R&D activities and to support its research programs at the central laboratory in Ottawa. As a consequence, the decentralization of R&D did not result in a scaling-down of R&D carried out in Canada. On the contrary, the positive spin-offs of decentralization had a stimulating effect on Canadian R&D programs.

Two other general conclusions can be drawn from analysis of Northern Telecom's development. Corporations that start out in small countries can benefit from continental competition, even though they do not face any real domestic rivals, provided, of course, that they succeed in establishing themselves in the larger and more competitive regional market. The Free Trade Agreement (FTA) will allow Canadian corporations to acquire North American competitive advantage, partly through the specialization and decentralization of strategic operations, particularly in high-tech fields. Northern Telecom provides an example of what can be achieved by following this path of expansion and excellence.

The impact of decentralized, specialized and coordinated R&D on the Canadian economy depends increasingly on the growth and dynamism of the Canadian telecommunications market and its ability to innovate or to use innovations profitably. In terms of public policy, the Northern Telecom case suggests above all else that the Canadian market is not yet competitive enough to produce world-class companies, although Canada can ready them for integration into the "North American diamond". Telecommunications regulation limits the ability of would-be competitors to offer new services to meet customer needs.

The Northern Telecom case underlines the reasons corporations make foreign investments. Northern's primary objective was to gain foreign market access for its products. In this connection, the company's decision to establish R&D facilities in foreign countries was *not* to support manufacturing in those countries. Initially, Northern Telecom's foreign investments were made to acquire knowledge of local markets so it could adapt its products accordingly. Although the R&D laboratories in the United States continue to adapt products, their mission has broadened since they were first established. Today their efforts are increasingly directed at developing new knowledge and new products.

FROM THE BEGINNINGS TO THE 1970S: DEVELOPING AN ORGANIZATION

THE HISTORY OF NORTHERN TELECOM can be traced back to 1882 when it was created by the merger of the Northern Electric and Manufacturing Co. and the Imperial Wire and Cable Co. It was incorporated in 1914 under the name Northern Electric Limited. At that time, Bell Canada held a 50 percent stake in the company, the Western Electric Company (an AT&T subsidiary) held 44 percent, and other shareholders held the remaining 6 percent.[5] On January 24, 1956, AT&T and the Federal Communications Commission (FCC) signed a consent decree barring AT&T from giving third parties exclusive access to patented technology. Western Electric's stake in Northern Electric therefore became much less attractive and so, in 1962, Bell Canada bought back Western Electric's share and in 1964 it became the sole owner of Northern Electric. Today Bell Canada Enterprises (BCE) holds 52.4 percent of Northern Telecom (Northern Telecom Limited, 1993, p. 6).

From its inception, Northern Electric relied on Western Electric for technological and product-development support. Northern Electric's role consisted essentially in adapting existing equipment to specific Canadian market requirements, especially those related to small urban centres. Northern Electric's business strategy was to meet the needs of its parent company, Bell Canada, within the Canadian market alone.

The 1956 change in ownership did not alter the special relationship between Northern Electric and Western Electric. Northern Electric's access to technology developed by Western Electric was guaranteed until 1970 by a service agreement, but the contract's limitations gradually led Northern Electric to start actively developing its own technological expertise. During the 1960s, Northern Electric continued to manufacture and adapt products designed by Bell Laboratories and Western Electric, but it became increasingly aware of the costs and inefficiencies of confining operations to a small market. The licensing agreements with Western Electric, which gave Northern Electric access to products designed by Bell Laboratories, severely limited its export opportunities to the United States.[6]

Northern Electric's R&D activities began on a very modest scale in 1958, with 42 employees divided between two small units in Montreal and Belleville. In 1960, however, Northern Electric decided to create a central research laboratory; its first priority was to acquire technological expertise for the development of a communications system to meet specific Canadian switching and transmission needs. That laboratory was established in Ottawa.[7]

Two product development projects confirmed Northern Electric's technological commitment in the 1960s and led to the creation of the Bell-Northern Research Limited (BNR) laboratories in their present form. In 1961, Bell Canada commissioned Northern Electric to develop a low-capacity switch. This development effort produced the SA-1, of which over 1,000 units would be sold in Canada and the United States.

In 1964, Northern Electric launched an ambitious project with a budget of over C$ 30 million and a research staff of over 120 people. This project led to the SP-1, a stored-program-controlled switching system for small urban centres, which was brought to market in 1971. In many respects, the SP-1 represents a turning point in the evolution of Northern Electric[8] because it marks the point at which electronics entered the world of telecommunications. The SP-1 was a semi-electronic switch combining electro-mechanical switch technology with computer-controlled switching. This integration of computers and electromechanical switching opened the way to space division switching. Electronics would henceforth increase the speed and complexity of switching technology. This new generation of switches constituted a transitional technology between the electromechanical technology of the previous 50 years and the fully digital technology, which became technically feasible in the 1970s. With this generation of switches, however, development costs increased substantially – to ten times what they had been for the preceding generation.[9]

In 1974, 25 percent of all SP-1 sales were to independent telephone companies in the United States, virtually all of which became major clients for Northern Electric. By 1975, all major Canadian telephone companies had adopted the SP-1. At that point, Northern Electric also controlled 90 percent of the Canadian market for space division switches.

The combined commitments of Northern Electric and Bell Canada to technological development in telecommunications led to the creation, on January 1, 1971, of Bell-Northern Research Limited (BNR). Initially BNR was 49 percent owned by Northern Electric and 51 percent by Bell Canada.[10] BNR's mandate was to pursue the efforts begun in the 1960s and to conduct an intensive ongoing R&D program in all sectors of telecommunications.

By the late 1960s Northern Electric had succeeded, to a large extent, in freeing itself from Western Electric's technological tutelage and in laying the bases for developing its own technologic potential. It had also adapted to the technological changes which led to the use of electronics in telecommunications products. Finally, it had begun to make inroads into the U.S. market by penetrating the only niche not yet occupied by competitors at that time – small switching systems designed for independent telephone companies. Nevertheless, Northern Electric remained an essentially Canadian company: its R&D and manufacturing operations were still undertaken entirely in Canada and Canada was still its main market.

DIGITAL SWITCHING PROPELS NORTHERN TELECOM INTO THE INTERNATIONAL MARKETPLACE[11]

FOLLOWING A REVIEW of their future prospects in world telecommunications, Bell Canada, Northern Telecom and BNR decided in 1973 to launch an ambitious R&D program of around C$ 140 million. As a result, Northern Telecom was able to offer, five years later, a complete line of fully digital switches, known as the Digital Multiplex System (DMS). In January 1976 Northern Telecom officially announced the advent of digital switching. (It had just launched the SL-1, the first digital PBX switch, in the business market a month earlier.) In October 1977 Northern Telecom brought the DMS-10, the first digital switch for public networks, into service. The DMS-10, a low-capacity switch for central offices serving rural areas, could handle 10,000 telephone lines. By 1979, Northern Telecom was able to offer a full line of digital switches.[12]

In terms of Ronstadt's (1977) model of gradual R&D centre evolution, Northern Telecom was little more than a technology transfer unit until 1958, given its U.S. Western Electric connection. Over the next 15 years, however, Northern Telecom evolved with increasing rapidity through successive stages of the technological development – beginning with local products, working through their design and improvement into world class products, and eventually becoming itself a developer of new technologies. These developments provide the key to why Northern Telecom became a world leader in telecommunications technology and a major player in North America: through its strategy of technological development, Northern Telecom acquired expertise in switching systems, which it was able to exploit through its organizational development and its sustained marketing efforts.

In the late 1960s, most of the leading telecommunications equipment manufacturers knew that electronics would have a major impact on new product development, particularly in the switching systems sector. Developments in micro-electronics and the introduction of very high-density circuits would make fully electronic switching technically feasible. However, this trend in technological development also entailed a number of uncertainties, the first of which was market-related. In the early 1970s, most manufacturers were either marketing space division switching systems or trying to catch up with the competition by developing systems of their own. Digital switching appeared too remote a technology to warrant immediate investment in its development and, in fact, many companies expected the shift to digital switching to take place in the mid rather than in the early 1980s. Additional uncertainties lay in the technical and financial challenges posed by the development of digital switching systems. The innovations involved were considerable, extremely costly and time-consuming. Any error could prove fatal to a company's financial health.

Of all the companies interested in this technology, only two, Northern Telecom and CIT-Alcatel, committed themselves fully to its development; they became its pioneers. AT&T and Ericsson were unable to bring their versions to market until 1992 and ITT reached that stage only in 1985, after overcoming a number of obstacles caused by poor R&D management and astronomical costs.[13]

Having played a pioneering role, Bell Canada, Northern Telecom and BNR could offer potential customers significant savings through the use of digital technology:

> Substantial trunking economies could be achieved through the introduction of digital switching in the toll/tandem applications. The relative reduction of capital expenditures in the interval 1982 to 1992 for Montreal was $36.5 million. Generalized over all of the Bell Canada metropolitan areas, the total could exceed $100 million. ("The BNR Story," p. 10)

According to some studies, where analog switching cost the customer $100, space division switching cost $84.20 and digital switching cost $62 (calculated on a base of 100).[14] It was therefore clear that digital switching would offer prospective customers significant savings, provided they were willing to invest in new and rapidly evolving equipment. Clearly, this called for a considerable marketing effort.

To minimize the technical risks and market- and cost-related uncertainties, Northern Telecom decided to apply digital technology first to small switching systems and then to undertake the development of a line of high-capacity switches. The first switch produced – the SL-1 – was launched for the business market in 1975. The project was successful in terms of the management of the technical risks associated with digitalization, and it yielded a new product which had the potential to give Northern Telecom access to a large segment of the North American market that was still open to competition – the PBX market. Risks related to innovation were also controlled during the subsequent development of small central office switches: the product was adapted to the needs of independent telephone companies serving mostly rural areas and small urban centres, the only segment of the public network market that was still genuinely competitive. It was not until 1984, when AT&T was required to divest itself of local telephone companies, that the U.S. public network market became truly accessible to Northern Telecom.

Northern Telecom's digital technology was decisive in the company's penetration of the U.S. market. By 1983, Northern Telecom controlled 19 percent of the U.S. PBX market, ranking just behind AT&T, which held 23 percent of the market.[15] In the public network market the shift to digital technology was more hesitant, with the result that the market grew more slowly. (Unitl 1983-1984, digital switches represented only 20 percent to 30 percent of total switch sales.)

On January 1, 1984, following anti-trust proceedings which had lasted for over a decade, AT&T's virtual monopoly was finally dismantled; AT&T had to divest itself of 22 local telephone companies. These were subsequently reorganized as seven 'Regional Bell Operating Companies' (RBOCs). Although these companies were henceforth free to choose their equipment suppliers, they were not permitted to manufacture their own equipment. Excluded also from providing new information services, they were to provide local and regional telephone service; AT&T retained the right to manufacture and sell equipment and to carry out R&D. AT&T's role was to serve the long distance market, which became fully competitive, and provide new information services. AT&T also recovered the right to operate internationally.[16] All of these developments prompted a rush to digitalization in a distinctly more accessible U.S. market.

This opening-up of the U.S. market was a boon to Northern Telecom in a number of ways. First, the creation of the seven RBOCs opened a market representing 78 percent of the 127 million main telephone lines in the United States. Of course Northern Telecom could not take this market for granted, but the RBOCs, who were now free to choose their suppliers, could choose between AT&T and Northern Telecom. AT&T was disinclined to market to independent customers aggressively and so its efforts were not impressive.

Second, when the long distance market was opened up in 1978, the companies that owned their own long distance plant (such as MCI, which owned a micro-wave transmission network) were able to expand and many other companies wanted to enter the market. Few were eager to buy equipment from Western Electric, a subsidiary of their long-distance rival, AT&T.

> Before divestiture, Bell Companies continued to order old generation electronic systems from AT&T because AT&T had not developed a Digital Class 5 switch. After divestiture, RHCs' [RBOCs'] dependence on AT&T significantly decreased from 92 percent of total equipment purchases in 1982 to 57.6 percent in 1986. (Zanfei, 1992, p. 235)

The RBOCs, which, for the most part, had not moved to digital switching, had to undertake the change quickly after AT&T was dismantled. By 1989, the digitalization of their networks had reached 36.9 percent. The RBOCs thus became major clients of Northern Telecom. "Seven regional holding companies, divested by American Telephone and Telegraph Company in January 1984, continue to be the company's largest U.S. customer category."[17]

Prior to 1977, Northern Telecom's international sales did not even appear as such in the company's financial statements. In 1977 they represented 23 percent of sales; in 1978 this increased to 41 percent. Subsequently, this figure fluctuated between 47 percent and 62 percent until 1983. In 1987, international sales reached 67 percent (Northern Telecom Limited, 1977 to 1983). As non-North American sales account for no more than 6 percent of Northern's total sales, the company achieved internationalization essentially by penetrating the U.S. market.

Northern Telecom grew from a marginal supplier to the U.S. market in the mid-1970s to become a major player currently holding a 40 percent market share in central office switches in the United States.[18] Its role as a technological pioneer in digital switching equipment undoubtedly contributed to the company's North American expansion. In turn, this continent-wide expansion made Northern's sustained technological thrust possible. The company's R&D spending rose from US $74 million in 1977 to $325 million in 1983. If foreign sales were excluded, R&D spending would have risen from 7.2 percent to 31.6 percent; as a proportion of total sales, however, they did not exceed 12 percent, which is comparable to the industry standard.

McFetridge (1993) posits a substitution effect and a scale effect stemming from innovation efforts by multinational firms in foreign countries. The North America-wide expansion of Northern Telecom's manufacturing and R&D was accompanied by phenomenal growth in overall sales and total R&D spending. Clearly, in this instance, the scale effect was decisive in driving the company's technological innovation. The North American expansion not only boosted Northern Telecom's sales, it also precipitated major changes in the organization of the company's manufacturing and R&D operations.

In 1971, Northern Telecom Inc. was incorporated in the United States. This was the parent company's first wholly-owned subsidiary outside Canada. The subsidiary's mandate was to produce and market Northern Telecom equipment in the United States. Numerous acquisitions followed in subsequent years – Northeast Electronics Corp. in 1973, Cook Electric Co. and Telecommunications Systems of America Inc. in 1976, Danray Inc., Sycor Inc., Data 100 Corp. and Eastern Data Industries Inc. in 1978.[19] In 1981, the company amalgamated all its manufacturing, marketing and service operations under Northern Telecom Inc. Table 3 sets out Northern Telecom investments for the period from 1969 to 1993, including acquisitions, mergers, acquisitions of interest in other companies, and investment in new companies. The table is incomplete, however, in that it does not include plant expansions and the opening of new plants within existing companies. Still, it is a good indication of the scope of Northern Telecom's internationalization during this period. In 1991, Northern Telecom Inc. had 20,000 employees, US$ 3 billion in sales and a net worth of US$ 1 billion; its operations were, and are still concentrated in North Carolina and Texas.[20]

In order to grow in the U.S. market, Northern Telecom not only needed to be able to serve customers from its plants, financing and leasing divisions and service units, it also had to collaborate closely with its main customers to adapt products and develop new ones. The North American expansion of business operations was therefore accompanied by a continental expansion of R&D, which now extends beyond North America. In 1992, Bell-Northern Research (BNR) had eight laboratories in four countries (Canada, the United States, the United Kingdom and Japan). In addition to these, Northern Telecom had R&D units within 24 facilities around the world, including Australia, France, the United States and Canada.[21] In all, approximately 8,000 people are employed in the BNR laboratory network, which comprises one central and seven regional labs[22] The central lab, built in Ottawa in 1971, remains the heart of BNR's technological operations, with close to 4,500 employees. This laboratory has overall responsibility for all research in the entire range of technologies and products of current and future interest within the framework of Northern Telecom's global strategy. It also plays a central role in transferring and developing new technologies and products to the seven regional labs. In addition, it often works with regional labs when direct collaboration can accelerate the development and adaptation of products for Northern Telecom customers.

All of BNR's regional laboratories were established primarily to adapt Northern Telecom products to local market conditions and specific customer needs. Each is located near a large manufacturing or marketing unit and employees work closely with major customers of the product lines made by the manufacturing unit. Cantwell's description of the decentralization of R&D fits the Northern Telecom case:

> A special case of this is the instance of user-producer interaction, by which the user of a technological input such as a piece of machinery feeds back the results of its learning-by-using experience to the producer to encourage

appropriate adaptation and the provision of supporting systems. The producers of such technological inputs may be compelled to disperse their research and production base in order to service their international customers. (Cantwell, 1991, p. 67)

BNR's first regional lab was set up in Montreal in 1974 for the specific purpose of responding to the particular needs of Bell Canada, who was then Northern Telecom's main client and who accounted for almost 50 percent of Northern's sales at the time. This laboratory also maintains close relations with Montreal's university community. The second and third regional laboratories were established in the United States. In 1982, BNR opened a lab in North Carolina's Research Triangle Park, located near a switch manufacturing facility, it maintains close relationships with regional telephone companies. (RBOCs). This laboratory currently employs 1,100 people – a reflection of the importance of the growing central office switch market to Northern Telecom in the 1980s.

In 1983, BNR opened another laboratory in Richardson, Texas. It, too, is located close to an electronic switching equipment plant and works closely with MCI and Sprint, both of whom are long distance interconnection service providers. This laboratory also expanded significantly during the 1980s and now employs approximately 750 people.

The latest BNR lab in the United States was opened in 1987 in Atlanta. It is located near a transmission product manufacturing plant. This laboratory collaborates closely with the central lab in Ottawa on the design and development of a complete family of fiber-based access, transport and switching products. Northern Telecom also opened the FiberWorld conference centre close to this laboratory to promote and demonstrate its new family of products. At present, the lab has a staff of 200. Northern Telecom announced its fiber-based line only in October 1989 and produced the first prototypes in 1990, which have been in telco trials and field testing since that time. The full product line became available and entered full production in 1992, but real market response may not be felt before 1995. In the circumstances, this lab does not yet have customers with whom it can collaborate.

In summary, Northern Telecom's expansion into the North American market was supported by stepped-up R&D efforts in the U.S. to ensure continuous product adaptation to specific customer needs. In 1992, more than 2,000 of 8,000 BNR lab employees worked at research facilities located in the United States.

Following the example of the vast majority of multinational firms,[23] Northern Telecom established R&D operations in the United States in order to improve and adjust its products and respond to the needs of its U.S. customers. Since the R&D laboratories in the U.S. were established, both their staffs and missions have expanded. Although they continue to adapt products, they are increasingly involved in developing new knowledge and new products.

TABLE 3

INVESTMENT ACTIVITIES OF NORTHERN TELECOM, 1967 TO 1993

DATE	TYPE OF INVESTMENT	COMPANY NAME	COUNTRY OF OWNERSHIP	FINANCIAL DETAILS	DESCRIPTION	INDUSTRY/ ACTIVITY
March 1993	Acquisition	NETAS-Northern Electric Telekomunikasyon A.S.	Turkey	51%	Increased interest from 31% to 51%	
1993	Acquisition	Lagardère Groupe S.C.A.	France			
January 1993	Partnership	Bell Atlantic Meridian Systems	U.S.	C$ 45 M	Partnership with Bell Atlantic Corp.	Markets, sales and service of in communications systems mid-Atlantic region
July 1992	Acquisition of Minority	Matra S.A.	France	20% C$ 140 M		Supplier of telecommunications equipment
April 1992	Acquisition	Novatel	Alberta	C$ 38 M		Telecommunications
March 1992	Joint Venture	Northern Telecom de Espana	Spain	50%	Joint venture with Agroman Inversiones S.A. (37.5%) and Radiotronica S.A. (12.5%)	
February 1992	Joint Venture	MOTOROLA-NORTEL Communications Co.	U.S.		Joint venture with Motorola Inc.	Sales and services cellular telephone networks in Canada, the Caribbean, Central and South America, Mexico and the U.S.
February 1992	Joint Venture	Northern Telecom Elwro	Poland		Joint venture with Elwro of Poland	Manufactures and supplies public switching equipment
1991	Divestiture	STC's subsidiary: International Computers Ltd. STC's Distributor Division STC's Land Cable Products Division STC's Electronics Division	U.K.	US$ 335 M		
February 1991	Greenfield	Northern Telecom Asia/Pacific	Asia			Marketing, sales and service organizations

TABLE 3 (CONT'D)

DATE	TYPE OF INVESTMENT	COMPANY NAME	COUNTRY OF OWNERSHIP	FINANCIAL DETAILS	DESCRIPTION	INDUSTRY/ACTIVITY
February 1991	Greenfield	Northern Telecom Europe	Europe			Marketing, sales and service organizations
November 1990	Acquisition	STC PLC	U.K.	US$2,560M	Purchase of all outstanding shares	
1989	Joint Venture	Microtel (subsidiary of B.C. Tel.)	Canada	51%	Joint venture with B.C. Tel to acquire Microtel	Central office switching business
1989	Acquisition	AWA-Nortel PTY	U.K.	40%	Purchase of AWA Ltd.'s interest in joint venture	
1988	Divestiture	Northern Telecom PLC	U.K.	C $70 M	Sold to STC PLC	Telecommunications and data systems operations
1987	Greenfield	NT Meridean S.A.	France			Manufacturing and R&D facility
October 1987	Acquisition	STC PLC	U.K.	24% US $728 M	Increased interest to 27.5 %	
1986	Greenfield	Northern Telecom Europe Ltd.	Europe			Manage operations in Europe, Near East and Africa
July 1985	Greenfield	Northern Telecom Pacific	Asia		Manage operations in Pacific region	
1983	Greenfield	U.K. subsidiary of Bell-Northern Research	U.K.			Laboratory
1983	Merger	Northern Telecom PLC	U.K.		Consolidated U.K. telecommunications and data systems operations	
1983	Greenfield	Northern Telecom Japan Inc.	Japan		Subsidiary	
February 1981	Divestiture	Intersil Inc.	U.S.	21.9% C $55 M		
January 1981	Merger	Northern Telecom, Inc.	U.S.		Merged Northern Telecom Industries and Northern Telecom Systems Corporation	

TABLE 3 (CONT'D)
INVESTMENT ACTIVITIES OF NORTHERN TELECOM, 1967 TO 1993

DATE	TYPE OF INVESTMENT	COMPANY NAME	COUNTRY OF OWNERSHIP	FINANCIAL DETAILS	DESCRIPTION	INDUSTRY/ACTIVITY
1981	Merger	B-N Software Research Inc.	Canada		Merged into Bell-Northern Research Inc.	
1981	Partial Divestiture	NETAS-Northern Electric Telekomurthern Telecom International Inc.				
November 1980	Joint Venture	Telko S.A.	Mexico		Joint venture with Alfa Industries of Monterrey	
1979	Divestiture	Zentronics Ltd.			Sold to Westburne International Industries Ltd.	
1979	Divestiture	Nedco Ltd.	Canada		Sold to Westburne International Industries Ltd.	
November 1978	Acquisition	Eastern Data Industries/Spectron Inc.	U.S.	100% C $21 M	Purchase of all outstanding shares	
1978	Acquisition/ Merger	DATA 100 Corporation	U.S.	100% C $164 M	Increased interest	
May 1978	Acquisition	Sycor Inc.	U.S.			
1978	Acquisition	Danray Inc.	U.S.	26%	Acquisition via Northern Telecom Inc.	Manufacturer of switching equipment
1977	Acquisition	DATA 100 Corporation	U.S.			Manufacturer of computer terminals
1977	Acquisition	Intersil Inc.	U.S.	24%	Acquisition via Northern Telecom Inc.	Semiconductor manufacturer
1977	Greenfield	Northern Telecom International Ltd.				Manages manufacturing and marketing activities outside North America
1976	Acquisition	Telecommunication Systems of America Inc.	U.S.			
December 1976	Acquisition	Cook Electric Company	U.S.			
October 1976	Greenfield	B-N Software Research Inc.	Canada	51%	Jointly owned with Bell Canada 49%	
1976	Greenfield	Northern Telecom Canada Ltd.	Canada			Manages Canadian manufacturing and marketing operations of parent company
1976	Acquisition	Bell Northern Research Ltd.	Canada	21%	Increased interest from 49% to 70%	

TABLE 3 (CONT'D)

DATE	TYPE OF INVESTMENT	COMPANY NAME	COUNTRY OF OWNERSHIP	FINANCIAL DETAILS	DESCRIPTION	INDUSTRY/ ACTIVITY
1975	Acquisition	Microsystems International Limited	Canada		Acquisition of all outstanding shares	
1974	Greenfield		The Netherlands		International subsidiaries	
1974	Greenfield		The Netherlands		International subsidiaries	
1974	Greenfield		Hong Kong		International subsidiaries	
1974	Acquisition	AVM Florida Inc.	U.S.			
1973	Acquisition	Zenith Electric Supply Ltd	Canada/Ontario		Acquired controlling interest via Nedco Ltd.	
1973	Acquisition	Northeast Electronics Corporation	U.S.		Acquisition via Northern Telecom Inc.	Manufactures power and test equipment
1973	Greenfield	Northern Electric (Ireland) Inc. (now Northern Telecom (Ireland) Ltd)	Ireland			Manufactures and distributes telephone sets and electrical equipment in Europe
1972	Greenfield	Nevron Industries Company Ltd.	Canada		Company later dissolved in 1980	Provides small companies with venture capital, technical assistance and marketing
1972	Greenfield	Nedco Limited	Canada		Wholly owned subsidiary	Distributes industrial, electric and electronic equipment in Canada
1971	Greenfield	Northern Telecom Inc.	U.S.		Wholly owned subsidiary	Manufacturing and distribution
1969	Greenfield	Bell Northern Research Ltd.	Canada	49%	With Bell Canada	R&D in telecommunications
1969	Greenfield	Microsystems International Limited	Canada		Wholly owned subsidiary	
1967	Greenfield	NETAS-Northern Electric Telekomunikasyon A.S.	Turkey		Jointly owned with the Post, Telegraph & Telephone Administration of the Republic of Turkey	Manufacturing and distribution

Source: Disclosure Inc. and the Financial Post Datagroup. Prepared by Marc Legault, Strategic Investment Analysis, Industry Canada.

Prior to 1991, BNR had only one regional laboratory outside North America – the Maidenhead lab set up in Great Britain in 1984 – established for essentially the same reasons that motivated Northern Telecom to set up labs in the United States. In 1983, Northern Telecom established a subsidiary in Great Britain (Northern Telecom PLC) to consolidate its European marketing, manufacturing and R&D operations. At the time, the British government was selling off 51 percent of British Telecom and deregulating the industry. In the first phase of deregulation, Mercury Communications (a subsidiary of Cable & Wireless) was allowed to compete with British Telecom, protected by a seven-year guaranteed duopoly.[24] The BNR laboratory was created primarily to work on the development of a fully digitalized network for Mercury Communications. This task was accomplished with the collaboration of the central laboratory in Ottawa and the regional lab in Richardson, Texas. Today, the Maidenhead laboratory also adapts Northern Telecom products to the specific needs and requirements of European customers. In 1992, it employed 250 people.

In 1991, Northern Telecom gave a clear signal of its intention to pursue a global strategy by setting up two regional laboratories outside North America. On March 5, 1991, Northern Telecom completed its purchase of STC PLC, in which it had acquired a 27.5 percent share in 1987. This major acquisition in the United Kingdom included a long-established R&D laboratory with a staff of 800 located in Harlow, which had once been ITT's largest European lab. As STC was one of British Telecom's chief suppliers, this new regional BNR lab was clearly intended to maintain and strengthen ties with British Telecom. At the time of its acquisition by Northern Telecom, the laboratory specialized in optical and optoelectronic transmission, wireless telephony and undersea communications. However, in 1993 Northern Telecom sold a large part of the STC facilities, including the Harlow laboratory, to Alcatel, probably because of Northern's poor financial results in 1992.

In November 1991, Northern Telecom announced plans to establish a BNR laboratory in Japan. The small team of 15 researchers and technicians already working there were to be moved into a research laboratory which was expected to have approximately 200 employees by 1995.[25] Northern Telecom's 1991 *Annual Report* outlined the functions of this newcomer to the BNR network as follows:

> The new BNR laboratory will develop enhanced features for switching systems in support of the Japanese and Asia/Pacific market. The initiative will help support the growing base of business in the region, which in Japan alone includes over 300 DMS-10 switches in the Nippon Telegraph and Telephone (NTT) network, as well as an eight-node network based on DMS SuperNode switches sold this year to INTEC, a new telecommunications services provider. Northern Telecom is already the sole switching equipment supplier to International Digital Communications (IDC) in Japan. (Northern Telecom Limited, 1991, p. 9)

The establishment of this laboratory[26] was an indication of Northern Telecom's plan to develop its markets in Asia – primarily in Japan, Australia and China – where it now has only modest sales totalling approximately C$ 400 million. With Japanese sales of C$ 200 million, Northern Telecom has become the chief foreign supplier in that market.[27]

A contract with NTT negotiated in 1986 accounts for two-thirds of Northern Telecom's Japanese sales. NTT's first large contract with a foreign supplier, it provided for the delivery (between 1986 and 1992) of DMS-10 switches manufactured in the United States. The purchase of these very low-capacity switches does not appear to have threatened the four Japanese suppliers with close ties to NTT. The remaining third of Northern's sales in Japan are to IDC and INTEC, two of the more than one thousand new companies that have established themselves in the Japanese market since deregulation in 1985.[28] Its laboratory in Japan gives Northern Telecom a presence throughout the triad countries. Not only will the laboratory serve to adapt Northern's products to the needs of Asian customers, it could also prove useful in acquiring technical expertise and assessing the technology of Japanese competitors. According to Dunning (1993b, p. 318), this is one of the motives influencing multinational firms to establish R&D laboratories abroad, especially in triad countries.

In recent years, therefore, BNR's R&D network has expanded well beyond North America and now comprises laboratories elsewhere in the world, which can support Northern Telecom's expansion into the European and Asian markets.

BNR has always intended its regional labs to work primarily on adapting products to specific market conditions and customer needs. However, as these laboratories acquire experience and begin to specialize, they tend to become centres of excellence for specific technologies. In addition to their role in product adaptation, they contribute to product development for all of Northern Telecom's markets. The changing mission of Northern's regional R&D facilities is consistent with the model proposed by Ronstadt (1977). It also supports Dunning's observation (1993b, p. 308) that specialized networked labs are the ones with the highest growth in industrialized countries in recent years. This trend stems from the impact of economies of scale on research centres of excellence (Cantwell, 1991). The establishment of R&D operations in foreign countries by multinational firms also results from the emergence of supply-side factors alongside market support influences (Pearce, 1992, p. 94).

In the course of performing both product adaptation and new product development functions effectively, a network grows increasingly complex and must develop knowledge transfer and co-ordination mechanisms. At BNR, these include cooperative projects, employee mobility, and a funding formula for R&D projects, all of which serve to maintain the linkage between R&D and market needs. Co-operative projects are, of course, quite common.

Moreover, when a new lab is established, personnel are often transferred in order to promote the transfer of expertise and the germination of new ideas.

> Fully two-thirds of the BNR Maidenhead staff have travelled to BNR's labs in North America, and nearly 200 BNR employees from other labs have come to Maidenhead to gain special knowledge about European and global markets. This important two-way cross-pollination of knowledge and ideas is vital in helping BNR and Northern Telecom develop truly global products and services. ("The BNR Story," p. 32)

BNR deals deftly with the technology-driven/market-driven tension which all high-tech companies must confront. The company promotes communication among its labs, manufacturing units and clients not only by locating labs close to large manufacturing units and major customers but also by the way it funds R&D.

> We originally arranged for BNR's funding to be supported directly from a central headquarters fund, in much the way most other research organizations operated. But, after BNR was established, we made a change that was destined to have a far-reaching effect on the way BNR carried out its business. We arranged for BNR's funding to come from Northern Telecom's individual manufacturing units.
>
> This decentralized funding structure had an important impact on BNR's approach to research. Because the company's funding came from the manufacturing divisions, its prime focus was on application-oriented products, rather than on the pure research done in other organizations. ("The BNR Story," p. 8)

The point of this approach to managing innovation is to ensure continuous product development and improvement and to focus greater concern on time pressures, in order to promote effective commercialization.

Northern Telecom's business strategy and success are grounded not only in technologically superior products but also in close interaction among R&D, manufacturing and the customer. The relationship seems to be growing closer still as the hardware side of switching shrinks and the development of customized software tailored to the customer's needs grows in importance. According to A. Zanfei, nearly one-third of RBOC purchase contracts between 1984 and 1988 included provisions for technical co-operation with the supplier. Northern Telecom also set up its Custom Programming Lab, which gives customers an opportunity to continue systems development to meet their own specific needs in co-operation with a BNR lab.[29] Some analysts suggest that in telecom equipment manufacturing, trailblazing companies have a substantial edge due to the enormous cost of R&D required to develop new generations of switching equipment (and then to adapt it to specific market conditions and customer needs) and the momentum generated by the supplier-customer relationships developed through continuous adaptation. In this context, Knickerbocker's "imitative entry" model (1973) of market entry by multinationals does not apply to the telecommunications equipment market.[30]

Due to its pioneering position in digital switching equipment and the gradual opening of the U.S. market, Northern Telecom has succeeded in becoming a North American multinational. Its success in the U.S. market-place is also attributable to the relatively decentralized operating system it has chosen for its manufacturing and R&D units which enables the company to establish close relationships with customers. According to G. Hewitt (1980), this type of "marketing" approach demands decentralized R&D.

THE GLOBALIZATION OF NORTHERN TELECOM

IN ITS OWN IDEA OF ITSELF AS WELL AS IN REALITY, Northern Telecom was, until 1988, an essentially North American company. It had a number of branch offices, a few plants and a few joint ventures outside North America, but these were of relatively minor importance; non-North American sales accounted for less than 5 percent of total sales. In 1987, however, Northern Telecom announced "Vision 2000", a new strategic orientation aimed at giving Northern a leadership position in the worldwide telecommunications marketplace. Indications are that the company continues to be guided by this vision. In 1991 and 1992, Northern Telecom revamped its divisional structure and marketing organization. In 1977, when Northern Telecom International was created, this division managed all Northern Telecom's manufacturing and marketing outside North America. Since 1992, however, Northern Telecom's international organization has been modified along product lines and geographical regions. The company now has four global product divisions (public networks, private networks, wireless systems and transmission), four regional marketing divisions (Canada, the United States, Europe and Asia-Pacific) and a regional marketing unit responsible for Latin America.[31]

Product design, development and manufacturing are expected to become more global in scope under the authority of the international product divisions. Northern Telecom's network of regional labs – which are capable of not only product adaptation but also, increasingly, simultaneous product development – supports this orientation. At the same time, the regional division of markets should enhance the company's presence in areas that are more dynamic than the United States – notably the Asian and European markets where growth rates are projected to be three times as high as in the United States. "The European telecom market is expected to grow at a rate three times that of the U.S. domestic market from 1991 to 1995."[32] Regional marketing should also raise Northern's profile in other potential but less certain markets such as Eastern Europe and Latin America.

Northern Telecom had made a major acquisition in 1991 with the purchase of STC in Great Britain. In the wake of this US$ 2.8 billion deal, 26 percent of Northern Telecom's sales were generated outside North America. The transaction made Northern Telecom a major player in Britain and the EC market, where STC was at the time the eighth-largest supplier of telecom equipment,[33] and consolidated Northern's involvement and competence in the transmission and wireless market segment. However, Northern Telecom has since sold off some of STC's facilities to Alcatel Cable.[34]

In 1992, Northern Telecom forged a strategic alliance with Motorola in cellular telephones. In the same year, it acquired a 20 percent interest in Matra Communication S.A. of France, which is rated ninth in the EC market.[35]

In Asia, Northern confirmed its interest in the Japanese market in 1991 by establishing a regional lab in Japan to strengthen its relationship with NTT and, even more so, with private telecommunications companies in Japan. In China, Northern's strategy is based on a joint venture with the China Tong Guang Electronics Corporation. However, Northern Telecom's efforts in Asia have not yet yielded a significant market share.

One cannot predict whether Northern Telecom will succeed in becoming a worldwide multinational. To be sure, the company is targeting world leadership by the year 2000 and some observers suggest that Northern may be one of only three surviving companies in the global telecommunications marketplace by the turn of the century. However, globalization promises to be played out in a far more complicated arena than was the case with North American expansion. In Europe, Northern Telecom must face rivals such as Alcatel, Ericsson and Siemens, who already enjoy market dominance. In Great Britain Northern was able to take advantage of deregulation to acquire a significant share of that market, and it has successfully carved out a leading position in the European PBX market, where it was the top-selling company in 1987.[36] In Europe, however, the market for central office switching equipment (which has been Northern's strong suit in North America) is not open for the moment. The same is true of the Japanese market, where NEC and a handful of other suppliers are firmly entrenched at NTT. Given this situation, Northern Telecom has recently begun to form alliances and acquire interests in other firms. However, a number of other major players are also very active in this field and competition using strategies of this type will be strong.[37]

> Among the leaders, Alcatel is still registering 80% of its sales in Europe. Northern Telecom's non-Canadian revenues come essentially from the United States. Only a few groups such as Ericsson and Motorola are really focussed on foreign markets. But most manufacturers are striving to expand beyond their borders. ("Dossier...," *Telecoms Magazine*, 1992, p. 36)

Northern Telecom has benefitted from AT&T's setbacks in the U.S. market but AT&T has since made major organizational changes. Although its drive toward internationalization – begun in 1984 with alliances with Philips and Italtel – was not successful, AT&T has renewed its efforts in the 1990s with the firm intention of becoming a global player.

> By the year 2000, AT&T hopes to generate some 20 percent to 25 percent of its revenues overseas. It has a long way to go. Last year [1988] only about 10 percent of its $35.2 billion in sales came from abroad, and most of that was from long-distance services, only $300 million from equipment sales. (Grigsby, 1989, p. 37)

CONCLUSIONS

THE NORTHERN TELECOM EXPERIENCE is particularly noteworthy in three respects: the company's use of R&D investment as FDI and the economic implications of this practise for purposes of analysis; Northern's relevance to the debate on Porterian clusters in Canada; and some implications for Canadian regulatory policy.

INTERNATIONALIZING NORTHERN TELECOM'S R&D: WINNERS AND LOSERS

DURING THE 1950S, Northern Telecom (then Northern Electric) was merely a supplier of telecommunications equipment to Bell Canada with operations confined to the Canadian market. The company relied heavily on the U.S.-based Western Electric Company (a subsidiary of AT&T) for its technology. After 1973, however, the conversion of public and private networks to digital technology ushered in a technological revolution for the industry as a whole and at Northern Telecom particularly. Northern Telecom's strategy for technological leadership involved substantial risk and demanded an enormous investment in R&D – which would have been entirely lost in the event of failure. Northern had virtually guaranteed sales in Canada, but that market was by itself clearly inadequate to support an R&D expenditure of C$ 1.375 billion over the period from 1973 to 1983. Northern Telecom had no alternative but to attack the U.S. market and attempt a breakthrough. Between 1973 and 1983, Northern's annual R&D spending increased ten-fold, but its sales increased five-fold. By 1983 U.S. sales accounted for 50 percent of Northern's total sales.

Northern Telecom had to develop a flawless strategy of market penetration for its central office and PBX switches – a strategy embracing the entire North American market. Its success in the U.S. marketplace was almost entirely due to the decentralization of its manufacturing and R&D operations which the company carried out in order to forge closer relationships with its major U.S. customers (RBOCs, MCI, Sprint, etc.). Until then, no foreign supplier had ever succeeded in winning a major share of the U.S. switching market using an export-based strategy. By setting up manufacturing facilities, R&D labs and sales and service offices in the United States and having them work closely with major customers, Northern Telecom created an interactive network in which manufacturing, engineering, product adaptation, financing and marketing were effectively integrated. The proximity of Northern Telecom's operations to its customers enabled this network to function smoothly. Rothwell (1993, pp. 4-6) calls this type of network a fourth-generation innovation model. According to Rothwell this model, which is widely used by Japanese companies, cuts the amount of both time and money required to carry out an innovation process. Freeman (1988, pp. 337-338) subscribes to this analysis of the distinctive characteristics of Japan's national innovation system and also cites Northern Telecom as an example.

McFetridge (1993) contends that decentralizing R&D produces a substitution effect (a reduction in R&D and innovation in the company's home country) and a scale effect (an increase in the company's R&D and innovation worldwide). Doz, Prahalad and Hamel (1990, p. 120) argue that trailblazing companies can achieve extensive benefits by regionalizing and globalizing their operations, and they cite the telecommunications equipment sector as one in which these factors play a major role. It was essential that Northern Telecom decentralize its R&D to the United States in order to adapt the company's products to specific market conditions and customer needs and thereby achieve substantial sales in the huge U.S. market. Those sales served to finance all of Northern Telecom's R&D and to support all R&D programs at the central lab in Ottawa. The scale effect was therefore much more significant than the substitution effect.

In 1991 the central lab employed 4,500 people, compared with 2,000 in the three regional U.S. labs; 69 percent of all Northern Telecom employees assigned to R&D in North America were therefore employed in Ottawa.

Northern Telecom's strong position in the North American market and enviable competitive posture in central office and PBX switches have prompted it to tackle the global telecommunications markets. This more recent strategy is an attempt to drive forward the process of diversification and globalization through acquisitions, joint ventures and active participation in other companies. Northern is therefore gradually developing a global network of integrated laboratories by setting up more and bigger labs with more diverse experiences and areas of competence.

The company's 1991-1992 reorganization into global product divisions with decentralized responsibility for design, development and production should support this more global approach. The central lab will be called upon to work closely with more specialized labs developing specific technologies. Technology flow should also become more multidirectional and Northern's regional labs will increasingly look for technological knowledge abroad, conducting what McFetridge (1993, p. 15) calls "knowledge-seeking R&D".

Northern Telecom faces a huge challenge. It must draw together specialized production techniques, R&D and marketing skills from throughout its network. Management experts are pointing to new demands being generated by increased competition and globalization: companies must create a world-wide mosaic of advantage (White & Poynter, 1990), put in place a trans-national organization (Bartlett & Ghoshal, 1989 and 1990) and a "heterarchy" (Hedlund, 1986 and Hedlund & Rolander, 1990) so as to implement a multi-focal strategy (Doz, 1986). Northern Telecom's probable development toward a networked organization can therefore be expected to complicate any analysis of the economic consequences of decentralized, specialized, co-ordinated R&D. The impact on the Canadian economy will increasingly depend on the dynamism of the Canadian telecommunications market and its ability to generate or pick up on innovations in technological innovations.

PORTERIAN CLUSTERS: CANADA'S TELECOMMUNICATIONS EQUIPMENT SECTOR

TRACING THE EVOLUTION OF NORTHERN TELECOM from a domestic supplier to an international leader in switching technology raises questions about what Michael Porter (1990 and 1991) calls an "industrial cluster". According to the model put forward by Porter in a stream of books and articles over the last twenty years, clusters of competitive companies within an industry are the keys to "the competitive advantage of nations". Porter argues that these clusters achieve world status through the intensity of domestic competition, which winnows out all but the best suppliers – suppliers who can satisfy the most demanding customers. Such is their excellence and command over process that they are able to keep new entrants at bay and stay on top of potential substitute products and technologies. Clusters derive from and, in turn, enhance the competitiveness "diamonds" of suppliers, customers, potential entrants and potential substitutes.[38]

Bell-Northern Research: The Incubator

Canada's telecommunications equipment sector approximates a Porterian cluster, with 154 firms supplying original equipment (according to Industry, Science and Technology Canada). Northern Telecom – specifically Bell Northern Research – has played a crucial role in the development of this cluster, particularly as an incubator company in which gifted engineers can acquire the contacts and learn the business side of telecommunications technology and then apply it to their own companies after leaving BNR. In any examination of R&D consequences, Northern Telecom's role as an incubator company for the high-technology cluster around Ottawa warrants special attention. The three companies owned by Northern Telecom between

1965 and 1982 – NT, BNR and Microsystems International – were identified by 15 high-technology company founders and co-founders of Ottawa-region companies as their incubator organizations. By comparison, Computing Devices of Canada was identified by ten. The federal government, by far the largest employer in the region, produced a larger number of start-ups – 17 of 30 such companies – but it took 12 departments to do so (Nichol, 1985).

The Competitive Dimension

Taking the competitive dimension into account, it is more accurate to say that Canada's cluster is actually an (increasingly) integral part of a North American cluster. Northern Telecom and the four or five other telecommunications "stars" in Canada are spectacular exceptions to what is generally a collection of tiny firms, not listed on any stock exchange and too small to make much difference. In other words, taken as an island, Canada has competitive companies, but weak clusters in telecommunications equipment.

There are several important differences between Canadian and U.S. telephone equipment suppliers. Apart from Northern Telecom and members of the Stentor Group, only six of Canada's 154 original equipment suppliers, (Dy-4 Systems, Gandalf Inc., Newbridge, Mitel, Spar and TIE Communications) are "made-in-Canada" original equipment manufacturers listed on a stock exchange. All the others are subsidiaries of foreign, (primarily U.S.) firms: Motorola Canada, Westinghouse, etc. Compare this with the 87 telephone equipment makers (including Mitel, Newbridge, Northern Telecom and TIE Communications) whose stocks are traded publicly in the United States. The other Canadians, Gandalf and Spar, also trade publicly in the United States, but are not telephone equipment makers. This suggests that access to the U.S. "competitive diamond" is a critical factor in helping Canadian companies achieve international competitiveness.

North American Diamonds

If the previous line of reasoning is pushed to its extreme, it might even be asked whether the Canadian "diamond" matters. Michael Porter's model for clusters, while a useful explanatory device, has a number of loose ends, especially where companies find their "diamonds" resulting from other than strictly national bases.[39] The Northern Telecom experience suggests that companies headquartered in small countries can profit from continental competition even though domestic competition is lacking, provided they can gain acceptance in the wider, competitive, market.

Porter alludes to the ability of Canadian firms to profit selectively from U.S. conditions, but stresses the importance of a Canadian diamond. Rugman & D'Cruz (1991 and 1993) counter that a North American diamond is essential for the competitive advantage of Canadian firms. With the free trade agreement, their argument goes, our most competitive firms will begin to create competitive advantage(s) on a North American basis. Arguably, this case study charts Northern Telecom's progress along this path.

Elsewhere in this volume, Rugman suggests that Northern Telecom be viewed as a company operating in a "double diamond" with different national strategies based on specific non-local advantages. In terms of this model, Northern Telecom pursues one strategy based on the advantages of the Canadian diamond in Canada and another strategy based on the advantages of the U.S. diamond in the United States. We argue, however, that different strategies can exist in the two diamonds only if they have different cost structures stemming from different industrial structures. These conditions must obtain for two economic spaces to be differentiated. This probably applies when we consider the triad, but is far from clear in the case of Canada and the United States. To develop and implement a viable strategy, a company such as Northern Telecom must set its sights on the entire North American market in order to remain competitive and to justify major investments in R&D and innovation.

Northern Telecom is now a major North American player in telecommunications equipment because of its cost leadership. Its clients in the United States are those companies who need leading-edge products to gain advantages themselves. Moreover, Northern's U.S. suppliers are also leading U.S. producers. It is noteworthy in this connection that Microsoft, not a Canadian company, supplied the software links for Northern's own networks. Pressure from its U.S. customers – not Stentor in Canada – is determining the research agenda at the central lab in Ottawa. On another strategic note, when Northern sold its STC transmission facility to Alcatel, it affected the competitive alignment between Northern Telecom and AT&T in Europe, in return for added liquidity – and thus added advantage – in North America. The question, therefore, is whether the "diamond" rhetoric obscures a more fundamental reality: the U.S. domestic market itself may well be the essential determinant of the "diamond", and in order to gain acceptance there, a company has at least to be perceived as being American (or somehow equivalent).

What About Outbound Foreign Direct Investment?

Another question arising from the Northern Telecom case is whether foreign investment by Canadian firms is "good". Porter tends to think it is better than foreign investment in Canada. Whatever one's position in this debate, however, it must be acknowledged that foreign direct investment (FDI) has been the major force shaping globalization. Although FDI is still tracked primarily in terms of capital flows, it now also takes the form of technology transfers and alliances aimed at more rapid market exploitation.[40] Northern Telecom's success has also been Canada's success. Thus, Canada is perceived as a major player in international telecommunications; most of the R&D in the country is performed in its service; and the largest Canadian corporations provide telecommunications equipment and services. Foreign investment by these companies creates competitive advantages from which they and their stakeholders benefit. Despite these considerations, Canada has not created a strong domestic base in the telecommunications equipment industry apart from the half-dozen leading firms (most of which are really U.S. firms which happen to be headquartered in Canada). The shortcoming is not investment, however, but public policy which constrains competition, obliging our best corporate "athletes" to train elsewhere to achieve excellence. In this connection, it is worth comparing Canada's experience in telecommunications equipment with its experience in aerospace. Through Northern Telecom (and recently a few other emerging companies), Canada has built a sustainable competitive advantage in telecommunications equipment. In aerospace, by contrast, Canada moved from a position of leadership in the 1950s to that of a follower. Subsequently, Canada has exited altogether from many segments of the aerospace market. The cancellation of the Avro Arrow and the resulting dispersal of Canadian aerospace capability to other centres in North America (mainly Boeing in Seattle and the Saturn project in Cape Canaveral) sealed Canada's failure in this sector.

PUBLIC POLICY IMPLICATIONS

THE MAIN POLICY-RELEVANT ASSERTION we can draw from the Northern Telecom case study is that the Canadian market is not yet sufficiently competitive to sustain its own world class players: at present it can only nurture them to the point of entry to the North American "diamond". True, there are advantages in "safe havens." Northern's majority shareholder, BCE, is well-known for its quiet support of innovative telecommunications technology suppliers.

As to what accounts for the competitive weakness of the vast majority of Canada's telecommunications suppliers, we submit that part of the answer lies with the structure of Canada's telecommunications services industry. About the same size as an RBOC, the Stentor Group sells long distance service, but it also enjoys a monopoly on local service. In Canada, the Stentor companies control Northern Telecom's access to the market. The Group has only recently begun to face limited competition from resellers; and it must also now contend with Unitel, which uses AT&T technology. Despite this competition, the Group still has a 90 percent market share. Its ability to introduce new services to meet customer needs (and now preempt services available in the United States before their arrival in Canada through Unitel's AT&T connection) is limited by regulation. Obviously this arrangement, combining market concentration and regulatory micro-management, makes it more difficult for any upstart company with a new and exciting product to sell to Stentor, the more so since there is no other RBOC for Stentor to compete with (except in the case of its business customers who are also active in the United States). In this context, consider the number of telephone equipment companies trading publicly: in the United States there are approximately 80 companies, or an average of 11 per RBOC – twice the Canadian average.[41] The difference between the number of publicly traded U.S. telephone equipment manufacturers and the corresponding number of Canadian companies is the price Canadians pay for acquiescing in a policy of closing the domestic market to competition in the name of efficiency.

In fact, there is an even steeper price to pay, for the U.S. market is now maturing and the heat is on for companies to provide enhanced value services such as find-me follow-me (or PCS for personal communications service), multimedia services, and better integration of voice and data handling. Northern Telecom's sales in the past were based on having the best hardware – the digital switch. Future sales will also be based on advanced switching technology, but the most important element is likely to be its programmability – i.e., the software that determines all the innovative things a provider can do that will win competitive advantage. In Canada, because of the aforementioned constraints, the pace of change is slower. The United States, not Canada, will be the laboratory of new techniques and technology. This means that previous competitive advantages – such as those enjoyed by Northern through its link to BCE – will diminish as the competitive focus shifts even further to the United States. Porter is clear about the dynamic relationship between competition, innovation and world-class performance. As he explains, "competitive advantage is created and sustained through a highly localized process". Clearly, when it comes to telecommunications equipment, it is easier to shape that advantage in the United States than in Canada. Indeed, Porter concludes that "the lack of local rivalry in Canada . . . will diminish the odds of sustained international success".[42]

Competitive Markets and Trade Balances

This brings us to the final issue: whether there is a trade-off between open markets and trade performance. Canada's telecommunications policies and industry structure have resulted in a Canadian trade surplus in telecommunications equipment throughout the 1980s, while the United States endured a large, chronic deficit. This reflects the relative openness of U.S. markets and the greater intensity of competition there (despite AT&T being both an equipment supplier and a service supplier). The beneficiaries have been the industry and the consumer, the first through technological advancement and the second through the availability of more services at lower prices – just as classical free trade theory predicts.

The U.S. experience poses a genuine dilemma for Canada: either accept more domestic competition (and thus narrower trade surpluses or even deficits) or witness the increasing pull of the U.S. "diamond" on innovation and excellence at home.

ENDNOTES

1 See "Dossier . . . ," *Telecoms Magazine*, 1992, pp. 31, 36 and 38.

2 See "Un club . . . " *Telecoms Magazine* , 1990, p. 47.

3 See "Un club très fermé de constructeurs face à l'inconnu," p. 48. The OECD (1991) reproduces Schnöring's data (1989). According to Schnöring, an investment of US $700 million to $1 billion is required to create a new generation of central office switches, and sales of at least US $14 billion are required to recoup the investment.

4 For example, "it took two and a half years and 300,000 hours of work to carry out the first two phases of adapting [Ericsson's Central Axe] to the French network....The third phase has yet to be completed" ("Un club très fermé de constructeurs face à l'inconnu," 1990, p. 55).

5 See Northern Telecom Limited, 1993, p. 6.

6 According to C.D. Hall, BNR's second president (1976-1981), "In those early days, the United States wasn't really on our minds because our technology licensing arrangements with Western Electric implied we couldn't sell Bell Lab-designed products into the United States" ("The BNR Story," p. 12). *Telesis*, a trade magazine published by Northern Telecom, devoted an issue to the organization of BNR's R&D facilities on the occasion of BNR's 20th anniversary. All the information on these facilities in this study has been drawn from this special issue, "The BNR Story", *Telesis*, Vol. 92, July 1991, pp. 5-66.

7 See "The BNR Story," p. 7.

8 *Ibid*, pp. 7, 10 and 12.

9 See Quelin, 1992, p. 145.

10 See Northern Telecom Limited, 1993, p. 6. On March 1, 1976, Northern Electric changed its name to Northern Telecom Ltd.

11 "The first sign that exchange switches built on a digital technology might replace recently introduced analog signal processing products occurred in the United States in the late 1970s when Northern Telecom's switch started creating what became referred to as "digital fever" in North America" (Bartlett and Ghoshal, 1990, p. 235).

12 "The BNR Story," pp. 11 and 22.

13 "As a result, duplication of effort and divergence of specifications began to emerge, and the cost of developing the switch ballooned to over US$ 1 billion. . . . After years of effort and hundreds of millions of costs, ITT acknowledged it was withdrawing from the US market. The largest and most successful international telecommunications company in the world was blocked from its home country by the inability to transfer and apply its leading edge technology in a timely fashion. It was a failure that eventually led to ITT's withdrawal from direct involvement in telecommunications" (Bartlett & Ghoshal, 1990, pp. 235-236).

14 See Doz, 1989, p. 258.

15 See Gattaz, 1985, p. 23.

16 See Grigsby, 1989, p. 36.

17 Northern Telecom Limited, 1993, p. 4.

18 See Northern Telecom Limited, 1992, p. 12.

19 See Northern Telecom Limited, 1993, pp. 6-7.

20 Dun & Bradstreet, 1992, pp. 1237-1238.

21 Northern Telecom Limited, 1991, p. 4, and 1992, p. 22.

22 See "The BNR Story," pp. 5-66.

23 See Dunning, 1993b, p. 307.

24 On this subject, see "Netting the Future; A Survey of Telecommunications," *The Economist*, March 10, 1990, p. 6 and "The New Boys; A Survey of Telecommunications," *The Economist*, October 5, 1991, p. 13.

25 See Terry, 1991, p. B1.

26 The Tokyo facility is the latest addition to the network of regional labs. However, on June 18, 1993, Northern Telecom signed a memorandum of understanding with the Chinese government providing for projects in that country, including the creation of a BNR research centre whose mission will be to develop new telecom software (Jannard, 1993, p. A16).

27 See Terry, 1991, p. B1.

28 *Ibid*, pp. B1 and B6, and Northern Telecom Limited, *Annual Report*, 1992, p. 9.

29 See Zanfei, 1992, p. 245-246.

30 See Doz (1979), p. 704, and Knickerbocker (1973).

31 See Northern Telecom Limited, 1991, p. 18, and 1992, pp. 6 and 10.

32 See *U.S. Industrial Outlook 1992*, p. 29-3.

33 See *Panorama of EC Industry 1991-1992*, p. 12-24.

34 See "Les grandes manoeuvres s'accélèrent," p. 24.

35 See *Panorama of EC Industry 1991-1992*, p. 12-24.

36 See Northern Telecom Limited, 1987, p. 3.

37 Telecommunications is one of the sectors with the most alliances. On this subject, see studies by Garrette & Quelin (1991) and Pisano, Russo & Teece (1988).

38 See Barrows, 1992, pp. 47-54.

39 See critiques of Porter by Rugman & D'Cruz (1991 and 1993) and by Dunning (1991 and 1993a).

40 See United Nations, *World Investment Report, 1992*.

41 Of the thirteen stocks listed as the technology component of the TSE 300, Gandalf, Mitel, Newbridge and Northern are telecom equipment suppliers and are listed in the United States as well. Only Newbridge and Northern have weights exceeding 1 percent (1.49 and 1.76 respectively). For an explanation of the TSE 300, see any issue of The Toronto Stock Exchange Review. The above weights were taken from the June 1993 issue.

42 See Porter, 1991, pp. 54 and 71.

ACKNOWLEDGEMENTS

THE AUTHORS WISH TO THANK editor Steven Globerman, John Knubley of Investment Canada, and discussant Jean-Guy Reins for their valuable advice and comments during the preparation of the final version of this case study.

BIBLIOGRAPHY

Barrows, D. "Canada's Global Competitiveness." In *Meeting the Global Challenge*. Edited by J. Dermer. Toronto: Captus Press, 1992, pp. 31-56.

Bartlett, C.A. "Building and Managing the Transnational: The New Organizational Challenge." In M. Porter, ed., *Competition in Global Industries*. Edited by M. Porter. Boston: Harvard Business School, 1986, pp. 367-401.

Bartlett, C.A. and S. Ghoshal, Managing Across Borders: The Transnational Solution (Boston: Harvard Business School, 1989).

Bartlett, C.A. and S. Ghoshal. "Managing Innovation in the Transnational Corporation." In *Managing the Global Firm*. Edited by C.A. Bartlett, Y. Doz and G. Hedlund. London: Routledge, 1990, pp. 215-255.

Cantwell, J. "The Theory of Technological Competence and Its Applications to International Production." In D. McFetridge, ed., *Foreign Investment, Technology and Economic Growth*, Investment Canada Research Series. Edited by D. McFetridge. Calgary: University of Calgary Press, 1991, pp. 41-84.

"Dossier, Les 100 qui font les Telecoms." *Telecoms Magazine* 18, (November-December 1992): 31-39.

Doz, Y.L. *Government Control and Multinational Strategic Management; Power Systems and Telecommunication Equipment*. New York: Praeger, 1979.

Doz, Y.L. "Italtel." In *Managing the Global Corporation; Case Studies in Strategy and Management*. Edited by W.H. Davidson and J. de la Torre. New York: McGraw-Hill, 1989, pp. 238-265.

Doz, Y.L. *Strategic Management in Multinational Companies*. New York: Pergamon, 1986.

Doz, Y., C.K. Prahalad and G. Hamel. "Control, Change and Flexibility: The Dilemma of Transnational Collaboration." In *Managing the Global Firm*. Edited by C.A. Bartlett, Y. Doz and G. Hedlund. London: Routledge, 1990, pp. 117-143.

Dun & Bradstreet. *America's Corporate Families 1992*. Parsippany: Dun & Bradstreet, 1992.

Dunning, J.H. "Internationalizing Porter's Diamond." *Management International Review* 33, (Special Issue 2/93, 1993a): 7-15.

_____. *The Competitive Advantage of Countries and TNC Activity: A Review Article*, Discussion Papers in International Investment and Business Studies No. 159. Reading: University of Reading, November 1991.

Dunning, J.H. *Multinational Enterprises and the Global Economy*.Wokingham: Addison-Wesley, 1993b.

_____. *Multinational Enterprises and the Globalization of Innovatory Capacity*, Discussion Papers in International Investment and Business Studies No. 143. Reading: University of Reading, Department of Economics, September 1990.

"Everybody's Favourite Monster; A Survey of Multinationals." *The Economist*, (March 27, 1993): 1-20.

Fortier, Y., (with C. Desranleau and L. Séguin-Dulude). *Northern Telecom et ses principaux concurrents dans l'industrie mondiale de l'équipement de télécommunications*. Cahier de recherche no 90-04. Montréal: Centre d'études en administration internationale, École des Hautes Études Commerciales, April 1990.

Freeman, C. "Japan: A New National System of Innovation?" In *Technical Change and Economic Theory*. Edited by G. Dosi, C. Freeman, R. Nelson, G. Silverberg and L. Soete. London: Pinter, 1988), pp. 330-348.

Garrette, B. and B. Quelin. "Les stratégies d'alliance des firmes d'équipements de télécommunication." In *Première conférence internationale de gestion stratégique*. Montréal: Centre d'études en administration internationale, École des Hautes Études Commerciales, October 20, 21 and 22, 1991, pp. 309-338.

Gattaz, P. *Le marché des télécommunications aux États-Unis*. Paris: Centre français du commerce extérieur, 1985.

Grigsby, J. "Global Report: Telecommunications." *Financial World*, 158, 8, (April 18, 1989): 32-39.

Hass, N. "Telecommunications, A Global Report; As Too Much Technology Competes for the Same Market, Warfare Looms." *Financial World*, 161, 18, (September 15, 1992): 30-38.

Hedlund, G. "The Hypermodern MNC – A Heterarchy?" *Human Resource Management*, 25, 1 (Spring 1986): 9-35.

Hedlund, G. and D. Rolander. "Action in Heterarchies – New Approaches to Managing the MNC." In *Managing the Global Firm*. Edited by C.A. Bartlett, Y. Doz and G. Hedlund. London: Routledge, 1990, pp. 15-46.

Hewitt, G. "Research and Development Performed by U.S. Manufacturing Multinationals." *Kyklos*. 33, 2, (1980): 308-327.

Jannard, M. "Northern Telecom signe une entente avec la Chine." *La Presse*, (June 19, 1993): A16.

Knickerbocker, F.T. *Oligopolistic Reaction and Multinational Enterprise*. Boston: Harvard University Press, 1973.

"Les grandes manoeuvres s'accélèrent." *Telecoms Magazine* 24, (August-September 1993): 24.

Light, W.F. "The Demands of Innovation in Northern Telecom." In *Managing Product Innovation*. Edited by C. Bolen, K. Durham, W. Light, C. Sadlow and V. Weir. Montréal: British-North American Committee, 1984: pp. 13-18.

McFetridge, D.G. Canadian Foreign Direct Investment, R&D and Technology Transfer, paper presented at the conference on Canadian-based multinationals, Industry Canada, Montréal, November 8-9, 1993.

Meyer, R. "Bait and Switch: The Japanese will Take a Hit in the U.S. Market to Protect their Global Franchise." *Financial World*, 161, 18, (September 15, 1992): 68-69.

"Netting the Future; A Survey of Telecommunications." *The Economist*, (March 10, 1990): 1-36.

NGL Consultants Ltd. (in co-operation with The Coopers & Lybrand Consulting Group and Collyn Managements). *A Proposal Towards a Strategic Plan for the Canadian Telecommunications Equipment Industry, Part I: The Canadian Telecommunications Equipment Industry in a Global Context*. Ottawa: January, 1991.

Nichol, L.J. Spin-offs and New Firm Formation: Entrepreneurship and High Technology in the Ottawa Area, unpublished Master's thesis in Geography, University of Ottawa, Ottawa, 1985.

Northern Telecom Limited, The Financial Post Datagroup, April 27, 1993, pp. 1-16.

Northern Telecom Limited, *Annual Reports*, 1977 to 1992.

Northern Telecom. *Interim Report, First Quarter*, 1993.

OECD. *Telecommunications Equipment: Changing Markets and Trade Structures*. Information Computer Communications Policy Series, No. 24. Paris: OECD, 1991.

OECD, *Communications Outlook 1993*. Paris: OECD, 1993.

Ohmae, K. *Triad Power; The Coming Shape of Global Competition*. New York: Free Press, 1985.

Panorama of EC Industry 1991-1992. Brussels: Commission of the European Communities, 1991.

Pearce, R.D. "Factors Influencing the Internalization of Research and Development in Multinational Enterprises." In *Multinational Enterprises in the World Economy, Essays in Honour of John Dunning*. Edited by P.J. Buckley and M. Casson. Aldershot: Edward Elgar, 1992, pp. 75-95.

Pisano, G.P., M.V. Russo and D.J. Teece. "Joint Ventures and Collaborative Arrangements in the Telecommunications Equipment Industry." In *International Collaborative Ventures in U.S. Manufacturing*. Edited by D.C. Mowery. Cambridge, Mass.: Ballinger, 1988) pp. 23-70.

Porter, M.E. *Canada at the Crossroads: The Reality of a New Competitive Environment*. Ottawa: Business Council on National Issues and Minister of Supply and Services, 1991.

Porter, M.E. *The Competitive Advantage of Nations*. New York: Free Press, 1990.

Quelin, B. "Trajectoires technologiques et diffusion de l'innovation : l'exemple des équipements de télécommunications." *Revue d'économie industrielle*, 59, (1st quarter, 1992): 132-153.

Ronstadt, R. *Research and Development Abroad by U.S. Multinationals*. New York: Praeger, 1977.

Rothwell, R. *Systems Integration and Networking: The Fifth Generation Innovation Process*. Montréal: Cahier de la Chaire Hydro-Québec en gestion de la technologie, Université du Québec à Montréal, May 1993.

Rugman, A.M. Strategic Management and Canadian Multinational Enterprises, paper presented at the conference on Canadian-based multinationals, Industry Canada, Montréal, November 8-9, 1993.

Rugman, A.M and J.R. D'Cruz. *Fast Forward: Improving Canada's Competitiveness*. Toronto: Kodak, 1991.

_____. "The 'Double Diamond' Model of International Competitiveness: The Canadian Experience." *Management International Review*, 33, (Special Issue 2/93): 17-39.

Ryans, A.B. "Northern Telecom." In *Canadian Marketing, Cases and Concepts*. Edited by K.G. Hardy, M.R. Pearce, T.H. Deutscher and A.B. Ryans. 3rd edition. Toronto: Allyn & Bacon, 1988, pp. 220-238.

Schnöring, T. *Research and Development in Telecommunications – An International Comparison*. Bad Honnef: Wissenschaftliches Institut für Kommunikationsdienste der Deutchen Bundespost, September 1989.

Symonds, W.C., J.B. Levine, N. Gross and P. Coy. "High-Tech Star, Northern Telecom Is Challenging Even AT&T." *Business Week*, (July 27, 1992): 54-58.

Teitelman, R. "How ITT Blew It, How the Greatest Businessman of the 1960s Turned His Back on the 1990s." *Financial World* 158, 8, (April 18, 1989): 61-62.

Terry, E. "Northern Telecom Has Asia's Number." *Globe and Mail*, (November 1991): B1 and B6.

"The BNR Story." *Telesis* 92, (July 1991): 5-63.

"The New Boys: A Survey of Telecommunications." *The Economist*, (October 5, 1991): 1-36.

"Un club très fermé de constructeurs face à l'inconnu." Les dossiers Télécoms Magazine Réseaux, *Telecoms Magazine* 34, (May 1990): 47-59.

United Nations Transnational Corporations and Management Division. *World Investment Report 1992: Transnational Corporations as Engines of Growth*. New York: United Nations, 1992.

U.S. Department of Commerce. *U.S. Industrial Outlook 1992*. Washington, D.C.: International Trade Administration, 1992.

White, R.E. and T.A. Poynter. "Organizing for World-Wide Advantage." In *Managing the Global Firm*. C.A. Bartlett, Y. Doz and G. Hedlund. London: Routledge, 1990, pp. 95-113.

Zanfei, A. "Collaborative Agreements and Innovation in the US Telephony Industry." In *The Economics of Information Networks*. Edited by C. Antonelli. Amsterdam: North-Holland, 1992, pp. 229-251.

Part VI   Lessons

André Raynauld O.C.
Professor Emeritus, Université de Montréal and
Senior Fellow, I.R.P.P.

Rapporteur's Comments

INTERNATIONAL INVESTMENT, as a topic for study, has received considerable attention in recent years. This volume on *Canadian-Based Multinationals* is the fourth in the Industry Canada Research Series and represents the fourth major installment from the department on issues related to foreign investment. There is also a flood of other independent research on issues related to direct investment abroad in addition to the papers presented in this volume. I refer to those books and papers which have already been, or are soon to be, published because direct investment abroad cannot be properly analyzed in isolation from related considerations having to do with technology, globalization, multinational enterprise strategies and alternatives to direct investment in achieving optimal economic performance.

My comments will be presented in three sections. The first highlights the main themes of the papers presented at the conference on Canadian Based Multinational Enterprises. The main focus of the presentations was the costs and benefits of Canadian direct investment abroad (CDIA). Related to this central theme, I touch on recent trends and patterns in CDIA, the rationale for CDIA and the impact of CDIA on the domestic economy. The second section draws out general implications for research and policy. The third and concluding section summarizes the main lessons from the conference.

COSTS AND BENEFITS OF CANADIAN DIRECT INVESTMENT ABROAD

THE PAPERS IN THIS VOLUME, diverse as they are, can be seen as making valuable contributions to the analysis of the costs and benefits of CDIA. In particular, the papers address such issues as the impact of direct investment abroad on the labour market, the balance of payments, innovation and technology transfer. There are also two country studies (on Japan and Sweden) as well as two case studies (Northern Telecom and MacMillan

Bloedel) which provide additional useful insights into direct investment abroad and suggest topics for further study.

TRENDS AND PATTERNS OF CDIA

THE FOCUS OF THIS CONFERENCE is on Canadian direct investment abroad and not on foreign direct investment, which is usually associated with inward direct investment. As a point of departure, therefore, researchers must be careful in their definitions of concepts: and they should not confuse stocks and flows of investment, and inward and outward investment.

Before addressing these main issues, it is useful to review the statistical trends and patterns in CDIA. The papers by Chow, McFetridge, and Rao, Legault & Ahmad are relevant here. The following points summarize the most significant trends in CDIA in recent years:

- There has been a substantial increase in CDIA between 1980 and 1992. The Canadian share of the world stock of direct investment went up from 4 percent in 1980 to 5 percent in 1992, while CDIA as a proportion of Canadian GDP increased from 8.7 percent to 14.4 percent over the same 12 year period.

- Outward flows of Canadian direct investment have increased faster than inward flows.

- The U.S. share of total CDIA is still dominant at 58 percent in 1991, but since 1986, it went down in favour of European countries and Asia.

- The industry composition of CDIA has changed appreciably, with financial services, such as banking and insurance, now representing 25 percent of the total. The shift has been at the expense of primary industries and manufacturing. However, the bulk of CDIA is still in traditional industries. It should come as no surprise, therefore, that CDIA has a rather low technological content.

- The comparisons between industry of origin in Canada and industry of destination abroad made by Gorecki in *Patterns of Canadian FDIA* (Statistics Canada, Analytical Branch, No. 33, 1990), are very revealing. Building on Gorecki's work, Chow similarly finds that 85 percent of CDIA belongs to the same industry in Canada and abroad. He attributes this pattern of horizontal linkages to the exploitation of established expertise in international markets and the small scale of the Canadian economy, which makes it difficult for firms to exploit economies of scale fully without going abroad.

- Foreign direct investment increases intra-firm trade. In work undertaken elsewhere, Lorraine Eden has shown that intra-firm trade accounts for 50 percent of trade flows between Canada and the United States.

- A last observation of considerable importance is the comparison of the relative performance of outwardly oriented and domestically oriented firms made in the Rao, Legault & Ahmad background paper. It shows clearly that firms having an international or global perspective fare much better than their counterparts in terms of growth, R&D spending, and rates of return on assets, to the obvious advantage, in my mind, of the economy as a whole.

THE RATIONALE FOR CDIA

I NOW COME TO THE APPROACHES taken to assess the effect of direct investment abroad on the home economy. With no criticism implied, most of the authors found it necessary to begin their analyses by outlining first the rationale or the objectives of a business firm when it decides to invest abroad.

There is, I believe, a broad consensus that for a relatively long time foreign direct investment was a substitute for trade because of trade barriers. Over the last 10 or 15 years, however, the world economy has changed dramatically; not only have trade barriers come down but there has also been a fantastic acceleration of structural change called globalization. Several papers presented at the conference describe the main manifestations of this phenomenon:

- The general policy orientations adopted by most governments have been more in favour of market mechanisms than government intervention. These in turn have led to the liberalization of trade, investment and financial flows, and to a substantial increase in international or global competition.

- The rapid pace of technological change has led to a substantial reduction in transportation and communications costs. As a result, product cycles are now shorter, new production methods have been developed, and there is more emphasis on investment in research and development.

- National economies are becoming less and less national and there has been a convergence of consumer tastes across countries and greater mobility of capital, labour and technologies.

- New players – particularly the Asian countries – have emerged on the world's economic stage.

- Finally, all these developments are shifting the comparative advantage positions of business firms and nations with attendant increases in uncertainty and risk.

It is in this environment that business strategies are developed and investment decisions are taken. In this context, direct investment abroad can be seen as one strategy among several, which a firm can use to position itself in the world economy. The main alternatives to direct investment abroad include trade, mergers and domestic acquisitions, minority ownership, joint ventures, alliances (Globerman & Wolf), subcontracting, and licensing.

Rugman, with his theory of "strategic strategies" has provided a framework for explaining investment decisions and direct investment abroad. Other papers in the volume, which adopt a more empirical approach, focus on what firms are trying to achieve with direct investment abroad. In the Vertinsky & Raizada paper on MacMillan Bloedel, direct investment abroad is described alternatively as a search for markets or customers, a search for a key resource, a search for efficiency and a search for strategic assets to reduce risk. (I have already referred to Gorecki's earlier work regarding horizontal linkages in CDIA.) In this instance, firms appear to be pursuing vertical linkages (looking for suppliers or customers) and conglomerate linkages based on diversification and risk reduction.

The last set of reasons for undertaking direct investment abroad, as well as alliances, is presented by Globerman & Wolf. The reasons they identify relate to the desire to acquire core competencies (which I interpret to mean technical know-how); to access new markets; to diversify and exploit economies of scale; to circumvent trade and investment restrictions, and finally (a very important consideration in my mind) to preempt competition.

THE EFFECT OF CDIA ON THE DOMESTIC ECONOMY

GIVEN THE GENERAL ENVIRONMENT of the world economy and the nature of the strategies adopted by multinational firms, several papers in this volume address the more immediate consequences of direct investment abroad.

The first to be considered is through financial flows. A direct investment abroad implies an outflow of capital with a negative effect on the capital account when it occurs. However, if that investment is successful, it will generate financial inflows in the form of dividends or royalties later, as Graham has shown. The Rao, Legault & Ahmad background paper presents estimates that direct investment income from abroad reached $4 billion per year in Canada during the period between 1986 and 1992. This is evidence that real income in Canada has increased as a result of CDIA.

Trade is another impact indicator. As mentioned previously, direct investment abroad used to be seen as a substitute for trade. Graham's review of the evidence on this issue leads to his guarded conclusion that, over all, trade is more likely to be a complement than a substitute. The Rao, Legault & Ahmad background paper produced new calculations of the elasticity of exports to direct investment abroad, showing that elasticity to be positive and relatively high. Therefore, the authors contend that the evidence suggests that exports are stimulated by direct investment abroad with additional benefits for the economy as a whole. In the Kokko & Blomström paper on Sweden, a similar if not stronger conclusion is reached on this point. The same can be said for Japan in the Ries & Head paper.

A third preoccupation with investment abroad is the labour-market effects and the potential loss of jobs. Gunderson & Verma investigate this issue thoroughly and look for the sources of potential losses and potential gains with the help of a systematic review of the literature. To reduce the argument to the essential, job losses are assumed to occur because the investment made abroad is seen as cutting domestic investment by the same proportion. It should be immediately obvious that this argument is untenable. The authors call this argument the "lump of labour fallacy", according to which there is a fixed number of jobs in an economy so that investing in another country becomes the equivalent of exporting jobs. Gunderson & Verma find that, in fact, direct investment abroad leads to a change in the employment structure of the home country, away from low-value-added jobs and toward higher-value-added jobs. Similar effects have also been attributed to trade liberalization in a country like Canada.

McFetridge uses a similar argument in another context. Even if direct investment abroad leads to some job losses in the home country, in one form or another the net benefit is still greater than not serving the foreign market at all. As an example, the Ries & Head study on Japan shows that multinational firms succeed better than domestic firms in maintaining or increasing employment and salaries in most industries, with the exception of textiles. This evidence is important. However, Wendy Dobson warns us that the Japanese experience is difficult to apply generally to other countries.

Gunderson & Verma raise another important issue related to the labour market effects of direct investment abroad – that direct investment abroad may have an additional indirect impact on employment and wages to the extent that it may lead to changes in labour laws and regulations. If existing regulations raise labour costs compared to other jurisdictions, direct investment abroad may be stimulated. In this context, direct investment is a proxy for capital mobility, and in essence, constrains the freedom of action of governments.

Gunderson & Verma also find that labour regulations are much more extensive in Canada than in the United States or Mexico. However, they believe that distinctions must be made among policy measures when it comes to determining the effects of regulation on labour costs. Some measures, such as job listings and training, increase the efficiency of the labour market and reduce costs accordingly, while several others, such as payroll taxes or minimum wages, do the opposite. Finally, one must consider whether labour costs are an important or negligible determinant of plant location decisions. The evidence on this point appears to be mixed.

A fourth and last set of considerations on the impact of direct investment abroad has to do with technology and innovation. On this subject, we have a remarkable paper of general interest by McFetridge and several more specific observations from the case studies.

This subject is more complex than the other effects of direct investment abroad. However, I have the rather strong feeling that in the Canadian case, technological considerations have very little to do with CDIA. It appears that CDIA is undertaken for essentially marketing and distribution purposes. The motivation is to reach new customers, not to develop new products or new processes. The revealed comparative advantage of Canadian direct investors in the United States, as given by McFetridge, is revealing indeed. The industries with comparative advantage are printing and publishing, retail trade, insurance and real estate. To say the least, these industries are not known to be the most dynamic and innovative in this day and age. Overall, no more than 10 percent of Canadian direct investment stock in the United States is technology-motivated. This is not to deny, however, that there is more direct investment abroad in research and development-intensive industries than in other industries. The difficulty is to identify the line of causality. It appears that research and development is not the driving force in foreign investment decisions. Research and development would be undertaken to the extent necessary to make the production unit work.

Whether technology transfers abroad occur, or do not occur, as a consequence of direct investment is much less important than it appears because there is so little to transfer out of Canada anyway. To the extent that transfers do occur, the benefits are not lost to the home country. The argument is that without foreign markets, the rate of return on research and development would be too low to justify any R&D at all being undertaken here in the first place. This argument is supported by the experience of Northern Telecom, as reported in the Amesse, Séguin-Dulude & Stanley paper.

This being said, I have a serious problem with the methodology in this area. In my view, R&D activity is not an adequate measure of high-tech intensity or innovative capacity. The critical test is not the production of new technologies, but rather the use of new technologies to improve efficiency and performance. One does not have to be a doctor to be in good health; one can buy medical services. The same is true of technology. A firm does not have to produce technology itself in order to use it; technology can be bought. If R&D is not a good indicator of technology intensity, then the question remains, how should we measure it empirically?

RESEARCH AND POLICY PERSPECTIVES

H ERE, I TURN TO SOME MORE GENERAL observations on research and policy perspectives associated with the topic of direct investment abroad.

RESEARCH

IT SEEMS TO ME THAT FOREIGN INVESTMENT and other transnational strategies are in the middle of a transition period where the rules of the game are still experimental, uncertain, and in a state of flux. The case studies, MacMillan Bloedel in particular, provide evidence that success with investment abroad is far from guaranteed and that the risks are very high. This is also one of the reasons why statistical data may be less conclusive than one would hope for in assessing direct investment abroad. In my view, the research effort in this field must be maintained to keep abreast of current and future developments. If I am right in thinking that we are in a transition stage, other changes have yet to occur, some of which cannot now be anticipated. More work is required to identify and describe the key relationships involving investment abroad.

One avenue of research to be pursued in this context could involve documenting the structural changes and restructuring that is taking place, not only in terms of direct investment abroad, but also in terms of the domestic economy as a whole. Indeed, we can be sure that one of the prime determinants of direct investment abroad is precisely what happens in the domestic economy. A structural change approach of this nature, focusing on changes in the sectoral allocation of resources, changes in the production functions, and changes in the availability and cost of resources of all kinds – natural, human, financial, technological – would help a great deal to increase our understanding of the future.

One additional area deserving further research is location determinants of investment decisions. There are several indirect or passing references to this issue in the papers in this volume, but there is no systematic analysis despite the fact that the world has already changed considerably in this respect. Distance from markets has almost disappeared as a determinant of plant location because of the shift in trade from goods to services and the reduction in transportation and communications costs. Marcel Côté made the same point in his comments at this conference. Unit labour cost differences, reflecting differences in productivity, still matter in an investment decision. The level of wages, however, has become irrelevant. Technology, in the broadest sense of the term, is the major factor of production as opposed to the stock of capital. Several other considerations could be mentioned, but these examples should be sufficient to show that a general reassessment of locational determinants is necessary. Rugman's paper would be an excellent starting point to a more empirical treatment of this issue.

Policy

THE POLICY IMPLICATIONS from existing research on direct investment abroad are numerous but relatively straightforward.

An overriding consideration to keep in mind is that no country – and that includes Canada – has any choice but to adapt to the new international economy. This may not sound very profound or scientific, but it is at the root of everything else one might want to do. For example, even if research led us to believe that direct investment abroad has a negative impact on the home economy, we would not be at liberty to stop it. This does not mean that our policy response would necessarily be the same in both cases; it does mean, however, that we must accept the reality of being part and parcel of the world.

One immediate consequence of this reality is that traditional protectionist measures will no longer protect anything. As several authors pointed out in their papers, trade and capital movement liberalization measures must be encouraged, both regionally (as we have begun to do with the FTA and the NAFTA) and worldwide (through the GATT as McFetridge suggests). We do not know with any certainty if Canadian direct investment abroad will increase or decrease as a result of more liberalization, but this consideration is not particularly important anyway. In her comments at the conference, Lorraine Eden recalled with good reason that there are still formidable barriers under the Free Trade Agreement in various industries, including finance, culture, energy, transportation and telecommunications. It would be in the Canadian interest to work toward removing them as far as possible.

The Northern Telecom study by Amesse, Séguin-Dulude & Stanley raises the issue of regulation and its negative impact on domestic competition, which in turn also impedes the company's competitiveness in global markets. Eden in her comments, and Graham, stressed the need for a more effective transnational competition policy following the model of the European Community. It is a fact that domestic regulation can have consequences very similar to protectionism. A reassessment of the regulatory framework should therefore be undertaken in Canada to stimulate competition and eventually to produce world leaders in fields where Canada should expect to have them.

My last observation addresses the issue of taxation, as raised in the highly technical paper by Donald Brean. Brean finds that the Canadian tax system treats CDIA favourably, virtually exempting it from taxation. He argues that this is reasonable, given the conflicting objectives of corporate taxation in an open economy where investment flows both into and out of countries.

He points out that Canada would risk causing CDIA to be taxed twice if it were more aggressive in its policy. But Jack Mintz, the discussant for Brean's paper, was more critical of the Canadian system. However, I think that both authors would agree that the over-all level of taxation in Canada should be competitive with foreign countries and therefore not higher than elsewhere – and preferably lower. Otherwise, the tax base itself will move abroad.

Canadian legislators and tax officials must recognize that the fiscal burden on individuals is higher in Canada than in the United States, and that highly skilled personnel have an incentive to work abroad.

For his part, Mintz offers several justifications to tax foreign source income effectively. One obvious reason is to protect the domestic revenue base in the same way as corporate tax protects the personal income tax base. Foreign source income could also be taxed according to the benefit principle to the extent that Governments incur costs and provide benefits to the corporations investing abroad.

The Canadian tax environment treats foreign source income and R&D favourably. Brean concludes, however, that Canada should not allow Canadian-based multinationals unlimited scope in writing off the full extent of headquarters costs and costs of R&D undertaken in Canada. The benefits associated with those expenditures, such as effective global management processes and intellectual property, are intangible assets, which are developed in Canada with fiscal support from governments and which result in streams of income from abroad that are untaxed in Canada. In Brean's view, Canada is entitled to recover at least part of the rents created with Canadian government assistance. The present situation implies that direct investment abroad is being subsidized compared with investment at home. An alternative would be to tax foreign source income but introduce export tax incentives as in the United States with their DISC and FISC programs.

The favourable tax treatment of research and development in Canada is seen by both Brean and Mintz as entirely justified by the existence of important spillovers associated with R&D. However, Mintz rightly adds a note of caution on R&D subsidization, since the conditions of success are not always present.

CONCLUSIONS

THE GENERAL PICTURE THAT EMERGES from this conference is that the increase in CDIA has been a favourable development for the Canadian economy. It is, indeed, a necessary response or adaptation to the new global environment. The benefits for Canada can be substantial in terms of financial flows over time, in terms of trade, and in terms of high value-added job creation. The results are less obvious with respect to technology and innovation. There appear to be no technology transfers abroad as a result of CDIA nor do we seem to gain very much.

The policy implications suggested at this conference are clear and unambiguous. We have no choice but to work toward a more open economy with further liberalization measures, both regionally and world wide. The same must be said for the regulatory framework, which must encourage rather than impede competition. These are seen as necessary conditions to reap the full benefits of Canadian direct investment abroad.

About the Contributors

Ashfaq Ahmad is Investment Analyst with the Strategic Investment Analysis group at Industry Canada. His research focus centres on global direct investment and merger and acquisition activity. He is co-author of a forthcoming Industry Canada Occasional Paper on Formal and Informal Investment Barriers in the G-7 Countries.

Fernand Amesse is Professor of Marketing at HEC in Montreal and member of the Center for International Business Studies (CETAI). His main areas of teaching are international marketing, technology and international technology transfer management, and market analysis. Current research topics are export management in small business firms, high technology industries in Canada, and international trade and marketing in business services.

Magnus Blomström is Professor of Economics at the Stockholm School of Economics and Research Associate at the National Bureau of Economic Research. His research focuses on foreign investment, international trade and economic growth and development. He is also a consultant to international organizations, governments and corporations. Recent publications include the books *Foreign Investment and Spillovers* and *Transnational Corporations and Manufacturing Exports from Developing Countries*.

Donald J. S. Brean is Associate Professor of Finance and Economics in the Faculty of Management, University of Toronto. He is a member of the International Panel of Tax Experts of the IMF and has advised numerous international agencies, including the World Bank, the European Community and the Canadian government. He has published extensively in the areas of international finance and investment, taxation, industrial organization, and economic policy.

Franklin Chow is a senior Economist in the Balance of Payments Division at Statistics Canada. In the Current Account and the International Investment Position Section of this Division, he has worked extensively on inward and outward direct investment flows and positions, and on acquisition activity in Canada and abroad. Recent work includes participation in the OECD project developing direct investment and globalization indicators.

467

Steven Globerman is Professor of Economics at Simon Fraser University and, in 1994, the Ross Distinguished Professor of Canada-U.S. Business and Economic Relations at Western Washington University. He has published numerous articles on foreign direct investment, consulted extensively on international business issues, and served on two federal Royal Commissions on the economy.

Edward M. Graham is Senior Fellow at the Institute for International Economics in Washington, D. C. Previously, he served on the faculties of MIT and the University of North Carolina and as an international economist at the U.S. Treasury. He has written extensively on international direct investment and multinational enterprises. His best known work, co-authored with Prof. Paul Krugman of MIT, is an analysis of the effects of foreign investment on the U.S. economy.

Morley Gunderson is Director of the Centre for Industrial Relations and professor in the Department of Economics at the University of Toronto. He is the author of numerous books and articles on work force issues. He is currently on the editorial advisory board of the *Journal of Labor Research* and the *International Journal of Manpower* and he is co-editor of the *Labour Arbitration Yearbook*. He has served as consultant on labour issues to major government bodies and international organizations.

Keith C. Head is Assistant Professor, Policy Analysis Division, in the Faculty of Commerce and Business Administration at the University of British Columbia. He teaches courses in international business management, commerce, international trade policy, and government and business.

Ari O. Kokko is Assistant Professor at the Stockholm School of Economics. His primary research interest is home-country effects of foreign direct investment, focusing on Sweden. He also has several ongoing projects on foreign direct investment related to particular countries, including Estonia, Vietnam, and Uruguay.

Marc Legault is an economist in the Strategic Investment Analysis Division of the Micro-Economic Policy Analysis Branch at Industry Canada. Recent work includes empirical analysis of the structure, characteristics and performance of the top 1,000 North American-based firms. He is currently engaged in research on "stateless" enterprises and corporate governance practices.

Donald G. McFetridge is Professor of Economics at Carleton University. He has taught at the University of Western Ontario, McGill University and Quing Hua University in Beijing and was also a Visiting Research Fellow at Harvard University. He is the author of numerous publications on various aspects of industrial economics and economic policy, and has served as advisor to corporations, government bodies and international organizations.

P. Someshwar Rao is Senior Policy Advisor in the Strategic Investment Analysis Division at Industry Canada. Recent work includes analyses of "stateless" corporations, and of North American multinational enterprises. Formerly at the Economic Council of Canada, he contributed substantially to major projects, including a report on Canadian competitiveness and development of a desegregated model of Canadian industry. He has published extensively on productivity, trade and macro-economic issues.

Rachana Raizada is a doctoral student in international business at the University of British Columbia. She holds a Bachelor of Arts degree in Economics from the University of Dehli and a Master of Business Administration degree from the University of Windsor. Her research interests focus on the international process through which multinational enterprises acquire the complex structural forms and interorganizational relationships they manifest today.

André Raynauld O.C. is Senior Fellow at the Institute for Research on Public Policy, an officer of the Order of Canada, and Research Fellow of the Development Centre of the OECD. He was named Professor Emeritus by the University of Montreal in 1993, after many years of distinguished service there as Professor of Economics. From 1971 to 1976, he was as Chairman of the Economic Council of Canada. He has published extensively and continues to be heavily involved in economic research.

John C. Ries is Assistant Professor in the Faculty of Commerce and Business Administration at the University of British Columbia. His teaching and research interests centre on international business, the Japanese economy and international trade issues. In 1988-1989 he was Foreign Scholar at the Research Institute of the Japanese Ministry of International Trade and Industry.

Alan M. Rugman is Professor of International Business at the University of Toronto. He has taught at Dalhousie, Winnipeg and Harvard universities, and at the Columbia and London Business Schools. He is also the author of numerous articles on the economic, managerial, and strategic aspects of MNEs and on trade and investment policy. He has served on Canada's International Trade Advisory Committee and on the sectoral trade advisory committee for forest products.

Louise Séguin-Dulude is Professor of Economics at the École des Hautes Études Commerciales in Montreal. At different times she has served as

Director of the Centre of International Business Studies and Director of the China-Montreal Management Programme at HEC. Her main teaching areas are international business, international economics and managerial economics. Her main research interests are the economic and managerial aspects of multi-national enterprises with an emphasis on technology management and R&D strategy.

Guy Stanley is a Senior Associate of the Centre for the Study of International Business at the École des Hautes Études Commerciales. He manages a number of CETAI's relations with industry and government in North America and teaches courses in international business, including graduate seminars on the Canada-U.S. FTA and global competitiveness. He has also taught at the University of Connecticut and the University of Western Ontario, the Canadian Foreign Service Institute, and the Institute for U.S.-Canada Business Studies at Pace University. He has written widely on international business matters.

Savita Verma teaches corporate and international finance in the Faculty of Administrative Studies at York University. She has taught at Northeastern, Boston and St. Francis Xavier universities and Nankai University (China), and at the Tecnologico de Monterrey (Mexico). Her extensive research interests include corporate dividend policy, comparative corporate-ownership structures, governance mechanisms, initial public offerings, and cross-border markets for corporate control.

Ilan Vertinsky is Professor of Management Science, Policy Analysis and Vinod Sood Professor of International Business Studies at the University of British Columbia. He is also a senior fellow and director of the Centre of International Business Studies, and director of the Forest Economics and Policy Analysis Research Unit at UBC. His current research focuses on strategic management, international trade and investment, and forest economics.

Bernard M. Wolf is Professor of Economics and International Business in the Faculty of Administrative Studies, York University. His research interests include the international monetary system, international trade, economic integration, foreign investment and strategic alliances. He is on the editorial board of the *North American Journal of Economics and Finance* and is a representative to the Pacific Asian Consortium of International Education and Research.